CREATING BUSINESS ADVANTAGE IN THE INFORMATION AGE

GW00494012

CREATING BUSINESS ADVANTAGE IN THE INFORMATION AGE

Lynda M. Applegate

Robert D. Austin

F. Warren McFarlan

All of the Graduate School of Business Administration
Harvard University

Boston   Burr Ridge, IL   Dubuque, IA   Madison, WI   New York   San Francisco   St. Louis
Bangkok   Bogotá   Caracas   Kuala Lumpur   Lisbon   London   Madrid   Mexico City
Milan   Montreal   New Delhi   Santiago   Seoul   Singapore   Sydney   Taipei   Toronto

McGraw-Hill Higher Education

A Division of The McGraw-Hill Companies

Publisher: *George Werthman*
Senior sponsoring editor: *Rick Williamson*
Developmental editor: *Kelly L. Delso*
Manager, Marketing and Sales: *Paul Murphy*
Project manager: *Karen J. Nelson*
Production supervisor: *Debra R. Sylvester*
Senior designer: *Jenny El-Shamy*
Media producer: *Greg Bates*
Lead supplement producer: *Marc Mattson*
Cover design: *Veronica Smith*
Typeface: *10 / 12 Century Schoolbook*
Compositor: *Carlisle Communications, Ltd.*
Printer: *R.R. Donnelley & Sons Company*

Library of Congress Cataloging-in-Publication Data

Applegate, Lynda M.
    Creating business advantage in the information age / Lynda M. Applegate, Robert D. Austin, F. Warren McFarlan.—1st ed.
        p. cm.
    Includes index.
        ISBN 0-07-252367-0 (alk. paper)
        1. Electronic commerce. 2. Business—Computer network resources. 3. Internet. I. Austin, Robert D. (Robert Daniel), 1962-II. McFarlan, F. Warren (Franklin Warren) III. Title.
HF5548.32.A666 2002
658′.054678—dc21

                                                                2001052201

http://www.mhhe.com

To Karen, Paul, Christopher, Laurel, Lillian, Evelyn, and Daniel

Lynda M. Applegate

Lynda M. Applegate is the MBA Class of 1952 Distinguished Professor of Business Administration at Harvard Business School, teaching courses in entrepreneurial management, managerial economics and business design, and serving as head of the school's Field-Based Learning program. Prior to joining the HBS faculty, she was on the faculty of the University of Michigan, University of Washington and University of Arizona. In addition to her academic positions, Lynda worked at Ford Motor Company in the 1960s and in the health care industry in the 1970s.

Lynda's research and recent publications focus on the impact of information technology-and more recently, the Internet-on industries, markets and organizations. She is the author of 2 books, over 40 articles and book chapters, and 200 published case studies on this subject. Her online course, Building E-Businesses, was the first distance learning program available through the school's newly-launched Harvard Business School Interactive unit and through HBS Publishing.

In 1999, Lynda was awarded Harvard Business School's prestigious Apgar Award for Innovation in Teaching, and in 1992, she was awarded the School's Berol Award for research excellence. A recent paper on 21st century business models was selected for presentation at the "Best Papers" session at the Academy of Management annual meeting, and a second paper was selected for presentation at the keynote session of the International Conference on Information Technology and Emergent Forms of Organization. She also won two "Best Paper" awards at the International Conference on System Sciences for papers describing the impact of information technology on group processes and decisions.

Lynda is an active international consultant, is on the board of directors of both public and venture-backed companies, and has served as an advisor and advisory board member for a number of entrepreneurial ventures. She is a member of the Advisory Council for NASDAQ and serves on the advisory board to Comptroller General of the U.S., David Walker. Lynda also serves on the advisory board for the World Bank's Global Development Gateway. During the late 1990s, Lynda participated on a Blue-Ribbon Panel to define a National Research Agenda on the Information Age Economy, and participated in a roundtable of advisors to President Clinton's Commission on Critical Infrastructure Protection.

Robert D. Austin

Robert D. Austin joined the Harvard Business School faculty in 1997 and currently teaches the first year course in Technology and Operations Management. During a recent leave of absence (2000-2001), he served as a senior executive for a new business being incubated by a leading technology company.

Before coming to Harvard, Robert was a technology implementation manager for the Ford Motor Company's European and Emerging Market operations. During ten years with Ford, he was involved in development, implementation, and support of IT applications in a variety of businesses, including aftersales service, parts operations, consumer credit, vehicle assembly, and technical support services. He has participated on Software Process Measurement and National Software Capacity Study teams at the Software Engineering Institute.

Robert earned his Ph.D. in Management and Decision Sciences from Carnegie Mellon University, where his dissertation received the Herbert A. Simon Award and was a finalist in the Association for Public Policy Analysis and Management's National Dissertation competition. He holds an M.S. in Industrial Engineering from Northwestern University and bachelors degrees in Engineering and English Literature from Swarthmore College, where he was elected to Phi Beta Kappa and Tau Beta Pi.

Robert's research focuses on information technology management, and more generally on management of knowledge intensive activities. He has written on these subjects in a book (*Measuring and Managing Performance in Organizations*) and in academic and trade journals.

F. Warren McFarlan

Warren McFarlan is Senior Associate Dean and Director of Harvard Business School's Asia-Pacific Initiative. He teaches in the Advanced Management Program, Delivering Information Services Program and several of the Social Sector programs.

In 1973, shortly after his appointment to full professor he, along with four other faculty members, was sent to Switzerland to set up the School's International Senior Management Program. He returned from Switzerland in 1975 to become Chairman of the Advanced Management Program, a position he held until 1978; and Chairman of all Executive Education Programs from 1977-1980. He was Senior Associate Dean and Director of Research from 1991 to 1995, and Senior Associate Dean and Director of External Relations from 1995-2000.

Warren earned his AB from Harvard University in 1959, and his MBA and DBA from the Harvard Business School in 1961 and 1965 respectively. He has had a significant role in introducing materials on Management Information Systems to all major programs at the Harvard Business School since the first course on the subject was offered in 1962.

Warren's newest book, *Corporate Information Systems Management: The Issues Facing Senior Executives,* (fifth edition), co-authored with Professors Lynda M. Applegate and James L. McKenney, appeared in 1999. "Working on Nonprofit Boards: Don't Assume the Shoe Fits" appeared in the November/December 1999 issue of the *Harvard Business Review.* He is editor of *Information Systems Research Challenge,* published by the *Harvard Business School Press,* 1984. He served a three-year term as Senior Editor of the MIS Quarterly (1986-1988). He is a member of several corporate and non-profit boards.

Creating Business Advantage in the Information Age examines how contemporary information technology (IT) enables organizations to conduct business in radically different and more effective ways. The commercialization of the Internet has created seismic change in the business environment. New channels of supply and distribution are emerging. New electronic marketplaces and exchanges are being created. The infrastructures of firms and the industries within which they operate have been permanently altered.

This is a fast moving and global phenomenon. For established companies the resulting challenges have been deep and pervasive. In many cases, the changes have threatened not just a firm's competitiveness but also its survival. Executives bear an enormous burden as they attempt to understand the challenges, keep abreast of events, and make intelligent decisions and plans.

The objective of the book is to provide readers with a better understanding of the influence of 21st century technologies on business decisions. The book discusses today's challenges from the point of view of the executives who are grappling with them. It recounts stories of success and failure, focusing on the issues faced and decisions made by executives in fifteeen different companies located around the world.

The cases presented here are organized in four Modules that correspond to issues that business and IT executives must confront. The first Module is aimed at understanding the challenges and opportunities embodied by IT and how these have changed in recent years. The second Module is concerned with the new business models, channels, and sources of value that derive from the new technologies and the emergence of the commercial Web. Module 3 focuses on issues of execution, on how to manage the tangled issues at the boundary of business and technology, so that everything works when it's supposed to. Module 4 concentrates on implementation—not a new IT issue, but more important than ever in an era where most work is project work. A final section and case pull it all together—the possibilities, the business models, the operations, and the implementation—into a summary discussion of the many and diverse global issues that face IT managers in the 21st century.

The material presented here is the outgrowth of direct field-based research we have conducted at the Harvard Business School since the early 1970s. To both Dean John McArthur and Dean Kim Clark we express our appreciation for making the time and resources available for us to complete this work.

We are particularly indebted to the companies and government organizations that provided so much time and insight during the course of our research. All of the cases in this book are based on observation of actual practice in real organizations. Without the cooperation of many executives, preparation of this book would not have been possible.

We are grateful as well for the many valuable suggestions and insights provided by our Harvard Business School colleagues, especially Jim Cash, Alan MacCormack, Andrew McAfee, Richard Nolan, Kash Rangan and David Upton. In addition, we acknowledge the valued work of our doctoral students, fellows, and researcher assistants. Our heartfelt thanks go to Nancy Bartlett, Meredith Collura, Mark Cotteleer, Melissa Dailey, Legrand Elebash, Cedric Escalle, Evelyn Goldman, Kristin Kohler, David Lane, Marc Mandel, Felipe Monteiro, Tom Rodd, Deb Sole, George Westerman, and Fred Young. We also acknowledge the support of the directors of HBS' research centers, including Christina Darwall of the California Research Center, Gustavo Herrero, Director of the Latin America Research Center, Camille Tang Yeh, Director of the Asia Pacific Center, and Carin Knoop, Executive Director of Global Research. Finally, we express our appreciation to our editor, Tom Cameron, and to Maureen Donovan, Brooke Spangler, and Maurie SuDock, who provided administrative support.

Lynda M. Applegate
Robert D. Austin
F. Warren McFarlan

BRIEF CONTENTS

CONTENTS

MODULE THREE

Information Age Operations

Cases

MODULE FOUR

Managing Information Age Projects and Programs

Cases

CONCLUDING THOUGHTS   381

Case

INTRODUCTION

Information technology has always been a wildcard in business, a source of opportunity and uncertainty, of advantage and risk. To business managers, IT has often seemed to be a realm of eye-glazing, mind-numbing, tech-speaking wizards with magic so powerful they cannot always control it. Since the 1970s (if not before), managers have encountered situations like one recently described by a technology company executive:

> We were two months into it, and I was on my hands and knees with the Chief Technology Officer saying, "Please, please, please, how can we get this launched on time?" None of that elegant business school theory seemed relevant. It was all about what we could get the technology to do.

Another business manager regarded her own similar experiences as an inevitable moment in the life of every manager foolhardy enough to become involved in an IT project:

> There's that point about two and a half months in when the IT guy comes to you sheepishly and says, "Well, you know what? This is going to be a little harder than I thought."

And yet we have, since the inception of business computing, tightened our embrace of IT, and for good reason. Despite exasperating in-process moments, it has been the most reliable font of transformational capabilities and revolutionary improvement for almost four decades.

The recent decade has added considerably to the mystique and the magic of IT. Something big happened to the world in the 1990s, although it is probably too early to discern the full impact. The first time we opened *Wired* and encountered pages of glossy ads for "nerdy" products, it struck us as incongruous, but it also told us that the world was changing.

Then came the boom of the late 1990s, when the tech market surged only skyward. Stories of IT businesses born on napkins, investors demanding that

1

their money be spent quickly, rapid-fire IPOs, and youthful billionaires left us perplexed. Then, as the new century dawned, everything came way, way back down. The tech-heavy NASDAQ lost more than half its value, and spending for IT equipment and services softened dramatically, ruthlessly culling the excesses of previous months and punishing even Cisco.

Some young managers came of age during the boom, and for a time it seemed they would have an advantage. When it all fell apart, though, managers young and old found themselves in pretty much the same situation, feeling a little like the drivers at a recent auto race in Texas on a new, steeply banked track: forces in excess of five Gs caused them to nearly black out while they were driving their cars.[1] Business managers can perhaps be excused if they feel as if they missed much of the backstretch.

Some things are clear. The world is forever changed. IT has burst forth from its safe containment in the IT department. The technology has become a core enabler, in some cases the conduit through which a new kind of business is done. The world is smaller and internationally more people are participating in online commerce. Physical location matters less than it did. Borders and boundaries, ownership and control have become more ambiguous. In areas like intellectual property, the development of commercial structures has far out-paced legal and regulatory structures. And there is much still to be done with the IT magic. The glossy ads in *Wired* are now commonplace and are now found in the business stalwarts like *The Wall Street Journal*.

Because so much has changed so quickly, because the ups and downs have come in such a short interval, now is a difficult time to engage in sense-making. And yet that is precisely what we are doing here, in this book. We're putting together "elegant business school theory" with decades of practical lessons learned from those who are creating the future. Our objective is to help executives get past the exasperating in-process moments and move on to the transformational capabilities and revolutionary improvements.

As we work toward this objective, we draw on years of research and experience, much of it in the field with companies in their transformational throes. This book is filled with their stories, cases from the front lines of the recent revolution. All are from the last decade. The vast majority are set in this new century. The last five years have been the richest vein of potential learning we have ever been positioned to mine. It was a period of intense experimentation. Many things were tried. Much of it failed. Some of it succeeded. We would be remiss if we did not set ourselves quickly to the task of understanding it all—the successes and the failures.

The content presented here is organized into the four modules. Each module includes an overview and a series of case studies that highlight the

---

[1] The 2001 Firestone Firehawk 600 at the Texas Motor Speedway was cancelled when 21 of 25 drivers experienced "disorientation" and "gray outs" during practice laps at more than 230 mph. See David Green, "Race Cancellation Justified," *The Sporting News,* April 30, 2001.

issues managers face when attempting to create business advantage in the Information Age.

- *Module 1: The Challenges of Managing in an Information Age* examines how the Internet and associated technologies of the 21st century influence market structure, market dynamics, and competitive positioning. It presents frameworks for analyzing IT-related opportunities and risks.
- *Module 2: Building Information Age Businesses* explores how emerging e-business models are revolutionizing the way business is conducted around the world. Portals, aggregators, exchanges, and marketplaces are but a few of the models examined. The in-depth analysis provides the foundation for discussion of business strategy, capabilities, value creation, and business model evolution in the Information Age.
- *Module 3: Information Age Operations* deals with hands-on, frontline issues of execution. It examines how the evolving IT infrastructure affects business operations and decisions and how executive priorities and responsibilities must shift to exploit opportunities and reduce operating risk.
- *Module 4: Managing Information Age Projects and Programs* provides a detailed look at factors that contribute to the success of projects and transformational programs. It includes advice and case material on managing major outsourcing programs that are an increasingly prevalent means of achieving organizational transformation.

A conclusion and a final case integrate the themes of the four modules and provide readers with an opportunity for synthesis.

We begin with Charles Schwab. The two Schwab cases[2] present a compelling and exciting story of strategic decision making, strategy execution, and risk. The cases show how Schwab, a mid-size player in the discount brokerage industry, was able to counter the threat of the new entrants, E-Trade and Ameritrade, while simultaneously and successfully competing against industry leader, Merrill Lynch.

---

[2]N. Tempest, and F.W. McFarlan, *Charles Schwab Corporation (A)*, (HBS Order No. 300-024) and *Charles Schwab Corporation (B)*, (HBS Order No. 300-025)

CASE I–1
CHARLES SCHWAB CORPORATION (A)[1]

David Pottruck, co-CEO of The Charles Schwab Corporation (Schwab), returned to his office in late 1997 after a long afternoon meeting with Charles Schwab—the company's founder, chairman, and co-CEO. It was the third meeting over the last several weeks on the same topic—should Schwab offer significantly discounted Internet trading to its entire customer base, accompanied by the full complement of Schwab customer service options? Schwab already offered customers two Internet trading options. The first option was Internet trading with full access to all of Schwab's customer service channels for around $64 per trade (a 20% discount off the standard retail commission of $80 per trade). The second option was Internet trading through the company's e.Schwab product, which offered a significantly discounted price of $29.95 per trade, but curtailed the level and type of customer service e.Schwab customers could receive. For example, e.Schwab customers were allowed only one free call per month to a live customer service representative; all other requests had to be handled via e-mail. Furthermore, Schwab's branch employees couldn't provide service to e.Schwab customers because they didn't have access to e.Schwab account information. Having helped Schwab earn a reputation for high-quality customer service, Schwab's customer service representatives weren't comfortable with the distinction in service that the e.Schwab product created. Interestingly, while some e.Schwab customers

also complained about it, most accepted it as the price they had to pay for low-priced trading. In fact, the total number of online accounts at Schwab[2] had doubled in the past year to 1.2 million, or 25% of Schwab's total, accounting for $81 billion in customer assets by December 1997.

Not only was Schwab's online business growing, but its offline business was also growing. In fact, Schwab's total revenues and net income had enjoyed annual growth rates of 24% and 23%, respectively, over the past four years. Even though a host of deep-discount online brokerages, such as E*Trade and AmeriTrade, had burst onto the scene beginning in 1995—with commissions as low as $8 per trade—Schwab had been able to grow its business by differentiating itself on the basis of innovative products and superior customer service. As a result, there appeared to be no immediate threat to Schwab's core business.

However, Pottruck and Charles Schwab wondered how long Schwab could justify its standard retail commission of $80[3] per trade—or its full-service Internet commission of $64 per trade—as more and more brokerages began to offer deeply discounted Internet trading, some for as low as $8 per trade. They were also concerned that the distinction in service created by their more heavily discounted e.Schwab product ran counter to the firm's founding proposition that customers shouldn't have to choose between price and service. Yet,

---

[1]This case was prepared by Associate Director of the HBS California Research Center Nicole Tempest under the supervision of Professor F. Warren McFarlan. Copyright © 1999 by the President and Fellows of Harvard College.
Harvard Business School case 300-024.

[2]Including e.Schwab and the company's other online products.
[3]Schwab's average commission for a trade placed through a "live" broker was $80 per trade. Customers trading via Schwab's automated touch-tonc phone, online software, or the Internet received a 10% to 20% discount from the "live broker" price. Customers trading via e.Schwab paid $29.95 per trade.

if Schwab decided to offer customers significantly discounted Internet trades *and* access to its full slate of customer service options, the firm risked enormous cannibalization of its offline business and its full-service online business, as customers migrated to the lower-priced Internet channel. In fact, an internal analysis suggested that projected cannibalization would cost the firm $125 million in revenue—most of which would fall directly to the bottom line—resulting in a pre-tax profit impact of at least $100 million the first year, or 22% of Schwab's projected 1997 pre-tax profit. Furthermore, due to a legacy commission system, Schwab had virtually no flexibility in the short term to tweak its commission structure in other areas to make up for the profit hit. While Schwab's experience with its e.Schwab product suggested that lower commissions did drive higher trading volume, it was not clear whether customers who were *given* the $29.95 option—rather than *asking* for it—would demonstrate this same behavior.

Pottruck knew that a projected $100 million hit to earnings would not be well received by Wall Street or Schwab's employees, who owned a substantial 40% of the company. However, as the brokerage industry moved increasingly toward the Internet, Pottruck wondered if it were just a matter of time before Schwab would have to take the plunge. If that were the case, acting quickly might give Schwab a competitive advantage.

Company Background

Based in San Francisco, Schwab was launched in 1975 by Charles Schwab, who seized the opportunity to start the world's first discount brokerage firm after the Securities and Exchange Commission abolished fixed-rate commissions on brokerage trades. Schwab's decision to pioneer the discount brokerage concept was driven by his objection to the conflict of interest inherent in the traditional full-service brokerage business—where brokers were paid a commission on each trade, as opposed to being rewarded for doing what was in the best interest of the customer. Schwab's strategy was to empower the individual investor by offering unbiased products and services at discounted prices. Unlike full-service brokerage firms, Schwab did not actively manage portfolios, make investment recommendations, offer proprietary research, or offer actively managed proprietary products. Rather, it offered a wide variety of third-party investment alternatives and provided generalized investment advice. To ensure that there was no conflict of interest between brokers' incentives and customer interests, Schwab paid its brokers a salary plus bonus, as opposed to commissions on trades. The bonus was determined by performance against a number of team-based measures, including business development, client satisfaction, and productivity. As a reflection of its strategy, Schwab's vision was "to be the most useful and ethical provider of financial services in the world."

While Schwab initially attracted customers who felt they had been "burned" by traditional full-service brokers, the company quickly developed a more mainstream following; by 1982 it had grown to $54 million in revenues. In 1983, BankAmerica bought Schwab for $57 million. However, a four-year clash between the entrepreneurial culture at Schwab and the more conservative culture at Bank of America persuaded Charles Schwab to lead a $280 million management-led buyout of the firm in 1987. Schwab went public later that year in a transaction that valued the firm at $450 million. Between 1988 and 1997 Schwab grew from $18 billion in customer assets to $354 billion—a 39% compound annual growth rate (CAGR)—and from $267 million in revenue to $2.3 billion—a 27% CAGR. Similarly, Schwab's full-time equivalent employees grew from 2,200 in 1988 to 12,700 in 1997 (see Exhibit 1 for selected financial and operating data). By December 1997, Schwab had a market value of almost $11 billion.

EXHIBIT 1 10-Year Selected Financial and Operating Data (in millions, except per share amounts, ratios, number of branches, average commissions, and as noted.)

	1997[a]	1996	1995
Operating results			
Revenues	$2,299	$1,851	$1,420
Expenses excluding interest	1,852	1,457	1,143
Net income	270	234	173
Basic earnings per share[b, c]	1.03	0.90	0.67
Diluted earnings per share[b, c]	0.99	0.87	0.64
Weighted-average number of common shares outstanding[b, d]			
Trading revenues as a % of revenues[e]	62%	65%	66%
Non-trading revenues as a % of revenues[e]	38%	35%	34%
Performance measures			
Revenue growth	24%	30%	33%
Pre-tax profit margin	19.5%	21.3%	19.5%
After-tax profit margin	11.8%	12.6%	12.2%
Return on stockholders' equity	27%	31%	31%
Financial condition (at year end)			
Total assets	$16,482	$13,779	$10,552
Borrowings	361	284	246
Stockholders' equity	1,145	855	633
Customer information (at year end)			
Schwab active customer accounts	4.8	4.0	3.4
Schwab customer assets ($Bil)	$354	$253	$182
SchwabFunds assets ($Bil)[f]	55.8	43.1	31.7
Mutual Fund OneSource assets ($Bil)[g]	56.6	39.2	23.9
Mutual Fund Marketplace assets ($Bil)[g]	104.6	74.6	50.0
Active independent investment managers (M)	5.3	4.8	5.6
Independent investment manager client accounts (M)	547.2	442.2	390.6
Independent investment manager client assets ($Bil)	105.8	72.9	50.6
Number of domestic branches	272	235	226
Employee information			
Full-time equivalent employees at year end (M)	12.7	10.4	9.2
Revenues per average full-time equivalent employee ($M)	198	190	185
Compensation and benefits expense as a % of revenues	41.8%	41.4%	41.8%
Customers' daily average trading volume[h]			
Daily average revenue trades	71.8	54.0	40.8
Mutual Fund OneSource trades	34.2	27.2	17.8
Total daily average trades	106.0	81.2	58.6
Average commission per revenue trade	$ 64.27	$ 69.08	$ 73.11

Certain prior years' revenues and expenses have been reclassified to conform to the 1997 presentation.

[a]1997 includes charges for a litigation settlement of $24 million after-tax ($.09 per share for both basic and diluted earnings per share).

[b]Reflects the September 1997 three-for-two common stock split.

[c]Both basic and diluted earnings per share are net of the effect of an extraordinary charge in 1993 of $.03 per share.

[d]Amounts shown are used to calculate diluted earnings per share.

[e]Trading revenues include commission and principal transaction revenues. Non-trading revenues include mutual fund service fees, net interest revenue, and other revenues.

1994	1993	1992	1991	1990	1989	1988
$1,065	$965	$750	$570	$387	$346	$267
841	758	604	482	358	313	254
135	118	81	49	17	19	7
0.53	0.45	0.31	0.19	0.07	0.07	0.03
0.51	0.44	0.31	0.19	0.06	0.07	0.03
67%	75%	76%	72%	64%	67%	70%
33%	25%	24%	28%	36%	33%	30%
10%	29%	32%	47%	12%	30%	−28%
21.1%	21.4%	19.5%	15.5%	7.5%	9.6%	5.0%
12.7%	12.2%	10.8%	8.7%	4.3%	5.5%	2.8%
32%	37%	35%	28%	10%	11%	5%
$7,918	$6,897	$5,905	$5,026	$4,188	$3,480	$2,533
171	185	152	119	126	131	132
467	379	259	200	154	172	159
3.0	2.5	2.0	1.6	1.4	1.3	1.2
$123	$96	$66	$48	$31	$25	$18
23.3	15.8	11.4	8.5	6.9	5.3	3.8
12.5	8.3	1.8				
31.0	24.9	11.5	6.1	2.6	2.1	1.4
4.8	4.3	3.2	2.3	2.0	0.8	0.3
301.1	216.4	133.3	87.1	57.5	29.9	15.2
32.6	22.9	13.3	8.3	4.2	2.3	1.0
208	198	175	158	129	110	110
6.5	6.5	4.6	3.9	3.0	2.8	2.2
170	179	169	162	131	132	117
41.1%	40.7%	40.9%	41.1%	40.0%	37.8%	35.6%
29.5	28.1	22.4	17.8	12.9	11.9	10.1
14.3	7.4	1.4	0.3			
43.8	35.5	23.8	18.1	12.9	11.9	10.1
$ 72.68	$ 76.75	$ 77.12	$ 77.18	$ 76.02	$ 77.23	$ 73.10

[f]Includes money market, equity, and bond funds. Schwab's money market funds were introduced in January 1990. Reporting periods prior to January 26, 1990 represent customer investments in certain money market funds of another mutual fund provider available through Schwab.

[g]Excludes money market funds and all of Schwab's proprietary money market, equity, and bond funds.

[h]Daily average revenue trades have been restated to include all customer trades (both domestic and international) that generate either commission revenue or revenue from principal markups. Mutual Fund OneSource trades are primarily executed through Schwab's Mutual Fund OneSource service. This data is reported in thousands on a trade date basis for 1995 to 1997, and settlement date basis prior to 1995.

Source: Charles Schwab 1997 Annual Report.

A number of other discount brokerages entered the market in the 1970s and 1980s, putting pressure on commissions. Schwab's response was to differentiate itself through innovative products and services and to use technology to both generate productivity improvements and to develop superior customer service. As part of its focus on customer service, Schwab pursued a multi-channel strategy—including branch offices, telephone-based brokerage services, and online trading—to address customers' needs for convenience.

Schwab opened its first branch in Sacramento, California in 1975. By December 1997, Schwab operated 272 domestic branch offices in 47 states; the company estimated that approximately 70% of the U.S. population lived within 10 miles of a Schwab branch. While the branches initially played an important servicing role, over time a significant percentage of routine customer service requests (e.g., quotes, balances, positions, trades) had migrated to the telephone and online service channels. As a result, the branches had more time to focus on opening accounts, assisting customers with more complex transactions, and providing customers with investment coaching. In fact, while 40% of all trades were made at branches in 1991, that figure had dropped to 5% by the end of 1997, resulting in a 50% reduction in the cost of processing trades. However, branches continued to play an important role in new account generation, even for customers signing up for online trading. Schwab estimated that 86% of its new online accounts were opened in a branch. Susanne Lyons, president of Schwab's retail client services division, explained:

> Customers want to kick the tires before opening an account. They want to see that there's a *real* building with *real* people who look reputable before handing over a check.

Pottruck added:

> Our branches distinguish us from the other online brokerages. Our customers have higher average balances

than customers of the pure[4] online brokerages do, and that's in part due to our branch system. People aren't going to put a $500,000 check in the mail; they just don't do that. New customers that come into our branches want to hand a real person their money, look that person in the eye, and know something about how that person is going to serve them. They want to have a sense of the company's commitment to them, and our branch personnel provide that.

To service its customers via phone, Schwab offered both an automated phone service and access to "live" customer service representatives. Schwab's automated TeleBroker phone service enabled customers to place trades, check account status, and get quotes without talking to a customer service representative. To provide live customer support, Schwab operated four 24-hour-a-day, 7-day-a-week regional customer service centers, located in Indianapolis, Denver, Phoenix, and Orlando. In 1997, over 1,500 employees worked in these centers, handling approximately 150,000 calls per week related to trading, quotes, and general inquiries. Customer service representatives were fully equipped with online computer terminals that enabled them to access account information and place orders online.

Industry Background

The abolishment of fixed-rate brokerage commissions opened the door to the discount delivery channel for retail trading services. Prior to this time, only one type of brokerage existed—the full service brokerage—that charged relatively high commissions, but offered investment recommendations, research, and proprietary products in return. Examples of the better known, full-service brokerages included Merrill Lynch and Paine Webber. After Schwab introduced the concept of a discount brokerage, a host of other players entered the market, including Quick & Reilly, Fidelity, and Waterhouse Securities. While

---

[4]Referring to online brokerages that did not have branch offices.

commissions varied by brokerage and by size of trade, a 1997 survey showed that a 200-share trade of a $20 stock cost on average $117 at a full-service brokerage, compared with $66 at a discount brokerage—representing a 44% discount.

As consumer interest in and comfort with "self-directed" investing grew, so too did discount brokerages. As a reflection of that trend, discount brokerage firms' share of total retail brokerage commissions grew from 1% in 1980 to 14% in 1997[5] (see Exhibit 2). Not only did discount brokerages gain share over this period, but they did so profitably. In fact, the average pre-tax margin for discount brokerages ranged from 15% to 19% between 1991 and 1996, while the pre-tax margin for the brokerage industry as a whole never exceeded 16% during the same period, and dropped to as low as 2% in 1994 (see Exhibit 3)[6] By 1997, there were an estimated 12 million to 14 million discount brokerage accounts, compared with 40 million to 45 million full-service brokerage accounts.

---

[5]Data limited to NYSE member discounters vs. all NYSE members. "Charles Schwab: Winning Through Asset Accumulation," Morgan Stanley Dean Witter U.S. Investment Research Report, May 8, 1998.

[6]"Online Brokerage," ABN AMRO Industry Research Report, August 13, 1997.

EXHIBIT 2   Discount Brokerage Firms' Share of Total Retail Brokerage Commissions[a]

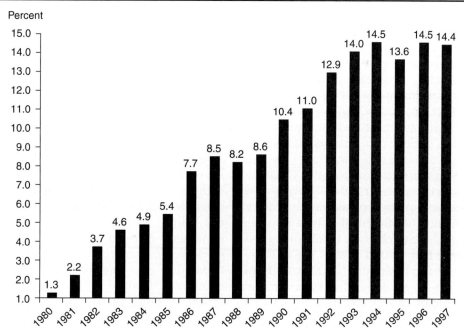

[a]Based on net revenue. NYSE member discounters vs. all other NYSE.
Source: "Charles Schwab: Winning Through Asset Accumulation." Morgan Stanley Dean Witter, May 18, 1998. From the SIA Fact Book.

EXHIBIT 3   Brokerage Pre-tax Profit Margins[a]

Year	Discounter	Total Brokerage
1989	9.4%	5.2%
1990	7.8%	−0.5%
1991	16.3%	14.0%
1992	16.0%	13.2%
1993	18.8%	15.3%
1994	15.1%	2.4%
1995	19.1%	12.7%
1996	16.7%	15.9%

[a]Based on net revenue.
Source: "Online Brokerage. Internet Leads to Secular Growth Opportunities for Online Brokers." ABN-AMRO Chicago Corporation. August 13, 1997.

Schwab's History of Innovation and Technology

Schwab's Role as a Product and Services Innovator. After pioneering the concept of a discount brokerage firm, Schwab continued to develop new products and services to meet its customers needs, earning the company a reputation for being highly innovative. As one industry analyst commented: "We view them [Schwab] as perpetually having next year's model. They see trends early, execute well, and get in with a sizable market position."[7]

Examples of Schwab's product and service innovations abounded. Schwab was the first discount brokerage to open a branch office and the first to offer 24-hour-a-day, 7-day-a-week order entry and quote services. Perhaps one of the best examples of Schwab's focus on innovation was the launch of its OneSource product. Schwab had offered a wide range of no-load mutual funds through its Mutual Fund Marketplace since 1984; however, Schwab charged customers a transaction fee on each purchase or sale of these funds to cover its accounting and processing costs. As investor interest in mutual funds soared, Schwab decided to augment its mutual fund offerings, and in 1992 the company introduced its OneSource product—the industry's first no-transaction-fee mutual fund "supermarket." OneSource gave customers access to hundreds of no-load mutual funds from dozens of fund families and simplified investor record keeping by consolidating mutual fund account information on one consolidated Schwab statement. Instead of charging a transaction fee, Schwab earned a 35-basis-point fee on assets under management from participating funds, in return for marketing, distribution, and accounting services. In less than five years, OneSource garnered the number three position among direct mutual fund distributors, behind industry heavyweights Fidelity and Vanguard. While Schwab's margins on its mutual fund business were lower than the commission rate it generated on trades, the increase in the volume of business that the mutual fund products generated more than made up for the lower margins. As Pottruck noted: "In the beginning, OneSource was not a very profitable product for us, but it brought a lot of business, which on the whole was quite profitable."[8]

This was not the only time Schwab succeeded by taking the lower margin route. In March 1992, Schwab dropped its $22 annual fee on Individual Retirement Accounts (IRA) with balances of $10,000 or more. By December 1994, Schwab's IRA assets had doubled to $33 billion. Later, in August 1994, Schwab announced it would reinvest dividends in any stock owned by one of its customers for free, as opposed to charging a fee for this service as many of Schwab's competitors did. While the company anticipated slightly higher costs

---

[7]"Doing it the Schwab Way," *US Banker,* July 1998, p. 47.

[8]"Cyber-Schwab," *Forbes,* May 5, 1997, p. 42.

from this service, Charles Schwab believed "it will attract more customers and, in the long run, we will get paid for it."[9]

Schwab's History of Technology Innovation. From its early days, Schwab took advantage of its proximity to Silicon Valley to embrace technology. As Dan Leemon, Schwab's chief strategy officer, noted, "At its core, Schwab is really a technology company that happens to be in the financial services business." Pottruck added:

> We have a culture that embraces technology as the core of our business. To us, technology is not a channel; it's the air we breathe. We think about our business as a human-technology partnership.

Schwab's use of technology helped the company develop state-of-the-art products and customer service. As Pottruck explained, "Schwab takes a high-tech, high-touch approach to the brokerage business." Technology also enabled the company to achieve significant productivity improvements over the years, which was necessary to maintain profits in the face of persistent downward pressure on commissions. For example, in 1992, each $100 of Schwab's customer assets generated $1.14 in revenue and $.92 in expenses. By 1997, revenue per $100 in assets had fallen to $.65—a 43% drop—but expenses had also declined by 43% to $.52, thereby maintaining Schwab's 20% margin.

Evidence of Schwab's technological leadership dates back to the 1970s. At that time, when a customer placed a trade, Schwab would have to wait for confirmation back from the relevant exchange that the trade had gone through, and then call the customer back to confirm. Schwab quickly realized that not only would customers prefer automatic trade confirmations, but the cost of making return confirmation phone calls was significant. As a

result, the company redesigned the system so that Schwab was in direct contact with the exchanges, allowing for immediate trade confirmations. Under the new system, Schwab brokers could let customers know immediately that the trade had gone through, eliminating the need for—and cost of—a follow-up phone call.

In 1979, Schwab made its first major investment in technology by bringing its entire trade clearing system in house. During the 1970s, many financial institutions, including Schwab, were outsourcing their information technology (IT) function. However, Charles Schwab realized that Schwab would never be an innovation leader if it continued to depend on third parties for technology. As a result, Charles Schwab made a "bet the company" decision to spend $500,000 to bring Schwab's back office software in house at a time when the company had a net worth of just $500,000.

In 1985, Schwab made its first foray into the electronic brokerage channel with the introduction of its Equalizer product. In keeping with Schwab's original goal of empowering individual investors, the Equalizer product gave individual investors the same timely information and trading capabilities as the Wall Street pros. Equalizer was a DOS-based proprietary software package that customers loaded onto their computers using diskettes. Customers would then use dial-up lines to access the Schwab system to get up-to-the-minute research information (e.g., news, quotes, fundamental data, and company narrative summaries), review account information, download trade confirmations and transaction details, and make trades. Bill Ginnis, then head of Schwab's Technology Services Group, noted: "This is a first for the individual investor."[10] Schwab sold the Equalizer software

---

[9]"The Schwab Revolution," *Business Week,* December 19, 1994, p. 88.

[10]"Charles Schwab Launches Two Financial Programs," *PC Magazine,* May 28, 1985, p. 62.

to customers for $199 and charged small additional fees for many of the third-party services offered through the system (e.g., Standard & Poor's Marketscope, Dow Jones News, and custom company reports composed of data from S&P, Zacks, and Market Guide). While there were other online trading products on the market at the time, *PC Week's* 1985 review of Equalizer concluded, "There are no other software packages that allow you to put it all together the way this package does."[11] While Schwab later introduced several more sophisticated online trading products, there were around 800 households still using the original Equalizer product by the end of 1997.

In 1989, Schwab developed TeleBroker—its automated brokerage phone service. Trades conducted via the TeleBroker service received a 10% commission discount. By 1997, the Tele-Broker service averaged 5.7 million calls per month and accounted for approximately 13% of Schwab's trading volume. That same year, Schwab augmented the telephone channel with its Voice Broker service—a proprietary speech recognition program for checking stock quotes and mutual fund prices.

It wasn't until the fall of 1993 that Schwab introduced its next major online trading program, StreetSmart—the first trading product designed for Windows.[12] StreetSmart took advantage of the user interface advantages offered by Windows—including icons, floating menu bars, and pull-down menus—to make it easier for customers to trade stocks, bonds, and mutual funds online. StreetSmart was also fully compatible with the popular financial management software, Quicken. Schwab charged $59 for the StreetSmart software, but offered customers a discount of 10% off standard commissions for using it to place trades. By the end of 1995, over 200,000 of Schwab's 3.4 million accounts, or 6%, were using Street-Smart. While the product was well received by customers, it was a relatively costly endeavor from Schwab's perspective, as customer service representatives spent a significant amount of time helping customers with "ancillary questions" related to the Windows operating system and modem configurations.

By 1995, Schwab executives observed several factors which highlighted the growing importance of the online channel: customer response to StreetSmart was strong; online services—such as America Online—were growing rapidly; and Schwab was facing new competition from a number of deep discount brokerages who were reportedly pursuing Internet trading. As a result, in the spring of 1995, Schwab's management team decided to make a greater commitment to its emerging online channel, forming a separate project team to work on it. The team was set up as a skunkworks operation, reporting directly to Pottruck. Leemon explained the rationale:

> The decision was made at a senior level that if we were going to really develop an online business, we couldn't have it buried in retail where it would have to compete for funds with new branches, because on a net present value basis, branches would always come out on top. Instead, the senior management team decided that the online project team should be raised to the level of all the other business units, so that it would get the management attention and funding it needed.

Pottruck reflected on how competition from the start-up online brokerages also affected the decision: "We had to figure out a way to compete with these small brokerages. So we felt we needed a group that felt like they did: nimble and unshackled from the larger bureaucracy."[13]

---

[11]"Charles Schwab & Co.'s 'Equalizer': Stock Trading System is Direct Line to Market," *PC Week,* July 9, 1985, p. 55.
[12]StreetSmart for Macintosh was released in mid-1994.

[13]"Schwab Puts it All Online," *Fortune,* December 7, 1998, p. 94.

Beth Sawi, who was running Schwab's mutual fund business, volunteered to lead the online team, which later evolved into a separate business enterprise called Electronic Brokerage. Sawi's direction from Pottruck was to develop a discounted—$39.95 per trade—online product by the fall of 1995. The rest of the management team was taken aback by the plan for a $39.95 price point, since $39.95 was almost half of Schwab's standard price point. However, based on the company's experience with low-priced mutual funds and IRAs, Pottruck believed that there was significant price elasticity in the financial services market. He was confident that a lower price would result in a higher volume of trades.

In the fall of 1995, the team piloted e.Schwab—a diskette-based electronic software package, similar in many ways to StreetSmart. e.Schwab enabled customers to trade any security available through a regular Schwab account—including stocks, mutual funds, and options—by dialing into the Schwab system on a proprietary 1-800 number. The e.Schwab product offered a flat $39.95 commission for any stock trade up to 1,000 shares. However, it curtailed the level of service its customers could receive. For example, while e.Schwab customers could receive unlimited free service via e-mail, they were only allowed *one* free call to a live customer service representative per month—after that they would be charged. They also could not receive customer service at a Schwab branch, because the branches didn't have access to e.Schwab customer account information. Moreover, Schwab set up several hurdles to enrolling in the e.Schwab service. Schwab customers had to first open a separate e.Schwab account, and then they had to call Schwab to transfer funds from their regular Schwab account into their e.Schwab account. Schwab designed these "speedbumps" to address an underlying concern that with such an attractive price, the e.Schwab business might quickly cannibalize Schwab's core business, resulting in a 50% reduction in top-line revenue with no benefits to show for it. After pilot testing the product in Florida, Texas, and California, Schwab went national with the product in January 1996. As Leemon quipped: "One of the great axioms around Schwab is that a 'pilot' is really just the first couple months of a rollout." The only publicity the product received was an announcement at the company's annual shareholders' meeting. Even so, within two weeks of its launch, 25,000 customers had signed up for e.Schwab—the company's goal for the entire year.

Concurrent with the pilot of e.Schwab, San Francisco-based Lombard Institutional Brokerage (Lombard) introduced an Internet trading program, called List On-Line which charged $34 for trades up to 1,700 shares. While Lombard wasn't the first to introduce Internet trading (the discount brokerage firm, Aufhauser & Co., was recognized as the first in 1994), its success took the industry by surprise; within 4 months, nearly 12% of Lombard's trades were being made through its Web site. In November 1995, Los Angeles-based Pacific Brokerage Services began offering online trading over the Internet for $25 per trade for trades under 1,000 shares. Then in February 1996, E*Trade—which was originally established in 1983 to clear trades for discount brokers—began offering Internet trading for $14.95 per trade for trades of 5,000 shares or less. Many industry observers viewed the emergence of Internet trading as a threat to Schwab. As one noted: "What Schwab did to the full-service firms, Lombard and E*Trade will do to Schwab and the full-service firms."[14]

Annoyed that Schwab hadn't pioneered the concept, Charles Schwab set forth a mandate to offer Internet trading by the end of the first quarter of 1996. In late March of that year,

---

[14]"With the World Wide Web, Who Needs Wall Street?" *Business Week,* April 29, 1996, p. 120.

Schwab introduced Internet trading to its e.Schwab customers for $39.95 per trade. Two months later, Schwab expanded its Internet channel by offering Internet trading to all of Schwab's full-service retail customers for a 10% discount off standard retail commissions. Then in August, Schwab lowered its e.Schwab commission from $39.95 to $29.95 to be more competitive with the new crop of online brokers. In a similar move, in December 1996, the company also increased the discount on its full-service Internet trading channel from 10% to 20% off standard retail commissions. Customer response to Schwab's Internet trading capability was strong—by December 1997, Schwab's online accounts had grown to 1.2 million (25% of the total), representing $81 billion in assets (23% of the total), up 94% in a one-year period[15] (see Exhibit 4).

Schwab's internal analysis on the impact of the $29.95 e.Schwab price point was encouraging. The company found that when customers went from paying $80 per trade to $29.95 per trade, their trading volume, on average, doubled (more for less active traders and less for more active traders). Where Schwab saw the greatest impact was in its moderate trading customers who went from making 4 to 5 trades per year to 10 to 11 trades per year. Of the new trades, about half

came from a "consolidation" of trades that previously had been made at other brokerages and the other half were truly new trades. Even more encouraging was the fact that the increase in trading volume appeared to remain consistent over time—it wasn't just a short-term "pop" due to the reduction in price.

Schwab's IT Infrastructure

IT Organization. In late 1997, Schwab's IT organization consisted of approximately 1,300 full-time equivalent employees. As a reflection of the importance of technology to the company, Dawn Lepore, the company's chief information officer (CIO), reported directly to Pottruck. Lepore shared "the office of the CIO" with Fred Matteson, executive vice president of technical services, and Geoffrey Penney, executive vice president of financial products and international technology. The IT organization was divided into two functional areas—a 700-person group that worked on centralized, corporate projects and a 600-person group of application engineers who aligned with Schwab's individual enterprises (e.g., electronic brokerage, retail, investment manager services). (See Exhibit 5 for Schwab's IT organization structure.) About 60% of the corporate project staff and almost all the application engineers worked in one of Schwab's offices in San Francisco. The remaining staff worked in the company's data centers and support centers across the United States.

---

[15]"Includes all of Schwab's online trading products.

EXHIBIT 4   Growth in Schwab's Online Accounts and Online Assets

Year	Total Active[a] Schwab Customer Accounts (mil)	Active[a] Online Customer Accounts (mil)	Total Assets in Schwab Customer Accounts ($Bil)	Assets in Schwab Online Customer Accounts ($Bil)
Dec–95	3.4	0.3	$181.7	$23.3
Dec–96	4.0	0.6	$253.2	$41.7
Dec–97	4.8	1.2	$353.7	$80.8

[a] "Active" defined as accounts that had balances or activity within the preceding 8 months.
Source: Charles Schwab 1997 Annual Report; Schwab Press Release July 31, 1997 and June 22, 1998.

EXHIBIT 5   Schwab's IT Organization

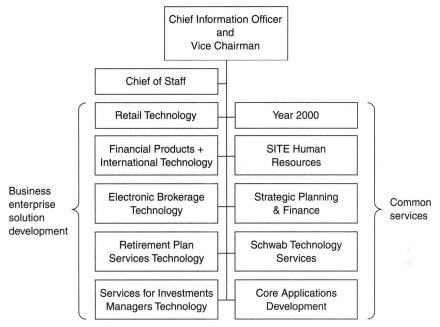

Source: Charles Schwab Corporation.

Schwab's IT organization operated under a two-pronged funding model. The centralized, corporate initiatives (e.g., networks, data centers, databases, distributed systems, desktops)—which accounted for approximately 80% of the total IT budget—were funded out of Schwab's corporate operating budget. The individual enterprise application initiatives were funded out of each enterprise's gross project dollars—defined as resources remaining after the enterprise had met its contribution commitment to the firm. As a result, the enterprises themselves could make their own decisions on whether to invest in additional IT applications. Matteson described the advantages of Schwab's IT's organizational structure: "We have a solid, well-funded, common infrastructure paired with nimble technology support groups that align with each individual enterprise's specific business requirements."

Schwab estimated that 70% of its IT staff were baby-boomers, 20% were "Gen-Xers," and the remaining 10% were from other demographic groups. The baby-boomer profile of Schwab's IT staff was somewhat unusual among Silicon Valley technology firms, which tended to be heavily staffed with Gen-Xers. Matteson explained the reason for the difference: "Schwab has grown so fast that our appetite for skilled talent has outstripped our ability to train it. As a result, we do very little hiring on college campuses; instead, we typically hire experienced staff from financial services firms and other high tech companies in the San Francisco Bay Area."

Responsibility for recruiting IT staff was shared by the vice president of human resources for technology—who reported to Schwab's centralized human resource department on a solid-line basis and into the IT group on a dotted-line basis—and the relevant hiring manager within the IT group. The vice president of human resources typically identified and screened candidates, while the hiring manager in the IT group typically conducted the interviews and made the final hiring decision. While Schwab favored hiring people with experience, the company still invested heavily in training, spending on average $2,000 per IT staff member per year.

IT Architecture.   Schwab's modular IT architecture was based on the premise that all front-end customer channels should access *consistent* back-end systems. Therefore, a key task of any application development project was to determine how to build a front-end system that could utilize existing back-end systems. The corporate projects IT group would then have to determine how to scale the back-end systems to handle the growth in front-end applications.

Schwab's back-end architecture consisted of three tiers: mainframes, middleware servers, and Web servers. In December 1997, Schwab had three "production" mainframes to handle transaction processing and back-office operations, one production mainframe for reporting purposes, and three other mainframes dedicated to functions such as back-up, development, and disaster recovery. The production mainframes were housed in two separate data centers, located 20 miles apart in Phoenix, Arizona. The company chose to co-locate the data centers in Phoenix in order to facilitate linking the two centers with high-speed fiber lines. In the event that one of the data centers went down, the high-speed fiber lines allowed transactions to be quickly re-routed to the other data center, thereby maintaining consistent customer service. To avoid the threat of both data centers going down simultaneously, Schwab designed them to be in separate power grids and flood plains, and to be routed through different telecommunication switching facilities. The company's goal was to design in as much diversity as possible so that the only way both data centers could go down simultaneously would be if something devastating happened to Phoenix as a whole.

Of Schwab's three mainframes dedicated to transaction processing and back-office operations, one ran on a legacy Datacom database and the other two ran on IBM's cutting edge DB2 database. The DB2 database leveraged IBM's "clustering technology," which allowed multiple mainframes to "look" like the same mainframe. This was especially important in situations where one of the mainframes went down; the DB2 database system allowed the workload to continue processing seamlessly on a different mainframe. Fortunately, Schwab's systems did not go down very often. In fact, Schwab's systems were available 99.2% of the time; unlike many firms, Schwab included both planned (e.g., site maintenance) and unplanned (e.g., technology failure) outages in its system downtime calculation.

The company also had eight middleware servers, which served as the conduit between all front-end applications and the corporate databases residing on the mainframes. One of the primary roles of the middleware servers was to validate a user's identity before granting access to the mainframe system. The final component of the back-end system was a series of 48 Web servers, which served two primary functions: processing communication with customers over the Web and conducting value-added processing on data obtained from the middleware servers and mainframes. (See Exhibit 6 for a diagram of Schwab's IT architecture.)

At the user level, all Schwab customer service representatives used desktop computers with the Windows NT operating system. In addition, all employees used the same e-mail and scheduling software. Finally, the company used one common voicemail system worldwide, which included a voice mail box for each employee.

EXHIBIT 6   Schwab's IT Architecture

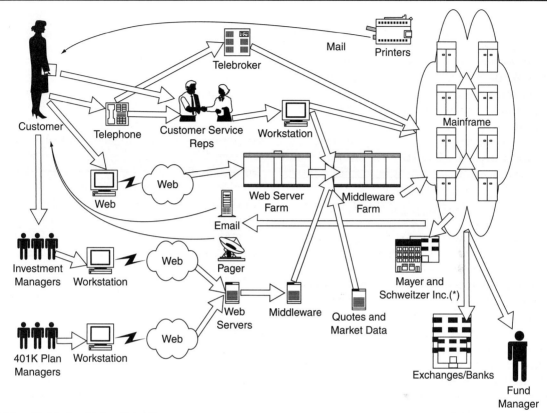

*Schwab's Market-Maker Subsidiary
Source: Charles Schwab Corporation

The Situation in 1997

Competition. By the end of 1997, as more and more investors gained Internet access and the longest-running bull market in history continued, interest in Internet trading soared. The number of firms offering Internet trading had increased from approximately 15 at the end of 1996 to almost 60 by the end of 1997. There were an estimated 3 million online brokerage accounts in 1997, and that number was projected to grow to 14.4 million by 2002, according to Forrester Research Inc. The firms that had gained the most notoriety in the Internet trading market were Schwab,

DLJdirect (a division of Donaldson Lufkin & Jenrette), E*Trade, Waterhouse Securities, AmeriTrade (which included the Accutrade, ebroker, and ceres brands), and Datek Securities. However, even with the entry of several online brokerage competitors, Schwab still maintained a healthy lead in terms of online accounts. Table A shows estimates for online account rankings in December 1997.

While the market was still early in its development, it was already segmenting into two categories: firms that were targeting the very price-sensitive Internet trader segment with deeply discounted commissions, and

TABLE A

	Number of Accounts
Online Brokerage	December 1997
Charles Schwab	1,200,000
DLJdirect	390,000
E*Trade	260,000
Waterhouse Securities	162,000
AmeriTrade	147,000
Datek Securities	55,000
Discover Brokerage Direct[a]	50,000[b]

[a]Formerly Lombard Brokerage. Dean Witter Discover acquired Lombard Brokerage in early 1997 and Dean Witter merged with Morgan Stanley later in 1997.
[b]As of June 1997.
Source: "Growth Surge Continues for Online Brokers," Credit Suisse First Boston Corporation, May 28, 1998.

TABLE B

Brokerage	*Commission*
Full-service average commission	$116.90[a]
Discount brokerage average commission	$66.09[b]
Commissions for Internet trades:	
Schwab	$29.95[c]
DLJdirect	$20.00[d]
E*Trade	$19.95/$14.95[e]
Quick & Reilly	$19.95/$14.95[f]
Fidelity	$19.95/$14.95[g]
Datek Securities	$9.99[h]
AmeriTrade	$8.00[i]
Suretrade	$7.95[j]

[a]On a 200-share trade of a $20 stock.
[b]On a 200-share trade of a $20 stock.
[c]$29.95 per trade for up to 1,000 shares; $.03 per share commission for every share over the first 1,000 shares.
[d]$20 for up to 1,000 shares; $.02 per share commission for every share over the first 1,000 shares.
[e]$14.95 for listed stocks; $19.95 for all OTC stock orders and limit orders on listed stocks; an additional $.01 per share on entire order for trades over 5,000 shares.
[f]$14.95 for market orders up to 1,000 shares; $19.95 for limit orders up to 1,000 shares; $.02 per share commission for every share over the first 1,000 shares.
[g]$19.95 for trades up to 1,000 shares for customers who make fewer than 36 trades per year; $14.95 for trades up to 1,000 shares for customers who make more than 36 trades per year and maintain an account balance of $20,000. An additional $.02 per share commission for each additional share over 1,000 shares.
[h]$9.99 for trades up to 5,000 shares; an additional $9.99 for each additional 5,000 shares.
[i]$8.00 per trade for market orders; $13 per trade for limit and stop orders.
[j]$7.95 per trade for market orders; $9.95 per trade for limit orders.
Source: CS First Boston, Company Reports; *Business Week,* December 8, 1997.

firms that were targeting the less price-sensitive Internet trader segment with slightly higher prices, but more value-added products and services. However, price competition was intensifying across the board. In June 1997, DLJdirect sparked a price war by cutting its commissions in half—to $20 per trade. In August, Fidelity set its first-ever Internet price at $28.95—about a third of its standard commission. Then in October, AmeriTrade ran an ad campaign promoting its $8 per trade commissions as "the lowest commission in the business." Soon after, Fidelity and Quick & Reilly cut their commissions to between $15–20 per trade. Later, in November, Quick & Reilly launched Suretrade—a deep-discount online brokerage that offered $7.95 commissions.

While many firms advertised a low "flat" rate commission, in reality additional charges were often assessed for trades over 1,000 shares, OTC trades, and limit orders. Prices were rapidly approaching the breakeven point; industry analysts believed that the marginal cost of completing a trade was between $3 to $5 for a self-clearing firm. Table B shows a comparison of commissions in December 1997.

While many new and existing players had entered the Internet trading market, the major Wall Street investment banks (with the exception of DLJ, which didn't have a large traditional broker force) had been notably absent. Investment banks had significantly higher cost structures than online brokers due to their large research, sales, and trading organizations. For example, Merrill Lynch had around 14,000 brokers and 600 professionals in its research group in 1997. As a result, they were very hesitant to offer lower-priced Internet trading due to fears of margin erosion resulting from large-scale cannibalization of their offline business. Moreover, the general sentiment among the major Wall Street investment banks was that their customers were more interested in the advice and proprietary products they could offer than the self-directed nature of online trading. Jay Mandelbaum, executive vice president for marketing at Smith Barney, voiced his opinion about Internet trading in 1996: "It's really not a concern. We find our investors want ongoing advice and service. Our clients don't want it [Internet trading]."[16]

John "Launny" Steffens, the head of Merrill Lynch's retail brokerage business, went so far as to say: "The do-it-yourself model of investing, centered on Internet trading, should be regarded as a serious threat to Americans' financial lives."[17]

The Wall Street investment banks also believed that their customer profile was different from the typical online investor profile. For example, the average Merrill Lynch customer was 52 years old and had $200,000 in household assets under management, whereas the average E*Trade customer was 39 years old and had an account balance of just $25,000. However, there were signs that a growing segment of full-service brokerage customers were also opening accounts at online brokerages to handle some of their trading. A Paine Webber

customer survey around this time showed that 8% of its customers had already opened an online account, and another 30% said they planned to open one within a year. Some industry analysts also believed that while younger and less wealthy, the online investor represented the next generation of investors.

The Internet Market. As one analyst summed up the Internet industry in 1997, "In biological terms, the industry morphed from infancy through childhood in 1997."[18] International Data Corp (IDC)—a leading research firm—estimated that the number of Internet users worldwide increased from 14 million in 1995 to 69 million in 1997—a five-fold increase over a two-year period.[19] No other mass medium in history had experienced the rapid adoption rate of the Internet.

While investors were interested in the Internet sector as a whole in late 1997, they were most enthralled with "portals"—Web sites that aggregated information and helped consumers navigate the Web. For most users, the first stop on the Internet was at a portal, such as AOL or Yahoo!. As a result, portals received a high number of visitors each day, which they depended on to support their primarily advertising-driven business models. Portals charged advertisers for placing ads on their site based on the number of consumer impressions the portal delivered. While portals were "hot" among investors in late 1997, e-commerce was just emerging as a credible channel. As one industry report noted:

> We look for a paltry $1 billion to $1.3 billion in e-commerce revenue for 1997. Compared with the trillion-dollar retail industry, this is barely a rounding error. While many traditional retailers have dipped their collective toes in the water, few have truly embraced the new medium. The competition between

[16]"With the World Wide Web, Who Needs Wall Street?" *Business Week,* April 29, 1996, p. 120.
[17]"Internet Trades Put Merrill Bull on Horns of Dilemma," *The Wall Street Journal,* February 12, 1999, p. C1.

[18]"The Second Annual Internet Top 10 List," Credit Suisse First Boston Research Report, January 21, 1998.
[19]IDC/LINK 1998.

Amazon and BarnesandNoble.com, the Internet's own version of Coke versus Pepsi, should have a positive effect on the medium as an e-commerce vehicle. We believe that these types of high-profile wars elevate the credibility of the industry.[20]

As a reflection of investor interest, portal companies were trading at an average of 14 times projected 1998 revenues compared with e-commerce companies (including online brokerages), which were trading at an average of 5 times 1998 revenues. In 1997, the two public "pure-play" online brokerages were E*Trade and AmeriTrade—both of which had generated profits, unlike many other companies competing in different Internet markets. E*Trade and AmeriTrade were trading at a multiple of 4.4 and 4.2 times revenue, respectively, compared to Schwab, which was trading at a multiple of 4.1 times revenue. Given the comparability of these multiples, it was not clear that Schwab would receive much of an "Internet trading premium" from pursuing an expanded Internet strategy. Furthermore, due to the intense price competition in the Internet trading market, the higher-priced players had come under pressure toward the end of 1997. For example, E*Trade—which went public in August 1996 at $10.50 per share—traded to a high of $47 per share in October 1997, before slipping to $20 per share in December 1997. Since AmeriTrade was already offering one of the lowest prices in the industry, the price war hadn't hurt it as much as E*Trade. After going public in March 1997 at $15 per share, AmeriTrade traded up to $33 per share before declining to $28 per share by mid-December.

Schwab's Performance. Schwab expected 1997 to be another good year for the firm. Revenues were projected to be $2.3 billion, and net income was projected to be 270 million, up 24% and 15%, respectively, from 1996. It was the third consecutive year that revenue growth had exceeded 20%. Customer accounts were projected to reach 4.8 million, up 20% from 1996, and customer assets were projected to reach $354 billion, up 40% from 1996. In fact, Schwab's customer assets had shown annual growth of 42% between 1990 and 1997, compared to 15% at Merrill Lynch and 18% at American Express Financial Advisors.[21] As a reflection of these results, Schwab's stock price had doubled during 1997, giving Schwab a market capitalization of almost $11 billion. Given Schwab's performance, there was no financial pressure pushing the company to take aggressive action in the Internet trading market.

The Decision on Whether to Take Action. However, by late 1997, Schwab's customer service representative had begun to voice their concern over the distinction in service created by the e.Schwab product. Sitting on the front lines, the customer service representatives were the ones who had to tell e.Schwab customers either that they couldn't help them or that they had to charge them for service. To Schwab's phone and branch representatives, the distinction in service ran counter to the company's values of being fair, empathetic, responsive, trustworthy, and teamwork-driven. Schwab had been founded on the idea that customers could get great service for a good price. Thus, forcing customers to choose between service and price ran counter to Schwab's founding principles.

Schwab believed that part of the customer confusion surrounding the e.Schwab product was due to the fact that it included the Schwab name in it. As a result, customers expected the product to come with Schwab's full menu of customer service options. As Len Short, Schwab's executive vice president of advertising and

---

[20]"The Second Annual Internet Top 10 List," Credit Suisse First Boston Research Report, January 21, 1998.

[21]"Charles Schwab: Winning through Asset Accumulation," Morgan Stanley Dean Witter U.S. Investment Research Report, May 18, 1998.

brand management, explained: "The moment the word Schwab was on it, that defined what we could do from a branding standpoint. If we had named it e.something else, we would have had an easier time marketing it as a discounted, limited-service channel, separate from Schwab."

Pottruck had also become increasingly uncomfortable with the distinction in service created by the e.Schwab product and believed that something needed to be done to resolve the situation. His instincts told him to do away with the distinction between e.Schwab and regular Schwab customers and offer *all* customers low-priced Internet trading with the full complement of Schwab's customer service options (e.g., branches, telephone, online). As he brainstormed the idea of an expanded Internet offering, Pottruck considered three price points—$39.95, $29.95, and $19.95. Interestingly, from a marketing standpoint, there appeared to be no room in between these prices. Pottruck's small team of advisors on the issue convinced him that Schwab's multichannel access, superior customer service, and broader selection of investment resources and products justified at least a $10 premium to the mid-priced online brokerages, such as E*Trade and DLJdirect, and a $20 premium to the bare-bones online players, such as Suretrade and AmeriTrade. As Tom Taggart, a Schwab spokesperson explained, "Schwab has no intention of entering a price war with an $8 broker. We have become the largest online broker through a combination of valued services at a fair price."[22] That left Pottruck with the option of a $39.95 or $29.95 price point. An internal analysis suggested that the revenue impact of moving to a $39.95 price would be comparable to moving to a $29.95 price, since the analysis projected less price elasticity at the $39.95 price point and more at the $29.95

price point. Hence, Pottruck decided that if the company were to introduce an expanded Internet offering, the preferred price point would be $29.95, since competitive pressures would likely force the price down over time, so why take the "thunder" out of the $29.95 price by taking an interim step toward it?

However, taking this approach was expected to cost the firm dearly. Schwab's strategy group estimated that the projected cannibalization of its offline and full-service online business would cost the firm $125 million in revenue in the first year. Schwab would have to make up for the revenue shortfall through increased trading and lower costs, which management knew would not come right away. The $125 million revenue hit would result in approximately $100 million in forgone profits, which represented 22% of the company's projected 1997 pre-tax profits. Wall Street was not likely to react favorably to an earnings decline of that magnitude, nor were Schwab's employees, who collectively owned 40% of the company.

Furthermore, the hit to earnings would result in less money available for marketing and advertising. Historically, Schwab had spent heavily on advertising, and many industry analysts credited Schwab's investment in this area as a leading factor behind the company's growth. As Short explained:

> We knew that if it took us a while to recover from the profit hit, we would have had very little money to invest in marketing and advertising at a critical time in the development of our brand and the market. Fidelity and others were ramping up and spending heavily on marketing their Internet offerings. Internet trading had quickly turned into a highly contested category, and it would have been devastating for us to be resource-constrained at a time when all these other companies were stepping up their budgets.

The other important marketing issue for Schwab was that, as the industry leader in the discount brokerage market, once it had set its price for a service-oriented Internet trading product, that price would rapidly become the

---

[22]"Do I Hear Two Bits a Trade?" *Business Week.* December 8, 1997, p. 112.

industry standard. As a result, there would be virtually no option of ever going back and raising the price.

However, there were also arguments in favor of taking aggressive action. Schwab was seeing some of its heavy traders migrate to the deep discount online brokers. While the numbers were small, it was still a concern to Schwab since the company generated 80% of its revenue from 20% of its customers. Schwab believed that improving its Internet trading capabilities would help retain its heavy traders and attract new investors from full-service brokerages who liked Schwab's combination of low prices and quality service.

Schwab also believed that it had the right core competencies to make an expanded Internet initiative a success. As Lyons explained:

> We are a very good technology company. We know a lot about technology and we've invested heavily in it over the years. We also had seen from the use of our Tele-Broker service and online products that we had a lot of customers who were very facile with technology. They were very independent and they wanted to be in control. So we believed that our customers would respond well to an expanded Internet offer.

From a technical standpoint, Schwab believed that it had the system capacity to handle the projected increase in online trading if it were to offer $29.95 Internet trading to all of its customers. Even with the growth of its online business, Schwab's system availability had remained surprisingly constant at 99.2% over the past two years. However, Schwab's commission-charging system was one of its few systems that was overdue for an upgrade. While the system had met the company's needs for over 20 years, by 1997, Schwab's need for additional pricing flexibility had outstripped the system's capabilities. The system's main drawback was that it could handle only one type of pricing structure (minimum charge plus cents-per-trade) and there were a limited number of pricing schedules it could handle within that structure. The company had developed a

"work-around" for its e.Schwab product, but it was clear that it would be "prohibitively difficult" to stretch the system much further. As a result, the company was working on an upgrade to the system in late 1997, but it was still several months away from being complete. Therefore, if Schwab decided to pursue an expanded Internet offering in the short term, it would not be able to offset the projected earnings shortfall by tinkering with commissions in other parts of its business.

The Decision

Numerous times throughout its history, Schwab had seen the long-term value of taking aggressive action and securing an early market position. Moreover, Pottruck believed that the Internet represented a transformational technology for the financial services industry. If that were the case, Schwab might derive a competitive advantage by fully embracing the technology early on. On the other hand, the Internet trading market was in the midst of intense price competition; was that a market that Schwab wanted to enter? Could Schwab ever compete on price given that its multi-channel approach gave it a higher cost structure than many of the "bare bones" online brokerages?

Furthermore, Schwab's management team wondered if it was the right time to pursue an expanded Internet strategy. With its existing online product offerings alone, Schwab had almost five times the online accounts of E*Trade, suggesting that Schwab was holding its own in the online channel. Investors were clearly pleased with Schwab's performance and were not assigning any significant trading premium to the pure-play Internet brokerage stocks. As a result, Wall Street was not likely to react well in the short run to a strategy that put Schwab in direct competition with the deep-discount Internet brokerages and resulted in a projected $100 million profit hit. Perhaps it made sense to hold off on an expanded Internet strategy until the market opportunity was clearer and until Schwab had a strategy for how to deal with the projected earnings impact.

Pottruck and Charles Schwab had discussed these issues during their meetings together over the previous weeks. While it was a complex issue that could be debated for months, Pottruck and Charles Schwab agreed that they needed to make a decision quickly on whether the company should combine its two existing Internet offerings into one new offering, with a significantly discounted $29.95 commission *and* access to Schwab's full slate of customer service options. They knew that any decision they made would have a significant impact on the future of the firm.

CASE I–2
CHARLES SCHWAB CORPORATION (B)[1]

*Great success in business is **not** about forcing customers to make difficult compromises on what they really want.*

—David Pottruck, *co-CEO Charles Schwab Corporation*

In late 1997, David Pottruck made one of the toughest decisions of his career—to offer *all* Schwab customers Internet trading for as low as $29.95 per trade[2] accompanied by the full complement of Schwab customer service options (e.g., branches, telephone, online)—thereby eliminating the previous distinction between the company's e.Schwab product and its traditional business. An internal analysis projected that taking this action could cost the firm $100 million in pre-tax profits on an annualized basis, at least in the short term. However, Pottruck believed that over the long term, increased trading volume and higher account balances would make up for the near-term profit shortfall. Pottruck reflected on the decision:

In 1997, we became convinced that the business models of both e.Schwab and Charles Schwab were not the business models for the long term. By now we've all read Clay Christensen's book[3] that advises companies to form a separate business unit to pursue an Internet strategy, and that's what we had done. But when that separate unit is growing at a pace that will make it as big as your traditional business, you have to put them back together. By doing so, we felt we would be merging the leading discount broker in the world with the leading online brokerage in the world.

I went to Chuck and said, 'Here's what we need to do. I'm convinced this is the right thing to do, but I've got to warn you that the benefits will not be immediate—they will accrue over time. Ultimately, we'll see more customers, more trades, fewer customers leaving, and a host of other benefits. But, in the short term, the pricing impact will be immediate and it will go straight to the bottom line. It's going to get ugly here fast. In fact, 1998 as a whole may be a pretty painful year. So, I need your support and the board's support on this.' And Chuck said, 'I think you're on the right track; it's the right thing to do. We'll take whatever pain comes.'

---

[2]$29.95 per trade for trades up to 1,000 shares, with a $.03 per share commission for every share over the first 1000.

[3]Referring to *The Innovator's Dilemma* by Clayton Christensen.

Executing the Internet Strategy

Pottruck moved quickly to identify a seasoned executive to head up the electronic brokerage unit, knowing that the first challenge for him or her would be to merge the proudly independent e.Schwab group into the rest of the organization—a task fraught with potential cultural and morale problems. However, these challenges did not dissuade Gideon Sasson, the head of technological development for e.Schwab, from stepping forward to declare himself a candidate for the position. While Pottruck considered a number of internal and external candidates, Sasson was ultimately selected. The decision marked the first time in Schwab's history that anyone other than a CIO had moved from a technical position to a general management position.

On January 15, 1998, Schwab launched its new expanded Internet offering. However, the company did very little in the way of advertising to build awareness of Schwab.com's new features and commission rates. This was primarily due to the fact that Len Short, the company's executive vice president of advertising and brand strategy, had spent years working on advertising campaigns for MCI and AT&T, and knew the danger of aggressively promoting price. Short was concerned that focusing on Schwab's commissions would validate price as the most important factor in selecting an online brokerage. In addition, since Schwab was not offering the lowest commissions, Short believed that focusing on price could work against them. In the short run, Schwab's decision not to aggressively promote its expanded Internet offering resulted in a lower increase in assets than the company had expected. In the long run, however, analysts hailed Schwab's decision to not actively market the Internet channel separately as one of the keys to its success. As Bill Doyle, director of online financial services at Forrester Research, reflected, "Schwab has done so well because they treat the Internet as just another channel."[4]

[4]"Schwab Treats the Web Like Any Other Channel." *Future Banker.* April 1999. p. 35.

To gain buy-in on the expanded Internet offering from its customer service representatives, Schwab gave each of its 4,000 phone and branch representatives Web access and training. Moreover, Schwab included a measure of customer migration to the Internet as one of a handful of components that determined team-based bonuses for its customer service representatives.

Schwab's goal was to introduce the expanded Schwab.com in waves so that the company could handle the volume of new accounts and trading activity from a customer service and systems standpoint. Schwab marketed the service first to its heavy traders and then to its customer base as a whole through phased direct mail campaigns. To further control the pace of migration, Schwab also required that customers go through an online enrollment process, which required that they agree to receive all their stock quotes electronically. While Schwab couldn't *really* monitor how customers received quotes, they purposefully included this constraint as a "speedbump" in the enrollment process to moderate the pace of migration.

Results

Despite the enrollment speedbumps and minimal advertising, customers signed up in droves. Within 5 months, Schwab had opened 500,000 new online accounts, representing $40 billion in assets. As Susanne Lyons reflected, "One of our mistakes was to assume we could temper the pace of migration to online trading. The world wanted the Web."

Schwab's first quarter (Q1) 1998 results reflected the impact of cannibalization. Schwab's average commission declined from $63 in Q4 1997 to $57 in Q1 1998. After having grown on average 6.5% per quarter over the previous four quarters, revenues declined 3% between Q4 1997 and Q1 1998. Similarly, pretax income declined 16% between Q4 1997 and Q1 1998, after having grown on average 8% per quarter in the previous four quarters (see Exhibit 1). In light of the company's performance, Schwab's stock sagged in the first half of 1998, declining from $40 per share in January to $33 per share at the end of June—an 18% decline. During the same period, Merrill Lynch's stock was up 29% and Paine Webber's stock was up 27%. Pottruck reflected on this period:

> The migration to Internet trading happened much faster than we had thought, and the elasticity we were expecting came more slowly than we had thought. So people were paying less and not trading significantly

more. As a result, the costs hit faster than we had thought and the benefits were slower to accrue, making it a very painful quarter for us.

However, by the end of 1998, Schwab's online bet was starting to pay off. Schwab's online accounts increased from 1.2 million in December 1997 to 2.2 million in December 1998, representing 40% of the company's total accounts (see Exhibit 2). By the end of 1998, online trades accounted for 61% of total trades—surprising even Schwab executives.

EXHIBIT 1   Selected Quarterly Financial and Operating Data

	Q4 1996	Q1 1997	Q2 1997	Q3 1997	Q4 1997	Q1 1998
Operating results (millions)						
Revenues	$ 482.3	$ 535.7	$ 530.7	$ 611.8	$ 620.6	$ 604.4
Total expenses	$ 383.1	$ 425.3	$ 425.0	$ 474.9	$ 487.3	$ 492.1
Pre-tax income	$ 99.2	$ 110.3	$ 105.8	$ 136.9	$ 133.3	$ 112.4
Net income	$ 59.7	$ 66.7	$ 64.0	$ 76.5	$ 63.1	$ 68.0
Performance measures						
Revenue growth		11%	−1%	15%	1%	−3%
Pre-tax income growth		11%	−4%	29%	−3%	−16%
Pre-tax profit margin	20.6%	20.6%	19.9%	22.4%	21.5%	18.6%
After-tax profit margin	12.4%	12.5%	12.1%	12.5%	10.2%	11.3%
Customer information (at year end)						
Schwab active customer accounts (millions)	4.0	4.2	4.4	4.6	4.8	5.0
Schwab customer assets (billions)	$ 253	$ 268	$ 306	$ 345	$ 354	$ 407
Customers' daily average trading volume (thousands)						
Daily average revenue trades	55.9	68.2	64.0	77.4	77.5	85.4
Mutual Fund OneSource trades	26.1	36.4	32.5	34.8	33.1	40.8
Total daily average trades	82.0	104.6	96.5	112.2	110.6	126.2
Average commission per revenue trade	$ 66.89	$ 65.55	$ 63.59	$ 64.61	$ 63.38	$ 56.88
Percent change in average commission per revenue trade		−2.0%	−3.0%	1.6%	−1.9%	−10.3%

Source: "Charles Schwab (SCH): Upgrade: Best is Yet to Come." Morgan Stanley Dean Witter Research Report. April 14, 1999; Charles Schwab 1998 Annual Report.

EXHIBIT 2   Growth in Schwab's Online Accounts and Online Assets

Year	Total Active[a] Schwab Customer Accounts (mil)	Active[a] Online Customer Accounts (mil)	Total Assets in Schwab Customer Accounts ($ Bil)	Assets in Schwab Online Customer Accounts ($ Bil)
Dec-95	3.4	0.3	$ 181.7	$ 23.3
Dec-96	4.0	0.6	$ 253.2	$ 41.7
Dec-97	4.8	1.2	$ 353.7	$ 80.8
Dec-98	5.6	2.2	$ 491.1	$ 174.1

[a]Active defined as accounts that had balances or activity within the preceding 8 months.
Source: Charles Schwab Quarterly Report. April 15, 1999; "Charles Schwab (SCH): Upgrade: Best is Yet to Come."
Morgan Stanley Dean Witter Research Report. April 14, 1999.

Moreover, Schwab's average number of daily trades rose to 115,300 by Q4 1998—representing a new high for the company and an increase of 49% over Q4 1997. While commissions continued to fall—reaching a low of $53 per trade in 1998—revenues increased 19% during the year to $2.7 billion and pre-tax profits increased 29% to $577 million (see Exhibit 3). Schwab's stock appreciated 158% between June and December 1998, giving the company a market value of $25.5 billion, just topping Merrill Lynch's $25.4 billion market value—a situation that astonished the securities industry given that Merrill Lynch had $1.4 trillion in client assets compared to Schwab's $491 billion.[5]

By the end of 1998, Schwab's online trades outnumbered trades made through its call centers by nearly a 4-to-1 margin, helping Schwab maintain its margins due to the efficiency advantages of the online channel. Schwab estimated that it would have needed four more call centers and 1,500 additional customer service representatives to handle the volume of business brought on by Internet trading—if those trades had not been made online. In total, Schwab estimated that the efficiencies gained from Internet trading resulted in annual savings of $100 million.[6]

Impact on Schwab's IT Infrastructure

In April 1999, Schwab's Web site reached a record high of 75 million hits per day, compared to just 6 million hits per day in early 1998. During normal trading hours, Schwab processed 4,000 transactions per second. Given this level of volume, Schwab's Web site was regarded as the most active, encrypted, secure site in the world. To meet the company's IT goal of "delighting our most demanding customer during the busiest hour of the day," Schwab invested between 15–17% of its annual revenue in technology.[7] Between January 1998 and June 1999, the company added five mainframes to its main production complex and increased its IT staff by 50%—from 1,300 to 2,000 full-time equivalents. Due to the pace at which Schwab had to scale its systems to handle its rapidly growing trading volume, the company had to endure more frequent and more complex technology installations than it

---

[5]"Schwab Tops Merrill in Market Value." *The Washington Post.* December 29, 1998. p. E01.

[6]"Schwab Puts It All Online." *Fortune.* December, 1998. p. 94.
[7]"Embarrassing Sights for E-commerce." *San Jose Mercury News.* June 20, 1999. p. E01.

EXHIBIT 3   **Selected Financial and Operating Data**

	1995	1996	1997	1998
Operating results (millions)				
Revenues	$1,420	$1,851	$2,299	$2,736
Expenses excluding interest	$1,143	$1,457	$1,852	$2,160
Pre-tax profits	$277	$394	$448	$577
Net Income	$173	$234	$270	$348
Performance measures				
Revenue growth		30%	24%	19%
Pre-tax profit growth		42%	14%	29%
Pre-tax profit margin	19.5%	21.3%	19.5%	21.1%
After-tax profit margin	12.2%	12.6%	11.7%	12.7%
Customer information (at year end)				
Schwab active customer accounts (millions)	3.4	4.0	4.8	5.6
Schwab customer assets (billions)	$182	$253	$354	$491
Customers' daily average trading volume (thousands)				
Daily average revenue trades	40.8	54.0	71.8	97.2
Mutual Fund OneSource trades	17.8	27.2	34.2	40.3
Total daily average trades	58.6	81.2	106.0	137.5
Average commission per revenue trade	$73.11	$69.08	$64.27	$53.44
Percent change in average commission per revenue trade		−5.5%	−7.0%	−16.9%

Source: Charles Schwab 1998 Annual Report.

had historically, increasing the risk of system outages. In addition, Schwab's online trading volume turned out to be "spikier" than its offline trading volume, which also increased the risk of system outages and highlighted the need for even more system capacity than had been projected. Pottruck explained:

> We thought we needed system capacity of three times the average daily trading volume. But we have come to realize that we actually need three times the average *hourly* trading volume, which can be three times the company's average *daily* volume. So we determined that we effectively needed ten times the average daily volume. So if we were doing 100,000 trades per day, we needed the capacity to do a million trades on a spiked day. That costs a lot of money.

While Schwab's system up-time remained consistent at 99.2%—even with the surge in volume—the impact and publicity associated with any period of downtime grew as a higher percentage of Schwab's business migrated to the Web. As Pottruck explained, "I didn't realize that a 15-minute outage would become major news in *The Wall Street Journal* and on CNN and CNBC. I missed that." To minimize outages, Pottruck made the decision to invest heavily in a powerful back-up system. As Pottruck explained:

> We're never going to completely eliminate outages, because in many cases, outages happen for reasons that are outside of our realm of control. So what we

have to do is make the functionality of our back-up system so robust that customers don't even know they're on a back-up system. We also need to reduce the cut-over time from 15 minutes to 10 minutes to 5 minutes to 2 minutes to a flicker; we'll have to do that incrementally over the course of 18 months to 2 years. It also implies an entirely different architecture for our system and an enormous differential in cost—in fact, it will almost double our costs.

In June 1999, Schwab announced its plan to strengthen its back-up system by working with IBM to add 32 new mainframes in a configuration that allowed them to all act as one computer. Thus, if one mainframe failed, another would take over instantly so that users would not even notice.[8]

Competitive Response

By 1999, Internet trading had grown to 30% to 35% of all stock trades by individuals—making it more and more difficult for the full service brokerage firms to ignore. Even Merrill Lynch—the leading full service brokerage firm in the United States—was reconsidering its stance on Internet trading. John "Launny" Steffens, head of Merrill Lynch's retail brokerage operations and a longtime opponent of Internet trading (he once referred to it as a "threat to Americans' financial lives"), restated his position for the public record in late 1998:

> Online trading in and of itself is not bad. In fact it is a refreshing wind in our industry and one we welcome and embrace.[9]

However, it was not easy for Merrill Lynch to respond to the Internet trading movement since the firm employed approximately 14,800 brokers who were certain to feel directly threatened by any move to offer it. Since Schwab did not pay its brokers on a commission basis, it did not face the same dilemma in launching its expanded Internet offering that Merrill Lynch and the other full service brokerages faced.

In June 1999, Merrill Lynch shocked the industry by announcing that it, too, would offer online trading for as little as $29.95 per trade—matching Schwab's price. As *The Wall Street Journal* reported:

> Indeed Merrill's decision—one that every full-service Wall Street brokerage firm will have to respond to—shows just how profoundly the Internet is transforming the competitive landscape in the U.S. economy. Rarely in history has the leader in an industry felt compelled to do an about-face and, virtually overnight, adopt what is essentially a new business model.[10]

Merrill Lynch planned to offer two Internet trading options. The first option, known as ML Direct, wouldn't be available until December 1999. ML Direct planned to offer customers $29.95 commissions on stock trades of up to 1,000 shares, with a $20,000 minimum balance requirement. For the same commission, customers could also place trades via telephone to an order taker at one of Merrill Lynch's service centers. ML Direct also included some additional services, including online access to cash management services and free access to Merrill Lynch research reports, but it did not include access to a Merrill Lynch broker. The second Internet trading option, known as the Unlimited Advantage account, offered customers unlimited free stock trades (either online, through a broker, or over the phone to an order taker) for an annual fee of .3% to 1.0% of the

[8]"Embarrassing Sights for E-commerce." *San Jose Mercury News.* June 20, 1999. p. E01.
[9]"Internet Trades Put Merrill Bull on Horns of Dilemma." *The Wall Street Journal.* February 12, 1999. p. C1.

[10]"Facing Internet Threat, Merrill to Offer Trading Online for Low Fees." *The Wall Street Journal.* June 1, 1999. p. A1.

account's assets[11]—with a minimum annual fee of $1,500. Unlimited Advantage account customers would also receive a number of additional services, including personalized service from a Merrill Lynch financial consultant with a periodic review of performance, free access to Merrill Lynch's research, and assistance with financial planning. Merrill Lynch was expected to make its core relationship accounts available by July 12, 1999.

Schwab executives were not completely surprised by Merrill Lynch's decision to introduce Internet trading; however, many questioned whether they could execute the new strategy successfully. Pottruck explained:

> I don't think Merrill will ever have two things that have been critical to our success. First, they will never embrace technology as the core of their business the way we do. Second, they will never have as low a cost structure as we do, which will make it hard for them to offer superior value.

At the same time that Merrill Lynch was taking steps to enter Schwab's territory, Schwab was taking steps to enter Merrill Lynch's territory in a strategy known as "reinventing full service." Reinventing full service entailed turning Schwab into a new type of brokerage firm that blended Internet-based trading with some of the investment advice offered by full-service brokerage firms. As Susanne Lyons, president of Schwab's retail client services division, explained: "We can't build a business on trading anymore because that service is a commodity."[12] One of the centerpieces of the reinventing full-service strategy was the introduction of a series of specialized services for active traders and investors with substantial portfolios. For cus-

tomers with $100,000 in assets, or who placed at least 12 trades per year,[13] Schwab offered its Signature Services account, which included a number of benefits, including priority service and online access to an enhanced library of research. For customers with $500,000 in assets, or who placed 24 trades per year,[14] Schwab offered its Schwab Signature Gold account, which offered customers a team of dedicated brokers who could give personalized investment advice on everything from portfolio planning to investment options. As Lyons described it, "Your team is your concierge."[15] Customers with over $1,000,000 in assets, or who placed over 48 trades per year,[16] could qualify for Schwab's Signature Platinum account, which offered even more benefits. Moreover, customers in any of Schwab's Signature accounts also received access to initial public offerings distributed through Schwab. *The New York Times* reported in June 1999 that Schwab would be taking things one step further, making buy and sell picks for individual stocks as well.[17]

Pottruck summarized the evolution of Schwab's strategy:

> When customers first open an account, they typically are simply looking for assurances that we can be trusted with their money and that we will be there to resolve any problems. Fulfilling those needs is what we have built the entire company around. But over time customers realize they need advice and help, and we are at a point now where we can provide that. We will educate customers and help them make choices. We're not going to invest for them, but we are going to empower them with tools, information, and perspective so that they can do it themselves.

---

[11]1% of equity and mutual fund assets; 30 basis points of cash and fixed income assets.
[12]"Remaking Schwab." *Business Week.* May 25, 1998. p. 122.
[13]And maintained a $10,000 minimum balance.
[14]And maintained a $25,000 minimum balance.
[15]"Remaking Schwab." *Business Week.* May 25, 1998. p. 122.
[16]And maintained a $50,000 minimum balance.
[17]"Low-Cost Trading Online is Planned by Merrill Lynch." *The New York Times.* June 2, 1999. p. 1.

1   THE CHALLENGES OF MANAGING IN THE INFORMATION AGE[1]

As the century closed, the world became smaller. The public rapidly gained access to new and dramatically faster communication technologies. Entrepreneurs, able to draw on unprecedented scale economics, built vast empires. Great fortunes were made . . . . Every day brought forth new technological advances to which old business models seemed no longer to apply. . . .

A prophecy for the 21st century? No. You have just read a description of what happened one hundred years ago when the 20th century industrial giants emerged.[2]

As this quote implies, new technologies can sometimes catch us off guard. In fact, when Rutherford B. Hayes, the nineteenth president of the United States, saw a demonstration of the telephone in the late 1800s, he reportedly commented that, while it was a wonderful invention, businessmen would never use it. Hayes believed that people had to meet face to face to conduct substantive business affairs—and he was not alone in his assessment.

Few of Hayes's contemporaries could foresee the profound changes that would be ushered in by the telephone and other technologies of the day— including steam engines and production machinery; railroads, automobiles,

---

[1]This module introduction is adapted from papers and materials from Professor Applegate's *Building E-Businesses* online course, which is available from Harvard Business School Publishing (Order No. 5238BN). This chapter draws on earlier work by Professor F. Warren McFarlan and James L. McKenney, which is summarized in McFarlan, F.W., McKenney, J.L., and Pyburn, P., "Information Archipelago: Plotting a Course," *Harvard Business Review*, January 1983.

[2]C. Shapiro and H. Varian, *Information Rules: A Strategic Guide to the Network Economy* (Boston: HBS Press, 1998).

FIGURE 1–1

The Impact of Technology on Business and Society During the Industrial Revolution

Figure reprinted with permission from Duke University Rare Book, Manuscript, and Special Collections Library

and other transportation technologies; and communication technologies, such the telegraph and telephone. (See Figure 1–1.) The exodus of people from rural to urban areas, the shift from craft-based work to mass production, and the decline of small, owner-operated firms in favor of large, vertically integrated multinationals; these transitions marked the shift from an agricultural to an industrial economy. In fact, while technological innovation served as one of many stimuli to change, it was the confluence of technological, business, and social changes that enabled passage from the agricultural to the industrial era.

In retrospect, these changes were revolutionary. But, they evolved incrementally through periods of evolution punctuated by intense periods of revolution.[3] Similarly, the shift from an industrial to an information economy began with a period of intense technological innovation during the 1940s, 1950s, and 1960s that built upon, yet significantly altered, the technologies of the industrial revolution.[4] And, today's Internet technologies both built upon and revolutionized computing and communication platforms introduced decades earlier. For example, the Internet servers that power Information Age businesses evolved from early mainframe computers and microprocessors commercialized in the mid-1950s and 1960s. In addition, the new computing and communication devices used to access the Internet to shop, pay bills, trade stocks, do business, and communicate with others around the world evolved from personal computers and cell phones introduced in the 1970s and 1980s. (See Figure 1–2.)

As we enter the 21st century, we are once again experiencing an intense period of technology-enabled innovation, creativity, and excitement that has been spurred by the commercialization of several core technologies and associated changes in work and society. The technological changes include:

- The ***Internet*** and ***Broadband Networks***—a low-cost, standardized, global alternative to the expensive, specialized communication platforms of the 1970s and 1980s. These technologies enable transmission of multimedia digital information on a common communication channel.
- The ***World Wide Web (WWW)*** and ***High Performance Servers***—a flexible, standardized, powerful platform for creating and storing information in all of its many forms (for example, text, data, voice, and video) on high-performance computers that can be located anywhere in the world.
- The ***Uniform Resource Locator (URL)*** and ***Browser***—a common approach for identifying and locating information anywhere on the Internet and an easy-to-use tool for accessing, packaging, and displaying multimedia information.

---

[3]Gersick, C., "Revolutionary change theories: A multilevel exploration of punctuated equilibrium paradigm," *Academy of Management Review,* 16, 10–36; Applegate, L.M., "In search of a new organizational model," *Shaping Organization Form,* (ed. DeSanctis and Fulk), Sage Publications, 1999; Applegate, L.M., "E-Business Models: Making Sense of the Internet Business Landscape," *Information Technology and the Future Enterprise,* (ed. Dickson and DeSanctis), Prentice-Hall, 2001.

[4]Interestingly today's sophisticated computers can actually trace their roots to mechanical tabulating machines and typewriters that heralded the start of the industrial revolution during the 1800s.

FIGURE 1–2

*Technology,
Business, and
Societal
Evolution
During the 20th
Century*

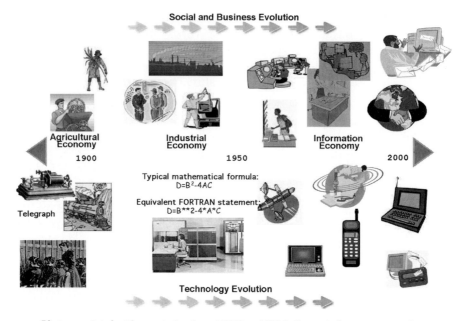

Photos reprinted with permission from AT&T and IBM; clip art is from www.arttoday.com
Source: AT&T and IBM

- ***Multimedia Digital Devices***—portable Internet access devices that provide a single point of entry to voice, television, and information. Today, the new devices include laptop computers, palm pilots, and interactive television and game consoles.

- ***Wireless Networks*** and ***Protocols***—the technology and supporting business infrastructure to enable access to the Internet, untethered by physical wires. While initially limited by a lack of common standards, performance, and useful applications, this "go anywhere" form of access is rapidly becoming a reality—especially in Europe and Japan. In Finland, for example, cell phone users can send e-mail, pay bills, check stock quotes, get traffic reports, and buy gas from a gas pump or a cup of espresso at a local café—all through a cell phone or wireless device. In Japan, the hottest new accessory for teens is the iMode phone. In the United Kingdom, British Telecom, Vodafone, and France Telecom have promised 3 gigabit wireless networks by 2002.[5]

---

[5]M. Alpert and G. Musser, "The Wireless Web," *Scientific American Special Report* (www.scientificamerican .com), October 2000. Note: A 3-gigabit network can transfer information at a speed of 3 trillion bits per second.

- *Java, Jini, XML* and other *Object-Oriented Programming Language and database technologies*—a powerful new approach to developing information systems that takes full advantage of the flexibility, modularity, connectivity, and multimedia features of the Internet.

Just as we saw during the technological revolution that gave rise to the Industrial Age, entrepreneurial firms—unfettered by the need to satisfy the expectations of entrenched shareholders—led the way as they defined innovative business models for the Information Age. In fact, during 1999, over $32 billion—90 percent of the total invested by venture capitalists—was invested in technology (including Internet-related) ventures.[6] As we entered the 21st century, investor confidence had hit an all time high. But, as annual and first quarter earnings reports hit the streets in late January through March of 2000, momentum buying was replaced by momentum selling and stock prices plummeted.[7] Venture capital investments in business-to-consumer (B2C), which had garnered 40 to 50 percent of private equity dollars during 1999,[8] declined to less than 3 percent of venture investments during 2Q2000.[9] E-commerce companies that only months earlier had been awarded valuations in excess of $1 billion went out of business in record numbers. In fact, over 360 Internet firms went out of business between January 2000 and March 2001.[10] (See Figures 1–3 and 1–4.)

While most were slow to get started, established firms have taken advantage of the decreased strength of new entrants and are taking a lead role in defining the information economy for the 21st century. Pioneering high tech firms (such as, Cisco, IBM, Microsoft, and Intuit) and established players in non-high-tech industries (such as General Electric, Charles Schwab, American Express, and Ford) have aggressively pursued Internet business initiatives—often building on e-business foundations begun decades

---

[6]M. Mowrey, "Financial Spotlight: Inside the Dot-Com VC Billions," *The Standard* (www.thestandard.com) February 21, 2000. This study reports the findings of three venture capital studies conducted by Price Waterhouse (www.pwcglobal.com), Venture Economics (www.ventureeconomics.com), and Venture One (www.ventureone.com).

[7]"NASDAQ's Near Meltdown," *TheStandard* (www.thestandard.com), April 4, 2000; J. Boudreau, "New Economy Reality Check," *SiliconValley.com* (www.sjmercury.com/svtech/news/indepth) April 16, 2000; S. Lorh, "Stocks' Slide May Spark Dot-Com Shakeout," *NY Times on the Web,* (www.nytimes.com), April 17, 2000; P. Wallace, "The Dog Days of E-Commerce," *TheStandard* (www.thestandard.com), June 1, 2000.

[8]M. Mowrey, op. cit.

[9]P. Bonanos, "Net VC: Past its Prime?," *The Standard* (www.thestandard.com), August 28, 2000.

[10]See Webmergers.com (www.webmergers.com) for a detailed report of dot-com mergers, acquisitions and failures. The data presented here were collected on April 4, 2001.

FIGURE 1–3

*Dot-Com
Shutdowns by
Month*

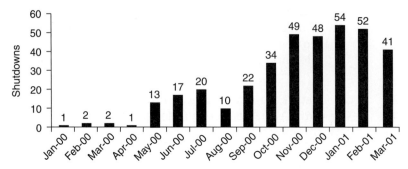

Source of data: www.webmergers.com, April 2001

FIGURE 1–4

*Dot-Com
Shutdowns by
Region*

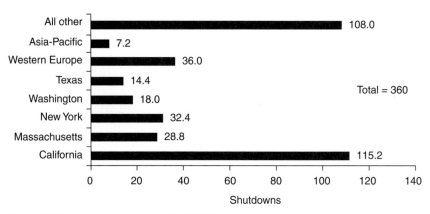

Source of data: www.webmergers.com, April 2001

earlier.[11] Non-U.S. firms (such as France Telecom, Vivendi Seagram, and Bertelsmann in Europe, Li & Fung, AdMart, and PSA in Asia, and Telefonica in Latin America, to name just a few) are also actively creating the global information economy.

This module draws on over two decades of research on the impact of information technology (IT) on industries, markets, and the organizations that operate within them. It examines the forces that shape strategic decision making in the 21st century and presents frameworks to analyze the impact of the Internet and associated technologies of the 21st century on

---

[11]We define e-business as the use of information and communications technology to support how business is conducted inside a firm and with customers, suppliers, and partners. As such, the concept of e-business is not new and lessons from history provide an important foundation upon which 21st century e-businesses are built. See Applegate, L.M., "Thought Leaders: An Interview with Lynda Applegate - E-Business Lessons from Planet Earth," *Strategy and Business,* 18:141–149, First Quarter 2000.

competitive and market forces. The module ends with a series of cases that enable discussion of the approaches executives use, the decisions they make, and the issues they face as they confront the many challenges of managing in an Information Age.

Forces That Shape Business Strategy

Companies that have deployed Internet technology have been confused by distorted market signals, often of their own creation. It is understandable, when confronted with a new business phenomenon, to look to marketplace outcomes for guidance. But in the early stages of the rollout of any important new technology, market signals can be unreliable. New technologies trigger rampant experimentation, by companies and their customers, and the experimentation is often economically unsustainable. As a result, market behavior is distorted and must be interpreted with caution.[12]

When the business environment is stable, strategic decision making is like a game of chess. One player studies an opponent's moves and then makes a counter move. During periods of business innovation, however, a competitor's moves may not necessarily reflect rational and reasonable business thinking. It then becomes necessary to return to the fundamental analyses of the forces that shape strategy.

In this section, we present three frameworks that can be used to guide analysis of the impacts of IT on strategy. Michael Porter's *Value Chain* and *Industry and Competitive Analysis* (ICA) frameworks, although not originally developed to examine the impact of the Internet and IT on strategic decision making, have proven very useful in this regard.[13,14] The third framework, Warren McFarlan's *Strategic Grid,* is a tool for characterizing the roles that the Internet and IT may play in specific firms and industries, and for deriving appropriate IT-related strategies and management practices.

Value Chain Analysis

For decades, the Value Chain framework (see Figure 1–5) has been a powerful tool for identifying and analyzing the stream of activities through which

---

[12]Porter, M., "Strategy and the Internet," *Harvard Business Review,* March 2001.

[13]Porter, M., *Competitive Advantage: Creating and Sustaining Performance,* New York: The Free Press, 1985. See Porter, M., "Strategy and the Internet," Harvard Business Review, March 2001 for a value chain analysis of Internet opportunities.

[14]Early pioneering work on the use of Porter's frameworks for analyzing the impact of IT on industries, markets, and firm strategies was conducted by Professors Jim Cash, Warren McFarlan, Jim McKenney, and Mike Vitale. The work was summarized in: Cash, J., McFarlan, W., McKenney, J., *Corporate Information Systems Management: The Issues Facing Senior Executives,* (3rd Edition), N.Y.: McGraw Hill-Irwin, 1988.

FIGURE 1–5

The Value Chain

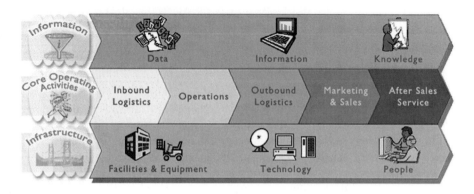

products and services are created and delivered to customers. Once activities are defined, it is then possible to analyze the economics at each step in the chain by identifying both costs incurred and value created. These activities can be located inside a firm or across firm boundaries. In the latter case, activities may involve customers, suppliers, partners, or other stakeholders. Accompanying the physical value chain is a related information value chain through which involved parties coordinate and control activities.

Participants within a business market assume one or more of four primary roles to carry out these value-creating activities (see Figure 1–6). The point within a value chain where maximum economies of scale and scope are created determines market power. *Economies of scale* are achieved when a market participant or network of participants are able to leverage capabilities and infrastructure to increase their revenues and profitability within a single product line or market. *Economies of scope* are achieved when a market participant or network of participants is able to leverage capabilities and infrastructure to launch new product lines or businesses, or enter new markets.

Industrial Age business innovations favored producers. The innovations included: physical/analog production and distribution technologies (machines, railroads, steam engines, telephones); an operating model (the assembly line, marketing, sales, and after-sales service channels); a management model (the hierarchy); and a social/regulatory system (specialized work, pay-for-performance incentives, worker education, unions, antitrust laws).

As we enter the 21st century, Information Age pioneers like AOL (now AOL Time Warner) are defining the business models that are reshaping the global business landscape and redefining power. Once again, emerging models exploit the power of technological, business, and social innovations within a regulatory and policy framework—the latter of which emerges over time.

FIGURE 1–6

Market Roles

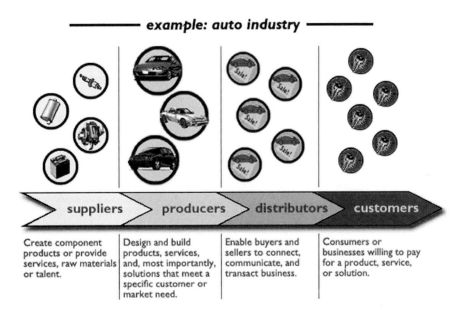

Information Age business innovations include: digital production and distribution technologies (broadband and wireless networks, sophisticated content creation, flexible knowledge management); an operating model (integrated supply chains and buy chains); a management model (teams, partnerships, consortia); and social/regulatory systems (ownership incentives, freelancing, virtual work, distance learning, digital copyright laws).

Although Industrial Age markets and power bases were built on proprietary infrastructure, participants within Information Age markets leverage a shared *digital business infrastructure* to enable new entrants and established firms to create and exploit *network* economies of scale and scope. Network economies of scale are achieved when a "community" of firms shares its infrastructure, capabilities, and customer base to produce and distribute products faster, better, and cheaper than competitors. Network economies of scope are achieved when the community uses its shared infrastructure to produce and distribute new products and services, enter new markets, or launch new businesses, more quickly, at less cost, and more successfully than competitors.

As we will see later in this section, the interorganizational IT systems of the 1980s and early 1990s (e.g., American Airlines' Sabre reservation system and American Hospital Supply Corporation's ASAP system) foreshadowed how network economics could create value. Because they were built using proprietary technologies, however, access, reach, and flexibility were limited. Table 1–1 compares Industrial Age and Information Age economics.

TABLE 1–1   Comparison of Industrial Age and Information Age Economics

Characteristics	Industrial Age	Information Age
Criteria for Economic Success	Internal, proprietary, and specialized economies of scale and scope; Economies of scope are limited by the level of infrastructure specialization required	External, networked and shared economies of scale and scope; Economies of scale and scope are dramatically increased by the ability to build new businesses on the nonproprietary, flexible, shared and ubiquitous Internet infrastructure
Core Technological Innovations	Production technologies	Distribution, communication and information technologies, and the ability to "assemble" component pieces
Core Operating Innovations	Standardization of work, job specialization, assembly line operations, value chain industry structure	Knowledge work, job expansion, work teams (face-to-face and virtual), extended enterprise, outsourcing and partnerships, value web industry and interindustry structures
Core Management Innovations	Hierarchical coordination structures and supervision, compliance-based control, pay-for-performance incentives, centralized planning & control	Networked coordinating structures, ownership incentives, information-based ("learning") models of control, distributed planning and control
Societal Innovations	Urban growth, mass transportation, social security and welfare, unions, federal regulations, domestic economy	Work-at-home, self-employment, personal pension and savings programs, global economy
Length of Time to Achieve Economies of Scale and Scope	Decades	Uncertain
Dominant Industry Power	Producers	Solution assemblers and channel managers

Industry and Competitive Analysis

Porter's ICA framework postulates that economic and competitive forces in an industry are the result of five basic forces: (1) bargaining power of suppliers; (2) bargaining power of buyers; (3) threat of new entrants; (4) threat of substitute products or services; and (5) competitive intensity and positioning among traditional business rivals. Figure 1–7 presents the ICA framework.

Porter describes three *generic strategies* for achieving proprietary advantage within an industry: cost leadership, differentiation, and focus.

FIGURE 1–7

*Forces
Influencing
Industry and
Competitive
Advantage*

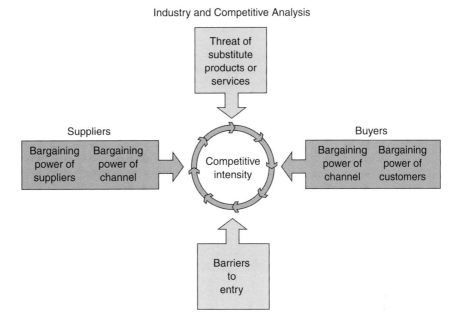

Industry and Competitive Analysis

Each generic strategy embodies two key choices: (1) the competitive mechanism (Should we lower cost or differentiate our products and services?); and (2) the competitive scope (Should we target a broad market or a narrow one?). Specific actions required to implement each generic strategy vary widely from industry to industry, as do feasible generic strategies within a particular industry. Selecting and implementing the appropriate strategy is central to achieving long-term competitive advantage in an industry.

Strategic Grid Analysis

The two levels of analysis discussed above help frame strategic decision making along the two dimensions depicted on McFarlan's Strategic Grid in Figure 1–8.

Along the vertical axis, executives assess the impact of IT on operations. For some organizations, the second-by-second, utterly reliable, precision execution of IT operations is crucial to survival. Even small interruptions in service or disruptions in quality have a profound impact. For other organizations, it would take a significant disturbance in IT operations over an extended period to have a major impact on an organization's ability to execute. In assessing the impact of IT on operations, it is no longer enough to merely consider Value Chain activities that take place inside organizational boundaries. In the past, the proprietary, sequential nature of Value Chain activities enabled executives to "wall off" IT operations within a firm. Given that Information Age Value Chain activities are performed on a shared, networked infrastructure,

FIGURE 1–8

The Impact of IT on Strategy and Operations

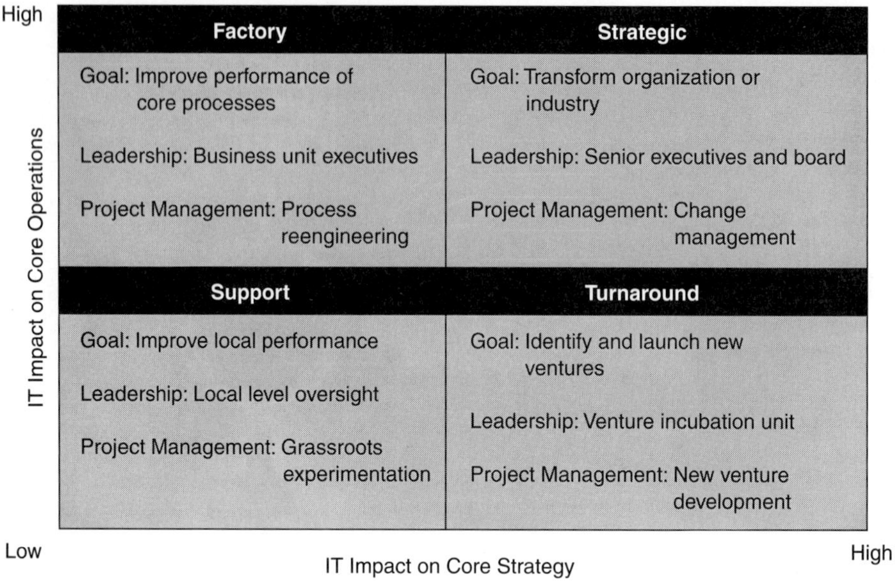

Factory	**Strategic**
Goal: Improve performance of core processes	Goal: Transform organization or industry
Leadership: Business unit executives	Leadership: Senior executives and board
Project Management: Process reengineering	Project Management: Change management
Support	**Turnaround**
Goal: Improve local performance	Goal: Identify and launch new ventures
Leadership: Local level oversight	Leadership: Venture incubation unit
Project Management: Grassroots experimentation	Project Management: New venture development

Axes: vertical — IT Impact on Core Operations (Low to High); horizontal — IT Impact on Core Strategy (Low to High)

Information Age executives must assess vulnerability and manage and control operations throughout the Value Chain.

Along the horizontal axis of the Strategic Grid, executives assess the strategic impact of IT on market forces that influence future sustainable business advantage. For some organizations, IT-enabled business initiatives are critical to future strategic positioning. For others, new IT applications provide local improvements but do not impact business strategy.

Analyzing the Impact of IT on Strategic Decision Making

Plotting the portfolio of IT applications and their impact within the Strategic Grid enables executives to choose the appropriate approach to organizing and managing IT-enabled business activities. Five key questions can be used to guide strategic decision making when evaluating the impact of 21st century IT on market structure, relationships, and positioning.

- Can IT be used to reengineer core value activities and change the basis of competition?
- Can IT change the nature of relationships and the balance of power among buyers and suppliers?
- Can IT build or reduce barriers to entry?
- Can IT increase or decrease switching costs?
- Can IT help firms add value to existing products and services or create new ones?

Can IT Be Used to Reengineer Core Value Activities and Change the Basis of Competition?

At its core, IT systems are used to automate activities—whether they take place inside an organization or across its boundaries. In the 1950s and 1960s, when IT was first introduced for commercial use, the primary target of IT applications was to automate routine, information-intensive "back office" transactions (for example, payroll processing, accounting, and general ledger postings). The primary goal was to increase efficiency and productivity.

Businesses quickly learned to apply these same benefits to "front office" activities that involved transactions with suppliers, distributors, customers, and other value chain participants. In fact, benefits increased dramatically when businesses used IT, not just to *automate,* but also to *transform* and *inform.* A streamlined and integrated value chain helped businesses eliminate redundancies, reduce cycle time, and achieve even greater efficiency and productivity. Information, a by-product of automation, also enabled executives, employees, partners, and other stakeholders to better understand fast-cycled operations. Moreover, timely real-time information could be used to improve coordination and control, to personalize products and services in meeting individual needs, to add value to—and differentiate—existing products and services, and to create new products and services that attract new market participants and generate new revenue streams.

American Hospital Supply Corporation (AHSC) and American Airlines (AA) are two early examples of using IT to reengineer value activities and transform the basis of competition.[15] The story began during the late 1960s when an entrepreneurial sales manager at AHSC created a system that enabled hospital purchasing clerks to order supplies across telephone lines using punch cards and primitive card-reading computers. At about the same time, enterprising sales managers at AA were also paving new ground by giving large travel agencies computer terminals that allowed them to check airline schedules posted within American's internal reservation systems. Indeed, from these entrepreneurial actions grew two legendary strategic IT applications that changed the basis of competition in their respective industries.

Both AHSC and AA built their strategic systems upon internal systems that were originally designed to automate back-office transaction processing. AHSC, for example, first installed computers to manage internal inventory and order processing activities; AA used computers to manage their internal reservation process. In both cases, the value of these early systems came from the ability to structure, simplify, and coordinate internal operations. But, once they had simplified and structured activities inside the firm,

---

[15]See McKenney, J.L. and Copeland, D.G., *Waves of Change,* Boston: HBS Press, 1995 and Applegate, L.M., "Electronic Commerce," *The Technology Management Handbook,* ed. Dorf, Richard C., CRC Press, 1999 for an in-depth discussion of the evolution of early strategic systems.

both AHSC and AA recognized that they could allow customers to take over performing the activities without fear of losing control. Because each firm had built its systems using proprietary technology, AHSC and AA owned the platform upon which business was conducted—and they also owned the information flowing from the automated transaction systems. This information enabled executives and front-line workers in both firms to coordinate and control activities whether they took place inside the firm or outside. And, by harnessing the power of the information, both firms were able to differentiate existing services and to offer new information-based services.

The benefit of conducting business online was so great that AHSC gave hospitals the card readers required to do business electronically and taught hospital supply clerks how to use them. AHSC even helped hospital personnel redesign their internal purchasing processes to fit with the new on-line process. AA did the same thing when they gave travel agents the computer reservation system terminals. Neither AHSC nor AA charged their customers for the computer equipment or the training. Why? The benefits to AHSC and AA from on-line purchasing, whether it was hospital supplies or seats on an airplane, more than offset the cost of giving away the terminals. For example, by 1985, AHSC saved over $11 million per year through on-line ordering and generated $4 to $5 million per year in additional revenue.

The AHSC and AA examples demonstrate how two firms used IT to fundamentally alter the basis of competition in their respective industries. This occurred when executives implemented strategies that radically changed both the cost structure for the industry and, at the same time, differentiated the product/service offering, causing massive shifts in market share and demand.

As we enter the 21st century, Internet pioneers are using today's technology innovations to reengineer value chains and fundamentally change the basis of competition. The Charles Schwab story, presented in the Introduction of this book, provides an example of how a firm built upon existing capabilities and technology infrastructure to radically transform the financial services industry. Founded in 1975, Schwab accomplished this feat—not once but twice. Initially Schwab executives placed a bet that a growing number of individual investors would prefer to save money and time by using low-cost local branch office brokerage services rather than high-priced personal brokers. They were correct, and by 1997 revenues for their discount brokerage had reached $2.3 billion. The industry was forced to adjust its practices in reaction to this new entrant, although full-service brokerages remained strong.

When the commercial Internet appeared in the mid 1990s, Schwab was poised to again segment the market. Already routine customer service requests (quotes, balances, positions) had migrated from Schwab branches to the telephone and a proprietary online service. By the time it launched its Internet online brokerage in January of 1998, only 5 percent of routine customer service was handled at a brokerage office. The Web-based service provided access to online and offline brokerage services for a single fee of $29.95 per trade (compared to an average $80 per trade for full-service brokerage commissions). By the end of the same year, sales were up 19 percent. And, since the online self-service business dramatically lowered costs, profits were also up 29 percent.

Full-service brokers, such as Merrill Lynch, were initially skeptical. But, as market penetration (and market value) of Charles Schwab soared, even the most stalwart critics were forced to launch their own online/offline integrated channels. The Merrill Lynch case, included in the concluding module, enables in-depth examination of the strategic decisions that Merrill Lynch executives faced during this challenging period.

Can IT Change the Nature of Relationships and the Balance of Power in Buyer-Supplier Relationships?

As mentioned above, AHSC rose to power within the hospital supplies industry by streamlining channels, dramatically decreasing cost, improving order accuracy, and increasing speed of fulfillment between suppliers (for example, Johnson and Johnson, Baxter, and Abbott) and hospital buyers. Initially, AHSC used traditional offline processes to buy supplies from manufacturers and to store them in AHSC-owned warehouses. But, once it succeeded in getting a large number of customers to buy online, AHSC sought to further streamline the supply chain. Sensing they were at risk from being excluded from the market and lacking the money, expertise, and time to respond, suppliers succumbed to the pressure to put their catalogs online and join the electronic market. Once electronic links to suppliers had been established, AHSC customers could order directly from supplier inventory. This enabled further reduction in cost and cycle time for all members of the online market.

Customers encouraged channel consolidation; they recognized the value of a multivendor marketplace but were unwilling to put up with the problems of using multiple different supplier systems to conduct business. Within a short time, AHSC became a powerful channel manager within the hospital supply industry, controlling both the physical and information channels for conducting business. In fact, this neutral, third-party distributor created such a significant shift in the balance of power away from hospital suppliers that, in 1985, it was bought by Baxter Healthcare Corporation, a hospital supplier in the industry. A few years later, responding to pressure from market participants, Baxter was forced to spin out its distribution business.

Initially, many believed that the Internet might similarly shift power from producers (e.g., manufacturers and service providers) to channel players (e.g., wholesalers, distributors, and retailers). Indeed, during the late 1990s, Internet-based channel players flourished, especially within fragmented markets and industries. Chemdex, for example, attracted much attention (and investment) by establishing a neutral, third-party virtual marketplace for the life-sciences industry.[16] Likewise, software services firms such as Commerce One, Oracle, and Ariba developed and operated electronic marketplaces that linked buyers and suppliers across multiple industries. By mid-2000, however, many independent marketplaces, such as Chemdex, were struggling or had closed, and software services firms were suffering from weakened demand. As neutral, independent channel players faltered, suppliers and buyers exploited the shared Internet online business infrastructure to launch initiatives to defend their respective positions. Once again, the healthcare industry provided an excellent view into shifting power dynamics.

In March 2000, five of the largest healthcare suppliers—Abbott, Baxter, GE Medical, Johnson and Johnson, and Medtronic—launched the Global Healthcare Exchange, LLC (GHX).[17] GHX promised to eliminate inefficiencies in every step in the healthcare supply chain, from placing orders to tracking delivery. These inefficiencies accounted for an estimated $11 billion in unnecessary purchasing costs.[18] The five founding companies supplied over 70 percent of all products and services purchased by hospitals and healthcare providers and did business with over 90 percent of potential buyers. By early 2001, over 70 additional suppliers had signed on. Consequently, GHX greatly increased bargaining power for suppliers.

Even before the launch of GHX, however, healthcare buyers had begun to form technology-enabled coalitions, called "Group Purchasing Organizations" (GPOs). HealthTrust Purchasing Group, L.P., founded in May 1999, was an example of a GPO established to provide member healthcare providers with the highest quality supplies, equipment, and other services at the most competitive prices. Between its founding and early 2001, HealthTrust Purchasing Group negotiated purchasing agreements with over 650 hospitals, surgical centers and clinics. During 2000, these member organizations purchased over $4 billion worth of healthcare equipment and supplies. In partnership with Medibuy—a CommerceOne E-Marketplace for

---

[16]Chemdex was launched in November 1998 to serve as an independent marketplace through which buyers and suppliers in the life sciences business could conduct business. In March 2000, the founders of Chemdex created a new corporate parent, Ventro, with the goal of creating multiple marketplaces. By late 2000, Chemdex had been forced to shut down and Ventro was struggling. See Collura, M. and Applegate, L.M., *Ventro Corporation: Builder of B2B Businesses,* HBS Publishing (Order No. 801-042).

[17]In addition to serving as a leading producer within a number of industries (for example, Medical, Appliances, Lighting, Power Systems, Capital/Financial Services), General Electric also served as an online marketplace software and services firm through its Global Exchange business. GE Global Exchange assumed responsibility for building, deploying, and hosting the Global Healthcare Exchange. Learn more about the Global Healthcare Exchange by visiting the company website at www.ghx.com. A case study that discusses the joint venture is also available: Applegate, L.M., *Medtronic: Transforming for the 21st Century,* Boston: Harvard Business School Publishing (Order #801-471).

[18]Winslow, R., "Baxter International, Others Plan Net Concern for Hospital Purchases," *Wall Street Journal Interactive,* March 30, 2000.

the healthcare industry—HealthTrust Purchasing Group provided Internet-based online capabilities and solutions to its member organizations.

As we entered the 21st century, the race was on to determine whether buyer-led or supplier-led coalitions would achieve a dominant power position within healthcare electronic commerce markets. By 2001, buyer-led coalitions like HealthTrust had begun to do business with supplier-led coalitions like GHX. In fact, GHX publicly stated that they considered the new GPOs to be important members of the exchange—not just as customers but also as partners. How buyer and seller power relationships will eventually stabilize is not yet clear. What is abundantly clear, however, is that enabling technologies have had significant impact on buyer-supplier relationships and that executives whose firms participate in a wide range of business markets are being forced to rethink strategic priorities and decisions.

Can IT Build or Reduce Barriers to Entry?

Companies erect entry barriers by offering customers and other market participants attractive products and services at a price and level of quality that competitors cannot match. Before the rise of the commercial Internet, first movers like AHSC and AA spent hundreds of millions of dollars over decades to establish a dominant position within electronic markets. The sheer magnitude of the investment to build and operate proprietary networks, transaction systems, and databases created significant barriers to entry. For example, American Airlines and archrival United Airlines each spent hundreds of millions of dollars during the late 1970s and early 1980s to build the proprietary networks and computer systems required to launch and run online customer reservation systems. By the time other airlines recognized the situation, they were forced to tie into these two dominant online channels or risk being cut off from customers.[19]

Over time, however, these technology-based advantages decreased. The more sustainable advantage came from second order barriers to entry created by exploiting the value of information generated by the technology and the value of the loyal community of suppliers, customers, and partners that did business using the company's proprietary digital infrastructure.

Today, many believe that the overall impact of the Internet technologies will be to lower entry barriers for all players in online markets.[20] This belief arises from the fact that Internet technologies dramatically lower the cost of participating in an electronic market. In addition, the shared, nonproprietary

---

[19]During the late 1980s and early 1990s, new entrant Southwest Airlines offered a regional service that offered a significant decrease in price and a corresponding increase in the number of flights to popular destinations within a local area. This niche market strategy enabled them to achieve a sustainable competitive advantage without tying into online reservation systems. By early 2000, Southwest was able to offer their own online reservation system that enabled customers to bypass travel agents and buy directly from Southwest.

[20]Porter, M., "Strategy and the Internet," *Harvard Business Review,* March 2001.

nature of the Internet makes it easy for market participants to link to a common, shared platform for conducting business online and, more importantly, to sever ties with one firm and link to another.

Indeed, the low cost and ease of penetration decreases the benefits to any one participant unless people within the firm are capable of learning and responding more quickly and more effectively than others, are able to build proprietary capabilities that are not easily replicable, and are able to build a large, loyal community that remains connected despite the availability of seemingly comparable alternatives. As we saw in the past, these "knowledge and community barriers" provide a more sustainable entry barrier within Internet-based electronic markets. In most cases, we see that incumbent firms with large investments in proprietary infrastructure and channels to market are at a particular disadvantage relative to new entrants when attempting to create and quickly deploy second order barriers to entry.

Amazon.com, one of the most celebrated new entrants of the dot-com era, provides an example of how new technology can lower entry barriers in an established industry. But, as we will see, while entry barriers were initially low, Amazon's original e-retail business model required the company to take ownership of physical inventory. This, in turn, required significant investment in building a "click and order" retail infrastructure, which, delayed profitability and, by late 2000, threatened the dominant position the company had achieved.

In July 1995, Jeff Bezos, Amazon's CEO and founder, launched the online bookstore from a 400-square foot warehouse (about the size of a one-car garage) with only a few servers and a high-speed connection to the Internet. The company quickly became the #1 online bookstore. Just two years after launch, sales had reached $148 million and the number of customers exceeded 2 million.

During its third year, Amazon executives demonstrated that the initial success in quickly dominating the online book market could be repeated. During the summer and fall of 1998, Amazon opened new online music and video "stores," and achieved the #1 position in online music sales within four months and the #1 position in online video sales within a record 45 days.[21]

The Amazon story demonstrates how the Internet can lower entry barriers to the detriment of established players. But there is also a deeper lesson here. Established competitors, such as Barnes and Noble, Borders, and Bertelsmann (in Europe), were not blind to Amazon's early success; they invested heavily but were unable to catch up. Why? Many erroneously believed that Amazon's dominance came from its first-mover advantage. While this was important, in other instances first movers have been quickly crushed. CDNow, for example, was overtaken by Amazon.com in short order.

---

[21]See Collura, M. and Applegate, L.M., *Amazon.com 2000,* HBS Publishing (Order No. 801-194) reprinted in Module 2.

The secret to Amazon's success was the knowledge and community barriers that Amazon.com executives built underneath its website. In fact, during 1999 and 2000, Amazon executives spent almost $500 million building a sophisticated, web-based order fulfillment capability that enabled the company to fulfill orders for over 31 million units during the 6-week 2000 holiday period from mid-November to the end of December. Over 99 percent of orders arrived on time.

The transaction infrastructure fed valuable information into a sophisticated knowledge management infrastructure that allowed executives and employees at all levels to develop a real-time understanding of the dynamics of the marketplace and of the needs of market participants. Amazon used this knowledge to coordinate and control operations—not only inside the firm but also across organizational boundaries. More importantly, it used its growing understanding of customer preferences to personalize its online services in a way that could not be matched by competitors and to feed valuable information to suppliers. The number of loyal customers increased quickly and by late 2000, over 25 million people shopped on Amazon. These proprietary knowledge and community barriers enabled Amazon to develop powerful barriers to entry that, to date, competitors have been unable to match. In Bezos' words:

> The Amazon.com platform is comprised of brand, customers, technology, distribution capability, deep e-commerce expertise, and a great team with a passion for innovation and serving customers well. We believe that we have reached a "tipping point," where this platform allows us to launch new e-commerce businesses faster, with a higher quality of customer experience, a lower incremental cost, a higher chance of success, and a clearer path to scale and profitability than perhaps any other company.[22]

By mid 2001, however, many wondered whether these proprietary advantages would be enough. After the rapid decline in the price of Internet stocks during 2000 and the loss of investor confidence in e-business models, the company found that sources of financing had dried up. Amazon executives altered the company's strategy and business model away from a dependence on retail product sales and toward a services model in an effort to reach profitability more quickly. This new strategy paralleled the approach used by AHSC and AA during the 1980s, as Amazon shifted from selling products to selling expertise to those established retailers that wished to tap into online markets while avoiding the risk and time required to develop, deploy, and manage equivalent capabilities. As of spring 2001, ToysRus.com and Borders had signed multiyear outsourcing contracts. At the time this book went to press, however, it was still unclear whether Amazon would be able to achieve its strategic goals before it ran through its rapidly-dwindling cash reserves.

---

[22]Amazon.com Annual Report, 1999.

Can IT Raise or Lower Switching Costs?

To provide a sustainable source of revenues, an IT system should ideally be easy to start using but difficult to stop using. Customers drawn into the system through a series of increasingly valuable enhancements should willingly become dependent on the system's functionality. Once use of the system becomes ingrained within day-to-day activities, switching to another system becomes difficult and costly.

In the past, when proprietary technologies were the norm, switching costs were often high because switching usually required buying into different proprietary networks and systems owned and operated by an online channel manager, such as American Airlines in the travel services industry, American Hospital Supply in the hospital supplies industry, or Wal-Mart in the retail industry. With the advent of the Internet, however, connecting costs little and technologies required to participate are not proprietary. Switching costs are, therefore, substantially reduced. For example, the cost to a customer of switching from shopping at Amazon to shopping at Barnes & Nobles is merely the effort required for a few keystrokes. Easy switching makes for easy price comparisons, which suggests that, over time, price will become the dominant factor determining customer loyalty.

While there appears to be a certain inevitability to this logic, savvy executives, for example, Scott Cook at Intuit, have identified ways to exploit the power of the Internet to increase, rather than decrease, switching costs. Launched in 1983, Intuit provided inexpensive financial services software (Quicken, TurboTax, and QuickBooks) designed to be easy-to-use by individuals with little to no background in finance or technology. Initially, the products "hooked" the user by providing a much simpler and easier way to complete time-consuming and repetitive tasks. By also providing a simple way to store personal information for re-use in the future, which would have to be re-entered if a customer switched to a different product, the company kept users hooked over time. Intuit quickly became the market leader for individual and small business financial software with over 80 percent market share across its product line and over 90 percent retention rates. The company continues to maintain this position despite aggressive competition by Microsoft.

A decade after launching its first software product, the company launched an online financial services portal, Quicken.com, to complement and extend its packaged software offerings. By linking its Internet business to the company's traditional desktop software, Intuit has been able to transition users from one product line to another while also offering an even easier to use and more useful set of services. By 2000, consumers and small business owners could pay bills and bank online, calculate and pay taxes, and manage a portfolio of investments. Small business owners also could manage payroll, customer accounts, purchase supplies, and inventory. As these features were added to the service, and as customers gained from their value and convenience, switching become more difficult. Changing an online bill paying service, for example, involved setting up relationships between the new online bill paying service and each company to be paid.

Intuit used the lessons learned from its successful software business to guide the launch and evolution of its Internet business. Careful attention was paid to create a service offering that provided a unique value proposition for customers and that "hooked" them to the company by providing a simple and easy-to-use way to complete time-consuming and repetitive tasks. And, once users invest the effort to store personal information, it becomes much harder to switch. Using these principles, within one year of launch, Intuit's online version of its TurboTax software gained over 80 percent market share in the highly competitive online tax preparation and filing market.

Can IT Create New Products or Add Value to Existing Ones?

In addition to lowering cost, improving quality, and changing power dynamics, IT also can add value to existing products or services and create new ones. For example, grocery stores used to be in the business of selling packaged goods and fresh food. But, now they are also in the business of selling information. Many market research firms purchase scanner data on consumer shopping behavior from large supermarket chains, analyze it, and then sell it back to the supermarkets along with aggregate competitor, industry, and demographic data from a wide variety of sources.

The information content of existing products also has increased markedly. Many are unaware that, in early 2000, there were more computer chips in a late-model car than were in the entire U.S. National Defense Department in 1960. Not only do these chips control everything from internal air temperature to the braking system, they provide valuable information to service mechanics and auto manufacturers to guide after-sales service and future product design.

Information technologies can alter or even completely transform a product from an analog to a digital form. Products particularly well-suited to digitization include books, magazines and other printed materials, music, video, and games. Over the past two years, established firms, such as Time Warner and Bertelsmann, Internet start-ups, like Napster and Amazon.com's e-books, and new coalitions of firms, such as MusicNet and Duet have proven that digital distribution of books, music, and video is here to stay.[23]

---

[23]On April 2, 2001, AOL Time Warner, Bertelsmann, EMI Group, and RealNetworks announced the formation of MusicNet, a joint venture that would create a "breakthrough platform" for an online music subscription service. On April 6, 2001, Yahoo! announced a non-exclusive partnership arrangement with Sony and Universal to make the latter two company's Duet online music service available through Yahoo!. See Cavallaro, M., "Yahoo and Duet: Déjà vu All Over Again," *The Standard* (www.thestandard.com) April 6, 2001.

Putting the Ideas to Work

Exploiting the opportunities afforded by the IT in the 21st century, while avoiding the pitfalls, requires vision, sound execution, and the ability to respond quickly. It also requires imagination—and a little luck.

The H.E. Butt Grocery case[24] shows how a U.S. grocery company moved to providing on-line ordering and delivery to customers thus changing the industry value chain. This case shows how key components of the industry value chain are disintermediated even in what on the surface looks to be a prosaic industry.

The next case features Admart,[25] a Hong Kong-based on-line grocery delivery service (similar to Webvan). The case captures the unique dynamics of change in a de novo start up, as well as capturing the special cultural issues involved in adapting an Internet approach to an environment very different from the United States.

The final case in this series shows the full nature of the global IT revolution today. Li & Fung,[26] a Hong Kong-based trading company with a deep network of supplier relationships, planned to use the Internet to move from selling just to its traditional large retailers to small- and mid-sized retail companies as well. Li & Fung implemented their strategy through software developed in a $200 million funded subsidiary in Silicon Valley. The case captures the challenges of the borderless world and shows how unknown competitors 8,000 miles away can suddenly appear and cause havoc for established players.

Collectively, these three cases address the powerful managerial issues that executives face and the decisions they must make when launching IT-enabled businesses and strategies.

---

[24]Dailey, M. and McFarlan, F.W., *H.E. Butt Grocery Company: The New Digital Strategy (A),* (HBS No. 300-106).
[25]Lane, D., McFarlan, F.W. and Knoop, C., *Admart,* (HBS No. 301-046).
[26]Young, F. and McFarlan, F.W., *Li & Fung,* (HBS No. 301-009).

CASE 1–1
H. E. BUTT GROCERY COMPANY: THE NEW DIGITAL STRATEGY (A)[1]

In the year 2000 the Internet promised to transform the retail grocery industry by providing a powerful communications network for the direct sale of groceries to consumers and for business-to-business electronic commerce. Fully Clingman, president and COO of HEB Butt Grocery Company (HEB), was placing renewed emphasis on technology in order to position the company in this new environment, while preserving HEB's consumer orientation and its trusted brand name. Specifically, in recent months, HEB had appointed a new director of e-retailing, John Sturm, to implement an electronic commerce strategy and a new chief information officer, Don Beaver, Sr., to inject new efficiencies into the supply chain. Clingman asked HEB managers to make Customer Relationship Management (CRM)—"nobody gets between HEB and the customer"—the theme of HEB's transition into the digital age. On March 8, a new organization structure was announced to intensify the organization's commitment to this rapidly evolving technology. Exhibit 1 is a memorandum describing the new structure.

The Competition

In 1999 HEB Grocery Company ranked 14th among leading grocery retailers, with $6.5 billion in sales from its 260 Texas store locations, but it was becoming clear that the company would have to navigate through a tumultuous period in order to maintain and improve its market position.[2] Consolidated grocery chains and mass merchants and were engaged in a steady market-by-market roll-up. U.S. retail grocery sales in 1998 totaled $449 billion, with the top four chains as of early 1999 (Kroger, Safeway, Albertson's, and Ahold USA) representing over 30% of the market.[3] Consolidation among traditional grocers had helped the top players create a concentration of market power and reduced operating expenses. Wal-Mart sold groceries in 564 super centers, with 150 more scheduled to open in 2000. The mass merchant's innovative "Neighborhood Markets" targeted a new customer base—buyers who wanted around-the-corner convenience and low prices. "In effect, Wal-Mart, once the icon for big-box retailing, is reinventing itself as the "small town" grocer for the new millennium," reported *Progressive Grocer.*[4]

A new breed of online grocers offered busy consumers a way of saving the time and trouble involved in going to the store. Customers shopped via computer for groceries that would be delivered straight to their kitchens. Investors rewarded rich valuations to early entrants in the online grocery industry—Webvan, Homegrocer and Peapod—despite the fact that profitability was considered a long-term goal. In addition to the grocery delivery services, the specialty dot-com retailers also posed a threat to the traditional grocer.

---

[1]This case was prepared by Research Associate Melissa Daily under the supervision of Professor F. Warren McFarlan.

Copyright © 2000 by the President and Fellows of Harvard College. Harvard Business School case 300-106.

---

[2]*2000 Marketing Guidebook,* (Wilton, CT: TradeDimensions, 1999).

[3]Mark Tosh, "Forever Changed: A wave of consolidation in 1998 has created a Big Three in food retailing: Kroger, Albertson's and Safeway," *Progressive Grocer Annual Report,* April, 1999.

[4]Len Lewis, "Markets in Motion: Supermarket sales hold their own, but labor, profit, and competitive issues loom large," *Progressive Grocer Annual Report,* April, 1999.

EXHIBIT 1   HEB Interoffice Memorandum

INTEROFFICE MEMORANDUM

TO: All Members of Management
FROM: Fully Clingman
Date: March 8, 2000

I'm excited to announce a new, big commitment for H-E-B. We are working "full-speed" ahead to create a new business . . . . selling Food, Drug Store and Pharmacy products and service to our customers over the Internet at **HEB.com!** Our goal is to be operational in this business, beginning with Austin, this fall.

In addition to giving H-E-B a new channel in which to sell products and services, our commitment is to use technology and 1:1 customer marketing, to transform the way ALL of H-E-B does business—-from the way we work with our suppliers to the way we interact with our customer—-on the Internet **AND** in our stores.

I am pleased to announce the following assignments and reporting relationships:

Bob Loeffler, formerly President of Pantry Foods & Dallas Divisions, will become President of a new division—-E-Commerce & Customer Relationship Marketing. Bob will continue to report to me.

Alan Markert will become VP of E-Commerce, and will transition out of his role as VP Finance over the next several months. Alan will report to Bob.

Harrison Lewis will become Director of Business-to-Business e-commerce, reporting jointly to Alan and our CIO, Don Beaver.

John Sturm will continue in his role as Director/General Manager of HEB.com, reporting to Alan.

Included in the new E-Commerce & Customer Relationship Marketing Division are:

*   **E-retailing.** This new way of doing business is gaining momentum daily, and we must be as competitive in this arena as we are in our H-E-B stores.

*   **Hal Collett,** VP/General Manager of the Central Texas Region, will add the first HEB.com fulfillment activities to his accountabilities in Austin, and will report to Bob for this operation. As the HEB.com pioneer, Hal will be intimately involved with the design of how e-retailing will work at H-E-B, and will be charged with developing this into a business we can quickly implement in other markets.

*   **Business-to-Business E-Commerce.** Where e-retailing deals with how H-E-B can satisfy the needs of customers, "B2B" e-commerce deals with our suppliers. Our objective is to conduct ALL routine business electronically, at Internet speeds, and without error.

*   **Customer Marketing.** As opposed to merchandising, which deals with the products we sell, how we display them, and how we promote them, Customer Marketing focuses on building the H-E-B brand, consumer research, and applying consumer insight across the company.

*   **Customer Relationship Management.** By building a customer database that allows us to know who are customers are and what they buy, we will be able to market effectively to each individual customer, and to create a relationship with each that generates loyalty to H-E-B.

Please join me in congratulating these Partners in their new roles and in supporting our efforts to build the greatest retailing company!

Would consumers continue to buy wine, coffee, flowers or camera film at the local grocery store, when they could shop online at wine.com, coffee.com, ftd.com or Kodak.com? HEB's market research showed that the pharmacy was the grocery department most vulnerable to specialty dot-com retailers, thanks to the rising popularity of commercial Web sites such as cvs.com, drugstore.com, planetrx. com, mothernature. com., and cybervitamin.com.

Forrester research predicted that online grocery sales would reach $10.8 billion by 2003, only 2% of total industry sales (see Exhibit 2).[5] The research firm predicted that supermarkets would ignore the online market until 2003, when sales were expected to surpass the $10 billion mark. But in 2000, leading food retailers were already making moves to win market share in cyberspace.

Online Grocery Shopping

Clingman intended to move quickly to protect HEB's markets. In a 1999 HEB survey of 800 customers in Austin, San Antonio and Houston, only 13% said they had made an online purchase. As Internet access and higher-speed bandwidths spread around the country, however, HEB estimated that one in five customers would become online shoppers by 2004. "This is as much a part of my grandchildren's lives as a wristwatch. As one generation moves through the pipeline to another, I think we're going to see a dramatic surge of activity."

HEB's new Director of E-Retailing, John Sturm, developed recommendations for the company's entry into the online market. In January, 2000 the HEB Executive Committee voted to move forward with the following three Internet initiatives, as a way of better understanding the issues.

1. Sturm would lead a redesign of the HEB Web site and the addition of several information services such as recipes, food safety information, and local store activities. Kiosks inside the stores would provide easy access to the Web site. Most importantly, the Web site would give HEB a new way to identify and communicate with the customer. "If, for instance, the customer comes to count on you for e-mail to let them

know when the fresh catch of shrimp or haddock comes in from the dock, then you've found a way to establish one more thread of the relationship beyond just the business," explained Bob Loeffler, president, e-commerce & customer relationship marketing.

2. HEB planned to launch a transactional pharmacy Web site in 2000, offering customers a new way to fill prescriptions. Customers would place their order online, and then receive the pharmaceutical product via direct mail. This plan would leverage the company's earlier investment in the construction of a new central facility for distribution of pharmaceuticals. Sturm argued that the creation of a transactional pharmacy would enable HEB to leverage existing assets, develop e-commerce expertise, and begin to build an online customer base that could be transitioned to online groceries.

3. HEB would enter the online grocery business by providing an Internet interface for online ordering and depot centers where customers could pick up their bagged goods. HEB's survey had revealed that most of their customers were not eager to have a delivery person in their kitchen but that they would welcome the opportunity to pick up bagged groceries from a store or other convenient location. HEB's proposed network of depots would include existing stores, new ministores, or even refrigerated trucks located in corporate parking lots. The company would have to place great emphasis on process engineering as it developed a system to fill up to 4,000 orders a day, seven days a week.

In spite of its eight-digit investment, HEB's executive committee voted to move forward

[5]"On-Line Grocery Exposed," The Forrester Report:, Volume One, Number Five, August 1998.

EXHIBIT 2 Total Electronic Grocery Spending

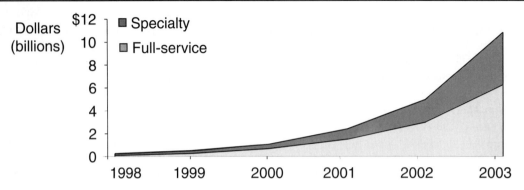

	1998	1999	2000	2001	2002	2003
Specialty	$79	$248	$659	$1,548	$3,058	$6,291
Full-service	156	265	473	911	1,951	4,545
Total revenue (millions)	$235	$513	$1,132	$2,459	$5,009	$10,836
Percent of industry total	0.05%	0.11%	0.23%	0.49%	0.98%	2.05%

		Online grocers	Specialty Online Retailers
Service providers	Example companies	• Peapod • Streamline • HomeRuns • ShopLink	• Kosher Supermarket • NetGrocer • Godiva • Hickory Farms
	Product selection	• All including perishables	• Gifts • Hard-to-find items • Build replenishment
Buyers	Demographics	• 80% female/20% male • Average age 35 • 65% with kids	• 35% female/65% male • Average age 40 • 36% with kids
	Location	• Urban area: ≥		• Nationwide/worldwide
	Primary motivation	• Convenience	• Convenience • Impulse/seasonality
Purchase behavior	Cost per order Items per order No. purchase per year Membership/delivery fee	• $105 average • ± 60 • 25–30 average • $10–$30 per month	• $50–$60 average • 1–2 • 2–3 • $5–$10 per order

Source: "On-Line Grocery Exposed," *The Forrester Report:,* Volume One, Number Five, August 1998.

with the depot model because they felt that in the long-term it would protect market share and overall profitability. In addition, the depots could be used as cross-docks to enable a home delivery model in the future.

In order to turn ideas into action, Sturm argued that his team would have to function with the speed and flexibility of an entrepreneurial group. "The e-commerce organization and culture must be designed to compete at digital speed," said Sturm in his report to management. "Deviation from traditional decision making processes may be needed for success." Clingman and other HEB senior executives were prepared to give its "dot-com" enterprise some independence from corporate structures in order to accelerate the development of Internet retail.

Strengthening the Supply Chain

HEB's successful Efficient Consumer Response (ECR) implementation had enabled the company to shorten and eliminate costs in the order cycle. Despite its successes, HEB managers agreed that there was still much work to do in streamlining efficiency. "A big interest of mine is getting rid of all the waste in handling cost, in storage of inventory on hand," said Clingman. HEB's Chief Accounting and Financial Officer, Jack Brouillard, explained that it was time to invest in new, integrated IT systems that would further streamline procurement and planning.

> From 1978 to 1996 HEB made a lot of money from the use of technology to improve operations. Now we are going to adopt strategies that would not be possible without technology. The cry for decision support is everywhere and in order to do it you must have a robust knowledge database. Within the year, we'll be doing a lot of work on data mining, hiring people for whom data is their life.

HEB planned to implement a new version of its store replenishment system (SRS) in the summer of 2000. SRS used point-of-sale (POS) data to produce a perpetual inventory, producing orders automatically to continuously replenish the store. The more advanced SRS would allow managers to judge stock-outs at the shelf level, rather than the warehouse level. Since HEB effectively owned only 10% of its warehouse inventory in 2000, information sharing with suppliers was becoming even more critical to supply chain efficiency.

A second upcoming HEB initiative was fast-slow warehousing. Profitable market baskets often contained slow-moving items. Yet 80% of HEB's product movement came from only 20% of its items—the "fast-movers." By managing its slow and fast-moving items from different distribution centers, with different acceptance and delivery systems, HEB hoped to deal more gracefully with all of its products and realize new efficiencies and cost savings.

HEB also planned to use Internet technologies to lower the cost of its internal and business-to-business communication. The company had developed a robust intranet for sharing a wide variety of data across the enterprise, including human resources and financial information. In 2000, HEB turned its attention to the development of an extranet for Web-based collaboration with suppliers. HEB would step beyond electronic data interchange (EDI) and provide a Web interface to its product databases. The company was becoming involved with UCC-Net, a nonprofit subsidiary of the Uniform Code Council, which was developing supermarket industry standards for extranet development. Standards for an industry-wide extranet were expected to be released in 2000.

Retail Store Operations

Managers agreed that the way to differentiate HEB from Wal-Mart was to continue building the relationship with the customer in every way possible. As part of its CRM initiative, HEB implemented a self-scanning pilot system, which allowed customers to ring up their own groceries. Shoppers would pass their own groceries through a scanner, which would read each item's bar code, total the cost of the order, and then accept customer payment with a debit or credit card. To ensure honesty, the scanners could check each item's weight to help ensure that customers did not exchange product bar codes.

In addition, HEB would begin to analyze POS data in order to identify the best-selling mix of merchandise and assess the effectiveness of promotions. While some leaders felt that CRM should be implemented in person (i.e., a wine steward assists the customer in making a selection), other executives also wanted to utilize POS data to keep in touch with individual customers. Loeffler explained: "We need to find a new way to go back to the 1950s where Mr. Whipple knew who you were as soon as you walked in the door. There are too many people now to do it the traditional way; but we can do it with integrated systems. What we're looking for is a deepening of the relationship that we have with the customer."

Although approximately 50% of HEB customers used some type of credit or debit card for their purchases, HEB had no way of identifying individual customers. Some industry retailers were planning to mine loyalty card data and direct promotions to customers based on their individual preferences. Clingman wanted to refrain from implementing a loyalty-card program because he felt that it might eventually lead to disloyalty. Pushing price promotions contradicted the stores' EDLP [Every Day Low Price] policy, he said. He was also concerned about the ethical questions around collection of data at the checkout counter: "We've decided to take the high road on that and not backdoor people and have them wonder, 'How did I get this information?' "

The company decided to postpone the implementation of electronic tagging until it was more affordable. The price of electronic tagging (over $4 per tag) was considered to be too expensive.

CASE 1–2
adM@rt (A)[1]

Our business has to be built with the bricks of innovation through the process of trial and error. Every time we make a mistake we learn what is not doable, and that shows us what probably is doable. Learning what is impossible shows us what is possible. And we use that negative information to discover a new way of doing business.

—Jimmy Lai Chee-ying, Owner, *Next Media Group*

[1]This case was prepared by Senior Researcher David Lane under the direction of Professor F. Warren McFarlan and Carin-Isabel Knoop, Executive Director, Global Research Group.

Jimmy Lai wondered if he had it right. No matter, the 51-year-old apparel magnate turned media-baron could always change it if it wasn't. Or could he? Lai had already reworked adM@rt, his e-commerce venture, three times in nine months. His freewheeling style had served him well in the past, but Lai wondered at what point trial and error would not suffice to satisfy investors now that his flagship Next Media assets[2] were listed on Hong Kong's stock exchange.

In addition to shareholders, Lai also needed to maintain the support of his various business managers, each of whom wanted the peace of mind to build and run a business without having to revamp, reorganize, and recapitalize to suit Lai's mercurial business visions. What kind of organization could promote the flexibility and experimentation on which Lai thrived without belittling the complexities and managerial challenges his employees faced in their day-to-day lines of business? Was "act first, ask questions later" the right management approach for an internet venture in which brand reputation, website loading times, and punctual, accurate delivery were critical elements of success?

A lively entrepreneur and charismatic salesman, Lai first came to prominence as the CEO of Hong Kong-based Giordano, a retail chain selling casual sportswear that gained a reputation for attentive customer service in Hong Kong and beyond. In 1995, Lai started *Apple Daily,* which quickly rose through Hong Kong's crowded newspaper market to become a bestseller. The popularity of *Apple*'s online edition led Lai in June 1999 to launch adM@rt ("ad" for *Apple Daily*), an e-commerce venture that first sold household staples and then consumer electronics, office supplies, and airplane tickets, with next day home delivery for orders placed by phone, fax, or over the Internet. (Exhibit 1 shows pages from adM@rt's website.) Lai had lost as much as HK$ 60 million a month[3] since adM@rt's launch in June 1999,

and planned to invest no more than a total of US$ 130 million of his own funds on the venture.[4] Even so, Lai had bigger plans afoot. With Next Media, a group of online consumer and lifestyle services established in 1999, Lai hoped to integrate his access to Hong Kong's consumers and small businesses with his offline content and brand strength. Though his final objectives were not yet clear, Lai assumed, as ever, that careful listening to his customers would show him the correct path.

Jimmy Lai and His Businesses

A former street urchin and grade-school dropout, Lai started out in a succession of garment factory jobs and picked up some English along the way. Smart and ambitious, he quickly rose through the ranks until, in 1975, he started his own clothing line. In 1980, Lai borrowed the notion of selling children inexpensive T-shirts and jeans from Gap Inc. in the United States, and built Giordano International Ltd. (named after a New York pizzeria) into a chain of 600 stores in a dozen Asian countries and over $400 million in annual sales.

But Lai became bored with retail. The offspring of his ennui was a ground-breaking weekly called *Next,* a glossy magazine he started in March 1991 that came in two parts: news, finance, and features, and an equally thick entertainment/lifestyle section. Stories included daring exposés of local Chinese criminal organizations known as triads, reports on prostitution, and investigations into alleged government corruption. By 1994 *Wired Magazine* called Lai the "coolest man in town,"[5] and with sales of

---

[2]Lai owned 88% of the magazine publishing unit, which also included online publications and 12 online consumer services.

[3]The Hong Kong dollar was pegged to the U.S. dollar at a rate of HK$ 7.8 to US$ 1.

[4]"Internet Retailing: Van Attack," *Economist,* September 18, 1999; Robin Paul Ajello and Ron Gluckman, "Inside Story: Hong Kong: The Maverick vs. the Establishment," *AsiaWeek,* December 3, 1999.

[5]Jeff Greenwald, "Media Typhoon," *Wired,* December 1994, p. 3.

EXHIBIT 1   adM@rt Web Pages, August 3, 2000

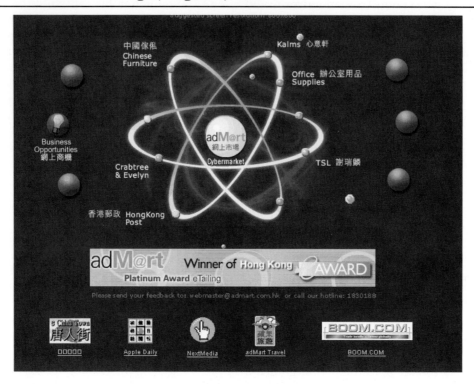

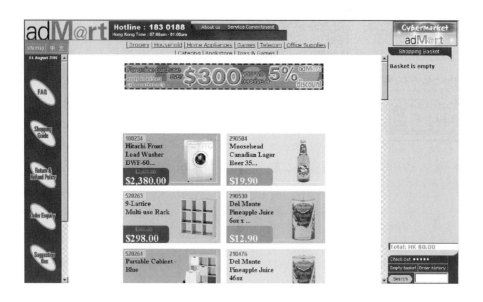

180,000 copies a week, *Next* had become Hong Kong's top-selling news magazine.

In 1995, he launched *Apple Daily,* a publication much like the British tabloids. (Exhibit 2 shows a recent page from *Apple Daily*'s online edition.) Though it faced dozens of competing Hong Kong newspapers, by 2000, *Apple Daily* led them all in advertising revenue and was second in circulation, selling some 430,000 copies daily. In addition to its sensationalist coverage, the newspaper had made its name with a fierce defense of Hong Kong's independence. Courting controversy was not riskless, however, and in 2000, an *Apple Daily* reporter

EXHIBIT 2   *Apple Daily* Online Edition, August 3, 2000

was fined for illicitly seeking news tips from the Hong Kong police. Other events had earlier forced Lai to sell his stake in Giordano in 1996 for US$ 280 million. That summer triad thugs had broken into *Next* offices and smashed the magazine's computers. The Hong Kong storefronts of Giordano were spray painted, and Lai's house was targeted by firebombs. Lai dismissed such tactics, however: "If they threaten me, they won't kill me," he had observed. "If they want to kill me, they won't threaten me."[6]

Meanwhile, Next Media prospered. Begun in 1994 as an internet offshoot of *Next Magazine* for overseas Chinese interested in Hong Kong life, by 2000, as Next Media.com it comprised print and online publications, as well as e-commerce services like local movie and restaurant reviews that catered to specific vertical segments of Lai's Hong Kong audience. By mid-2000, Next Media employed over 400 journalists across its magazines and newspapers, both print and digital. Its four magazines were *NEXT Magazine* ("for people with an edge"), *Sudden Weekly* (targeted to the 15- to 25-year old female population, with features on celebrities, health, fashion, and travel), *Easy Finder* (classified listings), and *Eden Travel*. About 200 staff focused on the web site, of whom 60% to 70% created online content. Advertising was the main source of revenue. (Exhibit 3 shows the Next Media.com home page.)

adM@rt Takes Shape

For some years, Lai had harbored hopes of creating a home-delivery retailing operation entirely separate from his online and offline publications. He started to build adM@rt early in 1999, realizing that growing internet use in Hong Kong had created a new marketing channel ideally suited to reach consumers with significant discretionary income. Hong Kong seemed perfect for the business: no other place had six million passionate consumers crammed into clusters of cheek-by-jowl apartment towers and connected by some of the most advanced telecom networks in the world.[7] Furthermore, though the dominant local supermarket chains, Park N' Shop and Wellcome, ran 182 and 228 stores respectively, most were cramped, dingy, and lacked parking lots. The largest might carry 10,000 items—half what a big U.S. store would display. In this environment, adM@rt seemed to have plenty of advantages. Following a model that had turned San Francisco-based Webvan, a similar home-delivery firm, into one of the most keenly followed Internet companies, adM@rt promised delivery of bulk staples like rice within a day in a cramped city with congested public transport and a perpetual parking shortage. adM@rt also had the benefit of being nearly fully virtual, in a city with some of the most expensive retail space in the world. Without a brick-and-mortar retail presence, adM@rt did not have to worry about cannibalizing any pre-existing sales. Finally, Lai could use groceries as an attention-getting market-entry device to sell higher-margin items like computers, telecom and other consumer electronics, as well as travel and financial services.

However, Lai had never sold groceries or electronics before. To create a credible business, he hired Philippe Ravelli on March 15, 1999 to be adM@rt CEO. Ravelli had spent 14 years with the giant French retailer Carrefour, six of them in Taiwan. Arriving to take charge of a six-person operation, Ravelli expanded adM@rt to almost 600 people within two months. At the time, skeptics abounded. Ravelli recalled the reactions of some:

> People said, "You're nuts! Hong Kong is the most convenient city in the world. Wellcome [supermarkets

---

[6]*Ibid.*

[7]This section draws upon "Internet Retailing: Van Attack," *Economist,* September 18, 1999.

EXHIBIT 3   Next Media.com Home Page, August 4, 2000

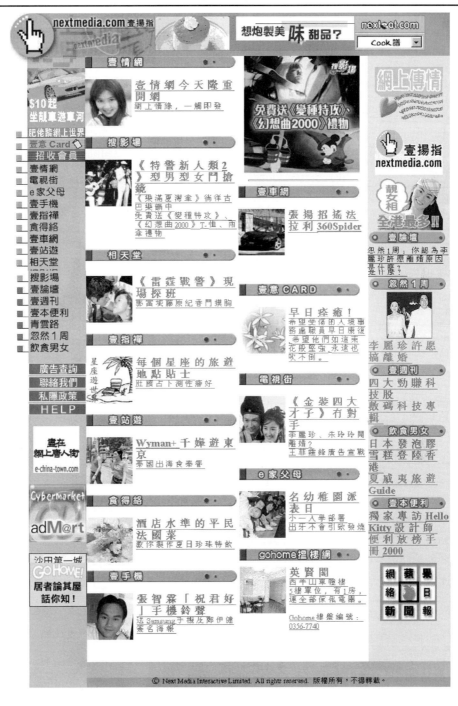

are] just downstairs [from most apartment blocks]. E-commerce works in the United States because people there have been mail ordering for 20 years, but in Hong Kong people have never done so."

Indeed, in a city where entire families crowded into one-bedroom concrete boxes, hanging out in shops and malls was a favorite, even necessary, pastime. Nor was home delivery an untried business: for several years Wellcome and Park N' Shop had offered home delivery of thousands of items ordered via the Internet or interactive TV. Nonetheless, Wellcome was averaging just 300 such orders a day in mid 1999; Hong Kong residents preferred to see and touch their groceries before buying. Even Ravelli was not immune to doubt. Internal calculations gave adM@rt just a one-in-seven chance of success.

adM@rt was officially launched on June 26th on a business to consumer (B2C) basis. Expectations were high. "It scares me," said adM@rt's Wilson Chu about the excitement surrounding the company. "I don't know if it scares Jimmy." Consumer interest in adM@rt was so intense that its website crashed upon opening. Ironically, press reports noted that frustrated would-be e-shoppers turned to Wellcome's site instead, temporarily swamping it as well. At launch "we were caught off-guard, but it reaffirmed our concept," Chu concluded.[8]

One early and persistent challenge was adM@rt's cost structure. Lai had spent heavily to create a logistics and delivery infrastructure. This investment was large even though adM@rt limited its initial product selection to 200 items. Though he had initially proposed starting with 30 warehouses, Lai settled instead on one central warehouse at Hong Kong's main container port of Kwai

Chung, and then leased warehouse space at inexpensive industrial sites to create a network of 16 separate satellite order-fulfillment centers across Hong Kong. Lai also bought a fleet of 220 delivery vans and set up a call center for phone orders and customer service.

Supply Challenges

Another significant challenge lay in lining up local suppliers, many of whom either sold to or had close ties to Wellcome and Park N' Shop. The two chains controlled around 70% of the US$ 2.4 billion market for supermarket sales in Hong Kong, and vendors were reluctant to alienate them. Nor could adM@rt afford to invest in large inventories of diverse products. As Lai remarked, "Without sales volume, we're dead, because we can't keep 4,000 items like the supermarkets do." Ravelli therefore felt compelled to rely on parallel imports[9]:

> When we talked to vendors, they first said, "We don't believe in the concept," and then they received instructions not to deliver to us. Nobody was willing to deliver merchandise to us. So we had to do it ourselves. We did it because we didn't have any choice. We had the business model. We had the people. We had the vans. But we couldn't get any merchandise to sell.

Parallel imports created savings by allowing adM@rt to take advantage of the unevenness in global supply and demand. For example, Coca-Cola was more inexpensive in Australia when it was winter there. But that coincided with summer in Hong Kong, a time of peak demand and pricing from Coca-Cola's official Hong Kong distributor.

Though their immediate problem was solved, Ravelli and his colleagues soon realized that reliance on parallel imports could imperil adM@rt's image. The supermarkets

---

[8]Joanna Slate, "The Net: Hong Kong Entrepreneur Jimmy Lai Returns to the Spotlight Armed with a New Listing and a New Concept," *Far Eastern Economic Review,* September 9, 1999.

[9]Parallel imports were goods adM@rt purchased from a manufacturer's subsidiary, or from other wholesalers and distributors, rather than directly from the original manufacturer or the manufacturer's local agents.

hit adM@rt hard when it was discovered that the company mistakenly had imported counterfeit French wine and cognac in October 1999. Newspapers competing with *Apple Daily* reported that 30,000 rice cookers sold by adM@rt had to be recalled. They also alleged that adM@rt was violating health codes and endangering consumers because it sold canned goods made for foreign markets, with labels local consumers could not read.[10]

Chain Reactions

adM@rt had made waves well before the counterfeit wine was discovered, however. The company's launch triggered an immediate, bruising battle with the supermarkets, thanks to amazing discounts and constant promotion in *Apple Daily*. AdM@rt proved adept at exploiting the parallel import market, bringing in cut-price Coca-Cola and beer, to the fury of Hong Kong's distributors and the glee of local consumers, who leapt to stock up during the ensuing price war. Park N' Shop began discounting 1,000 items a week indefinitely, and promised to refund twice the difference in price of any of those items found available elsewhere for less. Wellcome followed suit.[11] In some ways, adM@rt's launch couldn't have come at a worse time for Hong Kong's supermarkets: despite relatively generous margins of 6% to 7%,[12] their sales were stagnating in the continuing aftermath of the regional financial shock of 1997.

Wellcome and Park N' Shop remained Hong Kong's largest advertisers, however, and each had a powerful corporate parent. Park N' Shop was owned via Hutchinson Whampoa by developer Li Ka-shing, one of the world's richest men and one of Hong Kong's most powerful people, and as such, a frequent target of Lai's populist barbs. Wellcome was part of the Jardine Matheson group of companies. Each parent group could influence trade and wholesale distribution in Hong Kong. As soon as adM@rt began promoting its bargain prices, each supermarket pulled its ads from the *Apple Daily,* as did department stores affiliated with Jardines and Li Ka-shing's companies, among others: an unrelated group of property developers followed suit and pulled all of their advertising in September and October 1999, for undisclosed reasons.[13] The paper reportedly lost 20% to 30% of its ad revenue.

In the face of strong reaction from Hong Kong's close-knit business community, Lai played on the connections between his ventures, using *Apple Daily* to display adM@rt's toilet paper and IBM computers in big colorful ads, and printing consumer surveys in *Next* to tout how much less his computers cost. Most of the advertisers eventually returned anyway, he said:

> The department stores advertise with us [again], for example. I think the supermarkets will have to come back as well, because we're the number one newspaper in advertising. We have 28% more ad revenue as a newspaper than the number one, which is just 3% ahead of us in circulation.

---

[10]Michael Flagg, "Hong Kong Publisher Tries Online Retailing, Making Some Enemies, *Asian Wall Street Journal* August 6, 1999.

[11]Felix Chan, "Supermarket Unveils 1,000 Discounts in Price Battle," *South China Morning Post,* August 7, 1999; Rowan Callick, "Cyber Supermarket Lays HK Old Guard in the Aisles," *Australian Financial Review,* August 11, 1999.

[12]Morgan Stanley Asia estimate, cited in Dan Biers and G. Pierre Goad, "Wired for Change," *Far Eastern Economic Review,* July 6, 2000. In contrast, U.S. supermarkets typically had margins as low as 1% or 2%.

[13]One press report suggested that the developers were responding to the displeasure of the Hong Kong government with Lai. See Jessica Wong and Peter Wonacott, "In Hong Kong: Persuasion or Pressure?" *Wall Street Journal,* July 21, 2000.

Furthermore, despite his competitors' tactical leverage, Lai felt that his own opportunity lay in their failure to grasp the strategic implications of the new medium:

> A lot of people think that the online business is just business online, that it's valuable just because of its high growth. We agree with that thought, but we also think that it is too valuable an entity to look at as business alone. It has a change-agent element in it. . . . It's just too disruptive to mainstream business. And even if they're smart enough to have thought about it, they can't do it. Moreover, the online business experts normally don't have the experience of running an offline business, so they don't get it either.

Terence Ting, Next Media's Chief Operating Officer, also felt that the Hong Kong conglomerates' history of property dealings handicapped their cyberspace ventures: "Property is a zero sum game, where if I get the building, you don't. But the Web is all about win-win and partnerships, alliances, and affiliations. Not everyone understands the win-win picture." That didn't stop the supermarkets from trying. By autumn 1999 the competition was matching adM@rt's prices and no-charge delivery policy, though they had stopped competitive advertising against adM@rt after realizing the inferiority of their own logistics and delivery systems.

Handling Costs

In September 1999, adM@rt was losing an estimated US $130,000 a day. Needing 30,000 orders a day to break even, it was reportedly getting just 3,000 to 4,000.[14] Two months later, Lai revealed that losses were running at HK $50,000 to HK $60,000 per month.[15]

Not only had the website broken down within days of launch, but for some time thereafter the company had to close every Tuesday to repair the chaos of the previous week. A new server was ordered to replace a computer system that failed to process internet orders effectively, and adM@rt's communications system was expanded to handle the 50,000 daily calls it received. Only about 7% of orders were made over the Web, and the importance of hiring and training call center staff was not at first perceived. Contrary to expectations, 90% of adM@rt orders came through the call center, which was manned by operators between 7am and 10pm. "We have been working with customers to ask why they were using the phone," Ravelli reported, "and they explained clearly to us that placing orders by phone is easier than using the Web. It's easier and faster." Unfortunately, the call center was equipped to handle only 18,000 daily inquiries, and Lai began to feel that adM@rt could not rely on the Web to build critical mass because local PC penetration was too low (see Exhibit 4 for comparative data on PC penetration and web usage in the region and elsewhere).

Unanticipated spending was high and rising. What adM@rt saved in retail leases, it spent on transport, as its fleet of vans grew from 200 to 400. Detractors noted that adM@rt drivers spent most of their time carting around cases of Coca-Cola to small food shops and offices. Since adM@rt's grey-market retail prices were below those of the local Coke wholesaler, the effect was to make the company a wholesaler itself, with correspondingly thin wholesale margins. "The economics of moving Coke around Hong Kong in vans just don't work," warned one supermarket competitor.[16] Furthermore, Hong Kong's street congestion made it impossible for a driver to park at each site and deliver orders. Instead,

---

[14]"Internet Retailing: Van Attack," *Economist,* September 18, 1999.
[15]Denise Tsang, "Focus on Concept Despite Losses, AdMart Chief Says," *South China Morning Post,* January 20, 2000.

[16]"Internet Retailing: Van Attack," *Economist,* September 18, 1999.

EXHIBIT 4   Technology Penetration Statistics for Selected Countries and Regions

	Estimated PCs per 100 Inhabitants		Cellular Mobile Subscribers per 100 Inhabitants			Internet Users per 10,000 Inhabitants	
	1995	1998	1995	1998	2000e	1995	1998
Hong Kong	11.63	25.42	12.90	47.47	51.90	484.65	1,495.39
China	0.21	0.89	0.30	1.90	3.19	0.06	16.72
Singapore	17.24	45.84	9.77	34.60	46.95	301.36	1,738.58
Taiwan	8.32	15.86	3.62	21.56	36.04	117.35	1,373.07
Korea	12.08	15.68	3.66	30.19	50.43	64.66	668.32
Japan	15.25	23.72	8.15	37.38	51.18	71.88	1,323.42
Asia	1.23	2.17	0.62	3.05	4.83	7.59	87.20
United States	32.80	45.86	12.84	25.60	36.23	380.06	2,219.16
Europe	7.99	13.89	3.04	13.15	19.79	103.68	488.50

Source: International Telecommunications Union.

the driver would circle the block repeatedly in a yellow and grey adM@rt van while a delivery boy hopped out to run individual orders up to customer apartments.[17]

The additional delivery staff and call center personnel raised headcount significantly: by October 15, 1999, adM@rt employed 2,000 people. Lai incurred other unanticipated expenses as well. To raise adM@rt's profile, the company opened small shops around the city to display its merchandise. The showcases started simply with stacked cases of Pepsi, and subsequently offered consumers the chance to examine the mobile phones and electronics otherwise visible only online. The shops did not hand over any of these goods on-site, but accepted orders for home delivery.

[17]Though adM@rt's call center and delivery staff were taught to encourage people to be home for delivery, one fortunate fact of Hong Kong life voided the need for a Webvan-type lock box in the garage: 147,000 Filipinas worked throughout the city as household staff and could receive the goods, pay cash if necessary, and place orders. A maid cost about HK$3,600 a month, less than US$500, plus living expenses.

Lai decided that he had built adM@rt too many warehouses. "We tried to do things without thinking about their complexity. Even experienced trial-and-error guys like me still forget about something. Simplicity is the saving grace. At first we came out with about 200 items, then I cut it down to 70, but none of it was right anyway." Complexity came from more than the number of products on offer—supplying 16 warehouses kept adM@rt resources tied up in the logistics of fulfillment-center inventory rather than sales and delivery to consumers. The company moved quickly to slim its distribution system, retaining the central warehouse in Kwai Chung but spinning off, subletting, or settling its leases on the others. Savings were visible immediately, particularly as payroll fell with the rationalization of the warehouses, to 1,300 employees by mid-January 2000. Even so, over half of the remaining workforce handled logistics.

Ravelli, too, had drawn some conclusions, primarily about his reliance on parallel imports. "When the counterfeit cases were found," he recalled, "we started to realize that the company was at risk. So we started to really push the vendors to work with us. It took months," but by March 2000, about 80% of adM@rt's goods were supplied locally, and 20% via parallel import. His headaches did not disappear, however: "They give me merchandise, but they rape me on price." Unwilling to raise its low prices, adM@rt margins came under intense pressure. By April 2000, Ravelli was reconsidering the virtues of parallel imports, this time with closer attention to quality control.

A New Opportunity

Despite the warehouse consolidation in late 1999, by March 2000 Ravelli reported that adM@rt was selling almost 2,000 different products. What had changed? Ravelli explained:

> We started out as a B2C door-to-door delivery service just for fast moving products, no more than 200. But we started to get 1, 2, 10, 20, 50 phone calls from people who said, "I am an adM@rt customer—I order Coke and toilet paper from you. Can you do the same for office supplies?" They explained to us that when they order office supplies they need three or four different suppliers, which means three or four orders, three or four invoices, and so on. All they wanted from us was one-stop shopping. Had you come to talk to me about B2B[18] one year ago, I would have asked you to explain. Today we have B2B, B2C, and we have learned over the past nine months of operation that competition from the supermarkets means that B2B has the biggest potential.

In part because of the premium paid for well-located space, Hong Kong lacked large, warehouse-type office supply stores like the Staples or Office Depot chains found in the United States. Instead, adM@rt's competitors were the hundreds of small, family-run stationery shops scattered around the city. Ravelli elaborated:

---

[18]Business-to-business online sales.

B2B is much easier because we are facing a very fragmented market, with no competition or pressure on supply or on margins. With B2B we have a very clear strategy: we are looking for small businesses, not big corporate accounts. Today we have 6,000 accounts to which we offer office supplies, office equipment, etc. We also offer catering products for small restaurants and coffee shops.

"In B2B you are here to solve your customer problems," Ravelli noted. "When you have a small company or a small office, you are facing a lot of small problems every day."

> To solve them, you have to interact with many different players. So when we offer one-stop shopping, with everything under one roof, when we have a sales team able to resolve most problems, I think this makes their lives easier. In fact, for B2B we want to set up a small business page on adM@rt's website to handle whatever problems small businesses may contact us with.

In fact, Ravelli developed a sales force specifically to target Hong Kong's office secretaries. He explained why:

> A secretary is the most important person within a company. She can decide everything. She can decide who is going to talk to her boss. We're trying to define her needs, her fears, what can we do to solve her problems through focus groups and sales teams. We have 44 sales people who go out every day to meet secretaries and discuss their problems, or to follow up on our ordering process. It's their information that allows us to build something and own the secretary's desk.

B2B deliveries started in October 1999. By March 2000, daily B2B sales had reached HK $250,000, and grew in direct proportion to the number of accounts. To encourage new accounts, therefore, adM@rt offered 30-day terms for payment and instant credit when opening an account online. Thus, in spring 2000, B2C comprised 60% of adM@rt's business and B2B 40%, but the latter was growing much faster and offered better margins. (Exhibit 5 shows the projected online market for groceries and office supplies in the United States and Europe.)

EXHIBIT 5   Projected Market for Online Sales, United States and Europe, 1999–2003

	1999	*2000*	*2001*	*2002*	*2003*
Online users (millions)					
U.S.	104	122	138	153	168
as % of population	38%	44%	50%	55%	60%
Europe[a]	64.5	85.0	106.7	125.6	142.8
as % of population	17%	22%	27%	32%	36%
Online buyers (millions)					
U.S.	28.8	39.3	51.8	67.3	85.0
as % of online users	29%	34%	40%	47%	54%
Europe	11.8	20.4	31.9	45.2	58.7
as % of online users	18%	24%	30%	36%	41%
Online consumer spending, by category:[b]					
Total online spending					
U.S.	17.3	28.0	41.1	60.0	86.3
Europe	2.9	7.6	14.7	24.0	35.0
Groceries					
U.S.	0.2	0.8	2.0	4.6	7.5
Europe	0.2	0.8	1.8	3.3	5.2
Computers and software					
U.S.	5.4	7.4	9.5	12.2	15.8
Europe	0.7	2.1	4.1	6.4	8.7
Consumer electronics					
U.S.	0.4	0.6	1.0	1.4	2.1
Europe	0.1	0.2	0.4	0.6	0.8
Entertainment					
U.S.	1.7	2.7	4.1	6.0	8.6
Europe	0.6	1.1	1.8	2.7	3.6
Travel					
U.S.	6.5	11.0	14.8	18.3	21.7
Europe	0.8	2.3	4.4	6.9	10.0
Apparel					
U.S.	0.9	1.6	1.8	4.7	7.8
Europe	0.2	0.6	1.1	1.7	2.4
Additional U.S. spending on:					
Office supplies	0.1	0.2	0.3	0.6	1.2
Furniture/home appliances	0.1	0.3	0.7	1.6	3.6
Health & personal care	0.2	0.6	1.4	3.1	6.0

[a]Europe includes the 15 European Union members, Norway, and Switzerland.
[b]Figures in billions of U.S. dollars and Euros, as appropriate.
Source: Adapted from Jupiter Communications, Internet Shopping Model, March–April 2000.

Expansion

At the time of the case, Lai and his colleagues planned geographic expansion into regional markets and partnerships with other firms. By spring 2000, adM@rt was working on a regional rollout, first to urban centers in Taiwan, Korea, and perhaps Thailand. Speaking from his experience with Carrefour in Taiwan, Ravelli noted that conditions in Hong Kong were like those in Taipei and elsewhere in the region: "Our success is based on density of population. This is something we can find in Taipei." In addition to population density and a sizable middle class, Lai stressed a less tangible factor underpinning the demand for adM@rt's presence: "Only in the big city," he noted, "does time become a variable" whose allocation affected the quality of life. Lai emphasized the urban preference for the convenience that adM@rt supplied and felt that the prospects for adM@rt in Asia were limited only by its proficiency at fulfillment and delivery logistics. Ting emphasized that adM@rt would not pursue niche markets, however: "There'll be guys doing roses, chocolate, and diamonds. We probably won't. There will be someone doing dry cleaning. We probably won't. There's someone doing popcorn and a video. We probably won't. But we hope to hold the mainstream 60% to 80% of the market." But this would depend on local conditions, he noted:

> How do you deal with the fact that Taiwan doesn't have maids, that there might not be someone home at delivery time? How do you account for convenience store chains, something we've never had in Hong Kong? Is that a potential pick-up point or simply a payment point? We want to find local partners to brainstorm and work together through this so that we can roll a business out as a partnership. Locals are going to control the majority of this kind of operation. I'm there for my intellectual property and my experience and that might be worth 20% to 30% of the business.

Next Media

Lai was not standing still while awaiting the market's verdict on adM@rt. Beginning in early 1999, staff at *Apple Daily* and *Next,* excited by the potential of the internet, began rolling out online publications and services based around the lifestyles of their readers. At first these sites were not linked. T. T. Lim, Next Media CEO, came from big-box retailing, specifically Makro in Taiwan and Wal-Mart in China, and had noticed the potential that the combination of previously disparate sites and adM@rt's direct marketing ability could provide. Aside from integrating the sites with hyperlinks, Lim worked to create cross-selling opportunities wherever possible. One such idea was to give visitors HK $5 for each click on a Next Media site's banner ads, money usable for purchases from adM@rt.

By mid 2000, 12 sites were integrated under the Next Media.com umbrella and included NEXT Eat (restaurant information and reservations), NEXT Movie (reviews, reservations, and ticket sales), NEXT Motor (auto sales), each of which took a vertical cut across Lai's various publications. The other sites offered personal ads, horoscopes, e-greeting cards, news and entertainment chat rooms, and celebrity photos. "We set the website up not really knowing why, except that it was cheap to do," said Lai, adding, "Now we have the best content in town."[19] Next Media originated as a way for overseas Chinese to keep in touch with Chinese culture and with doings in Hong Kong. As Lai recalled:

> I said, "Tell me how much it costs us." And they said, "One-and-a-half million [Hong Kong] dollars for the magazine website and the same for the newspaper website." I said, "OK, give me three million dollars. It's containable. I don't know why we do it, but if it's good for the people who emigrate to keep in contact with Hong Kong, then we're doing something good." It turned out to be a gold mine.

---

[19]Michael Flagg, "Concept of an Umbrella of Web Sites Is the Apple of Jimmy Lai's Eye," *Wall Street Journal Europe,* February 29, 2000.

Until spring 2000, the site sold Chinese furniture and porcelain with a partner, and ad space to an online Chinese bookstore, a long-distance phone company, and others. Next Media.com also had links to *Apple Daily* and *Next*. In February 2000, with the gradual integration of the lifestyle services in progress, the Chinese-language-only site received seven million page views a day, one of the highest among Hong Kong websites. Lim estimated that up to three million visitors visited his sites daily, assuming that each visitor viewed two or three pages. Two-thirds of the visitors were Chinese emigrants tuning in from North America, and page views grew by as much as 7% a month. Though 1999 earnings were just HK $1 million, Next Media.com was one of the few media websites making any money at all.[20]

Similar sites were planned for other Asian nations in their own languages. Ting stressed the importance of catering to local tastes, though he noted the regional appeal of Hong Kong's popular culture:

> How do we extend this whole model outside of Hong Kong? I think the content side is relatively easy. Many content players approach us looking for content swap because one of our strongest content areas is entertainment and, in entertainment, Hong Kong is a hub for Asia. Our entertainment content extends to Taiwan and to other Chinese-speaking environments very nicely. It doesn't always work the other way around. People in Shanghai could not care less about what's happening in Beijing, so if you don't offer them something very local, they're not interested. So simply saying, "We're a China portal" is not good enough.

Eventually, all the country sites would be funneled to a gigantic cybermall able to sell merchandise to customers in their own language. Ultimately, Lai dreamed of buying television stations, TV channels, and movie studios to provide content for delivery via interactive broadband cable systems offering Internet access and TV-quality images.

Extending the adM@rt Franchise

Regardless of its ultimate likelihood of success, each new business idea further clarified to Lai and his managers the strengths and weaknesses of the infrastructure they already had built, and lay the basis for subsequent efforts to make use of those assets. Lai viewed the Internet as a crucial enabling mechanism in this quest. In *Apple Daily* and *Next* he already had successful offline businesses, each with a stable base of readers whom he hoped to attract to adM@rt and Next Media. By inserting hyperlinks to various subjects touched on by stories in the print and online versions of his publications, for example, Lai expected to draw readers to the internet, keep their attention longer, and thereby elicit further business for adM@rt and Next Media advertisers.

Lai's managers also saw many opportunities to create new businesses from adM@rt assets and infrastructure. In addition to bringing the adM@rt model to Taipei, Seoul, and Singapore, Ting proposed offering its services to brick-and-mortar clients in Hong Kong. To create some conceptual separation between adM@rt's B2C offerings and the B2B service he envisioned, Ting and Lim first created ezVan—a horizontal platform comprised of adM@rt's call center, warehouse, hubs, and 260 delivery vans—which they packaged for local retailers as an outsourced e-commerce solution. "That's where the real value is," Ting enthused, "and that's very, very exciting." The rationale, he explained, was that the high establishment costs for retail outlets in congested Asian cities made it almost certain that retailers with an existing presence of several dozen shops would open further shops only for the incremental revenue they could provide,

[20]Absent independent tracking as of mid 2000, however, there was no way to confirm the accuracy of these numbers.

not simply to raise the company's profile. Ting thought that for players like Nike and Warner Brothers, new shops might consume up to 40% of the annual sales they generated, making that incremental revenue quite costly. Instead, Ting suggested, ezVan could take over order fulfillment and delivery of online sales for the client, while articles and banner ads on Next Media.com sites would drive customers to the client website. The partner could use ezVan's transaction server and payment gateway, and receive an allotment of 10 linear feet of warehouse space for its own inventory that ezVan would use to pick and fill orders for client merchandise. Ting would offer the client a deal: "Now that we saved you all your establishment costs, we can split the proceeds of the online sales in half, or any way you want, but either way, I think both of us have a very nice value proposition here." Such deals would also help Next Media build its content community and increase the breadth of its offerings, while requiring little alteration to the adM@rt assets that ezVan used, save to augment their IT systems to account for profit, revenue, or data sharing with the merchants.

On the basis of many such deals, Ting expected to launch a community of merchants in mid June 2000. This would make shopping seamless to the consumer, who, once online, could pick something up from Nike, from adM@rt, from H₂O, from the Body Shop, put everything into one shopping cart, and pay for everything at one time. Delivery and billing would also be seamless: everything would arrive in one box with one bill.

Ting also considered wireless technology. "Hong Kong people hate down time. You can see people fidgeting even on short subway rides. Well, in the 10 minutes it takes to get from Quarry Bay to Central, why don't we give them the opportunity to buy their groceries?" Using voice recognition software on their portable phones, people could call in their grocery deliveries during their commute. They

could check on their mobile if a certain garage has space availability and reserve a space. "This is a far corner of our business model," Ting noted, "but we don't leave it out."

In spring 2000, Lai and his colleagues also were developing a HK$ 1 "lifestyle" broadsheet that would feature adM@rt products and condensed content from Lai's publications. To be sold at newsstands, it would differ from adM@rt flyers inserted in *Apple Daily* and would "display the menu" of adM@rt items available for order by phone or on the Internet. In so doing, Lai acknowledged, he would "eventually disintegrate our relationship with Apple. We will create a standalone tabloid, and also advertise in *Apple* at the same rate everybody else pays. Each business will be treated independently."

Further, Lai had announced Next Ventures in early 2000 to mentor new online enterprises and provide services in exchange for equity positions: "We want to use our online and offline advertising platform to build startups' brand names. And we can give them logistic, management, and marketing support as well." Go Home was Next Ventures' first client; it focused on Hong Kong's large but expensive market for apartments.

Integrating Online and Offline Worlds

Lai looked back on his e-commerce experience with adM@rt and considered its lessons:

> When we started this business, we knew only that the Internet created convenience for people. We did not have experience in online business. But something I do know from offline business that I don't want to repeat online is that traditional business is based on planning and projections. In other words, you are just repeating the future with the past. The attitude we should take for online business is trial and error. For instance, I think now that you need to focus on one business online, but that the mix of products in that one business doesn't have to be the traditional one. People don't care if you are selling groceries, hardware, and electronics all in one place, so long as what you are really selling—convenience, or whatever—is available. We

found that out the hard way, but we woke up and fixed the problem. We learned that the marketing attitudes of offline business don't work in the online world. That gave us a great insight: we now know that people have become amphibians, living online for convenience but offline for emotional and social satisfaction.

Ravelli had seen this unfold in practice:

E-commerce and brick-and-mortar retail are completely different. Not seeing this was my biggest mistake. I tried to put my brick-and-mortar experience on the Net. It didn't work because customer expectations online are completely different. The only common point is competitor response. Customers using the Web, or even a call center, are looking for convenience. They are not looking for choice, or price, or priorities. What do they order from us today? They order products that are heavy, bulky, and large. If tomorrow I started to sell cookies and chips, even at prices 50% cheaper than the competition, I will have no sales. Why not? Because that is much more like impulse buying, something people don't go to the Web or pick up their phone to do.

Having recognized that the internet was more than another place to sell things, Lai considered the implications of a new business model. Unlike his competitors, Lai viewed online sales not just as an extension of the offline business. Instead, he felt that an online presence should be used to push one's offline business into new directions.

You should take the online perspective and look back to your off-line business. Not the other way around. We believe that online business is a catalytic mechanism. We can transfer the convenience, democratization, and innovation-based culture from the online world to the offline. There are many ways to create convenience once you infuse online into offline business. Having the customer buy into the online model, and then packing that into the legacy business, and leading the customer to interact with the legacy business—that's what its all about.

That realization suggested a larger theme:

We have a mission in this business because Asia today is very similar to the United States in the early 1980s. Business was somnambulating, waiting to be restructured. At that time, people like Mike Milken took over companies and restructured them. Their downfall lay in burdening the companies they took over with bonds that required high interest [payouts]. We don't have this problem: we can use the high value of [equity attached to] our online business for us to take over failing businesses. Once it matures, our online business will be the catalyst we will pack into the legacy business. And we think that this is the way Asia should be restructured. Traditional businesses have P/E ratios averaging 3 to 4. If we take them over, change them, and raise their valuation to P/Es of 30 or 35, that's where we add new value. Asia is waiting for this catalyst. We know it's going to change everything, but we don't know how it's going to be changed.

CASE 1–3
LI & FUNG[1]

"I'm not an Internet guy, I'm a business guy," quipped William Fung, managing director of Li & Fung Trading Co. Clad in his chinos and black American Eagle T-shirt, Fung looked

much more like a new economy entrepreneur than the self-described offline, old economy relic: "I'm 51, I'm more than a grey hair in Internet terms, I'm a fossil."[2] Nor did lifung.com, his elder brother Victor's new online company, resemble a typical Internet

[1]This case was prepared by Senior Researcher Fred Young from the Asia-Pacific Research Office under the direction of Professor F. Warren McFarlan.

[2]Rahul Jacob, "Inside Track: Traditional Values at the Click of a Mouse," *Financial Times,* August 1, 2000, p. 14.

start-up, particularly with a 96-year parent born at the end of the Qing Dynasty. In August 2000, the day before beta launch of the new business-to-business (B2B) e-commerce portal, William described the challenges facing Li & Fung:

> About three or four years ago, Victor and I discussed the Internet and how it impacts us. Our starting point was a defensive posture: Would the Internet disintermediate us? Would we get Amazoned[3] by someone who will put together all of the information about buyers and factories online? After a lot of research, we realized that the Internet facilitates supply chain management and we weren't going to be disintermediated. The key is to have the old economy know-how and yet be open to new economy ideas.

With a press conference the following day, William was confident of the Group's performance and lifung.com's prospects. But he knew that important issues remained unresolved: Was there any chance of channel conflict or cannibalization between the offline business and the start-up? How would the market react to the start-up once it was launched the following year? And how specifically would e-commerce ultimately transform his family's century-old company?

Company Background[4]

Li & Fung was founded in 1906 by William's grandfather, Fung Pak-Liu and his partner, Li To-Ming in Guangzhou, China as an export trading company in Southern China selling to overseas merchants. In the 1920s and 1930s, the company diversified into warehousing and the manufacture of handicrafts. Shortly after Fung Pak-Liu passed away in 1943, his son Fung Hon-Chu assumed charge of the company. Two years later, silent partner Li To-Ming retired and sold his shares to the company. The company retained Li's surname, a homophone for "profit" in Chinese, which, along with "Fung," a homophone for "abundance," had an auspicious ring when combined.

Li & Fung relocated permanently to Hong Kong at the end of World War II, expanding its operations to include toys, garments, plastic flowers, and electronics. In the early 1970s, both Fung brothers had just returned from the United States: William had earned his MBA from Harvard Business School and returned to the business in 1972. Victor had recently completed his Ph.D. in economics at Harvard University and, following a two-year stint teaching at Harvard Business School, rejoined the business in 1974. Their return heralded Li & Fung's transition from a family-owned business to a professionally managed firm, with a planning and budgeting system in place for the first time. William and Victor, the third generation to run the company, felt that the next logical step in growing the company was to go public. In 1973, Li & Fung became the holding company for the Group and was listed on the Hong Kong Stock Exchange. Throughout the 1980s, Li & Fung expanded its regional network of offices throughout the Asia-Pacific region as more sources of supply emerged in the rapidly industrializing Asian economies. In 1988 the Group was privatized and streamlined, incorporated in Bermuda in 1991, and its trading activities were listed on the HKSE in July 1992. With the 1995 acquisition of Inchcape Buying Services (formerly Dodwell), Li & Fung expanded its customer base in Europe while simultaneously shifting its sourcing network beyond East Asia to include the Indian sub-continent, the Mediterranean, and Caribbean basins.

By 2000, Li & Fung was a $2 billion global export trading company with 3,600 staff

---

[3]Online bookseller Amazon.com had decimated the ranks of independent booksellers by aggregating services and offering a broader selection of stock at lower prices than the small bookstores could.
[4]Some information in this section comes from previous Harvard Business School Case Studies: "Li & Fung: Beyond "Filling in the Mosaic"—1995-98," Michael Y. Yoshino, Carin-Isabel Knoop, Anthony St. George; January 1, 1998; and "Li & Fung (Trading) Ltd.," Gary Loveman, Jamie O'Connell, October 26, 1995.

worldwide, sourcing and managing the global supply chain for high-volume, time-sensitive consumer goods. (Exhibit 1 shows recent Li & Fung financial data.) By 2000, 69% of Li & Fung's sales were in the United States and 27% in Europe. Key customers included The Limited, Gymboree, American Eagle, Warner Brothers, Abercrombie & Fitch, and Bed,

EXHIBIT 1   Li & Fung Consolidated Income Statement (December 31, 1999), in HK$[a]

	2000 (HK $'000 (June 30) Half-year	1999 HK $'000 (December 31) Full-year	1999 (HK $'000 (June 30) Half-year	1998 HK $'000 (December 31) Full-year
Turnover	10,267,606	16,297,501	6,583,730	14,312,618
Cost of sales	(9,262,171)	(14,585,881)	(5,895,432)	(12,891,709)
Selling expenses	(191,616)	(354,124)	(143,136)	(287,524)
Administrative expenses	(87,741)	(867,842)	(56,436)	(747,725)
Profits before taxation	328,943	613,861	208,936	471,098
Taxation	(29,805)	(36,638)	(14,536)	(16,425)
Profit after taxation	299,338	577,223	194,400	454,673

[a]In August 2000, $1 = HK $7.78.

Li & Fung Consolidated Balance Sheet (December 31, 1999), HK$

	1999 HK $'000	1998 HK $'000
Fixed assets	1,161,808	1,145,056
Investment securities	86,484	51,389
Current assets		
Inventories	110,014	72,267
Trade and bills receivable	1,488,780	1,089,011
Cash and bank balances	1,029,373	904,581
	2,961,634	2,234,490
Current liabilities		
	2,976,829	1,976,958
Net current (liabilities)/assets	(15,195)	257,532
	1,234,339	1,466,767
Financed by:		
Share capital	64,765	63,761
Reserves	749,346	1,030,295
Shareholders' funds	814,11	1,094,056
Minority interests	4,460	(24,595)
Long-term liabilities	414,868	397,058
Deferred taxation	900	248
	1,234,339	1,446,767

Source: Company documents.

Bath, & Beyond. Tesco, Avon Products, Levi-Strauss, and Reebok had become customers within the last two years; Royal Ahold, Guess Jeans, and Bebe had signed on in 2000.

Li & Fung's product mix included hard and soft goods. Soft goods referred to apparel, including woven and knit garments for men, women, and children. Hard goods included fashion accessories, festive or holiday products, furnishings, giftware, handicrafts, home products, fireworks, sporting goods, toys, and travel goods. Hard goods provided higher margins than soft goods because, despite a generally lower item value per unit, they required higher value-added services for orders that were also usually much smaller than soft goods orders. Hard goods items such as watches, shoes, suitcases, kitchenware, or teddy bears required an inspector for quality control evaluation for even the smallest batch order, thereby greatly increasing what Li & Fung could charge. Margins for soft goods were roughly 6% to 8%, while margins on hard goods ranged anywhere from 10% to 30%, depending upon the degree of complexity involved in sourcing raw materials. Li & Fung attempted to expand its sale of hard goods. In 1998, soft and hard goods contributed 77.5% and 22.5% of total sales, respectively, while the proportion of hard goods sales grew to 25% in 1999 and was projected to increase to 27% in 2001 and 29% in 2002.

Holistic Supply Chain Management. Although Li & Fung described itself as a trading company, by 2000, it was far more sophisticated than a typical Hong Kong import-export trading company and had come a long way from its roots in matching Chinese manufacturers with Western buyers:

> We have been changing. Now we're orchestrating a whole production process that starts from raw materials all the way through to finished product. If you look at the old days, language skills could guarantee you margins better than we have now. My grandfather

used to charge 15% or more, basically to be an interpreter. Those days are over.[5]

With 48 offices in 32 countries, the company provided value-added services across the entire supply chain in a so-called "borderless" manufacturing environment (see Exhibit 2). A down jacket's filling, for example, might come from China, the outer shell fabric from Korea, the zippers from Japan, the inner lining from Taiwan, and the elastics, label, Velcro, and other trim from Hong Kong. The garment might be dyed in South Asia, stitched in China, then sent back to Hong Kong for quality control and finally packaged for delivery to The Limited or Abercrombie & Fitch. Victor explained:

> Say we get an order from a European retailer to produce 10,000 garments. We determine that, because of quotas and labor conditions, the best place to make the garments is Thailand. So we ship everything from there. And because the customer needs quick delivery, we may divide the order across five factories in Thailand. Effectively we are customizing the value chain to best meet the customer's needs. Five weeks after we received the order, 10,000 garments arrive on the shelves in Europe, all looking like they came from one factory.[6]

Li & Fung clients benefited in several ways: supply chain customization could shorten order fulfillment from three months to five weeks, and this faster turnaround allowed clients to reduce inventory costs. Moreover, in its role as a middleman, Li & Fung reduced matching and credit risks, and also offered quality assurance to its customers. Furthermore, with a global sourcing network and

---

[5]Gren Manuel, "Technology Journal: Historic Trader Keeps Its Cool—Li & Fung Says It's Found a Place in the Internet Economy," *The Asian Wall Street Journal*, March 27, 2000, p. 15.
[6]Joan Magretta, "Fast, Global, and Entrepreneurial: Supply Chain Management, Hong Kong Style, An Interview with Victor Fung," *Harvard Business Review*, September-October 1998, p. 106.

Exhibit 2   Li & Fung Total Value Added Package

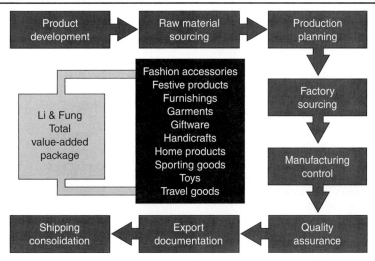

Source: Company documents.

economies of scale, Li & Fung could offer lower cost and more flexible sourcing than its competitors. In addition, through acquisitions and global expansion, Li & Fung was extending this knowledge base to sub-Saharan Africa, Eastern Europe, and the Caribbean. Finally, Li & Fung provided up-to-date fashion- and market-trend information to clients. As a result of its Camberley acquisition in 1999 it started offering clients virtual manufacturing, or product design services.

According to Victor, "Li & Fung does not own any of the boxes in the supply chain, rather we manage and orchestrate it from above. The creation of value is based on a holistic conception of the value chain." In recent years, however, Li & Fung had begun to improve operations by controlling or owning strategic links in the chain. In some cases, Li & Fung offered raw material sourcing. In the past, when clients placed an order, Li & Fung would determine the manufacturer best suited to supply the goods, and that factory would source its own raw materi-

als. But Li & Fung understood its clients' needs better than its manufacturing plants did, so by offering raw materials to its suppliers, the company both ensured greater quality control and bought larger, and thus more cost effective, amounts of raw materials, thereby producing cost savings for each manufacturer. In such cases, Li & Fung also earned revenue by charging its factories a commission on each raw material purchase they made. By mid-2000, nearly 15% of Group sales involved Li & Fung's raw material sourcing service.

Corporate Culture and Compensation. From the 1992 privatization on, the division of labor between the Fung brothers was clear-cut: as Group chairman, Victor was primarily concerned with the Group's strategic issues and long-term planning. As Group managing director, William attended to everyday operations of the publicly listed trading arm, or as he joked in a recent interview, "Victor is the deep thinker, and I just make the money."[7] In another interview, Victor joked that "William calls me the visionary, meaning that I don't really know what's going on."[8] But both brothers lived in the same apartment building as their mother and sisters and conversed every day to keep abreast of developments at Li & Fung. The duo created a strong synergy that was described by the CEO of the Group's e-commerce venture as:

> A combination of both thought leadership and execution, with the unique relationship between Victor and William cementing the entire organization. They create a very particular kind of culture that blends pragmatism and, at the same time, a recognition of and openness to innovation.

According to Victor, once the business was successful, it was essential to keep an open mind and rather than resting on their laurels, that the challenge was to move past success and look forward. Furthermore, Victor held that it was imperative to cultivate a corporate culture that not only tolerated but encouraged diversity, or in his words, "Keep the culture so that it remains humble, agile, and responsive all the time and keep the people externally focused." Bi-annual retreats were held in Hong Kong, senior management meetings attended by division-level managers in order to foster communication across the Group.

Li & Fung's 3,600 employees were spread around the globe in offices ranging in size from 6 staff in Saipan to 1,100 in the Hong Kong head office. Five of the 48 offices were hubs—Hong Kong, Taiwan, Korea, Thailand, and Turkey. Each (except the Hong Kong office) had 200 to 300 employees. Li & Fung was entrepreneurial, allowing senior managers to run 90 small, worldwide management teams as separate and individual companies. These dedicated teams of product specialists focused on the needs of specific customers and were grouped under a Li & Fung corporate umbrella that provided centralized IT, financial, and administrative support from Hong Kong. This decentralized corporate structure allowed for adaptability and rapid reaction to seasonal fashion shifts.

As a meritocracy, performance-based promotion and compensation were cardinal principles. Each of Li & Fung's top executives negotiated individual compensation packages. In contrast to companies that restricted executive bonuses to a fixed percentage of salary, Li & Fung bonuses were based on profits with no ceiling.

> It's not every company that calls its executives "little John Waynes." But for Li & Fung, the image captures perfectly the drive, dedication, and independence of the company's far-flung managers. As Li & Fung extended its geographic reach, it also expanded its mix of cultures. And to manage the mix it uses a simple formula: give managers the freedom to work as they see fit, so long as they get the job done.[9]

Tripartite Growth Strategy

In 2000, Li & Fung saw its future growth coming from a combination of organic growth, expansion through acquisition, and extension of its supply chain to new markets via the Internet.

Organic Growth. Since 1995, the Group had grown organically by receiving more orders from existing clients and by securing new mandates from strategic clients. Li & Fung further extended its network and diversified its sourcing around the globe with new offices in places as diverse as Bangladesh, Sub-Saharan Africa, and Manchester, England (see Exhibits 3 and 4).

---

[7] Louis Kraar, "The New Net Tigers," *Fortune Magazine,* May 15, 2000, p. 310.
[8] Joanna Slater, "Masters of the Trade," *Far Eastern Economic Review,* July 22, 2000, p. 10.

[9] Joanna Slater, "Corporate Culture," *Far Eastern Economic Review,* July 22, 1999, p. 12.

EXHIBIT 3　Li & Fung's Global Network

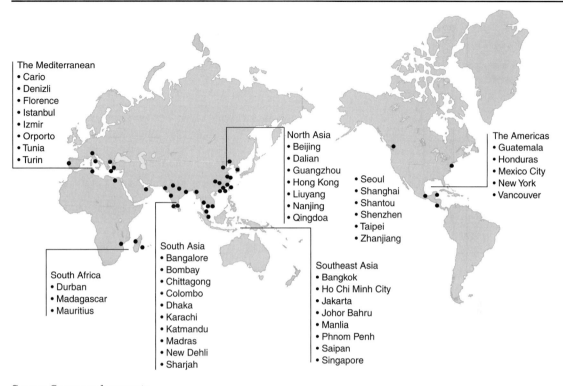

The Mediterranean
• Cario
• Denizli
• Florence
• Istanbul
• Izmir
• Orporto
• Tunia
• Turin

North Asia
• Beijing
• Dalian
• Guangzhou
• Hong Kong
• Liuyang
• Nanjing
• Qingdoa

• Seoul
• Shanghai
• Shantou
• Shenzhen
• Taipei
• Zhanjiang

The Americas
• Guatemala
• Honduras
• Mexico City
• New York
• Vancouver

South Africa
• Durban
• Madagascar
• Mauritius

South Asia
• Bangalore
• Bombay
• Chittagong
• Colombo
• Dhaka
• Karachi
• Katmandu
• Madras
• New Dehli
• Sharjah

Southeast Asia
• Bangkok
• Ho Chi Minh City
• Jakarta
• Johor Bahru
• Manlia
• Phnom Penh
• Saipan
• Singapore

Source: Company documents.

EXHIBIT 4　Li & Fung Sourcing Markets (Q1 and Q2, 2000)

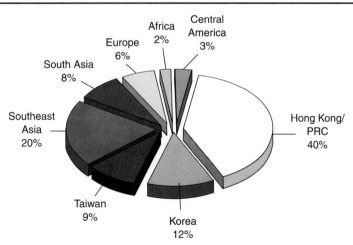

Central America 3%
Africa 2%
Europe 6%
South Asia 8%
Southeast Asia 20%
Taiwan 9%
Korea 12%
Hong Kong/PRC 40%

Source: Company documents.

In 1996, Li & Fung adopted a "three-year plan" system, one which William described as having been adopted directly from the economic planning system of the Chinese Communist Party, one that "allows the company to look ahead, but not too far ahead." William elaborated:

> We thought that the Chinese had a neat system. They have five-year plans, fixed; we have three-year plans, fixed. We don't want moving goalposts, we want set goals. At the beginning of every three-year plan we sit down and look at the business from its fundamentals. We use backwards planning, we recognize where we want to be in three years time, identify the gaps between that and where we are now, and see what we have to do to get there.

During its first three-year plan (FY1993–1995), entitled "Filling in the Mosaic," Li & Fung focused on filling in the gaps in its network of offices to cover new sourcing markets. The second three-year plan (1996–1998), "Margin Expansion," was launched immediately after the Inchcape acquisition to increase its profitability. A third three-year plan "Doubling Profits" (FY1999–2001), established the goals of doubling profits every three years and achieving $3 billion in annual sales.

Investors liked the results: Li & Fung outperformed the Hang Seng Index by over 75% in 2000. The reward was inclusion in the Morgan Stanley Country Index for Hong Kong in May 2000, subsequent inclusion in the HSI in August 2000, and on the FTSE World Index Hong Kong Section in September 2000. With a market capitalization of $6.6 billion, by mid-2000, Li & Fung was the nineteenth largest Hong Kong stock trading with a company record price to earnings (P/E) ratio of nearly 60x. A local newspaper declared:

> It is difficult to find a bad word [about Li & Fung]. It could be a poster-child for shareholder value, with a return-on-equity of 60.2% at the end of last year. The firm is well positioned to benefit from the opening of

the mainland market and Beijing's accession to the World Trade Organization, with 40% of sourcing on the mainland and Hong Kong.[10]

Acquisitions   Li & Fung's acquisition strategy was based on buying rival sourcing companies, thereby gaining new client accounts, integrating their operations, and eventually bringing the operating margins of these acquired units up to Li & Fung levels. In 1995 Li & Fung acquired Inchcape Buying Services, a 100 year-old company roughly the same size as Li & Fung and its closest competitor. The Dodwell acquisition brought access to sourcing markets on the Indian subcontinent and European export markets. This acquisition took nearly three years to be fully absorbed into Li & Fung's operations. Within three years, Dodwell's operating margins increased from 0.8% to 3%, primarily through the provision of Li & Fung value-added services to Dodwell customers.

In December 1999, Li & Fung acquired the export trading operations of the Swire Group, Swire & Maclaine and Camberley, which were Li & Fung's next two largest Hong Kong-based competitors, and in the process became the only listed supply chain management company in Hong Kong. Like Li & Fung, Camberley did not own its own factories. Instead, it provided "virtual manufacturing" in the form of in-house design, pattern and sample making, and raw material sourcing. Manufacturing was subcontracted to factories in China. Through Camberley, Li & Fung gained access to the design process—another link in the value chain—as well as access to new clients such as the Asia buying offices of Laura Ashley and Anne Taylor. As it had with Inchcape, Li & Fung expected to bolster its own bottom line by raising the operating margins of these two

---

[10]David Wilder, "Internet Key to More Gains for Li & Fung," *South China Morning Post,* September 4, 2000, Business Post, p. 1.

companies. With a robust cash flow and the solid financial performance of past acquisitions, Li & Fung was in position to continue growing its business by further acquisitions.

By August 2000, Li & Fung was nearly five times the size of its two closest local competitors, William E. Connor and Associates and Colby International, which had twice postponed the IPO of its B2B portal in 2000.

E-Commerce. A core element of Li & Fung's three-year planning system included an introspective look at "whether we are still relevant, including whether or not we are going to be disintermediated." Part of its response was an Internet initiative of its own. In 1995 Li & Fung launched an Intranet to link the Group's offices and manufacturing sites around the world, thereby expediting and simplifying internal communications. The progress of orders and shipments could be tracked in real time, and digital imagery allowed for online inspection and troubleshooting. For example, past quality problems with Bangladeshi production would require an on-site Li & Fung inspector to send physical samples to Hong Kong by express mail, whereas the Intranet now allowed a high resolution digital photo to be sent via the Intranet for real-time response and remedy.

In 1997, Li & Fung launched secure Extranet sites. Each site linked the company directly to a key customer and was customized to that customer's individual needs. By 2000, 10 such Extranets were in place, each taking nearly 6 to 9 months to fully implement, from design to testing of the user interface. Through each Internet site, Li & Fung could carry out online product development as well as order tracking, obviating much of the cost and time necessary to send hard copies of documents back and forth. Furthermore, with Li & Fung as the key link between manufacturers and retailers, the Extranet provided a platform for the two to interface, thus streamlining communications as the order moved through the supply chain. Customers could track an order online just as it was possible to track a UPS delivery. This monitoring of production also promoted quick-response manufacturing. Until the fabric was dyed, the customer could change the color; until the fabric was cut, the customer could change the styles or sizes offered, whether a pocket or a cuff would be added, and a number of other product specifications. According to William, some customers went as far as connecting their entire ERP (enterprise resource planning) system to Li & Fung's Extranet system.

Li & Fung's IT division had 60 people, all based in Hong Kong, but software development of both the Intranet in 1995 and its Extranets in 1997 was outsourced. Successful implementation of these systems provided the initial building blocks of Li & Fung's e-commerce solution and with them in place, the Fungs became further aware of the extent to which integration of Internet technology enhanced internal efficiency and improved communication between Li & Fung divisions and customers and began to consider extending the organization's online presence.

Competitive Threats

The Fung brothers said that they decided to go online to avoid being disintermediated. But a closer examination of local B2B portals and online exchanges led Victor to conclude that the online threat to their offline business was far less than first imagined. "People from the first wave were so far out and garbled in their thinking that we felt that there was no immediate threat," he noted. "Therefore, we needed to think through e-commerce properly, to formulate a proper response."

In Victor's words, B2B exchanges were: "a molecule thick and a mile wide," based on many depthless relationships. Li & Fung preferred "narrow and deep" relationships nurtured with fewer customers and including value-added services. As William professed, "The same reason why we were not disintermediated by the offline guys is going to be the reason why we're not going to be disintermediated by the online guys."

However, William discovered on a 1999 visit to the United States that Li & Fung's old economy retail customers felt seriously threatened by Internet pure plays. At first this hype did not make much sense:

> I asked my friend at Toys 'R' Us, "Why are you concerned about eToys? It does about $28 to $30 million in sales whereas you do $11 billion, and it loses as much as its entire turnover? How can you worry about them?" And the first lesson I learned was that it's not their size that is the threat but the fact that investors are throwing money at them.

William discovered that Internet companies could use the money that was pouring in to them to damage offline competitors, either by acquiring them or their key people. "They can hire away all of the talent that you have. The biggest weapon is the money they have. At one point, they could have hired away my entire management."

Other possible threats came from online companies acquiring an old economy trading company, or from offline companies like Japanese trading companies or local sourcing firms that could partner with a dot-com and become a competitor overnight. William hinted that the Swire & Maclaine acquisition was a defensive move to preempt acquisitions by new economy companies.

William gave his view of the Internet revolution:

> I started off saying that the Internet is just another technology that affects the way information is transferred and people communicate with each other. It has a very dramatic impact, more dramatic than the fax. But for me, it's yet another in a series of technological changes that affects our business that we have to be keenly aware of. It may be the most important change until now, but it is probably not the last.

According to Victor,

> The Internet is a revolutionary technology, but new technology is nevertheless still technology. Li & Fung always has been aggressive in adopting new technologies. When the telephone came along, my grandfather was shocked. When the fax came around, the technology changed our turnaround time into just days. With Internet technology, now we get answers within hours. When broadband and WAP comes online, there will be even less lag.

"Bubble In"

Once the Fungs determined that Li & Fung needed an e-commerce strategy, the remaining question was how and in what shape it would emerge, how specifically e-commerce would eventually add value to Li & Fung, and whether it would use the existing IT department of 60 or absorb a new team of "netrepreneurs." Victor felt strongly that their e-commerce strategy should come from within the company, not outsourced as the intra- and extranets were, or as he phrased it, "bubble in, *not* bubble out." According to Victor, only if the solution was an internal one could he be certain that "the technology would pervade the entire Li & Fung organization." Nor did Victor care to start a brand-new entity separate from the parent:

> I'm not interested in starting a dot-com division, getting a high valuation with a $13 million cash flow, and then spinning it off. I want Li & Fung to be around for another 100 years, not just 5 or 15. To start a pure Internet division is as equally absurd as starting a fax division, a division that exclusively uses faxes.

To better grasp the fundamentals of embarking on a new IT venture, Li & Fung added two new technical directors to its board, one a technology company CEO, the other an academic. According to William,

> The one thing certain about our business is that it will be constantly changing, so we need to install a mechanism for monitoring external environmental changes that impact our business. We decided a long time ago that we were an information and knowledge-based

services company, so anything to do with information technology is crucial to us. We keep up with what's happening with board members who can help us scan the horizon.

Enter Castling. In 1997, Michael Hsieh (HBS '84), president of LF International Inc., Li & Fung's venture capital arm and 15-year Li & Fung veteran, received a telephone call from John Suh (HBS '97), CEO of Castling Group, an Internet start-up company that, like the chess move "that allows you to defend your king and simultaneously position your rook for attack," used the Internet to both defend the offline, old economy companies against online companies' threat to their markets while simultaneously extending their own online presence. The two met in San Francisco to discuss "how a focused combination of technology and supply chain reform could transform retail."

Hsieh, well aware that Li & Fung was working on its own e-commerce strategy, noted:

> As a VC, I see numerous business plans that say that with Li & Fung behind an online exchange, we create significant value and therefore offer you 5% if you join us. However most of the plans do not make sense. They offer very little value and the founders lack either industry or technology expertise. John had the right blend of technology and business sense, the right mix of right and left brain.

Like the Fungs, Hsieh favored a "bubble in" approach. He compared outsourcing e-commerce implementation to a third-party consultant for a $10 million fee as "putting the fox in the chicken coop." It created a risky dependency on outsiders, particularly if future design changes were required, and also provided outsiders with proprietary information, strategy, and the entire business model. Finally, Hsieh remarked: "As a venture capitalist, I always have to think about the strength of the management team and what could go wrong with the venture. Can they deliver? Do they know the indus-

try? Is this a credible business proposition? What if there is a negative reaction?" By late 1999, the time was right to act on their initial meeting. Hsieh commented that "both the evolution of Castling from B2C to B2B and Li & Fung's needs complemented each other nicely; John had a real appreciation for the supply chain and a record for building successful e-commerce models." In December 1999 Hsieh joined Castling's board and LF International invested in Castling. They subsequently co-invested in an initial round of financing for lifung.com, and Castling committed key managerial staff to lifung.com. Suh described Li & Fung as "The perfect strategic partner. They have an entrepreneurial philosophy rooted at the core of their system. They've got an aggressive and visionary leadership team at the forefront of supply chain management. And they're ready to operate according to the rules of the new economy."

In one fell swoop, San Francisco-based lifung.com's management team was immediately staffed with Castling's professionals, serving as vice president of Business Development, vice president of Operations, director of Marketing, and CTO. Suh stepped down as CEO of Castling, retaining the position of Non-Executive Chairman, and signed on as CEO of lifung.com. Apart from Suh and CTO Derek Chen, 20% of lifung.com's initial staff came from Castling, amounting to an in-house e-commerce incubation team that represented a slight twist on Victor's "bubble in" strategy. Suh and Chen, the latter formerly of Andersen Consulting's Advanced Network Solutions Group, brought along their experience from Castling e-commerce strategy projects for jcrew.com, hifi.com, giftcertificate.com, and ferragamo.com. The rest of the team came from either within Li & Fung (e.g., the senior vice president of Merchandising) or from outside the Li & Fung organization (e.g., the vice presidents of Sales and of Marketing). To facilitate the integration of the new online entity into the Li & Fung fold, a senior manager was tasked to provide an interface between the two groups. By Q3 2000, lifung.com had 40 full-time professionals and 25 consultants, with 80 full-time staff expected by year's end. For B2B ventures, moving first and fast was often a prerequisite for dominance. Scarcely a year had passed since the initial meeting with Castling and its first round of financing. According to Suh, there were three stages of launching an online venture: the business strategy, the design-build-test phase, and then actual execution. "Moving quickly," Suh remarked,

> requires a fundamental trust in an organization that best arises from the experience of a team that has built things together, with members who know each other's strengths and weaknesses. We do a lot of team building, because without trust you cannot move at the speed required. There are certain elements critical to the success of a dotcom . . . openness and constant communication are essential because there are so many skills and inter-functional dependencies that must be navigated for a successful launch. At lifung.com we have a great mix of people, individuals with 30 years of merchandising experience, a deep operations staff, seasoned technologists, and wonderkids, rounded out by newly minted MBAs. It's truly a mix of old and new, but what's united through this mix is the culture, and that's what makes me most proud of our team.

However, before Li & Fung fully embarked on its e-commerce venture, William reminded analysts at a press conference that, "although the Group is developing along the lines of the new economy, we're still using an old economy mindset." At this juncture, William felt that it was essential to complete some traditional market research, something that most dotcoms simply did not do: "We cannot assume," he said, paraphrasing Kevin Costner in *Field of Dreams,* "that if you build it they will come. In building lifung.com we have to have a balance of the two mentalities, both old and new, there needs to be a happy medium. So let's do some top-down old economy market research first to find out how big the target market is,

some bottom-up focus group research to identify retailers' real needs, and then we'll see whether or not they will come."

SME Target Market: "B to small b"

Market research was well received by industry analysts, who unanimously endorsed Li & Fung's preliminary research of its target SME (small- and medium-sized enterprise) market. Given the proliferation of B2B portals in early 2000, it was important to foster initial investor confidence in the lifung.com business model. Li & Fung defined its target SMEs in the United States as primarily retailers with annual sales under $100 million and wholesalers with turnover of less than $50 million. According to William, 15 to 20 SME focus groups told him that the Li & Fung brand was well known as "the guys who work with The Gap and The Limited." More importantly, the market research pinpointed SME needs and determined the extent of demand for a "B2b" portal like lifung.com. According to William, "One of the beauties of B2B is the finite number of customers. You don't have to take out Super Bowl advertising time or plaster the New York subway system with ads. By and large, we knew just whom to target, we know the names and addresses of these retailers, we know how to reach them since they all read the same trade publications and go to the same trade shows."

Li & Fung's research determined that 20,000 retailers and 2,800 wholesalers in the United States with a total market size of $54 billion were potential customers, not including the more fragmented markets of Europe and Japan. Because SME orders were small and lacked economies of scale, SMEs traditionally had to pay importers high margins, ranging anywhere from 25% to 30% of the total order, compared with the 6% to 8% commission Li & Fung charged its key clients for apparel and 10% to 12% average commission for hard goods. Not only did the SMEs pay the most, but they were also served the least: these smaller firms were typically only offered a limited range of options in product specifications and were frequently overlooked by suppliers more concerned with serving larger clients. Furthermore, SMEs often lacked current information and lagged far behind large retailers in identifying fashion trends (see Table A). William summarized: "Not surprisingly, the small guys want what the big guys want, a differentiated product line at good prices. However, the SMEs do not have many options and have been poorly serviced in the past."

Historically it had not been cost effective for Li & Fung to trade with SMEs since orders were small and often below factory minimums. But by aggregating their smaller orders via its B2B portal, the Fungs projected that they could profitably offer SMEs an array of products with the option of limited mass customization. In other words, Li & Fung could offer a differentiated product to SMEs despite the small order size, providing them with the limited amount of customization that they required. Explained William, "The idea is to capture economies of scale by concurrently manufacturing the aggregated orders while giving SMEs enough differentiation of embellishment choice (i.e. color, pockets, label) to enable them to each have a different product."

Lifung.com planned to charge SMEs a 10% to 15% commission, far less than what these small retailers were used to paying. Limited mass customization represented a further extension of Li & Fung's supply chain customization and innovation, critical in the Internet age in which customers expected even greater speed and reliability of order fulfillment. With lifung.com's limited customization, a given China-sourced item might be available in one shape but with 10 different patterns and 15 different colors. The possible permutations were infinitely greater than what other online and offline competitors could efficiently offer (see Table B.)

In addition, by not requiring a minimum order, Li & Fung added further value by allowing SMEs to reduce their inventory levels and use the system for replenishment buying. This made it easier for them to respond to changing market conditions and fashion trends. If, for example, orange polo shirts were fashionable one season and light blue the next, orders could be placed in small quantities each month to avoid being stuck with a surplus inventory of orange polo shirts.

"B2B" Parameters. On March 27, 2000, Li & Fung announced 1999 final results and the creation of B2B portal lifung.com, as well as the start-up's management team. Li & Fung also acknowledged that it was committing $200 million to build the online business and proceeded to outline how the start-up would achieve $2 billion in sales by 2004 by targeting

---

TABLE A Needs and Realities for SMEs

	Needs	*Realities*
Product	Differentiation of product at competitive prices	No purchasing power
Service	Reliable procurement	No supplier leverage, no logistics for direct sourcing
Information	Up-to-date news, information	Starved for information

Source: Li & Fung analyst presentation.

TABLE B   SMEs' Sourcing Possibilities

	Product Differentiation	Competitive Price	Reliable Procurement	Information Flow
Importer	Poor	Poor	Strong	Poor
Small agent	Fair	Fair	Poor	Poor
Small buying office	Fair	Fair	Poor	Fair
Internet exchange	Poor	Fair	Poor	Fair
lifung.com	Strong	Strong	Strong	Strong

Source: Li & Fung analyst presentation

SME clients. The next day, Li & Fung raised $250 million by placement of 60-million shares through underwriter Goldman Sachs to fund the new online venture, fortuitously timed just before the mid-April 2000 dot-com crash in the U.S. stock market. According to Li & Fung management, $200 million of these funds were slated for lifung.com with the remaining $50 million devoted to acquisitions in the core business start-up.

William remarked on the old economy-style financing of lifung.com:

> Besides market research, the second atypical thing for Internet companies that we did was the way we approached financing: the typical way of financing Internet startups is that first you have some entrepreneurs who decide on a great idea. They have a lot of sweat equity in the beginning and don't want that diluted unless the value increases a lot. Consequently they finance themselves very short, up until the next stage where they have something new to show. However, they don't think about how much financing is required to make this a viable business.
>
> Our approach has been completely different: We come from a traditional background and don't want to think about that kind of financing at all, particularly since we are building this as part of our total business. Therefore, we want to know what it's going to cost us to take it all the way to the end. And that's why we went out into the market for $200 million and got $250 million.

Furthermore, according to the Fungs, two of the three guiding principles behind lifung.com

referred to as "B2B[3]" were old economy standards: the online company would adopt a "business-to-business" model that which took a "back-to-basics" approach by implementing Li & Fung's supply chain management know-how to SMEs on a "back-to-back" order basis, in other words, with no inventory risk for Li & Fung.

While its initial contribution to Group earnings were likely to be minimal for the first two years, lifung.com was expected to bolster earnings by an operating margin of roughly 6% or 14% of total revenue. Li & Fung expected that, by 2004, the online division would contribute as much as $2 billion in sales, or nearly up to one-third of the group's total revenues, with 1,000 new SME clients in the United States targeted for sales of $2 million each. As lifung.com gained credibility over time and its value proposition became known among SMEs, Li & Fung expected its operating margins to increase to 7% to 8%.

Located near Silicon Valley, lifung.com would not only be close to the heart of Internet culture, but also close to its SME clients in the United States. Nor was lifung.com a prodigal start-up that would be allowed to run at a loss for long; like the parent company, there was an unspoken mandate from the top which decreed that it would follow the three-year planning system with attention focused clearly on the bottom line. According to Suh, lifung.com was steeped in the pragmatic culture of Li & Fung Trading, which was "How does it affect my bottom line? What are the commission rates?" William dismissed the risk of channel conflict between the SMEs and key client business:

> The biggest conflict that our existing customers fear is us working in an old-fashioned way with their direct competitors. In other words, if I am Abercrombie & Fitch and you also work with American Eagle, which is a direct competitor, I normally should have a problem. But if you are big enough, like Li & Fung is, you can compartmentalize these customers, you put walls between them, which is also how banks work with clients who are competitors. We have a system of dedicated accounts and management to segregate the two. Our large customers' first concern will not be the SME competitors but large direct competitors.

E-commerce Execution. Lifung.com[11] offered a wide array of customization options to its clients. For example, with polo shirts, users could choose on screen from a limited variety of specifications such as pockets, collars, and buttons including that customers' own logo. The website would display a high-definition, rotating image of a polo shirt (see Exhibit 5), which the user can customize. When satisfied with its appearance, the user could then place an order online, 24 hours a day. Lifung.com used Sun Microsystems for its hardware platform; Selectica for online configuration of products; Oracle for its database software;

---

[11] On August 17, 2000, lifung.com was rebranded as StudioDirect.com (http://studiodirect.com/).

EXHIBIT 5 Limited Mass Customization (web page sample)

Source: Company documents.

Broadvision for its transaction system, an interface to CIT, the U.S.'s largest factor, to evaluate credit risk; an interface to Danzas AEI, a bulk freight specialist, that would allow door-to-door tracking; and Andersen Consulting, a leading systems integrator, to "wrap" the entire package for a seamless experience.

Moreover, lifung.com was developed and operated independently of Li & Fung's IT department, particularly since the two were based on separate continents. From time to time, four or five programmers from Li & Fung's IT department traveled to lifung.com in San Francisco in order to map the connection between the two units and to ensure that the order placement and fulfillment processes functioned seamlessly. In practice, lifung.com was designed to interact with Li & Fung in the same way as one of the Group's key customers, with orders placed through an Extranet. However, as part of Li & Fung Trading, lifung.com would enjoy a far closer interaction with its parent.

If there was any concern that it would be difficult to integrate an online venture into the corporate culture of a 96-year-old trading company, Victor was determined to "demystify" the technology among the offline staff with internal training courses and daily exposure to the new technology. Victor noted:

> The Internet is not black magic, there is no need to be afraid of it. Yes, it is a disruptive technology, but so what? I want to ensure that the technology pervades the entire organization, mainly because it is a technology that will be adopted sooner or later, and the sooner we do, everyone will be the wiser. Disruption comes from the real world, not cyberspace. For example, if the whole world goes into a trade war or China doesn't gain entry into the WTO, now those are real-world issues I worry about. Li & Fung has always been at the forefront of adopting new technology and that's why we are ahead of the game.

Just as Castling's e-commerce solution prescribed, lifung.com was not only a defensive move, protecting the traditional markets of Li & Fung from local online sourcing companies such as GlobalSources.com and Alibaba.com, but also offered an offensive thrust at new markets that these B2B pure plays were aiming for (see Exhibit 6). The Fungs believed that B2B exchanges did not constitute a tangible threat since they only offered a trading platform matching buyers and sellers. They could not add value in the same way that Li & Fung could through back-end logistics infrastructure, reliable procurement, market knowledge, and brand reputation, nor could they provide product differentiation. Referring to Li & Fung's historical relationships with suppliers, William believed that it would be difficult for any B2B portal to effectively compete with lifung.com: "You couldn't just have four recent MBAs put this all together."

Future Ventures

William indicated that Li & Fung was exploring ways in which the Internet could draw on the company's traditional strengths to enhance Li & Fung's existing business. Lifung.com was only the beginning. By 2001, Li & Fung planned to expand its online B2B penetration with a new platform known as "Electronic Stock Offer." Whereas lifung.com aspired to aggregate the orders of retailers, Electronic Stock Offer, code-named "eSO," would target the other side of the butterfly model (see Exhibit 7) and attempt to aggregate suppliers to post surplus inventory for sale on the Internet. According to William,

> What we've done on the buyer side, we're now doing on the supply side. We thought about what business we should be in with the suppliers that we haven't been in before that would actually help our business. Because we're in the quick-response fashion business, a business where there is very little machinery, we generate a lot of stock and this creates seconds for orders that are cancelled because of untimely delivery. What can the Internet do more efficiently than what

EXHIBIT 6   Li & Fung Competitive Positioning

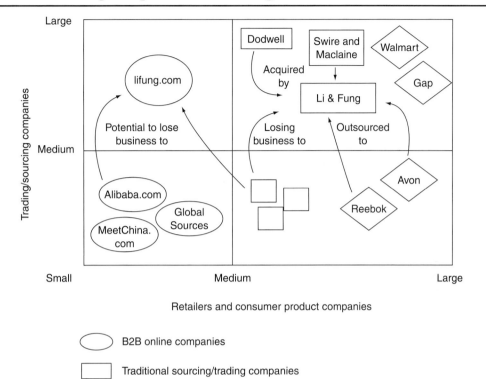

Source: Tristan Chua, Wui Kiat Heng, "Li & Fung," *Goldman Sachs Global Equity Research,* June 21, 2000, p. 10.

we do now? We view these stock problems as a nuisance and have a handful of buyers such as Value City, Ross Stores, and TJ Maxx and who do nothing but specialize in buying these goods.

In particular, eSO was aimed at creating an efficient system for reaching out into Li & Fung's supplier base and posting surplus stocks on the Internet. This, in turn, would provide a more efficient and cost-effective platform from which Li & Fung could sell to buyers primarily interested in purchasing seconds. Li & Fung maintained close contact with its suppliers, inspecting and certifying

each on an annual basis to ensure quality. Buyers trusted Li & Fung quality and price, and would readily join this online trading platform.

As William pointed out:

Because of our old economy history and our network, we can inspect suppliers' goods much easier. Buyers don't have confidence to buy from anonymous suppliers that they don't know. We think we can bring the two together within the Li & Fung network, we can build a business using the Internet to aggregate suppliers on their stock positions. You go back to the butterfly shape: We feel it's far too ambitious to create a virtual exchange inside this middle space that tries to

EXHIBIT 7   lifung.com Market Positioning

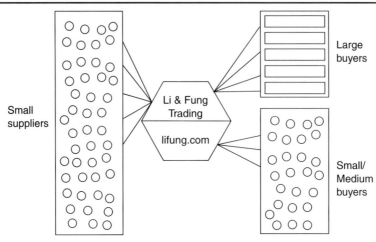

Source: Company documents.

be a clearinghouse for both sides. All I need to do is interpose Li & Fung and we can intermediate the whole process. This is the mirror position of what we are doing at lifung.com, using the Internet to aggregate thousands of small suppliers around the world and then have them post whatever stock they have available.

In contrast with vertical B2B portals, exchanges that proposed to match suppliers with buyers, Li & Fung aimed to add value to the e-commerce transaction by virtue of its old economy network, brand, and reputation. Through online ventures such as Electronic Stock Offer and lifung.com, the Group intended to exploit e-commerce as an integral constituent of its strategy of expanding and diversifying its traditional, offline business.

Outlook and Prospects

Thanks to robust macroeconomic conditions in the United States and Europe, the trend towards casual wear in the American workplace, and the rapid growth of private label in United States and Europe, the Group was expected to enjoy strong top-line growth for at

least the next few years. A survey by Levi-Strauss indicated that over half of the American white collar workforce now wore casual apparel to work every day.[12] The trend towards casual wear in the American workplace offered considerable upside for retailers of polo shirts and khakis and thus for sourcing agents such as Li & Fung. Even a downturn in the U.S. economy promised potential upside, as retailers would consolidate and turn to outsourcing to minimize costs and remain competitive. An increasing number of Li & Fung's key clients as well as SMEs had already begun outsourcing in order to minimize costs, which along with the rapid growth of private label in the United States and Europe provided lifung.com with a fertile market for limited mass customization.

"What if we do build it and no one comes?" William wondered. In other words, what if the 1,000 SMEs projected to procure customized goods through lifung.com and provide $2 billion in sales over the next four years did not

---

[12] "Retailing: General Industry Survey," *Standard & Poors,* May 25, 2000, p. 13.

flock to the B2B portal? If the online venture had a negative impact on share performance, at what point would Li & Fung cut its losses and shut it down? Suh had remarked in his presentation that: "Beta means never having to say you're sorry." The soft beta launch was intended to highlight bugs in the system. The company was on the verge of beta-testing with a select few American clients, but if the beta launch was a failure, would that undermine investor and SME confidence in the model?

When asked about competition, Suh pledged that: "We're going to run like we don't know who is chasing us."[13] But was there, in fact, a risk Li & Fung would not be able to see who

was chasing them, such as a copycat old economy sourcing company that would see the success of lifung.com and mimic its well-publicized model?

Finally, what was the chance that Li & Fung's offline operations would eventually migrate online after lifung.com had proven itself as a reliable and established model? This could potentially reduce many of the offline costs and enhance operating margins, but what of possible channel conflict? Although the online venture was based in San Francisco, how would its integration into the group be perceived by old economy Li & Fung veterans? What would be the future of the in-house e-commerce team once lifung.com was on-line? Would Li & Fung eventually spin off the clicks-and-mortar hybrid and take it public, or would it remain within the group?

---

[13] L. R. Scott, "Chess and the Wired Age," *Global Partnerships,* vol. 5, no. 2, p. 1.

2   BUILDING INFORMATION AGE BUSINESSES[1]

A fundamental shift in the economics of information is underway—a shift that is less about any specific new technology than about the fact that a new behavior is reaching critical mass. Millions of people at home and at work are communicating electronically using universal, open standards. This explosion in connectivity is the latest—and for business strategists—the most important wave in the information revolution. A new economics of information will precipitate changes in the structure of entire industries and in the ways companies compete.[2]

Few would dispute that rapid technological advancements over the latter half of the 20th century spawned dramatic worldwide socioeconomic changes. By the mid-1980s, a new economic paradigm was emerging that many called the Information Age. Its promise caused large, established firms to embark upon business transformation initiatives designed to shed static, rigid structures, processes, and business mind-sets that remained as legacy to the Industrial Age. Today, as we stand at the gateway to a new millennium, the Internet and associated technologies of the network era form the foundation upon which Information Age businesses are being built. Initially, entrepreneurs and executives in established firms approached the Internet in much the same way that fortune seekers of the 1800s prospected for gold. Although there are still frontiers to explore, the "gold rush" mentality has given way to a search for frameworks and analytics to guide us in building successful—and sustainable—Information Age businesses.

---

[1]This module is adapted from papers and materials in Professor Applegate's *Building E-Businesses* online course series (order #5238BN).

[2]P. Evans and T. Wurster, "Strategy and the Economics of Information," Boston: *Harvard Business Review,* 1997.

Drawing on over six years of work with hundreds of Internet pioneers, this module analyzes how emerging Information Age business models are revolutionizing how business is conducted around the world. Portals, aggregators, exchanges, and marketplaces are but a few of the models examined. The in-depth analysis provides the foundation for discussion of business strategy, capabilities, value creation, and business model evolution in a number of companies, including two established firms—American Express and Intuit—and a newly launched independent Internet venture—Amazon.com.

Business Models: Something Old and Something New

If there is one lesson we can learn from the continuing evolution of work and competition in the new economy, it's this. . . Change the question and you change the game. . . The old question was "What business am I in?" The new question is "What is my business model?"[3]

Why is a focus on business models so important today? If you think about it, we spent nearly a century building and perfecting the Industrial Age models that defined how companies conducted business throughout most of the 1900s. As a result, we knew what it meant if someone said, "I sell insurance" or "I sell cars." We had developed a shorthand way of describing how a business was structured, what type of people were needed, and what roles they filled. That shorthand told us how our company interacted with others in the industry and, most importantly, how it made money and delivered value to customers, suppliers, partners, employees, and owners. It also told everyone who did business with us what they could expect. The Industrial Age business models became so familiar that they no longer required explanation.

In contrast, the Internet enables us to create new business models and redefine existing ones. It provides a flexible channel for procuring and distributing products and services, and the tools needed to create and package content in all of its many forms, including data, voice, and video. This highly interactive and engaging channel offers new opportunities and enables development of new capabilities that were difficult to achieve before the commercialization of the Internet. Figure 2-1 shows the building blocks of a business model and the relationships among them. Table 2-1 highlights categories of analysis and representative outcomes for each category.

As you review the business model framework, it is important to recognize that the components and relationships depicted here are not new. Indeed, this basic approach has been used for decades to analyze a wide variety of industrial business models. What is new are the business rules and assumptions that form the *mental models* that, in turn, guide how we make

---

[3]A. Slywotzky and D. Morrison, *Profit Patterns.* New York: N.Y. Times Business, 1999.

FIGURE 2-1

*Building Blocks
of a Business
Model*

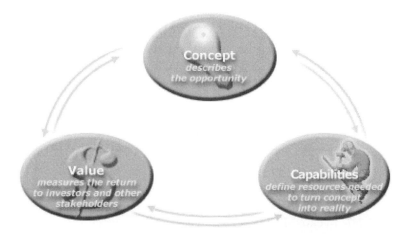

decisions and take actions. As we define new models we don't immediately throw out the old. In fact, the best inventions leverage old paradigms, relaxing assumptions to define new models that are both familiar, yet decidedly superior to the old.[4] Scott Cook, founder of Intuit, explained:

> Some of the best innovations involve a paradigm shift, a real mental change of assumptions and certainties. In fact, the process of innovating and entrepreneuring is much less about invention or new ideas. It's much more about rethinking and questioning the assumptions people already make...The ability to rethink fundamental assumptions and take what people accept as certain and question it, [is the *central*] talent of being a great entrepreneur.

Emerging E-Business Models

> *Consumers are looking for the ability to bundle the products they want in a fashion unique to each individual, and the Web will provide this capability...We believe that vertical portals will do the best job of providing the consumer empowerment that the Internet makes possible...Not only will vertical portals have a profound effect on traditional distribution networks, but because many vertical portals will have production capabilities, they may also pose a threat to specialty [producers] that choose to downplay the significance of the Internet channel.[5]*

For decades, executives have used the value chain framework, discussed in Module 1, to describe the set of activities through which a product or service is

[4]T. Kuhn, *The Structure of Scientific Revolution* (*Chicago:* University of Chicago Press, 1970).

[5]U.S. Internet and Financial Services Equity Research Team, "The Internet and Financial Services," Morgan Stanley Dean Witter, August 1999.

TABLE 2-1   **Analyzing a Business Model**

What is it?	*How will we?*
An organization's **business concept** defines its: • Market opportunity • Product and services offered • Competitive dynamics • Strategy for capturing a dominant position • Strategic options for evolving the business	• Attract a large and loyal community? • Deliver value to all community members? • Price our product to achieve rapid adoption? • Become #1 or #2? • Erect barriers to entry? • Evolve the business to "cash in on strategic options"? • Generate multiple revenue streams? • Manage risk and growth?
An organization's **capabilities** are built and delivered through its: • People and partners • Organization and culture • Operating model • Marketing/sales model • Management model • Business development model • Infrastructure model	• Achieve best-in-class operating performance? • Develop modular, scalable, and flexible infrastructure? • Build and manage strong partnerships with employees and the community? • Increase the lifetime value of all members of the community? • Build, nurture, and exploit knowledge assets? • Make informed decisions and take actions that increase value? • Organize for action and agility?
What is it?	*How will we?*
Value is measured by: • Benefits returned to all stakeholders • Benefits returned to the firm • Market share and performance • Brand and reputation • Financial performance	• Deliver value to all stakeholders? • Claim value from stakeholder relationships and transactions? • Increase market share and drive new revenues off existing customers? • Increase brand value and reputation? • Generate confidence and trust? • Ensure strong growth in earnings? • Generate positive equity cash flow? • Increase stock price and market value?

created and delivered to customers.[6] Once activities are defined, it is then possible to analyze the economics at each step by identifying costs incurred and value created.

As you recall from Module 1, participants within a business market assume one or more of four basic roles to carry out these value-creating activ-

---

[6]M. Porter, *Competitive Advantage: Creating and Sustaining Superior Performance,* New York: The Free Press, 1985.

FIGURE 2-2

Emerging E-Business Models

ities. *Suppliers* create component products or provide services, raw materials or talent. *Producers* design and build products, services, and, most importantly, *solutions* that meet a specific customer or market need. They may sell and maintain the product or may share that role with others in an industry or with those outside traditional industry boundaries. *Distributors* enable buyers and sellers to connect, communicate, and transact business. These distributors may connect suppliers to business customers, forming what is often called a *supply chain,* or they may connect producers to consumers, forming what may be called a *buy chain. Customers* may be either individual consumers or businesses willing to pay for a product, service, or solution. When selling to business customers, individual consumers—the actual end users — are often located inside the customer firm. This can create a two-stage adoption cycle — first the business must decide to purchase a product or service and then individuals must decide to use it.

The new e-business models emerging on the Internet can be classified within one or more of the four generic market roles. See Figure 2-2. In addition, the models can be grouped into two categories. First, and most relevant for our discussion in this note, are the *digital businesses* being built and launched on the Internet. The second major category of e-business models comprises *businesses that provide the platform* upon which digital businesses are built and operated. Appendix A describes the various emerging e-business models and Appendix B summarizes revenue, cost and asset models. It is recommended that you review these appendixes before proceeding to the next section.

The e-business model classification, presented above, suggests that there is a separation between companies that produce and sell technical infrastructure and businesses that use the technology to support business strategy and design. As we will see in this module, however, the distinction is blurring as adoption of Internet-based business models penetrates to the very core of how firms do business. IBM, AOL, Microsoft, and Intuit no longer just sell technology products; these companies are now content aggregators, portals, and media companies. At the same time, non-high-tech businesses, such as Charles Schwab, are becoming technology infrastructure providers. David Pottruck, co-CEO of Charles Schwab explained: "[Charles Schwab] is a technology company that just happens to be in the brokerage business. . . If we are going to be successful, [technology] is going to have to be built into our DNA."

Another interesting feature of emerging e-business models concerns relationships within an online market. Traditionally, market participants performed their roles sequentially. Each participant in a value chain received inputs from those downstream, added value, and delivered outputs to the next participant in the chain. As you will see in the next section, in emerging Internet markets, this orderly sequence of value-creating activities, transactions, and relationships may no longer apply. Participants in an e-business marketplace may assume more than one role and often relate through a complex series of interdependent transactions and relationships that are best modeled as a *value web*. An excellent example of a value web in action can be found by analyzing the multiple e-business models and relationships adopted by Citigroup. See Figure 2-3.

Initially each business unit within the Citigroup family of companies (for example, Citicard, Citibank, Travelers Insurance, and Salomon Smith Bar-

FIGURE 2-3

Information Age Value Webs

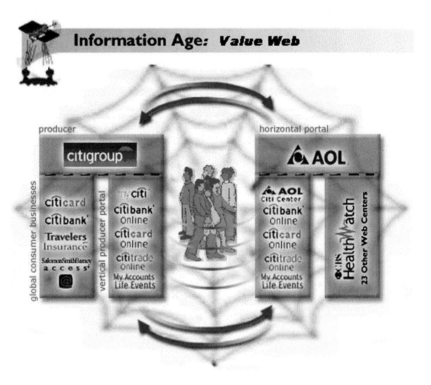

ney) strengthened offline channels and integrated them with new online channels to market. Thus, each business unit adopted a focused distributor business model. By 2000, the company had combined these independent focused distributors within two vertical portals that provided customers with an integrated solution — one portal, myCiti, could be accessed directly on the Citigroup website and the other, AOL Citi Center, was available to individuals with accounts on America Online (AOL).

Crafting Value Webs

The key to reconfiguring business models for the knowledge economy lies in understanding the new currencies of value. A value network [or value web] generates economic value through complex dynamic exchanges between one or more enterprises, and its customers, suppliers, strategic partners, and the community. These networks engage in more than just transactions [involving exchange] of goods and services, [they also exchange] knowledge and intangible value [for example, community, brand recognition, and reputation].[7]

E-Businesses are built by artfully combining a variety of business models. These businesses are then linked with others across multiple value chain networks to create what Frank Getman, CEO and president of HoustonStreet Exchange, refers to as a "web for the Web."[8] By incorporating multiple business models that generate separate revenue streams off of the same infrastructure, a network of businesses can more efficiently use resources, more effectively meet customer needs for integrated solutions, and drive additional value from the same level of investment. By linking the web of businesses inside a firm with a business network composed of a much larger web of businesses, an organization can leverage the resources of the community to further enhance value delivered to all members. The evolution of Quicken.com, Intuit's vertical portal for consumers, is an excellent example of how value webs are crafted within organizations, industries, and markets.

Intuit Crafts a Value Web Inside its Organization

In 1983, Intuit founders Scott Cook and Tom Proulx embarked on a quest to revolutionize the way individuals and small businesses managed their finances. A decade later, Intuit had emerged as the worldwide leader in the

---

[7]V. Allee, "Reconfiguring the value network," *Journal of Business Strategy,* 21 (4): 36–39, July/August 2000.
[8]"HoustonStreet Exchange weaves new round of investments and strategic partnerships into its web for the Web," HoustonStreet press release, March 23, 2000.

market for personal and small business finance software. Its Quicken (personal finance), QuickBooks (small business accounting), and TurboTax software accounted for 70 percent or more market share in their respective markets.

Intuit executives were quick to recognize the potential opportunities and threats presented by the commercialization of the Internet, the World Wide Web (WWW), and user-friendly browser software. They believed these technologies could be used to deliver new products and services and to dramatically expand the company's customer base and the range of products and services delivered. Although the market opportunity for Intuit's traditional software business was estimated as $300 million in 2002, the market opportunity for its online businesses was estimated to exceed $202 billion.[9] To exploit this opportunity, Intuit launched Quicken.com in 1996.

Initially, Quicken.com operated as an information aggregator through which consumers could access financial services news and information from a number of different information providers. Quicken.com added value by synthesizing the content, categorizing it for easy search and retrieval, packaging it, and then distributing it over the Internet to a rapidly growing network of consumers. In an effort to expand its customer base, Quicken.com executives decided not to charge consumers a subscription fee for its service, but instead, would generate revenues through advertising. The more consumers visited Quicken.com, the more the company learned about what those consumers wanted, and the more valuable the site became to advertisers.

Between 1996 and 1998, six focused distributors were launched under the Quicken.com umbrella brand. By summer 2000, Quicken.com logged an impressive 6 million visitors per month with 20 million regular users during the year. The business models adopted by the six focused distributors within the Quicken.com vertical portal are described below.

QuickenInsurance, QuickenLoan, and *Quicken Bill Manager* were marketplaces where consumers could purchase insurance, apply for and receive loans, and pay bills online. Revenues were primarily from suppliers that were charged a commission on each transaction. Suppliers were also charged development, consulting, and maintenance fees for system integration. Advertising and referral fees provided additional revenues.

QuickenRetirement and *QuickenInvestment* were aggregators. Consumers could access information but could not invest online. Revenues were generated primarily from sponsors that were charged advertising and referral fees.

QuickenShopping was a retailer. Consumers and small businesses could purchase Quicken's packaged software products online and could immediately download the software and all documentation to their personal computer. Alternatively, a consumer could request that Intuit ship the software in its traditional packaging that included printed documentation.

---

[9]Intuit Annual Report, 2000.

QuickenTurboTax enabled consumers to access information, tutorials and advice, prepare tax returns and file online. With the launch of Quicken-TurboTax, Intuit evolved its traditional packaged software business model to become an Application Service Provider (ASP).[10] But, Intuit did not eliminate its traditional packaged software when it adopted its online model. In early 2001, consumers could buy TurboTax packaged software for $39.95 and prepare their taxes on a personal computer. The tax forms could be printed out and submitted manually or they could be submitted online using Quicken-TurboTax. Alternatively, consumers could bypass purchasing the software package and could use QuickenTurboTax to prepare and submit their taxes online. Intuit saved money by shifting to the hosted online software model, and it passed the savings to the customer. There was no charge to prepare taxes online. A fee of $9.95 to $19.95 was charged to file online. Within one year of its launch in 1999, QuickenTurboTax for the web had captured 80 percent market share for online tax preparation.

Although not discussed in depth here, a second vertical portal, Quicken.com for Small Business was launched in the late 1990s. This vertical portal/ASP provided a wide range of online services (including payroll, bookkeeping, invoicing, and purchasing) to Intuit's installed base of over two million small business users of its packaged software, QuickBooks. By the summer of 2000, the Quicken for Small Business vertical portal/ASP had over five million users worldwide. Once again, Intuit found ways to link its packaged software to its online business and, as the number of Quicken for Small Business users grew, so too did the user base for QuickBooks packaged software, which increased to three million.

During 2000, Intuit earned almost $300 million from its online businesses and the majority of these businesses were profitable. Figure 2-4 provides an overview of Intuit's consumer business models in summer 2000.

Each Intuit online business leveraged a common infrastructure to generate multiple streams of revenues while also building knowledge assets and strengthening the brand — not just for Intuit but for all members of its value web. (See Figure 2-5.) Because the Internet and its associated technologies offered a common, standardized interface for linking value webs inside and outside the organization, Intuit's Internet-based digital infrastructure provided a modular platform upon which individual businesses could be integrated and built. The marginal cost of adding a new business to the infrastructure was low, and the revenue potential increased dramatically. Over time, new businesses could be built, launched, and grown to scale in months, dramatically increasing the company's agility and innovation potential while dramatically decreasing risk.

---

[10]An Application Service Provider, or ASP, provides online access to business software applications. Rather than buy a software package or build custom software that is then run on a personal computer or in a company's data center, an organization pays a fee to access software that runs on computers that are managed by an independent service provider.

FIGURE 2-4

Intuit's Consumer Business Models in Summer 2000

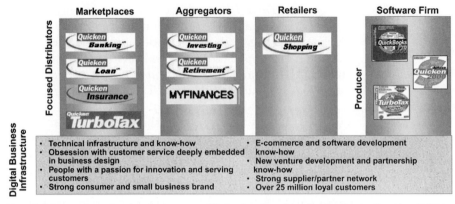

Note: Quicken.com's marketplace businesses could also function as Application Service Providers (ASPs). For example, insurance carriers could contract with QuickenInsurance to host the website and applications that were used by consumers to compare policies and apply for insurance, and Quicken TurboTax users logged into an online version of Intuit's TurboTax software.

FIGURE 2-5

Leveraging the Intuit Digital Business Infrastructure

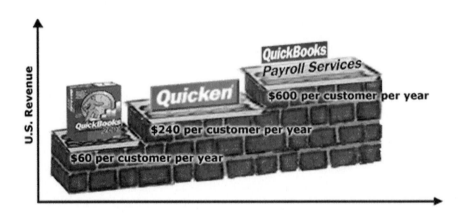

Intuit's Value Web Extends to its Business Community

The Quicken.com and Quicken for Small Business value webs do not stop at the door of the organization. Instead, these two vertical portals and the individual online businesses within them unite a network of suppliers, partners, and customers. For example, in the fall of 2000, QuickenInsurance linked 50 insurance carrier suppliers to over 500,000 visitors per month. Approximately 30 percent of its visitors came through Quicken.com, 20 percent through AOL, and 17 percent through its 55 other distribution partners.[11] Indeed, America Online was a key member of the Quicken.com value web and, as such, AOL's success increased the success of Quicken.com (see Figure 2-6).

---

[11]L.M. Applegate, *QuickenInsurance: The Race to Click and Close,* (HBS order #800-295).

FIGURE 2-6

Quicken.com and AOL Distribution Partnership

Founded in 1985 as Quantum Computer Services, the AOL.com online information service was launched in 1989 as a proprietary news, information, communication, and entertainment service. From the beginning, AOL also served as a network services provider, giving away its content and community services while charging per minute network access fees.

In summer 1995, AOL had approximately 500,000 members in the United States, revenues of $344.3 million, and was losing money. Losses continued as AOL shifted from a proprietary to an Internet infrastructure, and as it shifted its revenue model to a flat monthly fee. During 1997, the company lost almost $500 million, and many doubted that it would survive its painful evolution to an Internet business model. But survive it did, and by the summer of 2000 AOL had over 23 million members worldwide (approximately 35 percent of total worldwide Internet users), revenues of almost $7 billion, profits of almost $2 billion, and over $1.5 billion in cash. The completion of the merger with Time Warner in January 2001 was expected to generate an additional $1 billion in equity cash flow to investors by the end of 2001.[12]

Even before the merger with Time Warner, AOL had evolved a complex business model. To most consumers, it was a horizontal portal that enabled free access to the Internet and its "World Wide Web" of businesses, information, and services anywhere and anytime. Revenues for this component of the business model were collected from advertisers and sponsors. For example, Intuit paid AOL $16.2 million in 1998 to become the exclusive

---

[12]AOL Time Warner Annual Report, 2000.

provider of personal and small business financial services within AOL's Finance Web Center. It also paid a "click through" fee every time an AOL customer accessed its Quicken.com and Quicken for Small Business vertical portals through AOL. Finally, AOL received a percentage of every transaction conducted on Quicken.com by AOL customers. In early 2001, Quicken.com was one of 25 vertical portal web centers offered through AOL, and AOL commanded 20 to 25 percent of worldwide online advertising revenues.[13]

In addition to providing a gateway to content and services, AOL's business model also reflected its roots as a proprietary network services provider. With the launch of its Internet service in the mid-1990s, it quickly became a leading Internet Service Provider (ISP). In this role, it developed and maintained the network infrastructure and services that enabled individuals to access the Internet across telephone (dial-up) or high speed (broadband) networks. The completion of the merger of AOL and Time Warner on January 10, 2001, created the complex online/offline media conglomerate shown in Figure 2-7.[14]

Because it provides a common infrastructure for sharing information and coordinating business transactions, the Internet dramatically increases the ability to create value webs like those of Quicken.com and AOL Time Warner. And, like the spider webs upon which they were modeled, these networked value webs, although they may appear delicate on the surface, are surprisingly strong, "sticky," flexible, and resilient. But, as multiple new business webs are added, the complexity of managing these dense networks of relationships increases. It remains to be seen whether complex, multimodel businesses like AOL Time Warner will be able to achieve the synergies that appear so powerful on paper.

Putting the Ideas To Work

It is just an incredible time to be in business and have the rules of business changing. . . . For many years we operated under a pretty consistent set of rules. They evolved maybe. . .but now they're morphing and that presents a situation that challenges entrepreneurs to figure out: Are these rules real, or are they temporary? Should we respond to them? Do we create new rules? How do we run a company in a world like this when we have 13,000 employees trying to figure out where we are going and what we should do?[15]

---

[13]L.M. Applegate, QuickenInsurance: The Race to Click and Close, (HBS No. 800-295).

[14]Data on the AOL Time Warner business model are from The AOL Time Warner 2001 Fact Book.

[15]David Pottruck address to HBS executive class October 1999.

FIGURE 2-7

The AOL Time Warner Business Model in Early 2001

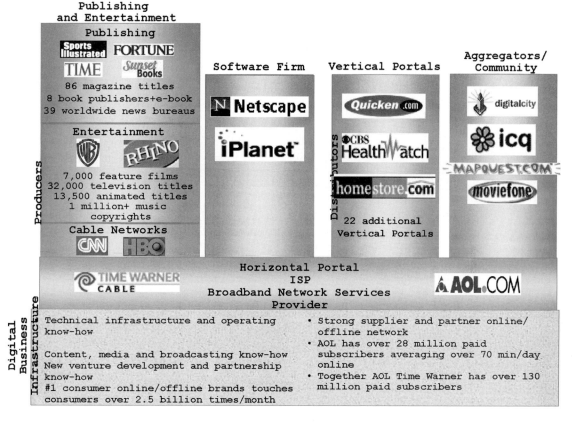

If you think about it, we spent most of the 20th century creating the business rules that were used to build and run a successful company in the Industrial Age. And, we spent the last two decades breaking those rules. Today, as we stand at the threshold of the 21st century, we're searching for new business models that enable a company to achieve the efficiency, power, resources, and reach of being big and the speed, agility, and responsiveness that comes from being small.

During the late 1990s, it was widely believed that new business models could not be built inside a traditional organization because the approaches and perspectives of the past would stifle innovation and creativity. Many believed that you had to "throw out" the old and build new businesses from the ground up. Although this approach was an important source of business

FIGURE 2-8

*E-Business
Implementation
Options*

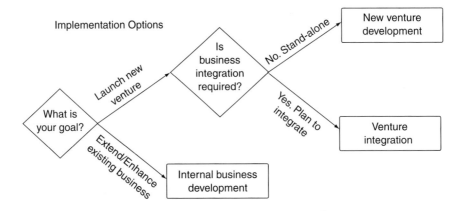

innovation, it was not the only approach used. In addition, it became increasingly clear that the ability to integrate old and new models was key to achieving both short-term and long-term success.

The decision tree presented in Figure 2-8 frames the choices executives and entrepreneurs must make when choosing an implementation approach. The cases in this module enable in-depth analysis of both business-to-consumer (B2C) and business-to-business (B2B) models, while also illustrating three key approaches to e-business implementation.

The first case in the series enables examination and comparison of the multiple business models and implementation approaches used by Intuit's Quicken.com. The case focuses on the evolution of one focused distributor, QuickenInsurance.[16] The initial business plan for QuickenInsurance — an online insurance broker — was developed by Steven Aldrich, a second year MBA student at Stanford's Graduate School of Business, as a project for an entrepreneurial management course. The company was founded in July 1995, one month after the hopeful entrepreneur graduated from business school. Less than one year later, after having trouble convincing insurance carriers to sign on, Aldrich sold his company to Intuit for $10 million.

Intuit provided instant credibility, access to a sophisticated online business infrastructure, and cash resources, but did not try to integrate the fledgling company into its organization and operations until the fall of 1999. Between 1995 and 2000 the business evolved from an idea on paper to a profitable online marketplace to a business offering within a tightly integrated vertical portal. The case, which enables examination of the evolution of the business model, strategy, and organization, also shows an interesting blend

---

[16]L.M. Applegate, *QuickenInsurance: The Race to Click and Close,* (HBS No. 800-295).

of the three different implementation approaches: new venture development, venture integration, and internal business development. It also enables comparison with the business model and implementation approach used by InsWeb — an online insurance competitor that evolved as a stand-alone new venture.

The Amazon.com[17] cases show how an entrepreneur — used the new venture development process to build an independent company. Amazon.com started as a U.S.-based online bookstore then added new product categories (e.g., music, video, consumer electronics, and toys) and entered European markets several years later. The case and valuation exercise enable in-depth examination of evolving business models and the complex value webs within which they operate. The case ends with the founder struggling to achieve profitability before rapidly dwindling cash reserves run out.

The case series end with the American Express Interactive case.[18] The case shows how executives used the new venture development and venture integration approaches when they built the firm's first e-business initiative, AXI Travel. In July 1997, senior executives announced that the company, in partnership with Microsoft, would build a new online travel business as an independent venture. At the same time, they declared their intention to integrate AXI Travel's "click and order" approach with the company's traditional "brick and mortar" travel business once the online service was launched in November 1997. To gain independence, the team moved to a Soho loft in New York City.[19] By February 1998, over 50,000 users in 225 companies were using AXI Travel and the team moved back into American Express corporate headquarters. But, rather than disband the members of the team to their original units, the group became the foundation for a new division, Corporate Services Interactive, that was charged with integrating the online/offline travel service and transferring ownership to the established travel business unit. The team was also charged with responsibility for leveraging the infrastructure built for AXI Travel to develop and launch other online services. The case enables in-depth examination of the evolving business model — from online marketplace to portal — and the challenges of integrating new online businesses with traditional operations, organizations, incentives, and cultures.

---

[17]M. Collura and L.M. Applegate, and M. Collura *Amazon.com 2000* (HBS No. 801-194); Applegate, L.M., *Amazon.com Valuation Exercise* (HBS No. 801-442).

[18]L.M. Applegate and P. Fischer, *American Express Interactive,* (HBS Order No. 399-014).

[19]Members of the software development team relocated to Redmond, Washington to enable them to work closely with Microsoft partners.

A E-BUSINESS MODELS

Focused Distributors

Focused distributors provide products and services within a specific industry or market niche. For example, E-Loan is a marketplace that connects buyers and sellers in the financial services industry and Lands' End.com is an online retailer that sells clothing and accessories. The five types of focused distributor business models—retailers, marketplaces, aggregators, infomediaries, and exchanges—are differentiated from each other by the following characteristics.

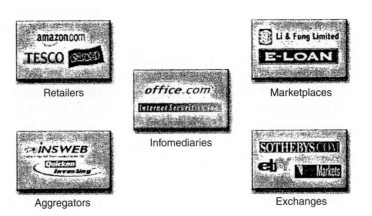

Retailers

Infomediaries

Marketplaces

Aggregators

Exchanges

Differentiating Features:

- Does the business assume control of inventory?
- Does the business sell online?
- Is the price set outside the market or is online price negotiation and bidding permitted?
- Is there a physical product or service that must be distributed?

Focused Distributor E-Business Trends:

- Focused distributors that do not allow customers and the business community to transact business online are losing power.
- Aggregators are evolving to marketplaces and/or vertical portals.
- Multiple business models are required to ensure flexibility and sustainability.
- Focused distributors must align closely with vertical and horizontal portals or evolve their model to become vertical portals.

Focused Distributor E-Business Models

Model & Examples	**Model Differentiators**					
	Own Inventory	*Sell Online*	*Price Set Online*	*Physical Product or Service*	*Likely Revenues*	*Likely Costs*
Retailer	Yes	Yes	No	Yes	Product/svc. sales	Advertising & marketing; Physical facilities, inventory & customer svc.; R&D; IT infrastructure
Marketplace	Possibly	Yes	No	No	Transaction fees; Service fees; Commissions	Advertising & marketing; R&D; IT infrastructure
Aggregator/ Infomediary	No	No	No	Possibly	Referral fees; Advertising & marketing fees	Advertising & marketing; R&D; IT infrastructure
Exchange	Possibly	Possibly	Yes	Possibly	Depends on model	Advertising & marketing; Staff support for auctions (especially B-2-B); Inventory & logistics if inventory control; R&D; Technical infrastructure

Portals

The American Heritage Dictionary of the English Language defines the term portal as "a doorway or gate—especially one that is large and imposing."[20] To many, this definition seems a fitting description of the portal business model that has emerged on the Web. Although the terminology is rather recent, the earliest online business portals (for example, American Hospital Supply's ASAP and American Airlines'

---

[20]*American Heritage Dictionary of the English Language.* Boston: Houghton Mifflin, 1971.

Horizontal
Portal

Vertical
Portal

Affinity or Life
Event Portal

Sabre) were first launched in the late 1960s and 1970s.[21] Online consumer portals (for example, America Online and CompuServe) emerged in the 1980s with the adoption of the personal computer. Built upon proprietary technology, these pre-Internet portals provided limited access. In fact, in late 1993, AOL's proprietary consumer portal had only 500,000 members. By early 2001, the number had grown to over 27 million.[22]

Differentiating Features

- Does the business provide gateway access to a full range of Internet information and services, including search, calendar, e-mail, instant messaging, chat, and other community-building tools?
- Does the business provide access to deep content, products, and services within a vertical industry (e.g., financial services) or related industries (e.g., travel)?
- Does the business provide information and services for all types of users or are the information and services specific to a well-defined affiliation group (e.g., women, the elderly, lawyers, families)?

Portal E-Business Trends

- Horizontal and vertical portals are emerging as dominant sources of power within e-business markets.
- Horizontal portals are joining forces with horizontal infrastructure portals to provide, not just access to content and services, but also access to network and hosting services.
- Large media and entertainment portals that represent convergence of data, telephone, television, and radio networks are emerging in the consumer space.
- B2B portals provide both horizontal access to business networks and vertical industry-wide solutions.

---

[21]See L.M. Applegate, F.W. McFarlan, and J.L. McKenney, "Electronic Commerce: Trends and Opportunities," Chapter 4 Corporate Information Systems Management, NY: McGraw-Hill Irwin, 1999.

[22]AOL company web site (www.corp.aol.com/who_timeline.html), March 2, 2000.

Portal E-Business Models

Model & Examples	Model Differentiators			Likely Revenues	Likely Costs
	Gateway Access	*Deep Content & Solutions*	*Affinity Group Focus*		
Horizontal Portals	Yes	Through partnerships with vertical & affinity portals	Possibly; Often through partnerships	Advertising, affiliation & slotting fees; Possibly subscription or access fees	Advertising, marketing & sales; Content/info asset mgmt.; R&D; IT infrastructure
Vertical Portals	Limited	Yes	No	Transaction fees; Commissions; Advertising, affiliation & slotting fees	Advertising, marketing & sales; Content/info asset mgmt.; R&D; IT infrastructure; Legacy system integration to support transactions
Affinity Portals	Possibly	Within affinity group	Yes	Referral fees; Advertising, affiliation & slotting fees	Advertising, marketing & sales; Content/info asset mgmt.; R&D; IT infrastructure

Producers

Producers design and make, and may also directly market, sell, and distribute, products and services. As mentioned earlier, producers often held the position of power within traditional business markets. During the late 1990s, many worried that new online entrants would dominate the Information Age. The demise of many once-powerful "dot-coms" shifted the balance of power in favor of established players.

Differentiating Features

- Does the business sell physical products and/or provide face-to-face services?
- Does the business sell information-based products and/or services?
- Does the business provide customized products and/or services?

Producer E-Business Trends

- Producers must be best-in-class — the #1 or #2 brand — to survive.
- Some large full service producers, like American Express and Citigroup in the financial services industry, are acquiring a full range of products and services

Manufacturers

Educators

Advisors

Publishers &
News Services

Service
Providers

Producer E-Business Models

Model & Examples	Model Differentiators				
	Sell/Serve Online	Sell/Serve Offline	Level of Customization	Likely Revenues	Likely Costs
Manufacturers	Yes	Yes	Low to Moderate	Product sales; Service fees	Advertising, marketing & sales; Content/info asset mgmt.; R&D; IT infrastructure
Service Providers	Yes	Possibly	Moderate to High	Commission, service or transaction fees;	Advertising, marketing & sales; Content/info asset mgmt.; R&D; IT infrastructure
Educators	Yes	Possibly	Moderate to High	Registration or event fee; Subscription fee; Hosting fee	Content/info asset mgmt.; R&D; IT infrastructure
Advisors	Yes	Usually	Moderate to High	Subscription fee; Registration or event fee; Membership fee; Commission, transaction or service fee	Content/info asset mgmt.; IT infrastructure
Information & News Services	Yes	Possibly	Moderate to High	Subscription fee; Commission, transaction or service fee	Content/info asset mgmt.; Advertising, marketing & sales; IT infrastructure

and then integrating them to provide vertical solutions required by customers.

- Industry supplier coalitions are forming to enable business-to-business commerce within industry groups and with key business customers.

Infrastructure Distributors

Infrastructure distributors enable technology buyers and sellers to transact business. Four categories of focused distributor, key differentiating features and trends are shown below.

Differentiating Features

- Does the business assume control of inventory?
- Does the business sell online?
- Is the price set outside the market or is online price negotiation and bidding permitted?
- Is there a physical product or service that must be distributed?

Infrastructure Distributor E-Business Trends

- The speed of obsolescence of the technology, coupled with the complexity of the solution and slim margins has forced massive consolidation in network and computing technology channels. For many, service revenues are driving profitability.
- Those distributors that take ownership of inventory are searching for inventory-less, just-in-time business models.
- Distributors that have the capability for custom configuration of products and services are gaining power.

Infrastructure
Retailers

Infrastructure
Aggregators

Infrastructure
Marketplaces

Infrastructure
Exchanges

Infrastructure Distributor E-Business Models

Models & Examples	Model Differentiators				Likely Revenues	Likely Costs
	Control Inventory	Sell Online	Price Set Online	Physical Product or Service		
Infrastructure Retailers	Yes	Yes	Not Usually	Yes	Product sales; Service fees	Advertising & marketing; Physical facilities, inventory & customer svc.; R&D; IT infrastructure
Infrastructure Marketplaces	Usually	Yes	Possibly	Yes	Transaction fees; Service fees; Commission	Advertising & marketing; R&D; IT infrastructure
Infrastructure Exchanges	Possibly	Possibly	Yes	Yes	Depends on model	Advertising & marketing; Staff support for auctions (especially B-2-B); Inventory & logistics if inventory control; R&D; Technical infrastructure

Infrastructure Portals

Infrastructure portals enable consumers and businesses to access online services and information. Five categories of infrastructure portal, key differentiating features and trends are shown below.

Differentiating Features

- Does the business enable users to connect to the Internet?
- Does the business enable users to outsource the operation and maintenance of websites?
- Does the business host applications and solutions?

Infrastructure Portal E-Business Trends

- Horizontal infrastructure portals (ISPs, Network Service Providers, and Web Hosting Providers) are merging or partnering with horizontal content portals to increase value created through intangible assets such as information, community and brand.
- Horizontal content portals such as AOL are vertically-integrating with horizontal infrastructure providers, such as Time-Warner's cable networks. (Note: Prior to the merger, AOL was an ISP.)
- Convergence of voice, data, and video channels and global acceptance of a common set of standards is leading to global industry convergence.

Producer
Application Service
Provider (ASP)

Network
Service Providers

Internet Service
Provider (ISP)

Distributor
Application Service
Provider (ASP)

Web Hosting

- Aggressive pursuit of growing market for hosted application services is leading to confusion as players with markedly different business models converge on the common space.
- Two competing Vertical Infrastructure Portal (ASP) models are emerging: producer-ASPs (for example, Oracle, Siebel, SAP) provide online access to their brand-name software; distributor-ASPs (for example, US Internetworking) offer application hosting of many software brands.

Infrastructure Portal E-Business Models

Models & Examples	Model Differentiators		Likely Revenues	Likely Costs
	Internet / Network Access and Hosting	*Hosted Applications and Solutions*	*Likely Revenues*	*Likely Costs*
Horizontal Infrastructure Portals Includes: Internet Service Providers (ISPs), Network Service Providers, and Web Hosting.	Yes	Through partnerships with non-infrastructure portals & ASPs	Access fees; Commission, service or transaction fees; Subscription fees; Hosting fees	R&D; IT infrastructure; Advertising, marketing and sales
Vertical Infrastructure Portals Includes: Producer and Distributor Application Service Providers (ASPs)	Often through partnerships with horizontal infrastructure portals	Yes	Licensing fees; Service & transaction fees; Maintenance & update fees; Hosting fees	Advertising, marketing & sales; Content/ info asset mgmt.; R&D; IT infrastructure

Infrastructure Producers

Infrastructure producers design, build, market and sell technology hardware, software, solutions, and services. Producers may sell and provide after-sales service directly or they may share this responsibility with online/offline channel partners including retailers, distributors, and portals.

Differentiating Features

- Does the business manufacture computer or network components or equipment?
- Does the business develop packaged software?
- Does the business provide infrastructure services or consulting?

Infrastructure Producer E-Business Trends

- Many hardware and software producers were early adopters of online commerce, selling directly to Internet-savvy customers and through online distributors. For example, in 1999, over 80% of Cisco's sales were through online channels-most of which was through online distribution partners.

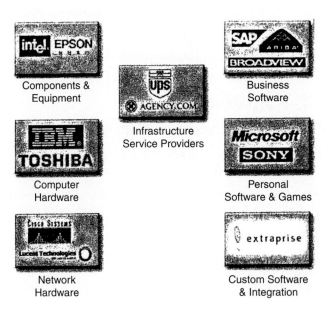

Components & Equipment

Infrastructure Service Providers

Business Software

Computer Hardware

Personal Software & Games

Network Hardware

Custom Software & Integration

Infrastructure Producer E-Business Models

Models & Examples	Model Differentiators			Likely Revenues	Likely Costs
	Sell/Serve Online	*Sell/Serve Offline*	*Level of Customization*		
Equipment/ Component Manufacturers	Yes	Yes	Low to Moderate	Product license or sales; Installation & integration fees; Maintenance, update & service fees	R&D; Advertising, marketing and sales; Production; Physical facilities & infrastructure; Specialized equipment, materials & supplies; IT infrastructure
Software Firms	Yes	Yes	Moderate to High	Product license or sales; Installation & integration fees; Maintenance, update & service fees	R&D; Advertising, marketing and sales; Production; Physical facilities & infrastructure; Specialized equipment, materials & supplies; IT infrastructure
Custom Software and Integration	No	Yes	High	Commission, service or transaction fee	Access to specialized talent; Professional development and training; Travel
Infrastructure Services Firms	Yes	Yes	High	Commission, service or transaction fee; Hosting fee	Content/info asset mgmt.; R&D; IT infrastructure

B   E-BUSINESS REVENUE AND COST MODELS

Sample Revenue Options

Commerce Revenues

Revenue Category	*Description*
Product Sales	Sell or license physical or information-based products.
Commission, Service or Transaction Fees	Charge a fee for services provided; can be a set fee or a % of the cost of a product or service.

Content Revenues

Revenue Category	*Description*
Subscription Fees	Charge for receipt of updated information on a particular topic or a broad range of topics for a specified period of time (e.g., annual).
Registration or Event Fees	Charge a fee for attendance at an online event, workshop or course.

Community Revenues

Revenue Category	*Description*
Advertising, Slotting, Affiliate & Referral Fees	Collect a fee for hosting a banner advertisement or special promotion.
	Collect a fee for an exclusive or non-exclusive partnership relationship.
	Collect a fee each time a visitor clicks through from your site to another company's site.
Membership Fees	Charge a fee to belong to a private group or service.

Infrastructure Revenues

Revenue Category	*Description*
Software/Hardware Sales	Sell or license a technology product.
Installation and Integration Fees	Charge either a set or variable fee for services provided; large-scale fixed price projects are often broken into a series of discrete projects with well-defined timeframes and deliverables; variable fees are often based on time, materials and expenses incurred while working on a project.
Maintenance & Update Fees	Charge a fee for software/hardware maintenance & updates.
Hosting Fees	Charge a fee for hosting a software application, website, data center or network.
Access Fees	Charge a fee for providing access to a network and/or to an Internet service.

Sample Cost Categories

Cost Category	Description
People & Partners	Cost to acquire, develop and retain skills and expertise needed to execute strategy; includes employees and partnerships.
Advertising, Marketing, Sales	Cost of offline and online advertising, marketing and sales.
Business Development	Cost of designing and launching new businesses, developing alliances and acquiring partners.
Materials & Supplies	Cost of physical materials used in production of products and delivery of services; includes general purpose and specialized supplies and components.
Specialized Equipment (does not include IT)	Cost of equipment—especially capital equipment—used in design, production, delivery, and distribution.
Research & Development	Cost of designing and developing digital business products and services; may overlap with IT infrastructure costs.
Physical Facilities and Infrastructure	Cost of corporate and regional headquarters, sales offices, factories, warehouses, distribution centers, retail stores, service centers etc.
Information Technology (IT) Infrastructure	Cost of computers and equipment (e.g., printers, data storage devices). Cost to operate and maintain data centers. Cost to design, develop, implement and maintain software. Cost of voice, data and video network equipment (e.g., physical cables, routers). Cost to operate and maintain networks.

Sample Asset Categories

Current Assets	
Asset Category	*Description*
Financial Assets	Accounts receivable. Cash and convertible notes.
Marketable Securities	Investments made as part of a cash management program.

Tangible Assets	
Asset Category	*Description*
Property, Plant and Equipment	Physical facilities. Fixed assets required to produce goods and services.
Inventory	Assets held for re-sale.

Investments	
Asset Category	*Description*
Securities	Stock held by one firm to enable joint control over shared business activities. Stock held by one firm in anticipation of a return at some time in the future.
Real Estate	Investment in property in anticipation of a future return.

Sample Asset Categories, *(Continued)*

Intangible Assets	
Asset Category	*Description*
Relationships	Breadth and depth of relationships with customers and the business community.
	Loyalty and commitment of customers and business community members.
Strength of Online & Offline Brand	Strong brand recognition among business and consumer communities (includes corporate brand, business unit brands, product brands and global brand).
	Ability to generate strong personal identification with brand.
	Ability to leverage "Internet" brand image.
	Reputation and image.
Knowledge & Expertise	Experience, skills and intellectual capabilities of employees and partners.
	Understanding of market and business dynamics.
	Scope and granularity of stored information.
	Flexibility and ease of accessing, customizing and distributing information.
	Information literacy.
	Understanding of technical and business evolution and ability to identify opportunities and threats.
Agility & Responsiveness	Ability to quickly recognize and act on new opportunities and threats.
	Ability to access and efficiently utilize resources required to execute strategy.
	Ability to capture the attention and mobilize the commitment of customers and members of the business community to implement new strategies.
Intellectual property	Patents, copyrights, etc. for which an objective measure of value can be assessed.
Goodwill	Value of an acquired company over and above current and tangible assets.
	The value of an acquired company's "franchise"—e.g., loyalty of its customers, the expertise of its employees—that can be objectively measured at the time of a sale or change of control.

CASE 2–1
QUICKENINSURANCE: THE RACE TO CLICK AND CLOSE[1]

We believe the vertical portal will become the most powerful long-term [financial services] distribution model . . . Among the vertical portals, we believe Schwab, Citigroup, Bank One, American Express, Intuit [Quicken.com], AOL, E*Trade and Yahoo! are, or will be, among the standouts long term.

Morgan Stanley Dean Witter Analysts, 1999[2]

In summer 2000, Steven Aldrich contemplated the immediate decisions that he would need to make as he transitioned from his role as General Manager, QuickenInsurance, to General Manager, Quicken.com (www.quicken.com). The need to make tough decisions seemed to be a fact of life these days. It began with his decision to launch an online insurance "dot-com" one-month after graduating from Stanford's Graduate School of Business in July 1995.[3] Less than one year after launch, his decision to sell the company to Intuit for $10 million had been equally tough.

In hindsight, Aldrich believed that both decisions were right. But at the time, the correct path seemed anything but clear. "When my partner and I first contemplated starting an online insurance business in 1994, the Internet was still uncharted territory," Aldrich recalled. "When we launched the business in 1995, we had a hard time convincing insurance carriers to join our service. The decision

to link our fledgling company with Intuit's well-known and well-respected brand dramatically increased our credibility with both suppliers and customers. Today, we have 50 of the largest, name-brand insurance carriers linked to our service." Aldrich also gained instant market reach as the exclusive online insurance marketplace on Intuit's popular Quicken.com, which by summer 2000 was receiving an average of 30 million visitors per month with over 20 million return visitors. He also gained access to other top financial services portals, and became the exclusive insurance broker for AOL Finance, Excite, Prodigy, CBS Marketwatch, CNNfn, Webcrawler, Motley Fool, The Wedding Channel, AutoTrader, and AutoWeb, among others.[4]

By October 1999, QuickenInsurance received over 500,000 visitors to its website. During 3Q99, it provided over 225,000 auto insurance quotes and 3,400 term life insurance applications to its insurance company suppliers.[5] And, unlike most other Internet competitors, QuickenInsurance's life and auto insurance businesses were already profitable.

While some initially argued that he had missed out on the high market capitalizations

---

[1]This case was prepared by Professor Lynda M. Applegate. Copyright © 2000 by the President and Fellows of Harvard College.
Harvard Business School case 800-295.
[2]U.S. Internet and Financial Services Equity Research Team, "The Internet and Financial Services," *Morgan Stanley Dean Witter Equity Research,* August 1999.
[3]The company that Aldrich founded was named Interactive Insurance, Inc., and it was headquartered in Alexandria, Virginia. Quicken.com was headquartered in Mountain View, California. The term "dot-com" refers to a business that was built and launched as an independent company that did business on the internet.

[4]A study by Media Metrix in May 1999 listed the top seven financial services vertical portals in terms of reach as: America Online Finance (12.7%); Yahoo! Finance (5.4%); Quicken.com (3.2%); E*Trade (2.9%), MSN Money (2.7%) and First USA (2.5%).
[5]Appleby, S. and Shane, R., "Intuit," *Robertson Stephens eFinance Research,* November 24, 1999.

afforded to Internet start-ups, Aldrich had always believed that, in the long term, the value created for *all* stakeholders would be much higher if he aligned his online insurance business with Intuit's Quicken.com brand and assets.[6] Analysts supported his view, giving both Intuit and Quicken.com high marks.

Not only is Intuit a highly profitable and growing software company, it also generates significant Internet revenues (almost $300 million in 2000). We believe this is a phenomenal franchise and that Intuit is a clear leader in the electronic finance space. The company has made it clear over the past nine months that it will invest aggressively to build its Internet business in lieu of passing upside through to the bottom line. [While] some investors could be disappointed, [we believe that] the time to act aggressively is now and Intuit is in a unique position of strength.

Hambrecht and Quist, Nov. 1999[7]

Once again, we are encouraged by Intuit's strong financial performance and recent announcements regarding its Internet strategy. We believe management is beginning to leverage the power of its strong brands into a powerful Internet presence. Coupled with [its] enhanced Internet products and services, we believe that Intuit is on track to build one of the first Super Financial Portals . . . which will cause Internet revenues to accelerate substantially in the back half of fiscal 2000.

Robertson Stephens, Nov. 1999[8]

Despite these words of praise for Quicken. com, Aldrich was concerned about the future of the QuickenInsurance business. Intuit's 2000 Annual Report (published in July 2000) noted that penetration and growth of the automobile insurance business had been slower than expected.

Users can currently receive quotes and apply for term life insurance from 12 national carriers in 50 states and Washington D.C. Auto insurance quotes are currently available from 2 carriers in 38 states (covering over 95% of the population), and online purchase of auto insurance is available from 8 carriers in 17 states (covering about 60% of the population) through the carriers' call centers. Progress for our auto insurance business has been slow. Future success will require that we offer a greater choice of quoting carriers in each state, and provide online purchase or call center fulfillment capabilities in more states. While we have plans in place to increase carrier and purchasing options, we expect to face continuing challenges in implementing these plans.

Slow growth for the auto insurance segment was of particular concern to Quicken.com executives since auto insurance was expected to represent the largest online insurance market segment. While the insurance market was large—over $1.2 trillion in insurance premiums were written in the U.S. in 1998[9]—only 700,000 households had purchased insurance online in 1999. This represented less than 1% of all insurance sales.[10]

A number of factors hampered the shift to online insurance sales. First, most industry insiders believed that insurance products were too complex for consumers to purchase online. Second, many insurance products were purchased infrequently and a recurring revenue stream could not be generated. Finally, a restrictive regulatory environment

---

[6]The dramatic decline in the market value of pure-play "dot-com" businesses during 2000 validated Aldrich's decision to align with Intuit.
[7]Combes, G., "Intuit, Inc.," *Hambrecht and Quist, Internet Research Note,* November 24, 1999.
[8]Appleby, S. and Shane, R., "Intuit, Inc.," *Robertson Stephens eFinance Research,* November 24, 1999.

[9]Zandi, R., and Vetto, M. L., "Insweb, Inc." *Salomon Smith Barney Equity Research,* November 24, 1999.
[10]During 1999, over 28 million households had purchased online. Clemmer, K. et.al., "Insurance's Researched Future," *Forrester Research Report,* March 2000.

hampered the entry of independent online marketplaces. Because of the relative simplicity of automobile insurance, the fact that it was renewed every year, and the overall size of the market, most analysts predicted much faster growth in online sales of automobile insurance than other insurance products. In fact, these predictions had been validated, and 76% of all online insurance purchases during 1999 were for auto insurance. Online auto insurance sales were estimated to grow to $11 billion by 2004 and online research of auto insurance would influence over $34 billion in additional sales. In contrast, sales of online term life insurance in 2004 were estimated to grow to approximately $375 million in sales and online research would influence an additional $1.4 billion in offline sales.[11]

By early 2000, established insurance carriers—especially those with significant investment in auto insurance products—were aggressively developing online sales channels. In fact, a Forrester Research study in early 2000 indicated that Geico (www.geico.com), Allstate (www.allstate.com), and State Farm (www.statefarm.com) drew more traffic to their web sites than independent online marketplaces, such as InsWeb (www.insweb.com), QuickenInsurance (www.quicken.com), 4freequotes.com (www.4freequotes.com) and Quotesmith.com (www.quotesmith.com).[12] But, while they trailed in traffic, customers rated 4freequotes.com and QuickenInsurance #1 and #2

respectively in customer satisfaction.[13] When asked to rate the most valuable features of an online insurance service, consumers chose: (1) the ability to compare multiple competing quotes from multiple carriers; (2) the availability of information about policies and terminology; and (3) the ability to use tools to calculate premiums, etc. Over 30% of the consumers rated their experience as "horrible" when they were forced to receive quotes by contacting the company via e-mail or "snail mail," or to leave the web site to contact an agent by phone. The ability to access an agent and purchase immediately through a web-enabled call center was considered by most to be at least as satisfactory—and for some it was more satisfactory—than purchasing online.

As established carriers turned up the pressure, so too did independent online marketplaces, like InsWeb. Fresh on the heels of its Initial Public Offering (IPO) in July 1999, InsWeb had spent heavily to increase its supplier and customer base, improve its customer service and reliability, and extend its business model to become an online insurance agent.[14] Having gone public at the height of the dot-com euphoria, InsWeb's stock price had surged to $44 in July 1999 giving the firm a market capitalization of $1.5 billion. Cash generated by the IPO was immediately used to fund a $75 million online and offline marketing campaign,

---

[11]Op Cit. Forrester Research, March 2000, page 14.

[12]Ibid, page 10. In fall 1999, Allstate announced a two-year $1 billion capital investment ($300 million for capital equipment and $700 million for systems development, advertising, and deployment—including hiring and training people) to build the digital infrastructure required to do business on the Internet and through web-enabled call centers. See Booker, E. and Schwartz, J., "Will Allstate Pull Insurers to the Web," *Internetweek,* November 22, 1999.

[13]While it received a lower customer satisfaction rating in the Forrester Research study (conducted in late 1999 and early 2000), InsWeb was rated the #1 online insurance site by independent web site rating service, Gomez.com (www.gomez.com) and was ranked one of the top 100 web sites by Yahoo! Internet Life's Top 100 Web Sites for 2001 (www.zdnet.com) May 2001. Gomez commended InsWeb for its "easy to use platform for requesting instant online quotes, wealth of educational content relating to insurance and a number of helpful calculators and tools for estimating an appropriate level of coverage." See InsWeb Press Release, January 4, 2001.

[14]Appleby, S.W., "InsWeb," *Robertson Stephens eFinance Research,* October 27, 1999.

to open a web-enabled call center and a back-up data center, and to launch an online insurance agency.

By 2000, InsWeb had signed distribution agreements with over 200 online sites, and was the exclusive online insurance provider for Yahoo! Finance, Microsoft Network (MSN), E*Trade and NextCard, among others.[15] The company offered auto insurance, term life, health, homeowner, and variable annuities quotes from 36 insurance carriers. In October 1999, InsWeb overcame regulatory hurdles preventing it from selling insurance and launched a wholly-owned subsidiary, InsWeb Insurance Services, that was licensed as an insurance agent in 39 states. In the remaining 11 states, InsWeb was licensed through its officers or resident agents. An April 4, 2000 InsWeb press release stated: "Today, licensed InsWeb agents are closing customer [transactions] and supporting policy fulfillment services on behalf of 7 auto insurers. . . . We have designed a comprehensive range of outsourcing services designed to help insurance carriers reduce paperwork and complete the entire business in record time."

Reflecting online insurance industry trends, auto insurance quotes represented the majority of InsWeb's 2000 revenues of $23.2 million, up from $21.8 million in 1999.[16] Revenues from two auto insurance carriers—State Farm and AIG—accounted for approximately 31% and 11%, respectively of InsWeb's total 1999 revenues. Revenues from State Farm, AIG, and GE Capital accounted for 14%, 11%, and 9%, respectively, of InsWeb's total revenues in 2000.

Effective May 1, 2000, however, State Farm stopped participating in the InsWeb online marketplace.

As confidence in pure-play Internet companies declined in summer 2000, so too did the price of InsWeb stock, which by fall 2000 had sunk to less than $2 per share. In an effort to cut costs, InsWeb announced plans to reduce its staff by approximately 40 percent by year-end 2000.[17] Hussein Enan, CEO and founder, commented: "These measures, combined with other cost-reduction efforts and our more than $75 million in cash and short-term investments as of March 31, make us confident that we will have more than enough cash to allow us to operate comfortably through 2002, at which point we expect to begin generating profits."

As he assumed his new role of general manager of Quicken.com, Aldrich knew that he must work with his successor to plan a strategy to address the threats to QuickenInsurance even as he looked forward to broadening his focus to define strategic direction for Quicken.com. As he did, he was forced to balance priorities for investment.

Could an independent vertical portal, like Quicken.com withstand the attacks of mega financial service providers, like Citigroup and American Express, while also countering focused attacks by brand-name niche providers, like Allstate and State Farm, across each of its six consumer businesses?[18] As independent dot-com players struggled, Aldrich and Quicken.com senior executives also wondered whether it was best to wait for firms to fail or to

---

[15]During 2000, InsWeb reported that it logged 8 million unique visitors and 2.1 million shopping sessions. See InsWeb 2000 Annual Report.

[16]As of March 2000, InsWeb offered auto insurance quotes to consumers in 49 states plus the District of Columbia. See InsWeb 2000 Annual Report.

[17]InsWeb Press Release, June 4, 2000. By year-end 2000, InsWeb had 137 employees, down from 297 in late 1999.

[18]In addition to offering online insurance, Quicken.com's consumer portal also provided access to QuickenLoan, QuickenBanking, QuickenInvestment, QuickenRetirement and QuickenTurboTax. (Visit the website at www.quicken.com.)

move quickly to snatch up assets before they fell into the hands of a competitor.

Recognizing that a vertical portal is only as strong as its independent business brands, Aldrich also wondered how aggressively to market Quicken.com's individual business brands, like QuickenInsurance. Until now, he had relied almost exclusively on Intuit and Quicken.com to market and drive traffic to the QuickenInsurance site. Should Steve Bruce, his successor as general manager of QuickenInsurance, step up efforts to independently market the QuickenInsurance brand? If so, how aggressively should he act? In his new role overseeing Quicken.com, Aldrich also questioned whether he should increase marketing for QuickenLoan, QuickenTurboTax, and the other Quicken.com businesses. Alternatively, should the company focus attention and resources on marketing Quicken.com as an umbrella brand?

Finally, Aldrich and Quicken.com senior executives wondered how to allocate investment priorities in evolving the Quicken.com business model. (See Exhibit 1 for Intuit financials.) All agreed that electronic bill payment and presentment, and personalization features that allowed consumers to enter and maintain personal finance information were "killer apps" that would increase customer retention. Indeed, in November 1999, Intuit signed a 5-year agreement to be the exclusive provider of integrated bill presentment and payment services for AOL. The service enabled AOL subscribers to use QuickenBanking to conduct a wide range of banking services and to view, track, and pay bills online. "We believe that EBPP [Electronic Bill Payment and Presentment] will be a [killer app for] online Super Financial Portals," Robinson Stephens continued. "Because Intuit and AOL are trusted providers, we expect that consumer acceptance of this service will develop quickly. With today's announcement, Intuit is positioned as a first mover in a space that For-

rester analysts estimate will reach 20 million U.S. households within 5 years."[19]

In early 2000, the company also announced the launch of a personalized information portal called MyProfile. While the new service was an instant hit with Quicken.com customers, the company's key distribution partner, AOL, decreased support for MyProfile to prevent conflict with its personalization portal, My AOL. In late 2000, if you entered Quicken.com through the Personal Finance Webcenter then clicked on the tab marked "My Portfolio," you received the following message. "**<u>Attention Quicken.com Portfolio Users:</u>** As part of the changes related to the launch of My AOL, we are no longer offering the 'snapshot' view of quicken.aol.com portfolios. Your portfolio remains intact and viewable through the AOL Anywhere Personal Finance Webcenter. To see and make changes to it, sign in on the boxes to the right and bookmark the page. We apologize for any inconvenience this may cause."

In 2000, Intuit also invested heavily in the launch of its Quicken.com for Small Business portal. The small- to mid-size business market was highly competitive and Intuit had demonstrated the appeal of its traditional software products for both consumers and small business owners. In 1998, more than 13 million home business owners had spent more than $22 billion on technology alone.[20] The ability to access a wide range of business services, such as payroll, business accounting, and procurement, was expected to represent a huge— and previously untapped—market for online service providers.

When Mark Goines, S.V.P. of Intuit's Consumer Finance Business, tapped Aldrich to become general manager of Quicken.com, he

---

[19]Appleby, S. and Shane, R., "Intuit," *Robertson Stephens eFinance Research,* November 24, 1999.
[20]Schmitt, E., et.al., "Unlocking Home Business," *Forrester Research Report,* December 1998.

EXHIBIT 1 Financial Overview

	Small Business Division	Tax Division	Consumer Finance Division	International Division	Other (1)	Consolidated
2000						
Net revenue	$394,264	$379,270	$225,930	$94,361	—	$1,093,825
Segment operating income/(loss)	112,275	165,400	(4,793)	14,042	—	286,924
Common expenses	=	=	=	=	(135,729)	(135,729)
Subtotal operating income (loss)	112,275	165,400	(4,793)	14,042	(135,729)	151,195
Realized gains/(losses) on marketable securities	—	—	—	—	481,130	481,130
Acquisition costs	—	—	—	—	(168,058)	(168,058)
Interest income/expense and other items	—	—	—	—	48,443	48,443
Net income (loss) before tax	$112,275	$165,400	$(4,793)	$14,042	$225,786	$512,710
1999						
Net revenue	$292,707	$337,734	$137,681	$79,446	$ —	$847,568
Segment operating income/(loss)	95,924	148,464	(6,621)	(2,252)	—	235,515
Common expenses		=			(114,938)	(114,938)
Subtotal operating income (loss)	95,924	148,464	(6,621)	(2,252)	(114,938)	120,577
Realized gains/(losses) on marketable securities	—	—	—	—	579,211	579,211
Acquisition costs	—	—	—	—	(100,692)	(100,692)
Interest income/expense and other items	—	—	—	—	18,253	18,253
Net income (loss) before tax	$ 95,924	$148,464	$(6,621)	$(2,252)	$381,834	$617,349

1998

Net revenue	$208,349	$192,789	$120,860	$ 70,738	—	$592,736
Segment operating income/(loss)	75,770	79,373	(16,414)	(11,472)	—	127,257
Common expenses	—	—	—	—	(66,776)	(66,776)
Subtotal operating income (loss)	75,770	79,373	(16,414)	(11,472)	(66,776)	60,481
Realized gains/(losses) on marketable securities	—	—	—	—	—	—
Acquisition costs	—	—	—	—	(80,909)	(80,909)
Interest income/expense and other items	—	—	—	—	605	605
Net income (loss) before tax	$75,770	$ 79,373	$(16,414)	$(11,472)	$(147,080)	$(19,823)

1997

Net revenue	$184,169	$170,223	$ 97,572	$ 73,537	—	$598,925
Segment operating income/(loss)	55,323	60,360	(17,487)	(1,560)	6,745	103,381
Common expenses	—	—	—	—	(54,024)	(54,024)
Subtotal operating income (loss)	55,323	60,360	(17,487)	(1,560)	(47,279)	49,257
Realized gains/(losses) on marketable securities	—	—	—	—	—	—
Acquisition costs	—	—	—	—	(39,041)	(39,041)
Interest income/expense and other items	—	—	—	—	(507)	(507)
Net income (loss) before tax	$55,323	$(60,360)	$(17,487)	$(1,560)	$(86,827)	$9,809

EXHIBIT 2   Intuit Organization Chart in February 2000

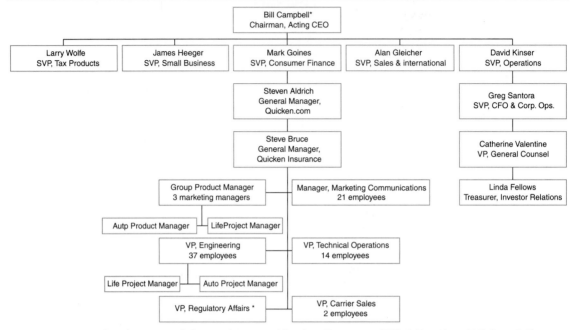

*On January 2000, Intuit announced the appointment of Stephen Bennett as CEO & President. Bill Campbell retired from day-to-day operations but remained Chairman.

**In addition to the personnel indicated on the QuickenInsurance organizational chart, there were three Administrative/HR/Accounting personnel.

In 2000, Intuit offered products and services through four principal business divisions.

- **Small Business Division:** Accounting software, financial supplies, employer services (such as online payroll), technical support consulting services, and other related services.
- **Tax Division:** Personal, professional, and small business tax preparation software, web-based tax preparation services, and electronic tax return filing.
- **Consumer Finance Division:** Personal finance software, marketplaces, and related services.
- **International Division:** Small business, tax, and consumer finance products, and services in selected foreign markets. With the primary focus on small business customers.

announced his intention to create tighter product and brand linkages among all of Intuit's online and offline consumer businesses. (See Exhibit 2.) As he contemplated his new role, Aldrich was convinced that the decision to unite Intuit's businesses into a seamless financial services vertical portal was right. But the path to take to address the many strategic,

operational, and organizational hurdles was much less apparent.

Industry Background

In 1995, when Aldrich first launched his online insurance venture, the U.S. insurance industry was a mature, $270 billion market. By 1996, growth of life insurance premiums had slowed to 2.9%, and growth of auto insurance had slowed to 4.3% per year.[21] With thousands of insurance providers in each product line, consolidation was inevitable. In fact, considerable consolidation had already taken place within the insurance industry, both within industry segments and across segments, as large players, such as Citigroup and American Express, positioned to become the financial services superstores of the 21st century.

The insurance industry in the 1990s was large, inefficient, and highly fragmented. From the consumer's perspective, the decision to purchase insurance was anything but straightforward; the process was time-consuming, and there were roadblocks at each step. Policy features, quality of service, and cost varied widely among the 1,100 property and casualty insurance providers—274 of which offered personal lines insurance[22]—and the nearly 1,200 life and health insurance companies. To support the decision-making process, insurance carriers traditionally sold their products through agents who received a commission for each product sold. Agents provided value to carriers by: (1) generating leads, (2) educating consumers about the need for insurance, (3) providing personalized customer service, (4) collecting information and processing applications, and (5) evaluating claims. To the extent that they were familiar with—and were able to sell—a wide range of insurance products, agents added value to consumers by: (1) providing a one-stop shop for insurance needs, (2) providing a single point of contact for selecting the right product at the right price that met individual

needs, (3) enabling a single point of data entry and storage of profiles, and (4) enabling efficient processing of applications and purchase.

By the mid-1990s, expenses for agent-based carriers often exceeded premiums, forcing insurance companies to rely more heavily on money made from investments. Estimates in 1998 indicated that over one million agents sold insurance to U.S. consumers. Independent agents sold policies for a number of insurance companies; dedicated agents sold the products of a single insurance company. Revenues from the sale of an insurance policy paid underwriting expenses—the cost of acquiring a customer, underwriting the policy, and paying the agent commission—and other operating expenses, which included claims. Income after expenses was invested.

As early as the 1980s, some insurance firms bypassed the agent channel and sold policies directly to consumers—usually through call centers. By the mid-1990s, USAA and GEICO had become the largest of these "direct response" carriers.

By 1999, agent and broker commissions during the first year of a term life insurance policy had risen to 40% to 70% of the revenues received. Over the life of the policy, commissions averaged 5% to 10%.[23] Morgan Stanley Dean Witter analysts estimated that the shift to an Internet distribution channel would save carriers at least 10% to 15% per policy per year by reducing the cost of selling and administering an insurance policy. (Exhibit 3 compares life insurance distribution costs by channel and projected distribution channel shifts.)

As the world entered the 21st century, the Internet was becoming an attractive alternative

---

[21]"Hitting the Open Road: Statistical Study of Passenger Auto Insurance," *Best Review—Property-Casualty Insurance Edition,* October 1997.

[22]Personal line insurance refers to insurance sold to consumers.

[23]U.S. Internet and Financial Services Equity Research Team, "The Internet and Financial Services," *Morgan Stanley Dean Witter Equity Research,* August 1999.

EXHIBIT 3   **Insurance Costs by Channel: Average Cost to Generate $100 in Insurance Policy Revenues**

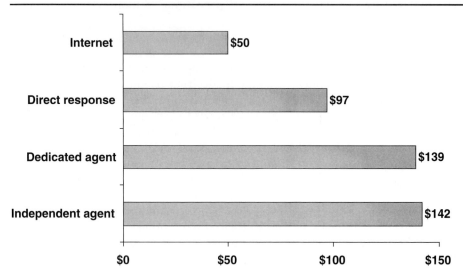

Adapted from: Booz-Allen Hamilton Insurance Industry Study, 1998, as reported in Salomon Smith Barney Research Report, October 24, 1999.

PROJECTED INSURANCE DISTRIBUTION CHANNEL SHIFTS*

Channel	Property/Casualty		Life/Health	
	1998	*2003*	*1998*	*2003*
Dedicated agents	56.5%	48.8%	45.0%	40.1%
Independent agents	27.0%	23.3%	35.5%	31.9%
Direct response	9.8%	10.0%	2.8%	3.9%
Banks	2.8%	8.1%	9.2%	14.9%
Internet	0.9%	7.3%	0.5%	2.9%
Other	3.0%	2.5%	7.0%	6.3%

*Source of data: Data Monitor Research. (As reported in *Salomon Smith Barney Research* by Zandi, R., Vetto, M. L., and Bokhari, Z., on InsWeb, Ocotber 14, 1999.)

distribution channel for less complex consumer insurance products, including automobile, term life, homeowner, individual health, and renter. But, unlike other financial services sectors, such as investing, the insurance industry was slow to take advantage of the Internet. (See Exhibit 4.)

Despite the slow start, many analysts predicted that the online insurance industry represented significant market potential. Firms that had established an online presence early were best positioned to benefit from the rapid growth.

EXHIBIT 4 Insurance Industry Market Data

Sector Breakdown of Insurance Industry Revenues

Industry Sector	1998 Market Size (Premium Revenues)	Industry Sub-Sector Market Size (Premiums)
Property and casualty	$281.5 billion	Commercial lines = 48% Consumer auto = 42% Homeowners/renters = 10%
Life and health	$453 billion	Annuities = 50.6% Consumer life = 21.9% Accident and health = 19.6% Group life = 5.4% Credit life = 0.4% Industrial = 0.1% Other = 2.1%

Source of data: A. M. Best, 1998 (as reported in Salomon Smith Barney Research Report on InsWeb, October 14, 1999).

U.S. Online Financial Services Revenues

Industry Sub-Sector	1998 ($ millions)	2003E ($ millions)
Consumer banking	$24,000	$235,000
Brokerage	2,500	32,000
Insurance		
Home	3	335
Term Life	38	601
Auto	114	3,198
Mortgage	75,000	147,200
Credit Card	100	3,500

Source of data on Banking, Brokerage, Mortgage, and Credit Card: U.S. Internet and Financial Services Equity Research Team., "The Internet and Financial Services," Morgan Stanley Dean Witter Equity Research, August 1999. Source of data on the Insurance industry: Temkin, B. D., Doyle, B., Valentine, L., "Insurers Wake Up the Net," Forrester, October 1998.

Traditional Brands Drive Traffic; Marketplaces Satisfy

Traditional Insurance Companies	Total Score	=	Reach Index	×	Satisfaction Index	×	Value Index
Geico	2.02		2.27		1.02		0.88
Allstate	1.68		1.77		1.04		0.93
State Farm	1.46		1.51		0.99		0.97
MetLife	1.24		0.84		1.02		1.47
Progressive	1.05		1.26		1.01		0.83

eMarketplaces	Total Score	=	Reach Index	×	Satisfaction Index	×	Value Index
Insweb	0.82		1.01		0.93		0.85
Free Insurance Quotes	0.77		0.73		0.98		1.07
Quotesmith.com	0.65		0.63		0.91		1.10
Quicken Insurance	0.52		0.50		1.04		1.00

Key:
Reach index = breadth of site reach.
Satisfaction index = customers' satisfaction with online experience.
Value index = dollar value of the online business.
Source: Adapted from Kenneth Clemmer et. al, "Insurance's Researched Future," *Forrester Research*, March 2000.

EXHIBIT 4 (CONTINUED)   **Forrester Online Insurance Forecast (All household (HH) and dollar values are in millions)**

Auto	1999	2000E	2001E	2002E	2003E	2004E
Number researched HH	8.0	12.8	18.8	25.3	30.3	34.2
Dollar value researched	$8,102	$12,936	$18,942	$25,417	$30,222	$33,882
Number bought HH	0.6	1.2	2.4	4.8	9.2	11.9
Dollar value bought	$633	$1,180	$2,471	$4,794	$9,121	$11,834
Percent of total market	0.5	1.0%	2.1%	4.1%	7.9%	10.2%
Homeowners						
Number researched HH	2.3	4.3	5.3	6.5	8.7	10.2
Dollar value researched	$1,081	$2,044	$2,557	$3,155	$4,219	$4,955
Number bought HH	0.6	1.0	1.2	1.4	1.9	2.4
Dollar value bought	$277	$474	$573	$679	$946	$1,163
Percent of total market	1.1%	1.8%	2.2%	2.6%	3.6%	4.5%
Renters						
Number researched HH	0.8	1.2	1.5	1.8	2.0	2.3
Dollar value researched	$166	$242	$314	$359	$399	$466
Number bought HH	0.2	0.2	0.3	0.3	0.4	0.5
Dollar value bought	$35	$47	$68	$68	$79	$106
Percent of total market	1.2%	1.6%	2.3%	2.3%	2.7%	3.7%
Term life						
Number researched HH	1.2	1.9	2.5	3.3	3.5	3.8
Dollar value researched	$429	$706	$934	$1,207	$1,300	$1,379
Number bought HH	0.3	0.46	0.5	0.7	0.7	0.8
Dollar value bought	$87	$203	$269	$348	$375	$410
Percent of total market	1.7%	2.8%	3.7	4.8%	5.2%	5.7%
Total						
Dollar value researched	$9,778	$15,928	$22,746	$30,138	$36,141	$40,682
Dollar value bought	$1,069	$1,905	$3,371	$5,889	$10,520	$13,513
Researched/bought ratio	9.1	8.4	6.7	5.1	3.4	3.0
Percent of total market	0.7%	1.2%	2.2%	3.8	6.9%	8.9

Numbers may not total due to rounding.
Source: Adapted from Kenneth Clemmer et. al, "Insurance's Researched Future," *Forrester Research,* March 2000.

Online Insurance Business Models

The financial services business has long been about gathering customers and their assets— note the well-documented success of American Express with credit cards; Merrill Lynch with its Cash Management Account; Fidelity with mutual funds for the masses; and Schwab with discount and now online brokers. [Today] a handful of Internet

EXHIBIT 5   Online Insurance Industry, 2000

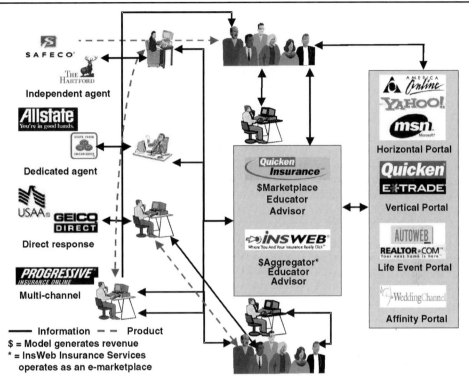

Source: Casewriter's original exhibit.

companies are deftly gathering customers and their assets.
Mary Meeker, 1999[24]

As Aldrich contemplated the insurance industry in the 21st century, five generic online business models had begun to play an important role: horizontal portals, vertical portals, aggregators, marketplaces and online insurance carriers.[25] In addition to online industry

players, there were also offline players, including offline agent-based insurance carriers and offline direct response carriers. (See Exhibit 5 for a summary of the online insurance.)

QuickenInsurance Business Model

In early 2000, QuickenInsurance, which operated as an independent online insurance agent, was licensed to sell life insurance in all 50 states and automobile insurance in 37 states. (See Exhibit 6 for an overview of the QuickenInsurance business model.) By summer 2000, QuickenInsurance had established relationships with 50 carriers—38 for automobile insurance and 12 for term life. Of these relationships, 13 carriers allowed QuickenInsurance to sell policies online—10 for auto and

---

[24]U.S. Internet and Financial Services Equity Research Team, "The Internet and Financial Services," *Morgan Stanley Dean Witter Equity Research,* August 1999.
[25]See Applegate, L.M., "Crafting E-Business Models," *Building E-Businesses Online,* Boston: Harvard Business School Publishing, (Order #5238P1).

EXHIBIT 6   QuickenInsurance Business Model (Fall 2000)

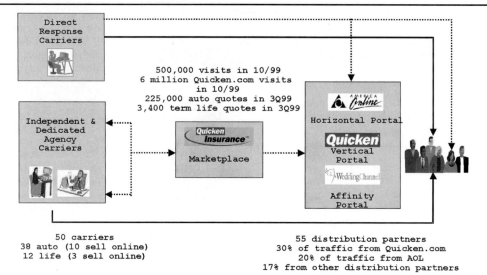

QuickenInsurance's major costs included:
Product development and carrier implementation (51 FTE in 1999)
Marketing and sales (26 FTE in 1999); its partnership with Intuit greatly reduced the cost of attracting
   traffic to its site

Revenues were generated by
Charging insurance carriers a commission for referrals that resulted in sales
Charging some agents commissions on offline sales referred to the agents
Charging carriers an up-front fee for installation and integration of the QuickenInsurance software and
   yearly fees for software maintenance
QuickenInsurance's service was free to consumers

QuickenInsurance offered unique value to the insurance carrier by:
Offering carriers the opportunity to reach a much larger base of consumers
Educating consumers and generating leads
Streamlining the quoting and application process at the carrier end
Providing 30–70% cost savings
Enabling carriers to move online in less time (2–3 months vs. years) and at less cost ($200,000 vs.
   millions of dollars)
Providing cost savings to offset industry price erosion, estimated at 10% in 1999
Providing value-added information on customer buying behavior and competitor pricing
Increasing the number of customers evaluating the carrier's products

QuickenInsurance offered unique value to the consumer by
Providing access to information, advice, quotes and price comparison
Lowering cost to the consumer by eliminating the need for an agent (one customer quoted savings of
   $4,000)
Enabling customers to conveniently purchase insurance directly online 24-hours per day
Streamlining the quoting and application process (In a test by an independent analyst, it took 4
   minutes to receive 9 quotes.)

EXHIBIT 6 (CONTINUED)   **QuickenInsurance Value Proposition to Carriers**

Key Metrics	InsWeb	Progressive	GEICO	QuickenInsurance
Average # of Quotes Returned	2	3	1	8
Types of Quotes Offered	Instant/Offline	Instant	Instant/Offline	Instant/Offline
Lowest # of Quotes Returned	0	2	0	0
Highest # of Quotes Returned	4	4	1	9
Average $ Disparity Between High & Low Quotes	$762	$2,093	$0	$1,884
Available for Online Purchase	No	9 cases	No	7 cases
Low-cost Provider	1 case	4 cases	0 cases	4 cases

Source of data: Salomon Smith Barney, 1999.

3 for term life. The company brought traffic to its site through vertical financial services portals (such as Quicken.com), horizontal portals (such as AOL.com), affinity portals (such as Women.com and WeddingChannel.com), and word of mouth.[26] In 2000, QuickenInsurance sold automobile and term life insurance and, in partnership with Quotesmith, provided quotes for medical and dental insurance. In addition, QuickenInsurance provided links to local agents selling disability insurance, annuities, small business insurance, and long-term care insurance. QuickenInsurance also provided information, analytical tools, and tutorials across a broad range of insurance products and services. "While most insurance products were designed from the actuarial point of view, QuickenInsurance is designed from the customer's perspective," Aldrich stated.

Revenue Model. QuickenInsurance charged carriers a commission on each product sold. In addition, when carriers signed up to distribute insurance through QuickenInsurance, they paid an upfront development and implementation fee to cover the cost of integrating the QuickenInsurance transaction

[26]In 2000, QuickenInsurance had agreements with 55 distribution partners.

systems and databases with those of the carrier. The amount charged depended on the level of integration required. In return for hosting each participating carrier's web site, QuickenInsurance charged carriers an additional annual maintenance fee. QuickenInsurance also generated revenue from referrals to agents. Aldrich explained:

> While some consumers are happy to buy online, some still want to talk with a person before they buy. If the question is simple, our customer support representatives—available 24 hours per day and 7 days per week—can answer it immediately. Today we offer a toll-free help line that is visible on every page of our site. In the future, we will open web-enabled call centers so that customers and our service representatives can work together online to ask questions and fill out applications. But, even with this interactive telephone support, we believe some people will still want to talk to an insurance agent face-to-face. To support those customers, we have developed relationships with local agents that sell our carriers' insurance products. We provide them with links to a special extranet that ties the agent directly to our transaction systems. When a customer fills out an application but wants to speak to an agent, we can send the application to them and our software keeps track of whether the customer goes on to purchase the policy. If they do, we get a portion of the commission.

Cost Model. In 2000, QuickenInsurance's major cost driver was the cost of hiring and retaining the technical talent required to develop the company's web-based insurance service and the custom-designed technical infrastructure needed to integrate it with participating carriers. "It often takes a team of technical specialists 2 to 3 months to bring a new carrier online," an account manager commented. "Today we have 80 people, with 37 devoted to product development and 14 to technical operations," Aldrich explained. "If you factor out our personnel costs, our budget is fairly lean. We leverage Intuit's data centers, call centers, and marketing staff, budget, and relationships." In 2000, Intuit operated 2 call centers—one in Fredricksburg, Virginia, and one in Tucson, Arizona. In each call center, total staff averaged 1,500 during peak times. QuickenInsurance's dedicated customer service representatives (CSRs) in Intuit's Fredricksburg call center handled approximately 500 telephone and e-mail requests per month.

Aldrich's decision to join forces with Intuit also enabled his firm to dramatically reduce the cost of driving traffic to the QuickenInsurance site. "Quicken.com has brand and reach on its own," Aldrich explained. "Over 30% of our traffic comes directly from the Quicken site, and we don't have to pay for it. In addition, because of Intuit's brand and customer base, our relationship with AOL provides very favorable terms."

In 2000, agreements with online partners—for example, vertical and horizontal portals that directed traffic to a destination site—typically required a company to share a portion of the revenues generated by customers who came to the site via the partners' links. Many large portals—such as AOL and Yahoo!—also charged their partners a fixed fee. These revenue-sharing agreements and fees were significant for firms that did business with the largest horizontal portals. For example, in summer of 1999, DrKoop.com announced an $89 million, 4-year deal with AOL to be the exclusive partner on AOL's Health Web Center.[27] In

2000, DrKoop.com was one of approximately 400 firms that declared bankruptcy between January 2000 and March 2001.[28]

InsWeb's Business Model

Until late 1999, InsWeb operated as an online insurance aggregator; the company provided quotes, educated customers, and generated leads for its 36 insurance carrier partners—automobile, term life, individual health, and homeowners/renters insurance—but did not sell policies online. (See Exhibit 7 for an overview of the InsWeb business model.) In 2000, 69% of annual revenues were generated by automobile insurance quotes. With the launch of its online and web-enabled call center insurance agency, InsWeb Insurance Services, InsWeb evolved its business model from an aggregator to a marketplace.[29]

Revenue Model. As an online aggregator, InsWeb could not collect fees for policies sold. Instead, the company received referral fees on every "qualified" lead. "While quotes . . . are provided free to consumers," the company's annual report stated, "insurance company partners pay fees [on] qualified leads." Qualified leads were produced in two ways:

- Insurance companies that offer consumers instant online quotes were charged for a qualified lead when a consumer requested insurance coverage based on a specific quote; and
- Insurance companies that provided e-mail or offline quotes were charged for a qualified lead when the consumer clicked to request the quote itself.

[27]Sacharow, A., "Dr. Koop Shortchanged for the Long Haul," *Jupiter Research Report,* July 12, 1999.

[28]Webmergers.com (www.webmergers.com), April 4, 2001.
[29]An online aggregator enables customers to shop—but not purchase—online. An online marketplace enables both online shopping and purchasing.

In either case, referral fees were paid whether or not the consumer actually purchased an insurance policy from the insurance company, and revenue from transaction fees was recognized when the qualified lead was delivered to the insurance company.

With the launch of insurance services, the company also began collecting transaction fees for the sale of online insurance policies and service fees from carriers that outsourced online insurance policy underwriting and fulfillment services to InsWeb.

Like QuickenInsurance, InsWeb also charged insurance company partners integration and maintenance fees. Integration of an insurance carrier into the InsWeb marketplace typically took three to six months and used 160 to 2000 person hours of effort.

EXHIBIT 7   InsWeb Business Model (Fall 2000)*

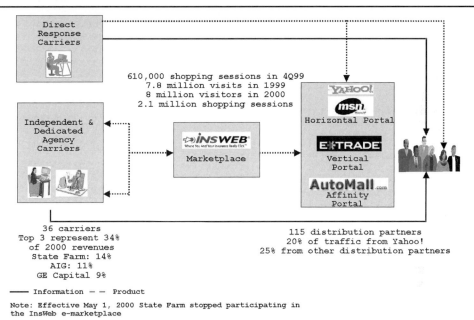

610,000 shopping sessions in 4Q99
7.8 million visits in 1999
8 million visitors in 2000
2.1 million shopping sessions

36 carriers
Top 3 represent 34%
of 2000 revenues
State Farm: 14%
AIG: 11%
GE Capital 9%

115 distribution partners
20% of traffic from Yahoo!
25% from other distribution partners

——— Information — — Product

Note: Effective May 1, 2000 State Farm stopped participating in the InsWeb e-marketplace

*The 1999 annual report states that, in late 1999, InsWeb began selling insurance through its affiliates.

InsWeb's major costs included:

Marketing and sales, including online and offline advertising and fees paid to other portals

Product development and carrier system implementation and integration with the InsWeb service: Integration of an insurance carrier into the InsWeb marketplace typically took 3-6 months (and used 160-2,000 person hours of effort)

Building and operating call centers and data centers

Revenues were generated through:

Referral fees on every "qualified" lead to each insurance carrier (or "click-throughs" to insurance carriers' sites), whether or not the lead results in an actual purchase

Advertising

Software integration and maintenance fees charged to each partner/carrier

(continued)

EXHIBIT 7 (CONTINUED)   InsWeb Financial Data (in thousands)

	1995 (1)	1996	1997	1998	1999	2000
CONSOLIDATED STATEMENT OF OPERATIONS DATA						
Revenues:						
Transaction fees	$ —	$ 7	$ 116	$ 3,151	$ 19,138	$ 19,561
Development and maintenance fees		199	551	789	2,673	3,598
Other revenues		42	83	370	29	51
Total revenues	—	248	750	4,310	21,840	23,210
Operating expenses:						
Product development	774	2,900	3,210	10,077	8,871	8,690
Sales and marketing	552	2,010	3,167	8,954	33,477	38,248
General and administrative	670	2,730	3,259	6,640	13,474	21,179
Amortization of stock based compensation	—	—	470	540	1,272	912
Amortization of intangible assets	—	—	—	—	3,129	1,150
Total operating expenses	2,025	7,640	10,106	26,211	60,223	76,764
Loss from operations	(2,025)	(7,392)	(9,356)	(21,901)	(38,383)	(53,554)
Other income (expense), net	—	—	—	600	(166)	56
Interest income (expense), net	(6)	122	293	(1,189)	2,348	4,286
Net loss	$ (2,031)	$ (7,270)	$ (9,063)	$ (22,490)	$ (36,201)	$ (50,847)
Net loss per share basic and diluted	$ (667.07)	$ (0.56)	$ (0.62)	$ (1.52)	$ (1.52)	$ (1.40)

	1995 (1)	1996	1997	1998	1999	2000
CONSOLIDATED BALANCE SHEET DATA						
Cash and equivalents	$ 6	$ 6,807	$ 2,360	$ 8,337	$ 25,689	$ 34,795
Short-term investments	—	—	—	—	64,063	26,331
Working capital (deficit)	(1,564)	6,739	2,040	5,497	91,361	51,657
Total assets	423	9,353	5,140	49,357	118,281	73,008
Long-term debt	—	—	—	2,089	1,464	1,312
Total stockholders' equity (deficit)	(1,184)	7,476	3,062	19,582	111,185	63,884

Source: Insweb 10-K, filed April 4, 2001

InsWeb's main data center was located in the company's Redwood City, California, corporate headquarters; a back-up data center was located in Irvine, California.

To generate traffic to its site, InsWeb entered into over 115 distribution agreements with portals, including Yahoo!, E*Trade, Snap.com and LookSmart.com.[30] In 1999, these online relationships generated approximately 45% of InsWeb's traffic. Each relationship was typically one year in length, could be terminated with one to three months notice, and was not automatically renewable. Approximately 20% of InsWeb's traffic was generated from its relationship with Yahoo!. Under the terms of the agreement, InsWeb paid Yahoo! a fixed fee plus approximately $.10 for each referral. As of June 30, 1999, Salomon Smith Barney analysts reported: "InsWeb paid Yahoo! fixed fees totaling $4.7 million and referral fees totaling $139,000. InsWeb was obligated to pay additional fees totaling $4.8 million through June 2000." In return, InsWeb was the exclusive merchant within Yahoo!'s Insurance Center.

Evolution of Quicken.com as a Vertical Portal

In 1983, Intuit founders Scott Cook and Tom Proulx embarked on a quest to revolutionize the way individuals and small businesses managed their finances. A decade later, Intuit had emerged as the worldwide leader in the market for personal and small business finance software; its Quicken (personal finance), QuickBooks (small business accounting) and Turbo-Tax software accounted for 70% or more market share in their respective markets.

Intuit executives were quick to recognize the potential opportunities and threats presented by the commercialization of the Inter-

net, the World Wide Web (WWW), and user-friendly browser software. They believed these technologies could be used to deliver new products and services and to dramatically expand the company's customer base and the range of products and services delivered. While the market opportunity for its traditional software business was estimated as $300 million in 2002, the market opportunity for its online businesses was estimated to exceed $202 billion.[31] To exploit this opportunity, Quicken.com was launched in 1996.

Initially, Quicken.com operated as an information aggregator through which consumers could access financial services news and information from a number of different information providers. Quicken.com added value by synthesizing the content, categorizing it for easy search and retrieval, packaging it, and then distributing it over the Internet to a rapidly growing network of consumers. In an effort to expand its customer base, Quicken.com executives decided not to charge consumers a subscription fee for its service, but instead, generated revenues through advertising. The more consumers visited Quicken.com, the more the company learned about what those consumers wanted, and the more valuable the site became to advertisers.

Between 1996 and 1998, six focused distributors were launched under the Quicken.com umbrella brand. The business models adopted by the six focused distributors within the Quicken.com vertical portal are described below.

QuickenRetirement and *QuickenInvestment* were aggregators. Consumers could access information but could not invest online. Revenues were generated primarily from sponsors that were charged advertising and referral fees.

QuickenInsurance, QuickenLoan, and *QuickenBanking* were marketplaces where consumers could purchase insurance, apply for and receive loans, and pay bills online. Revenues

---

[30]Zandi, R. and Vetto, M., "InsWeb, Inc.," *Salomon Smith Barney Equity Research,* November 24, 1999.

[31]Intuit Annual Report, 2000.

were primarily from suppliers that were charged a commission on each transaction. Suppliers were also charged development, consulting, and maintenance fees for system integration. Advertising and referral fees provided additional revenues.

QuickenTurboTax enabled consumers to access information, tutorials and advice, prepare tax returns, and file online. With the launch of QuickenTurboTax, Intuit evolved its traditional packaged software business model to become an Application Service Provider (ASP)[32] but did not eliminate it. In early 2001, consumers could use the online tax software to prepare their taxes for free but paid a service fee of $9.95 to $19.95 to file online. In comparison, the cost of the Quicken TurboTax packaged software was $39.95 + $5.95 shipping. Intuit saved money by shifting to the hosted online software model and it passed these savings to the customer. Within one year of its launch in 1999, QuickenTurboTax for the web had captured 80% market share.

A second vertical portal, Quicken.com for Small Business was launched in 1999. This portal provided a wide range of online services (including payroll, bookkeeping, invoicing, and purchasing) to Intuit's installed base of over two million small business users of its packaged software, QuickBooks. Many of these businesses adopted the ASP business model and by summer 2000 Quicken for Small Business had over five million users worldwide and use of its QuickBooks software package had increased to three million.

During 2000, Intuit earned almost $300 million from its online businesses and the majority of these businesses were profitable. Exhibit 8 provides an overview of Intuit's consumer business models in summer 2000.[33]

Each Intuit online business leveraged a common infrastructure to generate multiple streams of revenues while also building knowledge assets and strengthening the brand—not just for Intuit, but for also for its customers, suppliers, and business partners. (See Exhibit 9.) Because the Internet and its associated technologies offered a common, standardized interface for linking together business communities inside and outside the organization, Intuit's Internet-based digital infrastructure provided a modular platform upon which individual businesses could be integrated and built. The marginal cost of adding a new business to the infrastructure was low, and the revenue potential increased dramatically. Over time, new businesses could be built, launched and grown to scale in months, dramatically increasing the company's agility and innovation potential while dramatically decreasing the risk.

Intuit's Value Web Extends to its Business Community

The Quicken.com and Quicken for Small Business vertical portals did not stop at the door of the organization. Instead, these two vertical portals and the individual online businesses within them united a network of suppliers, partners, and customers. Indeed, America Online was a key member of the Quicken.com value web and, as such, AOL's success increased the success of Quicken.com (see Exhibit 10).

Founded in 1985 as Quantum Computer Services, the AOL.com online information service was launched in 1989 as a proprietary news, information, communication, and entertainment service. From the beginning, AOL

---

[32]An Application Service Provider, or ASP, provides online access to business software applications. Rather than buy a software package or build custom software and then run it on a personal computer or in a company's data center, an organization rents, leases, or provides a service fee to access software that is hosted on the service provider's computers.

[33]In November 2000, InsWeb acquired selected assets of QuickenInsurance and became the exclusive provider of insurance services on Quicken.com.

EXHIBIT 8 Quicken.com Business Model

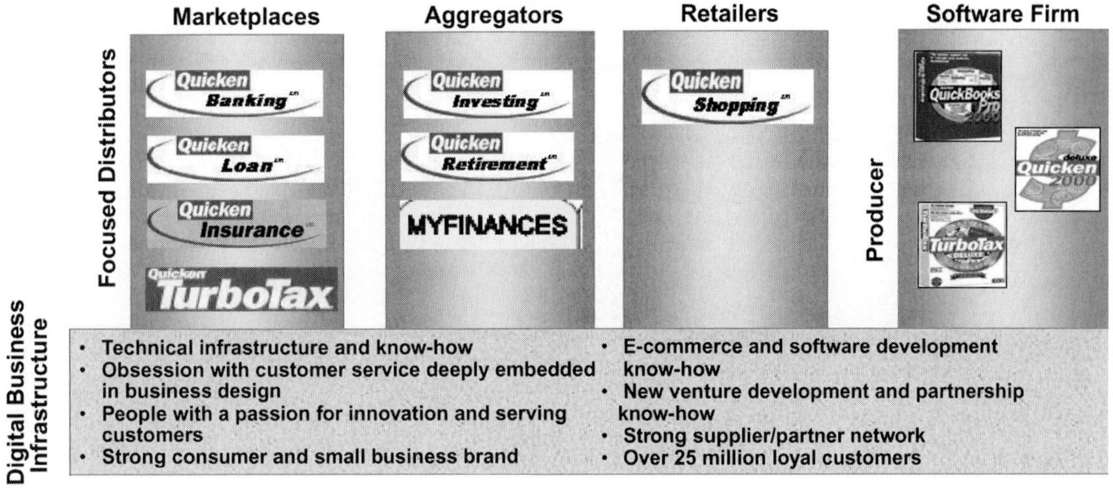

Quicken.com Revenue Model in 2000
Slotting fees & referral fees (Distribution Agreements)
Transaction Fees (Marketplaces)
Slotting fees & transaction fees (Retailers)

Quicken.com Cost Model in 2000
Web site development, implementation & maintenance
Sales & marketing
Slotting fees & referral fees paid to portals
Online & offline advertising
Call center operations
Data processing & network operations & hosting
Administration & management
Physical infrastructure

Intuit Profit Model in 2000
Intuit Revenues = $1.1 billion up from $567 million in 1996
Online revenues were $294 million in revenues in 2000 up 108% from 1999
75% of Internet businesses were profitable

Pro forma net income = $134.2 million up 35% from $99.6 million in 1999
Earnings per share − $0.64 up from $0.50 in 1999
Market value = $2.1 billion with $.15 billion in cash and short-term investments

EXHIBIT 9   Leveraging the Intuit Digital Business Infrastructure

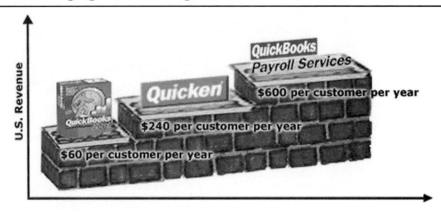

also served as a network services provider, giving away its content and community services while charging per minute network access fees.

In summer 1995, AOL had approximately 500,000 members in the United States, revenues of $344.3 million, and was losing money. Losses continued as the company shifted from a proprietary to an Internet infrastructure and as it shifted its revenue model to a flat monthly fee. During 1997, the company lost almost $500 million and many doubted that it would survive its painful evolution to an Internet business model. But survive it did, and by summer 2000 AOL had over 23 million members worldwide (approximately 35% of total worldwide Internet users), revenues of almost $7 billion, profits of almost $2 billion, and over $1.5 billion in cash. The completion of the merger with Time Warner in January 2001 was expected to generate an additional $1 billion in equity cash flow to investors by the end of 2001.[34]

Even before the merger with Time Warner, AOL had evolved a complex business model. To most consumers, it was a horizontal portal

that enabled free access to the Internet and its "World Wide Web" of businesses, information, and services anywhere and anytime. Revenues for this component of the business model were collected from advertisers and sponsors. For example, Intuit paid AOL $16.2 million in 1998 to become the exclusive provider of personal and small business financial services within AOL's Finance Web Center. It also paid a "click through" fee every time an AOL customer accessed its Quicken.com and Quicken for Small Business vertical portals through AOL. Finally, AOL received a percentage of every transaction conducted on Quicken.com by AOL customers. In early 2001, Quicken.com was one of 23 vertical portal web centers offered through AOL, and AOL commanded 20% to 25% of worldwide online advertising revenues.

In addition to providing a gateway to content and services, AOL's business model also reflected its roots as a proprietary network services provider. With the launch of its Internet service in the mid-1990s, it quickly became the leading Internet Service Provider (ISP). In this role, it developed and maintained the network infrastructure and services that enabled individuals to access the

---

[34]AOL Time Warner Annual Report, 2000.

EXHIBIT 10   AOL Business Model in 2000

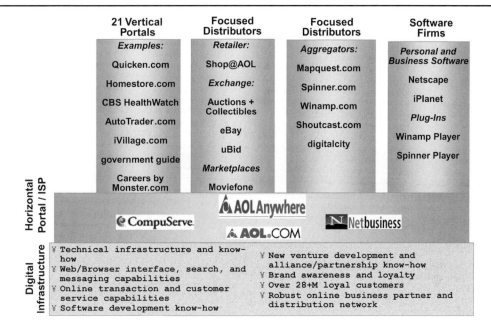

Revenue Model in 2000
Subscription fees = $4.8 billion; up from $3 billion in 1999
Advertising and commerce fees = $2.4 billion; up from $1 billion in 1999
Software licensing, sales and service fees = $557 million; down from $610 million in 1999

Cost Model in 2000
Operations = $3.9 billion; up from $3.3 billion in 1999
Sales and marketing = $1.9 billion; up from $1.4 billion
Includes advertising expenses of $829 million; up from $575 million in 1999
Property and equipment = $1 million; up from $895 million in 1999
Administration = $408 million

Profit Model in 2000
Total Revenues = $7.7 billion; up from $4.8 billion in 1999
Total costs = $5.8 billion; up from $4.3 billion in 2000
Operating Income = $1.8 billion; up from $819 million in 1999
Net Income = $1.2 billion; up from $1.0 billion in 1999
Income per share = $.50; up from $.47

EXHIBIT 11   AOL TimeWarner Business Model in 2000

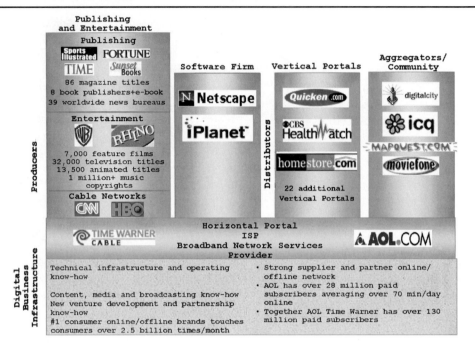

Internet across telephone ("dial-up") or high-speed ("broadband") networks. The merger of AOL Time Warner on January 10, 2001 created the complex online/offline media conglomerate shown in Exhibit 11.[35]

Winning in the Race to Click and Close

Only a small number of companies will be big winners in the online market. . . . We believe the vertical portal will become the most powerful long-term distribution model by offering the consumer superior value through choice, convenience and low prices. . . . A few aggregators may survive, despite our belief that many of them will be displaced by vertical portals. . . . [Producers] will continue to partner with vertical portals to provide best-in-

breed products at low cost. . . . We generally envision higher valuations for vertical portals than we would for [producers].[36]

Morgan Stanley Dean Witter, 1999

As the world stood at the gateway to a new millenium, the financial services industry was reeling from the one-two-three punch of technology, deregulation, and global consolidation. The opportunities for adding value and shifting the balance of power were enormous. Those prepared to take advantage of these opportunities stood to gain a significant market position.

---

[35]Data on the AOL Time Warner business model are from The AOL Time Warner 2001 Fact Book, available online at www.aoltimewarner.com.

[36]Using Morgan Stanley Dean Witter's (MSDW) generic business models, InsWeb was classified as an aggregator, while Quicken.com was a leading financial services portal. Allstate and State Farm were classified using the term "producers" in the quote used in the case. "The Internet and Financial Services," *Morgan Dean Witter Equity Research,* August, 1999.

CASE 2–2
AMAZON.COM, 2000[1]

The Amazon.com platform is comprised of brand, customers, technology, distribution capability, deep e-commerce expertise, and a great team with a passion for innovation and serving customers well . . . We believe that we have reached a "tipping point," where this platform allows us to launch new e-commerce businesses faster, with a higher quality of customer experience, a lower incremental cost, a higher chance of success, and a clearer path to scale and profitability than perhaps any other company.

Excerpt from Jeff Bezos' Letter to Shareholders, 1999 Annual Report[2]

Throughout 2000, Amazon.com's senior management, along with colleagues at other publicly traded dot-com companies, faced tremendous pressures from Wall Street and shareholders to generate profits.[3] While many struggled to attract customers and top talent, Amazon.com's success at defining online retailing was legendary. In fact, 1999 studies had shown that over 60% of U.S. consumers recognized the Amazon.com brand—making it the #1 Internet brand. Amazon.com was ranked as the 57th most valuable brand worldwide

between Pampers and Hilton. Amazon.com's leadership came from the most widely respected and well-managed firms in the world—General Electric, Wal-Mart, Microsoft, and Allied Signal to name a few—and its CEO and Founder, Jeff Bezos, had been named *Time Magazine's* "Man of the Year" in 1999.

While many Internet companies had fairly straightforward business models and limited revenue streams, Amazon.com had continued to evolve its model, pushing forward the boundaries of what could be accomplished online. Initially launched as an online book retailer in 1995, beginning in 1998 Amazon.com aggressively launched new retail categories, including music, DVDs, videos, consumer electronics, software, toys, video games, home improvement, and lawn and patio products. In 1999, it extended its business model further by launching two online auction stores—one low-end and another high-end—and an online marketplace for small merchants (called zShops).[4] In early 2000, it evolved once more, entering into a number of equity partnerships with brand-name online

---

[1]This case was prepared by E-Business Fellow Meredith Collura and Professor Lynda M. Applegate.
Copyright © 2000 by the President and Fellows of Harvard College.
Harvard Business School case 801-194.
[2]Amazon.com 1999 Annual Report (Seattle: Amazon.com, 2000).
[3]Friday, April 14, 2000, ended a week of major downslides for both technology and blue-chip stocks. The NASDAQ Composite tumbled 355.46 points (9.7%) and closed at 3321.32 (its largest one-day point decline and second-largest percentage drop since its inception in 1971). Amazon.com (stock symbol AMZN) was listed on the NASDAQ. The Dow Jones Industrial Average slipped 616.23 points (5.6%) to 10,307.32, its worst ever one-day point loss. Amazon's stock price closed at $46.875 per share, down from its fifty-two week high of $113.00 on December 9, 1999. Task, A., "Ruthless Selloff Hits All Sectors: This Was One for the Record Books," www.TheStreet.com (14 April 2000). Declines continued throughout 200 and by year-end, Amazon.com's stock price had sunk to less than $10 per share.

[4]Over 100 small merchants could "rent" space in Amazon.com zShops. As of late 1999, zShop merchants paid the company $9.99 a month to open a web store, selling up to 3,000 items or $.10 per individual item. In addition, the merchants paid Amazon a transaction fee of 5% for items priced less than $25, 2.5% for items worth $29 to $999, and 1.25% of items over $1,000.

retailers such as: Drugstore.com (health and beauty), Della.com (wedding and gift registry), Ashford.com (jewelry, watches, and gifts), and Greenlight.com (automobiles). It was estimated that these equity partnerships—which Amazon.com executives called its Commerce Network—would generate $1 billion in co-marketing revenues by 2005.[5] But, the majority of these partnerships were with newly-launched "dot-coms" that had yet to generate earnings, which dramatically increased the risk—especially since many of these deals included payments in the form of stock.

In summary, in less than two years Amazon.com's business model had evolved from a book, music, and video retailer to a consumer shopping portal where "anyone could buy anything, anywhere and anytime" at the "Earth's Biggest" online store.[6] And, while its online retail model required that the company assume control and risk of physical inventory, its new Commerce Network and zShop model enabled small, medium, and large merchants to leverage Amazon's investments in building its brand, attracting over 25+ million loyal customers and top talent, and building its e-commerce expertise and logistics infrastructure.

In 1999, Amazon.com spent $300 to $400 million to build the state-of-the-art digital retail infrastructure senior executives believed would be needed to execute the company's evolving strategy. By year-end 1999, Amazon.com had nine distribution centers and seven customer service centers in the U.S. and Europe. This infrastructure was built with rapid growth in mind, and the company started the year in January 2000 with 70% to 80% overcapacity in its distribution centers.

Amazon executives were convinced that the new strategy and e-commerce capabilities would enable the company to reach its "tipping point,"[7] and that rapid growth and profitability would soon follow. Its book business was reported profitable in the fourth quarter of 1999 and margins on its auction businesses were reported as 45%.[8] Likewise, the company estimated that its non-inventory businesses would have gross margins of 85% to 95% within a few short years.[9] But, losses continued to mount in 2000. As investors clamored for profits, stock price dropped from over $100 in late December 1999 to less than $15 in late December 2000.

Despite increasing investor dissatisfaction, the number of loyal customers continued to rise. In fact, the number of cumulative customer accounts rose from 17 million in March 2000 to 25 million by October 2000, and sales had increased from roughly $1.6 billion at year-end 1999 to over $2.8 billion in 2000.

PaineWebber analysts praised Amazon for the speed with which it entered and dominated new product categories:

> Several aspects lead Amazon to stand out as the e-retailer best positioned to capitalize on the growth of e-commerce. The first is Amazon's ability to extend the strength of its brand and customer base into new markets. Because of these strengths, we often refer to Amazon as a platform for e-commerce. This was clearly seen in late 1998 when Amazon began selling music and quickly rose to the leading market share

---

[5]Becker, H., Salomon Smith Barney. "Amazon.com" (8 December 1999). Available from Investext (www.bschool-investext.com), p 10.

[6]Wireless e-commerce allowed customers to securely shop and check the status of auction items using handheld devices and cellular phones.

[7]Economists define a market's "tipping point" as the point at which a dominant technology or player defines the standard for an industry resulting in "winner-take-all" economies of scale and scope. See Shapiro, C. and Varian, H., *Information Rules: A Strategic Guide to the Network Economy,* Boston: HBS Press, 1999 (pages 176–177 and 187–188) for a more in-depth discussion of market tipping in Internet markets.

[8]Farley, S. and Modi, N., PaineWebber. "Amazon.com" (23 February 2000). Available from Investext (www.bschool-investext.com), p 19.

[9]Ibid.

position in just four months. This success was followed by its experience in the video market, in which it rose to take the top spot in just 45 days.[10]

But, analysts and company executives grew increasingly concerned about whether the company could execute its complex strategy. An analyst commented:

> Having largely pioneered Internet retailing, Amazon needs to establish and secure the homestead. Growing a robust business will require Amazon to sell across categories at Wal-Mart levels of performance, fulfill at FedEx scale, and monetize eyeballs like AOL.[11]

Bezos agreed:

> [There has been a] big change over the past two years . . . [Today] our biggest challenge and our biggest risk is internal. It's this "simple execution risk," which is anything but simple. Think about what we're trying to do that [increases] execution risk. We're growing very rapidly—90% in three months [the fourth quarter of 1999], on a billion-dollar plus sales rate. At the same time, we are entering into new product categories, which is a strategy that's working—as validated by the fact that less than half of our sales are now U.S. books. We're investing in new business models altogether, things like auctions and zShops. And we're investing in new geographies, Amazon.com.de and Amazon.com.co.uk. And, all of that is in the context of trying to raise the bar everyday in terms of the customer experience.[12]

---

[10]Ries, D. and Truong, V., C.E. Unterberg, Towbin. "Amazon.com" (13 October 1999). Available from Investext (www.bschool-investext.com), p 4.
[11]Becker, p 27.
[12]Bezos, J., Keynote Speech at Harvard Business School Cyberposium, February 26, 2000.

Industrial Age giants learned through experience about the challenges of managing complex organizations with multiple lines of business; they spent most of the 1980s and 1990s downsizing, simplifying, and focusing their businesses. But new e-business powerhouses, like America Online/Time Warner and the new Amazon.com, were anything but simple. Ellen Roy, Managing Director of Softbank's e-business incubator, I-Group/Hotbank, believed that the Internet's flexible, shared, and ubiquitous platform would enable a new breed of "e-business mega-firm." Roy stated that successful mega-firms provided a state-of-the-art horizontal portal infrastructure and then expanded through partnerships with strong vertical portals and focused distributors. She explained:

> I distinguish between a horizontal [portal] that provides the infrastructure—the platform—and a vertical marketplace [that provides the content and commerce]. I think you can grow a very big company with the horizontal infrastructure and platform. . . [For example, companies like] Yahoo! and AOL don't take inventory, so they don't have to worry about [Industrial Age] problems [associated with physical goods] . . . The most powerful companies are bound to be the horizontal platforms.[13]

Would Amazon.com be able to flawlessly execute its aggressive growth strategy as the "Earth's Biggest," "most customer-centric" online company? Would the strategy enable the company to reach profitability? If so, when?

---

[13]Author interview with Ellen Roy, July 10, 2000.

EXHIBIT 1   Amazon.com Business Models in Fall 2000

	Retail	Exchange	Marketplace	ASP
Focused Distributors	U.S. Books	Amazon Auctions	zShops	Toys R Us
	Music	Sotheby's.com	Over 100 small merchants	
	Video/DVD		Drugstore.com	
	Software		Della.com	
	Kitchen		Greenlight.com	
	Lawn & Patio		Gear.com	
	Home Improvement		HomeGrocer.com	
	European Books		IMDb.com	

Digital Business Infrastructure	• E-Commerce Know-How • Technical Architecture and Know-How • Distribution, Order Fulfillment, Inventory and Customer Service Capabilites • People with a Passion for Innovation and Serving Customers	• New Venture Development and Partnership Know-How • Brand • 25+M Loyal Customers • Business Partner Network

Business Model Definitions[14]

Retailers assume control of inventory, set a non-negotiable price to the consumer, and sell physical products online. Therefore, the primary revenue model often is based on product/service sales, and the cost model includes procurement, inventory management, order fulfillment, and customer service (including returns). Because e-retailers assume control of physical goods, their ratio of tangible to intangible assets often is much higher than would be found in a firm that does not assume control of physical inventory.

Marketplaces sell products and services but do not take control of physical inventory. They do, however, sell products with a non-negotiable price and complete the sale online. Their revenue model often includes a commission or transaction fee on each sale. Because sales transactions take place online, e-marketplaces must often electronically link to supplier databases and transaction systems to ensure that transactions can be completed and revenue may be recognized. However, because marketplace companies do not assume control of physical inventory, procurement and inventory management costs often are lower than those of retailers.

(continued)

---

[14]See Applegate, L.M., "Overview of E-Business Models," HBS Publishing No. 800-390 for a detailed discussion of emerging e-business models. This note is also available as an online interactive e-learning program in Applegate, L., "Crafting E-Business Models," *Building E-Businesses Online,* HBS Publishing No. 5238P1.

EXHIBIT 1 (CONTINUED)   Amazon.com Business Models in Fall 2000

Exchanges may or may not take control of inventory—the tendency is to try and avoid assuming inventory carrying costs whenever feasible—and may or may not complete the final sales transaction online. The key differentiating feature of this model is that the price is not set; it is negotiated by the buyer and seller at the time of the sale. The revenue, cost, and asset models vary depending on whether the online exchange assumes control of inventory and completes the transaction as well as the level of human facilitation required. B2B auction exchanges, such as FreeMarkets, often charge transaction fees and supplement revenues with fees for consulting services. B2C and C2C exchanges often supplement transaction revenues with advertising revenues.

Portals provide gateway access to the Internet's vast store of content, and they also provide a broad range of tools for locating information and web sites, communicating with others, and developing online communities of interest. Like the broadcast networks upon which they were modeled, "pure-play" horizontal portals, like Yahoo!, initially depended on advertising as the primary revenue source. Development, maintenance, operation of infrastructure and content development and management were the primary costs. But, a pure content aggregation portal model proved hard to sustain. To decrease dependency on a single source of revenue, horizontal content portals like Yahoo! extended their business models, launching multiple vertical portals that enabled users to, not just shop, but also buy and transact other forms of business online. These transactions enabled portals to generate additional revenues through transaction fees. By early 2001, however, many questioned whether this would be enough as Yahoo!, once the darling of Wall Street and one of the only remaining independent content portals, came under fire; advertising revenues had declined by almost half in 1st quarter 2001 and the company reported that it expected to move from profitability to barely break-even.[15] CEO Tim Koogle and the company's top advertising executive resigned. The stock fell precipitously from a high of $237.50 per share on January 3, 2000 to less than $20 per share by March 2001. By comparison, America Online (AOL) combined horizontal content and infrastructure services portal. This approach gained favor with investors as the company surprised the street by reporting 1st quarter 2001 equity cash flow gains of 20%.[16]

Application Service Providers (also called ASPs) provide online access to software (for example, salesforce support, inventory management, payroll services, even word processing etc.) and network services (for example, e-mail, file sharing etc.) that used to be purchased and managed by individuals or companies. ASPs charge system integration, hosting, and maintenance fees. The key costs are related to operating and managing data centers, networks, and customer support call centers, software development, and system integration.

The tables on the next several pages summarize the e-business models discussed above, and also provide information on other e-business models not discussed in this case.

---

[15]Weinberg, A., "Early Market Movers: Yahoo Puts on the Hex," www.thestandard.com, March 8, 2001.

[16]In 2001, AOL derived revenues from multiple business models. As a horizontal content portal it generated advertising revenues, and its 23 vertical portals generated commerce revenues. In addition, AOL was also a horizontal infrastructure portal, charging subscription services as an Internet Service Provider (ISP) and, with its merger with Time Warner, as a broadband cable services provider.

EXHIBIT 1 (CONTINUED) **Business Model Comparisons**

Focused Distributor E-Business Models

Model & Examples (Visit each company web site to analyze online offerings.)	Model Differentiators				Likely Revenues	Likely Costs (Note: on the Internet, people, partners, and business development costs are universally high)
	Control Inventory	Sell Online	Price Set Online	Physical Product/ Svc		
Retailer Amazon.com LandsEnd.com Walmart.com	Yes	Yes	No	Yes	Product/svc. sales	Advertising & marketing; Physical facilities, inventory & customer svc.; R&D; IT infrastructure
Marketplace E-Loan AXI Travel	Possibly	Yes	No	No	Transaction fees; Service fees; Commissions	Advertising & marketing; R&D; IT infrastructure
Aggregator / Infomediary InsWeb AutoWeb.com	No	No	No	Possibly	Referral fees; Advertising & marketing fees	Advertising & marketing; R&D; IT infrastructure
Exchange Sothebys.com (B-2-C) EBay (C-2-C) PriceLine (C-2-B) FreeMarkets (B-2-B)	Possibly	Possibly	Yes	Possibly	Depends on model	Advertising & marketing; Staff support for auctions (especially B-2-B); Inventory & logistics if inventory control; R&D; Technical infrastructure

Trends
- Focused distributors that do not allow customers and the business community to transact business online are losing power. Aggregator and pure "info broker infomediary" models are at risk.
- Multiple business models are required to ensure flexibility and sustainability.
- Focused distributors must align closely with vertical and horizontal portals or evolve their model to become vertical portals.

EXHIBIT 1 (CONTINUED) Business Model Comparisons

Infrastructure Portal E-Business Models

Model & Examples (Visit each company web site to analyze online offerings.)	Model Differentiators			Likely Revenues	Likely Costs (Note: on the Internet, people, partners, and business development costs are universally high)
	Gateway Actess	Deep Content & Solutions	Affinity Group Focus		
Horizontal Portals AOL.com Yahoo!.com ¡Won.com Virgin.com	Yes	Through partnerships with vertical & affinity portals	Possibly; Often through partnerships	Advertising, affiliation & slotting fees; Possibly subscription or access fees	Advertising, marketing & sales; Content/info asset mgmt.; R&D; IT infrastructure
Vertical Portals Quicken.com Healtheon/WebMD	Limited	Yes	No	Transaction fees; Commissions; Advertising, affiliation & slotting fees	Advertising & marketing & sales; Content/info asset mgmt.; R&D; IT infrastructure
Affinity Portals IVillage.com TheKnot.com	Possibly	Within affinity group	Yes	Referral fees; Advertising, affiliation & slotting fees	Advertising & marketing & sales; Content/info asset mgmt.; R&D; IT infrastructure
Trends					

- Horizontal and vertical portals are emerging as dominant sources of power within e-business markets.
- Horizontal portals are joining forces with horizontal infrastructure portals to provide not just access to content but also access to network and hosting services.
- Mega broadcast portals that combine voice, video, data and entertainment are emerging in the consumer space.
- Mega B-2-B portals provide both horizontal access to business networks and vertical industry-wide solutions.

151

EXHIBIT 2   Amazon.com Statement of Operations (in thousands, except per share data)

	Three Months Ended December 31		Year Ended December 31	
	2000	*1999*	*2000*	*1999*
Net sales	$972,360	$676,042	$2,761,983	$ 1,639,839
Cost of sales	748,060	588,196	2,106,206	1,349,194
Gross profit	224,300	87,846	655,777	290,645
Operating expenses:				
Marketing, sales and fulfillment	186,233	179,424	594,489	413,150
Technology and content	69,791	57,720	269,326	159,722
General and administrative	28,232	26,051	108,962	70,144
Stock-based compensation	(1,112)	14,049	24,797	30,618
Amortization of goodwill and other intangibles	79,210	82,301	321,772	214,694
Impairment-related and other	184,052	2,085	200,311	8,072
Total operating expenses	546,396	361,630	1,519,657	896,400
Loss from operations	(322,096)	(273,784)	(863,880)	(605,755)
Interest income	10,979	8,972	40,821	45,451
Interest expense	(36,094)	(18,142)	(130,921)	(84,566)
Other income (expense), net	(5,365)	(366)	(10,058)	1,671
Non-cash investment gains and losses, net	(155,005)	—	(142,639)	—
Net interest expense and other	(185,485)	(9,536)	(242,797)	(37,444)
Loss before equity in losses of equity-method investees	(507,581)	(283,320)	(1,106,677)	(643,199)
Equity in losses of equity-method investees, net	(37,559)	(39,893)	(304,596)	(76,769)
Net loss	$(545,140)	$(323,213)	$(1,411,273)	$(719,968)
Basic and diluted loss per share	$ (1.53)	$ (0.96)	$ (4.02)	$ (2.20)
Shares used in computation of basic and diluted loss per share	355,681	338,389	350,873	326,753
Pro forma results:				
Pro forma loss from operations	$(59,946)	$(175,349)	$(317,000)	$(352,371)
Pro forma net loss	$(90,426)	$(184,885)	$(417,158)	$(389,815)
Pro forma basic and diluted loss per share	$ (0.25)	$ (0.55)	$ (1.19)	$ (1.19)
Shares used in computation of pro forma basic and diluted loss per share	355,681	338,389	350,873	326,753

Source: Amazon.com 8-K, filed February 2, 2001.

EXHIBIT 2 (CONTINUED)   **Balance Sheet (in thousands, except per share data)**

	December 31, 2000	December 31, 1999
Assets		
Current assets:		
Cash and cash equivalents	$822,435	$133,309
Marketable securities	278,087	572,879
Inventories	174,563	220,646
Prepaid expenses and other current assets	86,044	79,643
Total current assets	1,361,129	1,006,477
Fixed assets, net	366,416	317,613
Goodwill, net	158,990	534,699
Other intangibles, net	96,335	195,445
Investments in equity-method investees	52,073	226,727
Other investments	40,177	144,735
Other assets	60,049	40,154
Total assets	$2,135,169	$2,465,850
Liabilities and stockholders' equity (deficit)		
Current liabilities		
Accounts payable	$485,383	$463,026
Accrued expenses and other current liabilities	272,683	176,208
Unearned revenue	131,117	54,790
Interest payable	69,196	24,888
Current portion of long-term debt and other	16,577	14,322
Total current liabilities	974,956	733,234
Long-term debt	2,127,464	1,466,338
Stockholders' equity (deficit):		
Preferred stock, $0.01 par value:		
Authorized shares—500,000		
Issued and outstanding shares—none	—	—
Common stock, $0.01 par value:		
Authorized shares—5,000,000		
Issued and outstanding shares—357,140 and 345,155 shares at		3,452
December 31, 2000 and December 31, 1999, respectively	3,571	
Additional paid-in capital	1,338,303	1,194,369
Stock-based compensation	(13,448)	(47,806)
Accumulated other comprehensive loss	(2,376)	(1,709)
Accumulated deficit	(2,293,301)	(882,028)
Total stockholders' equity (deficit)	(967,251)	266,278
Total liabilities and stockholders' equity (deficit)	$2,135,169	$2,465,850

Source: Amazon.com 8-K, filed February 2, 2001.

EXHIBIT 2 (CONTINUED)   Segment Information (in thousands, except per share data)

	Year Ended December 31			
	1999	*2000*	*2001E*	*2002E*
US Books, Music and DVD/Video				
Net Sales	$1,308,292	$1,698,266	$1,842,650	$2,050,000
Gross profit (loss)	262,871	417,452	442,165	519,650
Operating income (loss)	(31,000)	71,441	83,491	98,700
Percent of revenues	79.5%	61.5%	54.4%	50.9%
Percent of gross profit	90.4%	63.7%	57.0%	55.4%
Gross margin	20.1%	24.6%	24.0%	25.3%
Operating margin	(2.4%)	4.2%	4.5%	4.8%
International				
Net Sales	$167,743	$381,075	601,269	767,000
Gross profit (loss)	35,574	77,435	132,569	159,000
Operating income (loss)	(79,223)	(145,071)	(120,476)	(92,000)
Percent of revenues	10.2%	13.8%	17.7%	19.0%
Percent of gross profit	12.2%	11.8%	17.1%	16.9%
Gross margin	21.2%	20.3%	22.0%	20.7%
Operating margin	(47.2%)	(38.1%)	(20.0%)	(12.0%)
US Early-Stage Businesses and Other				
Net Sales	$163,804	$682,642	945,081	1,209,800
Gross profit (loss)	(7,800)	160,890	200,781	259,948
Operating income (loss)	(242,147)	(243,370)	(173,920)	(165,258)
Percent of revenues	10.0%	24.7%	27.9%	30.0%
Percent of gross profit	(2.7%)	24.5%	25.9%	27.7%
Gross margin	(4.8%)	23.6%	21.2%	21.5%
Operating margin	(147.8%)	(35.7%)	(18.4%)	(13.7%)

Note: Operating expenses include fulfillment. Most retailers account for fulfillment as a cost of goods sold (COGS). Adding fulfillment to COGS above would decrease gross profit and gross profit margin.

Source: Amazon.com 8-K, filed February 2, 2001, Newman, A. and Kolb, D. "Amazon.com" *ABN AMRO Equity Research,* April 4, 2001.

EXHIBIT 2 (CONTINUED) Statement of Cash Flows (in thousands, except per share data)

	Quarter Ended 12/31		Year Ended 12/31	
	2000	1999	2000	1999
Cash and cash equivalents, beginning of period	$647,048	$73,543	$133,309	$71,583
Operating activities:				
Net loss	(545,140)	(323,213)	(1,411,273)	(719,968)

Adjustments to reconcile net loss to net cash provided by (used in) operating activities:

Depreciation of fixed assets	22,741	13,871	84,460	36,806
Amortization of deferred stock-based compensation	(1,112)	14,049	24,797	30,618
Equity in losses of equity-method investees, net	37,559	39,893	304,596	76,769
Amortization of goodwill and other intangibles	79,210	82,301	321,772	214,694
Impairment-related and other costs	184,052	2,085	200,311	8,072
Amortization of previously unearned revenue	(42,653)	(5,837)	(108,211)	(5,837)
Loss (gain) on sale of marketable securities	3,877	2,602	(280)	8,688
Non-cash investment gains and losses, net	155,005	—	142,639	—
Non-cash interest expense and other	6,450	3,055	24,766	29,171

Changes in operating assets and liabilities:

Inventories	(10,683)	(82,777)	46,083	(172,069)
Prepaid expenses and other current assets	3,412	(22,242)	(8,585)	(54,927)
Accounts payable	180,674	208,395	22,357	330,166
Accrued expense and other current liabilities	113,374	78,256	93,967	95,839
Unearned revenue	31,727	6,225	97,818	6,225
Interest payable	29,160	14,843	34,341	24,878
Net cash provided by (used in) operating activities	247,653	31,506	(130,442)	(90,875)

Investing activities:

Sales and maturities of marketable securities	23,811	403,728	545,724	2,064,101
Purchases of marketable securities	(88,715)	(150,114)	(184,455)	(2,359,398)
Purchases of fixed assets	(37,331)	(105,196)	(134,758)	(287,055)
Investments in equity-method investee and other investments	(691)	(146,754)	(62,533)	(369,607)
Net cash provided by (used in) investing activities	(102,926)	1,664	163,978	(951,959)

Financing activities:

Proceeds from exercise of stock options	4,980	27,539	44,697	64,469
Proceeds from long-term debt	—	3,000	681,499	1,263,639
Repayment of long-term debt	(3,930)	(4,176)	(16,927)	(188,886)
Financing costs	—	—	(16,122)	(35,151)
Net cash provided by financing activities	1,050	26,363	693,147	1,104,071
Effect of exchange rate changes on cash and cash equivalents	29,610	233	(37,557)	489
Net increase in cash and cash equivalents	175,387	59,766	689,126	61,726
Cash and cash equivalents at end of period	$822,435	$133,309	$822,435	$133,309
Supplemental cash flow information:				
Fixed assets acquired under capital leases	$113	$ —	$ 4,459	$ 25,850
Fixed assets acquired under financing agreements	—	—	4,844	5,608
Stock issued in connection with business acquisitions		139,066	32,130	774,409
Equity securities for commercial service agreements	—	54,402	106,848	54,402
Cash paid for interest	8,456	3,299	92,253	59,688

EXHIBIT 2 (CONTINUED)   **Supplemental Financial and Business Metrics Fourth Quarter 2000**

	Q4 99	Q1 00	Q2 00	Q3 00	Q4 00	Year-Over-Year Growth %
Results of operations:						
Net sales (MM)	$676	$574	$578	$638	$972	44%
Gross profit (MM)	$88	$128	$136	$167	$224	155%
Trailing twelve months net sales per active customer	$113	$117	$125	$130	$134	19%
U.S. Customers purchasing from non-Books, Music and Video/DVD (BMV) stores	24%	11%	13%	14%	36%	n/a
Cost per new customer	$19	$13	$17	$15	$13	(32)%
Fulfillment costs as a % of net sales	16%	17%	15%	15%	13%	n/a
Pro-forma operating loss (MM)	$175	$99	$89	$68	$60	(66)%
Pro-forma operating loss as a % of net sales	(26)%	(17)%	(15)%	(11)%	(6)%	n/a
U.S. BMV pro-forma operating profit (loss) as a % of BMV net sales	(4)%	(1)%	3%	6%	8%	n/a
U.S. pro-forma operating profit (loss) as a % of net sales	(24)%	(14)%	(11)%	(5)%	(2)%	n/a
Customer data:						
New customers (MM)	3.8	3.1	2.5	2.9	4.1	8%
Trailing twelve months active customers (MM)	14.1	15.9	17.0	18.2	19.8	40%
New customers—international (MM)	0.6	0.6	0.6	0.9	1.1	83%
Cumulative customers—international (MM)	1.8	2.4	3.0	3.9	5.0	178%
Balance sheet:						
Cash and marketable securities (MM)	$706	$1,009	$908	$900	$1,101	n/a
Cash generated by (used in) operations (MM)	$ 32	$(320)	$ (54)	$ (4)	$ 248	n/a
Inventory, net (MM):	$221	$172	$172	$164	$175	(21)%
Inventory turnover—annualized	14	9	10	11	18	n/a

Source: Amazon.com 8-K, filed February 2, 2001.

EXHIBIT 2 (CONTINUED)   **Notes to Accompany Fourth Quarter 2000 Earnings Release**

- Net sales included the retail price of products sold by Amazon.com, less returns and promotional gift certificates. It also included outbound shipping charges to customers and service revenue earned in connection with strategic partnerships (e.g. ToysRus). These partnership revenues were approximately $73 million (compared with $7 million in the fourth quarter of 1999). The percentage of cash-based service revenue was approximately 69 percent of total service revenues, of which $9 million was associated with the sale of inventory to ToysRus.com during the fourth quarter of 2000.

- Sales to customers outside the U.S., including export sales from Amazon.com and sales from Amazon.co.uk, Amazon.de, Amazon.fr, and Amazon.co.jp, represented approximately 21 percent and 19 percent of net sales for the quarter ended December 2000 and 1999 respectively.

- Orders from repeat customers represented 75 percent of total orders in the quarter ended December 31, 2000, up from 73 percent the previous year.

- Gross profit consisted of net sales less the cost of sales, including the cost of merchandise sold to customers, shipping costs, packaging supplies and costs associated with the service revenue. Gross profit from service revenue earned from strategic partnerships (e.g., ToysRus.com) was approximately $39 million and $7 million in the fourth quarter of 2000 and 1999, respectively. Gross profit from product sales, including shipping, Auctions, zShops and Marketplace, was approximately $186 million for the fourth quarter of 2000 and $81 million for the fourth quarter of 1999. Gross loss from shipping was approximately $17 million and $5 million in the fourth quarter of 2000 and 1999, respectively.

- Marketing, sales and fulfillment expenses consisted of advertising, promotional and public relations expenditures, credit card fees and payroll-related expenses for personnel engaged in marketing, selling and fulfillment activities.

- Fulfillment costs represented costs incurred in operating and staffing distribution and customer service centers (including costs attributable to receiving, inspecting and warehousing inventories; picking, packing and preparing customers' orders for shipment; and responding to inquiries from customers) and credit card fees. Fulfillment costs amounted to approximately $131 million, or 13 percent of net sales and 15 percent of product sales, in the fourth quarter of 2000, and $107 million, or 16 percent of net sales and product sales, for the fourth quarter of 1999. Fulfillment-related costs associated with the strategic partnership with ToysRus.com were included within gross profit.

- Technology and content expenses consisted principally of: payroll and related expenses for content development and editorial activities; systems and telecommunications operations personnel and consultants; systems and telecommunications infrastructure; and costs of acquired content, including freelance reviews. Fourth quarter 2000 technology and content expenses increased 21 percent over the prior year.

- General and administrative expenses consisted of payroll and related expenses for executive, finance and administrative personnel, recruiting, professional fees and other general corporate expenses.

- The company recorded impairment losses on goodwill and other intangible assets of approximately $184 million. No impairments of enterprise-wide goodwill (see below for definition) were identified. Impairment-related and other for the year ended December 31, 2000 also included a third-quarter charge of approximately $11 million. Amazon.com defines goodwill in two separate categories: enterprise-level and business-unit level. Enterprise-level goodwill resulted from acquisition of businesses that were fully integrated into the company's operations and no longer existed as discrete business unit. Business-unit goodwill and other intangibles resulted from business "combinations" where the acquired operations were managed as a separate business unit and were not fully absorbed into the company.

(continued)

EXHIBIT 2 (CONTINUED)   **Notes to Accompany Fourth Quarter 2000 Earnings Release**

- Other income (expenses) primarily consisted of net realized gains and losses on the sale of marketable securities and other investments, and net foreign exchange transaction gains and losses.

- Noncash investment gains and losses included other-than-temporary impairment losses totaling approximately $155 million to record certain of the company's investments at their fair values.

- Noncash investment gains and losses, net for the year ended December 31, 2000, included the following items: a gain of approximately $40 million related to the acquisition of HomeGrocer.com, Inc. by Webvan Group, Inc.; a gain of approximately $20 million representing the previously unearned revenue recognized upon the termination of the company's commercial agreement with living.com; a loss of approximately $14 million, representing the company's investment in living.com at the time of its bankruptcy; and other-than-temporary impairment losses totaling approximately $34 million and $155 million in the quarters ending September 30 and December 31, 2000, respectively, to record certain of the company's investments at their fair values.

- Pro forma results for the quarter and year ended December 31, 2000 and 1999 are presented for informational purposes only and are not prepared in accordance with U.S. generally accepted accounting principles. These results present the operating results of Amazon.com, excluding losses of approximately $455 million and $138 million for the fourth quarter, and $994 million and $330 million for the years ended December 31, 2000 and 1999, respectively. These losses were related to stock-based compensation; amortization of goodwill and other intangibles; impairment-related and other; noncash investment gains and losses; and equity in losses of equity-method investees.

- The number of shares used in calculating loss per share for the fourth quarter and year 2000 does not include the weighted average number of outstanding shares subject to repurchase. The effect of stock options is antidilutive and accordingly excluded from diluted loss per share. If the effect of stock options were included, the number of shares used in computation of basic and diluted loss per share would have been approximately $379 million for the fourth quarter of 2000.

- The company classified all highly liquid investments with an original maturity of three months or less as cash equivalents. This included marketable securities of approximately $36 million. These securities were stated at fair value, and consisted primarily of A-rated or higher short- to intermediate-term fixed income securities, as well as equity securities.

- Accounts payable days as of the end of the fourth quarter of 2000 were approximately 60 days, a decrease of approximately 12 days from the end of the fourth quarter of 1999.

First Quarter 2001 Expectations

- Net sales are expected to grow to between $650 million and $700 million.
- Gross margin is expected to be between 21 percent and 23 percent of net sales.
- Pro forma operating losses are expected to decrease year-over-year to between 10 percent and 13 percent of net sales.
- Cash and marketable securities are expected to be over $650 million as of March 31, 2001, which includes up to $50 million of cash outflow in connection with the restructuring.

2001 Expectations

- Net sales are expected to increase between 20 percent and 30 percent over 2000.
- Pro forma operating losses are expected to be between 4 percent and 7 percent of net sales for the year, with pro forma operating profitability expected in the fourth quarter.
- Cash and marketable securities are expected to be over $900 million at December 31, 2001. Unless the company chooses to raise cash to further strengthen its balance sheet or for strategic flexibility, it has no reason to do so.

EXHIBIT 3   Amazon.com's Stock Price and Market Capitalization

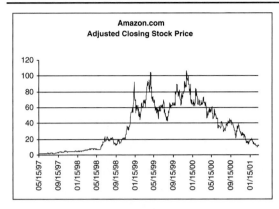

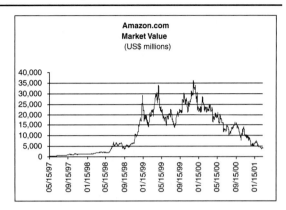

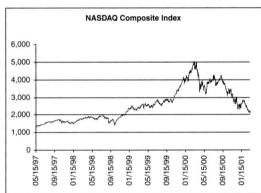

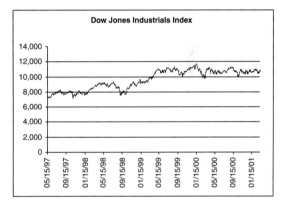

Source: Datastream International.

EXHIBIT 4   Timeline of Amazon.com Business and Revenue Models

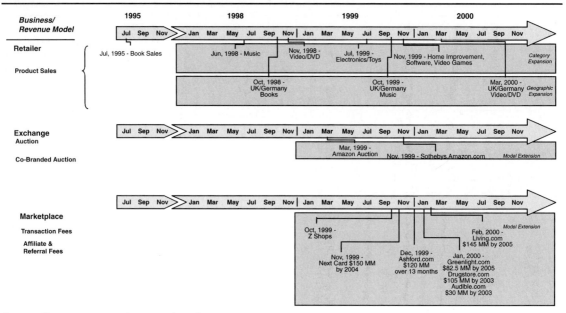

Source: Company press releases and analyst reports.

EXHIBIT 5   Amazon's Organizational Structure

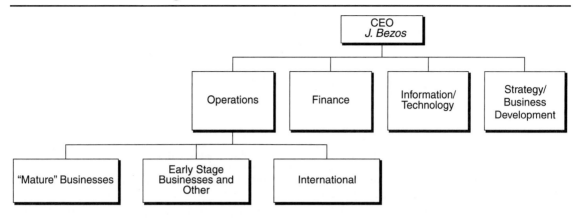

In 1999, Amazon.com offered products and services through 3 distinct operating units:
- "Mature" Businesses
  Retail:
    —*Books*
    —*Music*
    —*DVDs / Videos*
- Early Stage Businesses and Other:
  Retail:
    —*Electronics*
    —*Software*
    —*Video games*
    —*Toys*
    —*Home Improvement*
  Marketplace/Exchange:
    —*Auctions*
    —*zShops*
    —*Sothebys.Amazon*
  Aggregator / Portal:[17]
    —*Amazon Commerce Network*
- International
  Retail/Marketplace/Exchange/Aggregator/Portal:
    —UK and Germany operations

Source: Company reports and case writer's interpretation; Wolverton, T., "Amazon Moves into Home Services with Living.com." 1 February 2000, Available from www.cnet.com.

---

[17]A recent news press release stated that Amazon and its "Commerce Network" partners were updating their technical systems to enable customers to place items purchased from a Commerce Network partner in their Amazon.com shopping cart. Once this is completed, the business model will shift from an aggregator to a marketplace.

EXHIBIT 6   Background for Amazon.com's Key Personnel

Executive Officers

Jeffrey P. Bezos has served as Chairman of the Board since he founded the company in 1994, and Chief Executive Officer since May 1996. Bezos served as President from founding until June 1999 and Treasurer and Secretary from May 1996 to March 1997. Prior to launching Amazon.com, Bezos was employed by D.E. Shaw & Co., a Wall Street investment firm from 1990 to 1994. From April 1988 to December 1990, he was employed by Bankers Trust Company, becoming Vice President in February 1990. Bezos, who is also a director of drugstore.com, inc., received his B.S. in Electrical Engineering and Computer Science from Princeton University.

Joseph Galli, Jr. joined Amazon.com in June 1999 as President and Chief Operating Officer. Resigned in Summer 2000. From 1980 until June 1999, Galli held a variety of positions with The Black and Decker Corporation, culminating as president of Black and Decker's Worldwide Power Tools and Accessories. As president, he supervised the marketing, sales, manufacturing, engineering, finance, MIS, purchasing and product service departments. Galli received a B.S. in Business Administration from the University of North Carolina and an M.B.A. from Loyola College.

Warren C. Jenson joined Amazon.com in September 1999 as Senior Vice President, Chief Financial Officer and Chief Accounting Officer. Before joining Amazon.com, Jenson was the Chief Financial Officer and Executive Vice President for Delta Air Lines from April 1998 to September 1999. From September 1992 to April 1998, Jenson served as Chief Financial Officer and Senior Vice President for the National Broadcasting Company (NBC), a subsidiary of General Electric, and participated in efforts to develop MSNBC, the cable-Internet joint news venture between NBC and Microsoft. Jenson earned his Masters of Accountancy—Business Taxation, and B.S. in Accounting from Brigham Young University.

John D. Risher has served as Senior Vice President and General Manager, US Retail Group since February 2000. Risher joined Amazon.com in February 1997 as Vice President of Product Development. He served as Senior Vice President of Product Development from November 1997 to February 2000 and as Vice President of Product Development from February 1997 to November 1997. From July 1991 to February 1997, Risher held a variety of marketing and project management positions at Microsoft Corporation, including Team Manager for Microsoft Access and Founder and Product Unit Manager for MS Investor, Microsoft's Web site for personal investment. Risher received his B.A. in Comparative Literature from Princeton University and his M.B.A. from Harvard Business School.

Diego Piacentini joined Amazon.com as Senior Vice President and General Manager, International in February 2000. From April 1997 until joining Amazon.com, Piacentini was Vice President and General Manager, Europe, of Apple Computer, Inc., with responsibility for Apple Computer's operations in Europe, the Middle East and Africa. Piacentini joined Apple Computer in 1987. Prior to that time he was a financial manager at Fiatimpresit in Italy. Piacentini received a degree in Economics from Bocconi University in Milan, Italy in 1985.

Richard L. Dalzell joined Amazon.com in August 1997 as Vice President and Chief Information Officer. From February 1990 to August 1997, Dalzell held several management positions within the Information Systems Division at Wal-Mart Stores, Inc., including Vice President of Information Systems from January 1994 to August 1997. From 1987 to 1990, Dalzell served as the Business Development Manager for E-Systems, Inc. Prior to joining E-Systems, Inc. he served seven years in the United States Army as a teleprocessing officer. Dalzell received a B.S. in Engineering from the United States Military Academy, West Point.

EXHIBIT 6 (CONTINUED) **Background for Amazon.com's Key Personnel**

Mark J. Britto was appointed Vice President, Strategic Alliances in August 1999. From June 1999 to August 1999, Britto served as Director of Business Development. He joined Amazon.com in June 1999 as part of the acquisition of Accept.com, which he co-founded in October 1998. From October 1994 through October 1998, Britto was Executive Vice President of Credit Policy at FirstUSA Bank, where he was responsible for the company's credit risk management practice. Prior to that, he served as Senior Vice President of Risk Management at NationsBank. Britto received an M.S. in Operations Research and a B.S. in Industrial Engineering and Operations Research from the University of California at Berkeley.

Jeffrey A. Wilke has served as Vice President and General Manager, Operations since September 1999. Previously, Wilke held a variety of positions at AlliedSignal from 1995 to 1999, including Vice President and General Manager of the Pharmaceutical Fine Chemicals unit from March 1999 to September 1999 and General Manager of the Carbon Materials and Technologies unit from August 1997 to February 1999. Prior to his employment at AlliedSignal, he was an information technology consultant with Andersen Consulting. He received a B.S.E. in Chemical Engineering from Princeton University and an M.B.A. and Master of Science in Chemical Engineering from the Massachusetts Institute of Technology.

Mark S. Peek joined Amazon.com in March 2000 as Vice President, Finance, and was appointed Chief Accounting Officer in April 2000. Prior to joining Amazon.com, Peek served as a consultant at the public accounting firm of Deloitte & Touche LLP. He joined the firm in 1980, was promoted to partner in 1990, and served as lead partner for a number of the firm's multi-national technology clients. Peek received a B.S. in Accounting, Economics and International Business in 1980 from Minnesota State University.

Board of Directors

Name	Position
Jeffrey P. Bezos	Founder, Chief Executive Officer and Chairman of the Board
Tom A. Alberg	Managing Director of Madrona Venture Group, L.L.C.
Scott D. Cook	Chairman of the Executive Committee of Intuit, Inc.
L. John Doerr	General Partner, Kleiner Perkins Caufield & Byers
Patricia Q. Stonesifer	Co-Chair of the Bill and Melinda Gates Foundation

Source: Adapted from Amazon.com 1999 Annual Report/10-K, Seattle: Amazon.com, 2000.

EXHIBIT 7 Amazon.com Acquisitions and Strategic Investments (April 1998–April 2000)

Date	Company	Description	Stake	Amazon Commitment Value	What Amazon Will Receive
4/27/98	Internet Movie Database	Online database of movie and television information	100%	Total of $55 MM	—
	Bookpages	Online book seller in UK	100%		—
	Telebook	Online book seller in Germany	100%		—
8/4/98	Junglee	Online database technology that searches for products	100%	$180 MM	—
	PlanetAll	Address book, calendar and reminder service	100%	$100 MM	—
2/24/99	drugstore.com	Online health, beauty, vitamins, neutraceuticals	46%[18]	< $40 MM (E)	$105 MM over 3 years to create "tab" on Amazon's site
3/29/99	Pets.com	Online pet supplies	50%	$65 MM (E)	N/A
4/12/99	LiveBid	Web-enabled real-time auction technology	100%	$50 MM (E)	—
4/26/99	Alexa.com	Web navigation service to recommend related web sites	100%		—
	Exchange.com	Marketplace for rare books and music	100%	$645 MM	—
	Accept.com	Developer of software that simplifies online transactions	100%		—
5/18/99	HomeGrocer.com	Online, next-day home-delivery of groceries in Seattle, WA, Portland, OR and Southern CA	35%	$42.5 MM	N/A
6/16/99	Sotheby's	Legendary auction house	N/A	$45 MM	10 year alliance for co-branded Auction site
7/14/99	Gear.com	Discount retailer of sporting goods	49%	$120 MM (E)	N/A
9/23/99	Della.com	Online wedding/gift registry services	20% (E)	$60 MM (E)	N/A
10/4/99	Convergence	Software enabling Internet access for hand-held devices	100%	$20 MM	—

Date	Company	Description	Stake	Value	Additional commitment
11/9/99	Tool Crib of the North	Tool and equipment catalog company	100%	N/A	—
11/10/99	NextCard	Consumer credit card company	9.9% (E)	$112 MM (E)	Potentially $150 MM over 5 years (E)
11/30/99	Back to Basic Toys	Online and catalog retailer of hard to find classic toys	100%	N/A	—
12/1/99	Ashford.com	Retailer of online luxury goods and gifts	16.6%	$10 MM	$120 MM over 13 months
1/11/00	Kozmo.com	Online one-hour, "e-mmediate" delivery service for entertainment/convenience products	23% (E)	$60 MM	3 year alliance allowing customers to receive e-mmediate delivery in Kozmo markets[19]
1/22/00	Greenlight.com	Online auto purchasing through partnerships with local dealers	5%	$15 MM (E)	$82.5 MM over 5 years
1/24/00	drugstore.com	Online health, beauty, vitamins, neutraceuticals	27%	$30 MM	$105 MM over 3 years to create "tab" on Amazon's site
1/31/00	Audible.com	Internet-delivered spoken audio for PC-listening or playback devices	5%	$10 MM (E)	$30 MM over 3 years
2/1/00	Living.com	Online retailer of home products and services	18%	$18 MM (E)	$145 MM over 5 years
2/3/00	Greg Manning Auctions	Online auctions dealer of collectibles	4.5%	$5 to $6 MM	N/A
3/28/00	eZiba.com	Online retailer of handcrafts from around the world	20%	$17.5 MM	N/A
4/18/00	WineShopper.com	San Francisco-based online wine-seller	N/A	$30 MM	N/A

Key: N/A = Data not available; — = Not applicable (due to acquisition); E = estimated by analysts (not by company).
Source: Amazon press releases, except where noted as analyst or other estimates (ING Barings, Solomon Smith Barney, PaineWebber, McDonald Equity Research, CNET News, Wall Street Journal).

[18] Amazon's investment was worth roughly $375 million (27% stake) following a $30 million add-on investment in January 2000.
[19] As of April 1999, these included New York, Boston, DC, San Francisco, Seattle and Los Angeles.

EXHIBIT 8   Amazon.com Revenues and Gross Margins by Product Category

Product Category	Percent of Total Revenue (Fourth Quarter 1999)	Forecasted Percent of Total Revenue (Longer-term*)	Gross Margin (Fourth Quarter 1999)	Forecasted Gross Margin (Longer-term*)
Retail:				
Books	54%	40%	22%	30%
Music	14%	9%	13%	19%
Videos/DVDs	10%	7%	13%	19%
Consumer Electronics	5%	10%	−20%	12%
Software	1%	8%	14%	20%
Video Games/Toys	13%	11%	−15%	20%
Home Improvement	2%	6%	5%	20%
Auctions/zShops	1%	4%	45%	85%
Marketing/Equity Partnerships	0%	5%	N/A	95%
Total	100%	100%	13%	29%

*Timeframe not specified.

Note: The company reported that low margins in the video games/toys and consumer electronics categories were due in part to large inventory write-downs.

Source: Farley, S. and Modi, N., PaineWebber. "Amazon.com" (23 February 2000); Amazon.com company reports.

EXHIBIT 9   Amazon Book Sales vs. Other Sales

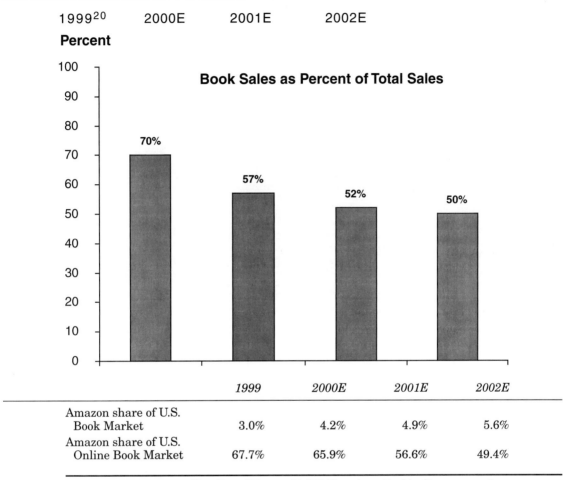

1999[20]   2000E   2001E   2002E

	1999	*2000E*	*2001E*	*2002E*
Amazon share of U.S. Book Market	3.0%	4.2%	4.9%	5.6%
Amazon share of U.S. Online Book Market	67.7%	65.9%	56.6%	49.4%

Source: Company reports; Ries, D. and Truong. V., C.E. Unterberg, Towbin. "Amazon.com."
13 October 1999. Available from Investext (www.bschool-investext.com).

---

[20]U.S. book sales represented less than half of total sales for 4Q99.

EXHIBIT 10   U.S. Book Contribution Per Order

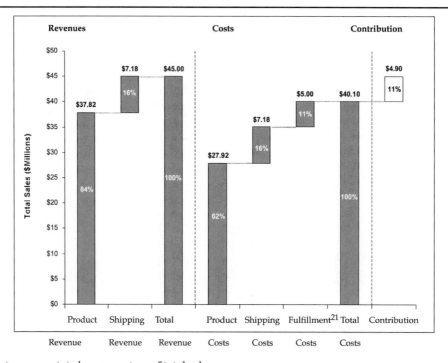

Note: Percentages are stated as percentage of total sales.

Assumptions:

90% of individual orders were shipped to same country, 2% shipped overnight and 28% were shipped via 2–3 day delivery.

40% of orders require customer contact.

Source: Adapted from Becker, H., Salomon Smith Barney. "Amazon.com." 9 December 1999. Available from Investext (www.bschool-investext.com), p 47.

---

[21]Includes credit card fees, warehousing/pick & pack, and customer support.

EXHIBIT 11   Addressable Market as of April 2000: Retail and Online Market Overview

Categories	1999 U.S. Market ($ billions)		2003 U.S. Market ($ billions)		Competition		
	Total Retail	Online Retail	Total Retail	Online Retail	"Brick and Mortar"	"Click and Mortar" (Cross Category)	"Click and Mortar" (Category Killer)
Books	30.5	1.4	38.1	5.4	Barnes and Noble Borders Wal-Mart Costco	Wal-Mart.com Costco.com Buy.com	Bn.com Buy.com Books.com
Music	13.0	0.3	15.8	2.2	Tower Records HMV Virgin Records Wal-Mart	Wal-Mart.com Costco.com Buy.com	CDNow GetMusic.com Bn.com BMGmusicservice.com
Videos/DVDs	8.6	0.2	10.5	1.1	Wal-Mart	Wal-Mart.com Costco.com Buy.com	Reel.com DVDExpress.com ToysRUs.com
Toys	24.1	0.5	29.6	3.0	Wal-Mart Toys-R-Us Kmart Target Stores KayBee's	Wal-Mart.com Costco.com Target.com JCPenney.com Bluelight.com (Kmart)	EToys.com ToysRUs.com FAO.com KbKids.com
Video Games	6.5	.1	7.9	.8	Wal-Mart Toys-R-Us Target	Wal-Mart.com Buy.com Beyond.com	Beyond.com Egghead.com
Software	7.0	1.1	8.5	3.6	Egghead Wal-Mart	Wal-Mart.com Buy.com	Egghead.com Beyond.com
Consumer Electronics	55.3	0.5	67.2	4.7	Best Buy Circuit City Wal-Mart Radio Shack	Wal-Mart.com Buy.com JCPenney.com	Outpost.com Crutchfield.com Egghead.com
Home Improvement	160.5	0.1	195.1	1.0	Home Depot Lowe's Companies Sears J.C. Penney	Wal-Mart.com Sears.com JCPenney.com	HomeDepot.com
Total Retail Categories	305.5	4.2	372.7	21.8			

EXHIBIT 11 (CONTINUED)   **Addressable Market as of April 2000: Retail and Online Market Overview**

Categories	1999 U.S. Market ($ billions)		2003 U.S. Market ($ billions)		Competition		
	Total Retail	Online Retail	Total Retail	Online Retail	"Brick and Mortar"	"Click and Mortar" (Cross Category)	"Click and Mortar" (Category Killer)
Auctions (Consumer only)	200–400	3.3	N/A	28.5[22]	Sotheby's Christie's	Yahoo! Auctions Excite Auctions AOL Auctions	EBay.com Priceline.com
Total (incl. Auctions)	505.5–705.5	7.5	N/A	50.3			

Source: Cassar, K. et al, "Shopping: Online Projections, Volume 2." November 1999. Available from Jupiter Communications (www.jup.com); Becker, H., Salomon Smith Barney. "Amazon.com." 9 December 1999. Available from Investext (www.bschool-investext.com); Rowen, M., Prudential Securities. "Amazon.com." 23 September 1999. Available from Investext (www.bschoolinvestext.com); and Farley, S. and Modi N., PaineWebber. "Amazon.com." 23 February 2000. Available from Investext (www.bschool-investext.com).

[22]Estimated online market size is for 2004.

EXHIBIT 11 (CONTINUED)   **Competitor Comparisons**

Top 10 E-Retailers	FY 2000								
	Revenues ($M)	Gross Profit[23] ($M)	Gross Margin (%)	SG&A ($M)	SG&A (%)	Operating Income ($M)	Operating Margin (%)	Unique Audience (000)	Purchaser Market Share
Amazon.com	$2,762	$241	9%	$558	20%	$(317)	-11%	22,751	15.1%
EBay	$431	$336	80%	$240	56%	$35	8%	18,987	14.5%
BMG.com	N/A	N/A	N/A	N/A	N/A	N/A	N/A	4,762	4.3%
Barnesandnoble.com	$320	$58	18%	$164	51%	$299	-93%	5,948	3.8%
Columbia House	N/A	N/A	N/A	N/A	N/A	N/A	N/A	2,723	3.7%
Half.com	N/A	N/A	N/A	N/A	N/A	N/A	N/A	4,939	3.1%
J.C. Penney	$31,846	$8,815	28%	$8,637	27%	$(886)	-3%	3,339	3.0%
Travelocity.com	$193	$121	63%	$137	71%	$(114)	-59%	7,966	2.5%
CDNow.com	$147	$29	20%	$101	69%	$(122)	-83%	5,295	2.2%
Southwest.com	$5,649	$1,021	18%	$1,843	33%	$1,021	18%	3,954	2.0%

[23]Data for J.C. Penney and Southwest reflect both online and offline operations. Data for CDNow.com is from 1999. Financial data from BMG.com, Columbia House, and Half.com are not available. BMG.com provides online marketing services for BMG/Music-a wholly-owned subsidiary of Bertelsmann A.G. Columbia House is a 50/50 joint venture between Time Warner and Sony, comprising the assets formerly owned and operated by The Columbia House Division of Sony Music Entertainment Inc. (formerly CBS Records Inc.) and the Time-Life Home Video Club. Founded in 1999, Half.com was acquired by eBay in 2000. The eBay audience and market share statistics do not include Half.com.

EXHIBIT 11 (CONTINUED) Competitor Comparisons

Online Retailers	Holiday Traffic (in 000) for the Week of:							
	11/5/2000	11/12/2000	11/19/2000	11/26/2000	12/3/2000	12/10/2000	12/17/2000	12/24/2000
amazon.com	4069	4673	5331	6201	6290	6806	6276	4372
walmart.com	321	657	829	1514	1337	1788	1578	697
bluelight.com	416	480	475	784	843	1051	1010	577
target.com	416	546	618	1109	983	1008	916	483
fingerhut.com	185	224	320	280	349	324	328	263

Holiday traffic table is adapted from: Amazon.com and T. Albright and L. Baker, "Amazon.com: Trading Growth for Profits in 2001," *Salomon Smith Barney*, 5 February 2001, p. 5. Top 10 E-Retailer data is taken from annual reports and Jupiter Media Metrix.

EXHIBIT 12 Amazon.com vs. Online Bookstore Competitors

Reach and Other Metrics, as of October 1999

	Amazon.com	BarnesandNoble.com	Borders.com
Reach[24]	17.8%	6.9%	1.2%
Unique Visitors	11,283	4,381	777
Average Usage Days/Visitor	1.8	1.4	1.2
Average Unique Pages/Visitor/Day	8.0	4.6	4.6
Average Minutes Spent/Usage Day	6.5	5.0	4.2

Source: Media Metrix; Adapted from Becker, H., Salomon Smith Barney. "Amazon.com." 9 December 1999. Available from Investext (www.bschool-investext.com).

[24]Reach was defined by Media Metrix as the percentage of web users that visited the site [during the month of October].

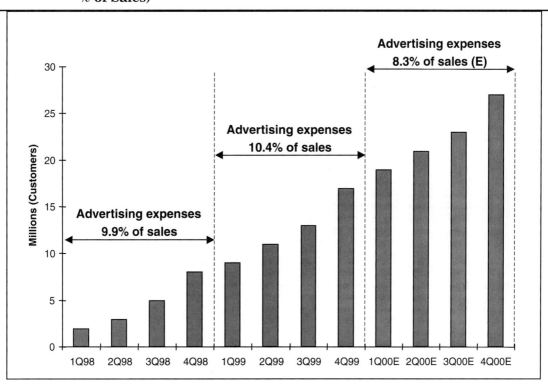

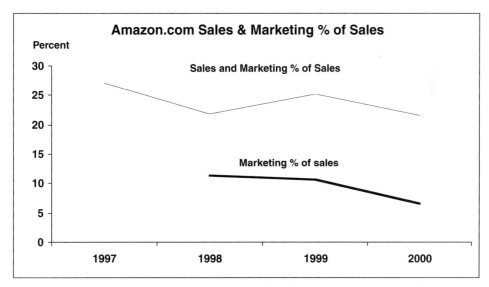

Source: Company data; Fogarty, T., ING Barings. "Amazon.com." 23 December 1999. Available from Investext
(www.bschool-investext.com), July 6, 2000.

EXHIBIT 14   Business/Operational Value Metrics

Fiscal Year 1999 Metrics
Traditional "Brick & Mortar" Retailers

	Wal-Mart	Toys R' Us	Barnes & Noble	Sears
Sales ($ MM)	165,013.00	11,862.00	3,486.04	41,071.00
COGS ($MM)	127,289.00	8,321.00	2,483.73	27,212.00
Gross Margin	22.86	29.852	28.75	33.744
Advertising as % Sales	0.003	N/A	N/A	0.04
SG&A (% of Sales)	.16	.23	.19	.23
Operating Margin	5.04	4.38	6.25	9.06
Employees (000's)	1,140	76	37.41	326
Sales/Employee ($)	144,748	156,079	100,347	125,985
Inventory Turnover	6.91	4.24	2.43	5.51
Working Capital Turnover	112.91	168.26	10.99	2.73

Fiscal Year 1999 Metrics
"Pure Play" Internet Retailers

	Amazon.com	eToys.com	BarnesandNoble.com	eBay.com
Sales ($ MM)	1,639.84	151.036	202.57	224.724
COGS	1,312.39	115.511	146.09	38.083
Gross Margin	19.99	23.521	27.88	83.053
Advertising as % Sales	0.09	0.37	0.21	0.20
SG&A (% of Sales)	0.41	1.286	0.816	0.72
Operating Margin	(36.45)	(127.80)	(60.54)	1.42
Employees (000's)	7.6	0.94	1.24	1.212
Sales/Employee	215,768	160,677	163,363	185,416
Inventory Turnover	10.49	3.53	53.46	N/A
Working Capital Turnover	6.12	1.62	0.8	1.01

Source: Standard & Poors' Research Insight.

EXHIBIT 15   Amazon Revenues: Repeat vs. New Customers

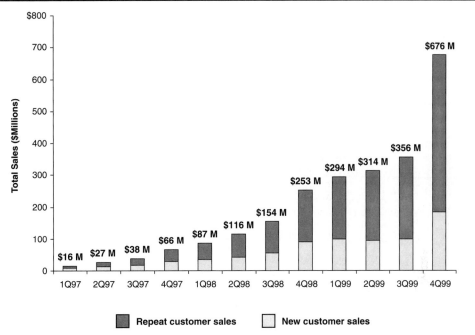

Source: Company reports; Rowen, M., Prudential Securities. "Amazon.com." 23 September 1999. Available from Investext (www.bschool-investext.com).

EXHIBIT 16   Jeff Bezos' 7 Myths About the Internet[25]

Myth #1: The Internet changes everything.

The Internet does change a lot. But there is something very fundamental that the Internet doesn't change: people. I've heard people talk about the fact that brand names are dead and that physical stores are going away. Brand names aren't dead, and physical stores aren't going away for the same reason that movie theaters didn't go away when you got television. People like to go outside, and that's going to continue. Stores are going to change in response to e-commerce. They're not going to compete on the basis of price with e-commerce because that's not possible but they're going—and they're going to become even more sort of entertainment-focused.

Myth #2: There are no barriers to entry in Internet businesses.

The barriers to entry keep going up and they're huge. How else do you explain the fact that we've invested hundreds of millions of dollars in our own business? And as those technology barriers keep going up, that's a great thing for companies who have a large base of customers to amortize those technology development costs. That is one of the key things about e-commerce: it's a technology business instead of a real-estate business, which makes it more of a fixed cost business and less of a variable cost business.

Myth #3: Intermediaries are dead.

Intermediaries are not dead. Intermediaries are going to change. There may not be a lot of them, and they may not be the same ones that exist today. It's much more precise if you focus instead on who adds value and who doesn't. Anybody who doesn't add value isn't long for this world, and anybody who adds value is going to be in a much better spot.

Myth #4: There are only going to be a few winners.

The world of e-commerce is going to be as diverse as the physical world because more business models will be possible online. Different people will be building brands, connecting with customers, building relationships with customers in different segments, and pursuing different strategies and niches, and thus many companies are going to be successful. There are also going to be a huge number of failures. I have been extremely impressed by how quickly and effectively the capital markets and the free market system have responded to embrace this new technology.

Myth #5: It's easy for bricks-and-mortar retailers to extend their business.

I have long maintained that it would have been easier back in 1997 for Barnes and Noble to open a chain of hardware stores than it was for them to build an online bookstore, because the set of skills that you need to expertly run their physical stores is actually much more similar to running a chain of hardware stores than it is to go online. The businesses are so different and the cultures that you need to support the businesses are different. One is a technology business, and the other a real-estate business; one is a variable cost business, and the other mostly a fixed-cost business.

Myth #6: The current leaders can't fail.

If you look at the history of pioneers, it's not that good. We [Amazon.com] could still be a footnote in the history of e-commerce. These early pioneers are good at risk-taking when they're small and then they get bad at risk-taking once they have something to lose. One of the things we try to do at Amazon.com to fight this is to continuously bet the company on things that we think are really important for customers.

Myth #7: Everybody needs an Internet strategy.

It is true that the Internet is an enabling horizontal layer, but it does not affect every industry. You actually see people making dumb business decisions because they force-fit an Internet strategy where one doesn't belong. If you get together with your Board of Directors to brainstorm, and you think about it and you can't figure out what to do, you should just do nothing for awhile. Not everybody needs an Internet strategy.

---

[25]Bezos, J., Keynote Speech at Harvard Business School Cyberposium. 26 February 2000.

CASE 2-3
AMAZON.COM VALUATION EXERCISE[1]

We do have to find new operations benchmarks. We do have to shift our expectations and stop just mapping the numbers we've chewed over for decades . . . to every web site we look at. how? I don't know yet. I still haven't found a way to value e-commerce that feels right. But I don't accept the idea that there are no such measures, that quantification is simply impossible.[2]

Traditional valuation techniques use a company's historical performance, standardized industry and company metrics, and forecasts of future market opportunity, and the impact of strategy execution to estimate free cash flow and discounted present value.[3] This approach is designed for companies and industries with a relatively stable capital structure. As such, the approach is less helpful if a company is operating in a high-growth, high-uncertainty, and rapidly changing environment. Furthermore, if a company has not yet generated earnings, the approach becomes highly unreliable and many of the measures cannot be calculated. Needless to say, these traditional techniques don't work when analyzing most new ventures on the Internet.

To address the problems with traditional measures, some analysts and executives developed revenue-based metrics (for example, price-to-sales and revenues-per-share). These measures, however, did not factor in costs or "cash burn" and, therefore, were not useful for measuring overall financial performance. In fact, many of the most "valuable" companies in terms of price-to-revenue and

revenue-per-share were among the firms listed as most likely to run out of cash in Barron's controversial study of "dot-com" balance sheets published in March 2000—immediately before the NASDAQ stock market plunge.[4]

The Business Value Framework, discussed in "Analyzing Business Value," enables a broad-based approach to measuring performance that unites the business fundamentals that drive shareholder value—Concept and Capabilities—with traditional financial measures. These measures are then used as input to a scenario-based approach to valuation that helps account for uncertainty and lack of comparability in the environment, technology, and business models.[5]

Example of a Scenario-Based Valuation of Amazon.com

In April 2001, analysts at ABN AMRO analyzed the value Amazon.com by separating its businesses into its profitable book, music and video division (BMV), and its international

---

[1]This case was prepared by Professor Lynda M. Applegate. Copyright 2000 by the President and Fellows of Harvard College.
Harvard Business School case 800-441
[2]Seymour, J., "How to Value the Web? Heck, There's *Gotta* Be a Way," (www.thestreet.com), October 18, 1999.
[3]For a good review, see: Simons, R. *Performance Measurement and Control Systems for Implementing Strategy.* Prentice Hall, 1999.

[4]Willoughby, J., "Burning up—Warning: Internet companies are running out of cash—fast," *Barron's Online,* March 21, 2000.
[5]The E-Business Value Framework is described in detail in, Applegate, L.M. "Analyzing Business Value," *Building E-Businesses Online,* Boston: HBS Publishing, 2000 (order #800-394). This approach is based on methodology developed by Harvard Business School Professor Paul Gompers and the work of McKinsey consultants published in: Copeland, et al., *Valuation: Measuring and Managing the Value of Companies,* N.Y.: John Wiley and Sons, 2000.

TABLE 1   Traditional Retailer Financial Overview

	Barnes & Noble	Best Buy	Circuit City	Wal-Mart	Amazon	
					Total	BMV
Revenues ($M)	$3,486	$12,494	$12,614	$165,013	$2,762	$1,698
Gross Profit ($M)	$1,002	$2,393	$2,863	$35,349	$241	$163
SG&A ($M)	$651	$1,854	$2,310	$27,040	$558	$91
Operating Income ($M)	$351	$539	$553	$8,309	$317	$71
Gross Margin (%)	29%	19%	23%	21%	9%	10%
SG&A (%)	19%	15%	18%	21%	20%	5%
Operating Margin (%)	10%	4%	4%	5%	−11%	4%
Stock Price ($/share as of close on 4/3/01)	$24.16	$40.06	$11.53	$49.19	$8.63	NM
Earnings per Share (2001 Estimate)	$1.61	$1.81	$0.53	$1.58	-$0.93	NM
P/E	15.0X	22.1X	21.8X	31.1X	NM	NM

Source of Data: ABN AMRO Equity Research, April 4, 2001; BigCharts.com (www.bigcharts.com).
NM = Not Meaningful

and early stage businesses.[6] To support the valuation, they compared Amazon.com with traditional retailers that were trading at between 15 and 30 times estimated earnings per share (see Tables 1, 2 & 3).

Critique the Valuation Scenarios and Adjust Your Value Estimates

Review the Amazon.com performance metrics, summarized in **Appendix A** at the end of this note. Do you agree with the scenarios developed by ABN AMRO analysts for the future state of Amazon.com's revenues and operating income? Do you agree with the decision to compare Amazon.com with traditional retailers? Adjust the scenarios to account for your assumptions about the value of Amazon's current strategy, execution capabilities, and P/E multiples. Using your revised scenarios and

forecasts, estimate the value of Amazon.com. Be prepared to support your value estimates based on your analysis of value drivers presented in Appendix A of this note and discussed in more detail in *Amazon.com 2000* (No. 801-194). It is recommended that readers who wish to conduct a deeper analysis review *Amazon.com: Exploiting the Value of a Digital Business Infrastructure* (No. 800-330).

Identify Strategic Options that Senior Executives Could Pursue to Increase Value

The valuations conducted by ABN AMRO assume that executives do not significantly change company strategy. Do you agree with this approach? What strategic options could the company pursue to increase value? Estimate the impact of different strategic initiatives on the company's value? How much time does the company have to implement these new initiatives? What capabilities and resources would be required?

---

[6]Newman, A., Kolb, D., "Amazon.com," ABN AMRO *Equity Research,* April 4, 2001.

TABLE 2   **Value of the BMV Division**

		Valuation	
		High Multiple (30X)	*Low Multiple (15X)*
Operating Income (01 E)	$83,491,000	$2,504,730,000	$1,252,365,000
Debt	$2,127,464,000		
Cash	$822,435,000		
Marketable Securities (liquid)	$242,087,000		
Net debt	$1,062,942,000		
BMV Allocation (40%)	$425,176,800		
Valuation		$2,079,553,000	$827,188,000
(Equity value per share)		($5.85)	($2.33)

355.7 million shares outstanding (39% = Institutional Ownership; 39% = Insider Ownership)

TABLE 3   **Value of International and Early Stage Businesses (Valuation scenarios are based on these businesses reaching profitability in 2004, 2005 or 2006.)**

	Valuation		
	Best Case	*Expected Case*	*Low Multiple*
Assume operating profit in (weighting)	2004 (25%)	2005 (50%)	2006 (25%)
Revenue in 2000	$1,063,717,000	$1,063,717,000	$1,063,717,000
Revenue growth until profitable	20%	15%	10%
Revenue at profitability	$2,205,724,000	$2,139,515,000	$1,884,440,000
Operating margin at profitability	5%	4%	3%
P/E Multiple	30X	25X	20X
Valuation	$3,308,585,000	$2,139,515,000	$1,130,664,000
Discount rate	12%	12%	12%
Valuation today	$2,354,986,000	$1,359,700,000	$641,569,000
Net debt	$1,062,942,000	$1,062,942,000	$1,062,942,000
Allocation (60%)	$637,765,200	$637,765,200	$637,765,200
Equity value per share	$4.83	$2.03	$0.01
Weighted average value	$791,224,000 ($2.22 per share)		

Source of data for Tables 2 and 3: ABN AMRO Equity Research, April 4, 2001.

A

APPENDIX A   **Amazon.com Value Metrics: Concept**

Business Concept

Market Opportunity

- Online sales of consumer goods in the U.S. in 2000 were $25.8 billion (0.8% of total retail sales), up nearly 50% from 1999. Amazon.com had 10.7% of online sales for 2000 and 11.5% for 4Q2000. Online sales were projected to increase to over $185 billion (or 7% of total retail sales) by 2005.
- Size of Amazon online markets served in early 2000 was $7 billion and projected to be $75.3 billion in 2003 (included 8 retail categories, auctions, zShops, and Commerce Network businesses.)
- 70% of Amazon's 1999 revenues came from U.S. book sales; by 2000, less than half came from U.S. book sales. Amazon's total revenues were $1.6 billion in 1999 and $2.8 billion in 2000.
- Partnered with ToysRus.com in August 2000, closed its online toy store, and opened a co-branded toy store. Amazon reported that 9 week revenues during the holiday season 2000 were $33.5 million and contribution margin was $4 million.

Value Proposition

- Provided customers with vast product selection, convenient and reliable service, easy-to-navigate site, easy-to-use 1-Click shopping, customer reviews, and personalized product recommendations.
- Offered customers discounts (initially, 10% off most books and 40% off New York Times bestsellers). Shipping costs could make products more expensive than if they were bought in the store.
- Offered breadth and depth of products (books, music, videos, DVDs, games, toys, software, garden, and tools, etc.).
- Suppliers (e.g., book publishers, distributors, and authors) gained access to customer information, lower display costs, lower book returns, and unlimited "shelf" space.
- Equity partners, such as Drugstore.com, leveraged Amazon's virtual store "real estate", customer base, brand name, supplier relationships, and knowledge and expertise in e-commerce.
- Amazon's "syndicated selling" partners (also referred to as members of the Associates Program) earned 15% of the value of sales transactions each time they referred a customer who, in turn, purchased on Amazon.com.

Competitive Position

- In 4Q2000, Amazon.com had 67% market share in online retail sales; became #1 online music retailer within one quarter of launch and #1 video retailer within 6 weeks of launch.
- Rivals were traditional book retailers (BN.com and Borders.com), traditional general merchandise retailers (Wal-Mart.com, Sears, Target), and category killers such as Circuit City, ToysRus, eBay, etc.
- In early 21st century, brick and mortar companies (e.g, Wal-Mart) were predicted to be the most significant threat, given powerful existing assets, relationships, and expertise.

Business Context and Risk

- During 2000, investor confidence in online businesses and technology stocks dropped precipitously. Having yet to achieve profitability, Amazon.com became a target for heavy criticism.

- Operating risks—standards indicate that online sites must perform with 99% up-time. During the 1999 holiday season, the Amazon.com site was up over 99% of the time and fulfilled 99% of its customers' orders on time.

- Amazon.com must take special precautions to guard against security risks (customer information, payments, credit card information etc.).

- Human resource talent risk (need to continue to attract and retain good people in the "war for talent"); Amazon.com executives believe that access to top talent is the single most important limiting factor.

- For its online retail businesses, Amazon.com takes on significant inventory risk. During the holiday season 1999, overstocking—especially in consumer electronics and video games/toys led to gross margins of -20% and -15% respectively. The ToysRus.com deal was designed to shift inventory risk to an established brick and mortar retailer while also improving capacity utilization in distribution centers.

- During 2000, Amazon took on significant equity risk by acquiring a percentage ownership of dot-com partners, for example, Drugstore.com, Della.com, living.com, Ashford.com, Sotheby's.com, etc. The decline in Nasdaq market value—especially within Internet sectors—increased equity risk. In August 2000, living.com declared bankruptcy forcing Amazon.com to close its Home Furnishings store just months after its grand opening on May 19, 2000. Amazon recorded a $14 million loss from the living.com bankruptcy.

- In 2000, Amazon.com recorded impairment losses on goodwill and other intangible assets of $184 million on acquisitions that continued to be operated as stand-alone businesses. The company also recorded non-cash investment losses of approximately $35 million (3Q2000) and $155 million (4Q2000) to record "certain investments at fair value."

Strategic Options

- Between summer 1998 and summer 2000, Amazon.com launched over 14 new businesses on its digital infrastructure built for books: 8 online retail stores (e.g., music, videos, toys, software, home improvement, lawn & patio, kitchen), high-end and low-end auctions, and a network of small, medium, and large affiliates—called its Commerce Network—that sold products over the Amazon digital infrastructure.

- In August 2000, Amazon.com and ToysRus.com announced a strategic alliance to create a co-branded toy and video games store. Under terms of the agreement, ToysRus.com, in collaboration with its majority shareholder, Toys "R" Us, Inc., would identify, buy, and manage inventory. Amazon.com would handle site development, order fulfillment, and customer service, housing both ToysRus.com's and its own inventory in Amazon.com's U.S. distribution centers. The agreement also allowed for global expansion of the arrangement. Under the terms of the 10-year agreement, Amazon.com would be compensated through a combination of periodic fixed payments, per-unit payments, and a "single-digit percentage" of revenue. Amazon.com would also receive warrants entitling it to acquire 5 percent of ToysRus.com. All parties, including Toys "R" Us, Inc., would market the co-branded store to their respective customers.

- In November 2000, Amazon.com launched its e-book store for distribution of books, audiobooks, and CDs. In January 2001, BN.com announced launch of BN Digital, which would source and sell e-books direct from authors; e-book prices would be between $5.95 to $7.95; BN Digital announced it would pay authors 35% royalties, up from 10% traditional royalty payment; Random House announced it would pay 50% royalties on its e-book offerings. In February 2001, Amazon and MGM Home Entertainment announced a partnership to distribute MGM films, many never before released on VHS, available exclusively on Amazon.com for $7.99. In February 2001, Amazon announced digital distribution of Intuit's popular TurboTax software. The war for digital distribution began heating up.

APPENDIX A (CONTINUED)   Amazon.com Sample Value Metrics: Capabilities

Operating Performance (except as indicated in the table, data are for 1999)

Operating Performance

- During 1999, Amazon.com spent $300 to $400 million building order fulfillment and customer service operating capabilities. By year-end, Amazon had 9 distribution centers and 7 customer service centers; all were state-of-the-art web-enabled operations that were electronically linked with suppliers, customers, and partners, enabling real-time transactions and information exchange.
- In early 2000, Amazon had roughly 70 to 80% overcapacity in its warehouse distribution centers (estimated to total 5 million square feet) and had capacity to ship an estimated $10 billion annually.
- Inventory turnover slowed to less than 9 in 1Q 2000 due to greater volumes of inventory in company distribution/warehouses. Inventory turns increased to 18 by 4Q 2000.
- Order fulfillment costs were 16% in 1999, compared with 11.4% at BN.com. Fulfillment costs decreased to 13% of sales in 2000; in early 2000, Barnesandnoble.com (BN.com) estimated that its fulfillment costs would rise from 11% to 13% in 2000.

Customer- & Community-Focused Quality

- While other retailers struggled, 99% of Amazon.com customer orders were fulfilled on time during the 1999 and 2000 holiday seasons and the site was up over 99% of the time.
- Amazon offered return rates to publishers/distributors of less than 10%; in 1998, average return rates of hardcover book returns to publishers were 30%, up from 15% in the 1980's.
- Very high quality standards; "Customer Obsession" was one of six "Core Values".

Information and Knowledge Assets

Strong Leadership

- Jeff Bezos, founder and CEO, was Time Magazine 1999 Man of the Year.
- Successful at attracting top talent.
- Warren Jensen, CFO, who joined in September 1999, was CFO and EVP at Delta Airlines, supervising restructuring, and CFO and SVP at NBC (a subsidiary of General Electric).
- David Risher, SVP and GM U.S. Retail, who joined in February 1997, was SVP of Product Development at Microsoft.
- Jeff Wilke, VP and GM Operations, who joined in September 1999, was VP and GM of Pharmaceutical Fine Chemicals at Allied Signal and a consultant at Andersen Consulting, now Accenture.
- Richard Dazell, CIO, and 14 others were recruited from Wal-Mart. In 1998, Wal-Mart sued Amazon for "improper recruitment of intellectual assets." The suit was dropped several months later.

Expertise and Skills

- Amazon had deep expertise and was considered "best-in-class" in e-business brand management, order fulfillment, customer service, technology infrastructure, and e-commerce.
- In 1999, Amazon had 7,600 full and part-time employees; labor relations difficulties had begun to be reported at distribution and customer service centers.
- Amazon.com's sales per employee were estimated to be $373,000 in 2000, compared to $161,000 at Wal-Mart and $104,000 at Barnes & Noble.
- Amazon had patents on its 1-Click shopping technology and its syndicated selling program. It's Bid-Click auction technology was trademarked.

APPENDIX A (CONTINUED)   Amazon.com Sample Value Metrics: Capabilities

Development & Retention of Employees, Partners and Expertise
- HR (called "Strategic Growth") spent a significant amount of time and energy hiring entrepreneurial, energetic, and customer-centric people and who had right fit for culture.
- Finding top talent was considered a key barrier to growth.
- Joe Galli, who joined as president and COO in summer 1999, left 1 year later to become CEO of VerticalNet.

Informed Decision Making and Action
- Because Amazon.com built and owned its own infrastructure, it controlled information collected on each and every activity for each and every transaction with suppliers, customers, partners, and internal employees.
- Sophisticated data mining was combined with real-time information to enable employees, customers, suppliers, and partners to make informed decisions, personalize products and services, and evolve the business model.

Information Value-Added Products & Services
- Information value-added—especially in the form of community reviews and personalized marketing and sales—was key to personalization and customer retention.
- Information on customer preferences and cross-selling opportunities was sold to publishers, key authors, distributors, and other category suppliers.
- Because real-time information and demand was shared with suppliers, Amazon.com was able to use the "Dell Computer" model for inventory management; most books were ordered from distributors at the time of purchase by consumers.
- Because of more frequent ordering, Amazon was able to give suppliers a better view of real-time demand.

Community Penetration and Loyalty (except as indicated in the table, data are for 1999)

Community Penetration
- Over 19.8 million active customers in December 2000; Up from 16 million in December 1999.
- Over 25 million unique visitors by October 2000.
- Over 31 million units were ordered and shipped between November 2 and December 23, 2000.
- Reach as of April 2000 was 18% vs. BN.com (7%) and Borders.com (1.2%).
- Equity partners in its "Commerce Network" included: online brand-name partners (e.g., Drugstore.com, Della.com) and traditional merchants (e.g., Sotheby's); These partners sold their products using the Amazon.com digital infrastructure. Also, thousands of small merchants sold products through Amazon.com's online mall (called its zShops), "renting space" on Amazon.com for $9.99 per month and paying a 1–5% transaction fee. In August 2000, Amazon.com outsourced its customer-facing and order fulfillment/inventory management/distribution capabilities to ToysRus.com to create a co-branded online toy and video game store.
- 350,000 distribution partnerships, including all major horizontal portals (e.g., AOL, Yahoo!, Excite, Netscape, MSN, and GeoCities), and a wide range of vertical portals and focused distributors (e.g., E*Trade, Quicken.com, Women.com); Amazon calls this its "Associate Network." These partners use Amazon's patented "Syndicated Selling" approach through which they offer Amazon.com books with personalized reviews to meet their community's unique interests. Amazon pays a referral fee of up to 15% for each book sold by a partner.

APPENDIX A (CONTINUED)   Amazon.com Sample Value Metrics: Capabilities

Personalization

- Online store and service were personalized for each registered user. In early 2000, Bezos commented: "If we have 17 million customers, we will have 17 million stores."
- Recognized as "best-in-class" in providing a personalized online experience.

Community Loyalty

- Repeat business was over 75% of sales in fourth quarter of 2000.
- In early 2000, 50% of polled Amazon consumer electronics shoppers said that their online experience was better than traditional offline experience; 90% responded that they would buy consumer electronics from the company again.
- Average sales per active customer in 2000 increased to $135, up from $116 in 1999 and $106 in 1998.
- "Commerce Network" equity partners were estimated to generate $1 billion in revenues through 2005. These partners paid a fee—for example, Greenlight.com paid $82.5 million over 5 years—to leverage Amazon's digital business infrastructure, including customers, suppliers, technology, brand, and expertise; Amazon also received a percentage of every transaction.

Cost to Acquire and Serve Customers and other Community Members

- During its first year of operations, the company did not spend money on advertising; the business grew by word-of-mouth—called "viral marketing."
- Traditionally, Amazon.com had much lower customer acquisition costs than other dot-coms— approximately $15 to $18 per customer during the second quarter of 1999 (depending on analyst report); during 2000, the company reported that its costs per customer decreased to $13.
- *The Industry Standard* (5/1/2000) reported that the average dot-com spent $82 to acquire a customer in 1999, up from an average of $42 in 1998. This compared with an average of $12 for traditional brick-and-mortar (or multi-channel) businesses. Forrester (2/2/2000) reported that E*Trade spent $289 per customer in acquisition costs in 1999.
- During 1998, Amazon spent only 10% of sales on advertising, whereas BN.com and eBay spent 52% and 26% respectively; marketing and sales costs increased from $413 million in 1999 (25% of sales) to $594 million in 2000 (21% of sales).
- *The Industry Standard* (5/1/2000) reported that overall 1999 marketing expenses as a % of revenues averaged: Dot-coms (119%); traditional catalog-based retailer (6%); and traditional store-based retailer (36%).
- Amazon's syndicated selling network (its "Associates Program") served as a low-cost sales force.

Lifetime Value of a Community Member

- In 1999, the average Amazon customer contributed $116 per year in revenues. Subtract $18 in acquisition costs and costs to serve of $129.07, which included roughly $52.70—operating expense per customer—and $76.47—cost of sales per customer.
- The lifetime value of "non-customer" community members—for example, publishers, distribution partners (Affiliates)—is not available.
- *The Industry Standard* (3/20/2000) reported that the gross income from a typical dot-com retail customer (after subtracting operating costs) was $24.50 during the first quarter of retention and $52.50 in each subsequent quarter that the customer purchases from the online retailer. But over two-thirds of all e-retail customers did not make repeat purchases. In addition, for each repeat buyer in 1999, an average dot-com spent $1,931 per year to keep its site up and running. (There was high variability in this number based on number of years of operation and technological sophistication of operations.)

APPENDIX A (CONTINUED)   Amazon.com Sample Value Metrics: Capabilities

Brand Equity

- In early 2001, Gomez rated Amazon the number one book, music, video, toy, electronics, and home improvement online store. Amazon was rated the number two auction site behind eBay.
- Opinion Research found that 60% of U.S. adults were aware of the Amazon brand, which ranked as the highest awareness of any e-commerce brand name.
- Interbrand ranked Amazon.com as the 57th most valuable brand, between Pampers and Hilton.

APPENDIX A   Amazon.com Sample Value Metrics: Shareholder Value

Shareholder Value

Shareholder Confidence and Trust

- Stock price closed at $46.875 on Friday, April 14, 2000, following its fifty-two week high on December 9, 1999 of $113.00 per share; stock price on 2/10/01 was $13 3/8 per share.
- $500 million market value at IPO in May 1997; $36 billion in December 1999; $25 billion in April 2000; $4.8 billion on 2/10/01.
- Earnings per share (12/31/2000): $-$4.02

Earnings and Margins

Net sales were $2.8 billion in 2000, up from $1.6 billion in 1999.

- Gross profit was $655.8 million in 2000, up from $290.6 million in 1999; gross profit margin in 2000 was 23.7%, up from 17.7% in 1999.
- Operating expenses were $1.5 billion in 2000, up from $896 million in 1999; operating margin was -11.5% in 2000, up from -21.5% in 1999.
- Operating loss (before interest and taxes) was $864 million in 2000, up from $600 million in 1999.
- Net loss was $1.4 billion in 2000, up from $720 million in 1999.
- Service revenues from Commerce Network Partners (including ToysRus.com) contributed only 6% to revenues in 2000 but generated over 17% gross profit.
- US Books, Music, DVD/Video represented 61.5% of sales in 2000 and $417.5 million in gross profit; gross profit margin was 24.6% and operating margin was 4.2%
- Early stage businesses represented 24.7% of sales in 2000 and $160.9 million in gross profit; gross profit margin was 23.6% and operating margin was -35.7%.
- International represented 13.8% of sales in 2000 and $77.4 million in gross profit; gross profit margin was 13.8% and operating margin was -38.1%.
- Reported gross margin for Amazon's online retail businesses in Q499 varied widely (from -20% to $+22\%$); 4Q99 gross margins for its auction business was reported as 45%. Overall gross margin in 2000 averaged 21% to 25%. By comparison, Barnesandnoble.com gross margin was 15% to 19% and Buy.com was 4% to 6%.
- Unlike most other retailers and many dot-coms, Amazon.com does not include fulfillment expenses in its cost of sales. When adjusted to include fulfillment costs, gross margin was 8.7% in 2000. (Newman, A. and Kolb, D., "Amazon.com," *ABN AMRO Investment Research*, April 4, 2001).
- Operating margin (excluding fulfillment costs) improved from -26% in 4Q1999 to -6% in 4Q2000.

APPENDIX A (CONTINUED)   Amazon.com Sample Value Metrics: Shareholder Value

Working Capital

As of year-end 2000:

• Working capital: $425 million.

• Current ratio: $1.44, up from $1.37 in 1999.

• $2.1 billion in total assets; down from $2.4 billion in 1999.

• $366 million fixed assets (net); up from $318 million in 1999.

• $96 million other purchased intangibles; down from $195 million in 1999.

• $52 million in equity-method investments; down from $226 million in 1999.

• $40 million in other investments.

• Long-term debt = $2.1 billion; up from $1.5 billion in 1999.

• In 4Q2000, total liabilities (long-term debt and capital leases) exceeded total assets. Analysts estimated that total liabilities could exceed total assets by as much as $500 million in 2001.

Ratios

• Return on equity: Not meaningful (due to negative earnings).

• Return on assets: −66.1%.

Free Cash Flow and Economic Profit

• Since going public in 1997, Amazon.com had not yet generated a profit.

CASE 2–4
AMERICAN EXPRESS INTERACTIVE[1]

American Express had its roots in the wild west of the 1850s. We started as the Wells Fargo stagecoach business, then we evolved into the pony express. For over 100 years, our company has been a pioneer. . . We invented Travelers Cheques for the business traveler and the corporate card and purchase card to help our corporate customers manage and control their expenses . . . Now we are developing a new Internet travel service that we believe will meet the needs of today's companies and business travelers and will, once more, redefine the world of corporate travel.

Senior Executive, *American Express, 1997*

In November 1997, American Express Corporation (AMEX) (www.americanexpress.com) launched its first Internet business, AXI Travel. With that bold move, the company announced its intention to integrate its traditional "brick and mortar" business model with the Internet's "click and order" approach. In a stirring 1997 speech, an AMEX senior executive called on corporate customers to work with the company to redefine corporate travel for the information age.

> Some people think that the new Internet technologies will be harmful to the industry. Some of you have raised the question that, given our investment in the current way of doing business, why do we want to change? Well the answer is simple. When change is inevitable you have a choice: you can either follow or you can lead. And we all know that nine times out of ten, the leader will get a disproportionate share of the gains. So we intend to lead. We know that we are better off working with you [our corporate customers] to define the game rather than to respond to someone else's standards.

With the support of existing and new customers, AXI Travel was launched in November 1997. By late 1999, the online/offline travel service had been adopted by over 240 corporations in the United States and abroad. Building on the success and momentum from AXI Travel, American Express launched other online businesses including AXI Expense (1998), AXI Purchasing Solutions (1999), and American Express @Work (1999). In November 1999, the company announced an alliance to develop its B2B Commerce Network—a business-to-business (B2B) marketplace designed to simplify corporate purchasing, create easy-to-use payment services, and enable a wide range of B2B suppliers to quickly and inexpensively participate in online commerce.

These new e-business initiatives were launched and operated by the company's Corporate Services Interactive (CSI) business unit, which was established in 1997 to develop and launch AXI Travel. During the development of AXI Travel, the CSI team, in partnership with Microsoft, moved to offices outside AMEX's corporate headquarters and was dedicated to building AXI Travel in the style of an entrepreneurial start-up company with its own marketing, sales, product development and business development resources.[2] This enabled the team to devote their attention to

---

[1]This case was prepared by Professor Lynda M. Applegate and High Tech Fellow Pauline Fischer. Copyright © 2001 by the President and Fellows of Harvard College. Harvard Business School case 399-014.

[2]Well-regarded and influential executives from Business Development, Marketing and Travel Related Services were chosen to serve on the AXI Travel e-business development team.

EXHIBIT 1   American Express Organization Chart, 1999 (Casewriter interpretation)

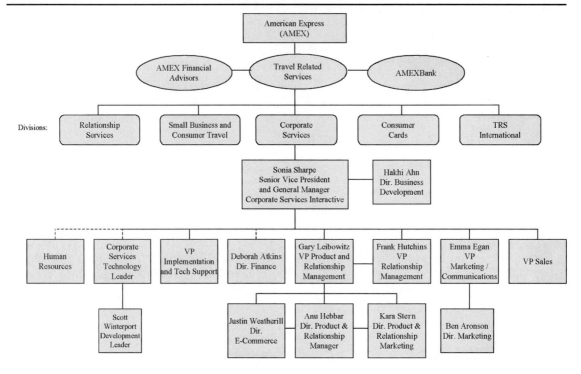

building the new venture. With the launch of AXI Travel, the team returned to corporate headquarters and became the CSI business unit. (See Exhibit 1 for an organization chart on June 1, 2000.) CSI was run by Sonia Sharpe who rejoined the company in July 1998 after the departure of the initial head of the CSI unit who left AMEX to become CEO of an Internet start-up. (See Exhibit 2 for short bios of CSI executives.)

Throughout the late 1990s, CSI served an important role—conceiving, incubating, and launching new e-businesses. But, as new businesses, like AXI Travel, gained traction in the marketplace, it became increasingly clear that they needed to be fully integrated with the company's traditional "brick and mortar" businesses or be spun off as separate businesses. By summer 2000, the company had begun an

extensive evaluation of the role of CSI within the company and of each e-business initiative that it had launched.

Company Background

Founded in 1850, American Express was a diversified, global travel and financial services company. In early 2000, the company was organized around three segments: Travel Related Services, Financial Advisors, and the American Express Bank. (See Exhibit 3 for financial information.) American Express Travel Related Services Company, Inc. (TRS), a wholly owned subsidiary of American Express Company, was a leader in charge and credit cards, Travelers Cheques, and travel services. TRS was composed of several product areas, including Consumer Cards, Small

Exhibit 2   Biographies of Key Personnel

Sonia Sharpe, General Manager

Sonia Sharpe was appointed General Manager of Corporate Services Interactive (CSI) on October 6, 1998. Sharpe led efforts to create and manage innovative technology products for travel, expense management and purchasing. In the three years preceding her role as head of CSI, Sharpe was President of Gemplus, U.S. and Canada, a French-based company specializing in smart card and magnetic strip technology. During Sharpe's tenure at Gemplus revenues of the U.S division increased from less than $5 million to more than $50 million. Before Gemplus, Sharpe worked at American Express Europe attaining the position of Corporate Services' Vice President of Marketing and Product Development. Sharpe has also worked as a consultant for McKinsey & Co. in Asia and Europe and worked for Rohm & HAAS Company as both Technical Sales Representative and Manufacturing Engineer/Supervisor. Ms. Sharpe has a BS in Chemical Engineering with honors from Tufts University and earned her MBA, concentrating in Corporate Finance, from the Wharton School.

Emma Egan, Vice President, Marketing

Emma Egan managed the marketing of AXI Travel, as well as Corporate Services Interactive's other product lines. Prior to joining AMEX, Egan worked at Berlitz International where she was Creative Director for the translation and publishing divisions and later Director of Business Development. Egan also worked as Director of New Business Development for AMEX's Relationship Services. She received a bachelor's degree from the University of Florida.

Frank Hutchins, Vice President, Relationship Management

Frank Hutchins led the original team that was stationed in Redmond to assist Microsoft with the development of AXI Travel. Prior to that, Hutchins was Director of Technology Consulting for American Express. Hutchins received a bachelor's degree from the University of Detroit.

Gary Leibowitz, Vice President, Product and Relationship Management

Gary Leibowitz was responsible for developing and bringing to market web-based business solutions, including AXI Travel, for the American Express corporate client base. Leibowitz received a masters degree in computer science from New York University and a MA from Columbia University.

Hakhi Ahn, Director of Business Development

Hakhi Ahn led business development for Corporate Services Interactive. Prior to this role, Ahn was Marketing Manager for the Expense Reporting Software group at AMEX, where she gained extensive experience in pricing products and marketing corporate applications software. Prior to joining AMEX in 1997, Ahn worked as a Product Manager and Marketing Manager for 3M, where she managed the diskette product line. Ahn received a bachelor of science degree in finance from the Wharton School, and an MBA from Carnegie Mellon University.

Deborah Atkins, Director of Finance

Deborah Atkins led the finance function at Corporate Services Interactive. Prior to that, Atkins was a Senior Manager for the Interactive Travel Group at Corporate Services, as well as a Business Development Manager for AERS. Atkins also spent time as an Analyst and Manager for the Consumer Card Group and the Travelers Cheque Group at AMEX. Atkins has a bachelor of science degree from the State University of New York at Albany, and a MBA from New York University.

(continued)

EXHIBIT 2 (CONTINUED)   Biographies of Key Personnel

Anu Hebbar, Director, Product and Relationship Management

Anu Hebbar played key role in working with Microsoft to design AXI Travel and in the global launch of AXI Travel. Hebbar received a masters degree in hotel, restaurant, and travel administration from the University of Massachusetts at Amherst.

Miriam Klein, Director of International Smartcard Division

Miriam Klein, who joined American Express in 1994, was a member of the original team that developed AXI Travel. Klein played a key role in analyzing competitive product offerings and in managing the relationship with Microsoft. From June 1996 to February 1998, Klein helped build AXI Travel, as George Cole's Director of Business Development. Klein received a bachelors degree from the College of William and Mary and a MBA from Columbia University.

Kara Stern, Director Product & Relationship Management

Kara Stern was an original member to the team that created AMEX's interactive travel strategy. Stern was particularly active in evaluating new partnership opportunities and competitive offerings. Prior to joining Corporate Services Interactive, Stern worked in Relationship Marketing for Corporate Services. Stern received a bachelor's degree from The George Washington University and a MBA from New York University.

Justin Weatherill, Director of Electronic Commerce

Justin Weatherill led the division's electronic commerce initiatives and played a key role in developing AMEX's corporate purchasing card. Weatherill received a bachelor of science degree from the University of Massachusetts at Amherst.

Scott Winterport, Development Leader

Scott Winterport managed the software and network architecture development. Prior to that, Winterport was the development manager for American Express' Management Information Systems group. Winterport has a BS from Texas A&M University, where he majored in computer science, and a MBA from Texas A&M University.

Business and Consumer travel, Corporate Services, TRS International, and American Express Consulting Services.

Corporate Services specialized in offering corporate charge cards, corporate purchasing cards, consulting on expense management strategies, and corporate travel services. Through its Corporate Services group, TRS had more than 70% of the Fortune 500 as customers of its business travel and/or Corporate Card programs. At the time of the AXI Travel launch in 1997, Corporate Services recorded $17.4 billion in worldwide travel sales, a large portion of which were from international markets, ranking it among the largest business travel agencies in the world. Travel sales included trip planning, reservations, ticketing and other incidental services. In addition, TRS provided corporate travel policy consultation and management. Supporting TRS throughout the world were 1,700 company-owned and affiliated owner-managed retail travel offices.

Corporate Services Interactive (CSI), a division of Corporate Services, focused on developing new ventures that leveraged the Internet and related technologies. In late

EXHIBIT 3   American Express Consolidated Statement of Income

Years Ended December 31, *(Millions, except per share amounts)*	*1999*	*1998*	*1997*
Revenues			
Discount revenue	$6,741	$6,115	$5,666
Interest and dividends, net	3,346	3,277	3,175
Management and distribution fees	2,269	1,851	1,486
Net card fees	1,599	1,587	1,604
Travel commissions and fees	1,802	1,647	1,489
Other commissions and fees	1,824	1,657	1,475
Cardmember lending net finance charge revenue	1,333	1,354	1,244
Life and other insurance premiums	517	469	424
Other commissions and fees	1,847	1,175	1,197
Total	21,278	19,132	17,760
Expenses			
Human resources	6,038	5,470	4,763
Provisions for losses and benefits:			
Annuities and investment certificates	1,377	1,425	1,414
Life insurance, international banking and other	639	822	567
Charge card	865	701	858
Cardmember lending	799	922	817
Interest	1,051	999	924
Marketing and promotion	1,424	1,228	1,118
Occupancy and equipment	1,328	1,250	1,139
Professional services	1,322	1,191	1,028
Communications	518	474	450
Other	2,479	1,725	1,932
Total	17,840	16,207	15,010
Pretax income	3,438	2,925	2,750
Income tax provision	963	784	759
Net income	$2,475	$2,141	$1,991
Earnings per Common Share			
Basic	$5.54	$4.71	$4.29
Diluted	$5.42	$4.63	$4.15
Average common shares outstanding **for earnings per common share (millions):**			
Basic	447	454	464
Diluted	456	463	479

EXHIBIT 3 (CONTINUED)   American Express Consolidated Statement of Income

December 31, (Millions, except share data)	1999	1998
Assets		
Cash and cash equivalents	$7,471	$4,092
Accounts receivable and accrued interest:		
Cardmember receivables, less reserves: 1999, $728; 1998, $524	22,541	19,176
Other receivables, less reserves: 1999, $169; 1998 $214	3,926	3,048
Investments	43,502	41,299
Loans		
Cardmember lending, less reserves: 1999, $581; 1998, $593	17,666	14,721
International banking, less reserves: 1999, $169; 1998, $214	4,928	5,404
Other, net	988	929
Separate account assets	35,895	27,349
Deferred acquisition costs	3,235	2,990
Land, buildings and equipment—at cost, less accumulated depreciation:		
1999, $2,109; 1998, $2,067	1,996	1,637
Other assets	6,819	6,288
Total assets	$148,517	$126,933
Liabilities and Shareholders' Equity		
Customers' deposits	$12,197	$10,398
Travelers Cheques outstanding	6,213	5,823
Accounts payable	7,309	5,373
Insurance and annuity reserves:		
Fixed annuities	20,552	21,172
Life and disability policies	4,459	4,261
Investment certificate reserve	5,951	4,854
Short-term debt	30,627	22,605
Long-term debt	5,995	7,019
Separate account liabilities	35,895	27,349
Other liabilities	8,724	7,881
Total liabilities	137,922	116,735
Guaranteed preferred beneficial interests in the company's junior subordinated deferrable interest debentures	500	500
Shareholders' Equity:		
Common shares, $.60 par value, authorized 1.2 billion shares; issued and outstanding 446.9 million shares in 1999 and 450.5 million shares in 1998	268	270
Capital surplus	5,196	4,809
Retained earnings	5,033	4,148
Other comprehensive income, net of tax:		
Net unrealized securities (losses)/gains	-296	583
Foreign currency translation adjustments	-106	-112
Accumulated other comprehensive (loss)/income	-402	471
Total shareholders' equity	10,095	9,698
Total liabilities and shareholders' equity	$148,517	$126,933

EXHIBIT 3 (CONTINUED)   **American Express Consolidated Statement of Income**

Years Ended Decemebr 31, (Millions)	1999	1998	1997
Cash Flows from Operating Activities			
Net income	2,475	2,141	1,991
Adjustments to reconcile net income to net cash provided by operating activities:			
Provisions for losses and benefits	2,392	2,491	2,307
Depreciation, amortization, deferred taxes and other	13	−212	187
Changes in operating assets and liabilities, net of effects of acquisitions and dispositions:			
Accounts receivable and accrued interest	−1,079	−665	−227
Other assets	−294	92	334
Accounts payable and other liabilities	3,313	131	517
Increase (decrease) in Travelers Cheques outstanding	392	253	−111
Increase in insurance reserves	173	182	172
Net cash provided by operating activities	7,385	4,413	5,170
Cash Flows from Investing Activities			
Sale of investments	3,031	1,656	1,778
Maturity and redemption of investments	5,279	7,331	4,827
Purchase of investments	−11,287	−10,176	−7,898
Net increase in Cardmember receivables	−3,988	−1,510	−2,575
Cardmember loans/receivables sold to trust, net	3,586	1,683	516
Proceeds from repayment of loans	22,148	224,791	25,591
Issuance of loans	−29,707	−27,587	−29,304
Purchase of land, buildings and equipment	−737	−392	−343
Sale of land, buildings and equipment	11	26	164
(Acquisitions) dispositions, net of cash acquired/sold	−82	−471	23
Net cash used in investing activities	−11,746	−4,648	−7,221
Cash Flows from Financing Activities			
Net increase in customers' deposits	1,911	1,039	733
Sale of annuities and investment certificates	5,719	5,337	5,888
Redemption of annuities and investment certificates	−5,504	−5,690	−4,965
Net increase in debt with maturities of 3 months or less	305	1,239	3,823
Issuance of debt	18,623	7,373	11,439
Principal payments on debt	−12,049	−7,426	−11,604
Issuance of Trust preferred securities	—	500	—
Issuance of American Express common shares	233	137	168
Repurchase of American Express common shares	−1,120	−1,890	−1,259
Dividends paid	−404	141	−423
Net cash provided by financing activities	7,714	205	3,800
Effect of exchange rate changes on cash	26	−247	−247
Net increase (decrease) in cash and cash equivalents	3,379	1,502	1,502
Cash and cash equivalents at beginning of year	4,092	2,677	2,677
Cash and cash equivalents at end of year	7,471	4,092	4,179

EXHIBIT 3 (CONTINUED)   American Express Consolidated Statement of Income

Years Ended December 31, ($Millions)	1999	1998	1997
Net Revenues			
Discount Revenue	6,741	6,115	5,666
Net Card Fees	1,604	1,584	1,609
Travel Commissions and Fees	1,802	1,647	1,489
Other Revenues	2,827	2,225	2,002
Lending:			
Finance Charge Revenue	2,884	2,470	2,105
Interest Expense	955	810	694
Net Finance Charge Revenue	1,929	1,660	1,411
Total Net Revenues	14,903	13,231	12,177
Expenses			
Marketing and Promotion	1,215	1,094	990
Provision for Losses and Claims:			
Charge Card	995	994	1,105
Lending:	1,186	1,093	937
Other	56	56	57
Total	2,237	2,143	2,099
Charge Card Interest Expense	1,055	1,040	973
Human Resources	3,860	3,544	3,076
Other Operating Expenses	4,149	3,346	3,254
Total Expenses	12,516	11,167	10,392
Pretax Income	2,387	2,064	1,785
Income Tax Provision	825	700	621
Net Income	1,562	1,364	1,164

1999, CSI had five main service offerings: AXI Travel, AXI Expense, AXI Purchasing Solutions, American Express@Work, and its B2B Commerce Network e-procurement portal. As General Manager of CSI, Sonia Sharpe was responsible for all five products.

Building AXI Travel

In the late 1800s when steamships were first coming in, a lot of the old time shippers resisted them because they were noisy, and they were smelly and they were pretty ugly. Some used existing technology to build sailboats to compete [with the steamships]. These boats were beautiful, and they were fast, but their range was small and they were made completely obsolete when the technology for the steamships advanced. I think the analogy for the travel business is pretty clear. We have an obligation to ourselves and to our customers to make our current systems as efficient as possible, but American Express is not going to get trapped with a dead technology. We intend to lead in defining the next generation of systems and to get there before our entrenched competitors do. So the question is how fast and how far do we want to go? And this is where we need some assistance from you. Sometimes a leader can get so far ahead that they don't have any followers. We don't want that to happen. And other times a leader gets so far off track that they get lost and shot, and we don't want that to happen either. We need to make sure we are moving forward on this new path, but we are moving at a pace, and tracking in a direction that makes sense.

Senior Executive, American Express, in a 1997 speech to corporate travel customers.

AMEX recognized the potential of the Internet and started to explore interactive travel options as early as 1995. Part of the impetus for AMEX's interest in interactive travel was internal and external research dating from August 1995 to March 1996 that found that a number of companies in the corporate travel industry were developing interactive travel products. AMEX needed to move quickly if it wanted to be a leader. In addition, the study highlighted that the profitability of AMEX's traditional business would continue to erode. At the time, AMEX Business Travel's primary revenue source was commissions paid to it by airlines. But, by the mid–1990s, airlines were cutting their commission rates. Simultaneously, the cost of providing travel service was increasing as competition for travel counselors increased due to travel industry growth and competition from other industries for skilled customer service labor. This added to the cost to recruit and train the nearly 12,000 travel counselors employed by AMEX. It was expected that an online travel product would reduce—but not replace—the cost of human travel counselors and of physical brick and mortar and administrative infrastructure. It would also help solve the problem of industry-wide travel counselor shortages.

While the team agreed with the analysis, they realized that another important reason for entering this market was to establish a leadership position in defining the standards for a new channel for B2B commerce. The team knew that to maintain its leadership in the corporate travel industry, AMEX would have to set the standard for corporate travel services on the Internet. In doing so, AMEX would establish a new channel to transact business, share information and interact with its corporate customers. While it was impossible to quantify the value of the "strategic options"[3] that could be pursued once an online channel to corporate customers was in place, all agreed that the follow-on business opportunities would be a significant component of the company's strategy in the years to come. Gary Leibowitz explained.

Once we have an electronic relationship, we have a great communication channel with a corporate customer. It allows us to create additional icons on the AXI Travel web site through which we can present driving directions and travel information. We can enable business travelers to make hotel, restaurant, and car service reservations, and we can even help them obtain passports. More importantly, it also allows us to offer other AXI products to provide one-stop shopping for expense management, purchasing and a wide variety of other business services. The possibilities are limitless.

Finding a Technology Partner

For the interactive travel product to "set the standard," Sharpe's predecessor believed it was critical to enter the market quickly with a product that linked to existing computer reservations systems (CRS) and that ran on most standard technology hardware and software.

---

[3]See Applegate, L. M., "Creating E-Business Value," an online course available from *Harvard Business School Publishing* (#5238P2), for an in-depth discussion of the "options value" of investments in a digital business infrastructure.

Because speed to market was important and its core competencies were not in software development, AMEX decided to partner with a technology firm. After evaluating partnership options in 1996, the company chose Microsoft to be its software development partner.

Given the experimental—and potentially disruptive—nature of the project, the AXI Travel team decided to find a separate location so that they could concentrate on building the new service without undue influence from the traditional AMEX businesses. Miriam Klein, director of International Corporate Services, commented: "It made a big difference in terms of focus and speed of implementation, and it separated us from the politics that were sure to surround the new business."

Once established in their New York City off-site office building, the AXI Travel team wasted no time in getting started. Some of the members of the development team immediately relocated to Redmond, Washington, where they worked side-by-side with the Microsoft developers. Anu Hebbar, director of product and relationship management, served as the Microsoft relationship manager and headed the team located in Redmond. "If you want to partner with Microsoft," he explained, "you have to work in Redmond."

It's important to be there day-to-day. We knew how the travel business worked and they knew how the technology worked. You can't design a new online business unless you have deep knowledge of both the business and the technology. But, we also needed to keep in direct contact with the team back in New York. So, every Wednesday morning we conducted a team meeting by teleconference so that we could exchange information and plan the next week's work.

Despite the fact that the AMEX/Microsoft development team did not start coding the system until January 1997,[4] AXI Travel was pre-announced with a great deal of fanfare at

the National Business Travel Association annual convention. Some questioned this decision fearing that pre-announcement would "tip the company's hand" and alert competitors to their plans. "Our critics didn't understand that AXI Travel was designed as a business-to-business travel service—not a consumer or leisure travel service," a member of the AXI Travel team explained.

Products and services for large corporate clients are sold very differently. Companies typically need to develop an RFP and—especially back then—it could take months to get it approved through the corporate budgeting process. Those delays actually worked to our advantage. By pre-announcing the product with Microsoft as a partner, we alerted our current and potential customers that we had an exciting new interactive travel service on the way. That enabled us to head people off from trying out a competitor's product. It also gave us time to develop a world-class, "industrial-strength" service that would integrate with our customers' existing business processes and technologies.

The relationship with Microsoft also enabled the AXI Travel team to capitalize on the excitement being generated by the emerging Internet economy. And, at the time, the West Coast was viewed as the place to be. "Everyone wanted to know what Microsoft was doing," an AXI Travel team member stated. In February 1997, AMEX and Microsoft jointly sponsored a client event in Redmond to which 150 corporate travel managers and CIO's from large global corporations were invited. "While 150 companies may not seem like a lot, the companies represented at that meeting accounted for 12% of the total volume of travel-related services in the U.S." Bill Gates, CEO of Microsoft, and Ed Gilligan, president, Corporate Services, gave the keynote addresses, visibly uniting the two firms' brands in the minds of the customers.

The purpose of the event was twofold. "It helped keep our corporate customers interested and aware of our progress and it also enabled us to get feedback on their expectations and our progress-to-date," an AMEX manager explained. "Everyone wanted to go to

---

[4]Up until that time, Microsoft developers were still building the travel engine that would power both Expedia (launched in late 1996) and AXI Travel.

Redmond in those days. In fact, we invited one company per day, four days per week, for almost 1½ years to come to Redmond and provide us feedback. We built a waiting list of customers and were able to pre-sell the product to them even before it was officially launched."

Following the Redmond event, Karen Stern, relationship manager of the corporate travel managers located at customer sites, launched a client-trial program. Initially 30 companies participated. Over the course of the rollout, the number of participating companies grew to 150. In March 1997, members of the trial program were given a password-protected demonstration site that provided users with a chance to preview AXI Travel and give feedback on it prior to implementing it in their respective companies. Feedback from the trial was incorporated into the product.

Continuing to keep the momentum alive, in July 1997, a beta version of AXI Travel was demonstrated at the National Business Travel Association annual meeting. It was at this event, that the first electronic ticket was issued to the Director of Monsanto's corporate travel program.

AXI Travel Version 1.0 was officially launched in November 1997, less than one year after the team began development. Updates were launched in March 1998 and June 1998, thus beginning a rapid period of product evolution and enhancement that continued throughout the time of the case.

By February 1998, 50,000 business travelers in 225 corporations were users of the online service, which accounted for $4.8 billion in total travel volume (online and traditional). Early adopters included Monsanto, Chrysler, Novartis and Polaroid.

AMEX and GetThere, Inc.

In March of 1999, AMEX's exclusive agreement with Microsoft expired, and the two companies jointly decided to renew the relationship on a non-exclusive basis. Sharpe sought out other

potential partners who met her criteria: solid technology, B2B e-commerce expertise, and willingness to form an equity relationship.

In January of 2000, American Express and GetThere, Inc. (www.getthere.com) entered into a *non-exclusive* relationship through which CSI marketed and sold a proprietary version of GetThere, Inc.'s system under the name Corporate Travel Online (CTO). Founded in 1996 as Internet Travel Network (ITN), Menlo Park-based GetThere, Inc. provided travel related technology and online booking services to some of the largest companies in the United States including Lucent, Xerox and Nike. GetThere, Inc. also powered online travel sites for many of the major airlines including United Airlines, TWA, and British Airways.[5] As part of the agreement, AMEX took a minority equity stake in Get-There, Inc. After closing the deal with Get-There, AMEX decided that it would support both the AXI Travel and CTO products.

Creating Value with AXI Travel

Marketing efforts began very early in the development process. The goal of pre-launch marketing was to prevent current customers from signing on to a competitive Internet travel service, while also encouraging users of competitor's services to become AMEX Business Travel Service customers. Leibowitz explained.

> When we first introduced AXI Travel, we made a decision that proved to be very important in helping us position the product in the market. In an effort to prevent cannibalization of our existing business, we stated that you had to be an AMEX Business Travel Service customer to use the new Internet service when it became available. We first mentioned this policy in July 1996 at the National Business Travel Association annual meeting. We repeated it when we brought current and potential customers into Redmond, and our 400-person field salesforce also explained the policy when they demonstrated our new Internet travel service to current and

---

[5]In mid-2000, United Airlines owned 28% of GetThere.com.

EXHIBIT 4   Cost to produce a ticket (1994 to 2001)

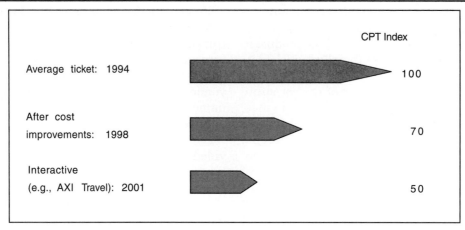

Source: Adapted from AMEX internal analysis.
Note: CPT stands for Average Industry Cost to Produce a Ticket—the average cost of an agency to service a customer. Numbers shown represent an index with 1994=100.

new customers. The result of this pre-marketing was that, between between 1996 and November 1997, we generated an additional 15% in our base business directly attributable to interest in AXI Travel.[6] This more than offset the cost of building the new service.

Pricing AXI Travel Service

Traditionally, the travel industry generated revenues from commissions. However, in the 1990s, in an attempt to lower the distribution cost of getting a ticket to the traveler, airlines reduced travel agent commissions from 10% to 8% for domestic tickets with a maximum commission capped at $25 each way. This significantly influenced AMEX Travel Service revenues. As a result even before the launch of AXI Travel, the company increasingly emphasized "fee-based arrangements" with corporate travel clients.

---

[6]Overall revenues grew by more than this amount during the period, but 15% were directly related to customers upgrading the level of service or new customers who switched from a competitor in anticipation of AXI Travel.

Hakhi Ahn, director of business development, and Deborah Atkins, director of finance, were in charge of developing the initial pricing policy for AXI Travel. Their goal was to develop a pricing model that motivated customers to shift an increasing%age of travel reservations and bookings from their traditional agent-based service to AXI Travel. "We found that AXI Travel decreased the cost of booking a travel reservation by over 50%," Ahn explained. (See Exhibit 4.) "30% of the savings come from streamlining the process before adding the Internet reservation system, and the additional 20% come directly from AXI Travel. These savings are spread across suppliers, our customers, and AMEX. But, to realize the savings, everyone needed to participate. We needed to encourage our customers to shift at least 30% of their travel arrangements to AXI Travel to ensure that both the customer and AMEX realized the savings from the click and mortar integrated service delivery system." (See Exhibit 5.)

EXHIBIT 5   **American Express "Click and Mortar" Service Delivery System (Casewriter Interpretation)**

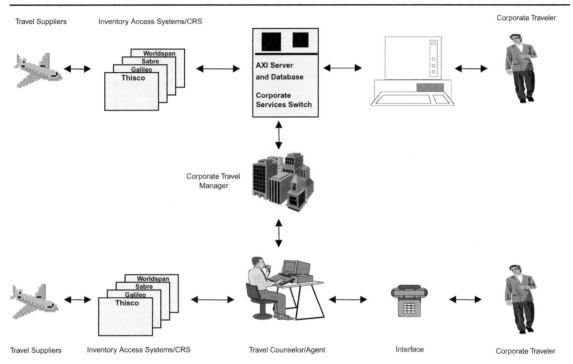

To encourage the shift, Ahn and Atkins offered discounts for transactions across AXI Travel. But, since AXI Travel would not replace the traditional travel service, it was also necessary to factor in the impact of the new pricing policy on the bottom line of the company. "AXI Travel was a new distribution channel for us," Atkins explained. "It did not replace our existing channels but instead served as an alternate channel. While we built the system outside the influence of the traditional business, once we launched AXI Travel, we needed to bring the two businesses together. While we wanted to encourage customers to adopt AXI Travel and to encourage business travelers to use it, we needed to carefully monitor the impact of our pricing policy on overall revenues, gross margins and

profitability." There were three different components to the initial AXI Travel pricing model.

- *Implementation fees* were charged when a company first adopted the service. These "one-time" fees included the cost of streamlining processes, integrating technical systems, and orienting and training employees. Several levels of implementation consulting and systems integration were offered to enable customers to choose the approach that best suited their business needs. *Consulting fees* were charged for process consulting and systems integration support after the implementation period. The Corporate Services consulting organization was extended to enable e-business consulting and technology support.

- *Transaction fees* were charged for each reservation booked on AXI Travel. These transaction fees were lower than the fees charged for booking a reservation using the traditional AMEX Business Travel Service. "While transaction fees varied widely for our traditional business travel service," Ahn, explained, "we wanted to standardize fees for use of AXI Travel and price the service to motivate companies and employees to book their travel online." Since cost savings increased when AMEX managed both agent-based and online reservations, the company waived all AXI Travel transaction fees for customers that outsourced management of their agent-based travel service to AMEX Corporate Services. In addition, we discounted their yearly service fee.[7] If a company decided to manage its own agent-based travel services, a $17.25 fee was charged for each reservation booked on AXI Travel.

- *Maintenance fees* varied based on the size of the company using AXI Travel and the type of computer systems. Large customers were typically charged a higher maintenance fee because of the sophisticated database management and storage requirements and processing requirements. Companies that wished to use dedicated, secure networks also paid a higher maintenance fee.

---

[7]With an outsource arrangement, customers paid AMEX to manage their agent-based and online business travel service. These services could be provided at the company location or in a shared call center facility. Facilities and technical systems may be dedicated to a single customer or shared. Because of the variety of options, service and transaction fees were negotiated on a customer-by-customer basis.

The AXI Travel team initially believed that some companies might wish to lease the AXI Travel software and run it in their data centers. This proved to not be the case. In May 1999, Leibowitz reported: "To date, all of our customers have been perfectly happy to let us host the AXI Travel service for them. In this sense, they are treating us as if we were one of the new breeds of Application Service Provider (often called an ASP). In fact, most of the business travelers that use our service don't have a clue where the actual software and computers reside."[8]

Benefits to the Corporate Travel Manager

The primary benefit of AXI Travel was that it addressed the need among corporations to control their travel expenses by incorporating the key ingredients for effective corporate travel management. At the time that AXI Travel was under development, U.S. companies spent approximately $156 billion on travel and entertainment (T&E). These expenses typically included airfare, lodging, car rental, entertainment, meals and other miscellaneous expenses. (See Exhibit 6.) In many Fortune 1000 companies, a corporate travel management department was responsible for managing T&E expenditures. At the time AXI Travel was launched, 39% of companies had a person or unit officially designated for corporate travel management.[9]

The corporate travel manager played an important role in controlling T&E expenses. Primary responsibilities included developing and monitoring corporate travel policy, negotiating with vendors, meeting planning, administering corporate credit and purchase card

---

[8]American Express outsourced data center and network operations to a web hosting partner.

[9]The 1998 American Express Survey of Business Travel Management.

EXHIBIT 6   Categories of T&E Spending

Travel & Entertainment Spending	1996	1998	2000
Air Travel	42%	44%	45%
Lodging	21%	22%	17%
Meals	14%	13%	10%
Car Rental	8%	8%	10%
Entertainment	8%	6%	8%
Telephone and Data Communications	5%	5%	8%
Other	2%	2%	2%

Source: American Express Travel Survey 2000.

programs, and controlling travel budgets. Traditionally, corporate travel management departments worked with a travel agency to meet the travel needs of corporate travelers. In 1997, there were over 30,000 travel agencies in the U.S. Travel agents accessed computer reservation systems (CRSs), for example, American Airlines' Sabre system, to check the availability of services from travel providers as well as make reservations. During the late 1990s, CRS access was increasingly available to business travelers and their travel arrangers through the Internet.

To meet the needs of the corporate travel manager, AXI Travel enabled them to streamline and simplify the corporate travel and expense reporting process. T&E policies, including negotiated supplier rates, preferred suppliers, and automated spending limits, could be embedded within the system, informing the business traveler and—when necessary, the corporate travel manager of problems at the time of booking. These features helped corporate travel managers to achieve better compliance with travel policy, thereby reducing corporate T&E costs.

In 1998, AXI Travel transaction fees were up to 40% less than the fees charged for agent-based travel booking. In addition, better compliance with negotiated rates and preferred supplier discounts further reduced the cost of

an airline ticket by 20% and the cost of a hotel by 10%. A corporate travel manager at Monsanto explained:[10]

> Instead of time on the phone with a travel agent, business travelers are able to book airline, hotel and car reservations directly from their desktop computer or laptop in the office, at home or on the road. In our company, the average agent-based travel reservation takes four phone calls, each of which lasts an average of 17 minutes. With AXI Travel, the entire process only takes a few minutes.

Benefits to the Business Traveler and Travel Arranger

While the corporate travel manager played a key role in deciding to adopt AXI Travel, the business traveler and their travel arrangers decided whether to use it to book travel. And, unless it was used, the company would not achieve the benefits. Satisfying both groups was a challenge, as Frank Hutchins, vice president of CSI relationship management,[11] explained:

> The two constituencies have different objectives. The corporate travel manager wants to manage the costs of

---

[10]In 1998, Monsanto spent over $100 million per year on T&E.

[11]With system launch, the AXI Travel development team returned to their home unit, Corporate Services Interactive.

travel and entertainment plus reduce the related administrative overhead. Most travelers, while they want to be good corporate citizens, are often more concerned with convenience and have definite personal preferences they want honored.

AXI Travel was designed to meet the business traveler's requirements for comfort and convenience. It allowed them to choose their own seat, locate the most convenient hotel, access destination information such as restaurant listings and weather forecasts, and confirm whether the flight was on time. While these features were designed to encourage business travelers to use AXI Travel, unless company policy mandated the use of AXI Travel, travelers and their travel arrangers always had the option of using the phone to talk directly to a travel counselor.

While the number of companies that initially adopted AXI Travel had exceeded the company's expectations, it proved to be a much more difficult task to get business travelers to use it. "Our travel agents are trained to provide high quality customer service, and their incentives reward them for delivering it," Emma Egan, vice president of CSI marketing, explained. Leibowicz explained:

> What's in it for the traveler when they can pick up the phone and get a very high level of service? That's the way they've done it in the past. How do we change their behavior without compromising the quality of our agent-based travel service?

Realizing that special features would probably not be enough, in late 1998, Egan and her team drew on their travel business experience and developed a set of loyalty programs designed to encourage business travelers to begin booking their reservations through AXI Travel. One such program, the "AXI Travel Bonus" gave points for each ticket booked through AXI Travel. After a certain number of points had been accumulated, the traveler received a free ticket.

In addition to providing incentives for business travelers, it soon became clear that travel arrangers (for examples, secretaries and administrative assistants) should also be trained on the system and motivated to use it. In fact, many companies chose to target their initial training and incentive programs toward these travel arrangers. Ben Aronson, director of marketing explained.

> If there's a secretary who books travel for 15 people and they travel, on average, 12 times per year, that's 180 transactions with one person. We need to get to that person. They are a key link in the distribution channel. We want to be sure that they receive direct benefits by going online. As a result, we developed a special promotion for these important users; if they book a ticket for the traveler they get credit toward a free ticket—not the traveler.

Benefits to the CIO

Initially, the AXI Travel team believed that CIOs would be primary decision makers for the adoption of AXI Travel. However, they soon found that this was not the case. "If we approached the CIO first," Leibowicz explained, "the sales process often stalled. While they were an important decision maker, we had greater success by initiating the sales process with the corporate travel manager or another corporate administrative officer responsible for corporate purchasing and expense management." To close the sale, however, the cooperation of the CIO was usually required.

Benefits to the Travel Agents

AXI Travel had been designed to support travel agents, not to replace them. In fact, by May 1999, the company still had many open positions for travel agents that they were actively trying to fill. While American Express' Travel Operations group had been involved in the development of the online service, it was still a tough sell to get them to embrace—and actively sell—the online service to their business customers. However, over time, the operations group became more supportive, as they started to realize the benefits of shifting low-value-added activities, such as answering travel research questions and booking simple itineraries, onto AXI Travel. By freeing up time, the Operations group could spend more time doing the higher-value, more interesting work for travel counselors. This also relieved the stress of ongoing personnel shortages.

Cashing in on the Options Value of AXI Travel

AXI Travel was the perfect lead product because it was built from the beginning to be a hybrid product. Customers could still call up on the phone to make a travel reservation or they could use the computer. We've tried to make the barriers to using and adopting AXI Travel very low, because we think the leverage is in getting AXI Travel on as many desktops as possible and then launching additional products and services.

Sonia Sharpe, 1998

The success in attracting corporate customers to implement AXI Travel convinced CSI to create new e-business offerings that leveraged the same skills, processes and supporting infrastructure and benefited from the experience the group had gained from AXI Travel. In early 1998, the CSI team partnered with Concur Technologies, Inc. to sell an AMEX-branded version of its Xpense Management Solution (XMS).[12] XMS/AX enabled employees to complete and file expense reports from their PCs and laptops. By integrating Amex Corporate Card data and a customer's in-house expense management and general ledger, AXI Expense enabled efficient and accurate reimbursement. By automating the expense management process, corporate clients could further reduce their administrative costs. It also encouraged greater use of the AMEX Corporate Card because both travel and charge data could be fed directly into corporate databases and expense reports.

In May 1999, AMEX once more expanded its network of e-commerce alliances with the launch of AXI Purchasing Solutions.[13] "Bridging an important gap in the emerging e-commerce marketplace," an AMEX press release announced, "American Express has enhanced its Corporate Purchasing Card [first launched in 1994] with a set of features for online purchasing. The new AXI Purchasing Solutions facilitate the process of order management, fulfillment, reconciliation, data management and program maintenance." E-commerce alliances were established with the leading vendors of e-purchasing software, including Ariba, Commerce One, SAP, Right-Works, Intellisys and Extensity.

A 1999 AMEX/Ernst and Young study found that adoption of a purchasing card enabled a company to save up to 95% of the costs associated with manual purchase order processing.[14] Firms using manual purchase orders to buy low cost, high volume supplies and services incurred an average processing cost of $90 for each transaction – with some firms spending as much as $200 on certain transactions. In comparison, companies using purchasing cards incurred a significantly lower average processing cost of $21.71. Firms that employed Internet-based and other electronic procurement systems to buy supplies, combined with a purchasing card for payment and accounting tasks, spent from $4.44 to $15 in processing costs per purchase.

"The win-win for leading-edge companies is to implement an electronic purchasing system for order efficiency and the American Express Corporate Purchasing Card for payment and

---

[12]AMEX Press Release, January 6, 1998.

[13]AMEX Press Release, May 25, 1999.
[14]AMEX Press Release, May 25, 1999.

reconciliation ease," said Sharpe in 1999. "Unfortunately, as companies move to install a new online system, they often resort to paper invoices and payment by check, which actually creates extra manual labor. In addition, traditional electronic data interchange (EDI) links are one-to-one connections, which are expensive to build and maintain. Our Corporate Purchasing Card, by servicing multiple suppliers and buyers on a uniform platform with the AXI Purchasing Solutions, is better suited to the Internet's many-to-many network business model."

More critical to its corporate card customers was the development of an online gateway into all of their many relationships with American Express. As they became more web-savvy, travel and purchasing managers and corporate card program administrators asked American Express to shift its priorities to development of a portal, which the CSI named American Express@Work. Corporate customers were eager to have anytime, anywhere access into AMEX's corporate card databases so that they could make routine changes to their card programs. In the past, these changes (for example, address changes, approving new cards or canceling cards of departing employees, changing the spending limits on purchasing cards, etc.) were made by telephone or fax. In addition, customers, tired of receiving mountains of paper reports, also wanted to be able to customize their own reports and receive them online. The Global Information Services group worked with the CSI team to develop simple-to-use e-mail and web-based formats for the travel and card management information reports, and CSI developed the online channels in American Express@Work. A pilot site went live in fall of 1999 with a few eager early adopter clients. Within the first quarter after launch, several hundred program administrators had learned of the new service by word of mouth and asked to be added to the pilot. By the end of 2000, American Express@Work enabled fully one-

third of eligible customer service transactions and over 75% of the MIS report delivery to be handled online.

B2B Commerce Network

Another product for which there was great marketplace demand was an e-purchasing marketplace through which buyers and suppliers could do business. Once more, AMEX teamed with technology partners to help build a robust, full-featured e-business marketplace. TRADEX Technologies, a provider of digital marketplace platforms and *ec*-Content, Inc., a provider of B2B supplier catalogs and content, were chosen as partners. The three companies worked together to create a product that would "simplify corporate purchasing processes, create easy-to-use payment services, and bring B2B suppliers onto the Web quickly and easily," a November 1999 AMEX press release stated.[15]

By mid-2000, AMEX recognized from its experience with the B2B Commerce Network pilot that it needed a partner with more skills than simply building the technology platform. In August, it announced a new partner, Ventro, a B2B e-commerce service provider. Ventro brought years of experience in building and running marketplaces and used the Tradex/Ariba platform as part of its core.[16] The new venture would be a separate start-up company, MarketMile™, jointly-owned by both firms and with board members from both parent companies. The new company was positioned to seek additional funding from venture capital and other potential stakeholders in the marketplace. MarketMile™ was scheduled to launch during first quarter 2001, providing "an open digital marketplace solution for purchasing and catalog management designed to

---

[15]American Express Press Release, November 15, 1999.
[16]Tradex was acquired by Ariba in December 1999. See "Ariba Acquires Tradex," *Ariba Press Release,* December 16, 1999 (www.ariba.com).

transform the way businesses and suppliers conduct e-commerce."[17] Sharpe explained:

> MarketMile™ enables companies to access customizable procurement applications with online payment tools, robust supplier services, content management services and advanced sourcing capabilities. American Express intends to use this new network to connect its corporate customers and suppliers with other horizontal and vertical marketplaces on the Internet. MarketMile™ was designed to be integrated into existing e-procurement solutions or used as a stand-alone e-procurement service. The network enables small, mid-sized, and large suppliers to create an online presence quickly and to maintain customizable catalogs efficiently.

21st Century Challenges and Opportunities

Years ago, AMEX understood its industry and the firms that competed within it. For instance, in their credit card business, Visa and Master Card were well-known competitors who shared similar business models and competitive pressures. While pre-Internet electronic commerce had complicated the competitive landscape in the travel industry, by the early 1990s the industry had begun to stabilize into three dominant, yet increasingly inter-related, channels: (1) traditional airline booking agents; (2) airline-owned computer reservation systems, also called CRS, (for example, American Airlines' Sabre System and Galileo, a CRS owned by a coalition of airlines led by United Airlines); and (3) travel agencies (for example, Carlson, Rosenbluth, BTI Americas, World Travel Partners, and Sato).[18]

However, the launch of AXI Travel and the multiple follow-on e-business initiatives dramatically changed the company's business landscape. No longer were AMEX's competitors clearly defined. The era of coopetition had

begun. The company now competed directly with and, in some cases, also partnered with newly emerging and established technology firms and B2B e-commerce firms (for example, Ariba, CommerceOne, FreeMarkets, GE Global Exchange, Oracle, and Ventro).[19] No longer were industry boundaries fixed and stable. They were expanding and changing as quickly as the Internet. Despite the uncertainties, executives at AMEX believed that the opportunities were enormous. In a February 2000 report, Forrester analysts had predicted that the market for B2B trade would exceed $2.7 trillion worldwide by 2004, with eMarketplaces, like MarketMile™, accounting for up to 53% of all trade and fueling most of the growth.[20] Yet progress was slow on penetration and use of its individual e-producers, such as AXI Travel/CTO, within corporate customers who had already purchased the online services.

By summer 2000, Sharpe was becoming convinced that the businesses CSI had developed were ready to be either integrated back into AMEX's traditional businesses, like AXI Travel and CTO, or be spun out to form new companies, like MarketMile™. But some, like American Express @ Work, did not fit neatly within any one AMEX business unit. Should CSI continue to operate and run some of AMEX's e-businesses or should any business that didn't easily migrate to an existing business be spun out? Clearly it was time to re-examine the role of CSI and the e-business venture development process at AMEX.

---

[17]American Express Press Release, November 15, 1999.
[18]See Applegate, L.M., "Electronic Commerce," *Handbook of Technology Management,* (ed. Richard Dorf), Boca Raton, FL.: CRC Press, 1998; Applegate, M., "Thought Leaders: An Interview with Lynda Applegate," *Strategy and Business,* First Quarter 2000.

[19]Visit these companies' websites to compare business models: Ariba (www.ariba.com), Commerce One (www.commerceone.com); FreeMarkets (www.freemarkets.com), GE Global Exchange, (www.geis.com), Oracle (www.oracle.com), Ventro (www.ventro.com). Current industry analyst reports include: Yates, S. et. al., "Demystifying B2B Integration," *Forrester Research Report,* September 2000; Walker, J. et. al., "Commerce Platforms," *Forrester Research Reports,* October 2000.
[20]Kafka, S. et al., "eMarketplaces Boost B2B Trade," *Forrester Research Reports,* February 2000.

3   INFORMATION AGE OPERATIONS[1]

In this new age, IT is not about business—it is the business. What is a bank other than a computer with a marketing department?[2]

As we enter the 21st century, computing infrastructure[3] lies at the heart of operating capabilities of most companies. One can quibble with Geoffrey Moore's assertion that many businesses *are* computers, but few would deny that changes in computing technologies lead to fundamental changes in how businesses can and do operate. More than that, many companies now depend on computers. No longer is computing infrastructure just nice to have. No longer is it just value adding. It is vital. Without effective IT operations, most companies cannot conduct business very well or for very long or—in an increasing number of instances—at all.

Recent technological advances have driven major changes in how IT services are delivered. For some time now, low-cost computing power has been driving a shift toward more distributed processing. The more recent rise to commercial prominence of "internetworking" technologies, which provide a low-cost way to connect virtually everyone on the same network, offers vast new possibilities for addressing the computing needs of businesses. The computing systems at the heart of many businesses are evolving into a new kind of mechanism.

---

[1]This module is adapted from papers and materials in Professor Austin's *Managing Business Technology Infrastructure* course module (Harvard Business School case 601-181).

[2]Geoffrey Moore, *Living on the Fault Line: Managing for Shareholder Value in the Age of the Internet,* Harper Business, 2000.

[3]In this module overview, we use the word "infrastructure" to refer to the entire layered fabric of hardware, software, systems, and media that collectively deliver IT-based services.

This evolution of computing infrastructure brings with it many benefits. IT services few envisioned several years ago have become commonplace. Older services can be delivered in entirely new ways. The cost structures that underlie new service delivery methods are superior to those on which older methods were based. Entirely new business models have emerged, enabled by advancing technologies, shifting infrastructures, and new possibilities. At a macro level, industries are restructuring to realize greater efficiencies and capabilities, as part of a long-term trend that will continue and accelerate, regardless of occasional technology market slumps.

Along with benefits, however, come challenges. Conveying an understanding of how to effectively address these challenges is the ultimate aim of this module. Drawing on years of field research with new and old companies, this module confronts hands-on, frontline issues of execution. Grand visions are of little use unless they can be translated into reality. New business models and systems cannot succeed unless they can be relied upon to operate at key moments. The cases and exercises here—Arepa, Selecting a Hosting Provider (and its technical note Web and IT Hosting Facilities), Trilogy, and iPremier—provide a basis for discussing how evolving IT infrastructure affects business, how management priorities should shift, and how the risks that impact day-to-day operations can be reduced.

The Drivers of Change: Cheaper Chips, Bigger Pipes

In this diluvian age, when bandwidth is at flood tide, bandwidth growth is a given, driven by a super Moore's Law, doubling every four- to-six months.[4]

In 1965, Gordon Moore, who would later co-found Intel, noted that the performance of memory chips was doubling every 18 to 24 months while their cost remained roughly constant. He predicted that the trend would continue and that the impact on the world would be profound. Nearly four decades later, most people are familiar with changes wrought by the continuing downward spiral in the cost of processing power predicted by "Moore's Law."

With the emergence of Personal Computers (PCs) in the 1980s, computing that had resided in centralized enclaves staffed by esoteric specialists spread throughout the organization and into the eager hands of business users. Financial analysts embraced spreadsheets. Marketers designed and analyzed their own databases. Engineers adopted drawing packages. For many computing tasks, response time delays and extensive reliance on "techies" became distant memories.

---

[4]George Gilder, in his opening address to the 2000 Gilder/Forbes Telecosm Conference, September 13–15, 2000.

As newly empowered computer users sought to share their work, new communications infrastructure emerged. Local area networks (LANs) allowed business users to share spreadsheets, word processing, and other documents, and to use common printers to obtain hard copies of their work. PCs and LANs became more sophisticated as user's computing needs evolved and as underlying technologies—fundamentally different from earlier mainframe technologies—advanced. The "client-server" movement was the culmination of this model: higher-powered but still distributed computers and more elaborate networks combined to provide IT services formerly provided by mainframe systems.

In the early 1990s, the rise to commercial prominence of the Internet, the Web, and underlying protocols (rules for how data would be moved across networks) led to new stages of evolution in computing infrastructure.[5] Transmission Control Protocol and Internet Protocol, together known as TCP/IP, provided a robust method of routing messages between LANs and created the potential to connect all computers on an ever-larger Wide Area Network (WAN). Because TCP/IP and other Internet protocols were open standards, not owned by any person or company, computers could be connected at low cost and with minimal central orchestration. Self-service hookup facilitated rapid growth in the worldwide Internet. Figure 3–1 depicts the corporate IT infrastructure evolution over the past few decades.

At first, the Internet was primarily useful for exchanging e-mail and large data files, but the Web, with its graphical user interfaces, made Internet communication much more valuable to those who were not computer specialists. Just as PCs had made computing accessible for a wide variety of non-technical users, now the Web made network resources (such as distant databases) and capabilities (such as virtual collaboration) accessible. It became apparent that the Internet had great commercial potential. The number of connected computers shot upward and the value of the network increased according to "Metcalfe's Law," which states that the usefulness of a network increases with the square of the number of users connected to the network.[6] As the number of users increased, commercial potential mounted and network capacity expanded. Cost reduction in network capacity abided by a Moore's Law-like curve steeper than the one that applied to chips. The combination of cheapening chips and data "pipes" fueled a process that would lead to qualitatively different computing infrastructures.

These related exponential trends—the reduction in the cost of computing power and the reduction in the cost of exchanging information between computers—have been the fundamental drivers of changes in the business landscape that we are just beginning to understand. Gaining an appreciation

---

[5]The Internet was not new in the 1990s. It had been in use by the military and by researchers since the 1960s. But commercial uses of these technologies accelerated dramatically in the 1990s.

[6]"Metcalfe's Law" is commonly attributed to Robert Metcalfe, founder of 3Com Corporation.

FIGURE 3–1

*The Evolution of
Corporate IT
Infrastructure*

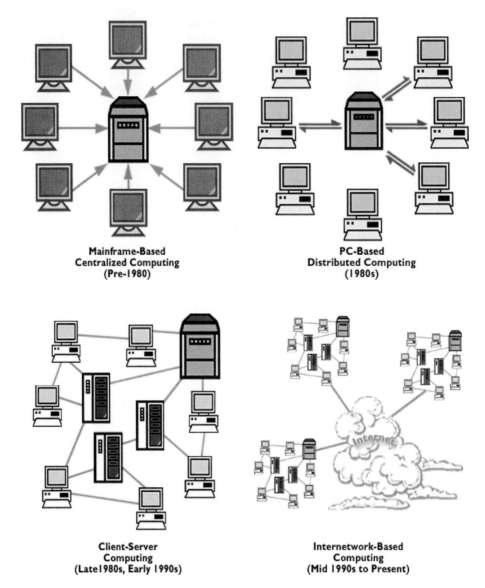

**Mainframe-Based
Centralized Computing
(Pre-1980)**

**PC-Based
Distributed Computing
(1980s)**

**Client-Server
Computing
(Late1980s, Early 1990s)**

**Internetwork-Based
Computing
(Mid 1990s to Present)**

for how shifting technology might result in changes in business capabilities, in the choices facing businesses, and in the structures of industries, is a prerequisite for understanding how to manage enabling IT infrastructures.

The Basic Components of Internetworking Infrastructures

Network, facilities, and processing systems are the three basic components of internetworking infrastructures. Network refers to the medium and supporting technologies (hardware and software) that permit exchange of information between processing units and organizations. As network capacity increases, the network takes on greater importance as a component of IT infrastructure. Facilities, the physical systems that house and protect computing and network devices, are perhaps the least glamorous of infrastructure components. But they, too, are increasing in importance as greater network capacity makes new facilities models viable. Processing systems encompass the hardware and software that together provide an organization's ability to handle business transactions. They are newly interesting in the age of internetworking because they are being redesigned to better capitalize on the advantages offered by Internet technologies.

Each of these infrastructure components generates opportunities and issues that managers must understand and be able to effectively address. Table 3–1 lists some of the core technologies that support each component and identifies some of the key management issues that arise for each component. The major trend underlying the evolution of these components is that internetworking creates many more degrees of freedom in how components can be arranged and managed. More degrees of freedom create possibilities for specialization, cost reduction, new capabilities, and new business models, but also pose more substantial challenges in understanding the full implications of new infrastructure arrangements.

TABLE 3–1   Fundamental Components of Internetworking Infrastructure

	Core Technologies	*Key Management Questions*
Network	Fiber optics, cable systems, DSL, satellite, wireless, Internetworking hardware (routers, switches, firewalls), content delivery software, identity management, net monitoring	• How to select partners • How to manage partner relationships • How to assure reliability • How to maintain security
Facilities	Corporate data centers, co-location data centers, managed services data centers, data closets	• Internal or external management? • Choosing a facilities model suited to your company • How to assure reliability • How to maintain security
Processing Systems	Transaction software (enterprise systems offered by companies such as SAP or Oracle; or more targeted solutions offered by companies such as Trilogy and i2), servers, server appliances, client devices (PCs, handhelds)	• What to keep internal and what to outsource • How to deploy, grow, and modify • Enterprise system or best-of-breed hybrid? • Relationships with legacies • How to manage incidents • How to recover after a "disaster"

Business Implications of the Rise of Internetworking

If the Internet had existed in the 1960s and 1970s, the packaged software industry would never have emerged. It would have been an online services industry from the beginning. What's happening now is that the entire software industry is being rebuilt around the concept of network services.[7]

Eric Schmidt, Google CEO, former Novell CEO and Sun Microsystems CTO, has observed that high-speed networks can enable a computer chip to interact just as well with another physically distant chip as with a chip only inches away. Given so much "bandwidth," physical location of computer processors ceases to matter very much. Operationally, the communication pathways inside a computer become indistinguishable from the pathways that connect computers. The network itself becomes a potential component of a larger processor composed of the network and all of its connected computers.

For most business computer users who do not have access to this level of network bandwidth, Schmidt's observation remains largely theoretical. Nevertheless, the idea of an increasingly connected network, both inside and beyond the boundaries of organizations, in which physical location of processors matters less and less, is of major practical importance. Improved technical connections between machines, departments, companies, and customers mean quicker realization of economic value when parties interact. Transactions are initiated and consummated quickly. Activities that were sequential occur simultaneously. Because the physical location of processing is less important, new possibilities for outsourcing and industry restructuring emerge. But along with these largely beneficial outcomes come drawbacks: increased complexity, unpredictable interactions, and new categories of threats to businesses and consumers.

The Emergence of Real Time Infrastructures

Historically, scarcity of processing and communication capacity required business transactions to be accumulated and processed in "batches" at a time later than they were initiated. A telephone calling card account might, for example, be updated by a "batch run" once each day. A stranded traveler, needing to reactivate a mistakenly deactivated card, might have to wait for the once-a-day batch run for the card to be reactivated. As processing and communication capacity become more abundant, however, batch processing becomes less necessary. Delays between initiating a transaction and completing of its processing are greatly reduced. With real-time infrastructures,

[7]Marc Andreessen, cofounder of Netscape and Loudcloud, "Features Interview," *Internet World,* 15 October 2000. Purists will note that the Internet *did* exist in the 1960s and 1970s. Andreessen, of course, refers to the commercial Internet.

customers are serviced and economic value is realized immediately rather than over periods of hours, days, or weeks. The potential benefits of real-time infrastructures do not end here, however.

Better data, better decisions.   In most companies, people in different parts of the organization and in disparate locations need access to the same data. Previously organizations had to keep copies of the same data in many places. But keeping the data synchronized was difficult and frequently not achieved. Discrepancies between instances of data presumed to be the same often led to errors, inefficiencies, and poor decision-making. Although abundant communication capacity has not completely eliminated the need for multiple copies, it has reduced the need and made it easier to keep copies synchronized. For the first time, it is becoming feasible to run the enterprise from a single, trusted set of numbers.

Improved process visibility.   Older IT systems based on proprietary technologies often communicated poorly with each other. Consequently, viewing the progress of orders or other transactions across system boundaries was difficult. People in a company's sales organization could not access data in manufacturing, for example, to obtain information about the status of an order. New communication technologies, based on open standards and compatible back-office transaction systems, now let users view transactions throughout supply and fulfillment, beyond specific system boundaries, and even beyond the boundaries of a company into partners' systems.

Improved process efficiency.   Many efficiency improvements result directly from enhanced process visibility. In manufacturing, workers who can see what supplies and orders are coming their way tend to hold less buffer stock ("just-in-case" inventory) to guard against uncertainty. Holding less buffer stock reduces working capital, shortens cycle times, and improves ROI. In both manufacturing and service industries, operational managers make better frontline decisions and make them sooner. A bank manager, for example, can see more information about a customer's account before making a credit decision. A manager in charge of supplying plastic cases for portable radios can see that orange is not selling well and can quickly reduce orange in the color mix.

From make-and-sell to sense-and-respond.[8]   Real-time infrastructures are a prerequisite for achieving highly responsive operations, those based on "sense-and-respond" principles rather than make-to-sell principles. The fundamental insight here is that if operating infrastructures can come close enough to real-time, then value-adding activities can be performed in

---

[8] See Richard L. Nolan and Steven P. Bradley, *Sense and Respond: Capturing Value in the Network Era,* Harvard Business School Press, Boston, MA, 1998.

response to *actual* customer demand, rather than *forecasted* customer demand. When organizations operate as sense-and-respond systems, there are no losses due to differences between actual and forecasted demand. The most celebrated example of a sense-and-respond operation is probably Dell Computer Corporation's make-to-order manufacturing process, in which manufacturing a computer is always a response to an actual customer order. But many other companies, in both manufacturing and service industries, have expressed intentions of moving to such models, including some with very complex products, such as automobiles. Companies that are able to reduce losses due to forecasting error and, ultimately, to move to a sense-and-respond paradigm for operations will tend to out-perform their rivals.

In many companies, especially older ones, moving to real-time systems involves re-engineering transaction systems to take advantage of greater processing and network capacities. Some companies have chosen to renew transaction infrastructure by implementing large "enterprise systems" made, for example, by SAP, Oracle, Peoplesoft, and Baan. Others have chosen to design "best-of-breed" transaction infrastructures by connecting what they see as the best products from a variety of niche vendors. Whichever approach a company takes, the objective is to remove batch processing and other non-real-time elements from the transaction infrastructure, to take advantage of the enhanced process visibility provided by increased network capacity, and to realize almost immediate economic value from transactions.

New Models of Service Delivery

In the early days of electric power generation, companies owned and managed their own power plants. Later, as standardization and technological advances made it possible to deliver power reliably via a more centralized model, companies began to purchase electric power from external providers. A similar shift is underway in the IT industry.

In today's companies, as more reliable networks make the physical location of computers less important, services traditionally provided by internal IT departments can be acquired externally, across internetworks, from service providers. Fundamental economic forces, for example, the scarcity of IT resources and the desire to reduce costs, are driving this shift. The shift, which parallels the maturation of other industries, reveals a common pattern: standardization and technological advance permit specialization by individual firms in value chains, resulting in economies of scale and higher service levels.

Since the advent of PC and client-server computing, end-user software has been designed to execute locally on your PC or on a computer down the hall. Saved work—documents or other forms of data—usually remain local on a PC's hard drive or on storage devices connected to a nearby computer (e.g., a server). In this scenario, when the software malfunctions the user contacts his or her IT department, which operates most (if not all) of the involved IT infrastructure.

With the advent of reliable, high capacity networks, local execution of software is no longer the only alternative, nor is it necessarily the best alternative from a business standpoint. Increasingly software is being designed to execute in geographically distant facilities that belong to specialized service providers, each of whom deliver software services across the Internet to many different customers. In this scenario, data is stored in a distant location and the end-user's company owns little of the infrastructure involved in service delivery. The end-user's company pays a monthly fee for a service bundle, which might also include technical support services.

The transition underway is analogous to the move from telephone answering machines to voice mail. Telephone answering machines were purchased by companies and attached to individual telephones. When they broke, it was the company's job to fix or replace the machines. Messages were stored locally, on magnetic tape inside the machine on the desktop. In contrast, companies acquire voice mail from service providers for a monthly fee. The hardware that supports the service is owned by the provider and physically resides in a central location unknown to most voice mail users. When voice mail breaks, the service provider is responsible for fixing it. The potentially sensitive contents of voice mail messages no longer reside on the end-users desk; rather, the service provider is entrusted with their care and security.

The move to over-the-Net service delivery is gradual. As supporting infrastructure matures, however, the economic advantages become more compelling. Even if actual software functionality is not acquired externally, external infrastructure management can still make sense. For example, a company may rent space in a vendor-owned IT hosting facility rather than incur the capital expenses required to build a data center, even when it retains internal management of the software. As technology advances and infrastructure becomes more secure and reliable, the benefits of outsourcing more elements that underlie IT service delivery mount.

Managing the shortage of skilled IT workers.   According to U.S. government statistics, there will be four million unfilled IT jobs in the United States by 2003. Outsourcing IT infrastructure management helps individual firms overcome the shortage of IT skills by reducing the need for internal staff. This benefit is especially important to small- and medium-sized businesses that have difficulty attracting and retaining IT talent.

Reduced time-to-market.   With the rise of the Web, many companies now use IT to enhance revenues by creating new business models, products, and services. New revenue opportunities frequently offer first-mover advantages. Seizing these advantages depends on a rapid deployment of business plans. Network-based service delivery models help companies develop new businesses quickly. For example, existing companies can use externally hosted e-commerce packages to become e-retailers, without purchasing any equipment or writing any software.

Increasing availability: the shift to 24 × 7 operations.   In the age of the commercial Web, consumers expect company sites always to be up. Real-time operations require computers always to be on. But the facilities and equipment in most enterprises were not designed for the 99.999% availability expected of modern IT services. Such high availability and reliability requires large capital investments in highly redundant power, connectivity, and environmental controls. Because specialized infrastructure vendors (such as hosting providers) are able to spread capital investments across many customers, they are able to achieve scale economies that justify large investments.

Favorable cash-flow profiles.   Traditionally, IT investments have required large up-front cash outlays and yielded only eventual and uncertain (because of high IT project failure rates) benefits. Subscription-based IT services have a more favorable cash-flow profile. Not much needs to be purchased up front and payback flows in more quickly. This benefit is particularly important to small- and medium-sized companies that cannot afford the large up-front investments associated with some IT services. Figure 3–2 compares the cash-flow profile of a subscription-based service delivered largely through prebuilt external infrastructure with the cash-flow profile of a traditional IT investment.

Cost reduction in IT services supply chains.   Centralized service delivery management can reduce support costs in a number of areas. Upgrades to new versions of software can be done on a central server, thereby eliminating the need for support personnel to upgrade individual client computers. Software that runs on centralized infrastructure reduces the overhead associated with moving a worker from one location to another. The worker can access the same central functionality from his or her new location, so little or no local equipment or data need be moved. This model of service delivery also reduces software piracy, because the software does not get physically distributed. There is no physical inventory for distributors to worry about or manage, because all services are distributed in real-time, on demand from end users.[9]

Figure 3–3 shows a possible supply chain for network service delivery. Independent software vendors (ISVs) develop software designed to operate over-the-Net. The software is hosted in secure, 24 × 7 facilities dedicated to running such systems. Aggregators (distributors) collect the offerings of ISVs and hosters into

---

[9]Studies from numerous sources have verified these savings. Morgan Stanley Dean Witter estimates that costs can be reduced by as much as 80% to 90% by outsourcing management of IT infrastructure (Jeff Camp, April Henry, Jaime Gomezjurado, and Kristen Olsavsky, "The Internet Hosting Report," November 2000). IDC estimates that the ROI from outsourcing services infrastructure can reach 300% with a payback on the investment of only 120 days (Melanie Posey, Beryl Muscarella, and Randy Perry, "Achieving Rapid Return on Investment in Outsourced Web Hosting," White Paper, 2000).

FIGURE 3–2

Purchase versus Subscribe Cash Flows

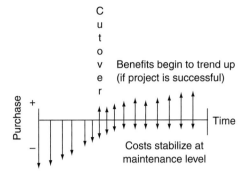

FIGURE 3–3

The IT Service Delivery Supply Chain

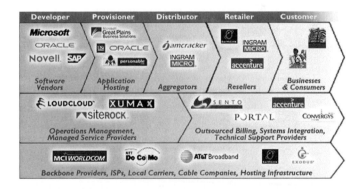

coherent packages, which they sell through resellers (retailers) who offer additional value-added services (such as tech support or consulting). Supporting players include network providers and outsourcing partners who specialize in back-office businesses such as billing or help-desk services. This is just one possible version of an IT services supply chain. Others are possible.

FIGURE 3–4

*Internal versus
External Service
Delivery*

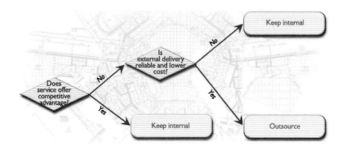

The advantage in a supply chain made up of specialized players is that each player can focus on what he or she does well, thereby realizing economies of scale and scope. Resellers focus on managing relationships with end customers. Aggregators focus on combining the offerings of different software vendors so that they interoperate. Hosters focus on reliable and secure operation of a type of system (e.g., e-mail). ISVs focus on developing their software.

This model is not hypothetical; players already conduct business in each of these roles. For example, Microsoft (an ISV) has cooperated with Personable (an Application Service Provider or ASP) in developing an over-the-Net version of Microsoft's Office™ productivity suite. Personable, which offers this version of Office to customers for $19.95 per month, runs the software in a data center owned by a hosting services provider. Jamcracker (an aggregator) combines the offerings of many ISVs/hosters into coherent packages. Accenture resells Jamcracker's packages.

As IT "service chains" proliferate and mature, companies will often face the question of which services to outsource. Figure 3–4 outlines the steps many companies consider in making this decision. IT services that are unique to a company and provide it with significant advantages over competitors will not be outsourced, at least not to vendors who are trying to sell similar services to all of their customers. Such services are so core to a company's business that an internal capability to manage and extend them must be maintained. But many IT services do not provide competitive advantage and probably never will. These services may be essential in running a modern business, but there may be no reason one company's service must be different from its competitors. For example, a company probably needs e-mail and word processing software. But the success or failure of a company usually has little to do with the features of these products. For such commodity-like services, the priorities are that they be delivered reliably and at lower cost (or with more favorable cash-flow profiles).

Management Challenges in the Age of Internetworking

We find that [the Worldwide Web and the Internet] display an unexpected degree of robustness, the ability of their nodes to communicate being unaffected even by unrealistically high failure rates. However, error tolerance comes at a high price in that these networks are extremely vulnerable to attacks (that is, to the selection and removal of a few nodes that play a vital role in maintaining the network's connectivity). Such error tolerance and attack vulnerability are generic properties of communication networks.[10]

Along with their advantages and possibilities, IT infrastructures based on internetworking technologies also generate challenges. To maintain robust operations, new priorities must emerge. Real-time infrastructures and new service delivery models have dark sides that do not offset their benefits, but that must be managed. The challenges of operational management in the internetworking age fall into several major categories.

Rapid Change, Complex Interactions, and Unpredictable Outcomes

The rise of internetworking technologies makes it possible to arrange IT infrastructure in an increasing number of configurations. The degrees of freedom in design choices are expanding rapidly. As businesses seek new capabilities and cost reduction by experimenting with different infrastructure configurations, unexpected and complex interactions are also on the rise. There are no precise models for anticipating the outcomes that result from efforts to combine new technologies in new ways.

Traditional planning and investment decision-making do not always work well in the presence of such unpredictability. Required actions and expenditures cannot always be identified in advance. The emerging response to these conditions of increasing complexity and uncertainty is "adaptive methods"—approaches to design, deployment, implementation, and investment that presume the need to gather information and to learn as we go.

The IT industry's most recent and intense experiences with combining technology components into real-time infrastructures have come in implementing large enterprise systems (also known as Enterprise Resource Planning or ERP systems). These systems, which emerged in the 1980s, became popular in the 1990s. They were an order of magnitude larger, more expensive, and complex than systems typically implemented up until that time. The details of managing implementation of these systems are left until Module 4, but enterprise systems projects do illustrate the advantages of emerging adaptive methods when faced with uncertainty borne of technological complexity.

The problem with large, complex systems as business propositions is they require large up-front investments to produce highly uncertain and

---

[10]Reka Albert, Hawoong Jeong, and Albert-Laszlo Barabasi, *Nature* 406, 378–382 (2000) © Macmillan Publishers Ltd.

occasionally disastrous results. Unintended consequences have flowed voluminously from these projects. FoxMeyer Drug was the fourth largest pharmaceutical products distributor in the United States until an abortive attempt to install an enterprise system forced them into bankruptcy. Dell Computer gave up their implementation after two years and $200 million spent. Dow Chemical considers their project a success now, but it took them seven years and more than $500 million to make it so. Nike, Hershey, Whirlpool, and W. L. Gore are other companies that have experienced embarrassing and expensive problems with enterprise systems.

Companies that have successfully implemented enterprise systems, as well as other complex new technologies, are achieving favorable outcomes by using adaptive methods. These methods, emerging only gradually, vary in how they are being used. Sometimes they are not even identified specifically as adaptive methods but are rather the result of processes evolving to take more uncertainty into account. However they appear, they tend to have the following five characteristics in common:

1. They are iterative, forcing infrastructure deployment to occur in small increments, so that outcomes and interactions can be better understood as they appear.
2. They rely on fast cycles and insist on frequent delivery of value so that incremental deployment does not slow deployment; long lead times and highly variable delivery timing are discouraged.
3. They emphasize early delivery to end-users of functionality, however limited, so that feedback can be incorporated into learning and improvement cycles.
4. They require highly-skilled people who are capable of learning and making mid-course adjustments in the midst of deployment.
5. They often resist ROI and other similar tools for investment decision making that implicitly assume predictability of outcomes, instead emphasizing "buying of information" about outcomes as a legitimate expenditure.

The common aim of such methods is that they permit rapid and controlled experimentation and incorporate learning from experiments immediately into deployment activities. Figure 3–5 shows a comparison between traditional planning-intensive approaches and more adaptive learning-intensive approaches.

Adaptive methods do not always fit comfortably with new technology deployment, especially large-scale deployment. Products must be designed for incremental deployment if such approaches are to be fully realized. Increasingly, software and equipment vendors are making less monolithic and more modular products, so that smaller chunks can be installed and changes can be made more gradually. Subscription-based external service delivery, as illustrated in Figure 3–2, fits well with adaptive approaches,

FIGURE 3–5

Traditional versus Adaptive Methods

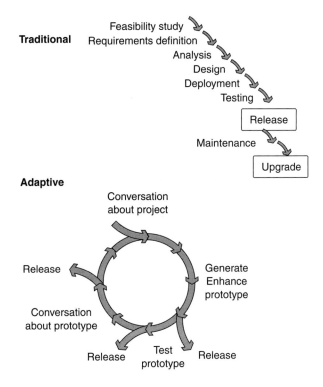

because subscription models are designed to be more incremental than traditional models.

Software development is one area where adaptive methods have developed a following. "Extreme Programming" (or "XP")[11] and "Adaptive Software Development"[12] are two examples of formal approaches of this kind. Open source software development, a technique that has led to the development of widely used infrastructure components, such as the Linux operating system and the Apache web server, also has adaptive characteristics.[13] The trend toward adaptive methods in software development is important in its own right, but there is also a broader trend exemplified by the efforts of companies such as Cisco and Tektronix as they deploy new IT infrastructure. Cisco very deliberately adopted "rapid, iterative prototyping," and Tektronix formalized their enterprise system deployment into "waves" that supported learning and adjustment.

A primary contribution of adaptive methods has been to legitimize the idea that plans will necessarily change during the course of a project, and

---

[11]Kent Beck, *Extreme Programming Explained: Embrace Change,* Addison-Wesley, 1999.

[12]James A. Highsmith, III, *Adaptive Software Development: A Collaborative Approach to Managing Complex Systems,* Dorset House, NY, 1999.

[13]Eric S. Raymond, *Cathedral & the Bazaar: Musings on Linux & Open Source by an Accidental Revolutionary,* O'Reilly & Associates, 2001.

that conformance to plans is not necessarily the measure of success for managers. In this approach, planning is not avoided. Detailed and rigorous planning remains one of the best ways to anticipate possible outcomes. But plans themselves are viewed by proponents of adaptive methods as tentative and always evolving.

Partner Selection and Relationship Management

As internetworking service models proliferate, IT service delivery depends on a growing number of service providers and other partners. One implication of this is that the reliability of vital services is only as good as the weakest link in the service provider chain. Selecting strong partners and managing relationships are vital, then, to reliable service delivery.

The prevalent contractual tool at the center of relationships with service providers is the "Service Level Agreement" (SLA). SLAs describe the specific conditions in which the service provider is held liable for a service interruption, and the penalties that the service provider will incur as a result. Figure 3–6 illustrates the kinds of contractual terms one might find in an SLA. Notice that failure is specifically defined, that penalties apply only in the case where the service provider is responsible for the service interruption, and penalties are prespecified and limited. But, the reason why a service provider might insist on these specifics is clear. The specific nature of the agreement complicates service delivery for the client company. What matters to the client company from a business standpoint is any failure, regardless of which service provider is the source of the problem.

What this means for most companies is that they need to manage a web of SLAs with many service providers. SLAs in the web must interlock so that penalty payments flow through the service chain in a way that provides appropriate incentives. For example: Suppose a software-on-demand company agrees with a client to pay a penalty if software is not available on demand for longer than 10 minutes. Suppose also that the actual cause of a failure is a different vendor, say an Internet Service Provider (ISP). Then, the SLA in place between the software company and ISP should specify that the software company will be reimbursed by the ISP for the penalty it owes to the client company. Although the SLA arrangement between the software company and the ISP might seem a matter best left to these two entities, it is to the client company's advantage to take an interest in how SLAs interlock. Disputes between partners in a service chain can have implications for the end user of the service.

The conventional wisdom in defining SLAs calls for designing them with "teeth"—that is, so that service providers feel pain when failures occur. In practice, however, determining appropriate penalty levels is difficult. SLAs provide service providers with both an incentive and a way of credibly expressing their intention to deliver reliable service, so it is important that they are in place. But setting penalties too low has insufficient effect in either regard. Setting them too high, so they are extremely punitive, has a detrimental effect

FIGURE 3–6

Example of Service Level Agreement Terms (for a hosting provider)

Downtime—defined as sustained packet loss in excess of 50% for 15 consecutive minutes due to the failure of the hosting provider to provide services for that period (does not include scheduled maintenance time).

Excess latency—defined as transmission latency in excess of 120 milliseconds round-trip time between any two points within the hosting provider's U.S. network.

Excess packet loss—defined as packet loss in excess of 1% between any two points in the hosting provider's network.

Each downtime period entitles customer to receive a credit equal to one day's recurring connectivity charge.

Hosting provider guarantees two-hour response time in diagnosing problems within hosting provider and customer network.

If problem is not within hosting provider and customer network, hosting provider will determine source within an additional two hours.

Customer will be advised of reason for problem within one hour of hosting provider discovering the reason for the problem.

If problem is within control of hosting provider, remedy for problem is guaranteed in two hours from diagnosis of the problem.

Inability to deliver diagnosis or remedies within the times stated above entitles customer to an additional service credit for each two-hour period of delay.

Customer can collect credits for no more than seven days charges in a calendar month.

Customer must request credits in writing within seven days of the event for which credits are compensation.

Credits are granted at the sole discretion of the hosting provider.

on a provider's willingness (and, if penalties are high enough, ability) to be a strong partner. So, while SLAs are important, it would be a mistake to consider them the primary means by which partners are managed.

The most successful relationships emphasize shared objectives and letting all partners earn a reasonable return. Relationships in which one partner obtains all the benefit, or worse, in which one partner is forced into a money-losing situation, are not stable in the long run.

Managing Legacies

Few companies are so new that they have no artifacts left over from earlier times that must be managed as they move forward with new technologies. Legacy systems present one set of challenges. They are often old and creaky, based on obsolete and proprietary technologies, and vital to the business as it operates from day-to-day. Fitting new infrastructure into complex legacy infrastructure, or vice versa, makes for formidable challenges and uncertain outcomes.

But systems are not the only legacies companies must manage. Even more significant are legacy processes, organizations, and cultures. The act of changing the IT infrastructure has unavoidable effects on non-technical elements of a company's operations. New technologies change how people work and interact. Managers have important decisions to make about how much they want the company's culture to drive the design of its infrastructure, or vice versa. There are companies whose managers have gone to great lengths to make sure IT infrastructure does not constrain culture or process. There are other companies whose managers intend to use IT systems as "sledge hammers" to bring about organizational change. Both approaches can work, but the issues and decisions involved are complex. Table 3–2 summarizes some of the concerns that must be addressed in successfully managing legacies.

Decisions about new technologies and how they should interact with legacies vary greatly from company to company, and depend on a large number of factors. Difficulties with legacy systems are part of the rationale for new infrastructure deployment. So with systems, replacing old with new is usually viewed as a plus. But this is not necessarily so with legacy organizational issues. At some companies, legacy organizational culture is viewed as an asset to be protected from the effects of new technology imposition. At others, legacy culture is viewed as a problem as great or greater than the legacy systems.

TABLE 3–2   Key Questions in Managing Legacies

Legacy Systems	• How will new infrastructure exchange data with legacy systems? • Will new infrastructure obtain needed real-time interaction with legacy systems? • What work-arounds are necessary? Are they sustainable? • What is long-term strategy for replacing legacy systems?
Legacy Organizations and Cultures	• How will new infrastructure affect ways of working and communicating? Are anticipated changes acceptable? • Should technology drive organizational and cultural change? • Should organization and culture be protected from technology effects? • What are organizational expectations about common processes in different parts of the organization? • What are criteria for deciding whether systems or process will change when the two are not compatible?

Broader Exposure to Operational Threats

On October 19, 1987, the Dow Jones Industrial Average plummeted more than 500 points in the single largest percentage decrease in history. The plunge of 22.6% was almost double the 12.9% drop in 1929 that foreshadowed the Great Depression. Unlike in 1929, the market quickly recovered in 1987, posting major gains in the two days following the crash and regaining its pre-crash level by September 1989. Nevertheless, the suddenness of these events prompted a search for explanations.

In identifying causes of the 1987 crash, many singled out the role of computerized "program trading" by large institutional investors. In program trading, computers initiate market transactions automatically, without human intervention, when triggering conditions appear in the markets. What no one anticipated, however, was the degree to which automatic trades could lead to more automatic trades. Automatic trades created market conditions that set off more automatic trades, which created conditions that set off more automatic trades and so on, in a rapid fire chain-reaction that was unexpected and difficult to understand while it was in progress.

This example reveals a dark side of real-time computing that extends to emergent real-time infrastructures. As batch-processing delays are eliminated and more transactions move from initiation to completion without intervention by human operators, the potential grows for computerized chain-reactions that produce unanticipated effects. Malfunctions and errors propagate faster and have potentially broader impacts. Diagnosis and remediation of rapid and complex interactions can present a major challenge for business managers.

Because of this reality of the internetworking age, it is essential that senior business managers be involved in decisions that in the past might have been left to "techies." Responsible managers must think in advance and in detail about how to respond to incidents and how to recover from failures. The importance of anticipating incidents and even practicing incident response is heightened by the presence of new and malicious threats to IT infrastructures. For example, the number of people trying to intentionally trigger real-time infrastructure failures is growing.

Proprietary technologies of the past were designed to deny access to systems unless someone intervened specifically to authorize access. Internet-based systems are different. Because they evolved in an arena not oriented toward commerce, primarily to support communities of researchers, Internet technologies allow access unless someone (or some system) intervenes specifically to disallow access. Security measures to support commercial relationships must therefore be retrofitted onto base technologies. Moreover, the universality of Internet connections—the fact that every computer is connected to every other computer—makes every computer a potential target for attack and every computer a potential base from which attacks can be launched. The average computer is connected to the Internet for only a few minutes before it is "port scanned"—probed for vulnerability to intrusion or attack. The vast majority of attempted incursions are the cyberspace equivalent of school kids playing a prank. But recent evidence shows that more serious criminals have begun to explore the possibilities presented by the Internet. The threat is real enough even from pranksters because simple-to-execute attack and intrusion methods are proliferating on the Internet.

"Denial of Service" (DoS) attacks, for example, are surprisingly simple. They bring an e-business operation to its knees in roughly the same way that a full tour bus swamps a fast food restaurant by unloading its passengers for dinner. The difference is that in a DoS attack, it is as if the bus passengers are standing in line, taking up the time of the fast food workers, but not actually ordering anything. Paying customers cannot make their way to the front of the line where they might order and pay. The insidious nature of such attacks derives from the difficulty in telling decoy customers from real cus-

TABLE 3–3   Wake-Up Call: Denial of Service Attacks in February 2000

Date	Target Company	Comments
February 7	Yahoo	• Overwhelming spike in traffic that lasted 3 hours. • Network availability dropped from 98% to 0%. • Attack originated from 50 different locations and was timed to occur during middle of business day. • Stock was down 3.2% for week in which NASDAQ rose almost 3%.
February 8	Buy.com	• Attack occurred within an hour of the company's Initial Public Offering (IPO) • Stock was down at week's end more than 20% from IPO price.
	EBay	• Stock was down 7.3% for week in which NASDAQ rose almost 3%.
	CNN.com	Service interrupted
February 9	E*Trade	• Attacked during peak trading hours. • Stock was down 7.6% for week in which NASDAQ rose almost 3%.
	ZDNet	Service interrupted
February 18	Federal Bureau of Investigation (FBI)	Website shutdown
February 24	National Discount Brokers Group (NDB)	• Attacked during peak trading hours. • Operators accidentally crashed site as they attempted to defend against the attack.

Overall performance of the Internet degraded by as much as 25% during the peak of the attacks as computers re-sent messages repeatedly and automatically, trying to recover interrupted transactions.
(Source: NetworkWorldFusion, www.nwfusion.com.)

tomers. Novice hackers (called "script kiddies") often launch these attacks using easy-to-use weaponry that is easy to find on the web.

In February 2000, the e-business community received a wake-up call concerning its vulnerability to e-attacks. Total damages from a series of high profile, centrally orchestrated attacks were estimated to be in excess of $100 million. As the Internet and the Web have risen to commercial prominence, computer security problems have progressed from being tactical nuisances that could be left to technicians into strategic infrastructure problems that require involvement of business managers up to the CEO level. Table 3–3 summarizes a series of attacks and their effects.

Putting the Ideas to Work

In an age of rapidly advancing technology and fast-changing business conditions, operational capabilities have an expanded, even strategic, role to play in successful companies. Operational considerations often have been regarded as primarily tactical, as ways of executing already formed strategies. But in times of great change, strategies have short useful lives. There is little time for top-down approaches that call for formulating strategy, then building operational capabilities to execute the strategy. Rather, a company's capabilities determine what strategies it is possible for a company to pursue. As conditions change, what a company is capable of—what possibilities it can realize that are appropriate new business environments—becomes the key determinant of what a company can reasonably attempt.[14] Even when strategy-making proceeds in a more traditional top-down manner, the ability to understand and forecast the technological possibilities remains important.

"Arepa,"[15] the company described in the first case in this module, is trying to envision what a successful future service delivery infrastructure will look like. The company's technology allows delivery of IT services via a software-on-demand model. Its managers are trying to build a successful business model around the technology. But this kind of service delivery is hypothetical for most of Arepa's prospective customers. The young company is selling not only a new service but also a new kind of service. Managers are trying to figure out how to package their offerings so that potential customers are most likely to buy. Intertwined with questions about what customers will buy are questions about how to structure the business model. Figuring out what customers will buy and how to capture economic value from selling it to them are the keys to accessing the financing Arepa will need to grow. Arepa offers an opportunity to discuss the viability of new, internetworking-enabled service delivery models. Deciding how to mount a successful business model atop a complex IT infrastructure requires detailed exploration of the infrastructure itself. The case makes very clear how business and technical issues

---

[14]Robert H. Hayes wrote about this sort of "reverse strategic planning" in 1985 (*Harvard Business Review*); his advice has become newly relevant in IT world of the early 21st century.

[15]D. Green and J. Light, *Arepa,* (HBS No. 201-008)

can interact in important ways, and how technical possibilities or impossibilities can enable or inhibit exiting new ways of doing business.

The "Selecting a Hosting Provider" exercise[16] in this module, with its accompanying technology note "Web and IT Hosting Facilities,"[17] focuses on the details of how to build reliable real-time infrastructures. Examining how hosting facilities are designed leads to a detailed understanding of the issues involved in assuring the levels of availability and reliability required by real-time operations. The exercise shifts the emphasis of discussion from the operations-enabled strategy concerns of Arepa toward issues of execution, but strategic elements remain in the decision of which hosting partner to select. The exercise is designed to elicit criteria for selecting infrastructure providers for each of two different companies, one a mature industrial age company, the other a young startup. By comparing the derived criteria for the two client companies, and through discussion of whether the choice of hosting partner might be different for the industrial age firm than it is for the startup, it is possible to arrive at a detailed understanding of the issues involved in outsourcing infrastructure management.

"Trilogy"[18] raises a number of provocative questions about the deep nature of operational capabilities. The company's founder and CEO has highly unconventional ideas about management and puts his beliefs into practice with a vengeance. In particular, he believes in a radical form of empowerment that calls for hiring the very best people and then letting them work without much management structure. He views traditional emphases on operational process as too constraining for his highly-talented and innovative employees. Critics of the company's approach call it chaotic. But a closer look at Trilogy and its dynamic leader reveals that there *are* processes at work in the company. Primarily, they are adaptive processes. Whether or not such processes can achieve the levels of reliability and consistency required of modern operations is a central question. The case serves as an excellent example of a company that has geared every aspect of its operations around the ability to adapt.

"The iPremier Company"[19] depicts a crisis in progress. A luxury goods retailer with high-income customers finds itself under attack from an unknown "hacker." The case describes the events as they unfold and demonstrates conclusively how decisions involved in securing IT infrastructures are, despite their technical complexity, necessarily in the mainstream of general management. How managers handled the 75 minute company shutdown, how they might have been more ready for the attack, and what they might do to prepare for the next attack are all issues discussed. A crucial general man-

---

[16]R.D. Austin, *Selecting a Hosting Provider: Exercise,* (HBS No 601-171)

[17]R.D. Austin, *Web and IT Hosting Facilities,* (HBS No 601-134).

[18]R.D. Austin, *Trilogy,* (HBS No 699-034)

[19]R.D. Austin, L. Leibrock, and A. Murray, *The iPremier Company: Denial of Service Attack (A),* (HBS No 601-114).

agement issue has to do with what the company should disclose publicly after the attack. Because iPremier was unprepared for the attack, its managers were unable to determine exactly what happened. Weighing the interests of customers, whose credit card numbers have been trusted to the company, against those of shareholders, whose investments might be impacted by unnecessarily alarmist disclosures, is clearly an issue for the CEO.

Taken together these four cases and a technology note provide an excellent overview of the challenges of managing e-business infrastructure for the 21st century.

CASE 3–1
AREPA[1]

"Arepa" is named after a Venezuelan breakfast burrito. I figured that at least I'd be famous in Venezuela if it didn't work.

—Ric Fulop, *founder and president of Arepa*

Ric Fulop checked his custom-built MP3 player to see if his tunes had downloaded from his home's wireless LAN. He then disconnected the wireless modem and tucked it under the passenger seat, plugged the player into his car's cassette slot, and pulled out of his garage. Before long, he was on Fresh Pond Parkway in Cambridge, Massachusetts, headed to work on a bright summer morning in June 1999. Fulop found that the ride cleared his thoughts. It gave him the opportunity to think about the difficult alternatives that he, Vinnie Grosso, and the Arepa leadership team would discuss at this afternoon's meeting.

The company he had founded, Arepa, planned to deliver "software on demand" to broadband subscribers. Arepa's exciting new technology would allow subscribers to access and use software online without having to suf-

[1]This case was prepared by High Tech Fellow Dan Green under the supervision of Professor Jay Light. Copyright © 2000 by the President and Fellows of Harvard College. Harvard Business School case 201-008.

fer through a frustrating purchasing experience and a time-consuming download, installation, and rebooting process. If successful, the Arepa system would almost surely take market share away from conventional software sales channels, replacing them with Internet-based sales and delivery.

For the moment, though, Arepa was still an embryonic company that needed to strike deals with partners on all sides. It needed broadband distribution channels, and would have to negotiate agreements with Broadband Service Providers (BSPs) such as @Home and RoadRunner that provided broadband over enhanced cable systems owned by Multiple Systems Operators (MSOs) such as AT&T Cable and Time Warner Cable. In addition, it might try to strike distribution deals with Digital Subscriber Line (DSL) providers. Arepa also had to strike deals with content providers, including a well-known group of software publishers such as Electronic Arts, Hasbro, Mattel, and Disney, some of which had assembled a broad array of software titles. These tasks could entail potentially difficult negotiations—the details of which could be dependent upon Arepa's selection of a business model.

Although the company had originally planned merely to license its technology (the server software) to various broadband service providers, the new CEO, Vinnie Grosso, believed that Arepa had to choose between a couple of alternative business models. Those alternatives had quite different cash flow characteristics and risk-reward patterns, and implied different negotiating stances and perhaps different sets of investors.

The intertwining negotiations and business model decisions threatened to confuse an already complicated business. Arepa's idea was a "category changer," one that would change an industry if it became successful. But Grosso worried that Arepa would try to do too much. Already the company was gearing up to participate in many adjacent but different links of the value chain. The company was getting hard to understand, and Grosso was concerned that it might not bode well for the next round of financing.

In terms of financing, Arepa needed to expand beyond its existing investor base of Intel and Venrock. It had to determine the usual questions about how much money it needed and how much the company was worth (the pre-money valuation), but these decisions were complicated by a new wrinkle. Arepa could pursue another round of venture capital, or it could attempt to raise a round from strategic corporate investors. If it pursued strategic investors, there were many companies that Arepa could approach for financing. Arepa would need to decide which potential investors would be the most valuable allies as it executed its business plan.

Software on Demand

Hey, you've got broadband . . . why aren't you using it? It's fine to get your email faster and
it's fine to get your downloads quicker, but what about all the other really great things you can do with broadband, like instantly download and play software?
—Bill Holding, *VP of Marketing, Arepa*

The consumer retail software market in the United States could be divided into three principal segments (see Exhibits 1A and 1B). PC-based games comprised $1.3 billion of the market. Productivity software, such as tax preparation and home finance titles, totaled $2.3 billion of sales, and "edutainment" titles for children and adults—that taught children reading skills, for example, or taught adults how to do home improvement projects—rounded out the market with another $0.6 billion annually. Altogether, over 107 million single-copies of titles were sold in 1998. In addition, the Web-based learning and small office/home office (SOHO) markets for software were very large.

In recent years, software titles had been sold on compact discs (CD-ROMs) in retail stores or through catalogues. Downloading an entire program from the Internet had not been practical for most titles because a dialup Internet connection was far too slow. Indeed, in most cases, even a broadband connection was too slow. At 600 megabytes in size, for example, a typical software title could clog a broadband pipe for an hour or more. The resulting need for physical distribution created a costly problem for software publishers. About 50% of the retail cost of the software was "lost" to the sales channel; it was used to provide retailer margins and to cover costs such as packaging, shipping, and inventory. Inventory presented a special challenge to publishers, since software often rapidly became obsolete. Game or simulation titles, for example, stayed in print for less than a year, after which they were retired because of declining sales. For obsolete titles,

EXHIBIT 1A Retail Consumer Software Market

	1999E Sales, ($ billions)	1999E Units Sold (millions)	1998 Sales ($ billions)	1998 Units Sold (millions)
Games	1.4	61	1.3	55
Productivity	2.6	28	2.3	25
Edutainment	0.6	28	0.6	27

Source: Arepa.

EXHIBIT 1B Expected Distribution of Revenues in the $30 Billion 1999 U.S. Consumers, Small Office, Home Office (SOHO), and School Web-based Learning Software Markets

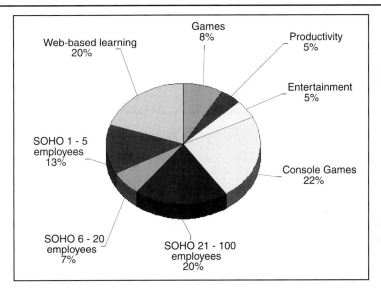

Source: Arepa.

publishers were presented with unattractive alternatives. They could allow the retailer to drop the price and reimburse the retailer for the lost profits on each title sold at the lower price, or they could allow the retailer to return the titles. If they allowed the retailer to return unsold titles, the publisher could either sell the returned titles to a liquidator or carry the titles indefinitely in inventory. Because of unpredictability, substantial inventory was often carried throughout the channel to prepare for periods of peak demand—in the first month of a game's release, at Christmastime, or during tax season, for example.

From the consumer's perspective, the process was no better. "Everyone knows today that the software purchase experience is a lousy experience," remarked Bill Holding, vice president of Marketing for Arepa.

Think about buying a music CD versus buying software today. If you hear a good song on the radio, you go down to Tower Records, and you can go in there and they've hired people who know something about music. You can see what the top titles are, you can talk to someone, and you can even put on headphones and listen to the new Santana album before you buy it.

But if you're buying software today, you walk into Circuit City or CompUSA. They sell everything from video cameras to televisions to software. So you make your way over to the software titles, and you find it's almost impossible to find someone who's knowledgeable about software, particularly about the titles that you want. And, of course, you can't try it before you buy it. So half the time you get it home and it doesn't install because you don't have the right video card or whatever. And then when you install more than a few titles, it resets your settings and your computer doesn't work any more. It's a terrible experience.

Arepa's technology for online delivery of software would dramatically improve the way software was sold. Online access reduced the risk that settings would be corrupted on the user's PC, because no installation process was needed. It also eliminated returns, and gave the publishers the flexibility to grant users limited-use access to titles so that they could try them before purchasing.

By cleaning up the customer purchasing experience, Arepa's technology would also help software publishers. The technology allowed the publisher to update the software frequently—in principle, even daily—adding new modules to a game or a piece of do-it-yourself software, for example. This would allow software titles to become adaptable, "living" programs, changing with up-to-date programming instead of remaining frozen at the time the CD is created. Arepa's unique way of dividing and encrypting programs also ensured that the user would not be able to copy and redistribute the software, enabling Arepa to offer software publishers anti-piracy guarantees that were just not possible in the CD channel. Also, because the distribution cost would be reduced (perhaps by up to 50%), publishers could set the prices for software

lower than they could through physical retail channels. Doc Honan, Arepa's CFO, suggested how the availability of software online would change consumer behavior. He suggested that because software would become much less expensive and easier to use, the publisher would see an increase in sales:

> My favorite example is TurboTax. You do your return once a year. You buy your TurboTax for forty bucks and do your return. You save the copy because, well, you never throw software away, even though you know it's going to be useless next year, because the tax code keeps changing. So you spend forty bucks a year buying TurboTax, and then all you do is store it and waste disk space. Suppose you could get it online for a few bucks per use. Wherever and whenever you called it up, you could be certain you had the latest version that included the most recent changes to the tax code.

Perhaps most important, online titles suffered no shelf space restrictions and incurred no inventory risk. As a result, all titles, no matter how old, could theoretically be made available to anyone at any time. Arepa's technology could exhume older "backlist" titles—games, for example—and make them available at very low rates. In theory, the new distribution mechanism could thus extend the useful life of a title, in much the same way that the invention of videotape had revolutionized the movie business by allowing movie producers to realize aftermarket revenues from motion pictures (see Exhibits 2 and 3). Honan explained:

> This thing, at least at a blackboard level, should obliterate the bricks-and-mortar store. It doesn't need inventory, and it doesn't need shelf space. How many titles can Circuit City fit in a store? There are 50,000 titles out there, and 49,500 of those are dead because there's not enough shelf space. Well, with Arepa, there's new life. Not *everybody's* going to want these backlist titles, but *somebody's* going to want them, especially if you let them try the titles first.

Finally, the Broadband Service Provider (BSP) would benefit, since the availability of the novel service would attract subscribers. Arepa would likely be the first true broadband-

EXHIBIT 2 **Value Generation for Video and Software Titles in the Secondary Market**

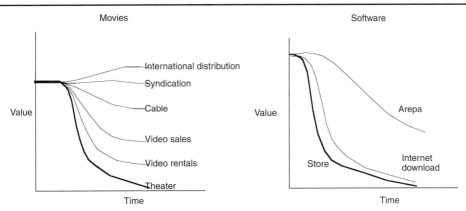

Source: Arepa.

EXHIBIT 3 **Typical Consumer Price Points**

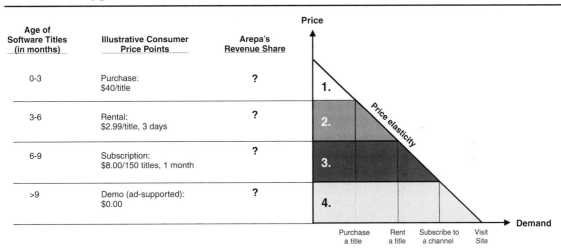

Note: Prices are hypothetical.
Source: Arepa.

only consumer application. "For the BSP," remarked Don Rogers, director of New Business Development for Arepa, "it's about providing a value-added service to their customers. Today, the BSPs are trying to differentiate themselves from narrowband beyond just delivering faster HTML pages. They may be able to deliver Yahoo! really fast, but if they want to attract new customers, they really need new and value-added services like us."

Technology

Because a typical software game with rich graphics could take over an hour to download, software-on-demand required that titles be delivered in an entirely different way. Arepa divided software into consumable portions that could be called from a hierarchy of regional and local data caches in the network as the user needed them. Arepa's technology enabled the user to begin playing a game just seconds after requesting it. An Arepa-enabled game would play without delays, just as it would if it were already sitting on a PC user's hard disk.

Arepa planned to deploy repurposed software in a national network of servers (see Exhibit 4). Broadband subscribers could use Arepa's proprietary technology to download compressed and encrypted segments—called *briqs*—of desired software from a cache run by Inktomi software in a local cable headend.[2]

---

[2]A cable headend housed equipment such as routers, switches, servers, and caches that connected subscribers to the network. Headends could be as small as a room or as large as a building, depending on the number of subscribers served from the location and the type of equipment it housed.

EXHIBIT 4   Arepa's Server Hierarchy

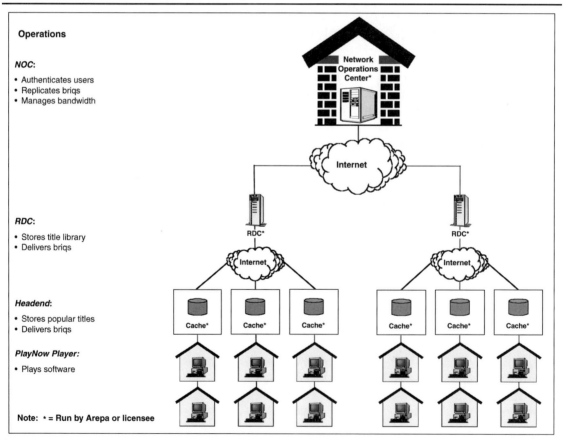

Source: Arepa.

Unused briqs of the program remained cached, and were downloaded to the user's PC only when needed—for example, when the user progressed to the next level of a game. Headend caches stored only the most popular titles. If the local cache did not have a current copy of the needed briq, the briq was retrieved from the next step up in the hierarchy—the nearest Regional Data Center (RDC). RDCs stored copies of the complete library of titles available under license by Arepa. Arepa might own and operate 150 RDCs nationwide, and would upload content to the RDCs from its central replication server—called a *briq house*—at the company's headquarters. Each RDC would serve approximately 20 cable headends and would be collocated at the BSP's facilities.

Essentially the same hierarchical architecture would be used to support DSL service—but instead of locating equipment in a cable headend, Arepa would install its servers in RBOC (local phone company) central offices that were provisioned for DSL.

Arepa would manage the entire network from its headquarter's Network Operations Center (NOC) and perform certain routine network tasks such as authenticating users as they requested access to titles.[3] It would also manage bandwidth availability on its network. Bandwidth management was an important service to BSPs, who worried about the effect on their networks of thousands of subscribers attempting simultaneous access to a particular server; redundant user requests for content delivery consumed valuable space on the broadband pipes and overloaded the server. The hierarchy of Arepa's network helped alleviate this, but in addition, Arepa could tweak its network to help prevent crashes during peak usage.

Historical Information on Arepa

Growing up in Venezuela, Fulop used his personal savings to found his first company in 1991 at age 16. The company distributed boxed software, and it quickly grew to become one of the largest software distributors in Venezuela. At age 18, he sold his interest in the venture to his partner for about $1 million in cash and founded a second company that created parametric modeling software to enable complex visualization of three-dimensional models. Although located in Venezuela, most of his customer base was in the United States; his customers included the Port Authority of New York and New Jersey and the National Aeronautics and Space Administration. In 1994, he sold this company to Deneba, a Florida-based developer and publisher of graphics and moved to the United States to join the company. Soon after, he moved to Boston to be with his girlfriend and, looking for another challenge, he enrolled in Babson's entrepreneurship program. By the summer of 1996, however, he was restless, and he had dropped out to start Arepa.

For the first year, Arepa was funded from Fulop's profits on his first two ventures. Then, in July 1997, he ran out of money. Down to his last $1,000, Fulop had 10 employees on his payroll, and somehow, they had to be paid. Fulop decided to call Rouzbeh Yassini, the inventor of the cable modem, to ask for an investment. Yassini was the founder of LANCity, and had sold the company to Bay Networks[4] a year earlier. Yassini left LANCity in late 1996, joined a cable industry standards group, and formed a venture to fund broadband startups. Fulop knew Yassini from a broadband conference that they had both attended earlier that year, and called him at work on a Friday. The two agreed to meet the next day at a Japanese restaurant on Newbury Street in Boston. When

[3]Arepa could similarly build in a set of controls to allow parents to restrict access to titles.

[4]Northern Telecom acquired Bay Networks in 1997. The combined company was renamed Nortel Networks.

EXHIBIT 5   Arepa's Financing History

Date	Investor	Investment ($mm)	Pre-Money Valuation ($mm)
	Ric Fulop	~ 1	—
July 1997	Rouzbeh Yassini	n/a	n/a
August 1997	Fidelity	0.5	1.0
June 1998	Intel, Venrock	5.0	10.0

Source: Arepa.
n/a = not available.

the appointed hour arrived, however, Yassini had not shown up. Fulop waited three hours, then hunted through all the Boston-area phone books to find Yassini's home phone number. Fulop finally reached him at his home, and after explaining his payroll problem, persuaded Yassini to meet the next day for lunch again. This time, Yassini showed up and agreed to fund Arepa's operations for a while in exchange for a portion of equity in the company.

Saved for the moment, Fulop continued his search for funding. Three weeks later, Fulop secured $500,000 of financing from Fidelity at a $2 million pre-money valuation. This allowed him to continue the development work on the basic technology for another year. By June 1998, Arepa had proven the technology concept on a limited scale, and closed on a $5 million investment from Intel and Venrock (a widely respected venture capital firm) at a $15 million pre-money valuation (see Exhibit 5).

Potential Competitors[5]

There was currently only one direct competitor planning to provide software on demand in the United States. Other large and successful companies, however, were in adjacent spaces, and could potentially step into the market if Arepa did not move quickly.

[5]Source: Company websites and press releases.

MediaStation was a 40-person Ann Arbor development and publishing firm that was primarily dedicated to generating some CD-ROMs for Mattel and Hasbro. It had published numerous children's entertainment titles, including Disney's Animated Storybooks for *101 Dalmatians* and *Winnie the Pooh and the Honey Tree,* as well as for Hasbro Interactive's Tonka Workshop, Tonka Garage, and Tonka Search and Rescue. It had begun to implement a cached-content business model as it worried about the viability of CDs as a distribution mechanism. It was not likely that Arepa would be able to secure distribution licenses for MediaStation titles. MediaStation planned trials of its service with Sprint in October 1999 over Sprint's DSL access lines in Orlando. MediaStation had announced plans for a two-tier pricing plan: It would charge $3.95 per title for access to new titles for a 48-hour period. Most titles in this category would be less than a year old. MediaStation planned to aggregate software older than a year into a small library of some 75 titles. For access to the library, the company planned to charge $6.95 to $9.95 per month (depending on connection bandwidth). The content would be turned over about 10% to 20% per month, depending on consumer demand. MediaStation's technology was quite awkward from a user's perspective, however. Unlike Arepa's, it required the user to download each title, install it, and reboot before being able to use it. MediaStation planned to supply BSPs with headend servers, priced under $10,000, that could download and deploy not just MediaStation's own titles but other companies' titles as well. So far, it was internally financed and had not received venture backing.

ARMT Multimedia and Telecommunication was a five-person Israeli company that had inked deals with Deutsche Telekom, Singapore Telecom, and Telia to deliver games-on-demand to residential customers. The company also provided an online software platform to enable real-time, remote consulting for open-heart surgery operations and an online video surveillance platform for bank security applications. It was funded in part by a cable television operator—Giltek, Ltd.—that was also Israel's largest cable television and wireless construction contractor. Most of its activity appeared to be in Europe.

Akamai had a network of 600 servers that delivered bandwidth-intensive web-page objects over the Internet. Akamai could deliver either entire web pages or just portions of pages, depending on the requirements of the web page's owner. Akamai's servers cached frequently used objects locally so that when users called up a page, the objects would not have to travel through the Internet. Akamai's servers also had a proprietary network management system that could reroute packets dynamically to avoid network congestion. Akamai managed its network of servers from a sophisticated network operations center (NOC) in Cambridge, Massachusetts. The technology cut download time in half for some web pages, allowing web page owners to deliver richer media to their users. Although Akamai was not focused on delivering CD-ROM software, it was possible that at some point in the future, its services could overlap Arepa's. For example, Akamai could conceivably use its technology to deliver Arepa's briqs for software publishers. Akamai had raised over $43 million from a syndicate led by Bat-

tery Ventures. Its COO, Paul Sagan, was a founder of RoadRunner. Its CEO, George Conrades, was formerly CEO of BBN, the first backbone provider on the Internet. The company's advisory board included such luminaries as Tim Berners-Lee, director of the World Wide Web Consortium, and Amos Hostetter, founder of Continental Cablevision.

Real Networks was a public company that sold broadcast servers that were designed to carry streaming audio and video content on demand. It also maintained a consumer destination site that allowed users to access audio and video content over the web. It had an 85% share of the streaming media server business and had not yet appeared to be contemplating delivery of interactive applications such as edutainment software.

Microsoft, as early as 1996, had sold a product called NetShow that streamed audio and video on demand inside corporate networks. By 1999, Microsoft's streaming technology had evolved to compete with Real Networks' server software on the Internet. Microsoft had signaled in press releases that it had contemplated setting up a software-on-demand service, and in fact, had signed an agreement in March 1999 with Hong Kong Telecom Broadband Services to develop interactive television services, including video-on-demand and software-on-demand. It was difficult to know how serious Microsoft would be about any of this.

The Broadband Channels

Broadband service was delivered either over cable TV infrastructure or through local phone lines, both of which were being upgraded to carry data.[6] Only 46% of the nation's cable

---

[6]Satellites are not considered here since their broadband "pipes" were one-way; only downloads were broadband. The user had to be dialed in on a phone line to send data upstream.

infrastructure had been upgraded to allow high-speed data services by the end of 1998, and the rollout of DSL service on local phone lines had just begun. In 1998, there were approximately 37 million residential Internet user accounts in the United States, of which 3% accessed the Internet through some form of broadband service. The potential to grow this channel by delivering data over cable, however, was enormous. Approximately 65% of the 100 million residences in the United States were passed by cable infrastructure. RBOCs and their emerging competitors had begun to provision local phone lines to deliver DSL service in 1998, but lagged cable deployment significantly. Virtually every home in the United States had a phone line, however, making the potential similarly enormous, and all of the RBOCs had announced that DSL deployment would be a future priority. By 2003, it was expected that there would be 75 million residential Internet accounts, 36% of which would have broadband access (26% cable, and 10% DSL).[7] While there were technical distinctions between the two types of service,[8] a broadband user could achieve several hundred kilobits per second and sometimes as many as 1.5 megabits per second—an appealing increase over the more conventional 56 kilobits per second available from a dialup modem.

Cable.   MSOs were granted local monopoly franchises to install coaxial cable infrastructure and set-top boxes and deliver programming services to local residences. MSOs had generally become accustomed to handling cus-

tomer billing and service and outsourcing all of their content needs. To adapt to broadband, however, a group of very large MSOs (including Tele-Communications, Inc.—which later merged with AT&T—Comcast, and Cox), invested in a BSP, @Home, which in turn provided exclusive broadband data connectivity to the MSO subscribers. MSOs installed the customers' cable modems and charged each @Home subscriber about $100 for a one-time setup fee (the cable modem itself cost several hundred dollars and was heavily subsidized by the MSO). Thereafter, @Home charged about $40 per month for the service—approximately twice the prevailing narrowband ISP monthly rate. The affiliated MSOs received between 65% and 79% of @Home's revenues, and they kept the entire cable modem installation fee. When it acquired Tele-communications, Inc. and the Media One Group, AT&T became the largest investor in @Home (see Exhibit 6), although other cable operators had veto power over board-level decisions. In 1999, @Home purchased the narrowband portal Excite and by mid-year, announced that it had reached 330,000 subscribers. Excite@Home was projected to reach nearly 1 million subscribers by the end of 1999. Through the exclusive distribution deals it had struck with MSOs, @Home was the only BSP available to 65 million households in the United States and Canada.

Time Warner and Media One (acquisition by AT&T was pending in 1999) had invested in and affiliated with a similar competitive BSP, RoadRunner (see Exhibit 7).[9] The number-two cable broadband provider, RoadRunner announced that it had signed up 250,000 subscribers by mid-1999. Its service was available to 30 million households in the United States and Canada through its affiliated MSOs, which included MediaOne (soon to be merged

---

[7]James Lindsay Freeze, "Internet Services Hypergrowth," Forrester Research, February 1999; Bruce Kasrel, "From Dialup to Broadband," Forrester Research, April 1999.

[8]The bandwidth available to cable broadband subscribers decreased as the number of users connected to the neighborhood cable increased. By contrast, the bandwidth available to DSL subscribers decreased with the distance to the local phone company's central office.

---

[9]Other RoadRunner investors included Microsoft, Compaq, and Advance/Newhouse.

EXHIBIT 6   Ownership Stakes in Excite@Home

Company	Percent of Common Stock, Fully Diluted
AT&T[a]	25.9%
Cox Communications, Inc.	8.0%
Comcast Corp.	8.0%
Cablevision Systems Corp.[b]	5.7%
Janus Corp	4.4%
Intuit Inc.	3.1%
Janus 20 Fund	1.8%
Thomas A. Jermoluk	1.7%
Vinod Khosla for Kleiner Perkins Caufield & Byers	1.0%
Others	Balance

[a]Because of differences in the voting rights of Series A and Series B common stock, Tele-Communications, Inc. (TCI) controlled approximately 57% of Excite@Home's voting power with its 25.9% stake in Excite@Home. AT&T owned TCI and therefore controlled this voting power. AT&T had the right to elect five directors, one of which was designated by Comcast and one of which was designated by Cox. Excite@Home's board could take action only if the action was approved both by a majority of the entire board and by at least four of the five AT&T-elected directors. As a result, corporate actions generally required the approval of AT&T's three directors and one, or in some cases both, of the directors designated by Comcast and Cox. Therefore, Comcast and Cox, acting together, could veto any board action. In 1999, four of eleven Excite@Home directors were also directors, officers or employees of AT&T or its affiliates.
[b]AT&T owned 37% of Cablevision Systems Corp.
Source: Schroder & Co. Inc., *Excite@Home* 10Q filing, 15 November 1999.

EXHIBIT 7   MSO Affiliation with BSPs

MSO	Basic Cable Subscribers[a] (at end of 1998)	Exclusive Broadband Service Provider
AT&T/Tele-Communications, Inc.	10,600,000	@Home
Time Warner[b]	12,300,000	RoadRunner
Media One[b]	5,000,000	RoadRunner
Comcast	5,600,000	@Home
Cox	3,700,000	@Home
Cablevision	3,400,000	@Home
Rogers[c]	2,225,000	@Home
Adelphia	2,150,000	Powerlink
Charter	2,150,000	@Home/Charter Pipeline
Shaw[c]	1,500,000	@Home

[a]Did not include broadband subscribers.
[b]AT&T's acquisition of MediaOne was pending in 1999. If it were completed, AT&T would own a 25% stake in Time Warner Cable and a 34% stake in RoadRunner.
[c]National legislation was passed in Canada in 1998 to force cable operators to void their exclusivity clauses with Broadband Service Providers and provide access to competing BSPs.
Source: BT Alex. Brown, Schroder & Co. Inc.

into AT&T), and Time Warner. Between them, therefore, these two BSPs covered most of the United States.

BSPs offered portal-like services as part of their basic connectivity package. A subscriber who signed up to use @Home's service, for example, was given access to a proprietary portal populated with third-party content. Most of this content was traditional, in that it was narrowband Web content delivered with higher quality at higher connection speeds. Few applications used the added bandwidth of cable to offer a higher tier of services such as video-on-demand or software-on-demand, in part because the bandwidth and the server capacity required to process a large number of parallel requests was just beginning to develop. From Arepa's perspective, this mirrored the development of the cable industry itself. Fulop remarked, "One of the main reasons to have cable in the early days was to get reception in remote areas. It was only after entrepreneurs like Ted Turner came along and added unique services that cable really took off, that people really wanted it. *We're* the reason people will want to get broadband."

DSL. Regional Bell Operating Companies (RBOCs), prodded to action by the threat of cable operators offering telephony over coaxial cable, began to deploy residential broadband data service via DSL on a wide scale in 1999. RBOCs were the monopoly owners of local phone lines. Although they didn't own a monopoly franchise, the economics of laying new phone lines to homes was prohibitive and tended to insulate their asset from competition—until it was shown that coaxial cable could be repurposed to deliver similar services. Also, RBOCs faced another group of competitors that leased equipment from them to deliver telephony and broadband data service to local residences or businesses. Many companies, such as Northpoint and Covad, had taken up the challenge. For the most part,

RBOCs in the past had handled all aspects of the customer relationship, from installation and service management to billing. They did not, however, have affiliated BSPs or exclusive portal relationships as the MSOs did.

Business Model Choices

The Technology Licensing Model. Arepa had three principal business model options. The original business model—and certainly the easiest to execute—was to license the server software to BSPs, DSL providers, and perhaps software publishers. The licenses would cover standalone software applications (designed to run on Sun Microsystems' Solaris operating system) that would be needed to operate the entire caching system.

Running a software licensing business would require by far the smallest amount of startup capital, since it would not require that Arepa own and operate a network. Moreover, the business model required fewer and less complicated negotiations because of the limited business interactions with BSPs and software publishers. Because of consolidation in the customer base, however, the license market was extremely limited in size (just a few BSPs and DSL providers, and a somewhat larger number of software publishers), and the market demand for the technology did not yet exist at the consumer level. As it tried to license server software, Arepa had found that it had to perform numerous functions unrelated to selling licenses. As Ian Edmundson, VP of Strategic Development, had noted, "We're really in a market vertical where we have to create the consumer marketplace first. If it's just the technology that gets licensed and thrown over the wall, it's kind of technology without a real mission behind it, and it doesn't have a marketplace yet to get dropped into." Because the market had not yet developed, Arepa knew that their technology stood a good chance of dying on the vine if they went with this simple business model. Vinnie Grosso, Arepa's CEO, added, "In order to make this business work, we have to invent and sustain great technology. But someone has to deploy a server network and operate it, and manage a consumer brand. All of this has to be in place to prove the concept and ramp up demand. It's tough to get our partner to do it, if all we do is sell software licenses."

The Consumer Portal Model.   At the other end of the spectrum, Arepa could develop a consumer-branded destination website. Home users could select software titles from the site and launch them using the PlayNow player on their desktop machines, much as users selected streaming-media content from a directory of branded services on a RealPlayer by Real Networks. Arepa could set up one consumer portal or different vertical portals for each of the education, gaming, and productivity markets. A tiered pricing system would allow consumers to rent older titles at lower prices or even provide very old titles for free. Arepa would earn revenues from individual rentals of new titles, subscriptions to huge libraries of old titles, and ads sold to support the (really old) free titles. The total revenues available in this business model would be shared with the BSP in order to allow placement of servers in their networks, as well as with the software publishers in order to allow usage of their software titles. Arepa would own and operate the network used to deliver the software, or it could outsource the management of the network to a third party (such as Akamai). Arepa would have to design and maintain a sophisticated and compelling consumer site and manage consumer functions like customer service, billing, and perhaps most importantly, direct marketing.

Developing its own consumer-branded portal would allow Arepa to more or less create and develop the consumer marketplace itself. To encourage users to sign up for the service,

for example, Arepa could embark on a nationwide ad campaign and offer free trials for certain titles to prompt the user to rent or buy. A direct-to-consumer marketing campaign could stimulate demand and help the company grow faster. The name-brand recognition could give the company a tactical edge in negotiations with business partners, much as consumer demand for Home Box Office gave HBO added pricing power with MSOs. "Having our own brand," Grosso noted, "throws grease on the wheel. Because we can control the development of the market, we can drive penetration of broadband subscriptions; in the endgame, the customers would belong to us, not the BSP."

It would mean, however, that Arepa would have to learn to deal with the added costs of a consumer business—such as subscription churn and the operation of a call center. It would have to briq all the software it distributed, instead of merely providing publishers with a briq developer toolkit so that they could do it themselves. Perhaps most significantly, Arepa would face the eventual challenge of raising money for a national consumer marketing campaign, which could certainly run into the tens or even hundreds of millions of dollars (see Exhibit 8).

The consumer portal model was the most vertically integrated of the business models. Arepa would be doing everything. Edmundson had noted,

> With the portal model, we would be doing every piece of the value chain. We would be doing the authoring tools to encode existing content and the server technology. We would deploy the servers inside the broadband network, we would deliver the content to the edge of the network from our network operations center. We would have a player that sits on the user's desktop, we would have systems that support the publishing of the content, then we would have a destination site.

The Enabler Model.   As a third and intermediate alternative, Arepa could decide to own and operate the infrastructure for broadband service

EXHIBIT 8   Typical Marketing Outlay for Consumer Destination Sites

	1996	1997	1998	1999	2000E	2001E	2002E
Amazon							
Sales, Marketing & Other ($MM)	$6.1	$40.5	$132.9	$393.2	$525.0	$750.0	$1,100.0
Customer Accounts		1,510,000	6,200,000	15,900,000	25,300,000	34,300,000	43,300,000
New Customer Accounts		1,510,000	4,690,000	9,700,000	9,400,000	9,000,000	9,000,000
Sales, Marketing & Other/Customer Account		$26.81	$21.44	$24.73	$20.75	$21.87	$25.40
Sales, Marketing & Other/New Customer Account		$26.81	$28.34	$40.54	$55.85	$83.33	$122.22
AOL ($ MM)							
Marketing	$297.0	$608.0	$623.0	$796.0	$904.0	$940.0	
Subscribers	6,193,000	8,635,000	14,605,000	19,620,000	25,686,000	32,164,000	
New Subscribers	3,336,000	2,442,000	5,970,000	5,015,000	6,066,000	6,478,000	
Marketing/Subscriber	$47.96	$70.41	$42.66	$40.57	$35.19	$29.23	
Marketing/New Subscriber	$89.03	$248.98	$104.36	$158.72	$149.03	$145.11	
CDNow							
Sales & Marketing ($MM)	$0.6	$9.5	$44.3				
Cumulative Customers	87,000	296,000	983,000				
Customers Added in Period		209,000	687,000				
Sales & Marketing/Customer		$31.99	$45.06				
Sales & Marketing/Customer Added		$45.30	$64.48				
Drugstore							
Sales & Marketing ($MM)				$63.0	$126.5	$84.0	$104.0
Repeat Customers				108,000	185,000	887,000	2,140,000
New Customers				709,000	1,380,000	3,344,000	6,564,000
Total Customers				817,000	1,565,000	4,231,000	8,704,000
Unique Customers				709,000	2,089,000	5,433,000	11,997,000
Sales & Marketing/New Customer				$77.10	$80.83	$19.85	$11.95
Sales & Marketing/Customer				$88.84	$91.67	$25.12	$15.84
Sales & Marketing/Unique Customer				$88.84	$60.56	$15.46	$8.67

EXHIBIT 8 (CONTINUED) Typical Marketing Outlay for Consumer Destination Sites

	1996	1997	1998	1999	2000E	2001E	2002E
eBay							
Sales & Marketing ($MM)	$13.1	$15.6	$36.0	$99.5	$125.0	$185.0	
Registered Users		341,000	2,181,000	9,500,000	14,729,085	20,031,556	
New Registered Users			1,840,000	7,319,000	5,229,085	5,302,471	
Sales & Marketing/Registered Users		$45.80	$16.50	$10.48	$8.49	$9.24	
Sales & Marketing/New Registered User			$19.55	$13.60	$23.90	$34.89	
Onsale							
Sales & Marketing ($MM)	$0.9	$7.9	$20.8				
Registered Customers			971,000				
New Registered Customers							
Sales & Marketing/Registered Customer			$21.40				
Sales & Marketing/New Registered Customer							
Yahoo!							
Sales & Marketing ($MM)	$16.2	$58.5	$124.7	$206.2	$296.0	$375.0	
Registered Users				85,000,000	100,000,000		
New Registered Users					15,000,000		
Sales & Marketing/Registered User				$2.43	$2.96		
Sales & Marketing/New Registered User					$19.73		

Source: Morgan Stanley Dean Witter.

providers, effectively becoming a software-on-demand Applications Service Provider (ASP). In this business model, Arepa would own and operate the network, including the Regional Data Centers and the data caches. It would sign up a variety of software publishers to distribute titles directly from their own individually branded homepages (such as the Electronic Arts homepage) but through Arepa's network. A broadband subscriber then would access an Electronic Arts game by going to the Electronic Arts page, either on the web or within @Home (or another BSP). An Arepa utility (a plug-in to the user's browser) would be used in the background to manage the user's session with the publisher. Arepa would invisibly operate the back end of the software publisher's branded service. Holding explained:

> The idea would be to go capture the value on a lot of these other software sites, where there is already significant brand identification, so that we don't have to spend the marketing dollars ourselves. The consumer could connect with a major software homepage, where we would recognize his machine as Arepa-enabled. Software titles would pop up there and the consumer could play the titles from those sites. Behind the scenes, over our servers, over our network, over our distribution partner's Web sites, the consumer's getting that same experience he would get if we had an Arepa-branded portal.

In this model, as with the Arepa-branded portal model, Arepa would share revenue with both the BSP and publisher, but the revenue shares might be quite different. Terms would be negotiated individually with each as part of a multiyear contract. Arepa would need to buy, set up, and maintain the 150 RDC servers and local caches and would need to collect the billing and usage information on its own centrally located authentication server. It was expected that constructing the network and these support functions would cost an initial one-time outlay of some $50 million. The BSP or publisher would perform the very costly "front office" functions like marketing, customer acquisition, customer support, and billing.

The enabler model had two principal advantages: first, relative to the consumer portal model, Arepa would need to raise and invest far less money in developing and maintaining a base of loyal consumers. Second, Arepa would still own a network, the resources of which it might be able to leverage in Akamai-like ways in the future to provide other specialized bandwidth-intensive services. Grosso commented on the advantages:

> Consider what's happening on TV today. Broadcast networks are repurposing soap operas, news, and even Jay Leno's monologues for resale through other networks or radio. No single sales channel can reach all eyeballs today. In this environment, every studio wants to cobrand its content to maintain its identity. So there's real potential for us to let software publishers distribute their content over Arepa's network, and then in addition, to build that network out by accommodating new services such as video rentals, distance learning, shopping catalogues, or on-demand TV. The enabler model could place us at vanguard of a new era of coopetition in media.

Of course, Arepa could pursue a mixed mode of business models, using primarily the enabler model in some markets and primarily the consumer destination model in others.

Negotiations

Arepa's team believed that software-on-demand could be one of the "killer apps" for the longer-run future of broadband, but the array of negotiations that lay before them in the short run was daunting. Positioned with great and compelling technology and a first-mover advantage (at least for now), management was nevertheless concerned about its ability to obtain the array of agreements it needed to operate. Honan explained:

> We have marvelous and fun technology that has to run on somebody else's pipes. The thing that runs on these pipes is content, and the content isn't ours, either. So here we are, a smallish startup company with the technical ability to take all of that content and get it to all of those consumers out there through somebody else's pipes. Even though we have all the technology,

we have no ability to deploy it, and even though we can deliver all the content, we have no ability to create it.

Arepa would have to negotiate with sets of companies controlling both the pipes and the content and would have to share revenues with these companies. The business model Arepa picked could affect the deals and the share of revenues Arepa could claim in the negotiation. With this in mind, the management team had prepared a financial model and used it to anticipate the impact of revenue sharing on Arepa's net income for both the enabler and consumer destination site models. Given the more uncertain outlook associated with the consumer destination site model, the management team prepared both an optimistic and pessimistic forecast (see Exhibits 9A and 9B). Detailed *pro forma* results were shown for each year for each scenario. Summary matrices then displayed and graphed the forecasts of income in year 7 (2006), as a function of various negotiated revenue shares.

Distribution.   Arepa needed to negotiate the right to distribute its content through the networks. As Grosso noted,

> There are a limited number of ways to get into the home. Broadband today resembles narrowcasting in the early days: there was a limited amount of spectrum, and the audience was captive to just a few networks. If you were a content provider and wanted to get on those networks, you quickly discovered that they had significant negotiating power. Today, distribution is owned by just a few broadband providers (the BSPs and the RBOCs). It's a significant bottleneck.

Edmundson anticipated that the BSPs had several motivations for working with Arepa. "The value to them is in subscriber acquisition," he remarked,

> ... in using the content to attract the mass middle to come to broadband. It's also in retention of subscribers—having content that makes a sticky site. It's also in transactional revenue. And then, potentially, it's also in equity, if we bring them into our next round

of investment or give them warrants. That would give them four potential reasons to do business with us.

"The cable companies," Rogers noted about the MSOs, "have traditionally controlled the content over their pipes, and they've traditionally extracted a lot of value from the people who have distributed content over their pipes, but they serve as one possible benchmark for assessing possible revenue sharing arrangements." MSOs had two distinct types of content available on their networks: Basic and Premium services. MSOs collected an average of $40 per subscriber per month for a basic package and typically paid very little for the programming content provided as part of this basic service.

Premium services operated differently. Movie wholesalers such as HBO sold an after-market movie service to MSOs, for example, for an average of $5 to $7 per subscriber per month.[10] While the MSO could resell HBO service to the consumer for any markup it wanted, a typical markup was about 100%.[11]

For Arepa's software-on-demand service, a variety of distribution deal structures could be used. Regardless of whether the portal or enabler model were selected, the BSP would likely demand the same revenue share. Arepa feared that a comparison with HBO economics suggested that for a straight revenue-sharing deal, the BSP would likely begin the negotiation with a number like 50% in mind. This was supported by Grosso's recollection of the cable industry: "Studios that supplied programming to MSOs were very happy to keep 50% of the gross revenues. The cable guys still have that mindset." Management feared that at Blockbuster-like consumer price points of a few dollars per title, Arepa would not be able

---

[10]The wholesale price for the movie service was often increased as more subscribers signed up.

[11]To guard against price gouging by the MSO, HBO often stipulated that it would get half of revenues received above a certain markup threshold.

EXHIBIT 9A *Pro Forma* Comparison of the Portal and Enabler Models

Enabler Model

Assumptions

20% Share of revenues to distribution partners
31% Share of "Revenues, net of distribution partner share" given to content partner

$29.95 Price for a purchased title
$2.99 Price for a rental
$8.99 Price per month for a subscription

	1999	2000	2001	2002	2003	2004	2005	2006
Broadband Subs	3,500,000	5,000,000	10,000,000	15,000,000	22,000,000	28,000,000	32,000,000	37,000,000
% of Broadband Subscribers enabled with Arepa player	1%	15%	30%	35%	38%	42%	46%	50%
Purchases per year per enabled broadband sub	0.002	0.002	0.006	0.018	0.05	0.08	0.1	0.12
Purchases per year	70	1,500	18,000	94,500	418,000	940,800	1,472,000	2,220,000
Rentals per year per enabled broadband sub	0.1	0.01	0.03	0.09	0.4	0.55	0.6	0.65
Rentals per_year	3,500	7,500	90,000	472,500	3,344,000	6,468,000	8,832,000	12,025,000
Subscribers, % of enabled broadband subs	3	0.3	2	5	7	8	9	10
Subscribers	1,050	2,250	60,000	262,500	585,200	940,800	1,324,800	1,850,000
Advertising Revenue ($mm)	$ 0.0	$ 0.2	$ 8.0	$ 14.0	$ 17.0	$ 18.0	$ 19.0	$ 20.0

($ millions)

Revenues	1999	2000	2001	2002	2003	2004	2005	2006
Purchases	$ 0.0	$ 0.0	$ 0.5	$ 2.8	$ 12.5	$ 28.2	$ 44.1	$ 66.5
Rentals	0.0	0.0	0.3	1.4	10.0	19.3	26.4	36.0
Subscriptions	0.1	0.2	6.5	28.3	63.1	101.5	142.9	199.6
Advertising	0.0	0.2	8.0	14.0	17.0	18.0	19.0	20.0
Total Gross Revenues	$ 0.1	$ 0.5	$ 15.3	$ 46.6	$ 102.6	$ 167.0	$ 232.4	$ 322.0
Distribution Partner Share	$ (0.0)	$ (0.1)	$ (3.1)	$ (9.3)	$ (20.5)	$ (33.4)	$ (46.5)	$ (64.4)
Revenues, Net of Distribution Partner Share	$ 0.1	$ 0.4	$ 12.2	$ 37.2	$ 82.1	$ 133.6	$ 185.9	$ 257.6
Content Partner Share	$ (0.0)	$ (0.1)	$ (3.8)	$ (11.5)	$ (25.5)	$ (41.4)	$ (57.6)	$ (79.9)
Net Revenues	$ 0.1	$ 0.3	$ 8.4	$ 25.7	$ 56.7	$ 92.2	$ 128.3	$ 177.8
Expenses								
Promotion	$ -	$ -	$ -	$ -	$ -	$ -	$ -	$ -
Content Aggregation	2.0	2.0	2.0	2.0	2.0	1.0	1.0	1.0
Network	20.0	20.0	20.0	20.0	20.0	10.0	10.0	10.0
Encoding/Profiling	-	-	-	-	-	-	-	-
SG&A	5.0	5.0	5.0	5.0	5.0	5.0	5.0	5.0
Other OH	30.0	30.0	30.0	30.0	30.0	30.0	30.0	30.0
Total Expense	$ 57.0	$ 57.0	$ 57.0	$ 57.0	$ 57.0	$ 46.0	$ 46.0	$ 46.0
Net Income	$ (56.9)	$ (56.7)	$ (48.6)	$ (31.3)	$ (0.3)	$ 46.2	$ 82.3	$ 131.8

Valuation
15 P/E × Net Income in 2005, discounted to 1999 at 40% = $ 166.1

EXHIBIT 9A (CONTINUED) Pro Forma Comparison of the Portal and Enabler Models

Consumer Destination Site Model—favorable outcome

Assumptions

20% Share of revenues to distribution partners
16% Share of "Revenues, net of distribution partner share" given to content partner

$29.95 Price for a purchased title
$2.99 Price for a rental
$8.99 Price per month for a subscription

	1999	2000	2001	2002	2003	2004	2005	2006
Broadband Subs	3,500,000	5,000,000	10,000,000	15,000,000	22,000,000	28,000,000	32,000,000	37,000,000
% of Broadband Subscribers enabled with Arepa player	1%	2%	3%	4%	8%	12%	18%	20%
Purchases per year per enabled broadband	0.006	0.006	0.018	0.054	0.15	0.24	0.3	0.36
Purchases per year	*210*	*600*	*5,400*	*32,400*	*264,000*	*806,400*	*1,728,000*	*2,664,000*
Rentals per week per enabled broadband	0.3	0.03	0.09	0.27	1.2	1.65	1.8	1.95
Rentals per year	*10,500*	*3,000*	*27,000*	*162,000*	*2,112,000*	*5,544,000*	*10,368,000*	*14,430,000*
Subscribers, % of enabled broadband subs	3	0.9	6	15	21	24	27	30
Subscribers	*1,050*	*950*	*18,000*	*90,000*	*369,600*	*806,400*	*1,555,200*	*2,220,000*
Advertising Revenue ($mm)	$ 0.0	$ 0.3	$ 16.0	$ 28.0	$ 34.0	$ 36.0	$ 38.0	$ 40.0
Titles briqd	100	500	1000	2000	3000	5000	5000	4000

($ millions)

Revenues	1999	2000	2001	2002	2003	2004	2005	2006
Purchases	$ 0.0	$ 0.0	$ 0.2	$ 1.0	$ 7.9	$ 24.2	$ 51.8	$ 79.8
Rentals	$ 0.0	$ 0.0	$ 0.1	$ 0.5	$ 6.3	$ 16.6	$ 31.0	$ 43.1
Subscriptions	$ 0.1	$ 0.1	$ 1.9	$ 9.7	$ 39.9	$ 87.0	$ 167.8	$ 239.5
Advertising	$ 0.0	$ 0.3	$ 16.0	$ 28.0	$ 34.0	$ 36.0	$ 38.0	$ 40.0
Total Gross Revenues	$ 0.2	$ 0.4	$ 18.2	$ 39.2	$ 88.1	$ 163.7	$ 288.5	$ 402.4
Distribution Partner	$ (0.0)	$ (0.1)	$ (3.6)	$ (7.8)	$ (17.6)	$ (32.7)	$ (57.7)	$ (80.5)
Revenues, Net of Distribution Partner	$ 0.1	$ 0.3	$ 14.5	$ 31.3	$ 70.5	$ 131.0	$ 230.8	$ 321.9
Content Partner	$ (0.0)	$ (0.1)	$ (2.4)	$ (5.1)	$ (11.5)	$ (21.3)	$ (37.5)	$ (52.3)
Net Revenues	$ 0.1	$ 0.3	$ 12.2	$ 26.2	$ 59.0	$ 109.7	$ 193.3	$ 269.6
Expenses								
Promotion	$ 20.0	$ 30.0	$ 50.0	$ 80.0	$ 100.0	$ 60.0	$ 60.0	$ 60.0
Content Aggregation	$ 2.0	$ 2.0	$ 2.0	$ 2.0	$ 2.0	$ 1.0	$ 1.0	$ 1.0
Network	$ 20.0	$ 20.0	$ 20.0	$ 20.0	$ 20.0	$ 10.0	$ 10.0	$ 10.0
Encoding/Profiling	$ 0.3	$ 1.3	$ 2.5	$ 5.0	$ 7.5	$ 12.5	$ 12.5	$ 10.0
SG&A	$ 7.5	$ 7.5	$ 7.5	$ 7.5	$ 7.5	$ 7.5	$ 7.5	$ 7.5
Other OH	$ 30.0	$ 30.0	$ 30.0	$ 30.0	$ 30.0	$ 30.0	$ 30.0	$ 30.0
Total Expense	$ 79.8	$ 90.8	$ 112.0	$ 144.5	$ 167.0	$ 121.0	$ 121.0	$ 118.5
Net Income	$ (79.6)	$ (90.5)	$ (99.8)	$ (118.3)	$ (108.0)	$ (11.3)	$ 72.3	$ 151.1

Valuation

30 P/E × Net Income in 2005,
discounted to 1999   60%   = $ 121.1

(Continued)

EXHIBIT 9A (CONTINUED) Pro Forma Comparison of the Portal and Enabler Models

Consumer Destination Site Model—unfavorable outcome

Assumptions

20% Share of revenues to distribution partners
16% Share of "Revenues, net of distribution partner share" given to content partner

$29.95 Price for a purchased title
$2.99 Price for a rental
$8.99 Price per month for a subscription

	1999	2000	2001	2002	2003	2004	2005	2006
Broadband Subs	3,500,000	5,000,000	10,000,000	15,000,000	22,000,000	28,000,000	32,000,000	37,000,000
% of Broadband Subscribers enabled with Arepa player	1%	2%	3%	4%	8%	12%	18%	20%
Purchases per year per enabled broadband sub	0.003	0.004	0.012	0.036	0.1	0.16	0.2	0.24
Purchases per year	*105*	*400*	*3,600*	*21,600*	*176,000*	*537,600*	*1,152,000*	*1,776,000*
Rentals per week per enabled broadband sub	0.15	0.02	0.06	0.18	0.8	1.1	1.2	1.3
Rentals per year	*5,250*	*2,000*	*18,000*	*108,000*	*1,408,000*	*3,696,000*	*6,912,000*	*9,620,000*
Subscribers, % of enabled broadband subs	1	0.6	4	10	14	16	18	20
Subscribers	*350*	*600*	*12,000*	*60,000*	*246,400*	*537,600*	*1,036,800*	*1,480,000*
Advertising Revenue ($mm)	$ 0.0	$ 0.3	$ 16.0	$ 28.0	$ 34.0	$ 36.0	$ 38.0	$ 40.0
Titles briqd	100	500	1000	2000	3000	5000	5000	4000
($ millions)								
Revenues	*1999*	*2000*	*2001*	*2002*	*2003*	*2004*	*2005*	*2006*
Purchases	$ 0.0	$ 0.0	$ 0.1	$ 0.6	$ 5.3	$ 16.1	$ 34.5	$ 53.2
Rentals	$ 0.0	$ 0.0	$ 0.1	$ 0.3	$ 4.2	$ 11.1	$ 20.7	$ 28.8
Subscriptions	$ 0.0	$ 0.1	$ 1.3	$ 6.5	$ 26.6	$ 58.0	$ 111.8	$ 159.7
Advertising	$ 0.0	$ 0.3	$ 16.0	$ 28.0	$ 34.0	$ 36.0	$ 38.0	$ 40.0
Total Gross Revenues	$ 0.1	$ 0.4	$ 17.5	$ 35.4	$ 70.1	$ 121.1	$ 205.0	$ 281.6
Distribution Partner Share	$ (0.0)	$ (0.1)	$ (3.5)	$ (7.1)	$ (14.0)	$ (24.2)	$ (41.0)	$ (56.3)
Revenues, Net of Distribution Partner Share	$ 0.1	$ 0.3	$ 14.0	$ 28.4	$ 56.1	$ 96.9	$ 164.0	$ 225.3
Content Partner Share	$ (0.0)	$ (0.1)	$ (2.3)	$ (4.6)	$ (9.1)	$ (15.7)	$ (26.7)	$ (36.6)
Net Revenues	$ 0.0	$ 0.3	$ 11.7	$ 23.7	$ 46.9	$ 81.2	$ 137.4	$ 188.7
Expenses								
Promotion	$ 20.0	$ 35.0	$ 60.0	$ 90.0	$ 110.0	$ 90.0	$ 80.0	$ 70.0
Content Aggregation	$ 2.0	$ 2.0	$ 2.0	$ 2.0	$ 2.0	$ 1.0	$ 1.0	$ 1.0
Network	$ 20.0	$ 20.0	$ 20.0	$ 20.0	$ 20.0	$ 10.0	$ 10.0	$ 10.0
Encoding/Profiling	$ 0.3	$ 1.3	$ 2.5	$ 5.0	$ 7.5	$ 12.5	$ 12.5	$ 10.0
SG&A	$ 7.5	$ 7.5	$ 7.5	$ 7.5	$ 7.5	$ 7.5	$ 7.5	$ 7.5
Other OH	$ 30.0	$ 30.0	$ 30.0	$ 30.0	$ 30.0	$ 30.0	$ 30.0	$ 30.0
Total Expense	$ 79.8	$ 95.8	$ 122.0	$ 154.5	$ 177.0	$ 151.0	$ 141.0	$ 128.5
Net Income	$ (79.7)	$ (95.5)	$ (110.3)	$ (130.8)	$ (130.1)	$ (69.8)	$ (3.6)	$ 60.2
Valuation								
30 P/E × Net Income in 2005, discounted to 1999 at	60%		= $ (6.1)					

Note: Network and Content aggregation costs include amortizations of $50 million network build and other start-up expense until 2003. Financial data have been disguised and are for discussion purpose only. Numbers reported here do not reflect actual projections contained within Arepa's business plan. Source: Arepa.

EXHIBIT 9B 2006 *Pro Forma* Net Income, Under Various Revenue Share Assumptions

Net Income in 2006
Different Revenue Share Arrangements for each model

Consumer Destination Site Model, Favorable Outcome

Legend:
- □ $200.0 - $300.0
- □ $100.0 - $200.0
- □ $- - $100.0
- ■ $(100.0)- $-

Percentage shared with Publishers after BSPs claim their share	Share of revenues to BSPs									
	5%	10%	15%	20%	25%	30%	35%	40%	45%	50%
5%	$ 244.7	$ 225.6	$ 206.5	$ 187.3	$ 168.2	$ 149.1	$ 130.0	$ 110.9	$ 91.8	$ 72.7
12%	$ 219.2	$ 201.4	$ 183.7	$ 165.9	$ 148.1	$ 130.3	$ 112.6	$ 94.8	$ 77.0	$ 59.2
18%	$ 193.7	$ 177.3	$ 160.9	$ 144.4	$ 128.0	$ 111.6	$ 95.1	$ 78.7	$ 62.3	$ 45.8
25%	$ 168.2	$ 153.1	$ 138.0	$ 123.0	$ 107.9	$ 92.8	$ 77.7	$ 62.6	$ 47.5	$ 32.4
32%	$ 142.7	$ 129.0	$ 115.2	$ 101.5	$ 87.7	$ 74.0	$ 60.2	$ 46.5	$ 32.7	$ 19.0
38%	$ 117.3	$ 104.8	$ 92.4	$ 80.0	$ 67.6	$ 55.2	$ 42.8	$ 30.4	$ 18.0	$ 5.6
45%	$ 91.8	$ 80.7	$ 69.6	$ 58.6	$ 47.5	$ 36.4	$ 25.4	$ 14.3	$ 3.2	$ (7.8)
52%	$ 66.3	$ 56.6	$ 46.8	$ 37.1	$ 27.4	$ 17.7	$ 7.9	$ (1.8)	$ (11.5)	$ (21.2)
58%	$ 40.8	$ 32.4	$ 24.0	$ 15.6	$ 7.3	$ (1.1)	$ (9.5)	$ (17.9)	$ (26.3)	$ (34.7)
65%	$ 15.3	$ 8.3	$ 1.2	$ (5.8)	$ (12.9)	$ (19.9)	$ (26.9)	$ (34.0)	$ (41.0)	$ (48.1)

Consumer Destination Site Model, Unfavorable Outcome

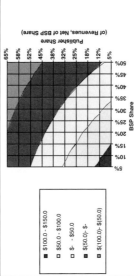

Legend:
- ■ $100.0 - $150.0
- □ $50.0 - $100.0
- □ $- - $50.0
- □ $(50.0)- $-
- ■ $(100.0)- $(50.0)

Percentage shared with Publishers after BSPs claim their share	Share of revenues to BSPs									
	5%	10%	15%	20%	25%	30%	35%	40%	45%	50%
5%	$ 127.7	$ 112.3	$ 98.9	$ 85.5	$ 72.2	$ 58.8	$ 45.4	$ 32.0	$ 18.6	$ 5.3
12%	$ 107.8	$ 95.4	$ 82.9	$ 70.5	$ 58.1	$ 45.6	$ 33.2	$ 20.8	$ 8.3	$ (4.1)
18%	$ 90.0	$ 78.5	$ 67.0	$ 55.5	$ 44.0	$ 32.5	$ 21.0	$ 9.5	$ (2.0)	$ (13.5)
25%	$ 72.2	$ 61.6	$ 51.0	$ 40.5	$ 29.9	$ 19.3	$ 8.8	$ (1.8)	$ (12.3)	$ (22.9)
32%	$ 54.3	$ 44.7	$ 35.1	$ 25.5	$ 15.8	$ 6.2	$ (3.4)	$ (13.0)	$ (22.7)	$ (32.3)
38%	$ 36.5	$ 27.8	$ 19.1	$ 10.4	$ 1.7	$ (6.9)	$ (15.6)	$ (24.3)	$ (33.0)	$ (41.7)
45%	$ 18.6	$ 10.9	$ 3.2	$ (4.6)	$ (12.3)	$ (20.1)	$ (27.8)	$ (35.6)	$ (43.3)	$ (51.1)
52%	$ 0.8	$ (6.0)	$ (12.8)	$ (19.6)	$ (26.4)	$ (33.2)	$ (40.0)	$ (46.8)	$ (53.6)	$ (60.4)
58%	$ (17.0)	$ (22.9)	$ (28.8)	$ (34.6)	$ (40.5)	$ (46.4)	$ (52.2)	$ (58.1)	$ (64.0)	$ (69.8)
65%	$ (34.9)	$ (39.8)	$ (44.7)	$ (49.6)	$ (54.6)	$ (59.5)	$ (64.4)	$ (69.4)	$ (74.3)	$ (79.2)

Enabler Model

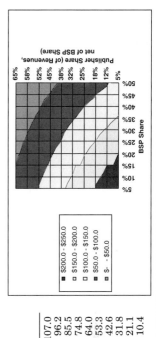

Legend:
- ■ $200.0 - $250.0
- □ $150.0 - $200.0
- □ $100.0 - $150.0
- ■ $50.0 - $100.0
- ■ $- - $50.0

Percentage shared with Publishers after BSPs claim their share	Share of revenues to BSPs									
	5%	10%	15%	20%	25%	30%	35%	40%	45%	50%
5%	$ 244.6	$ 229.3	$ 214.0	$ 198.7	$ 183.4	$ 168.1	$ 152.8	$ 137.6	$ 122.3	$ 107.0
12%	$ 224.2	$ 210.0	$ 195.8	$ 181.6	$ 167.3	$ 153.1	$ 138.9	$ 124.7	$ 110.4	$ 96.2
18%	$ 203.8	$ 190.7	$ 177.5	$ 164.4	$ 151.2	$ 138.1	$ 124.9	$ 111.8	$ 98.6	$ 85.5
25%	$ 183.4	$ 171.4	$ 159.3	$ 147.2	$ 135.1	$ 123.1	$ 111.0	$ 98.9	$ 86.8	$ 74.8
32%	$ 163.0	$ 152.0	$ 141.0	$ 130.0	$ 119.0	$ 108.0	$ 97.0	$ 86.0	$ 75.0	$ 64.0
38%	$ 142.7	$ 132.7	$ 122.8	$ 112.9	$ 102.9	$ 93.0	$ 83.1	$ 73.1	$ 63.2	$ 53.3
45%	$ 122.3	$ 113.4	$ 104.5	$ 95.7	$ 86.8	$ 78.0	$ 69.1	$ 60.3	$ 51.4	$ 42.6
52%	$ 101.9	$ 94.1	$ 86.3	$ 78.5	$ 70.7	$ 63.0	$ 55.2	$ 47.4	$ 39.6	$ 31.8
58%	$ 81.5	$ 74.8	$ 68.0	$ 61.3	$ 54.6	$ 47.9	$ 41.2	$ 34.5	$ 27.8	$ 21.1
65%	$ 61.1	$ 55.4	$ 49.8	$ 44.2	$ 38.5	$ 32.9	$ 27.3	$ 21.6	$ 16.0	$ 10.4

Note: Financial data have been disguised.
Source: Arepa.

to cover its significant network costs if it ceded 50% of the revenues to the BSP. Instead, they hoped to pay the BSP around 20%. Arepa might be able to keep the BSP's revenue share low by paying up-front tenancy fees. It could minimize the BSP's revenue share by issuing warrants to the BSP as a part of the deal. @Home and RoadRunner were both "new economy" firms, and as such might be particularly interested in warrants. "If it's a warrant or any sort of up-front payment," Rogers remarked, "I want it tied to the number of people to which they're giving access to our service. I also want payments or warrant issues staged, contingent on operational milestones, so that they have an incentive to keep Arepa out there and keep servicing it. If it's a one-time, up-front payment or warrant, I'll lose all leverage."

A BSP (or MSO) negotiation, Grosso had warned his team, could well degenerate into a series of price concessions by Arepa and in the worst case, equity concessions, too. In the cable industry, some cable operators had demanded up to 15% equity interest in their content providers, on top of revenue shares of 50% or more. Of course, if all failed with the BSPs, Arepa could still pursue deals with DSL providers, but the lack of BSPs and nascent state of DSL rollout was likely to multiply the marketing burden on the company while it popularized its product. It would be far better if Arepa could negotiate a deal with the two principal BSPs (Excite@ Home and RoadRunner).

Content

Arepa also needed to negotiate with software publishers for the right to distribute their titles. Arepa's distribution rights would almost certainly be nonexclusive. Many of the most popular titles were published by a handful of large companies, including Mattel, Hasbro, GT Interactive, Electronic Arts, and The Havas Group (see Exhibit 10). Arepa could use the "old-world" sales channel as a point of comparison to anchor its pricing assumptions. Publishers sold through bricks-and-mortar channels to stores like CompUSA or Electronics Boutique—as well as through Internet-based retailers like Egghead. A typical wholesale price for a newly released title was around $20 to $32. The retailer marked the price up to about $30 to $50 (implying that the publisher typically received 40% to 67% of the retail price). Unfortunately for the publisher, the software business was hit-driven; many new titles never sold successfully and some new titles were huge hits and suffered stock-outs. As a result, the retailer was often protected by a retroactively applied publisher discount in the event of overstocks. Titles were rarely returned to the publisher; more com-

EXHIBIT 10   Recent Software Industry Acquisition

Acquirer	Acquired Companies
Electronic Arts	Origin, Maxis, Westwood
Mattel	Softkey
Softkey	Broderbund, The Learning Company, MECC
Havas Group (Vivendi)	Cendant
Cendant	Sierra, Davidson/Blizzard, Knowledge Adventure
Hasbro	MicroProse, Tiger, Avalon Hill, Atari, Namco

Source: William Blair & Company.

monly, retailers were allowed to sell the old titles from a "bargain bin" at a steep discount, and to claim a reimbursement (an "overstock discount") from the publisher. The publisher's overstock discount, when it was used, was highly variable and almost discretionary, but often ranged from $10 to $20 per title. Backlist titles, by contrast, were often sold out of publisher warehouses for as little as $12 and resold in retail channels for around $20. Arepa management feared that the software publishers, using the bricks-and-mortar channel as a reference point, might demand a high revenue share, perhaps up to half of the revenues that remained after the BSP claimed its share. Arepa might expect the publisher's demand for revenue share to be considerably less in the consumer destination site model than in the enabler model, but management knew from its *pro formas* that it could certainly not afford to cede a very large share to the publishers. It hoped to be able to cede something like only 15% to the publishers in the consumer destination model, and up to twice that in the enabler model.

Funding.   Also, Arepa needed to raise money in the midst of these content and distribution negotiations. It had several options, all made more complicated by the fact that its business model was still in flux. The software licensing model would require very limited new funding (perhaps only $5 million). Both the enabler and consumer destination model would require at least $50 million up front to build out the network, and of course, required ongoing network operating expenses. The consumer destination model would also require huge ongoing consumer advertising and promotions expense, and would therefore reach cash breakeven much later than the enabler model.

It also wasn't clear what pre-money valuation would be possible for the company. Arepa's current venture capital investors thought that $30 to $40 million would be an appropriate pre-money valuation. Honan, however, was able to derive a much higher number by multiplying his expected earnings four or five years in the future by a conservative price/earnings ratio. Discounted back to mid-1999, Honan's figures suggested Arepa's pre-money valuation might be about $100 million if it adopted the enabler model. The consumer destination model offered a longer time to breakeven with higher risk, but industry comparables suggested would likely be valued at a higher multiple because of its faster growth rate and closer relationship with retail customers. Even this model, by Honan's estimation, could be worth over $100 million (see Exhibit 9A). Honan thought that he might hope to achieve a similar valuation in negotiations with investors. In fact, he realized that some groups of investors—strategic partners with whom Arepa intended to have a business relationship—might be willing to accept a higher valuation if other benefits—such as an attractive revenue share—could come with a financing deal.

If it chose to raise money from venture capital funds, Arepa would likely receive offers to invest from Fidelity and Venrock, its two current investors, as well as some technology-focused funds. Because of the risk, venture capitalists were likely to request a relatively large share of the company.

Corporate investing partners might include companies of strategic significance, including BSPs such as @Home or RoadRunner; MSOs such as AT&T or Time-Warner; local phone companies such as Bell Atlantic, SBC, U.S. West, or Bell South; or software publishers such as Disney, Electronic Arts, Mattel, or Hasbro. Entities such as the Republic of Singapore could prove to be valuable contacts for international deployments, and infrastructure companies such as Inktomi (for whose products it could be argued Arepa would increase demand) might have an interest in helping to shape the company. Equipment companies such as Cisco might also be interested in investing to get a glimpse of future applications on the network.

The idea of securing corporate investment was seductive, but potentially dangerous. Arepa had needs for strategic relationships to execute each business model. The company might, for example, be able to get a higher revenue share from @Home or Electronic Arts if they were investors. Fulop realized that if he could sign up a particular group of investors, it could tip the scales in favor of one of the business models. It was difficult to know how strategic investments could affect the business model decisions, but it was clear that they would be linked in a complicated way. Fulop made a mental note to map out the likely negotiating stances of the potential corporate investors. At the same time, he wondered whether he wanted to have his potential strategic partners—with whom he would have to strike distribution and content deals—on his board of directors. "Board members know a lot about our cost structure," Rogers had noted the other day. "If we have a potential distribution partner on the board, it changes the dynamic for the distribution negotiation a lot." Even if Arepa gave up a lot on valuation, it would be far less complicated to do a traditional venture-capital round. It wasn't clear which group Arepa should choose to approach first, how much funding it should request, and what pre-money valuation should comprise its reservation price.

Opportunity

Arepa was on the cusp of emerging into an entirely new market category, but it had to make decisions about its business model and its negotiating strategy soon. From this point, Arepa's selection of a business model would change its character profoundly; the talent it needed to recruit, the business partners it chose, and the investments it accepted would all be different on each path. Arepa had a lot of options, and none of them seemed simple. Fulop wondered if the negatives of the original licensing model were really so limiting after all.

CASE 3–2
SELECTING A HOSTING PROVIDER[1]

Exercise

You have been assigned to a team that will choose a hosting facility for your company's new web-based infrastructure. Your task is to examine the information summarized in the exhibits on the next several pages about the three hosting providers under consideration, and to recommend one of them. The choice has been narrowed to these three because they have space available on the timetable required by your project in your metropolitan area (Cincinnati). Information in the exhibits has come from public sources, from proposals submitted by each vendor, from visits by your technical experts to the facilities under consideration, and from a presentation/Q&A session with vendor representatives. Your recommendation should be accompanied by 1) a list of the criteria you used in making your selection and, 2) an explanation of why the recommended service provider is best positioned to meet your company's needs.

As you undertake this selection process, you will represent *one* of the following two compa-

[1]This exercise was prepared by Professor Robert D. Austin. Copyright © 2001 by the President and Fellows of Harvard College. Harvard Business School case 601-171.

nies, as assigned by your instructor. Prepare your recommendations only for the company that is assigned to you. Other members of the class will prepare recommendations for the other company. By coincidence, both companies happen to be in the Cincinnati area, and both intend to house the same starting equipment configurations (summarized in Exhibit 1).

EXHIBIT 1 Requirements for Infrastructure Facility

Equipment to Be Housed in Facility

Application System/Oracle Database
- 3 Sun 200 series servers, rack mountable
- 1 Sun Enterprise 6000 series server with 2 CPUs
- 2 Compaq PIII servers, rack mountable, low profile

Web Server
- 2 Compaq PIII servers, rack mountable, low profile

Firewall/Acceleration/Load Balancing
- Compaq Caching Server
- 2 Cisco PIX firewalls
- 2 Cisco Local Directors

DNS
- 2 Compaq PIII servers, rack mountable, low profile

Network Infrastructure
- 2 Cisco Catalyst 6000 series Ethernet Switches
- 2 Cisco 7000 series routers
- 2 Cisco 3000 series routers

Backup
- DLT Array (manufacturer TBD)

Disk Array Chassis
- 10 × 9 GB (OS) *housed inside Sun E6000 cabinet
- 10 × 36 GB (DB) *housed inside Sun E6000 cabinet

Customer Support System
- 2 Sun 200 series servers, rack mountable

Space, Power, Connectivity

6 racks of enclosed space in the Cincinnati metro area

Rights of first refusal on 6 more racks adjacent to first 6 racks

Physical 24×7 security, with live guards, access control, closed-circuit TV (CCTV), disaster protection

HVAC and AC/DC power to handle at 75% capacity handle redundant power connections to each machine list above

Power connection to two separate utility power grids; Uninterruptible Power Supplies (UPSs); Generator backup with 36 hours of reserve fuel

10 mbps Full Duplex Ethernet (upgradeable to Fast Ethernet burstable to 100 mbps)

TCP/IP addressing sufficient for twice this starting configuration

DNS support

Company A: International Equipment Company. The roots of the International Equipment Company (IEC) are deeply planted in the industrial age, but its progressive senior managers are eager to capitalize on the technologies of the information age. The $3 billion company based in Cincinnati, Ohio, is a leading manufacturer of lifting and loading equipment, in both standard versions (e.g., forklifts) and customized configurations. Although the company's manufacturing facilities are based primarily in the American Midwest, it has sales offices all over the world and achieves 29% of its sales outside the United States. Founded in 1931, IEC has experienced ups and downs over the years, but heading into 2001 it has averaged after tax earnings of just over $170 million for five straight years. This period of success has left the company in a strong financial position, but IEC senior managers are trying to avoid complacency and to leverage current financial strength into enduring competitive advantage.

In late 2000, a team studying the potential of Internet technologies to streamline supply and distribution channels concluded that significant advantage could be gained in this area. The team recommended, therefore, that IEC begin to build a new Web-based information technology (IT) infrastructure, first to sit atop and "web-enable" the legacy infrastructure but eventually (over a period of several years) to replace legacy systems. This group also recommended that the physical infrastructure—servers, network and storage devices, etc.—be housed off IEC premises in a modern IT hosting facility owned by a hosting services provider.

The basis for the hosting recommendation was fourfold. First, existing IEC data centers, built in the mainframe era, are not prepared to support the high levels of availability that the study team thinks will be required of web-based applications; data center staff are already nervous about a very small number of high-availability servers that they have been compelled to house for the marketing department. Second, the complexity and limitations of legacy systems suggested to the team that the existing IT infrastructure would eventually need to be replaced, not just enhanced, and they preferred a "green field" location in which to construct the new infrastructure. Third, the team argued that hosting providers, which provide services for many customers, are able to specialize and realize economies of scale far in excess of what IEC could realize on its own; this meant, team members believed, that external hosting services would, in the long run, be less expensive and higher in quality than anything IEC could achieve internally. Finally, the team noted, external hosting facilities are already constructed, so the new infrastructure project could get going immediately, without waiting for physical renovations or additions to any existing IEC data centers.

The IEC Network Services department has agreed reluctantly to go along with the study team's recommendations. But they insist that the hosting provider chosen should be one based on the co-location model. The co-location model, unlike the managed services model, would permit IEC technical staff to remain in design control of the new infrastructure. This fact has assuaged some of the concerns raised by technical staff about security and reliability of commercial hosting facilities.

The initial application to be constructed as a pilot for the overall infrastructure replacement effort is a basic transaction hub that would permit dealers to submit and view the status of orders of IEC's highest volume product via a web-based system. If the pilot project is successful, the hub will provide a basis for extending similar functionality backward through the supply chain to suppliers, and also for broadening the functionality to include other products and other kinds of functionality (e.g., after sales support). Eventually, when the new infrastructure has proven itself and when everyone is agreed that the time is right, IEC will migrate its lifeblood transaction systems to the new infrastructure.

Company B: The Web Billing Company. The young, ambitious managers of the Web Billing Company (WBC) succeeded in landing a round of financing for their startup company just before the tech market swoon of early 2000 struck with full force. In spring of 2001, as they prepare to launch with their first customers, the 50 person company retains more than $16 million of the $25 million it had received from venture investors in February 2000. Their monthly burn rate stands at about $550,000, but that will increase to nearly $700,000 as they staff up for full operations in the next quarter.

WBC plans to offer outsourced billing services to Internet companies who want to focus on their core service delivery businesses and leave the hassles of billing services to specialists. The innovative WBC technology platform interfaces over the Internet with the service provisioning and delivery functionality of its clients to capture billable events in real-time. By using WBC services, an Internet company can offer a tremendous variety of billing options to customers, such as monthly subscription fees, time-based usage fees, messaged-based usage fees, volume discounts, free-trial periods, etc. WBC will handle everything to do with billing and collection from end user customers;

moreover, WBC has developed methods and technologies that facilitate taking over billing from companies with existing billing operations. Market research suggests that billing has been an afterthought for many Internet companies and that many are doing a bad job of it. WBC has fielded interested inquiries from broadband providers, ASPs, ISPs, and many others who are eager to turn over their billing difficulties to another company. Two customer companies have been identified to begin pilot projects in ten weeks time. WBC managers hope that success with these clients will entice numerous companies waiting in the wings to quickly sign up for billing services also.

WBC technology has so far been developed in a laboratory setting and now must be translated to production. The company owns no facilities suitable for hosting production operations, so commercial hosting facilities are the only real option. The CTO, whose talents extend to computer security, wants to retain design control over the production infrastructure and therefore insists on a hosting provider in the co-location model. To capture billing information in real-time, WBC infrastructure will have to be highly available on a $24 \times 7 \times 365$ basis. Downtime will result in failure to capture billable events and customers are expected to have very low tolerance for such failures. Already, clients and prospective clients are negotiating for Service Level Agreements (SLAs) with big penalties for downtime. Worse, spectacular failures early on will likely cause prospective customers to rethink outsourcing their billing to WBC.

EXHIBIT 2   Provider Overviews

Provider 1

Provider 1 is a regional company founded in 1997 to provide co-location services and broadband connectivity in the Midwest region. It is a venture backed, privately held company with a gold-plated list of investors, including Microsoft and Cisco executives. The company owns three data centers of 40,000, 55,000 and 75,000 square feet as well as a regional network of high capacity backbone communication lines that extend outward from Cincinnati in a 100 mile radius (connections with other backbone providers offer robust, worldwide connectivity). The two smaller data centers are officially fully booked, although there has been recent speculation that some dot-com customers may not be paying their bills. The company is known to have a handful of large, financially solid customers, however. The 75,000 sq. ft. data center is about 60% booked, and it is in this facility that IEC/WBC is considering renting space. Provider 1 recently laid off 16% of its workforce (about 260 people) in its division that focuses on DSL deployment. In its response to the RFP, Provider 1 declined to provide any financial data citing its status as a private firm.

Provider 2

Provider 2 was an early entrant (in 1994) into the hosting market and is now the U.S. market leader in co-location hosting. By year-end 2001, the company expects to have 38 data centers in North America accounting for more than 2.8 million square feet. The company owns redundant network backbone capacity sufficient to connect its data centers to each other and its representatives noted that a large percentage of traffic exchanged between companies whose infrastructure is housed by Provider 2 never leaves Provider 2 equipment (relationships with several other backbone providers provide robust, worldwide connectivity should traffic need to leave Provider 2). The company experienced financial losses in 2000 of about $180 million on sales of almost $600 million. Provider 2 attributes its losses to the rapid rate at which it has been adding data centers and asserts that its individual data centers become profitable after a year to eighteen months. In the tech-unfriendly market of 2001, the stock price has fallen to $14/share from a 12 month high of $83/share. Partly this is due to the perception that the company has considerable exposure to failing dot-coms. Provider 2 acknowledges that more than 40% of its customers were dot-coms in 2000, but notes that it is successfully working to reduce that dependency by focusing more emphatically on the needs of enterprise customers.

Provider 3

Provider 3 is a recent entrant into the hosting market but a veteran in telecomms and networks services. Formed from mergers of two telcos, an ISP, and a variety of other networking service companies, Provider 3 still obtains a significant amount of its revenues from older lines of business, such as long distance services and sale of business T1 lines. The company's recent initiative to leverage its telco operating capabilities and infrastructure into the hosting business have resulted in a buying spree during which Provider 3 has acquired several tier 2 or 3 hosting facilities with the intention of improving them. The facility in Cincinnati is a warehouse that another company had already partly converted to a hosting facility before Provider 3 purchased it. Renovation plans now call for updating the facility into a modern, 60,000 square foot hosting site; there are already some customers who have live operations (mostly inherited from the facility's previous owner). Provider 3 is a $13 billion company with after tax earnings of just under $1.1 billion in 2000 and little dot-com exposure. Its network resources make it a backbone provider to numerous other companies; like other hosting companies, though, Provider 3 also acquires backbone services from other providers. The company's stock price has recently declined to a level 43% lower than its 12 month high.

EXHIBIT 3   Selected, Summarized Information from RFP Responses

RFP Question	Provider 1	Provider 2	Provider 3
Company Description	Regional hosting and broadband comms (backbone, DSL) service provider	National hosting service provider, market leader	Regional telco, backbone, broadband service provider
Employees	1600	3300	28,000
Financial Profile	Declined to provide (private company)	After tax loss $180 mil on sales of $600 mil; strong cash position; rapidly building new facilities; historically, individual data centers profitable within 18 months of opening	After tax profit of $1.1 billion on sales of $13 billion (most not from hosting business)
Profit structure of account	Declined to provide data	Declined to provide data	Declined to provide data
Business partners to be involved in service provision to IEC/WBC	Electrical contractors	None	Physical security firm
Last six months account of loss of availability or intrusion events for this facility	None	No loss of availability for this facility during last six months	No data; new facility
Space offered	3 8′ × 8′ cages (192 sq ft), partitions removed to provide contiguous space	3 8′ × 7′ cages (168 sq ft), partitions removed to provide contiguous space	280 sq ft enclosed room
Right of first refusal on adjoining space	Not available	Not available without acquiring adjoining space now	Available
Physical security	Fully meets requirement	Fully meets requirement	See notes from site visit
Power	Fully meets requirement	Fully meets requirement	Should fully meet requirement in 6 weeks; now connected to only one power grid
Connectivity	Fully meets requirement	Fully meets requirement	Should fully meet requirement in 6 weeks; not redundant yet

EXHIBIT 4   Summary Notes from Network Services Visits to Hosting Facilities

Provider 1

Initial walk around exterior: Facility is housed in building wholly owned and dedicated to use by provider. Second floor of building is data center. Other floors (1st and 3rd) are offices. Conventional brick structure (not structurally hardened) in urban setting, adjacent to some sort of manufacturing facility (although physically separate by several hundred yards distance). One loading dock in rear; we were able to walk right up to it; did not try to enter facility this way, but saw nothing that would prevent it (no guard apparent, but there might have been CCTV we did not see). Diesel generators securely enclosed. HVAC units not visible (probably on roof).

Entering facility: Very modern facility, with lots of biometrics. Saw palm readers and voice recognition in use. Did, however, observe maintenance worker "piggy-back" entrance into mantrap area, bypassing voice recognition (another worker held the door for him). Enter into data center through large mantrap. Interact with security guard through bullet proof glass; lots of CCTV monitors visible through glass, although no one watching them when we entered facility. Another guard on duty had apparently stepped out to let someone into a cage. Picture ID required for entry, access badges issued.

Cages: Standard issue, chain link, enclosed at top. Raised floor, power comes in from underneath. Patch panel for comms in location of our choice. Comms cross connects come from above trays. Basic bolt in racks and shelves provided.

Verification of Redundancy, Security, etc: Redundant power and connectivity configurations check out. Had network security conversation with a very savvy engineer. There is one key technical guy who seems to field all the deep technical questions, although there are other quiet staff members who also seem attuned. Conversation with one of those in hallway revealed him to be a CCIE (very expert certification in internetworking).

Concerns: Lots of technology and flash, but saw a couple of apparent procedural lapses (like piggy-back access to data center). Lots of people in data center apparently doing contracting work. Not necessarily a concern, but these are not Provider 1 employees.

Overall Assessment: Looked pretty solid. Saw nothing that constituted reason for serious concern. This facility would be a reasonable choice and would meet our technical requirements.

Provider 2

Initial walk around exterior: Facility is housed in building wholly owned and dedicated to use by provider. Data center and offices all on one floor. Conventional brick structure in suburban setting has been physically hardened by apparently erecting a steel inner structure inside walls of original building. Suspect this would survive even a close proximity bomb blast (learned later that building is hardened against earthquakes, also). No adjacent buildings in sight. One loading dock we were able to walk right up to; saw nothing that would prevent us from entering (no guard apparent), but there may have been concealed CCTV that we did not see. On tour of facility, discovered that there is a constantly manned security station just inside loading dock door (were several guards there when we toured). Diesel generators securely enclosed. HVAC units on roof.

Entering facility: Mantrap with Kevlar lined walls and guard seated inside. Security guard behind bullet proof glass, several others visible watching CCTV monitors. Biometrics palm readers visible but used only after 6 PM. Lots of physical presence of guards. Strict procedures (made one of us finish his candy bar before they would let us through mantrap). Guards inspected a bag one of us was carrying. Picture ID required for entry, access badges issued. Guard had to meet us to open (an empty!) cage for our examination.

Cages: Standard issue, chain link, enclosed at top. Raised floor, power comes in from underneath. Patch panel for comms in location of our choice. Comms cross connects come from above trays. Basic bolt in racks and shelves provided.

Verification of Redundancy, Security, etc: Redundant power and connectivity configurations check out. Sophisticated NOC visible behind glass. All facility level networking, power distribution, and HVAC equipment was in access controlled enclosed area (we were not permitted to enter during tour even, although we could see some through reinforced glass). Talked to several obviously competent technical people.

Concerns: None, really.

Overall Assessment: Very impressive. This company appears to focus on this business and they appear to do a very good job. Could a seriously motivated terrorist or the like get in and cause mischief here? Probably, but these guys have it covered as well as anyone.

Provider 3

Initial walk around exterior: Facility is housed in a renovated warehouse building (conventional brick, not hardened) shared with some sort of delivery service. The data center is on the third floor. First floor and basement include a garage used by the delivery service. Panel trucks come and go on the lower levels on the north side. Second floor includes some offices and appears to be largely empty. We never spoke to anyone who could tell us definitively how the second floor would be built out, or if even that was the plan. CCTV cameras are visible around the perimeter of the facility. Diesel generators are enclosed in 12-foot high chain link enclosures, HVAC on roof. The west side of the building is composed of a series of loading doors. On the day we were visiting, three of the doors were open. As we walked around the building, we succeeded in climbing up onto the loading dock and walking right into a power infrastructure room where many of the facility's UPSs resided. We waited, expecting CCTV or some other kind of alarm to summon security, but no one ever showed up. (Later, when we asked why we had been able to walk right in to such a critical part of the facility, they explained that the door was open to facilitate construction and renovation, and that the guard who was supposed to be posted there had been reprimanded). Urban setting amid a complex of warehouses. City workers were doing roadwork near the facility, with heavy duty digging (i.e., potentially fiber cable slicing) equipment.

Entering facility: First level security is building security. Guard appeared not to realize that there was a data center in the building. He ushered us up to the third floor where we encountered an unoccupied security desk behind a sliding (regular) glass partition. One CCTV console was visible at desk. It would have been easy to literally climb through the opening to the security desk so that we could buzz ourselves into the facility. Biometric palm reader visible, but dust covered, at door. Security guard who had walked us up stairs called someone on his radio and someone came to let us in. The person who let us in came from somewhere down the hallway outside the data facility. He let us in by leaning through the opening and hitting the buzzer, which was in reach. We stood inside the door while he made out visitor badges for us. He did ask to see picture IDs at this point, but it was kind of a farce by this point and everyone was a little embarrassed (including us for them). The room we were standing in while he prepared badges approximated a mantrap in that there was another door about 20 feet away that opened into the data center proper. Unfortunately, that door was propped open.

Cages: No cages. Everyone gets their own enclosed room (drywall and everything) with keypad access to room. No raised floor, power comes in from above, as do comms. Basic bolt-in racks and shelves provided. Walls of rooms do not extend to high warehouse roof, so it would be possible to climb over walls, or to toss something over a wall into an enclosed room.

(Continued)

EXHIBIT 4 (CONTINUED) Summary Notes from Network Services Visits to Hosting Facilities

Verification of Redundancy, Security, etc: Redundant power and connectivity are not yet in place, although they are promised within six weeks. Network hardware for facility was exposed, in an open area that anyone walking to his or her own enclosed space would need to pass by. There was no onsite NOC, although they expressed willingness to provide specific network monitoring on site on a contract basis; they noted too that network operations were monitored from a regional NOC. The guy giving us the tour kept apologizing for the construction (although he was a bright guy and knew his stuff).

Concerns: This facility is not fully built yet (although some customers are operational). Provider promises to have it in shape in time to remain consistent with our project, but the fact is that we cannot compare this facility on an equal basis with the others. The facility being under construction did not explain all of the lapses we saw.

Overall Assessment: These guys don't appear to have the hosting business figured out yet. Maybe it's just that they are in a construction phase. But there was little that we saw that offered warm feelings during our tour.

EXHIBIT 5 Service Level Agreements Offered by Hosting Providers

Provider 1

"Downtime" is defined as sustained packet loss in excess of 50% for 15 consecutive minutes due to the failure of the hosting provider to provide services for that period (does not include scheduled maintenance time). "Excess latency" is defined as transmission latency in excess of 100 milliseconds round-trip time between any two points within the hosting provider's U.S. network. "Excess packet loss" is defined as packet loss in excess of 1% between any two points in the hosting provider's network.

Each downtime period entitles customer to receive a credit equal to one day's recurring connectivity charge. Hosting provider guarantees two-hour response time in diagnosing problems within hosting provider and customer network. Customer will be advised of reason for problem within one hour of hosting provider discovering the reason for the problem. If problem is within control of hosting provider, remedy for problem is guaranteed in four hours from diagnosis of the problem. Inability to deliver diagnosis or remedies within the times stated above entitles customer to an additional service credit for each four-hour period of delay. Customer can collect credits for no more than ten days charges in a calendar month. Credits are granted at the sole discretion of the hosting provider.

Provider 2

"Downtime" is defined as sustained packet loss in excess of 50% for 15 consecutive minutes due to the failure of the hosting provider to provide services for that period (does not include scheduled maintenance time). "Excess latency" is defined as transmission latency in excess of 120 milliseconds round-trip time between any two points within the hosting provider's U.S. network. "Excess packet loss" is defined as packet loss in excess of 1% between any two points in the hosting provider's network.

Each downtime period entitles customer to receive a credit equal to one day's recurring connectivity charge. Hosting provider guarantees two-hour response time in diagnosing problems within hosting provider and customer network. If problem is not within hosting provider and customer network, hosting provider will determine source within an additional two hours. Customer will be advised of reason for problem within one hour of hosting provider discovering the reason for the problem. If problem is within control of hosting provider, remedy for problem is guaranteed in two hours from diagnosis of the problem. Inability to deliver diagnosis or remedies within the times stated above entitles customer to an additional service credit for each two-hour period of delay. Customer can collect credits for no more than seven days charges in a calendar month. Customer must request credits in writing within seven days of the event for which credits are compensation. Credits are granted at the sole discretion of the hosting provider.

Provider 3

"Downtime" is defined as sustained packet loss in excess of 30% for 15 consecutive minutes due to the failure of the hosting provider to provide services for that period (does not include scheduled maintenance time). "Excess latency" is defined as transmission latency in excess of 100 milliseconds round-trip time between any two points within the hosting provider's U.S. network. "Excess packet loss" is defined as packet loss in excess of 1% between any two points in the hosting provider's network.

Each downtime period entitles customer to receive a credit equal to three day's recurring connectivity charge. Hosting provider guarantees two-hour response time in diagnosing problems within hosting provider and customer network. Customer will be advised of reason for problem within one-half hour of hosting provider discovering the reason for the problem. If problem is within control of hosting provider, remedy for problem is guaranteed in two hours from diagnosis of the problem. Inability to deliver diagnosis or remedies within the times stated above entitles customer to an additional service credit for each two-hour period of delay. Total credits in a month will be limited to total amount of recurring payment to hosting provider for month of SLA triggering events (full refund for the month).

Exhibit 6 Pricing

	Provider 1	Provider 2	Provider 3
Space	3 8'×8' cages (192 sq ft), partitions removed to provide contiguous space	3 8'×7' cages (168 sq ft), partitions removed to provide contiguous space	280 sq ft enclosed room
Set up cost for space	$6500 one time fee	$7800 one time fee	$10,800 one time fee
Recurring cost for space	3 × $6500 per month	3 × $6800 per month	$9,800 per month
Set up cost for connectivity	$1200 one time fee	$1500 one time fee	$1600 one time fee
Connectivity	$1200 per month plus $525 per month for each mbps above 10	$1500 per month plus $589 per month for each mbps above 10	$900 per month plus $412 per month for each mbps above 10
Rights of first refusal on adjoining space	Not available	Same as above (must acquire adjoining space now to reserve it)	$1,500 per month (good for six months, renewable if both parties agree)

EXHIBIT 7   Services Offered by Hosting Provider for Additional Cost

Provider 1
Enhanced network monitoring
Consulting and professional services on a project basis

Provider 2
Enhanced network monitoring
Intrusion detection services
Security audit and security hardening
Performance diagnostics
Load testing
Consulting and professional services on a project basis

Provider 3
Consulting, monitoring, and professional services on a project basis

CASE 3–3
WEB AND IT HOSTING FACILITIES[1]

Technology Note

The emergence of the commercial Web has accelerated creation of a worldwide computer network capable of transmitting large volumes of data reliably across vast geographic distances. As the network grows in capacity and reliability, companies gain more options for delivering IT services to end users, whether they are customers or employees. Managers are faced with new decisions about how underlying IT infrastructure should be designed and managed. Making the wrong decision can have severe impact on a business that relies on IT services to operate. Unsatisfied customers, unplanned outages, or security breaches that shatter customer confidence are among the disasters that can readily result from poor infrastructure design or management.

This technology note focuses on decisions about where to physically locate a company's computer systems. More specifically, this note introduces readers to emerging Web and IT hosting technologies which make it possible to move computer systems outside a company's own walls and into data centers belonging to companies that specialize in data center management. Hosting companies, such as Exodus, Qwest, Genuity, and Digex, contend that their facilities are the best places to physically locate mission-critical computer systems. Outsourcing mission-critical systems in this way generates new management challenges; not least of which is assuring that IT services are available and perform well enough to satisfy end users.

[1]This note was prepared by Professor Robert D. Austin. Copyright © 2001 by the President and Fellows of Harvard College.
Harvard Business School case 601-134.

Hosting facilities physically house Web, application, and database servers, storage devices, and networking equipment in a robust environment that enables network-based computer systems to function in a secure and reliable manner. These facilities are designed to provide space, power, and Internet connectivity, as well as a range of supporting services that varies across hosting providers. Although hosting centers are often referred to as data centers, they should not be confused with the mainframe data centers built by many enterprises during the last three decades to house their own computer applications. Enterprise data centers were typically designed around a different set of platforms (mainframes) and performance expectations; they are usually only partially able to meet the requirements of a modern hosting facility.

Proponents of hosting based infrastructures describe a future in which companies routinely obtain much of the IT functionality they need for day-to-day business "over the Net" from a variety of service providers. Services accessed in this way, they suggest, will replace many services that have traditionally been provided by internal IT departments. Hosting companies play a vital role in this picture, by owning and managing the facilities to house computers that provide over-the-Net services. This vision is already a reality in business-to-customer (B2C) e-commerce. The back-office functionality (shopping cart, checkout, credit card processing, etc.) that enables Web-based consumer purchases typically resides on computing platforms in hosting facilities rather than on the selling company's premises or local to the consumer. The nascent Application Service Provider (ASP) industry seeks to extend this concept to delivering all the IT services needed to support many (especially small- and medium-sized) businesses with very little computing hardware (e.g., just PCs) located physically near end users.

The Hosting Value Proposition

Using a hosting provider to house and manage computer applications can potentially help companies meet several important challenges as they seek to maximize the return on IT investments. These challenges include:

The Shortage of Skilled IT Workers. According to the US government, there will be 4 million unfilled IT jobs in the US by 2003. By outsourcing management of computer system infrastructure to hosting providers, companies can potentially reduce their need for IT staff, or at least reduce the number of very skilled employees that they must hire. Such benefits are especially important to the small and medium-sized businesses that have the most difficulty attracting and retaining IT talent. Hosting companies can also realize savings, which can be passed on to customers, from economies of scale in the use of IT staff. For example: according to IT Centrix, the number of gigabytes of storage that an IT manager can manage ramps rapidly as the storage infrastructure becomes more centralized and shared.[2]

The Need for 24 × 7 Operation. Unlike traditional business operations, Web-based businesses are expected to operate around the clock. Consumers expect Web-based retailers to always be up. Businesses seeking efficiencies from the Web derive them partly from the real-time and "always on" nature of the Web. But most companies lack in-house infrastructure capable of assuring 24 × 7 operation. Some enterprises have their own data centers, but most of those facilities were designed for different computing platforms (mainframes) and different performance and availability expectations. In contrast, hosting company data

---

[2]"The Internet Hosting Report." Jeff Camp, April Henry, Jaime Gomezjurado, Kristen Olsavsky. Morgan Stanley Dean Witter. November 2000.

centers are designed for modern (server-based) computing architectures and high availability. Because their facilities are shared across many customers, hosting companies can justify larger investments in performance and availability than their customers can individually. A recent IDC study found that companies reduce downtime by an average of 87% when they move Web servers into centralized hosting facilities.[3]

The Drive to Reduce Costs Throughout the IT Service Supply Chain.   Hosted services offer cost-saving benefits to hosting customers as well as to numerous other service providers. In addition to the staffing economies of scale that have already been mentioned, cost savings can also be generated by sharing computing infrastructure across customers. Hosting-based models reduce the cost of making changes in a client company's software because fixes or upgrades only need to be applied to platforms within the hosting facility. Packaged software vendors favor the hosting service model because it reduces the potential for software piracy by keeping most software resident inside secure hosting facilities even while it is being used. Distributors of software can benefit from the reduced need to transport physical media for software (e.g., CD-ROM) and the smaller inventory of packaged software "boxes" that need to be managed. Studies to date have shown that moving applications to hosting providers tends to lower costs and increase returns. Morgan Stanley Dean Witter estimates that costs can be reduced by as much as 80% to 90%.[4]IDC estimates that the ROI from outsourcing to hosting companies can reach 300% with a payback on the investment of only 120 days.[5]

[3]"Achieving Rapid Return on Investment in Outsourced Web Hosting." Melanie Posey, Beryl Muscarella, and Randy Perry. IDC white paper, 2000.
[4]Camp, et al., ibid.
[5]Posey, et al., ibid.

The Need to Reduce Time-to-Market.   In recent years, businesses have increased their emphasis on using IT to enhance revenues by creating new business models, products, services, and industries. Revenue-side opportunities often offer significant early mover advantages. Seizing these opportunities depends on getting functionality up and running quickly. Here hosting helps by providing an immediately available physical facility to house new applications. Hosting companies also partner with Web systems integrators to offer standardized quick start packages. For example, hosted e-commerce packages can allow companies to become e-retailers almost overnight. Signing up for some e-commerce services requires only an Internet connection, a Web browser, and a valid credit card.

The Unfavorable Cash-Flow Profile of IT Investments.   IT investments have traditionally required large up-front cash outlays and yielded only eventual and uncertain (because of high IT project failure rates) benefits. Hosted services typically require relatively small up-front setup fees and allow for subscription-based payment for specific IT services. Furthermore, hosting customers can decide to add additional services in relatively small increments and relatively quickly. Adding a new service or increasing the level of an existing service can happen in hours or days.

The Need to Make Applications Globally Accessible.   Hosted IT services are designed to make geography relatively unimportant to service delivery capability so that centralized data centers can serve large geographic areas. A side benefit of this design is that services can easily be available from any computer with a Web browser and the ability to authenticate. Traveling employees can access the same virtual "workspace" regardless of where they are physically in the world. The IT overhead associated with moving a worker from one location to another is eliminated because the IT infrastructure is geography neutral.

Inside a Hosting Facility

Although there is much variation in what are sometimes called hosting facilities, there are well-defined data center features to which providers aspire and that constitute a de facto standard. Particular facilities may fall short on one or more "standard features," but in the mainstream of the hosting industry providers tend to offer at least the following on a 24 × 7 basis:

Uninterruptible Electric Power Delivery. Facility design typically allows for redundant power delivery to each piece of computing equipment housed in the facility (i.e., two power cables for each computer—high availability computing equipment often accepts two power inputs). Power distribution inside the walls of the facility avoids single points of failure and includes uninterruptible power supplies (UPSs) to maintain power to computing equipment even in the event of a sudden loss of power to the facility. Connections to external sources of primary power are also redundant; typical facilities can access two power grids. Redundant diesel generators are available for backup power generation with on-site fuel tanks containing fuel for a day or more of operation. There is usually a plan for high-priority access to additional fuel in the event of a prolonged primary power outage. All components in the facility that are critical to continuing service delivery have at least one redundant stand-by unit.

Physical Security. Security guards are posted in protected ("bulletproof") enclaves at all points of entry and exit, and they patrol the facility regularly. Closed-circuit TV monitors all critical infrastructure at all times and can provide immediate visibility into any area of the facility from a central security desk that is constantly attended. Access to internal areas of the facility requires picture ID and must be pre-arranged (i.e., there is a list of people authorized to enter the facility that is checked against the picture ID). Anyone entering the facility must cross through a "mantrap" buffer zone that can be locked down. Items (e.g., boxes, equipment) brought into the facility are opened and inspected. The building that physically houses the data center is dedicated to that use and is not shared with other aspects of the hosting company's businesses.

Climate Control and Fire Suppression. Facilities typically contain redundant heating, ventilating, and air conditioning (HVAC) equipment capable of maintaining temperatures in ranges suitable for computing and network equipment in all areas of the facility that house computing and network equipment. Mobile cooling units are often used to alleviate "hot spots." Integrated fire suppression systems include smoke detection, alarming, and gas-based (i.e., no equipment damaging water-based) fire suppression.

Network Connectivity. External connections to Internet backbone providers[6] are redundant, involving at least two backbone providers, and typically connect into the building through two physically separate points of entry. Hosting companies have agreements with private peering partners that permit significant percentages (say, 50%) of network traffic to travel from origin to destination without having to traverse often-congested public Internet junctions. There is a 24 × 7 network operations center (NOC) staffed with network engineers who monitor the connectivity infrastructure of the facility; a redundant or mirrored NOC on another

[6]"Backbone providers" own the very large data transmission lines via which large quantities of data are moved long distances.

site is usually capable of providing most of the services provided by the primary NOC.

Help Desk.   Customers are able to contact facility staff for assistance at any time. The facility has procedures for responding to unplanned incidents that can be invoked regardless of the time of day or night. Automated trouble ticketing systems are integrated with similar systems at service delivery partners so that complex problems involving interactions between multiple service providers can be quickly tracked down and alleviated.

Additional Hosting Facility Features

In addition to de facto standard features, some facilities provide further measures of protection. As hosting providers add these enhancements, the de facto standard seems to be rising. It appears likely that some of these additional features will become de facto standards in the not-too-distant future:

Hardened Physical Structure.   Facility structure is hardened against external explosions, earthquakes, and other disasters. Entry into facilities is through multiple, single-person capacity ("hostage proof") mantraps with integrated metal and explosive detection. Access to zones within the facility is controlled by biometric scanning technologies.[7] Internal private rooms and high-security vaults are available to house the most sensitive equipment. Motion sensors supplement video monitoring. Perimeter fencing surrounds the facility.

Enhanced Network Infrastructure.   This may include one or more of the following: mirrored NOCs, greater capacity for private peering traffic (up to 90%), three or more Internet backbone providers, placement of all mission-critical network components in segregated enclosures.

Enhanced Power Delivery Infrastructure. This could include primary power generation by an independent power plant with first level of backup power from local utility power grids and redundant diesel generators for second level backup. UPSs might employ batteryless, flywheel-based technologies.

A Note Concerning Redundancy and Availability

The level of redundancy of mission-critical components that is commonly implemented today within a hosting facility is designated "N+1." This means that for each type of critical component, there should be at least one extra component of that type standing by. For example, if a facility requires four diesel generators to meet its power demands in the event of a primary power outage, N+1 redundancy would require that the facility have five such generators in total (four to operate, one to stand-by). Obviously, N+1 redundancy provides a higher level of availability if the underlying number of components (the N in the N+1) is small.

Increasingly, hosting companies are aspiring to a higher level of redundancy, designated "N+N." This level of redundancy requires that there are twice as many mission-critical components as are necessary to run the facility at any one time. For example, a facility that requires four diesel generators to meet its power demands in the event of a primary power outage would need eight such generators on-site to achieve N+N redundancy. Where N+1 facilities are typically able to commit to service levels in the 99.9% availability range, N+N facilities can ensure availability levels in the 99.999% level. Not surprisingly, this very high level of availability is very costly. Forrester Research estimates that

---

[7]"Biometric" technologies identify people by their biological characteristics; examples include retina scanners, palm readers, and technologies that recognize individual voices.

increasing the availability of a Web site from 99% to 99.999%—that is, reducing downtime from 90 hours per year to less than 5 minutes per year—will require additional initial spending of $3.7 million and additional annual fees of $1.8 million.[8] Morgan Stanley Dean Witter estimates that the cost of building a 99.999% availability data center is in the $400 to $550 per square foot range. For comparison, a data center capable of 99% to 99.9% uptime costs about $150 per square foot to build.[9]

Hosting facilities are often categorized according to the level of uptime they are able to support. Level 1 data center infrastructure is available 99% to 99.9% of the time. Level 2 is commonly equated to 99.9% to 99.99%. Level 3 ensures uptime in the 99.99% to 99.999% range. Level 4, the highest level of availability in current common usage, equates to 99.999% to 99.9999% uptime. A Level 4 facility experiences downtime that is unnoticeable by most end users, literally seconds per year.

---

[8]"The Best of Retail Site Design," Randy K. Souza with Harley Manning, Hollie Goldman and Joyce Tong, October 2000.
[9]Camp, et al., ibid.

Managed Services

Guarantees of power, connectivity, climate control, and security do not in themselves guarantee reliable and secure operation of a computer system within a hosting facility. An e-commerce application, for example, will not necessarily run well just because it is housed within a state-of-the-art data center. Rather, a computer application requires ongoing administration and tuning of the software, databases, and other elements of the computing infrastructure. Table 1 shows the layers of services that can be provided to a customer to support a computer application.

Notice that previously discussed hosting facility features are all at the network or real estate services level. This fact prompts a question: who should provide higher-level services? Customers can of course, provide platform, application and business operating services for themselves, but some may wish to outsource these services as well. Hosting companies are arguably well positioned to provide some of these "managed services" along with their facilities related offerings. Because high value-add managed services offer potentially high margins to hosting companies, almost all

TABLE 1   Levels and Descriptions of Services

Level of Service	Description of Service
Business operating services*	Administering and operating an application.
Application support services*	Support for software above the operating system level; application support; application performance monitoring and tuning; design of applications for scalability, reliability, security.
Platform services*	Support for hardware, operating system; reboot services; data backup and disaster recovery services; URL monitoring.
Network services	Connectivity within the facility and externally to the public Internet and to private peering networks; monitoring of network traffic at the transport layer; service level assurances at the packet loss and network availability layer; network security.
Real estate services (lowest level)	Suitable floor space and physical facilities; maintenance of the space and facilities.

*"Managed Services"—Business operating, Application support and Platform services

have begun aggressively pursuing this lucrative revenue source.

The managed services business segment has been largely defined, however, by a different kind of company that calls itself a "managed service provider" (MSP). Loudcloud is a high-profile entrant in this category (Marc Andreessen, of Netscape fame, is chairman). Loudcloud bills itself as a complete substitute for the operations department of a client company. It provides clients with the services that would otherwise be provided by the client's own network administrators, database administrators, security experts, network architects, and systems administrators. MSPs work with Web systems integrators to offer standardized functionality and a managed services package. Some MSPs will stage, test, and deploy applications.

MSPs often partner with multiple hosting providers but they do not typically own hosting facilities. The advantage in this arrangement is that MSPs can target a lucrative segment of the hosting industry without having to invest the huge sums required to build data centers. The disadvantage, however, is that MSPs generally require the cooperation of hosting providers who also want to capture managed service revenues. MSPs often find themselves managing crucial but delicate relationships with hosting companies. Some MSPs private-label their services to hosting providers. These kinds of partnerships can be mutually beneficial by helping hosting providers enter the managed services business quickly and helping MSPs maintain access to data centers.

Hosting Models

Hosting companies design their facilities based on one of three hosting models: shared, dedicated, and co-location. Each model assumes different levels of customer involvement in managing the computer systems housed in the facility. The hosting model also directly influences the degree of operational robustness that can be supported and the cost to the customer of the hosting service.

Shared Hosting. In shared hosting, servers are owned and operated by the hosting provider and customers purchase space on servers. Multiple customers share a single physical server. Some providers use sophisticated clustering technologies to achieve highly secure and reliable performance. But this model is usually considered best suited to non-mission-critical hosting for small companies or individuals for whom low cost is an important requirement. Large customers are often wary of the degree of sharing implicit in this model, because of its perceived negative implications for security and reliability. Shared hosting typically provides entry-level Web site hosting for companies that want to post static content or mount basic applications, such as functionality to support basic e-commerce transactions.

Dedicated Hosting. As with shared hosting, servers are owned and operated by the hosting provider. Unlike the shared model, however, there is no sharing of servers between customers; servers are "dedicated" to individual customers. Other infrastructure components that provide network, storage, and some other services are shared across customers. Dedicated hosting providers usually offer a complete managed services package that includes everything needed to run the customer's systems at the required level of security and availability. Dedicated servers are able to support very high levels of security and availability. Hence, this model is suited to hosting the mission-critical application of large and medium-sized customers.

IDC separates the dedicated hosting category into three sub-categories called simple, complex, and custom dedicated hosting, defined as follows.[10]

Simple dedicated hosting.   This option relies on Web server appliances to deliver a narrow menu of highly standardized functionality, such as basic kinds of Web hosting. Web server appliances do not require complex configuration and are very simple and inexpensive to operate. In this dedicated hosting model, server appliances are typically allocated one per customer. Simple dedicated hosting is inexpensive but limited.

Complex dedicated hosting.   This option relies on two or more servers with different functions (e.g., Web, application, database) to meet a single customer's business needs. The offering supports a wider range of functionality than does simple dedicated hosting, but there is still an emphasis on standardized hardware and software configurations. The hosting company partners with manufacturers and developers of components that comprise the hoster's standard offerings; the hosting provider's staff becomes vendor-certified to support these components. By focusing on standard configurations that are more complex than those in simple dedicated hosting, this model facilitates reliable and economical operation of larger, but still somewhat limited, computer systems.

Custom dedicated hosting.   As the name suggests, hosting offerings in this category are designed specifically to support custom functionality. Custom architectures usually involve multiple servers of types that go beyond the hosting company's established standards. To reliably design, build, and operate custom functionality, hosting providers often team with systems integrators, MSPs,

---

[10]"Web Hosting Service: US Web Hosting Market Forecast, 1999-2004," Melanie A. Posey and Courtney Munroe, December 2000.

and other professional service providers, who work and bill on a one-time, project basis to design and deploy custom infrastructure.

Co-location Hosting.   Co-location hosting companies provide no-frills access to a facility and its infrastructure. Customers rent floor space, connectivity, and power inside a facility. Everything beyond these basics is provided à la carte and not necessarily by the hosting provider. Customer space is usually enclosed inside floor-to-ceiling cages, and the customer owns and retains responsibility for all servers and equipment inside the cages. The hosting company often knows very little about what is running inside customer cages. Needless to say, this model requires that the customer has (or acquires from a third party) the IT expertise to design, maintain, and operate the equipment inside the cages. This model supports a wide range of architectural possibilities and is generally capable of offering high availability. Large and medium-sized businesses are typical users of services in this category.

The Market for Hosting Services

Most analysts expect strong long-term growth in the hosting market (see Table 2). Demand for hosting facility space is expected to outpace supply as we move into the future. Large enterprises do not yet outsource to hosting facilities at a very high rate and may therefore represent a very large and untapped source of additional demand. As the IT staff shortage worsens and cost advantages of outsourcing to hosting providers become more apparent, many believe that large companies will begin to outsource their IT infrastructure at an increasing rate. The nascent ASP industry is another potential source of hosting services demand. The Phillips Group estimates that the ASP market will grow from $1 billion in

TABLE 2   Predicted Growth Rates for Hosting Services Market

Source	Growth Projection for Hosting Service Market
Morgan Stanley Dean Witter	From $5.5 billion in 2000 to $74.5 billion in 2005[12]
International Data Corporation	
—shared hosting	From $534 million in 1999 to $3.4 billion in 2004
—dedicated hosting	From $1 billion in 1999 to $17.2 billion in 2004
—co-location hosting	From $343 million in 1999 to $4.2 billion in 2004
Total hosting services	From $1.9 billion in 1999 to $24.8 billion in 2004
Gartner Dataquest	From $2.0 billion in 1999 to $9.3 billion in 2004
Forrester Research	$20 billion by 2004

[12]MSDW forecast is worldwide. Others are for U.S. market only. MSDW expects 63% of this growth will be in the United States.

1999 to $13 billion in 2004.[11] Other analyst projections are comparable. As the ASP industry grows, most of its computing infrastructure will be housed in hosting facilities.

Such strong demand factors create the potential for attractive profit margins. Moreover, revenues from hosting are annuity-like and persistent. Once customers move into a data center, they rarely leave. Churn rate for the industry is estimated at less than 2%.[13]

Morgan Stanley Dean Witter estimates that building a Level 2 or 3 data center of 50,000 square feet requires an investment of about $20 million. The revenue potential for that data center is about $1,200 per square foot per year, or $60 million per year when the data center is full. Payback periods for individual data centers are reported to be short. Exodus targets 15 months as time to EBITDA (earnings before interest, taxes, depreciation, and amortization) profitability for each of its data centers. In practice, it has beaten that target by an average of five

months. One facility, Santa Clara IV, reportedly reached breakeven in only four months.[14]

Hosting Market Threats.   The outlook for the hosting industry is not uniformly positive. Some risk factors and potential risk factors are identified below:

Dot-com fallout.   Most hosting companies have been adversely affected by the "dot-com crash" of 2000 and 2001. Hosted services are popular with startups because they provide a quick route to getting a business up and running. Consequently, dot-com companies have been present in hosting facilities in numbers disproportionate to their presence in the overall business market. As these dot-coms fail, hosting providers experience collections difficulties. Major players in the hosting provider industry have worked to reduce their dot-com exposure and it appears that many will survive the tech market malaise.

Commoditization.   The basic, no-frills hosting business based on a co-location model is essentially a high-end real estate market. As

[11]"Network Hosted Applications: US Market Demand and Segmentation Analysis," The Phillips Group, June 2000.
[13]Camp, et al., ibid.

[14]Camp, et al., ibid.

supply catches up with demand, such non-differentiated offerings could commoditize. Commodity providers would compete primarily on price and would experience significant pressure on margins. That would be an unwelcome development for companies that have invested heavily in data center construction. Clearly, pure co-location is the hosting model most vulnerable to this problem. Most hosting providers are defending against the possibility of commoditization by bundling their facilities offerings with more differentiated managed services. Forrester Research estimates that of the $20 billion in revenues they believe the market will generate in 2004, the majority, about $11 billion, will go to providers of managed services. Only a little over $1 billion will go toward base co-location provision.[15]

Large Enterprises might remain reluctant to outsource to hosting providers. Surveys have indicated that the top reason firms do not outsource their IT infrastructures to hosting providers is that they have concerns about data and transaction security as they move to an outsourcing model. Other reasons for outsourcing reluctance include concerns about the flexibility of hosting provider service offerings, the customer service capabilities of the hosting provider, and concerns about cost and performance. Hosting providers suggest that technological advances and compelling economics will soon overcome these concerns. Whereas now the reflex of the CIO may be to keep sensitive data close, argue hosting providers, in the future his or her reflex will be to rely on a trusted hosting provider; just as he or she keeps money in a bank, so will they trust reputable hosting providers to safeguard their sensitive data. Even if hosting companies are right, however, a slower than expected change in CIO attitudes could generate risks.

Brief Profiles: Two Prominent Hosting Companies

Exodus and Digex, two leading hosting providers at the time of this chapter represent illustrative differences in their approach to the hosting business. Exodus is far larger than Digex, but Digex has been an innovator in dedicated hosting.

Exodus Communications. Exodus was the pioneering company in the hosting business. As of year-end 2000, there were 46 open Exodus data centers worldwide, which accounted for more than 25% share of the co-location market. The company provides high-quality hosting infrastructure that satisfies large, demanding customers. Internationally, the company has moved aggressively into Europe and Japan. Projected revenues for the company were in the $2 billion to $5 billion range for 2002 and 2003.

Exodus hosting facilities are based primarily on a co-location model. Customers' primary purchase is space in a data center. Connectivity and managed services are sold as add-ons to the base space, power and environment service. Customers frequently enter data centers to manage their own equipment that is housed inside private cages. A primary challenge facing Exodus is expanding high value-add and high-margin managed service offerings. The company appears to be succeeding in this effort, as annual revenues per customer have increased from less than $100,000 in early 1998 to almost $300,000 at the end of 2000.[16] Exodus has experienced significant dot-com exposure; 47% of their customers were dot-coms at year-end 2000.[17]

[15]"Hosting's Moving On Up, " Jeanne M. Schaaf, with Mark Zohar, Gregory J. Scaffidi, Theo Dolan, and Susan Lee, Forrester Research, May 2000.

[16]It should be noted, however, that some of this per-customer growth surely arises from customers buying more data center floor space as their businesses grow.
[17]Camp, et al., ibid.

Digex.   Digex is newer and smaller than Exodus, but its dedicated hosting model embodies some interesting trends. As of year-end 2000, Digex had only four data centers operating compared to Exodus's 46, and less than 250,000 square feet of data center space, compared with Exodus' more than 5 million. Like Exodus, Digex targets large, demanding customers who want very high quality hosting offerings. Even more than Exodus, though, Digex focuses on differentiating itself by the quality of its data centers. Digex builds N+N redundancy data centers that cost $525 per square foot to build; in comparison, Exodus data centers have N+1 redundancy and cost $300 per square foot to build. The Digex emphasis on quality has landed some very large customers. The company's revenues are projected to approach $500 million in 2002.

At the heart of the difference between Digex and Exodus is that Digex is designed from the ground up to support dedicated hosting, including high levels of managed services. The company does not offer pure co-location. Whereas a large segment of Exodus' customers still buy primarily space and connectivity, Digex offers only fully-managed solutions. Customers rarely enter data centers and do not have their own cages (although they do have Digex-owned servers dedicated to them). One advantage of this arrangement is that data centers do not need to be physically near customers' sites. Digex captures substantially more revenue per server than does Exodus; in the most recent quarter for which data was available, revenues per server were $4,100 per month at Digex versus $1,300 per month at Exodus. The Digex high-end orientation translates into a favorable revenue mix in which only about a third of its customers have been dot-coms.[18]

_____

[18]Camp, et al., ibid.

CASE 3–4
TRILOGY (A)[1]

"Everything about Trilogy, from its company ski boat moored at a nearby marina to its 24–7 work ethic, shrieks a single message: Live fast or die."
–Rolling Stone[2]

Joe Liemandt, Trilogy's 30-year-old CEO, shouted encouragement to 36 of his newest employees as each placed a $2,000 bet at the roulette wheel. The unmistakable tension in the special room for high-stakes gamblers was heightened by an anxious drone from just out-

_____

[1]This case was prepared by Professor Robert D. Austin. Copyright © 1998 by the President and Fellows of Harvard College Harvard Business School case 699-034
[2]"The Seduction of Bryon Krug," by Jeff Goodell, *Rolling Stone,* October 15, 1998.

side, where 230 more recent hires waited eagerly to hear of winners and losers.

Coming to Vegas was their reward for getting halfway through "Trilogy University," (TU) the company's grueling three-month training program for college recruits. Except for betting, the trip was all-expenses-paid for the TU participants, most of who were barely old enough to get into a casino. The big bets that were causing so much commotion resulted from a challenge Liemandt had issued a few moments earlier: Trilogy would front money to anyone willing to place a $2,000 bet. Losers would have $400 deducted from their paychecks for the next five months. Who would accept the challenge? *It's enough to hurt if they lose*, Liemandt reasoned, *but not so much that it would wreck anyone*. That was the level of risk taking he wanted them to adopt as Trilogy employees.

The wheel spun. The ball dropped, then settled. One of the 36 high rollers won $72,000.[3]

As the winner celebrated and the rest commiserated, Liemandt's thoughts turned to the bets he and his management team were placing as year-end 1998 approached, bets intended to make Trilogy the "next great software company." Some of their choices looked unconventional to outside observers. For example: the company resisted traditional management structures, choosing to rely instead on superstar performers and an extreme form of empowerment that some felt bordered on chaos, even as these 260-plus new employees nearly doubled the company's size. Plans called for hiring 1,000 more next year. There were plenty who doubted that Trilogy could grow so fast, maintain its "anything goes" culture, and still remain successful. Liemandt realized all this, but it did not bother him. Given their incredibly ambitious goals for Trilogy, he and his colleagues were taking the only possible course. Big bets were necessary. Only time would tell how big the payoff would be.

Company Background[4]

In early 1990, at age 21, Joe Liemandt dropped out of Stanford to start a software company, just months before he would have graduated. He convinced one other Stanford senior, John Lynch, to drop out also, but failed to persuade Christie Jones, Chris Porch, and Seth Stratton. These three stayed involved in the effort while they finished up their school work, however, and Jones and Porch continued as part of the team after their graduation. Stratton was replaced by Thomas Carter, another recent Stanford grad, in the spring of that year. All five turned away lucrative job opportunities to instead form the core group that was to become Trilogy. Liemandt describes some of the fallout from their decisions:

> My parents were calling me up thinking I'm a wacko, telling me "When are you going to quit this ridiculousness." Their parents were calling them up saying "You didn't go to Stanford to waste your life away." *Their* parents were calling *me* up and yelling at *me* about it.

One consequence of adverse parental reactions was that no seed money was forthcoming from family sources. The team had *no* funding, except for the modest revenues generated by small consulting jobs they did on the side. What they did have, however, was a big idea.

Liemandt had come to Stanford knowing he wanted to start a software company. As an undergraduate, he had spent many hours researching the industry and thinking about where the best opportunities might be. In and around school work, he did consulting to pay bills and to stay on top of the latest in information technology practices. Eventually, experiences from consulting clicked with the research.

It seemed to Liemandt that hardware vendors had difficulty delivering their products with the right equipment. His consulting clients frequently received computers with missing or incompatible components. Selling and delivery processes for these complex products appeared to be largely manual and fraught with error. This observation prompted Liemandt to analyze the income statements of

[3]See also, for another account of this event, "High Rollers: How Trilogy Software Trains Its Raw Recruits To Be Risk Takers," by Evan Ramstad, *The Wall Street Journal*, September 21, 1998.

[4]Some of the factual material in this section was found in "Dream On," by Karen E. Starr, *Selling Power*, October, 1997, Vol. 17, No. 8; and "Holy Cow, No One's Done This!" by Josh McHugh, *Forbes*, June 3, 1996.

Exhibit 1   Liemandt's Analysis of Computer Product Companies' Spending

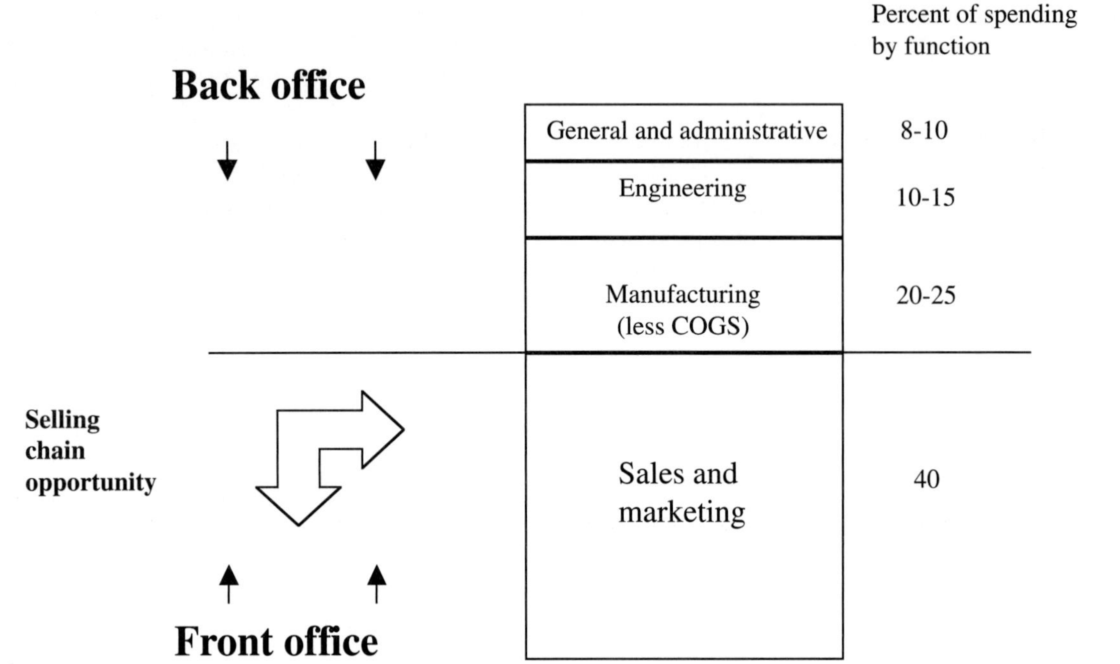

Percent of spending
by function

Back office

	Percent of spending by function
General and administrative	8-10
Engineering	10-15
Manufacturing (less COGS)	20-25
Sales and marketing	40

Selling chain opportunity

Front office

Source: "Holy cow, no one's done this!" *Forbes,* June 3, 1996.

computer product companies, comparing spending patterns with the degree of automation in each company function. What he found surprised him (see Exhibit 1).

Companies typically spent only 8% to 10% on General and Administrative costs, which had been extensively automated over the years. Research and Development, also highly automated in most high-tech companies, accounted for slightly more spending, about 10% to 15%. Manufacturing was a similar story: mature cost-saving technologies had been applied to reduce spending (less cost of goods sold) to 20% to 25% of the firm's total expenses. What remained after deducting these major categories was the more than 40% of expenditures that were mostly related to Sales and Marketing—an area which, surprisingly, was *not* very automated. If automa-

tion of the "selling chain" allowed companies to put an additional 2% of revenues on the bottom line (a number which Liemandt considered reasonable), that would be worth literally billions of dollars. It was a potentially huge market that had not yet been targeted by anyone.

While still in school, Liemandt and the others had begun working on configuration software, which incorporated complex if-then rules into a tool that would prevent mismatches between incompatible product parts. They continued this work after school, into 1991, always sure they were on the verge of solving the configuration problem that would finally give them a completed product. Companies like Hewlett-Packard (HP) and Digital were working on their own "configurators," which added urgency to Trilogy's efforts. Liemandt presented their ideas to venture capitalists, but none would invest in a company composed entirely of barely 20-years-olds. To stay afloat, the team leveraged more than 20 credit cards, managing to borrow almost half a million dollars in cash advances. Liemandt describes the mood in the days before the company had revenues or product:

> At the beginning, nothing worked. We lived failure every quarter. The product never worked. We'd sit around thinking "this is just ridiculous, why are we continuing?" We were living in a state of failure, but we had this hope, this shining star that wouldn't go out. What kept us together was the vision that this was a huge opportunity; we just needed to make it work. That, or the fact that we were yelling at each other the whole time.

In 1991 the company moved to Austin, Texas, so that Liemandt could spend more time with his father, Gregory Liemandt, who had been diagnosed with a fatal illness. By this time Trilogy had an early product and had applied for patents covering its algorithms, but the company still had no customers. They were working hard to generate interest in their software, but nothing was working. HP, a key potential customer, sent a particularly discouraging letter saying, in essence, "we already have a configurator and don't need your product."

Meanwhile, however, being in Austin enabled Trilogy to hire David Franke, a software developer with an industry-wide reputation, from a research consortium in Austin. With Franke on board, the company suddenly had new-found credibility. Silicon Graphics became the first customer, signing a small deal. Within months, HP was back, this time offering $3.5 million for software and support services. The deal was consummated in March of 1992. At the time, Trilogy had eight employees.

When HP signed, everything changed for Trilogy. Software that was good enough for HP was good enough for a lot of other big companies, also. The floodgates opened and Boeing, AT&T, and, eventually, IBM and Chrysler became customers (the IBM deal alone was worth $25 million). Also significant: Liemandt's father, a former GE executive and chairman of UCCELL, who had called his son a moron for squandering his Stanford education, agreed to become Trilogy's chairman, a position he retained until he passed away in 1993. Trilogy accepted funding from two venture capitalists, not because the company needed the money, but because it needed the expertise on how to grow a company that those firms could offer. Venture investors who had refused to fund Trilogy in the early days came calling—and were turned away. Liemandt retained more than 50% ownership.

As orders rolled in, Trilogy staffed up. The company grew rapidly to around 100 employees. They hired experienced executives to head Development, Consulting, and Sales. But by late 1994, Liemandt was not happy with the way things were going. Things were good at present, but he worried about the future:

> Between '92 and '95 these experienced executives built mediocre organizations. They weren't passionate about building the company. Their goal set was lower than the rest of Trilogy's. It was "Let me get this thing to $30 million, IPO it, we're done." That will work for next year, but then what do you do? What do you do when you're at $30 million and SAP's trying to take your market away and you don't have a development team that can build another product as good as the original one?

By 1995 it was clear to Liemandt that he needed to change the way the company was being built. He conferred with Jack Welch, CEO of General Electric, a longtime family friend from the days when Liemandt's father was at GE. Welch advised him to keep relying on "kids" to run the company, and to avoid building a traditional organization. To achieve this, John Price, a trusted Liemandt lieutenant, took over recruiting, created Trilogy University, and set out to hire the very best people from the nation's top universities. Some employees, including experienced executives, were let go.

Exhibit 2   Some of Trilogy's Customers

Allegiance Health Care
Bay Networks
BMC Software
Boeing
EJ Gallo
General Electric
Goodyear
Haworth
Hewlett-Packard
IBM
Lucent
Norand
Volvo
Whirlpool

Source: Trilogy Website (www.trilogy.com), as of
November 30, 1998.

Over the next three years, Trilogy focused on building the organization, expanding the customer base, and broadening the product line to support all elements of sales and marketing. They successfully acquired new, young talent and made key industry hires. Large companies, recognizing that configurator software was a key to delivering customized products and services to their own customers, beat a path to Trilogy's door (see Exhibit 2 for a list of Trilogy customers). The increasingly talented development team continued to enhance the product. As Trilogy entered 1998, estimates of the privately-held company's revenues exceeded $100 million annually. The workforce, by then totaling nearly 400, with an average age of less than 26, operated in constant overdrive to keep up with demand for Trilogy's products and services.

Industry and Competition

Liemandt's original analysis of spending patterns versus degree of automation in computer product firms had identified a wide-open market worth at least $10 billion. The few companies that were in that market at the time were bit players, selling things like contact management software for salespeople. Most of the functionality that constitutes the bulk of the "selling chain"—catalog updating, configuration, pricing, bid preparation, commission calculation—was performed manually or by software written by product firms themselves. Trilogy had pushed rapidly and successfully into this mostly empty space.

But Trilogy's success did not go unnoticed. Beginning in about 1993, new companies like Aurum, Brightware, Calico, Clarify, Remedy, Scopus, Siebel Systems, and Vantive entered the general area of sales and marketing automation. Some of these companies targeted niches that were not in immediate competition with Trilogy. But all were operating in the same general space, going after that 40+% of P&L spending that Liemandt had first noticed as a student. More worrying than these small players, however, was the awakening interest of the giants of Enterprise Resource Planning (ERP)—rapidly growing companies that were many times larger than Trilogy, such as SAP, Oracle, Peoplesoft, and Baan (see Exhibit 3 for profiles of these companies).

Trilogy had intentionally positioned itself as an "enterprise software" company, meaning that its products were designed to work together to provide end-to-end functionality for a major segment of a customer's business (the selling chain). This was necessary because Trilogy's corporate customers were increasingly looking to build or buy integrated systems. Companies that did not sell enterprise products risked losing out to companies with more integrated and broader product offerings. But ERP vendors saw the enterprise software market as *their* turf. One company's supply chain, reasoned the ERP giants, was another company's selling chain. As the experts on integrating a customer's "back office"—the value stream from procurement through production to delivery—it seemed

Exhibit 3   Profile of Leading ERP Companies

Company (1997 data)	Sales (in $ millions)	Market Share	Employees
SAP	3,461.2	30%	12,856
Oracle Financials	1,400[a]	10%	7,000[a]
PeopleSoft	815.7	7%	4,452
Baan	679.6	6%	4,254
J.D. Edwards	647.8	9%	3,577

[a]Estimate

Sources: OneSource website (GlobalBB.onesource.com) as of November 5, 1998; "Baan's Voyage," *Red Herring,* August 1998.

only natural to the ERP vendors that they should also integrate the "front office"—the selling chain. Liemandt summarized the threat to his company in stark terms:

> They decided that Trilogy had done some fantastic research for them and that they'd just come in and take it over. The question was (and still is) "can we withstand the onslaught of giants ten times as big who want to move into our space?"

As early as 1993, Trilogy had realized that the number one threat to its long-term well-being was SAP, the largest of the ERP vendors, which by 1998 owned 70% of the back office automation business for *Fortune* 500 customers. In 1997 and 1998, the threat from SAP and the other ERP vendors became more immediate. Baan purchased Aurum. Peoplesoft announced partnerships with Vantive and Siebel Systems (which itself bought Scopus). SAP pointedly failed to invite Trilogy to exhibit at Sapphire 1998, the SAP-sponsored tradeshow for its own customers, even though the company had participated in earlier years.[5]

---

[5]Trilogy responded to not being invited to Sapphire 98 by renting a parking lot across the street from the convention center where Sapphire 98 was being held, erecting a structure with Trilogy's name all over it, and raffling off Porsche Boxsters to Sapphire attendees who stopped in to talk to Trilogy reps. This guerilla marketing maneuver won favorable mention for Trilogy in many press accounts of Sapphire 98.

At that same tradeshow, Hasso Plattner, SAP's chairman and co-founder, announced to his customers that 80% of the company's R&D going forward would be aimed at building front office products.

Trilogy had a considerable head start on ERP vendors in the development of key technologies, especially configuration software, some of which was by then protected by patents. But the protection provided by patents would be short-lived. Whether Trilogy would remain a factor would depend far less on past accomplishments than on what they could accomplish in the future.

Trilogy Places Its Bets

Trilogy's business strategy was driven by the ambitious goals of Liemandt and the rest of his team. By 1998, anyone willing to settle for less than becoming the next great software company was gone from the company's management. Microsoft, the reigning champ of software companies, was a model that Trilogy employees readily acknowledged. The drive to be distinctive was a central element in the company culture. It led them to develop a set of strategies in specific areas that they believed would move them most rapidly toward their goals, but which had noticeable differences from the paths being pursued by their competitors.

Marketing the Product. SAP chairman Plattner's use of the term "front office" in declaring his company's intention to go after the sales automation market was a victory of sorts for Trilogy. Trilogy had been working to create this distinction between front and back offices in press releases, with their customers, and anywhere else an opportunity appeared. Customers who took for granted that there was a difference between front and back office software would be more open to suggestions that there was something special about the front office. Step one in holding off SAP was positioning Trilogy reps so that they could say to a VP of sales and marketing: "You don't want decisions already made by the manufacturing VP to drive the way you sell and market your products—do you?"

Focusing on Trilogy's strength in the front office worked well to negate customers' inclinations to get selling and supply chain software from the same vendor. But SAP had another huge advantage over Trilogy. Ajay Agarwal (MBA 1995), Trilogy's senior marketing executive, described the advantage and its implications:

> They've got an installed base of nearly 10,000 customers and they've got thousands of reps out there in the field. Our view is that if we try to build the same model as SAP, they're going to win because we cannot achieve the scale required fast enough. We're never going to hire enough direct sales people to have the *Fortune* 500 and Big Six relationships they already have. So we've had to look at an alternative set of models.

To counter SAP's advantage, Trilogy concentrated on building distribution through indirect channels. By establishing formal relationships with systems integrators and other software firms, Trilogy had access to a sales force that was already growing past 1,500 people—other companies' employees selling Trilogy's products. Agarwal further explained Trilogy's decision to not scale a large direct sales force:

> Our fundamental belief is that there is excess direct sales capacity in the enterprise software market. The companies in the space are able to support the capacity with differentiated products that provide premium pricing and profits. However, as competition in a given space intensifies, massive pricing pressure causes profits to collapse. In this scenario, only the biggest players (e.g., SAP) survive, because their product breadth, installed base, and massive distribution provides them with enough defendable market space to fund the competitive battles. Trilogy's approach in this environment is to be the "component" supplier, funneling our differentiated technology through the sales channels of the other players.

Trilogy's industry-best configuration software helped them establish indirect sales channels. Because no products were true peers to Trilogy's configurator, many companies found it convenient to incorporate Trilogy products into their own offerings. This allowed Trilogy, as the component supplier, to be the arms dealer in the ever-escalating enterprise software war.

Trilogy maintained a small direct sales force to manage large customer accounts and relationships with other companies (such as vendors) who were deemed key to Trilogy's distribution aims. How this sales force worked pointed out another aspect of the Trilogy approach, their intention to be "marketing led" rather than "sales led." Liemandt explains:

> We've broken down the tasks of customer acquisition and minimized the amount of work the sales rep has to do. In a traditional enterprise software sale, a sales rep is in charge of lead generation, lots of marketing activities, account development, and sales. We just focus them on the relationship and sales execution. Lead generation is done by marketing. Account development is done by another organization, working with sales. The result is that our sales reps are ten to twenty times more productive on a revenue basis than the average ERP rep.

Being marketing led meant that Trilogy would maintain a highly developed capability for finding new opportunities and for adjusting to events in the market place. Not all of the changes in selling the product over the next few years would fall within the traditional sales realms. Trilogy's goal was to be ready for opportunities in any form.

The company's primary distribution objective going forward was to move down market, to sell profitably to smaller customers. The company's channel for large companies—say $5 billion or more in revenues—was well developed and successful. If your name was Lucent, IBM, or GE, Trilogy could offer the best technology to solve a variety of very large problems. Such large companies were able and willing to pay top dollar and deals were sized at a level that would support considerable marketing and business development overhead. But Trilogy's managers did not believe the company could survive with only the *Fortune* 500 as a customer base. Liemandt was prepared to go to considerable lengths to broaden Trilogy's distribution:

> The reason Trilogy might die is if we don't figure out how to get to the *Fortune* 50,000. We are like Cray, Silicon Graphics, Apple were in their early days. They were the esoteric high end with great technology, but no distribution. We are determined not to end up like them. We are focused on developing a large distribution channel. We have to get volume to prosper long-term. If you're a technical company, you can't protect the crown jewels. High-tech companies die because they're run by high-tech people who think that the stuff they wrote is great. If you really trust your high end engineering team, you give away what they did to get what you don't have. So at Trilogy, we're now trading our high-end technology for distribution. Under the assumption that our engineering team will deliver just like they delivered in the past.

If SAP began giving away selling chain functionality to win broader business from its customers, Trilogy could find itself playing Netscape to SAP's Microsoft. Liemandt and his colleagues wanted to achieve as broad as possible distribution before that had time to happen.

Developing the Product. Trilogy's marketing goals depended vitally on the company's product development capability. Specifically, marketing objectives required that developers sustain the competitive advantage Trilogy enjoyed in configurator technology while dramatically broadening the product to fill the enterprise needs of large and small customers in a variety of industries.

Trilogy aspired to maintain a software development capability that was second to none. Their comparison set for evaluating themselves in this area was not their direct competitors, but other world class development organizations, especially Microsoft. In their aim to be the best, they believed that they had largely succeeded. Liemandt was convinced that no other enterprise software vendor was even a close second to Trilogy in development capability. Scott Snyder, Trilogy's senior development VP, estimated that 15 or 20 successful software companies could be built around the talent in Trilogy's development organization.

Central to the company's development capability was the "rule of the super coders," which held that 1 superstar programmer could do the work of 10 average programmers. "Getting the most out of great developers," remarked Snyder, "is one of the things Trilogy does amazingly well." The development process was geared toward giving Trilogy's superstar programmers the support and freedom they needed to produce great products. Snyder described some of the company's fundamental philosophies of software development:

> Our development is based around four basic philosophies. *Small teams*, very small from a traditional development standpoint. We expect entire new products to be created by one or two superstar programmers you can count on to deliver great products quickly. *Complete ownership* of the product at the developer level from initial product requirements

gathering through product support. We don't have a separate change team that insulates the developers from the impact of producing poor quality products. Intense focus on *automation* in order to free the developers (or anyone else) from having to spend their time manually performing frequently repeated tasks like regression tests. Finally, a focus on *incremental development* model that allows us to deliver new functionality quickly and provides us the flexibility to react to changes in the market quickly.

A key feature of the development process was that it evolved to maintain responsiveness to the market, becoming more structured as the product matured. As the product grew beyond a certain size, explained Snyder, maintaining responsiveness and high product quality depended on some key disciplines:

> The goal is to maintain your code at ship level quality on a weekly basis. When a developer drops code for a new feature or bug fix into the build, it must be accompanied by the appropriate suite of automated tests to validate that the changes work as expected. These tests are added to the existing suite and the entire set is executed every time the product is built, whether that was a weekly or nightly build.
>
> If you had to develop a feature that took longer than the weekly build cycle, you branch your development, develop the feature, develop tests, merge it all back into the main build, then rerun all the tests on the integrated code. In addition to the individual product tests, we also have automated system tests which test the interactions between products. The goal is to constantly improve the quality of the product as you increase its functionality. Again, a very incremental model. It's awesome and brilliantly suited for an environment which requires you to react quickly to any new requirement or change in market direction as long as you maintain the quality discipline.

As the product grew in complexity, programmers retained absolute freedom to add features in whatever way they saw fit, but they were obliged to maintain quality. As interdependencies developed between different developers' programs, the build and release cycle became more structured, with decisions being made about the timing of the release of new features on a feature-by-feature basis. New features were scheduled around a plan that

used 60% to 70% of Trilogy's development capacity with the remaining 30% to 40% held in reserve for late-breaking and urgent fixes.

The process for identifying customer requirements for new products or new major features was largely unstructured and based on rapid development of a prototype. A developer would be assigned the task of creating a live screen prototype, which was not fully functional but would provide users with a good approximation of the experience of using an eventual system. Prototypes could be constructed very quickly, without much advance requirements gathering or specification. Customers could then be shown the prototype and valuable feedback could be obtained. Even if prototypes were far off the mark, the feedback provided would be far better than reaction to a paper document describing what a future system might do. "Customers will say," observed Snyder, "uh-uh, this isn't what I want, but if I could just do that with this screen it would be awesome."

The primary challenge Trilogy faced in maintaining its development capability was in pulling new talent into the process. Universities produced unrefined development talent, super coders who were not yet super developers. Making the leap to super developer from super coder required an understanding and appreciation of the disciplines required for producing sellable product. Trilogy University played a major role in effecting the transformation from coder to developer, but not everyone made the transition with equal ease.

Developers who reached superstar status at Trilogy were amply rewarded. As in all areas of the company, the bonus plan for developers was extremely generous at the very top. Being among the very best at anything at Trilogy would result in annual cash bonuses (some of which could be taken in the form of stock) that were multiples of base salary. The Developer of the Year award conferred recognition and a valuable gift that was specially matched to the winner's interests (for example, a seat at a high stakes Las Vegas poker game was purchased for the 1998 winner who was a poker enthusiast). Liemandt also sometimes issued challenges to individual developers in the form of bets. If accepted, bets typically required a person to commit money (say, $1,000) to be paid *to* the company if a certain objective was not met in exchange for a larger sum (say, $10,000) to be paid *by* the company to the person if the target was met.

Growing the Company[6]   The number of Trilogy employees doubled in 1998, and the company had plans to more than double the number again in the following year. There were two major motivations for such rapid growth. First, Trilogy had only begun to fill the huge market for front office software, and now the competitors (especially SAP) were coming. Big chunks of the market would be seized by the major players over the next year or two. Trilogy needed to be big enough to be considered a major player, to capture as much of that market as possible. Second, there was much more demand for Trilogy's products and services than could be met. Important initiatives were languishing for lack of anyone to work on them. Opportunities were there for Trilogy's taking, but the company literally lacked the bodies to grab them.

Liemandt and his team believed that the ability to manage rapid growth was a required competency for a "software powerhouse." But such rapid growth did generate concerns. Chief among these was whether Trilogy could maintain its high standard of individual talent as it increased its hiring volume. To address this concern, the company refined its hiring processes in an effort to reduce the likelihood of bad hires. The company tended to

retain its best employees and, unlike many companies, to lose people at the bottom rather than the top of the performance scale.

Other concerns had to do with continuing to execute effectively while growing rapidly, maintaining company culture in the face of the new hire onslaught, and more mundane (but still very important) issues of logistics and communications. Trilogy University was an effective mechanism for dealing with some of these concerns. It instructed new hires in the Trilogy way of doing things, dosed them with the Trilogy culture, and oriented them so that they were able to become contributors more quickly.

Growth was accomplished primarily via university hiring for which Trilogy was developing a formidable reputation. Job candidates were interviewed several times on campus by recruiters who remained resident at top universities for extended periods. Prospects who passed the rigorous screening were flown to Austin for numerous interviews there. From September through May, the company hosted 20 or more candidates a week at Trilogy's headquarters.

Once Trilogy decided to go after a candidate, the recruiting machine kicked into high gear. Consistent with the company's emphasis on empowerment, recruiters were encouraged to think of new ways to attract candidates. Potential employees received not only the usual treatment consisting of nice hotels and fancy dinners, but also a variety of novel inducements. Some were taken on afternoon spins in the company ski boat. Many spent hours on the phone with Trilogy recruiters, talking about career choices and decisions. Most received gifts ranging from clothing (invariably with "Trilogy" printed or embroidered on it), to CDs and books (targeted to specific candidate interests), to Tiffany writing pens (to make signing with the company easier). According to *Rolling Stone* magazine, Trilogy marketed itself to students "like a garage

[6]Some of the factual material in this section was found in "The Seduction of Bryon Krug," by Jeff Goodell, *Rolling Stone,* October 15, 1998.

band."[7] The tactics so impressed an official at Carnegie Mellon University's computer science school that he was prompted to declare Trilogy the savviest recruiter on campus.[8]

The company was also refining its processes for hiring from industry and from top business schools. Increasingly, people were coming to Trilogy from companies like HP, IBM, McKinsey, and Microsoft. In the 1997–1998 recruiting year, Trilogy interviewed 250 MBAs from top schools, made 11 offers, and succeeded in hiring nine of those (eight were from Harvard). These older employees, relative "gray hairs" in the very young company, were expected to assume vital roles in managing the creative chaos as Trilogy grew. The gray hairs also shored up the company's reputation, clearly establishing it as an owner of first rate management talent as well as technical talent. Unlike the previous generation of experienced managers (which had needed to be replaced), this new generation was not hired to immediately assume VP level responsibilities. Rather, they were placed in initiative leadership positions and given broad opportunities that would allow them prove themselves and then advance quickly as the company grew.

The Trilogy Culture. As new employees were absorbed by Trilogy, Liemandt and his management team worked at preserving vital elements of the company culture. The culture expressed itself in phrases that were often repeated by employees throughout the company: "Take risks." "Change the world." "The next great software company." "Question everything." The culture also expressed itself in a way of doing things that stuck some outside observers as chaotic. Liemandt remarked on

perceptions of his company and its management style:

> Some people do view Trilogy as a bunch of kids out of control. But we put these kids into an organization that very much understands 'this is the way you get product out.' We're trying to hire stars, we're trying to change the world, so those are the people who come to Trilogy. We're building an organization and process that can handle that. Which means very wide latitude in what you let them do. Your risk factors in managing this way have to do with how well your process can handle fault conditions. Can you handle breakage along the way? Breakage is fine as long as the process is telling you there is breakage. We're more into reporting than enforcement mechanisms.
>
> I push empowerment to the limit. I say, "Get outside your comfort zone. Go make a big impact. Look at your global scope and ask how you can make the biggest impact." Our culture is about pushing that. If a side effect is chaos, well okay. I don't see that as chaos. Software is all about people. And if you have the best people you have to stretch them, give them opportunity. The more you box them, the more the process becomes a regimen, the less you are using the people. Trilogy management makes very few decisions. Individuals make their own calls.

This policy of total empowerment was reflected in the company's lack of certain policies that were routinely present in most companies. There was no vacation policy. People took time off as they saw fit. There were no standard working hours. Most people worked very long days and weeks anyway.

The Trilogy culture was also maintained by evolved practices. Every Friday afternoon at five, employees wandered down from their offices to the ground floor of the Trilogy building for "Party on the Patio." Developers' offices were strewn with mattresses, old furniture, etc. Floor-to-ceiling office windows with spectacular views of the Colorado River valley were used as whiteboards, covered with scrawls in blue marker. On the day of the X-Files movie premier, the company was shut down so that everyone could catch the matinee (see Exhibit 4).

As the company grew larger, Trilogy University became an increasingly important

---

[7]Ibid.
[8]Ibid.

Exhibit 4 Excerpt from Trilogy Recruiting Brochure

Searching for *Relief*?

It's here. Looking for something different? Some adventure? A break from the norm? Trilogy is where you'll find it. Not convinced? We didn't think so. Check this out. It's 1PM on a weekday afternoon. You're in the middle of building a software demo. Everyone starts leaving the office and heading to the parking garage. They are buzzing about something. You hear words like "aliens," "government conspiracy," " kidnapping," "cancer man" . . . And then it hits you. Today is the premier of the new X-Files movie, and the whole company has tickets, including you. What an awesome way to spend your afternoon.

Source: Trilogy 1999 recruiting brochure, page 1.

conduit for the company culture. Participants in the program considered it rigorous and intense, often using phrases like "boot camp" to describe it. Amanda Terry, a 1998 TU graduate, related her impressions of the three-month training experience:

> Two hundred and sixty plus recent college graduates together on one floor, working long hours to produce the next great software product, being mentored by star performers at Trilogy—that begins to give you an idea of what Trilogy University is like. It's like a fresh-

man dorm colliding with a Wall Street trading floor. It's intense yet social, a combination of high energy and constant learning.

Looking Forward

As the end of 1998 approached, Trilogy was juggling a series of objectives that contained obvious tensions. Grow extremely rapidly. Maintain business success and culture. Rapidly broaden product offerings. Maintain product quality. Dramatically increase distribution. Without adding fixed cost.

Perhaps the most pressing objective, however, was to remain capable of dealing with whatever happened in the enterprise software market. Liemandt summarized the company's predicament:

> You cannot predict the market even two years out. Which market segments will the big guys go after? What will SAP do? Where are they not going to go? What matters very much is being nimble on your feet. We do no long-term strategic planning except for the very global vision: be a dominant player in the front office. Truth is, I'm not willing to lock in a plan today, because the odds of being right are extremely low. So you're building an organization that's incredibly flexible with incredibly good people who are able to create new markets, who are able to change on a dime, who are used to lots of different variables coming in, or one of their main variables changing 180 degrees. Our flexibility is what will keep us alive and prosperous.

CASE 3–5
THE iPREMIER COMPANY: DENIAL OF SERVICE ATTACK (A)[1]

[1]This case was prepared by Professor Robert D. Austin; Dr. Larry Leibrock, Chief Technology Officer, McCoombs School of Business, University of Texas at Austin; and Alan Murray, Chief Scientist, Novell Service Provider Network.
Copyright © 2001 by the President and Fellows of Harvard College. Harvard Business School case 601-114.

January 12, 2001, 4:31 AM

Somewhere a telephone was chirping. Bob Turley, CIO of the iPremier Company, turned beneath the bed sheets, wishing the sound would go away. It didn't. Lifting his head, he tried to make sense of his surroundings. Where was he?

The Westin in Times Square. New York City. That's right. He was there to meet with Wall Street analysts. He'd gotten in late. By the time his head had hit the pillow it was nearly 1:30 AM. Now the digital display on the nearby clock made no sense. Who would be calling him at this hour? Why would the hotel operator put the call through?

He reached for the phone at bedside and placed it against his ear. Dial tone. Huh? The chirping was coming from his cell phone. Hanging up the hotel phone, he staggered out of bed. No sooner had his feet met the floor than his pager went off. Almost simultaneously, the hotel phone erupted, as if protesting being placed back in its cradle. Fumbling in his briefcase, he located the cell phone and hit "answer" on the tiny keypad.

"This is Bob Turley."

"Mr. Turley?" There was panic in the voice at the other end of the line. "I'm sorry to wake you, Joanne told me to call you."

The pager was still sounding. He found it in his briefcase and silenced it. The hotel phone stopped ringing as suddenly as it had started.

"Who is this?"

"It's Leon. Leon Ledbetter. I'm in Ops. We met last week. I'm new. I mean I was new, last month."

"Why are you calling me at 4:30 in the morning, Leon?"

"I'm really sorry about that Mr. Turley, Joanne said—"

"No, I mean what's wrong? Why are you calling?"

"It's our web site, sir. It's completely locked up. I've tried it now from three different browsers and nothing's happening. Our customers can't access it either; the help desk is getting flooded with support calls."

"What's causing it?"

"Joanne thinks—if we could only—well, someone might have hacked into us. Someone else might be controlling our site. Support has been getting these e-mails—We thought it was just the web server, but I can't even telnet[2] to anything over there. Joanne is on her way to the colo.[3] She said to call you. These weird e-mails, they're coming in about one per second."

"What do the e-mails say?"

"They say 'ha.'"

"Ha?"

"Yes, sir. Each one of them has one word in the subject line, 'ha.' It's like 'ha, ha, ha, ha.' Coming from an anonymous source. That's why we're thinking—."

"When you say they might have hacked into us—could they be stealing customer information? Credit cards?"

"Well, I guess no firewall[4]—Joanne says—actually we're using a firewall service we purchase from the colo, so—."

"Can you call someone at the colo? We pay them for monitoring 24 × 7, don't we?"

"Joanne is calling them. I'm pretty sure. Is there anything you want me to do?"

"Does Joanne have her cell?"

"Yes sir, she's on her way to the colo. I just talked to her."

"Call me back if anything else happens."

"Yes sir."

Turley stood up, realizing only then that he had been sitting on the floor. His eyes were bleary but adrenaline was now cranking in his bloodstream. Steadying himself against a chair, he felt a vague wave of nausea. This was no way to wake up.

---

[2]"Telnet" is a network service that permits access to a computer from a remote location.

[3]"Colo" is short for "co-location facility," where Internet companies often house their vital computing hardware. Co-location facilities are sometimes called "Internet Data Centers" or simply "hosting facilities." They provide floor space, redundant power supplies, high-speed connectivity to the Internet, and a variety of other services to their customers.

[4]A "firewall" is a combination hardware/software platform that is designed to protect a local network and the computers that reside on it against unauthorized access.

He made his way to the bathroom and splashed water on his face. This trip to New York was a great assignment for someone who had been with the company such a short time. It demonstrated the great confidence CEO Jack Samuelson had in him as the new CIO. For a moment Turley savored a memory of the meeting in which Samuelson had told him he would be the one to go to New York. As that memory passed another emerged, this one from an earlier session with the CEO. Samuelson was worried that the company might eventually suffer from "a deficit in operating procedures." "Make it one of your top priorities," he had said. "We need to run things professionally. I've hired you to take us to the next level."

Looking himself over in the mirror, seeing his hair tussled and his face wet, Turley lodged a protest with no one in particular: "But I've barely been here three months."

The iPremier Company

Founded in 1994 by two students at Swarthmore College, the iPremier Company had evolved into one of the few success stories of web-based commerce. From its humble beginnings, it had risen to become one of the top two retail businesses selling luxury, rare, and vintage goods on the web. It was also one of the few profitable entities in the so-called "new economy." Based in Seattle, Washington, the firm had grown at a rapid rate and held its own against incursions into its space from a number of well-funded challengers. For the fiscal year 1999, profits were $2.1 million on sales of $32 million. Sales had grown at more than a 50% annual rate for more than three years, and profits had begun to trend favorably.

Immediately following its Initial Public Offering in early 1998, the company's stock price had nearly tripled. It had continued up from there amid the euphoria of the 1999 markets, eventually tripling again. A follow-on offering had left the company in very strong cash position. During the NASDAQ bloodbath of 2000, the stock had fallen dramatically but it had eventually stabilized. In the treacherous Business-to-Consumer (B2C) segment, the iPremier Company was one of a very few survivors. Several respected analysts rated the firm a "Buy" despite overall weakness in the B2C sector.

Most of the company's products were priced between fifty and a few hundred dollars, but there were a small number of items priced in the thousands of dollars. Customers paid for items on-line using their credit cards. The company had flexible return policies, intended to allow customers to thoroughly examine products before deciding whether to keep them. The iPremier Company's customer base was very high-end, so much so that credit limits on charge cards were rarely an issue, even for the highest priced products.

Management and Culture.   The management team at the iPremier Company was a mix of talented young people who had been with the company for some time and more experienced managers who were gradually being hired as the firm grew. Recruitment had focused on well-educated technical and business professionals with reputations for high performance. Getting hired into a senior management position required excelling in an intense series of three-on-one interviews. The CEO interviewed every prospective manager at the director level and above. The reward, for those who made the grade, was base compensation above the average of managers at similar firms, and variable compensation that could be a significant multiple of the base. All employees had options based on the company stock price and managers received particularly lucrative incentives. When the share price had fallen off in 2000, senior management had gone to the company's board of directors twice, to reorganize the option plans and maintain strong employee incentives. All employees were subject to quarterly performance reviews that were tied directly to their compensation. Unsuccessful managers did not usually last long.

Most managers at the iPremier Company described the environment as "intense." The company formally stated its governing values in terms of "discipline, professionalism, commitment to delivering results, and partnership for achieving profits." Unlike many Internet companies, the iPremier Company had emphasized a balanced approach to growth and profitability, although growth had tended to rule the day. Throughout the company, there was a strong orientation toward doing "whatever it takes" to get projects done on schedule, especially when it came to system features that would benefit customers. The software development team was proud of its record of consistently launching new features and programs a few months ahead of major competitor, MarketTop. Value statements aside, it was well understood by senior managers that their compensation and future prospect with the company depended primarily on executing to plan. Manager pursued "their numbers" with almost obsessive zeal.

Technical Architecture. The company had historically tended to outsource management of its technical architecture and had a long-standing relationship with Qdata, a company that hosted most of the iPremier Company's computer equipment and provided connectivity to the Internet. Qdata was an early entrant into the Internet hosting and "co-location" business, but it had lost any prospect of market leadership. The facility was close to the corporate offices of the iPremier Company, but some felt there was little else to recommend it. Qdata was a steady provider of basic floor space, power, connectivity, environmental control, and physical security, and it offered some higher level "management services," such as

monitoring of web sites for customers at its Network Operations Center (NOC) and some Internet security services (such as the firewall service used by the iPremier Company). But Qdata had not been quick to invest in advanced UNIX server technology, and had experienced difficulty in retaining staff.

The iPremier Company had a longstanding initiative aimed at eventually moving its computing to another facility, but several factors had conspired to keep this from happening. First, and most significant, the iPremier Company had been very busy growing; hence the move to a better facility had never quite made it to the top of the priority list. Second, the cost of more modern facilities was considerably higher, two-to-three times as expensive on a per square foot basis. iPremier Company computers occupied a good deal of space, so a move to another facility would have increased costs significantly enough to affect the slender but increasing profit trend the company was eager to maintain. Third, there was a perception—not necessarily supported by fact according to the operations staff—that a move might risk service interruption to customers. The operations staff maintained that with appropriate modernization of the computing infrastructure, growth could be accomplished by adding installations in other facilities, rather than by expanding floor space in the existing facility. The work of planning how this might be carried out had never been done, though. Finally, one of the founders of the iPremier Company felt a personal commitment to the owners of Qdata because the latter company had been willing to renegotiate their contract at a particularly difficult time in iPremier's early days.

Exhibit 1 provides a diagram of the iPremier Company's technical architecture.

4:39 AM

Turley situated himself at the desk in his hotel room and began paging through the dig-

EXHIBIT 1   The iPremier Company's Technical Architecture

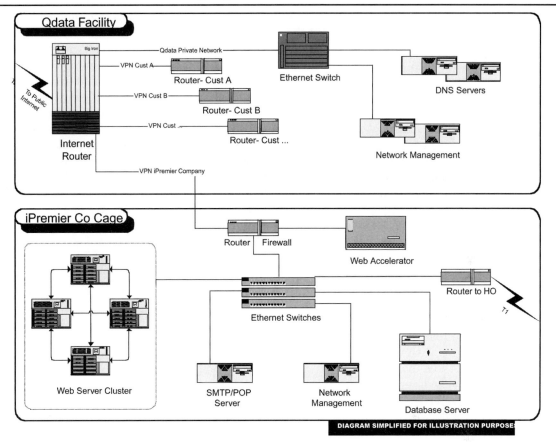

ital phonebook on his cell phone. Before he could find the number for Joanne Ripley, his technical operations team leader, the phone began to chirp. The incoming call was from Ripley. Turley tapped the answer key.

"Hello, Joanne. How are you this morning?"

A cautious laugh came from the other end of the circuit. "About the same as you, I'm guessing. I assume Leon got a hold of you."

"He did, but he doesn't know anything. What's going on?"

"I don't know much either, yet. I'm in the car, on my way to the colo."

"You can't do anything from home?"

"Well—no." She paused for a moment, as if deciding whether to say more. "I've been wanting to put secure shell access[5] in place so we could do things remotely, but that has performance implications. It would slow down customer traffic. Every time I've brought it up, the answer has been 'not now.' Besides, Leon

---

[5]"Secure shell access" allows authorized users to remotely access a computer via an encrypted connection. Without such access, connecting remotely to the computer would require sending information across the network in a format that could be intercepted and read by third parties.

can't telnet into any of the boxes behind the firewall via the T1 line at the office,[6] so something is screwy with our connectivity to the colo. Sounds like a problem outside the perimeter of our architecture. I called Qdata, but they assure me that there is no problem with connectivity into or out of the building. They're looking into it further, but their night shift is on duty. I don't know where they get those bozos. I haven't talked to anyone yet who knows what he's doing."

"How long till you get there?"

"I'm driving fast and running red lights. I ought to be there in five minutes."

"How long after that until we are back up and running?"

"Depends on what's wrong. I'll try restarting the web server as soon as I get there, but if someone has hacked us, or if there's some kind of attack going on, that might not do it. Did Leon tell you about the e-mails?"

"The 'ha, ha' e-mails? Yeah. Makes it sound like something deliberate."

"I'd have to agree with that."

"Can we track the e-mails?"

"Not soon enough. They're coming through an anonymizer that's probably in Europe or Asia. If we're lucky we'll find out who sent them sometime in the next 18 months. Then we'll discover they're originating from some DSL-connected PC in Podunk, Idaho and that the Joe Schmo who owns it has no idea that it's been compromised by hackers."

"Any chance they're stealing credit cards?"

There was a long pause at the other end of the phone.

"There's really no way of knowing without more info."

"Can we pull the plug? Literally disconnect the power? Or the communications lines?"

"We can, but I don't recommend it. If we start pulling cables out of the wall it may take us a while to put things back together. The database server takes a minimum of 40 minutes to restart after a controlled shutdown. If we bring it down hard, we could end up with a mess. Data corruption, that sort of thing. Then we'd be down for a long time. Major customer impact. Right now most of our customers are asleep. Whoops." There was a pause while Ripley negotiated a traffic obstacle. "Sorry. Anyway, let me restart the web server and see what happens. Maybe we can get out of this without too much customer impact."

Turley thought about it for a moment. "Okay. But if you see something that makes you think credit cards are being stolen, I want to know that as soon as possible. We may have to take drastic actions."

"Understood. I'll call you back as soon as I know anything."

"Good. One more thing: who else knows this is going on?"

"I haven't called anyone else. Leon might have. I'll call him and call you right back."

"Thanks."

Turley flipped his cell closed then picked up the hotel phone. After a series of transfers, he found someone who would bring coffee to his room, despite the odd hour. Never before had he so desperately wanted coffee.

Just as he replaced the hotel phone his cell rang again. He looked at the display to see who was calling.

"Damn." It was Warren Spangler, VP of business development. Turley remembered vaguely that Leon Ledbetter had come into the organization via a recommendation by Spangler. They were old high school buddies or something. Ledbetter had almost certainly called Spangler.

"Hi, Warren," said Turley, flipping the phone open.

---

[6]The hosting facility where the production computer equipment was housed was connected to the iPremier Company's offices via a leased "T1" line. This line would ordinarily permit people at the office to connect to production computers without traversing the public Internet.

"Hi, Bob. I hear we've got some kind of incident going on. What's the story?"

"Something's definitely going on, but we're not sure what yet. We're trying to minimize customer impact. Fortunately for us it's the middle of the night."

"Wow. So is it just a technical problem or is somebody actually doing it to us?"

Turley was eager to call the chief technology officer (CTO), so he didn't really have time to continue this discussion. But he didn't want to be abrupt. He was still getting to know his colleagues.

"We don't know. Look, I've got to—"

"Leon said something about e-mails—"

"Yes, there are suspicious e-mails coming in so it could be someone doing it."

"Oh, man. The stock is going to take a hit tomorrow. Just when I was going to exercise some options, too. Shouldn't we call the police?"

"Sure, why don't you see what you can do there, that'd be a big help. Look, I've got to—"

"Seattle police? Do we know where the e-mails are coming from? Maybe we should call the FBI? No. Wait. If we call the police, the press might hear about this from them. Whoa. Then our stock would really take a hit."

"I've really got to go, Warren."

"Sure thing. I'll start thinking about PR. And I'll work with Leon on this end. We got you covered here, bro. Keep the faith."

"Will do, Warren. Thanks."

Turley ended that call and began paging to find the number for Tim Mandel, the company's CTO. He and Mandel had already cemented a great working relationship. Turley wanted his opinion. Just as Turley was about to initiate the call, though, another call came in from Ripley.

Turley flipped the phone open and said: "Leon called Spangler, I know. Anything else?"

"That's it for now. Bye."

Turley dialed Mandel. At first the call switched over to voice mail, but he retried

immediately. This time Mandel answered sleepily. It took five full minutes to wake Mandel and tell him what was happening.

"So what do you think, should we just pull the plug? Shut off the power?"

"That'd be a mess. You'd lose logging data that would help us figure out what happened. Whatever we do, we want to preserve evidence of what has happened or else we may never know exactly."

"I'm not sure that's the most important thing to me right now, knowing exactly what is happening."

"I suggest you change your mind about that. If you don't know what happened this time, it can happen again. Worse than that, if you don't know what happened you won't know what, if anything, you need to disclose publicly."

Turley thought about that for a moment. What if they halted the attack but he could not be sure of the danger, if any, to customer information? What would the company need to say publicly? It was too much to sort out on the fly. Mandel was saying something else.

"Come to think of it, Bob, preserving the logs is irrelevant because I'm pretty sure logging is not enabled. Logging takes up a lot of disk space on the web server. To run with logging enabled, we would have to add significantly to our storage arrays and I've never been able to convince Linda that the expenditure was necessary. Plus logging adds a performance penalty of about 20% and nobody's been game for that."

"So we aren't going to have evidence of what happened anyway."

"There'll be some, but not as much as we'll want."

Another call was coming in.

"Hold on, Tim." Turley kicked the phone over to the waiting call. It was Peter Stewart, the company's legal counsel. What was he doing awake?

"This is Turley."

"Hey, Bob, it's Pete. Pull the plug, Bob. Shut off the power, pull the comm lines out of their sockets, everything. We can't risk having credit cards stolen."

"Spangler call you?"

"Huh? No, Jack. Samuelson. He called me three minutes ago, said hackers had control of our web site. Told me in no uncertain terms to call you and 'provide a legal perspective.'

That's just what he said: 'provide a legal perspective.' "

So the CEO was awake. The result, no doubt, of Spangler's "helping" from that end. Stewart continued to speak legalese at him for what seemed like an eternity. By this time, Turley was incapable of paying attention to him.

"Thanks for your thoughts, Pete. I've got to go, I've got Tim on the other line."

"Okay. For the record, though, I say pull the plug. I'll let Jack know you and I spoke."

"Thanks, Pete."

Turley switched back over to the call with Mandel.

"Spangler's got bloody everybody awake, including Jack. I recommend you get dressed and head in to the office, my friend."

"Is Joanne on this?"

"Yes, she's at the colo by now." Turley's phone rang. "Got a call coming in from her now."

He switched the phone.

"What's up Joanne?"

"Well I'm at Qdata," she said in an angry voice, "and they won't let me into the NOC. There's no one here who knows anything about the network monitoring software and that's what I need to use to see the traffic coming into our site. The Qdata guy who can do it is vacationing in Aruba. I tried rebooting the web server, but we've still got a problem. My current theory is an attack directed at our firewall, but to be sure I've got to see the packets coming in, and the firewall is their equipment. You got an escalation contact to get these dudes off their butts?"

"I'm in New York, Joanne. I've got zip for Qdata contact information with me. But let me see what I can do."

"Okay. I'll keep working it from this end. The security guard doesn't look too fierce. I think I could take him."

"Do what you can."

Turley hung up. He noticed that Mandel had disconnected also. For a moment Turley just sat back in the chair, not sure what to do next. There was a knock at the door. Coffee. Good news, for a change.

5:27 AM

He had just taken his first sip of hot coffee when he got the call he'd been dreading. It was from Jack Samuelson, the CEO.

"Hi Jack."

"Bob. Exciting morning?"

"More than I like it."

"Are we working a plan?"

"Yes, sir. Not everything is going according to plan, but we are working a plan."

"Is there anything I can do?"

"Actually, Jack, there is. Call someone senior at Qdata and tell them we need their full and immediate support. They're giving Joanne the runaround about access to their NOC."

"I'll do that right now, Bob."

"Thanks, Jack."

"Bob, the stock is probably going to take a hit and we'll have to put a solid PR face on this, but that's not your concern right now. You focus on getting us back up and running. Understand?"

"I do."

The call ended. It had gone better than Turley had feared. He avoided the temptation to analyze Samuelson's every word for clues to his innermost thoughts. Instead, he dialed Joanne.

"Hi, Bob," she said, sounding mildly cheerful. "They let me in. I'm sitting in front of the console right now. It looks like a SYN flood[7] from multiple sites directed at the router[8] that runs our firewall service. It's not a proper firewall, Bob, we need to work on something better."

"Fine, but what can we do right now?"

"Well, looks like the attack is coming from about ten sites. A classic distributed denial of service (DoS) attack. If the guys here will let me, I'm going to start shutting down traffic from those IP addresses."[9]

"Samuelson is waking up the senior guys at Qdata. If the night shift gives you any trouble, tell them it's going to be raining executives really soon."

"Samuelson, huh? So everybody's up for our little party. Okay, I'm going to try shutting off traffic from the attacking IP addresses. I'll have to set the phone down for a minute."

There was a pause of a couple of minutes. Turley heard some muffled conversation in the background, then several exclamations. Ripley came back on the line.

"Damn it, Bob, they're spawning zombies. It's Dawn of the Dead out there."

"You're going to have to translate that one for me, Ripley."

"Every time we shut down traffic from an IP address, the zombie we've shut off automatically triggers attacks from two other sites. I'll try it a few more times, but right now it looks like that's just going to make things worse."

"If it's a denial of service attack, they haven't hacked us, right? It means it's an attack, not an intrusion. They haven't gained entry to our system. So the credit cards and other customer data are safe. Can we say that?"

"That'd be my first take on it, yeah. There's nothing that makes a DoS attack and a intrusion mutually exclusive, of course. But, yeah, the script kiddy[10] hackers who usually launch these kinds of attacks aren't sophisticated enough to get inside our firewall." She paused for a moment as if reconsidering what she had just said. "On the other hand, targeting the firewall strikes me as a fairly sophisticated attack."

It was not the straight answer he had hoped for, but it would have to do for the time being. "I'll let you get back to it. Call me with an update when there is something to tell."

Turley hung up and thought about whether to call Samuelson and what to tell him. He could say that it was a DoS attack. He could say that it therefore probably didn't put customer information at risk. But Turley wanted to think before we went on record with that position. He'd talk to Tim, see what he thought.

For a moment, everything was quiet. He put the cell phone down on the desk and poured another cup of coffee. Pacing across the room, he picked up the TV remote and hit the "ON" button. A movie appeared, an old Hitchcock film. An airplane was chasing Cary Grant. He muted the sound then walked to the window and pulled the curtain aside. There was a red glow below the horizon in the east.

---

[7]Each "conversation" with a web server begins with a sequence of "handshake" interactions. The initiating computer first sends a "SYNCHRONIZE" or "SYN." The contacted web server responds with a "SYNCHRONIZE-ACKNOWLEDGE" or "SYN-ACK." The initiating computer then completes the handshake with an "ACKNOWLEDGE" or "ACK." A "SYN flood" is an attack on a web server intended to make it think a very large number of "conversations" are being initiated in rapid succession. Because each interaction looks like real traffic to the web site, the web server expends resources dealing with each one. By flooding the site, an attacker can effectively paralyze the web server by trying to start too many conversations with it.

[8]As the name suggests, a "router" is a hardware platform that routes traffic across internal networks and the Internet.

[9]An "IP address" corresponds to a particular machine located somewhere on the Internet.

[10]"Script kiddies" are relatively unsophisticated hackers who use automated routines—"scripts"—written by other more sophisticated hackers. These scripts are generally available to anyone willing to spend a little time searching for them on the Internet.

His cell phone rang. He went to it and picked it up. It was Ripley.

"It stopped," she said excitedly. "The attack is over."

"What did you do?"

"Nothing. It just stopped. The attack just stopped at 5:46 AM."

"So—what do we do now?"

"The website is running. A customer who visits our site now wouldn't know anything had ever been wrong. We can resume business as usual."

"Business as usual?"

"Actually, I'd recommend that we give everything a proper going over after an attack like this. We really ought to do a thorough audit. I've been thinking about how they targeted the firewall, and I don't think it sounds like script kiddies."

"Sit down when you get a chance and write me an e-mail that summarizes what you think we should do. Tell me how whatever you recommend will impact on customers, if at all. I've got to figure out what to tell Samuelson."

M   O   D   U   L   E

4   MANAGING INFORMATION AGE PROJECTS AND PROGRAMS

Although glitch-plagued software implementations are nothing new, the growing number of brand-name firms reporting big troubles with their multimillion-dollar projects is starting to look like a Who's Who of the Fortune 500.[1]

In 1996, pharmaceutical company FoxMeyer Drug filed for bankruptcy and cited a failed enterprise software implementation project as the primary cause. Bankruptcy trustees sued both the implementation consulting firm and the software company, seeking $500 million in damages from each. The targeted vendors called the suit "preposterous." But trustees argued that the system, which vendors (allegedly) said would save $50 million annually, had "messed up" orders. It "could handle no more than 10,000 orders per night" compared with the legacy system that "could process 420,000 orders."[2] Before this IT project, the company had been the fourth largest distributor of pharmacy and medical products in the United States with annual sales of more than $5 billion.

The era of big IT project disasters is still with us. Problems with IT projects at Nike, Whirlpool, W.L. Gore, and Hershey have generated high-profile news coverage. In a Harvard Business School survey of executives involved in enterprise systems implementation,[3] more than two-thirds estimated

---

[1]Kim Girard and Melanie Farmer, "Business Software Firms Sued Over Implementation," *CNET News.com,* November 3, 1999.

[2]*Drug Store News,* July 20, 1998, page 4.

[3]The survey was administered to participants in the Harvard Business School "Delivering Information Services" executive program from 1998 through 2000. The program is targeted at CIO level executives and draws a mix of CIOs, CIO direct reports, and IT-interested executives from other business functions. These results are from the 1998 and 1999 surveys. The 2000 survey showed similar estimates of risk but a modestly improved situation for completed projects.

293

implementation risk as moderate or higher in all three survey categories: (1) risk that the software would be unable to meet business requirements, (2) risk that the organization would be unable to change to permit realization of benefits, and (3) risk that the project would hurt rather than help the business. The subset of respondents whose firms had completed implementations indicated that projects overwhelmingly overran budgets and schedules and under performed relative to the expected benefit.

Although the failure rate for IT projects is debated, many believe it remains in excess of 50 percent. The number, disturbing on its own, becomes alarming when we consider that in the past decade projects have grown much larger and more expensive. In the 1980s, an IT project with a $10 or $20 million budget was considered large. By 1996 or 1997, the prospect of a $10 million dollar project barely warranted a return phone call from large systems integration firms. The stakes had been raised.

Clearly, implementing IT projects remains a challenge for companies that want to reinvent themselves for the Information Age. Strategic vision, while terribly important, accounts for only 15 percent of the effort and the risk in managing IT strategically. The remaining 85 percent is related to execution. As projects grow into major transformational programs with price tags that often reach into the hundreds of millions of U.S. dollars, and as technological change renders more day-to-day IT effort into nonrecurring project work, seamless project and program execution becomes increasingly vital.

Determining the appropriate combination of internal and external management adds another dimension to the project and program evaluation. Today, nearly all companies outsource some elements of their IT operations. Module 3 showed how firms increasingly acquire IT services in the same way they acquire phone service, via a utility model. But many companies go well beyond selective outsourcing and adopt a large-scale, programmatic approach. Rather than outsource specific services, these organizations turn over all or the majority of IT functions to companies that specialize in end-to-end IT support. Outsourcing on this scale often entails transfer of equipment, facilities, and employees formerly belonging to the client company, to one or more vendors. This intimate intercompany partnership creates a strategic business linkage. Not surprisingly, the intense interactions in these relationships generate business opportunities and risks that, like those involved in major project implementations, can translate into spectacular success or failure.

This Module focuses on how companies evaluate and control IT project risk, determine when and what to outsource, and manage relationships with project and program partners. Like Module 3, this module discusses operational execution and reliability. Here, though, we address these factors primarily as they pertain to the high-stakes activities involved in implementation. The cases included in this Module—Tektronix, BAE, Cisco Systems, and General Dynamics/Computer Science Corporation—provide a cross section of industries, business situations, and technologies and support rich discussion of the essential elements of managing IT projects and programs.

Implementation Risk

"You know," he said, "careers are lost over much less money than this." We were as white as a sheet of paper. We knew that if we failed that we were going to get shot.[4]

Projects fail in numerous ways and in varying degrees. The most severe failure occurs when a project is completely written off—thrown away without delivering any value at all—often after much implementation effort and expense.[5] But projects can also be considered failures when they are finished so late that their business value is greatly diminished, or when they cost far more than their budgets, or when they fall well short of delivering the promised benefit. Astute business executives evaluate the potential for such failure and see that projects are managed in a way that minimizes the prospect of failure.

Three important dimensions of an IT project influence its inherent implementation risk: project size, experience with the technology, and project structure.

Project size. The larger a project in monetary terms, staffing levels, elapsed time, and number of departments affected, the greater its inherent risk. Multimillion-dollar projects carry more risk than $50,000 efforts and, if adverse situations actually materialize, affect the company more. Project size relative to the average size of an IT group's past projects also is important. A $1 million project in a department whose average undertaking costs $2 to $3 million, for example, usually has lower implicit risk than a $250,000 project in a department whose projects have never cost more than $50,000.

Experience with the technology project. Risk increases as the project team's and organization's familiarity with the hardware, operating systems, database packages, and project application languages decreases. Leading-edge technology projects are intrinsically more risky than more mature technologies. A project posing a slight risk for a large, leading-edge systems development group may be highly risky for a smaller, less technically advanced group.

Project structure. In some projects, the nature of the task to be automated completely defines the required result of the project from the very beginning. When project requirements are not subject to change during the

---

[4]Randy Pond, a Cisco implementation team leader, describing a meeting with CEO John Morgridge before taking their enterprise systems project to the board for approval. For more details, see Cotteleer, Mark, Austin, Robert D., and Nolan, Richard L. "Cisco Systems, Inc.: Implementing ERP," Harvard Business School case no. 699-022, October 1998, page 6.

[5]One could argue that the FoxMeyer case illustrates an even more severe failure—one that creates serious collateral damage on the way to a write-off.

TABLE 4–1   Effect of Degree of Structure, Company-Relative Technology, and Project Size on Project Implementation Risk

		High Structure	*Low Structure*
Low Technology	Large Project	Low risk	Low risk (very susceptible to mismanagement)
	Small Project	Very low risk	Very low risk (very susceptible to mismanagement)
High Technology	Large Project	Medium risk	Very high risk
	Small Project	Medium-low risk	High risk

project's lifetime, the project is easier to manage. Similarly, projects that require little organizational change are much less risky than projects that require substantial modification of the organization and employee work habits.

Project Categories and the Impact on Implementation Risk

Table 4–1, which combines the various dimensions influencing risk, identifies eight distinct project categories with varying degrees of implementation risk. Even at a basic level, this classification helps separate projects for different types of management review. Innumerable IT organizations use the matrix to understand the relative implementation risk and to communicate that risk to users and senior executives. It is a proven, useful tool as well for making sure that all people involved in a project will have the same understanding of its risks. In addition, a company should develop a profile of the aggregate implementation risk for its portfolio of IT projects. By determining the number (and proportion) of its projects that fall into each category, a firm can make decisions based on a better understanding of the overall risk implicit in the project portfolio.

Project Management

"Ready, ready, ready, aim, aim, aim . . . fire" is the approach we have traditionally taken to project management. A better approach for some projects, especially e-business projects, would be, as Gary Hamel puts it, "fire, fire, fire, fire, aim again, fire, fire, fire—there is no time for 'ready.'"[6]

---

[6]Jim Highsmith, from his "Order Out of Chaos" symposium; these remarks were made during a presentation sponsored by the Cutter Consortium, Cambridge, MA, November 2000. See also Highsmith's book, *Adaptive Software Development: A Collaborative Approach to Managing Complex Systems,* Dorset House, January 2000. The quotation attributed to Gary Hamel is from *Leading the Revolution,* Harvard Business School Press, Boston, MA, August 2000.

Is there a single "right approach" to project management? Conventional wisdom holds that managers should apply a cluster of tools, project management methods, and organizational linkages uniformly to all projects. While there are general tools that can be used in managing IT implementation projects, the contribution each makes to project planning and control varies widely according to the project's characteristics. The tools can be categorized into four principal types:

Formal Planning. Designed to ensure clear definition of project goals, formal planning tools are essential in obtaining commitment to those goals. They help identify and structure the sequence of tasks required to meet those goals. This category also includes tools to identify and contract with partners and to estimate the time, money, and technical resources the team will need to complete the project.

External Integration. These coordination and communication tools and techniques help a project team manage activities that involve key stakeholder groups and partners. This category also includes communication ("boundary spanning") tools to enable the team to collect information from stakeholders and to keep stakeholders informed of progress.

Internal Integration. These coordination and communication tools and techniques help a project team manage activities that take place within the team. Included here as well are communication tools that enable the team to share information and keep team members and others informed of progress.

Formal Results Control. These tools help managers evaluate progress and spot potential problems so that corrective action can be taken.

Table 4–2 gives examples of commonly used types of planning, integration, and control tools. Table 4–3 shows the relative contribution that these tools can make for different types of projects. The core concept here is that there is no "right way" to manage all projects, but rather project management approach flows from the nature of the project.

Emergence of Adaptive Project Management Methods

The trend in the recent decade has been toward projects that entail very high implementation risks. For example, enterprise systems –large computer systems that promise to replace major chunks of a company's applications infrastructure with an off-the-shelf third-party package[7]—involve

---

[7]In the early-to-mid 1990s, enterprise systems were primarily Enterprise Resource Planning (ERP) systems that focused on integrating the back-office, transaction-based systems required to run modern companies. For the last few years, however, the phrase "enterprise system" has broadened to include front-office systems engaged in Customer Relationship Management (CRM), e-commerce, as well as some more specialized packages that undertake to replace major chunks of a company's application portfolio.

TABLE 4–2   Tools of Project Management

Integration Tools / Techniques, External	*Integration Tools / Techniques, Internal*
Selection of user as project manager.	Selection of experienced IT professional to lead team.
User steering committee (which meets frequently).	Team meetings.
User-managed change control process.	Distribution within team of info on key design decisions.
Distribution of project team info to key users.	Technical status reviews/Inspections.
Selection of users as team members.	HR techniques to maintain low turnover of team members.
User approval process for system specifications.	Selection of high percentage of team members with significant previous work relationships.
Prototyping with users.	Participation of team members in goal setting and deadline establishment.
Progress reports.	Obtaining outside technical assistance.
User involvement/responsibility in other key decisions and actions.	

Formal Planning Tools	*Formal Control Tools*
Project management software.	Status-versus-plan reports.
PERT, CPM.	Change control disciplines and systems.
Milestone selection.	Milestone review meetings.
Systems specifications.	Analysis of deviations from plan.
Project approval processes.	
Post-project audit procedures.	

TABLE 4–3   Relative Contribution of Tools to Ensuring Project Success by Project Type

		Contribution			
Project Type	*Project Description*	*External Integration*	*Internal Integration*	*Formal Planning*	*Formal Results Control*
I	High structure—low technology, large	Low	Medium	High	High
II	High structure—low technology, small	Low	Low	Medium	High
III	High structure—high technology, large	Low	High	Medium	Medium
IV	High structure—high technology, small	Low	High	Low	Low
V	Low structure—low technology, large	High	Medium	High	High
VI	Low structure—low technology, small	High	Low	Medium	High
VII	Low structure—high technology, large	High	High	Low+	Low+
VIII	Low structure—high technology, small	High	High	Low	Low

new technologies, and impose high structure on business operations. These systems also have unattractive investment profiles: they require large investments, most of which must be made up-front, to achieve uncertain (because of their inherently high implementation risk) benefit. An increasingly common approach to managing such difficult projects involves an extension of the adaptive methods introduced in Module 3. Cisco and Tektronix, for example, have successfully implemented large enterprise systems by restructuring projects to make them more iterative, and formally incorporating in-progress learning and mid-course adjustment. Adaptive projects are implemented in a wide variety of specific ways, but they share five basic characteristics:

1. They are iterative; implementation occurs in increments that result from each iteration, so that outcomes and interactions can be tested and understood as they appear.
2. They rely on fast cycles and on delivery of some value, however limited, at the end of each iteration, so that incremental implementation does not mean slow implementation.
3. They deliver functionality, however limited, to end-users early in the project, so that feedback can be incorporated into learning and improvement cycles.
4. They require highly skilled project personnel who are capable of learning and making mid-course adjustments during a project.
5. They often resist ROI and other similar tools for investment decision making that implicitly assume predictability of outcomes, instead emphasizing "buying of information" about outcomes as a legitimate expenditure.

Although Cisco's managers did not explicitly identify their project management approach as "adaptive," they did explicitly emphasize "rapid, iterative prototyping." Tektronix divided their project into more than 20 "waves" that provided formal opportunities for deliberation, adjustment, and learning.[8] Although the approaches these two companies adopted were different in detail, they shared the five characteristics of adaptive projects.

Note that traditional results-oriented controls are not only inappropriate for large, risky projects, but actually can lead to dysfunction and disaster. For example, insisting that schedule commitments set early in a project be met regardless of unexpected complications creates an incentive to downplay or

---

[8]Robert D. Austin and Richard L. Nolan have suggested, in a paper called "Manage ERP Initiatives as New Ventures, Not IT Projects," (Harvard Business School Working Paper 99-024) that very large IT projects have risk profiles that resemble those of new ventures more than those of traditional IT projects. Venture investors cope with risky venture profiles via a variety of adaptive techniques that legitimize the notion of buying information about the new venture. Large IT projects must adopt a similar approach that recognizes the impossibility of knowing everything in advance and the importance of in-progress learning.

ignore the complications. Within an adaptive framework, unexpected complications become inputs to learning that prompt mid-course adjustments. In a traditional results-oriented framework, complications often are "swept under the rug" because they interfere with achievement of preset project milestones and because implementation team members are reluctant to admit they failed to anticipate complications.

This dysfunctional dynamic can be especially problematic if a company has hired expert consultants to assist with implementation (consultants hired as experts especially dread admitting that they did not foresee complications). Client company managers often presume that experts must have anticipated all possible complications (sometimes they presume this in menacing tones—e.g., "as experts in this area, surely you anticipated . . ."). Under these conditions, an unexpected complication can lead to systemic lack of communication between consultants, who do not want to admit what they did not anticipate, and client managers, who have unrealistic expectations about what consultants should have foreseen.

Lack of communication is a major factor in a large number of failed projects. When the first major unexpected complication arises, a favorable pattern is set if project team members react by communicating the complication to all stakeholders, seeking to understand it, and engaging in collaborative problem solving. A dysfunctional pattern is set if the team fails to communicate the complication to others and instead downplays it and engages in overly optimistic assumptions about the impact of the complication on the project. The longer the dysfunctional pattern prevails, the harder it is to reverse. The best approach is to plan for unexpected complications and have a predetermined way of handling them when they appear.

Process Consistency and Process Agility in Project Management

In practice, project management always involves balancing tensions between process consistency and process agility. Project managers must ensure a thorough and disciplined approach, to make sure that no balls are dropped, that all requirements are adequately met, and that no important details go unnoticed. Usually consistency develops through formal specification of project steps, required documentation, and compliance mechanisms (such as reviews or progress reports). At the same time, however, companies need to retain the flexibility to change direction, in the middle of a project if necessary, when business conditions require it. Tension arises because the very tools used to improve consistency—specifications, documentation, compliance mechanisms—often are perceived as encumbrances that work against project responsiveness and agility. A firm that is well-practiced and expert in its established routines may have trouble changing them. Equally, a firm that has grown accustomed to using certain tools may continue to try to use them in business conditions in which they are less effective.

In the 1990s, many companies struggled with process consistency versus agility, including many in fast-changing industries for whom responsiveness-to-market and time-to-market were overriding concerns. For the most part, these companies resisted fully adopting traditional project methodologies, which were perceived as too harmful to project and organizational agility. Instead, many Information Age companies developed "light" methodologies that contained the essential elements of traditional methodologies but were not as cumbersome.

A Minimalist Approach to Process Formalization

Companies that have been most successful in balancing consistency and agility have not eschewed process formalization altogether, nor have they let process formalization overwhelm them. Rather, they have developed simple process management tools based on the idea that *the best balance is one that includes the minimum formal specification that is critical to success of a project.* The tools fall into three categories:

Flow. Project teams need to understand the relationships between their activities and those of others. That is, they need to understand the overall process "flow." Process tools in this category are depictions of the overall process context, intended to give decisionmakers at specific points in the process a sense of the overall business picture, including the sequence of major events and important dependencies. Project activity flow charts are simple tools in this category.

Completeness. Project teams need to be sure everything is being done and no ball is dropped. All details must be covered to assure that essential tasks are not neglected. Checklists that convey what needs to be done, when it needs to be done, by whom, and whether or not it is complete are simple tools in this category.

Visibility. Team members need to be able to review projects while they are being executed to obtain status information. Ideally anyone, whether from engineering, marketing, or elsewhere, can review the same "picture" and come away with needed information. This ideal of visibility is not easy to achieve. Elaborate computerized project tracking systems provide this kind of visibility. So do simple wall charts that track project status in a way that everyone (in one physical location, anyway) can see.

Some projects, for example, government projects or projects involving safety-related systems, require another category of tools to ensure that project activities can be *audited.*

The level of process specification needed to produce a successful outcome varies greatly across projects and business situations. For a small team working in a fast-changing industry in which time-to-market is essential, very simple tools in each of these categories might work well. For a large project in a safety-related industry, more elaborate tools (although still in the same categories) might well be required. Hence, just as useful tools are highly variable across projects, so too is the *methodological intensity*. Sometimes extensive documentation and control is appropriate. Sometimes only light methods are needed for a project.

Managing the tension between consistency and agility is, for most companies, a general issue that extends well beyond project management. Earlier process frameworks, developed when systems were proprietary and the common Internet platform was not available for commerce, significantly encumber many Industrial Age firms. As these companies work to transform themselves into the Information Age, they will face the difficult task of distilling processes down to essential elements, to reclaim lost project and organizational agility.

Outsourcing

The business and technology cycles for most businesses have grown shorter while depreciation schedules have remained constant. Consequently, that which used to enable may now inhibit. Owning resources in house may inhibit business agility.[9]

In 1989, Katherine Hudson, VP of Information Systems at Eastman Kodak, announced that the company would outsource management of its data center, networks, and desktop PCs to IBM, Digital Equipment, and Business Land, respectively.[10] The magnitude of the program was unprecedented. Never before had a company turned over management of so much of its IT capabilities to another firm. Other companies quickly followed similar paths, including General Dynamics in 1991, whose program with Computer Sciences Corporation is described in this Module.[11] Today, program outsourcing of the IT function has become an accepted management option. Most major companies have at least considered outsourcing management of major components of IT capability.

Selective outsourcing has become commonplace in this new century. Many firms have, for example, outsourced the management of employee ben-

---

[9]Wendell Jones, former VP, Worldwide Service Delivery for Compaq Computer Corporation, during a presentation at the Cutter Consortium Summit 2001, Cambridge, MA, May 2001.

[10]For more information about this outsourcing initiative, see Applegate, Lynda M and Montealegre, Ramiro "Eastman Kodak Co.: Managing Information Systems Through Strategic Alliances," HBS case no. 192-030, September 1995.

[11]F. Warren McFarlan and Katherine N. Seger, "General Dynamics and Computer Sciences Corporation: Outsourcing the IS Function (A) and (B) (Abridged)," HBS case no. 193-178, June 1993.

efits administration. Employees who wish to make adjustments to their retirement savings accounts often access systems run by financial services firms on behalf of the employee's own firm. The potential for creating value through this kind of selective outsourcing increases as new service companies, such as Application Service Providers (ASPs) and Web hosting facilities proliferate.

As was described in Module 3, ASPs provide online hosting, support, and maintenance of software functionality and network services. Hosting facilities physically house Web, application, and database servers, storage devices, and networking equipment in a robust environment. Proponents of hosting-based infrastructures describe a future in which companies routinely obtain much of the IT functionality they need for day-to-day business "over the Net" from a variety of service providers. Services accessed in this way, they suggest, will replace many services that traditionally have been provided by internal IT departments.[12]

Driving Forces for Outsourcing

The circumstances that lead companies to consider outsourcing vary widely from one company to another. Underlying the circumstances, however, are a series of common themes that seem to explain the pressures to outsource.

General manager's concerns about IT costs and quality of service. To the general manager concerned about the costs and level of capability associated with the internal IT department, the outsourcing operations to service companies offers numerous apparent advantages:

> **Lower overhead cost.** On balance, outsourcing service companies run leaner overhead and management structures than do many of their customers. This translates into more efficient and less costly operations for customers.
>
> **Aggressive use of low-cost labor and creative use of geography.** Outsourcing service companies often leverage communications capabilities by locating data centers and development activity in low-cost areas (developing countries, for example). This too leads to enhanced economic efficiency for customers.
>
> **World-class skill standards.** Employees of companies that outsource often have skill sets not well matched to leading-edge technologies and management practices. Outsourcing service companies are more motivated and successful in keeping employee skill sets current. Because outsourcing service companies focus on the IT business, they are able to attract talented IT staff with scarce, in-demand skills.

---

[12]R.D. Austin, *Web and IT Hosting Facilities* (HBS No. 601-134).

Bulk purchasing and leasing. Vendors who perform similar outsourcing services for many companies can negotiate better deals with equipment suppliers because they can buy in greater volume.

Better management of excess hardware and service capacity. By combining many firms' work in the same operations center, outsourcing service companies can sell or use hardware and services that would otherwise be idle.

Better control over software licenses. Outsourcing companies buy licenses in greater volume and therefore can negotiate better pricing. Once in possession of licenses, they are positioned to manage licenses efficiently, sometimes by reallocating licenses between client companies.

Aggressive quality of service management. Quality of service is a primary basis on which outsourcing firms compete, hence they are highly motivated to achieve high quality of service levels. Because they are able to achieve economies of scale across numerous customers, outsourcing service companies are better positioned to invest in quality of service than any single customer.

Hustle. Outsourcing vendors are professional firms focused on delivering outsourcing services. That is their only business and success is measured by satisfied customers who recommend them to others, by bottom-line profitability, and by stock-market performance.

A crisis or breakdown in internal IT performance.   Program outsourcing is sometimes motivated by a traumatic problem with the existing IT organization or infrastructure. In many instances, the breakdown convinces general managers of the need to retool a backward IT capability. When the breakdown is internal, the outsourcing option becomes more attractive.

Proliferation of service supply options.   Kodak's decision to outsource data center and network management occurred as suppliers, such as IBM and DEC, sought ways to add new value-added services. Today, a growing number of new delivery and service players are looking for ways to provide new kinds of value-adding services.

Desire to simplify the general management agenda.   To a firm under intense cost or competitive pressures, outsourcing is a way to delegate a time-consuming, non-core activity so managers can focus on the core business. This rationale is contingent on the assumption that the outsourced functions do not provide or have the potential to provide long-term competitive advantage.

Financial factors.   Financial issues sometimes make outsourcing an appealing option. For example:

Cash transfers at the beginning of a program. Program outsourcing deals often involve transferring physical assets (e.g., computer hardware) to the outsourcing service company in exchange for cash. The outsourcing vendor effectively buys assets (including, sometimes, intangible assets, such as the human capital inherent in IT employees transitioning to the outsourcing service company) from the client firm. Such a transaction generates cash for the client company and improves its balance sheet by reducing physical assets.

Translating fixed into variable cost. Outsourcing can turn a largely fixed-cost activity into a variable-cost activity. For firms whose IT activity volume varies widely from year to year, or that face significant downsizing, this change is particularly important.

Making IT expenditures real. A third-party relationship brings an entirely different set of dynamics to a firm's view of IT expenditures. The firm is now dealing with a hard-dollar expenditure that all users must take seriously (no longer is it a soft-dollar allocation). With hard-dollar expenditures, firms develop a sense of discipline and tough-mindedness that an arm's-length, fully charged-out internal cost center has trouble achieving.

For a firm considering divestiture or outright sale of one or more of its divisions, outsourcing has special advantages. For example, a firm can obtain cash value for an asset unlikely to be recognized in a divestiture. Additionally, it gives the acquirer fewer problems to deal with in assimilating the firm. And the outsourcing contract may provide the acquirer a very nice dowry, particularly if the firm is small in relation to the acquirer. The contract can be phased out neatly, and the IT transaction volume can be added to the firm's internal IT activities with little or no additional expense. In the 1990s, several mid-sized banks used this as their guiding rationale for outsourcing. It gave them access to reliable IT support while making their eventual sale (which they saw as inevitable) more attractive from the acquirers' viewpoint.

Corporate culture.   A company's culture and values can make it very hard for managers to take appropriate action. For example, the internal IT department of a major defense company simply lacked the clout to pull off a centralized IT strategy in what was a highly decentralized firm built up over the years by acquisitions. Company managers saw the decentralized culture as a major strength, and the matter was not subject to reconsideration. Outsourcing all divisional IT activities provided the fulcrum for overcoming this impasse.

Eliminating an internal irritant.   No matter how competent and adaptive existing IT management and staff are (and usually they are very good), tensions develop between the users of computing resources and the IT staff.

Often, the tensions are exacerbated by perceptions that IT costs are too high, that the IT organization is unresponsive, that internal skill sets are obsolete, and even IT personnel speak a different language and are not attuned to business issues. In such contexts, the notion of a remote, efficient, experienced outsourcing vendor is particularly compelling.

Reports of outsourcing success.   One large company felt it was getting a level of commitment and energy from an outsourcing vendor that would be difficult to obtain from an in-house unit. Another firm, frustrated by its inability to get products to market faster, found that outsourcing gave it an adrenaline boost that lead to achieving a two-thirds improvement in time to market. As program outsourcing becomes more common, and as long as success stories proliferate, companies will continue to explore major outsourcing options.

When Should a Firm Outsource IT?

The outsourcing option can be evaluated relative to an organization's position on the Strategic Grid (Table 4–4). Outsourcing operational activities is generally attractive, particularly as the budget grows and the contract becomes more important to the outsourcing vendor. The more the firm is operationally dependent on IT, the more sense outsourcing makes. The bigger the firm's IT budget, however, the higher in the organization the decision will be made, and thus the more careful the analysis must be. At the superlarge scale, the burden falls on the outsourcing service company, which must show it can bring more intellectual firepower to the task.

When the application's development portfolio is filled with maintenance work or projects, that are valuable but not vitally important to the firm, transferring these tasks to a partner holds few strategic risks. However, as new systems and processes increasingly come to deliver potentially significant differentiation and/or massive cost reduction, the outsourcing decision comes under greater scrutiny, particularly when the firm possesses a large, technically innovative, well-run IT organization. The potential loss of control and flexibility and inherent delays in dealing with a project management structure that cuts across two (or more) organizations become of greater concern.

As shown in Table 4–4, for companies in the support quadrant, the outsourcing presumption is yes, particularly for large firms. For companies in the factory quadrant, again the presumption is yes, unless they are huge and perceived as exceptionally well managed. For firms in the turnaround quadrant, the presumption is mixed; outsourcing may represent an unnecessary, unacceptable delegation of competitiveness, although conversely, it may be the only way to access the latest IT skills. For companies in the strategic quadrant, the presumption is also mixed. Some companies in the strategic quad-

TABLE 4–4   Strategic Impact—Applications Development Portfolio

High	*Factory*	*Strategic*
Strategic Dependence on Operating Systems	*Outsourcing Presumption:* **YES,** unless company is huge and well managed. Reasons to consider outsourcing: • Economies of scale possibilities for small & mid-size firms. • Higher quality of service. • Facilitates management focus. • Access to international IT solutions facilitated by advanced communications technologies.	*Outsourcing Presumption:* **MIXED** Reasons to consider outsourcing: • Access to leading edge technology application and industry skills. • Assure bulletproof reliability. • Rescue an out-of-control internal IT unit. • Reduce risk of inappropriate IT architectures.
Low	*Support* *Outsourcing Presumption:* **YES** Reasons to consider outsourcing: • Access to higher IT professionalism. • Possibility of off-loading a low priority, perhaps problem-laden part of the firm. • Access to current IT technologies.	*Turnaround* *Outsourcing Presumption:* **MIXED** Reasons to consider outsourcing: • Access to leading edge technology application and industry skills.
	Low	**High**

**Importance of Sustained, Innovative
Information Resource Development**

rant not facing a crisis of IT competence find it hard to justify outsourcing; others find it indispensable in gaining access to otherwise unavailable skills. Also, not having a critical mass of potentially differentiating skills is an important driver that has moved companies to consider outsourcing.

For larger multidivisional firms, the strategic analysis suggests that various divisions and clusters of application systems can be treated differently (i.e., strategic differentiated outsourcing). Similarly, because of the dynamic nature of the grid, firms under profit pressures after a period of sustained strategic innovation (in either the turnaround or the strategic quadrant) are good candidates for outsourcing as a means to reorganize their shop and procedures.

Managing Outsourcing Relationships

Outsourcing programs involve two or more organizations in a close, long-term relationship. Contracts with terms of five or more years are common. As with other close, long-term relationships, outsourcing relationships benefit from being constructed on a sound foundation and from ongoing attention. In the decade or so since Kodak announced the first large-scale outsourcing program, we have learned some things about how to build and manage such programs.

Built-to-last relationships.   For an outsourcing relationship to endure through the long time span that is typical of an outsourcing program, both parties must perceive the terms as fair. It is not unusual for outsourcing contracts to have disproportionate benefits for one party to the relationship early in the life of the contract (usually the customer). But it is important that the other party believe that it too will eventually benefit. One manager of a troubled outsourcing program reported that he could pinpoint the exact origin of the relationship's difficulties: a meeting in which it became clear that the outsourcing vendor had miscalculated its bid and would never make money on the project. A partner that feels wronged and is constantly looking for ways to eke out some small profit from a one-sided deal will be inclined to cut corners, to meet the letter but not always the intent of the agreement.

The relationship must be based on reasonable expectations. As discussed earlier in this Module overview, unrealistic expectations often lead to communication failures, as the constituent parties become defensive. In a sense, an outsourcing program is an attempt to synthesize an effective organization out of two already existing organizations. This complex task does not lend itself to completion or perfection on the first try. Most successful outsourcing relationships go through numerous stages of organization and governance before the relationship stabilizes. Managers of successful outsourcing programs devote much time to managing expectations and, especially, to frequently synchronizing the expectations of all involved in the program.

The role of contracts.   Contracts, extremely important in outsourcing relationships, specify the roles and terms of interaction between the firms. They define what performance means within the program and provide a way for the service provider to credibly commit to performance levels. If well negotiated, they also outline transition processes, such as the conditions and terms under which the contract may be renewed, terminated, or renegotiated. And they define procedures for escalating concerns beyond the first level of program management.

But by themselves contracts are never adequate to define an effective long-term relationship. Kodak managers, in putting together their historic program, aspired to develop "fluid" contracts that would encourage "collaborative problem solving." They wanted to create a "framework for the relationship," not just a document that specified deliverables and penalties for compliance failures. The Harvard Business School survey on enterprise system implementation found that almost a third of companies that completed large projects found contracts to be of limited importance, ultimately. Although contracts always specify penalties for vendors' failure to perform, no client company wants to invoke these clauses. When a penalty clause is invoked, it means something already has failed.

As one of the divisions of Tektronix implemented its enterprise system, managers actually abandoned unilaterally some of the conditions of its contract that they thought were forcing vendor personnel into tasks that were contracted for but no longer relevant. The Tektronix and vendor teams had begun to function very effectively as if they were all part of the same organization. They had internalized shared project objectives and formed binding personal relationships. At that point, the contract became a distraction.

Outsourcing program oversight and governance.   A committee of senior managers that represent all parties to the relationship often governs large outsourcing programs. The committee meets on a regular basis to review program status, using agreed to performance metrics. Mid-course program corrections and directives, designed to bring about organizational transformation as required by the evolving program, are common outputs of such meetings.

Some of the most important personal relationships occur at this senior committee level. When it implemented its enterprise system in the mid 1990s, Cisco formed a steering committee that included VPs from the software vendor and partners from the systems integration firm. Lower level managers in all the involved companies knew that steering committee members had strong personal relationships and had made commitments to each other. Project employees were therefore motivated to resolve conflicts before they made it to the steering committee level. Ironically, it was because the relationships on the steering committee were known to be strong that they were rarely tested.

In composing a management oversight committee for this kind of program (or for any large, transformational program, for that matter), it is essential that senior management in all involved companies be genuinely committed to the program, and that they communicate their commitment to their organizations. The oversight committee not only monitors the program, but also, through its composition, signals to all levels of the organization that senior management believes in the program objectives. In programs that fail, lack of across-the-board management commitment often is a factor.

A common but subtle form of lack of commitment arises when some senior managers commit conditionally only. In one company, all employees knew that an influential senior manager was committed to a program "as long as it did not interfere with manufacturing." Manufacturing employees regarded the conditional commitment as license to ignore aspects of the program they did not like. As a result, the program developed serious, though predictable, problems.

Keeping relationships healthy.   Keeping relationships healthy requires active attention and constant effort. Kodak managers hired a relationship consultant to help structure their relationships with outsourcing vendors, and to nurture the relationship in the long-term. Outside expertise often is helpful, especially at critical junctures, for example, when a contract is renegotiated. Co-locating vendor and client personnel is a positive factor in maintaining relationships. Many outsourcing programs orchestrate events that bring personnel together for social interaction. The ideal is to create a sense of shared objectives and organizational unity, even though not everyone works for the same company. When conflict occurs, as it inevitably will, organizations with strong ties are able to work through the difficulties.

In many outsourcing programs, renegotiations begin again soon after the program is initiated, as all parties learn better what needs to be done and how. Such negotiations usually go smoothly, if they occur in the context of a healthy relationship. Wise program managers have predetermined and agreed upon plans for how to proceed when renegotiation becomes necessary. They also are constantly looking for ways to improve the relationship.

Putting the Ideas to Work

The cases in the Module depict both failures and successes as firms attempt to manage the risks inherent in implementing IT projects. The failures provide detailed examples of what can go wrong, thereby making project risks concrete. The successes offer models for managing the implementation of IT-enabled strategies. Issues involved in outsourcing are present to some extent in most of the cases.

The Tektronix case[13] describes the company's implementation of an Enterprise Resource Planning (ERP) solution in three global business divisions. The company's managers needed to balance the requirements of each division with the company's overall need to standardize business practices and its desire to adhere to a common business model across the enterprise. Each division used a different mix of internal and external project personnel. The case details the difficulty of major business change in a mature business and technical environment.

The BAE case[14] describes events surrounding the construction of the baggage-handling system at the Denver International Airport. In examining the complete failure of the automation system, the case addresses the politics of project management, including decisions regarding budget, scheduling, and overall project structure. The case is approached from the point of view of BAE—the company hired to develop the automated system—as it struggled to fulfill its contract, work well with airport project management

---

[13]Austin, R.D., Nolan, R.L., Cotteleer, M.; *Tektronix, Inc.: Global ERP Implementation,* (HBS No. 699-043).
    [14]R. Montealegre, H.J. Nelson, C.I. Knoop, and L.M. Applegate,; *BAE Automated Systems (A): Denver International Airport Baggage-Handling System,* (HBS No. 396-311).

and other contractors, and deal with numerous supply, scheduling, and engineering difficulties.

The Cisco Systems case presents a spectacular implementation success story.[15] The company placed big bets early in its corporate life by investing more than $100 million to create a standardized IT platform for carrying out all of its business. The bet paid off to the tune of estimated $1.3 billion in benefits for FY2000. The case demonstrates unequivocally the power of getting implementation right.

The General Dynamics and Computer Sciences Corporation agreement was the largest outsourcing agreement in the industry at the time of the case.[16] The case captures key issues in IT outsourcing, which provides interesting discussion points and a useful context in which to discuss other significant IT outsourcing arrangements.

Taken together, the stories of these four companies provide an excellent overview of challenges of managing IT project implementation in the 21st century.

---

[15]K.A. Porter, C. Akers, R.L. Nolan, and C.L. Darwell; *Cisco Systems Architecture: ERP and Web-enabled IT,* (HBS No. 301-099).

[16]K.N. Seger, and F.W. McFarlan; *General Dynamics and Computer Sciences Corporation: Outsourcing the IS Function (A),* (HBS No. 193-178).

CASE 4–1
TEKTRONIX, INC.: GLOBAL ERP IMPLEMENTATION[1]

When Carl Neun started his new position as CFO of Tektronix, Inc., in 1993 he knew he had his work cut out for him. A Silicon Valley transplant, he arrived at the Tektronix campus in Wilsonville, Oregon[2], assumed broad responsibilities and immediately began shaking things up. After 50 years of success, the high-tech producer of electronic equipment was facing increased global competition. Among the company's challenges were management and information systems that lacked integration and suffered from decades of uncoordinated evolution. Of particular importance was the fact that the financial performance of the company was suffering (see Exhibit 1). The company was in the middle of a five-year recovery program aimed at solidifying its competitive footing.

Neun believed that the company's future success would depend on his ability to simplify and restructure its operations. His first acts as CFO included selling off businesses, changing business processes, and increasing visibility into operations. A key enabler for sustaining these changes was the implementation of improved information technology (IT).

---

[1]This case was prepared by Doctoral Candidates George Westerman and Mark J. Cotteleer under the supervision of Professors Robert D. Austin and Richard L. Nolan. Copyright © 1999 by the President and Fellows of Harvard College. Harvard Business School case 699-043.
[2]Tektronix maintained corporate campuses in Wilsonville, OR , and in Beaverton, OR 20 miles away.

EXHIBIT 1 Selected Financial Data*

	1998	1997	1996	1995	1994
Net sales	$2,085.8	$1,940.1	$1,768.9	$1,498.0	$1,342.5
Gross margin	41.5%	42.9%	41.9%	45.3%	46.1%
Excluding non-recurring charges(1)	43.3%	42.9%	41.9%4	45.3%	46.1%
Research and development expenses	9.7%	9.7%	9.3%	11.1%	11.9%
Selling, general and admin expenses	24.4%	24.8%	24.8%	26.7%	27.6%
Operating margin	5.5%	8.5%	8.1%	7.7%	6.5%
Excluding non-recurring charges(1)	9.3%	8.5%	8.1%	7.7%	6.5%
Pretax margin	5.9%	8.7%	8.0%	7.4%	6.5%
Excluding non-recurring charges(1)	9.7%	8.7%	8.0%	7.4%	6.5%
Earnings margin	3.9%	5.9%	5.6%	5.4%	4.6%
Excluding non-recurring charges(1)	6.5%	5.9%	5.6%	5.4%	4.6%
Net earnings	$82.3	$114.8	$99.6	$81.6	$61.5
Excluding non-recurring charges(1)	$135.2	$114.8	$99.6	$81.6	$61.5
Basic earnings per share	$1.63	$2.32	$2.00	$1.67	$1.27
Excluding non-recurring charges(1)	$2.68	$2.32	$2.00	$1.67	$1.27
Diluted earnings per share	$1.60	$2.29	$1.95	$1.64	$1.25
Excluding non-recurring charges(1)	$2.63	$2.29	$1.95	$1.64	$1.25
Weighted average shares outstanding:					
Basic	50.4	49.5	49.8	48.9	48.5
Diluted	51.3	50.2	51.0	49.8	49.3
Dividends per share	$0.46	$0.40	$0.40	$0.40	$0.40
Cash and cash equivalents	$120.5	$142.7	$36.6	$31.8	$43.0
Total assets	$1,376.8	$1,316.7	$1,328.5	$1,218.3	$1,002.8
Long-term debt	$150.7	$151.6	$202.0	$105.0	$104.9
Total debt	$156.1	$157.7	$246.6	$192.6	$124.0
Total capitalization	$784.9	$771.3	$675.3	$604.2	$472.8
Return on equity	10.6%	15.9%	15.6%	15.2%	13.5%
Excluding non-recurring charges(1)	16.8%	15.9%	15.6%	15.2%	13.5%
Ending shares outstanding	50.3	50.1	49.0	49.6	48.3
Book value per share	$15.59	$15.39	$13.77	$12.18	$9.79
Closing share price	$38.25	$38.25	$25.25	$30.67	$19.17
Capital expenditures	$155.1	$112.0	$106.7	$103.8	$71.9
Depreciation expense	$65.9	$59.6	$47.1	$40.9	$55.3
Square feet in use	4.0	3.8	4.1	4.3	5.0
Employees	8,630	8,392	7,929	7,712	8,591
Net sales per employee (in thousands)	$241.7	$231.2	$223.1	$194.2	$156.3
Revenue from new products(2)	74%	73%	67%	62%	50%

* Some earlier year financial comparisons are not available due to changes in financial practices and corporate structure.

Notes: Amounts are in millions, except per share and employees. Returns are based on average net assets.

(1) Amounts for 1998 do not include non-recurring charges of $79.0 million pre-tax, $52.9 million net of tax ($1.05 per basic share, $1.03 per diluted share).

(2) Represents percentage of total product sales generated by products introduced within the last two years.

Source: Tektronix internal financial data.

Neun knew that in order to achieve improvements, he would need to bring a strong CIO on board to help guide the effort. His choice was Bob Vance, a technology manager with whom he had worked in the past. Together Neun and Vance assessed the 1970s-vintage information architecture and made their plans. Fixing Tektronix's IT was crucial to the long-term success of the company. They knew what they wanted and they had the support of their Board of Directors. While it was not clear exactly how they would get there, both Neun and Vance knew they were in for an exciting ride.

Tektronix History

Founded in 1946 as a maker of electronic test equipment, Tektronix had grown by 1993 to be a $1.3 billion manufacturer of electronic tools and devices. The company's business was split into three autonomous divisions: Measurement Business Division (MBD); Color Printing and Imaging Division (CPID); and Video and Networking Division (VND) (see Exhibit 2). Tektronix divisions were based in the United States and had an international presence in nearly 60 countries.

The company was the worldwide leader in oscilloscopes with a market share of more than twice that of its next largest competitor. It was also the worldwide leader in television test, measurement and monitoring equipment and a leader in the market for workgroup color printers. Despite occupying a strong and stable position in its markets, however, the company was hampered by a fifty-year legacy that limited its flexibility and growth opportunities.

One of Tektronix's major issues was its IT infrastructure. The company had many different application systems and technologies[3] around the world. Gary Allen, IT director—

---

[3]See Exhibit 3 for a brief history on the technical path Tektronix took to replace its IT hardware and communications infrastructure.

Finance & HR Systems, called it "a spaghetti factory."

> There was a lot of 'not invented here' mentality at Tektronix. Everyone made it sound like Tektronix was unique. The systems reflected that as well. We had over 460 legacy systems just in the United States. None of the systems was standardized globally. Business processes were not common anywhere in the world. We had no visibility of inventory once products were shipped from Beaverton to any of our sites around the world. If we wanted to divest any portions of our business, it was all caught up into this big mainframe system and very difficult to even identify the data that could be spun off. This didn't leave us very much flexibility.

The architectural problems embedded in Tektronix's IT manifested themselves in a variety of ways. Shortcomings made it impossible for the company to ship "up to the minute" or on a Saturday. The patchwork of legacy systems—a holdover from the days when Tektronix was operated as 26 independent divisions—also created the need for a sales order to be entered multiple times in different systems as it made its way through the order cycle. This slowed processing and customer service and introduced the opportunity for order errors to creep into the system. Expediting an order required extensive manual coordination, leading to the saying "five calls does it all." Additional weaknesses in Tektronix's information architecture meant that the company lacked accurate information on performance, did not have the capacity to effectively manage customer accounts and credit on a global basis, and could not calculate an invoice total for a customer at order creation.

The financial systems also suffered from a lack of integration. Multiple charts of accounts existed across the firm. Closing the books each month took weeks. It was extremely difficult to know which products and divisions were profitable and which were not. Neun felt that he needed better information so that he could cut costs and find efficiencies. He also needed clear

EXHIBIT 2   Major Lines of Business (Source: www.Tektronix.com)

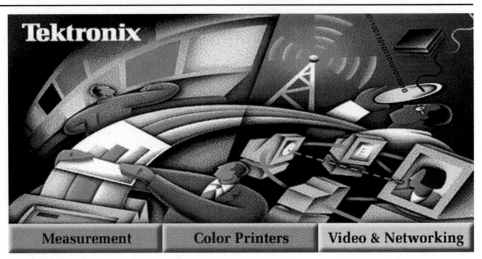

	Measurement	Color Printers	Video & Networking
Major products	A broad range of instruments for virtually every measurement application. They include sophisticated oscilloscope solutions, logic analyzers, instruments on a card, intelligent hand-held tools, spectrum analyzers, cable testers, stimulus devices, communications transmission tests and television and audio test equipment.	The Phaser™ family of workgroup color printers, selling into the office, graphic arts and engineering/scientific markets.	Video production, editing and transmission products, as well as disk-based storage and playback systems. Tektronix also offers a complete line of Windows-based terminals hardware and software products for the lowest-cost desktop access to PC, mainframe and Unix applications, as well as distributed digital multimedia hardware and software and high-speed remote connect protocols.
Sales (1996)	$812.3 Million	$561.6 Million	$395.0 Million
Sales (1997)	$852.8	$638.5	$448.8
Sales (1998)	$962.9	$728.7	$394.2

information to be able to sell off unprofitable businesses and integrate new acquisitions.

Because Tektronix had previously had difficulty implementing other IT projects,[4] the company needed both a vision and a justification for undertaking a project to replace legacy systems. Neun provided the vision:

> It was pretty clear that the whole world from an information point of view was going to get really small. Pricing disparities around the world were going to collapse. . . . We came up with our own vision and said we needed to be able to see right through the businesses worldwide. We needed to strip out all of the infrastructure that existed around the world. And we needed a common template in which to do all of this. [In order to accomplish this] I came up with this concept, which I labeled 'Frankfurt is Orlando.' It says that these are sales and distribution businesses. Why is it any different, other than language and local laws, to do business in Germany than in Florida? That was the concept that we began to launch off on.

Moving Toward Enterprise Resource Planning (ERP)

Justifying the Change. Neun's vision could provide only part of the impetus for a project of this magnitude. The business justification came from Roy Barker, president of CPID. CPID's business had been growing quickly and its legacy systems were not projected to be able to support the division much longer. CPID had considered replacing its systems a few years before, but a strong business case for the investment was not seen to exist. Kathy Goeddel, IT director for CPID, remarked that this lack of a business case might have had more to do with the ability of a skilled workforce to cover for system deficiencies than with the strength of the systems in place at the time. She wondered whether any level of employee skill could maintain service

---

[4]In the previous decade Tektronix had tried to replace its Order Management systems five times. Each time they ended up canceling the project, failing to progress beyond requirements definition.

delivery if the company continued to grow as expected.

Under Barker, CPID adopted a new business model with a goal of doubling the division's size. Barker's plan was to take CPID from niche player in the printer industry, supporting graphics terminals in mainframe engineering environments, to a mass-marketer targeting high-volume sales to PC-based corporate customers. Barker was very clear with everyone in the company that he felt the future of the color printer business would be "a volume game." In the new, more competitive environment systems could not be an inhibiting factor. CPID needed to have an IT capability that would grow with the business.

Barker's call for change echoed Vance and Neun's desire to revamp the systems at Tektronix. The company immediately began to plan for the new implementation. Management spent no time formally justifying the investment. Allen recounted the company's rationale:

> There was hardly any desire on Carl Neun's part to do some big return on investment analysis. That's not even close to his strategy. He knew that we needed to put some industrial strength processes in and had enough experience to know that, by driving standardization and keeping things simple, the costs would go down automatically. He didn't need analysis to demonstrate that — he knew intuitively.

Expanding the Vision. After Barker raised the issue, other managers joined the cause. Implementation would start with CPID, and then move to the other divisions. Neun and Vance pushed to change the company's processes rapidly. Neun's vision for the enterprise had three components: separability of the businesses; leveraging shared services; and staying as "plain vanilla" as possible. The first component, separability, was key to the vision. Each of the three divisions had different distribution and selling methods. Neun's approach called for each division to have its own instance of the system that managed its customer fulfillment process. He wanted to be sure that Tektronix didn't have the requirements of one organization driving the practices of another. However, within each division he demanded standardization. In the case of CPID, no matter where somebody ordered a color printer from, the transaction would be executed in the same system, using the same database. In short, Frankfurt would equal Orlando.

Implementation of shared services was also key. While the divisions needed separability from each other, they also needed to be comparable to one another and to provide a global, up-to-date view of their financial status. Tektronix management needed a way to make "apples to apples" comparisons among them. Neun and his team believed that substantial cost reductions could be achieved by consolidating certain functions. Accounts Payable, General Ledger, Fixed Assets, and some portions of Procurement were among the easy targets for this treatment. This meant implementing a single financial and accounts receivable system worldwide. Introducing this type of commonality would be difficult because charts of accounts varied from division to division and country to country, and many countries had specific language and legal requirements.

The third tenet of Neun's vision was the concept of "plain vanilla" implementation. Tektronix would minimize the number of changes required to the software package it purchased. In this way, processes would be standardized and software maintenance and upgrades would be easier. Neun felt that maintaining the integrity of the software was critical and that, in cases where business processes did not match software functions, the default response must be to change the process. Changes to the software would be allowed only if the package simply could not execute a process as required, or if a "non-

vanilla" approach constituted a key competitive advantage for the company.

Planning for ERP

Selecting Software. Implementation planning began with software selection. There was never a question about whether Tektronix should purchase a package or build the system in-house. Neun commented:

> Buying a package is a real outsourcing advantage. We're not in the business of developing all this code. We don't see all of the issues and the business problems that software developers do. The package vendors get to see so much more diversity and so much more opportunity that ultimately they're going to have a much more robust system. They will be able to leverage their R&D investment over thousands and thousands of users versus us leveraging it over our single company.

Tektronix already had a manufacturing package developed by a smaller player in the ERP market. Given that the company had only recently completed implementation of this package, management did not have the desire to put Manufacturing through the pain of another implementation so soon. Tektronix considered implementing the package's order management functionality but in the end did not consider it to be a viable long-term solution.[5] According to Steve Rees, Director of IT Computer Services, "the technical people felt very certain that [the database] could not scale to meet our requirements."

Vance made the decision to keep the manufacturing system in place. For the rest of Tektronix's systems, however, he pushed the company to embrace a single vendor ERP strategy rather than to take a "best of breed" approach.

---

[5]In the case of CPID, the division went so far as to use the manufacturing package's order management functionality as the basis for reengineering its business processes.

EXHIBIT 3   Brief History of Tektronix Technical Upgrade Path.

The Tektronix ERP implementation required more than process change and software customization. It also required a complete rework of the global hardware and communications infrastructure. While most of the major applications previously ran on dumb terminals attached to IBM mainframes and DEC VAX machines, the new system would use PCs attached to Unix machines. Luckily, the company had begun rebuilding its infrastructure several years before.

In 1992, Tektronix had seven separate data centers, running a combination of IBM mainframe, DEC VAX, and IBM minicomputers. These were decentralized, segregated by division. Prior to Vance's arrival, the then CIO had begun a data center consolidation. When Vance arrived, the company was down to three data centers. Vance pushed the change farther, consolidating to a single data center and vowing to get rid of the mainframes as soon as possible. In 1996, Tektronix outsourced its mainframe processing and shut down its last in-house mainframe. The goal was to shut down all mainframe processing by 1999.

Tektronix had a few Unix machines, made by Sun and IBM, before the changes took place. It wasn't until early 1993 that Unix machines entered the data centers. Prior to that, the main data center support staff had only minor Unix experience. Yet, the company's new manufacturing system ran only on Unix. Tektronix had to launch a major effort to retrain its mainframe-oriented support staff on Unix. Difficulties remained because there were many Unix machines located around the data center. The only way to monitor their operation was to walk around the data center and watch each machine's console. Tektronix purchased an integrated Unix-based systems management package (CA Unicenter) to monitor usage and provide mainframe-class computer operations support functions. By 1996, Tektronix could continuously monitor all of its Unix machines from a single operator console. This reduced staffing needs and increased system uptime.

The communications infrastructure also needed rework. Previously, each manufacturer had its own standard communications protocol. Thus, Tektronix had to install multiple lines and several protocol converters around its global network. In the early 1990s, Tektronix decided to standardize on Internet Protocol (IP). By 1994, all machines on the network, regardless of manufacturer, were using IP. This made it much easier to monitor network status, install new machines, and communicate between all machines on the network. During this time, the Tektronix global network grew from approximately 20 locations to over 100 sites around the world.

If Tektronix was to grow in the way managers wanted it to, it was not in the best interests of the company to fight with the maintenance, integration, and upgrade issues brought on by implementing multiple packages.

In selecting a specific package, Tektronix spent little time comparing features and costs. Neun and Vance both had previous experience with the ERP solution offered by Oracle. They felt that the need to move quickly combined with the lack of maturity among competing ERP packages justified a fast selection.

Rather than spending resources evaluating alternatives, the company instead formed a small team of people who spent one to two months ensuring that Oracle could do what Tektronix needed. Satisfied, they set to work planning the implementation.

Worldwide Business Model. Tektronix's first implementation move was to create a steering committee. The committee's job was to refine the company's vision and to develop a "global business model" (see Exhibit 4) that set out

---

EXHIBIT 4   Global Business Model for the ERP Implementation

1. Order entry and fulfillment at business division
2. Business division owns customer relationship
3. Division chooses where order entry occurs
4. Business division stipulates distribution channels and inventory sourcing
5. Management information at both corporate and business division levels, worldwide
6. AR and GL at the corporate and regional level
7. Corporate owns the customer data
8. Credit exposure managed globally
9. Customs and trade administration controlled at the corporate level
10. Regional distribution and accounting centers utilized

EXHIBIT 5   Business Practice Changes and Guiding Principles

1. Change business practices, not the Oracle application.
2. One Oracle Order Management, Accounts Receivable system by business division, worldwide, using common code, synchronized periodically, with custom selectable, optional portions to meet unique business requirements by business unit and/or geography.
3. All finished inventory to be maintained in Oracle, using common item nomenclature, and visible, by business division, worldwide.
4. Cross region selling transactions, in U.S. dollars, will go through a U.S. based holding company with branches throughout the world.
5. The base currency is U.S. Dollars. Inventory, cross-region sales, and management reporting will be in U.S. Dollars, but orders and invoices will be in the local currency.
6. One standard cost, worldwide.
7. English will be the system language worldwide, except for customer facing documents.
8. Only one business division's products will be placed on any order.
9. Customers will be registered worldwide.
10. Every order will go through the worldwide credit logic.
11. One order per transaction that reflects the end customer (no back-to-back orders).
12. Orders on credit hold will not be shipped.
13. All invoicing, collection, and cashiering will be done in Oracle.

---

the overarching guidelines to which the system must adhere in order to be successful. At a slightly lower level a set of "Business Practice Changes and Guiding Principles" (see Exhibit 5) were developed to provide more concrete direction for the implementation. Jeanne Gordon, director of Worldwide Customer Fulfillment Systems, believed that this guidance was essential:

> Since there were going to be major changes to the way the countries and regions had to operate, it was very valuable to have these principles clearly identified, articulated, and reiterated by management, ahead of the detailed work on the project. While some of these

Exhibit 6   ERP System Architecture

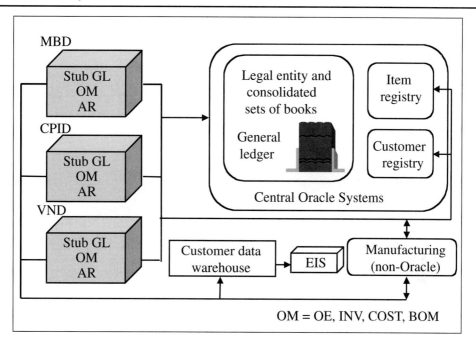

MBD

Stub GL
OM
AR

CPID

Stub GL
OM
AR

VND

Stub GL
OM
AR

Legal entity and
consolidated
sets of books

General
ledger

Item
registry

Customer
registry

Central Oracle Systems

Customer data
warehouse

EIS

Manufacturing
(non-Oracle)

OM = OE, INV, COST, BOM

principles were challenged frequently, management's consistent support of them helped simplify the worldwide implementation, and promoted our ability to meet our schedules.

Implementation of the business model necessitated a complex architecture (see Exhibit 6), in which each of the three divisions had its own worldwide implementation of Order Management. There was to be one worldwide implementation of Accounts Receivable[6] and the General Ledger. A common, worldwide chart of accounts, a central customer registry, and a single item-master table would tie divisions together. Using a single definition for each piece of data, the company would build a data ware-

house to provide near-real-time visibility into worldwide operations.

Project Organization and Management.   The project management and communications infrastructure was built upon a number of key roles (see Exhibit 7). Roles were important from more than just a technical standpoint. Key players in each functional and geographic area ran interference and acted as negotiators when business change was needed. Project participants had to develop both business process expertise as well as depth in the Oracle package. It was only through a combination of technical and functional strength that critical project issues could be resolved.

At the top of the project sat Neun, who acted as the final arbiter of all disputes. Lacking detailed knowledge of every issue, Neun led by establishing a "set of fundamentals"

---

[6]While Accounts Receivable was to ultimately exist as a single rather than divisionalized entity, the implementation plan called for it to be rolled out by division with Order Management functionality.

EXHIBIT 7   Project Team Structure and Roles

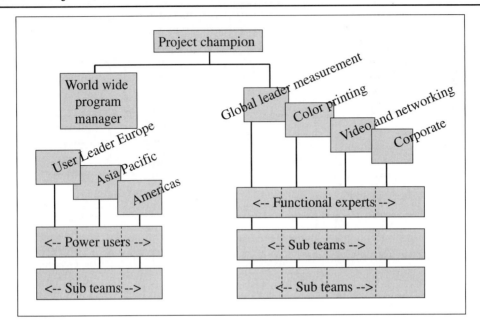

- **Sponsor / Champion:** Carl Neun served as sponsor/champion. As CFO, he was considered a neutral party by the three business divisions. His role was to force decisions, influence compliance with the project goals and principles, break log jams, challenge current processes, help maintain schedules and momentum, and authorize funding.
- **Program Management:** Program management was provided by a single person who was responsible for mustering all forces to ensure a successful roll out.
- **User Project Leader:** Each geography had a user project leader, who was an advocate for the businesses and the region. Most often this person was from the region or had long-time ties there. The role was to provide a balance between the business principles as set down by enterprise management, with their most critical business challenges. In addition, this person helped ensure that targets were met, resource levels were sufficient, and issues got aired and resolved. This role also helped smooth the cultural and language differences that occasionally cropped up in the diverse, cross-geography teams.
- **Global Leader:** In addition to the team members described previously, each business division had a global leader who had been with the project throughout all phases of the rollout. They functioned as global business advocates, who helped prioritize requirements, assisted the countries in understanding the division business model and helped determine what business practice changes were required.
- **Power User:** In order to have hands-on users knowledgeable on the generic system, "power users" for each key area, i.e. order entry, logistics, credit, invoicing, were identified for each major implementation wave. These power users received training, provided input into requirements, assisted in coming up with solutions for gaps, developed procedures, played a heavyweight role in system testing, and helped in training their colleagues.

- **Functional Expert:** Functional experts were allocated to each wave to ensure enough system and business knowledge remained with the implementation teams up to the final wave. This was difficult, since the most knowledgeable resources were in demand for other initiatives, which had to be postponed.
- **Change Control:** To ensure that proposed changes to the system did not disrupt business functionality in the production system, rigorous concept review and change control mechanisms were put in place. Any proposed system changes, after passing initial research and reasonableness checks, were reviewed, using a worldwide email distribution list. This was followed up with review in a bimonthly global meeting. Once approved for development, the actual migration to production was timed to minimize disruption of the production system and ongoing implementation rollout dates.
- **Functional Sub-team:** Small groups were formed for each wave to focus attention on major implementation activities or issue areas. These included conversion, system testing, training, and procedures teams. Often, local interfaces, customs documentation, or tax also required a team. The teams were chartered to research requirements, propose solutions, test the system and ensure the procedures were updated.
- **Test Team:** Cross-business and cross-geography test teams, with standard membership, were organized worldwide. These teams tested new functionality. They also developed test scripts to regression test most critical or fragile functions. These test teams still operate today for post-implementation enhancements.

based on the business model. Neun's authority derived directly from the CEO's office and he used it to accelerate the implementation process. Neun described the situation:

> [The CEO] gave me unlimited authority on the implementation and nobody questioned that authority. I never had to ask him to step in on anything of that nature. That made a big difference of being able to cut through issues and say, 'I'm sorry, we're not going to do this.'

Neun was flanked by strong leaders in each business division, as well as by Vance in IT. Vance spent nearly 60% of his time on the project, and dedicated over half of his best people to the task. He made tough decisions, from outsourcing the mainframe to retraining and sometimes removing his staff. The presidents of each division were also important in driving the project, making key people available, and removing political obstacles. Rob Nichols, senior program manager at MBD, highlighted the role of his division president: "He did a great job of setting up the team for success. He gave us credibility. Every time he touched one of the local sales offices, he was endorsing what we were doing and doing a sell job for us."

Project Schedule. The implementation was considered to be a single change program, consisting of many "waves." Each wave delivered a specific set of functionality for a particular division or geographic region. While the waves were managed independently, the program management team watched all interdependencies carefully to ensure that the entire change program remained on course.

The concept of waves was important. They gave regular feedback that could only be obtained by implementing a part of the system in the real world. In addition, the wave concept gave the program managers some flexibility in scheduling. For example, as new releases of Oracle became available, the program managers could add a wave to upgrade software before implementing new functionality. As an added bonus, the wave concept yielded frequent victories. This was considered important, both to keep team morale high, and to ensure that the Board continued to support the high cost and long timeline of implementation.

Neun held to one principle that was never published in the business model. He believed strongly that schedule was much more important than budget in an implementation of this magnitude. He was willing to spend extra resources to keep projects on track. According to Neun:

> The momentum behind the project becomes so powerful that, if you don't get your hands around it, it can run away with you from a cost perspective. It's cheaper to add a couple more resources and stick to a schedule than it is to let the schedule slip.

Implementation

Tektronix's ERP implementation was split into five major sub-projects. The first, led by Allen, was the implementation of the financial management system (Financials). Subprojects two through four, led by each of the divisional IT Directors, consisted of the Order Management/Accounts Receivable (OMAR) implementations in the three divisions. The final subproject was the global rollout led by Gordon.

Financials were implemented in parallel with OMAR at CPID. The other OMAR projects followed after CPID. For both Financials and OMAR, Tektronix decided to implement the United States first, and then roll the systems out to the rest of the world. This would allow them to get basic functionality working for a single country before adding the complexity of the international business.

Financials
We did this to gain information visibility and drive out cost. There's no value-added in doing accounts payable really well. You have to do it so you can have good relationships with your suppliers and all of that, but it is not value.
— CFO Carl Neun

Neun's goal for the financial system was to have a single view of all financial information worldwide. The financial system installation emphasized the part of Neun's vision calling for a "plain vanilla" approach. This emphasis required a number of changes in business processes around the world. It also provided the stimulus to implement business process improvements.

Standardization and Simplification.   The first steps were to standardize charts-of-accounts and to eliminate most of the complex transfer pricing practices that were in place. These changes made it easier for the company to roll up financials and close its books. More importantly, they allowed managers to see up-to-date information about financial status, rather than having to wait for end-of-period reports.

In Europe, even larger changes were required. Neun decided that the existing organizational structure, based on independent managers in each country, was not working. The marketing director for Europe shared this view. Both Neun and the European director wanted a pan-European focus, with a single language and a single measurement basis. Their first move was to eliminate all of the country managers. Next they decreed that English would be the single language used for business inside Tektronix. Sales people would work with their customers in the local language, but internally all would speak English.

Neun reinforced this approach by moving each country from a profit-center to a straight commission basis. With the country managers gone, Neun could hire non-executive "office managers," who were responsible for physical facilities and administration without having supervisory or managerial duties. He also changed the financial transaction processes. The financial back offices in each country were closed. All transactions throughout Europe were processed through a single location in Marlow, England.

Adoption of the "plain vanilla" implementation approach required the implementation team to address many issues of local importance. In many cases the team faced apparent requirements that were not satisfied by the Oracle package. The project team had to deal with each issue one by one. By carefully analyzing true requirements, team members found that in most cases the local differences were tradition and business practice rather than legal requirements. These practices were changed in the name of standardization. Only in cases of extreme need were modifications to the financial system approved.

Implementation Support. Tektronix relied heavily on consulting support for its financial implementation. They used a combination of large and small consulting firms as well as independent consultants. Of particular importance to the financial implementation team was the relationship formed with Aris Consulting. Aris was a small but rapidly growing firm that specialized in Oracle implementations. Its founders had worked at Oracle before leaving to form their own firm in 1990. Aris was initially engaged on a fixed-price basis to provide functional support for the implementation of general ledger and chart-of-accounts functionality. Over time, Tektronix built confidence in Aris' capabilities and ended up changing the consultant's role in the implementation. Allen described the situation:

> As we got more comfortable with Aris, we decided we were spending too much time managing the scope of the application, and just went to a time and materials basis. This worked out better. We ended up bringing in an Aris functional expert for each of the major modules and teamed them with user and IT leads from Tektronix.

For roles that required less functional and business expertise Tektronix brought in lower cost technical consultants. These contractors wrote conversion programs and did routine customizations to reports. Tektronix also hired a small firm to develop an interface between its manufacturing package and Oracle. In order to reduce costs in this area, Tektronix granted the contractor the right to resell this interface to other companies.

Order Management/Accounts Receivable (OMAR)

Order management is very much oriented to the business. We couldn't push back as much. In addition, there was no one person at Tektronix responsible for the whole Order Management process.

—Director of Worldwide Customer Fulfillment Systems
Jeanne Gordon

The OMAR implementation was similar to Financials in its approach, but different in execution. The overriding principles of separability, shared services, and "plain vanilla" implementation were adhered to wherever possible. In many ways, however, the problems faced during the implementation were more difficult. Much more customization was required. The need to deviate from the core principles of the implementation and/or to customize the software was driven by two realities. First, Tektronix managers felt that, in contrast to many financial functions, the way the company faced its customers was a competitive factor. To the extent that the firm could not meet customer requirements, they would lose business. Given differences in the types of customers that each business line faced, divisional differences seemed necessary.

The second reason had to do with the capability of the package itself. Despite being seen as an overall fit for Tektronix, Oracle did not have some of the functionality that was required for OMAR. In some cases, functionality was planned in later releases of the package. However, for the most part Tektronix chose not to risk delays in release and opted to modify the software itself.

One example of a significant customization was local language support. While the corporate language was English, Tektronix could not compete if its customer-facing documents were not in the local language. In addition, each country had slightly different legal language for official documents. In order to deal with these differences, the OMAR team built a "multilingual engine" which rode on the outside of the core package. When printing was needed, the engine read the required data from the database, formatted it appropriately, and printed it on electronic forms tailored to the particular country's language and business practices. This allowed the rest of the systems to work in a single language, and eliminated the need for a different system implementation for each country.

Implementing OMAR at CPID. CPID was the logical candidate for starting the OMAR implementations. The division represented the business with the highest velocity, the most commodity-type business, and the greatest need to deal with growth. Division President Roy Barker had been an advocate for the initiative. He was able to articulate a strong business need for new IT. In addition, Barker viewed IT as a key enabler for the redesign of new business processes that would make CPID more responsive to its customers.

CPID was also a good fit from the IT side. Its shift in business models led the division to adopt a product strategy that focused on a relatively small number of standard, built-to-stock products. As a result, CPID represented the simplest operational scenario. In contrast, MBD had literally thousands of parts, and VND dealt with a small number of large, highly-complex orders that required validation and coordination. Both MBD and VND built made-to-order products. By starting with CPID, Tektronix could build the basic order management functionality and work out many technical issues before tackling the more difficult business challenges from the other divisions.

Although the CPID implementation was considered more straightforward from a business standpoint, the newness of the technology and the challenge of executing the first implementation meant the task was still very difficult. For implementation, Tektronix had decided to go with a "beta" version of the package.[7] The instability of this version forced the implementation team to spend months "debugging" the package.[8]

Tektronix needed to build internal skills in project management, as well as technical and functional skills with the Oracle application. In response to these difficulties, the OMAR team turned initially to a large consulting firm for assistance. Their experience was less than fulfilling. One manager was extremely critical of the consultant's contribution: "I don't think they produced a damn thing for CPID. I think at the end of the day, what we were left with was a cancelled check." Allen was more diplomatic in his assessment:

> [The consulting firm] added a lot in the areas of project management and process reengineering, but they had absolutely no idea how Oracle order management worked. They didn't really bring any functional expertise to the table and clearly did not help us through the issues of implementing [a newer release] of Oracle.

---

[7] A "beta" software release is one that has passed through development at the vendor but is not considered ready for general distribution. Companies implementing beta software versions often do so in an attempt to access greater functionality or in exchange for additional support or price considerations from the vendor. However, working with beta software releases often requires a company to deal with a large number of software bugs in the package.

[8] Note that by the time implementation was complete, the "beta" designation had been dropped from the version of Oracle CPID implemented. The division went live with a general release version of the package.

Unhappy with their initial choice, and seeing what the financial implementation team was doing with consultants, the OMAR team hired Aris, Oracle, and other consultants. Once again, they paired consultants with functional expertise with a large number of Tektronix staff. Tektronix took responsibility for much of the business change, and asked the consultants to handle the system details. Where additional bodies were required, Tektronix hired contractors from other small firms. In hiring any contractor, the company protected itself by rigorously interviewing candidates and specifying a "probation period" during which any individual could be released for no charge.[9]

While the implementation at CPID took longer than expected, it was considered successful. With this first domestic implementation, Tektronix was able to learn powerful lessons, build internal skills, and establish practices that helped with all of the future implementation waves.

Implementing OMAR at MBD
CPID proved that the software worked for a limited set of business processes. However, at MBD we run a large field organization, our orders are not centralized but distributed, and we don't have six printers, we have 1500 products. There's a much higher level of complexity here.

—MBD IT Manager Larry Bunyard

The implementation at MBD was able to leverage much of what CPID accomplished. However, in adapting CPID processes to a relatively more complex environment, the team uncovered some problems not previously encountered. For example, where CPID assembled products domestically and relied heavily on local distribution centers, MBD's new business model demanded direct shipment to end customers. Direct shipment represented a huge change, especially for Tektronix's international offices that were used to buying inventory from Tektronix, holding it and then reselling it as the customer required. Bunyard recounted the difficulties that the organization had with the changes: "We met a lot of resistance. We had to go back to the business model again and again to show why we were doing this."

MBD adopted an early reliance on Oracle consultants. Managers felt strongly that the use of these consultants gave Tektronix better visibility within Oracle's technical support organization. Bunyard described the advantages of using the vendor consultants:

> Oracle knows their code better than anybody else. They can go into the code, which we can't do. They can say 'Look right here. Here's your problem.' They also can validate our problem, reproduce it, and talk to the tech people in their own language. It gives us credibility with the tech support people in Oracle, and also gives me a scapegoat. If a problem comes up, it's Oracle, either consulting or software. That's powerful leverage.

Because of their complexity, MBD decided to pursue a vigorous testing program. Managers emphasized the need to test the system doing "actual work, with actual load." The testing program included four independent test conversions,[10] and six system tests. System tests took place on Saturdays when the rest of Tektronix was shut down. Participants in five cities[11] simulated full system load

---

[9]It should be noted that even in turning to outside consultants for support, the OMAR team found itself critically short on functional software expertise. In general, skilled Oracle order management implementers were not available in the market at any price.

[10]Test conversions were aimed at ensuring that operational data (e.g., customer records, item records, bills of materials, etc.) would not be corrupted when transferred from one system format to the other.
[11] Washington D.C., Dallas, Chicago, Santa Clara, and Beaverton.

conditions for four hours. After its final data conversion, MBD even shut down its entire $190 million order management system for a week so they could reconcile each open line item.

The MBD implementation took nearly twice as long as originally anticipated. Much of the time was spent in learning how to work with the system. Another large part was spent in testing. Despite strong schedule pressure from the executive level, MBD delayed their implementation several times in order to do additional cycles of testing. The result was a launch that was delayed but relatively free of problems. According to Bunyard, "We did not have the startup problems that CPID had. When we came live, we had acceptable processes and cycles."

Implementing OMAR at VND
They just slammed it in . . .
—CFO Carl Neun

The last wave to begin for OMAR in the United States was the implementation at VND.[12] The implementation team had two advantages when starting this wave. First, VND was the smallest of the three divisions at Tektronix. Second, the implementation team was in a position to benefit from all the prior work that had been done in the other two divisions. Despite these advantages, however, VND had its own issues, not the least of which was the fact that it had the most complex products. Rob Blaskowsky, VND IT director described the environment:

> We introduce new products regularly, but the big problem is complexity. You have to put rules into the

Bills of Material that prevent somebody ordering options that don't work together. It's tough to structure the system in a manner that not only does that but also is simple enough for one order entry person to enter.

Another issue for VND was the fact that the division was in the process of absorbing a recent acquisition and integrating a subsidiary component manufacturer based in California. Half of VND's workforce was in Oregon and half in California. Facing this issue, division management placed relatively less emphasis on the implementation of ERP. To VND executives, the ERP project was just something that had to get done. In order to avoid an extended distraction from the implementation, the VND president established a firm implementation date. According to one manager: "She drew the line and said 'It's going to be done by this date.'"

VND went for a rapid implementation, with much less preliminary work than the other divisions. They were helped by their small size, since few people needed training and few people could mount aggressive resistance. The project team encountered problems, but managed to work through them. In the end, the fast, high-risk approach worked for VND. They were able to implement quickly, with less involvement from the executive level. Blaskowsky described some of the consequences of their rapid implementation approach:

> We clearly didn't anticipate the level of resources this was going to consume. The complexity of entering orders required more order entry people than we originally planned. Also, in the area of item maintenance [configuring the products in the system], it's taking a higher skill set in the people than was originally planned. They're no longer just data entry requirements.

Global Rollout.   As the OMAR implementation at CPID began to wrap up, the Tektronix management team began to consider the best

---

[12]Note that even though the VND implementation began after MBD, it actually "went live" before MBD due to a shorter implementation time.

approach to a global rollout of Oracle ERP.[13] The team planned to extend its "wave" approach to Tektronix's international sites, starting with Europe. In the same way that the CPID implementation was relied upon for early business process learning, it was hoped that a European implementation would address the majority of international implementation issues. Gordon described the team's decision process:

> We had many, many, many meetings about how we would roll out. We had months of elapsed time, and days of meetings trying to decide that. We said 'We don't know exactly how we're going to do this. Let's start with something in common—the distribution center (DC) in Holland. Everybody uses that. It was a smart thing to do. It gave us a win and it accommodated some of the skepticism. It proved to people that we wouldn't hurt their business. They were still able to ship just as quickly, or even more quickly. Beyond that we decided to plan incrementally, and roll out future waves as we learned more about the process.'

In the aftermath of the Holland DC implementation, the Tektronix team opted to implement Oracle in a pilot set of countries representing both EU and Non-EU nations. This was followed by a "big bang" for the rest of the European countries. This "big bang" implemented all three divisional systems together. The team then moved on to implementations in the Americas and Asia/Pacific.

Leveraging the experiences in Europe, the Americas implementation adopted a similar, multi-divisional "big-bang" approach. There was, however, one difference. Because of the geographic distances between Canada, Mexico, and Brazil (the major, non-U.S. countries in the Americas), and the lack of business synergies between them, Tektronix rolled out all three divisional systems to each country in turn.

The Tektronix team addressed the challenges of implementing the Asia/Pacific region by first going after the English-speaking countries of Singapore and India. Following these two countries they tackled the language difficulties in Korea, Taiwan, and Hong Kong.[14] The final country to be implemented was Australia, which had older, mature business processes, and complex legacy systems needing simplification.

The rollout schedule for OMAR is shown in Exhibit 8. Starting with the EU pilot, and ending with Australia, the rollout covered 23 countries in less than 500 days. At the end of the rollout, the company had full information visibility, by division, of all inventory and transactions worldwide.

Results

Hell yes, it was worth it. We're able to do business at a level that wasn't possible with the old systems. They were totally out of steam. As far as cost is concerned, we paid for the entire project just on the fact that we've avoided the Year 2000 and Euro problems.
— CIO Bob Vance

Without question the team responsible for implementing Oracle at Tektronix felt that the time, effort and expense had been worth it. Operationally, managers could point to specific improvements enabled by the new technology. Measures such as Days Sales Outstanding and inventory levels showed

---

[13]Note that the global rollout did not begin until after all domestic sites were implemented.

[14]One of the major challenges of implementing in the non-English speaking Asian companies had to do with the complex character set used in each language. These character sets consist of two computer bytes per character rather than the one required for most other languages. The multilingual engine needed customization to allow the customer facing documents to use these "double-byte" languages.

EXHIBIT 8   Global Rollout Schedule for OMAR

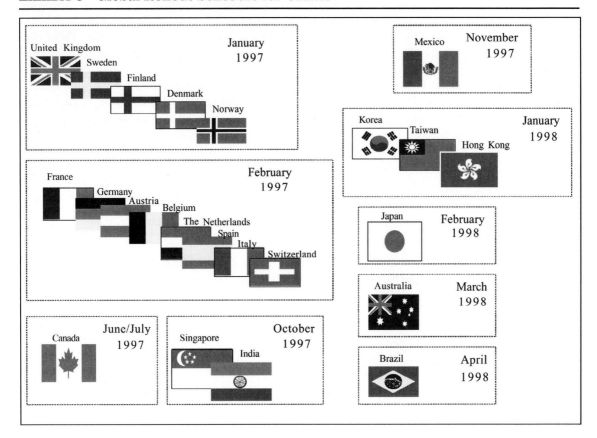

improvement. Tektronix now had finished goods inventory visibility regardless of where in the world it was located. In at least one division, same day shipments had risen from 15% prior to implementation to nearly 75%. Cycle time expended in obtaining credit approvals, over 24 hours pre-implementation, had been virtually eliminated.

Beyond the "hard" benefits of the implementation, managers felt that there were many non-quantifiable benefits.[15] Allen's per-

spective exemplified the attitude of most managers:

> There are a lot of operational improvement initiatives going on around here. How much cost savings is directly related to the system? I don't know, and we don't really care. We know ERP is an enabler, and [these improvements] wouldn't have happened without it.

Improved data integration allowed financial analysts to drill down to several levels of detail in a single account. This allowed better visibility into sales trends and internal performance. Closing the books at the end of a financial period was accelerated substantially. In addition, managers felt the stan-

[15]The capture of many of these benefits was facilitated through the use of a web-based executive information system made available to executives at all levels of the organization.

dardization of business processes leveraged improved information to make even better decisions. Neun characterized the impact on operations:

> We began to emphasize the think, not the do. This was exciting to our people. In the past, they had been "green eyeshades oriented," and seen as a necessary evil. Now, they were becoming more integral to the operation of the business.

Users lower in the organization were also pleased with the results. Personnel felt more effective in their jobs. One user described the results of the implementation in the following way:

> Suddenly, our job is just different. Instead of spending 90% of our time collecting data and 10% of the time turning it into information, we spend 10% of our time getting the data and 90% our figuring out how to turn it into something management wants. The information is more timely, it's better, and we get it faster.

Despite strong feelings about the benefits of implementing ERP, team members felt it was also important to recognize that it came at a cost. The project was expensive, totaling approximately $55 million in software, internal and contract labor. Gordon described the team's perspective:

> We know that the implementation was expensive, but that was not really our focus. We didn't spend a lot of time on budgeting or reporting variance to plan. We spent most of our time reporting progress to plan against the time schedule.

Looking Back

Neun and Vance shared a table at lunch and discussed their years with the company. Tektronix had completely changed the way it handled information. It was in a much better position to manage its existing business, and now had the capacity to grow its business substantially. Tektronix's business processes benefited from increased efficiency and standardization. There was better visibility into customers and products than ever before. The new infrastructure also met the goal of giving the company more flexibility to acquire new businesses and divest others.[16]

Looking back, the two men remembered the hard decisions and long hours spent implementing the system and reengineering the company's processes. They remembered pitfalls and successes on the road. The company was better off now. But, the effort had cost many millions of dollars and countless lost hours of sleep. What did they learn, they wondered, that would help with another major implementation?

---

[16] An example of this was the way Tektronix had integrated a new German acquisition in less than two months.

CASE 4–2
BAE AUTOMATED SYSTEMS (A): DENVER INTERNATIONAL AIRPORT BAGGAGE-HANDLING SYSTEM[1]

No airport anywhere in the world is as technologically advanced as the Denver International Airport.[2]

It's dramatic. If your bag [got] on the track, your bag [was] in pieces.[3]

In November 1989 ground was broken to build the Denver International Airport (DIA). Located 25 miles from downtown Denver, Colorado, it was the first major airport to be built in the United States since the opening of the Dallas-Fort Worth Airport in 1974. In 1992, two years into construction, the project's top managers recommended inclusion of an airport-wide integrated baggage-handling system that could dramatically improve the efficiency of luggage delivery. Originally contracted by United Airlines to cover its operations, the system was to be expanded to serve the entire airport. It was expected that the integrated system would improve ground time efficiency, reduce close-out time for hub operations, and decrease time-consuming manual baggage sorting and handling. There were, however, a number of risks inherent in the endeavor: the scale of the large project size; the enormous complexity of the expanded system; the newness of the technology; the large number of resident entities to be served by the same system; the high degree of technical and project definition uncertainty; and the short time span for completion. Due to its significant experience implementing baggage-handling technology on a smaller scale, BAE Automated Systems Inc., an engineering consulting and manufacturing company based in Carollton, Texas, was awarded the contract.

Construction problems kept the new airport from opening on the originally scheduled opening date in October 1993. Subsequently, problems with the implementation of the baggage system forced delays in the opening of the airport another three times in seven months. In May 1994, under growing pressure from shareholders, the business community, Denver residents, Federal Aviation Administration (FAA) commissioners, and the tenant airlines and concessionaires, Denver mayor Wellington Webb announced that he was hiring the German firm Logplan to help assess the state of the automated baggage system. In July, Logplan issued an 11-page report to the City of Denver that characterized BAE's system as "highly advanced" and "theoretically" capable of living up to its promised "capacities, services and performances," but acknowledged mechanical and electrical problems that "make it most improbable to achieve a stable and reliable operation." Logplan suggested that it would take approximately five months to get the complete BAE system working reliably. It also suggested that a backup system of tugs, carts, and conveyor belts could be constructed in less than five months.

[1]This case was prepared by Research Associate H. James Nelson and Assistant Professor Ramiro Montealegre of the University of Colorado at Boulder, and Research Associate Carin Isabel Knoop, and Professor Lynda M. Applegate.
Copyright 1996 by the President and Fellows of Harvard College.
Harvard Business School case 396-311.
[2]Fred Isaac, Federal Aviation Administration regional administrator, quoted in "Denver Still Working Out Kinks as Its First Birthday Arrives," *USA Today* (February 28, 1996), p. 4b.
[3]Fred Renville, United Airlines employee quoted in "Denver Still Working Out Kinks as Its First Birthday Arrives," *USA Today* (February 28, 1996), p. 4b.

In August 1994, Mayor Webb approved the construction of a backup baggage system. At the same time, he notified BAE of a $12,000-a-day penalty for not finishing the baggage system by DIA's original October 29, 1993 completion date. Webb also demanded that BAE pay for the $50 million conventional tug-and-cart baggage system. Gene Di Fonso, President of BAE, knew that his company could demonstrate that flaws in the overall design of the airport and an unsystematic approach to project changes had affected implementation of the integrated baggage system. He wondered whether he should just cancel the contract and cut his losses, or attempt to negotiate with the city for the support required to finish the system as specified, despite the severe deterioration in communication and rising hostility. Could the problems with the automated system be overcome with the dedication of additional resources? Given that the system represented a significant departure from conventional technology, would reducing its size and complexity facilitate resolution of the problems that plagued it? And, if the city could be persuaded to accept a simplified system, would the tenant airlines, particularly those with hubbing operations that had been promised more advanced functionality and better performance, be likely to sue?

Building the Most Efficient Airport in the World

Until about 1970, Denver's Stapleton Airport had managed to accommodate an ever-growing number of airplanes and passengers. Its operational capacity was severely limited by runway layout; Stapleton had two parallel north-south runways and two additional parallel east-west runways that accommodated only commuter air carriers.

Denver's economy grew and expanded greatly in the early 1980s, consequent to booms in the oil, real estate, and tourism industries. An aging and saturated Stapleton Airport was increasingly seen as a liability that limited the attractiveness of the region to the many businesses that were flocking to it. Delays had become chronic. Neither the north-south nor east-west parallel runways had sufficient lateral separation to accommodate simultaneous parallel arrival streams during poor weather conditions when instrument flight rules were in effect. This lack of runway separation and the layout of Stapleton's taxiways tended to cause delays during high-traffic periods, even when weather conditions were good.

Denver's geographic location and the growing size of its population and commerce made it an attractive location for airline hubbing operations. At one point, Stapleton had housed four airline hubs, more than any other airport in the United States. In poor weather and during periods of high-traffic volume, however, its limitations disrupted connection schedules that were important to maintaining these operations. A local storm could easily congest air traffic across the entire United States.[4]

The City and County of Denver had determined in the mid-1970s that Stapleton International Airport was in need of expansion or replacement. In July 1979, a study to assess the airport's needs was commissioned by the City of Denver to the Denver Regional Council of Governments. Upon completion of the study in 1983, a report was issued saying that, due to its size and geographic location, and strong commitments by United and Continental Airlines, Denver would remain a significant hub for at least one major U.S. carrier. The study recommended expansion of Stapleton's capacity.

---

[4]According to James Barnes [1993], "By 1994, Stapleton was one of the top five most constrained airports in the US. There were over 50,000 hours of delay in 1988 and by 1997 the FAA had projected that Stapleton would experience over 100,000 hours of delay per year."

Political Situation.[5] The City of Denver's 1983 mayoral race precipitated initiatives to improve the airfield infrastructure. Three candidates were vying for mayor: Monte Pascoe, Dale Tooley, and Frederico Peña. Pascoe, a prominent Denver attorney and former State Democratic Party co-chair, seized upon the airport issue, forcing other candidates to adopt stronger positions on airport expansion than they might have otherwise.[6] Peña and Tooley, however, drew the highest numbers of votes in the general election, and were forced into a runoff. At the persistent urging of the Colorado Forum (a collection of 50 of the state's top business executives), Peña and Tooley signed a joint statement committing themselves to airport expansion. Peña won the runoff. Committed by a public promise that could have been enforced, if necessary, by the most highly-motivated members of the region's business leadership, Peña immediately restated his intent to expand Stapleton.

The City of Denver and neighboring Adams County began to develop plans for long-term airport development in 1984. In 1985, a new site northeast of Denver was chosen. Consummation of the airport siting issue, however, was left to Adams County voters, which had to vote to permit the City of Denver to annex property therein. The city hired a consulting firm to help organize its resources and its efforts to work through the legal process. The data that was gathered through the master planning and environmental assessment later proved useful for public education.

An "Annexation Agreement" between Adams County and the City of Denver was reached on April 21, 1988. Adams County voters approved a plan to let Denver annex 43.3 square miles for the construction of an airport. In a special election on May 16, 1989, voters of Denver endorsed a "New Airport" by a margin of 62.7% to 37.3%. According to Edmond, "Those two referendums passed largely on the merits of the economic benefits: jobs and sales tax revenues."

Economic Considerations. A number of trends and events in the mid-1980s alarmed bank economists and other of the region's business leaders in the mid-1980s. The collapse of oil shale ventures between 1982 and 1986 saw mining employment fall from 42,000 to 26,000 jobs, while service support jobs fell from 25,300 jobs to 13,700.[7] Construction jobs fell from 50,700 to 36,600 jobs, and the value of private construction plummeted from $24 billion to $9.5 billion.[8]

A lackluster economy led many government officials in counties and municipalities as well as in Denver to embark upon an unprecedented policy of massive public construction to save the region from what was regarded in 1987 as an economic free-fall. A $180 million-plus municipal bond was issued for public improvements, including a new downtown library, neighborhood and major roadway improvements, and a host of overdue infrastructure investments. During the same period, the Peña administration moved decisively to confront an increasingly aggressive Chamber of Commerce leadership that was promoting airport relocation.

The determination of the "pro-New-Airport" clan was growing. The project was being marketed as a technologically advanced, state-of-the-art structure to draw businesses, import federal capital, and fund the creation of new

[5]Extracted from: Moore, S.T.: "Between Growth Machine and Garbage Can: Determining Whether to Expand the Denver Airport, 1982–1988," Annual Meeting of the Southern Political Science Association, Atlanta, Georgia, November 4, 1994.
[6]Ibid.

[7]*Colorado Business Outlook Forum,* University of Colorado School of Business, 1990.
[8]*Small Area Employment Estimates; Construction Review,* U.S. Department of Commerce, 1990

jobs with bonded debts to overcome the short-term decline in the economy. The airport was to become a grandiose project to revive the Colorado economy and a master showcase for the Public Works Department. "The entire business community was behind it," recalled a member of the Mayor's administrative team:

> The Chamber of Commerce, members of the city council, the mayor, and state legislators, participated in informational discussions with other cities that had recently built airports. [This enabled] everybody to understand the magnitude of the project. So we studied the other two airports that had been built in the United States in the last 50 years and said, "Tell us everything that you went through and all the places you think there will be problems." We were not going into it blindly.

Forecasts of aviation activity at Stapleton by the Airport Consultant team, the FAA, and others, however, did not anticipate events such as a new phase of post-deregulation consolidation, the acquisition in 1986 of Frontier Airlines by Texas Air (the owner of Continental), significant increases in air fares for flights in and out of Stapleton, and the bankruptcy of Continental. Consequently, the level of aviation activity in Denver was overestimated. Instead of rising, Stapleton's share of total U.S. domestic passenger enplanements fell 4% per year from 1986 through 1989.[9]

The Master Plan

The City of Denver's approach to preparing a master plan for the airport was typical. "One hires the best consultants on airfield layout, noise impacts, terminal layout, on-site roadways, off-site roadways, cost estimating, finan-

cial analysis, and forecasting," observed DIA administrator Gail Edmond. "They brainstorm and generate as many alternate layouts as possible." Alternatives were discussed and eliminated at periodic joint working sessions, and a technical subcommittee was organized to gather input from the eventual airport users, airlines, pilots, and the FAA. "Everybody knows how to begin an airport master plan," Edmond added.

Following a bidding process, the consulting contract was awarded to the joint venture of Greiner, Inc. and Morrison-Knudsen Engineers for their combined expertise in the fields of transportation and construction. The consulting team, working under the direction of the DIA Director of Aviation, focused first on four elements: site selection; the master plan; the environmental assessment; and developing support by educating the public on economic benefit. The final master plan presented to the city by the team in the fall of 1987 called for the construction of the world's most efficient airport. It was to be created from the ground up with no predetermined limitations.

The plan was to allow the airport to grow and expand without compromising efficiency. Twice the size of Manhattan at 53 square miles, the nation's largest airport was to be designed for steady traffic flow in all weather conditions. It was to comprise a terminal with east and west buildings joined by an atrium structure, three concourses, an automated underground people mover, and five parallel 12,000-foot-long runways on which as many as 1,750 planes could take off and land daily. Its flow-through traffic patterns would allow planes to land, taxi to concourse gates, and take off again all in one direction. The ultimate buildout, projected for the year 2020, was to include up to 12 full service runways, more than 200 gates, and a capacity of 110 million passengers annually. Estimated cost (excluding land acquisition and pre-1990 planning costs) was $2 billion. By the end of

---

[9]Furthermore, when selling the project to voters, planners at one point forecast up to 36 weekly flights to Europe by 1993. The number recorded in 1993, however, was four. The number of passengers departing from Denver was to rise from 16 million in 1985 to some 26 million by 1995. The 1994 figure, however, was about the same as the number of passengers in 1985, or half of Stapleton's capacity.

1991, the estimated cost had increased to $2.66 billion. Plans called for the project's completion by the fall of 1993.

In September 1989, federal officials signed a $60 million grant agreement for the new airport, which was to be financed in multiple ways—by issuing revenue bonds and securing federal grants—supplemented by a sizable investment by the city [county of Denver 1991]. Estimated federal grants for the new airport originally totaled $501 million. Portions of these were forthcoming from the FAA, for federal fiscal year 1990 in the amount of $90 million and for federal fiscal year 1991 in the amount of $25 million. The remainder of the $501 million letter of intent was to be received on an annual basis through fiscal year 1997. The revenue bonds assumed the "Date of Beneficial Occupancy" (DBO) to be January 1, 1994, with bond repayments to begin on that date. At that time, the city determined that DIA would meet the DBO no later than October 31, 1993. A member of the Mayor's administrative team described the approach.

> What we did was plan the DBO date and then we planned an extra six months just in case there was a lag in the opening, which, in essence, allowed us to create stability in the market. The other thing we did was that we conservatively financed and filled every reserve account to the maximum. So we borrowed as much money as we could at the lower interest rate and were able to average the debt cost down, not up, as we thought it would be.

A Build-Design Project. By the time construction began at DIA in November 1989, a transfer of authority was taking place in the City of Denver. Wellington Webb was elected the new mayor. According to one of his assistants, the Peña administration had announced that the airport would be operational in October 1993. "This was a build-design project, which means that we were building the airport [while] we were designing it," he explained. "Because of the delays early on in

the project, we had to accelerate construction immediately. There was a lot of pressure and too many players. This was an airport built by committee. We had regular meetings to straighten things out, but it didn't always work."

Although the Webb administration inherited the airport project without a commitment on the part of the major carriers, the support and input of concerned airlines were absolutely key, not only financially but also in terms of input on overall airport layout, scope, and capacity, and supporting systems such as fueling and baggage handling. Denver launched the DIA program without specific commitments from either of Stapleton airport's two major tenant airlines, United and Continental, which together accounted for more than 70% of existing passenger traffic. Continental committed to the new airport in February 1990, United in December 1991. Fundamental changes were made to the airport layout plan and facilities (some already under construction) to accommodate the operational needs of these carriers.

The Webb administration followed the predecessor administration's emphasis on assuring that the project's greatest beneficiaries would be local businesses. The desire was to involve as many individual firms as practicable and to use Denver area talent. It was reasoned that local talent was easily accessible to the program management team (PMT), knew Denver building codes and practices, and had available the necessary professional labor pool to accomplish the design in accordance with the demanding schedule. In addition, existing law stated that 30% minority-owned firms and 6% women-owned firms had to participate in a public works program. The result was a contracting philosophy that maximized opportunities for regional businesses and the local workforce to compete for the work. At least five of 60 contracts awarded for the design of DIA went to Denver-area firms.

These 60 design contracts generated 110 construction contracts. Eighty-eight professional service contracts also had to be coordinated. Many local firms had to be hired and the program was chopped up into many small projects. Involvement totaled 200 to 300 firms and reached 400 during the construction phase. Five different firms designed the runways, four the terminal. The city's emphasis on encouraging everyone to compete and yet be part of the project increased the potential for interface and coordination problems.

Denver's flat economy led the administration to keep construction money within the city. Although this benefited the city, it introduced an additional burden on administration. As many as 40 to 50 concurrent contracts involved many interrelated milestones and contiguous or overlapping operational areas. The estimated daily on-site work force population exceeded 2,500 workers for a 15- to 18-month period beginning in mid-1991 and peaked at between 9,000 and 10,000 in mid-1992. Adding to the human resource coordination problems was a forecasted 4,000 deliveries daily. Construction volume for six months in mid-1992 exceeded $100 million per month.

The prolonged period of assessment and negotiation prior to final approval of the project, and the financial plan selected (which required that bond repayments begin on January 1, 1994), pressured the PMT to push the project ahead at all cost. Because the project had to assume the characteristics of a "fast-track" project early in the construction startup, the compressed design period precipitated a more dynamic construction effort than might be anticipated for a "competitively bid, fixed price" program. Reliance on a design/build method for the project was, according to one DIA official, "unusual because projects this complex normally happen during separate stages. For example, you need to finish up the site selection before you begin the master planning."

Moreover, communication channels between the city, project management team, and consultants were neither well defined or controlled. "If a contractor fell behind," a resident engineer who reported to one of the area managers said,

> the resident engineer would alert the contractor and document this. The resident engineer would document what would have to be done and what additional resources were necessary to get back on schedule and finish the contract on time. As a public agency, the amount of documentation that we did was enormous. I don't know how many trees we cut down just for this project. The resident engineer had about five to eight 12-drawer filing cabinets of documentation and this was nothing compared to what the area manager had. It was just incredible. There were at least four to six copies of everything.

The scheduling manager described the evolution of the tracking system that was used.

> One of the biggest problems we had was keeping track of all the changes. So we developed a database system that was installed at each one of the resident engineer's trailers and each contract administrator was then charged with keeping that system up to date and feeding us disks, which we would then merge together periodically to produce an integrated report. But every party had developed their own tracking system before the start of the project. That worked well for each group, but there was no way to take each one of these divergent systems and combine it into one, comprehensive report. So when we introduced the change tracking system everybody said, "fine, that's wonderful, and I'll update it when I get to it and when I get time." It took three years to implement the tracking system.

Project Management. In a fast-moving, ever-changing environment such as the development of a new airport, the management structure must be able to rapidly produce engineering alternatives and the supporting cost and schedule data.[10] But because DIA was financed by many sources and was a public

---

[10]The DIA project used the so-called "fast-tracking" method, which made it possible to compress some activities along the critical path and manage the construction project as a series of overlapping tasks.

works program, project administrators had to balance administrative, political, and social imperatives.[11]

The City of Denver staff and consultant team shared leadership of the project and coordinated the initial facets of DIA design. "The initial thought," reflected one staff member, "was that the city staff would do their thing and the consulting staff do theirs and later we would coordinate. It became evident within a very short time that we were doing duplicate duties, which was inefficient. Finally the city decided to coordinate resources."

The city selected a team of city employees and consultants and drafted a work scope document that clearly separated the city's from the consultants' responsibilities. The elements the city did not delegate to consultants included ultimate policy and facility decisions, approval of payments, negotiation and execution of contracts, facilitation of FAA approvals, affirmative action, settlement of contractor claims and disputes, selection of consultants, and utility agreements. The city delegated some elements such as value engineering, construction market analysis, claim management, on-site staff and organization, and state-of-the-art project control (computerized management of budget and schedule). Exhibit 1 depicts the DIA management structure.

The program management team became the organization dedicated to overseeing planning and development for the new airport. Headed by the associate director of aviation, the team was partially staffed by city career service employees. To add experience and capability, the city augmented the PMT with personnel from the joint venture of Greiner Engineering and Morrison-Knudsen Engi-

neers, the consulting team. Observed one program management team member, "This working partnership of the City of Denver and consulting joint venture team developed into a fully integrated single organization, capitalizing on the best to be offered by all participants, and optimizing the use of personnel resources."

DIA's operational project structure comprised five different areas subdivided into smaller units. The working areas were: site development (earthmoving, grading, and drainage); roadways and on-grade parking (service roads, on-airport roads, and off-airport roads connecting to highways); airfield paving; building design (people-mover/baggage-handler, tunnel, concourses, passenger bridge, terminal, and parking); and utility/special systems and other facilities (electrical transmission, oil, and gas line removal and relocation). An area manager controlled construction within each area. Area managers were responsible for the administration of all assigned contracts and, in coordination with other area managers, for management of the portion of the overall site in which their work took place.

United Airlines' Baggage System

From the public's perspective, the "friendliness" of any airport is measured by time. No matter how architecturally stimulating a new airport structure, the perception of business or leisure travelers is often registered in terms of efficiency in checking luggage at the departure area or waiting to claim a bag in the arrival area. The larger the airport, the more critical the efficient handling of baggage. Remote concourses connected by underground tunnels present special problems for airport planners and operators because of the great distances passengers and baggage must travel. The purpose of an airport being to move passengers as efficiently as possible, moving bags quickly is part and parcel of that

---

[11]These included considerations such as affirmative action, local participation, neighborhood concerns, civic pride, input from the disabled community, art, secondary employment benefits of contract packaging, concern for the environment, and political interest.

EXHIBIT 1   Organization Chart

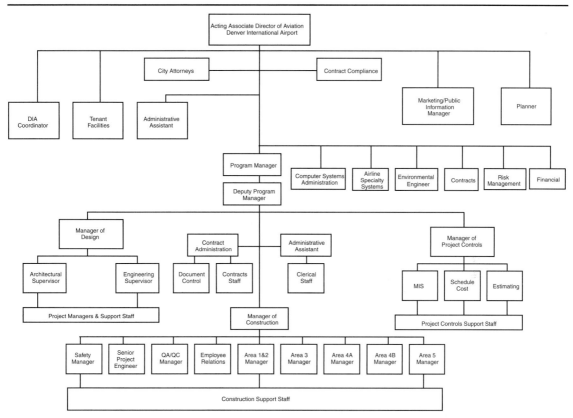

Source: City and County of Denver, Colorado, Airport System Review Bonds, Series 1991D, October 1991.

responsibility. Rapid transport of frequent flyers accomplishes very little if bags are left behind.

DIA's Concourse A, which was to house Continental Airlines, was situated some 400 meters, and United Airlines' Concourse B nearly 1,000 meters, north of the main terminal. Concourse C, home to other carriers including American, Delta, Northwest, America West, and TWA, sat parallel to the other two concourses more than 1,600 meters north of the main terminal. The initial project design did not incorporate an airport-wide baggage system; the airport expected the individual airlines to build their own systems as in most other American airports.[12] United Airlines, which in June 1991 signed on to use DIA as its second-largest hub airport, proceeded to do just that.

Needing an automated baggage handling system if it was to turn aircraft around in less than 30 minutes, United, in December 1991, commissioned BAE Automatic Systems, Inc., a world leader in the design and implementation of material handling systems, to develop an automated baggage handling system for its B Concourse at DIA. The contract, which

---

[12]Rifkin, G.: "What Really Happened at Denver's Airport," *Forbes,* SAP Supplement, August 29, 1994.

included engineering and early parts procurement only, was valued at $20 million; and the task was estimated to be completed in two and one-half years. "We began working at DIA under a contract directly with United Airlines," recalled Di Fonso. "Obviously, United Airlines has experience with airports. They concluded that the schedule had gotten totally out of control from the standpoint of baggage and they acted to serve their own needs, basically to protect themselves. We contracted with United and were already designing their portion of the system before the city went out for competitive bidding."

BAE was founded as a division of Docutel Corporation in 1968. Docutel, which had developed the Telecar (a track-mounted automated baggage system), constructed an automated baggage system for United Airlines at San Francisco airport in 1978. When Docutel ran into financial difficulties during this installation, United asked Boeing, a major supplier of its aircraft, to take over the company. Boeing agreed and the new company, a wholly-owned subsidiary dubbed Boeing Airport Equipment, completed the San Francisco installation. In 1982, Boeing sold the company to its senior management, which renamed it BAE Automated Systems. In August 1985, BAE became an operating unit of Clarkson Industries, a wholly-owned subsidiary of London-based BTR plc. BTR plc (formerly British Tire and Rubber), was a $10 billion conglomerate with global interests in building, paper and printing products, and agricultural and aircraft equipment.

In 1994, BAE's 365 employees worked on projects across the United States and in Europe and Australia. In-house engineering, manufacturing, and field support capabilities enabled BAE to develop, design, manufacture, install, and support every project it undertook from start to finish. BAE also provided consulting, engineering, and management services for airport projects and a variety of material handling applications.

With sales of $100 million in 1994, up from approximately $40 million in 1991, BAE accounted for 90% of U.S. baggage sorting equipment sales. Between 1972 and 1994, the company had successfully designed, manufactured, and installed nearly 70 automated baggage handling systems (worth almost $500 million dollars) at major airports in the United States, in New York, Dallas-Fort Worth, Chicago, San Francisco, Atlanta, Miami, Newark, and Pittsburgh. It had also installed systems in Vancouver and London and was selected, in 1992, as a consultant to the $550 million main terminal for the New Seoul Metropolitan Airport in South Korea.

BAE was a very self-contained, integrated company structured along two business lines: manufacturing and engineering. Its approximately 200,000 square foot manufacturing facility was capable of producing nearly all of the components required by BAE systems save motors, gearboxes, and bearings. The engineering department was structured according to major projects. Each project was assigned a project manager who reported directly to the company president.

Implementing an Integrated Baggage-Handling System

BAE had already commenced work on United's baggage system when the PMT recognized the potential benefits of an airport-wide integrated baggage system. Moreover, as one DIA senior manager explained, "airlines other than United simply were not coming forward with plans to develop their own baggage systems." Airport planners and consultants began to draw up specifications and the city sent out a request for bids. Of 16 companies contacted, both in the United States and abroad, only three responded. A consulting firm recommended against the submitted designs, on the grounds that the configurations would not meet the airport's needs.

BAE was among the companies that had decided not to bid for the job. BAE had installed the Telecar system at a number of other airports and the basic technologies of the Telecar, laser barcode readers, and conveyor belt systems were not new. What was new was the size and complexity of the system. "A grand airport like DIA needs a complex baggage system," explained Di Fonso,

> Therefore the type of technology to be used for such a system is the kind of decision that must be made very early in a project. If there is a surprise like no bidders there is still time to react. At DIA, this never happened. Working with United Airlines, we had concluded that destination-coded vehicles moving at high speed was the technology needed. But quite honestly, although we had that technology developed, its implementation in a complex project like this would have required significantly greater time than the city had left available.

A United project manager concurred: "BAE told them from the beginning that they were going to need at least one more year to get the system up and running, but no one wanted to hear that." The City of Denver was getting the same story from the technical advisers to the Franz Josef Strauss Airport in Munich. The Munich Airport had an automated baggage system, but one far less complex than DIA's. Nevertheless, Munich's technical advisors had spent two years testing the system and the system had been running 24 hours a day for six months before the airport opened.

Formulating Intentions. As BAE was already working on United's automated baggage handling system and enjoyed a world-wide reputation as a superior baggage system builder, Denver approached the company. BAE was asked to study how the United concept could be expanded into an integrated airport system that could serve the other carriers in the various concourses. BAE presented the City of Denver with a proposal to develop the "most

complex automated baggage system ever built," according to Di Fonso. It was to be effective in delivering bags to and from passengers, and efficient in terms of operating reliability, maintainability, and future flexibility. The system was to be capable of directing bags (including suitcases of all sizes, skis, and golf clubs) from the main terminal through a tunnel into a remote concourse and directly to a gate. Such efficient delivery would save precious ground time, reduce close-out time for hub operations, and cut time-consuming manual baggage sorting and handling.

Although an automated system was more expensive initially than simple tugs and baggage carts, it was expected that it would reduce the manpower which was required to distribute bags to the correct locations. Bags unloaded from an aircraft arriving at a particular concourse would barely be touched by human hands. Moved through the airport at speeds up to 20 mph, they would be waiting when passengers arrived at the terminal. To prove the capability of its mechanical aspects, and demonstrate the proposed system to the airlines and politicians, BAE built a prototype automated baggage handling system in a 50,000 square foot warehouse near its manufacturing plant in Carrollton, Texas. The prototype system convinced Chief Airport Engineer Walter Slinger that the automated system would work. "[The City of Denver] approached us based on one core concept," recalled Di Fonso. "They wanted to have a fully integrated, airport-wide baggage system. The city had two major concerns. First, they had no acceptable proposal. Second, United was probably going to go ahead and build what it needed and the rest of the airport would have been equipped with something else." Di Fonso continued,

> When we arrived on the scene, we were faced with fully defined project specs, which obviously in the long run proved to be a major planning error. The city had fallen into a trap, which historically architects and

engineers tend to fall into as they severely underplay the importance and significance of some of the requirements of a baggage system, that is, arranging things for the space into which it must fit, accommodating the weight it may impose on the building structure, the power it requires to run, and the ventilation and air conditioning that may be necessary to dissipate the heat it generates.

In April 1992, BAE was awarded the $175.6 million contract to build the entire airport system. According to Di Fonso, company executives and city officials hammered out a deal in three intense working sessions. "We placed a number of conditions on accepting the job," he observed.

> The design was not to be changed beyond a given date and there would be a number of freeze dates for mechanical design, software design, permanent power requirements and the like. The contract made it obvious that both signatory parties were very concerned about the ability to complete on time. The provisions dealt mostly with all-around access, timely completion of certain areas, provision of permanent power, provision of computer rooms. All these elements were delineated as milestones.

Denver officials accepted these requirements and, in addition, committed to unrestricted access for BAE equipment. Because of the tight deadlines, BAE would have priority in any area where it needed to install the system. Di Fonso elaborated,

> When we entered into the contract, Continental Airlines was still under bankruptcy law protection. The city was very concerned that they would be unable to pay for their concourse. They only contracted for about 40% of the equipment that is now in concourse A, which was the concourse that Continental had leased. Beyond that, concourse C had no signatory airlines as leaseholders at the time. The city, therefore, wanted the simplest, most elementary baggage system possible for concourse C. The outputs and inputs were very, very crude, intentionally crude to keep the costs down because the city had no assurance of revenue stream at that point in time. The city did not get the airlines together or ask them what they wanted or needed to operate. The approach was more along the lines of "we will build the apartment building and then you come in and rent a set of rooms."

Project Organization and Management. No major organizational changes to accommodate the new baggage system were deemed necessary, although some managerial adjustments were made on the DIA project. Design of the United baggage system was frozen on May 15, 1992, when the PMT assumed managerial responsibility for the integrated baggage system. The direct relationship with BAE was delegated to Working Area 4, which also had responsibility for building design efforts such as the people-mover, airside concourse building, passenger bridge main landside building complex and parking garage, and various other smaller structures. The area manager, although he had no experience in airport construction, baggage system technologies, or the introduction of new technologies, possessed vast experience in construction project control management.

BAE had to change its working structure to conform to DIA's project management structure. Di Fonso explained,

> There was a senior manager for each of the concourses and a manager for the main terminal. The bag system, however, traversed all of them. If I had to argue a case for right of way I would have to go to all the managers because I was traversing all four empires. In addition, because changes were happening fast at each of these sites, there was no time to have an information system to see what is concourse A deciding and what is concourse B deciding. We had to be personally involved to understand what was going on. There was no one to tie it all together and overlap all these effects because the basic organization was to manage it as discrete areas. It was pandemonium. We would keep saying that over and over again. Who is in charge?

For the first two years of the project, Di Fonso was the project manager. The project was divided into three general areas of expertise: mechanical engineering, industrial control, and software design. Mechanical engineering was responsible for all mechanical components and their installation, industrial control for industrial control design, logic controller programming, and motor control panels, and software design for writing real-time process control software to manage the system.

At the time the contract with BAE was signed, construction had already begun on the terminal and concourses. Substantial changes had to be made to the overall design of the terminal and some construction already completed had to be taken out and reinstalled to accommodate the expanded system. Installation of the expanded system was initially estimated to require more than $100 million in construction work. Walls had to be removed and a new floor installed in the terminal building to support the new system. Moreover, major changes in project governance were taking place during the baggage system negotiations. In May 1992, shortly after the baggage system negotiations commenced, the head of the DIA project resigned.

The death in October 1992 of Chief Airport Engineer Slinger, who had been a strong proponent of the baggage system and closely involved in negotiations with BAE, also exerted a significant impact on the project. His cooperation had been essential because of the amount of heavy machinery and track that had to be moved and installed and the amount of construction work required to accommodate the system. His replacement, Gail Edmond, was selected because she had worked closely with him and knew all the players. Her managerial style, however, was quite different from Slinger's. A Public Works manager recalled his first reaction to the change: "[The airport] is not going to be open on time." A United Airlines project manager summarized Edmond's challenge thus:

> Slinger was a real problem solver. He was controversial because of his attitude, but he was never afraid to address problems. He had a lot of autonomy and could get things done. Gail was in a completely different position. Basically, she had a good understanding of how the project was organized and who the key players were, but didn't know much about the actual construction. Also, the city council didn't give her anywhere near the autonomy and the authority that

Slinger had and she had to get approval from the council on just about all decisions. They really tied her hands and everyone knew it.

Di Fonso echoed the project manager's assessment:

> Walter [Slinger] understood that one of the things we had to have was unrestricted access. I think he clearly understood the problem the city was facing and he understood the short timeframe under which we were operating. He was the one that accepted all of the contractual conditions, all the milestones of the original contract. He really had no opportunity to influence the outcome of this project, however, because he died within months after the contract was signed. I think Gail did an excellent job [but] she was overwhelmed.[13] She just had too much. The layers below focused inward, worrying about their own little corners of the world.

"Not only did we not get the unrestricted access that was agreed upon," Di Fonso emphasized, "we didn't even have reasonable access." Ten days after Slinger's death, a BAE millwright found a truck from Hensel Phelps, the contractor building Concourse C, blocking her work site. She asked someone to move the truck or leave the keys so it could be moved. According to a BAE superintendent, "she was told that 'This is not a BAE job and we can park anywhere we please: is that clear?'" Elsewhere, BAE electricians had to leave work areas where concrete grinders were creating clouds of dust. Fumes from chemical sealants forced other BAE workers to flee. Di Fonso pleaded with the city for help. "We ask that the city take prompt action to assure BAE the ability to continue its work in an uninterrupted manner," he wrote. "Without the city's help, the delays to BAE's work will quickly become unrecoverable."[14]

To further complicate matters, the airlines began requesting changes to the system's

---

[13]In addition to her role as Chief Airport Engineer, Edmond kept her previous responsibilities as Chief of Construction and Acting Director of Aviation.
[14]*Rocky Mountain News,* January 29, 1995

design even though the mechanical and software designs were supposed to be frozen. "Six months prior to opening the airport," Di Fonso recalled, "we were still moving equipment around, changing controls, changing software design."

In August 1992, for example, United altered plans for a transfer system for bags changing planes, requesting that BAE eliminate an entire loop of track from Concourse B. Rather than two complete loops of track, United would have only one. This change saved approximately $20 million, but required a system redesign. Additional ski-claim devices and odd-size baggage elevators added in four of the six sections of the terminal added $1.61 million to the cost of the system. One month later, Continental requested that automated baggage sorting systems be added to its west basement at an additional cost of $4.67 million. The ski claim area length was first changed from 94 feet to 127 feet, then in January 1993, shortened to 112 feet. The first change added $295,800, the second subtracted $125,000, from the cost. The same month, maintenance tracks were added to permit the Telecars to be serviced without having to lift them off the main tracks at an additional cost of $912,000. One year later, United requested alterations to its odd-size baggage inputs—cost of the change: $432,000.

Another problem was the city's inability to supply "clean" electricity to the baggage system. The motors and circuitry used in the system were extremely sensitive to power surges and fluctuations. When electrical feedback tripped circuit breakers on hundreds of motors, an engineer was called in to design filters to correct the problem. Although ordered at that time, the filters still had not arrived several months later. A city worker had canceled a contract without realizing that the filters were part of it. The filters finally arrived in March 1994.

A third, albeit disputed, complication related to Denver's requirement, and city law, that a certain percentage of jobs be contracted to minority-owned companies. The City of Denver had denied BAE's original contract because it did not comply with hiring requirements, where upon BAE engaged some outside contractors in lieu of BAE employees. Di Fonso estimated that this increased costs by approximately $6 million, a claim rejected by the Mayor's Office of Contract Compliance. Then, in September 1993, BAE's contract negotiations with the City of Denver over maintenance of the system resulted in a two-day strike of 300 millwrights that was joined by some 200 electricians. BAE negotiated with Denver for maintenance workers to earn $12 per hour on certain jobs that the union contended should be worth $20 per hour. As a result, BAE lost the maintenance contract.

Project Relations. Much of the effort for implementing the baggage system was directed within one of the four working areas. "The relationship with the management team was very poor," recalled Di Fonso.

> The management team had no prior baggage handling competence or experience. This was treated as a major public works project. The management team treated the baggage system as similar to pouring concrete or putting in air-conditioning ducts. When we would make our complaints about delays and access and so forth, other contractors would argue their position. The standard answer was, "Go work it out among yourselves." . . . With contractors basically on their own, this led almost to anarchy. Everyone was doing his or her own thing.

Another perspective was offered by a project manager from Stone & Webster, a consultant to the PMT, reflecting on the work done by BAE: "This contractor simply did not respond to the obvious incredible workload they were faced with. Their inexperienced project management vastly underestimated their task. Their work ethic was deplorable."[15] PMT man-

---

[15]*Forbes,* ASAP Supplement, August 29, 1994.

agement insisted that access and mechanical issues weren't the problem. "They were running cars in Concourse B all summer (1993)," Edmund observed. "The problem was that the programming was not done and BAE had full control of the programming."[16]

Lawsuits and a Backup Baggage System

In February 1993, Mayor Webb delayed the scheduled October 1993 airport opening to December 19, 1993. Later, this December date was changed to March 9, 1994. "Everybody got into the panic mode of trying to get to this magical date that nobody was ready for," a senior vice-president for BAE recalled. In September 1993, the opening was again postponed—this time until May 15, 1994. In late April 1994, the City of Denver invited reporters to observe the first test of the baggage system, without notifying BAE. Seven thousand bags were to be moved to Continental's Concourse A and United's Concourse B. So many problems were discovered that testing had to be halted. Reporters saw piles of disgorged clothes and other personal items lying beneath the Telecar's tracks.

Most of the problems related to errors in the system's computer software, but mechanical problems also played a part. The software that controlled the delivery of empty cars to the terminal building, for example, often sent the cars back to the waiting pool. Another problem was "jam logic" software, which was designed to shut down a section of track behind a jammed car, but instead shut down an entire loop of track. Optical sensors designed to detect and monitor cars were dirty causing the system to believe that a section of track was empty when, in fact, it had held a stopped car. Collisions between cars dumped baggage on tracks and on the floor; jammed cars jumped the track and bent the rails; faulty

---

[16]*Forbes,* ASAP Supplement, August 29, 1994.

switches caused the Telecars to dump luggage onto the tracks or against the walls of the tunnels.

After the test, Mayor Webb delayed the airport's opening yet again, this time indefinitely. "Clearly, the automated baggage system now underway at DIA is not yet at a level that meets the requirements of the city, the airlines, or the traveling public," the mayor stated. The city set the costs of the delay at $330,000 per month. Recognizing that his reputation was staked on his ability to have a baggage system performing to a point at which the new airport could be opened, Mayor Webb engaged, in May 1994, the German firm Logplan to assess the state of the automated baggage system. In July, Logplan isolated a loop of track that contained every feature of the automated baggage system and intended to run it for an extended period to test the reliability of the Telecars. Jams on the conveyor belts and collisions between cars caused the test to be halted. The system did not run long enough to determine if there was a basic design flaw or to analyze where the problems were. Logplan recommended construction of a backup baggage system, and suggested using Rapistan Demag, a firm it had worked with in the past. Construction of a backup system was announced in August 1994. The system itself cost $10.5 million, but electrical upgrades and major building modifications raised the projected cost to $50 million.

In the meantime, the City of Denver, as well as many major airlines, hired legal firms to assist with negotiations and future litigation. "We will have enough legal action for the rest of this century," a city administrator mused. The City of Denver had to communicate with such parties as the United States Federal grand jury, Securities Exchange Commission, and the General Accounting Office. The federal grand jury was conducting a general investigation concerning DIA. The SEC was investigating the sale of $3.2 billion in bonds to finance DIA's construction, and GAO the use of Congressional funds.

Di Fonso, reviewing Mayor Webb's letter and requests that BAE pay a $12,000-a-day penalty for missing DIA's original October 29, 1993 completion date, as well as assuming the costs of building the $50 million conventional tug-and-cart baggage system, summed up the situation thus: "We have gotten to the point with the city that literally we are not talking to each other. Consultants recommended a backup baggage system, and the minute that the decision was made, the city had to defend it. We are left out in limbo."

CASE 4–3
CISCO SYSTEMS ARCHITECTURE: ERP AND WEB-ENABLED IT[1]

Cisco CEO John Chamber's vision of a "New World Network"—where voice calls over the Internet will be free—is as far-reaching as Microsoft Chairman Bill Gates' decade-ago vision of "information at your finger tips, with a computer on every desk and in every home."

The vision is core to our perception of the marketplace. We carry these cards in our wallets with our goal printed on them: "Internet experts: the Global Internet Company".

—Pete Solvik Cisco CIO

Founded by two Stanford computer scientists in 1984 and brought public in 1990, Cisco Systems, Inc. dominated the exploding "Internetworking" market. In 1997—its first year on the Fortune 500—Cisco ranked in the top five companies in return on revenues and return on assets. (See Exhibit 1 for Cisco's

financial performance). Only two other companies, Intel and Microsoft, had matched this feat. On July 17, 1998, just 14 years after being founded, Cisco's market capitalization passed the significant $100 billion mark. Less than two years later, on March 27, 2000, Cisco overtook Microsoft as the most valuable business on earth with a market cap of $531 billion.

Cisco's core technology began with routers. Routers are what make the Internet work. They act as multilingual translators tying the disparate computer networks of the world together on the Internet, in much the same way that telephone networks in different countries pass calls to each other.

Cisco was at the forefront of challenging a world of three independent proprietary networks: (1) the phone networks for voice, (2) the local area and wide area networks for data, and (3) the broadcast networks for video. Digitization enabled the convergence of the three networks on the Internet, whereby the Internet acted as a global network of networks. The Internet (as a single network) made it possible to transmit voice, data, and video in a more efficient and economical manner than transmitting these signals over the three independent and proprietary networks. The Internet and its open

---

[1]This case was prepared by Research Associates Kelley A. Porter and Christina Akers, Professor Richard L. Nolan with assistance from Christina L. Darwall. This case also draws on *Cisco Systems Inc.: Implementing ERP,* (HBS No 699-022). Revised March 24, 1999. Copyright © 2001 by the President and Fellows of Harvard College. Harvard Business School Case 301-099.

EXHIBIT 1 Financials and Other Cisco Statistics

Year ending (Fiscal year runs September–August)	2000	1999	1998	1997	1996	1995
Net Sales (m)	$ 18,928[a]	$ 12,154	$ 8,459	$ 6,440	$ 4,096	$ 1,979
Income before provisions for income taxes (m)	$ 4,343[a]	$ 3,316	$ 2,302	$ 1,889	$ 1,465	$ 679
Net Income (m)	$ 2,668[a]	$ 2,096	$ 1,350	$ 1,048	$ 913	$ 412
Common Equity — Total (m)	$ 26,497[a]	$ 11,678	$ 7,107	$ 4,290	$ 2,820	$ 1,379
Total Assets (m)	$ 32,870[a]	$ 14,725	$ 8,917	$ 5,452	$ 3,630	$ 1,757
Stock price (at close of fiscal year)	$ 61.75[b]	$30.81	$ 15.958	48.84	$5.75	$ 3.097
Number of employees	31,140	21,000	15,000	11,000	8,782	4.086
Net sales per employee	$607,835	$578,762	$563,918	$585,470	$466,490	$546,415
Net income per employee	$485,678	$ 99,809	$ 90,005	$ 95,334	$103,999	$111,720

[a]www.cisco.com, August 28, 2000
[b]www.bloomberg.com, August 28, 2000
Source: Compustat, except for:

standards created a new competitive battle-ground for the entrenched telecommunications (telecom) players including AT&T, Verizon (GTE & Bell Atlantic), British Telecom, and Deutsche Telecom.

Challengers to the incumbents have spear-headed their attacks through the Internet by offering services such as Internet access, hosting, extranets, e-mail, and search capabilities. Many—including UUNet, PSINET, GTE/BBN, and over 5,000 other Internet Service Providers (ISPs)—were competing on price in providing fax, messaging, and electronic data interchange (EDI).[2]

All of this activity signaled the acceleration of the trend to Internet Protocol (IP)-based networks. This market did not exist three to five years ago. In 2000, more than 275 million people were on the Internet and it was projected to be more than a billion by 2005. More than 75% of all Internet traffic traveled over Cisco products. It was estimated that in the United States in 2001, data network traffic exceeded voice network traffic.

Lucent Technologies had not stood idle since its 1996 spin-off from AT&T. In 2001, Lucent Technologies was the leader for telecom gear with 2001 revenues of $33.8 million and a market capitalization of $60.1 million. As phone companies shifted their traffic from overstretched networks, which were designed to carry voice versus the 0s and 1s of computers, Lucent had been remaking itself to transition with its customers.

IP-based networks had cost advantages over traditional phone networks. In addition, the new IP-based technology providers, such as Cisco, were better equipped to address performance and security issues due to their constant influx of venture capital and talent. Many of the IP-based technology companies benefited from being located in Silicon Valley where there was

an incredible spirit of innovation in both technology and management. Juniper Networks competed directly with Cisco by providing next generation Internet backbone routers that were specifically designed for service providers. Juniper Networks floated their IPO on June 25, 1999, and with revenues of about $100 million had a market value of $2.1 billion. Juniper's 2000 revenues were $673.5 million and they had a market capitalization of over $40 billion in January 2001.[3]

But neither Cisco nor Lucent had the products they needed to ensure a big win, nor did any of the other network companies including Northern Telecom (Nortel), Bay Networks (now a part of Nortel), or 3Com.[4] All of the network companies were racing to develop a new hybrid product that would have the speed and efficiency of a router and the precision of a telephone switch—a switched router or a routing switch.

The Top Management Team at Cisco

The two founders of Cisco were long on innovation acumen. Don Valentine, partner of Sequoia Capital and vice chairman of the Board of Cisco[5] was the initial venture capitalist who invested in Cisco; believing that Cisco would be a success, he took a chance when other venture capitalists were more cautious. Valentine wanted to protect his initial $2.5 million investment thus he reserved the right to bring in professional management when he deemed it appropriate.

---

[2]McKinsey 1997 Report on the Computer Industry, pp. 1–55.

[3]OneSource, February 2001.
[4]Nortel acquired Bay Networks in June 1998 for $9.1 billion in stock. At the time, Nortel had annual revenue of $15.4 billion, and a market value of $28 billion compared to Cisco's annual revenue of $6.4 billion and a market value of $85 billion.
[5]Don Valentine was previously the outside executive Chairman of the Board of Cisco. Cisco has maintained its Chairman of the Board as an outside director. Currently, John Morgridge serves as an outside director and Chairman of the Board.

In 1988, Valentine hired John Morgridge as Cisco's CEO. Morgridge, an experienced executive in the computer industry who had worked at Grid Systems, Stratus Computers, and Honeywell, immediately began to build a professional management team. This team soon clashed with the founders, and after Cisco's IPO in 1990, both founders sold all of their stock and left the company. Some observers felt that this early exit of the founders provided a receptive environment for laying the groundwork for disciplined management, which in turn let the company capitalize on market opportunities and grow at a phenomenal rate without derailing its focus or losing control.

Morgridge believed that many Silicon Valley firms decentralized too quickly. He felt that many companies did not appreciate that the functional organizational structure had a proven ability to scale during levels of rapid growth without sacrificing control. Accordingly, Morgridge maintained a centralized functional organization at Cisco that still existed in 2001. Although product marketing and R&D were decentralized into three "Lines of Business" (Enterprise, Small/Medium Business, and Service Provider), the manufacturing, customer support, finance, human resources, information technology (IT) and the sales organizations remained centralized. For example, the only responsibility of each sales country manager was to sell the three market segment products. They were not responsible for non-sales activities (e.g., accounting, IT, manufacturing, etc.) within a country or geography. There was a belief within Cisco that consistency of strategy, goals, organization, and management provided a huge stable benefit to a fast growing, fast moving company.

Cisco's Business Strategy

In 1991 Morgridge hired John Chambers from Wang Laboratories (Chambers had also worked for IBM for six years), and turned over the duties of CEO to Chambers in 1995. Morgridge reflected: "When Chambers took over, Cisco never lost a beat."[6] Chambers continued to execute a plan that he jointly created with Ed Kozel, chief technical officer, and Morgridge in 1993. The plan consists of four elements:[7]

1. *Assemble a broad product line so Cisco can serve as one-stop shopping for business networks.* Exhibit 2 shows how information is routed through the Internet; Cisco's revenues and market shares for those products are also stated.

2. *Systematize acquisitions as an efficient business process.* Cisco had made more than 70 acquisitions and key strategic alliances since 1993 to fill out its product line.

3. *Set industry-wide software standards for networking.* Cisco has issued IOS (Internetwork Operating System) licenses to Alcatel, Ericcson, Northern Telecom, Compaq, Hewlett-Packard (HP), Bay Networks, 3Com, Microsoft, Intel and 12 Japanese companies.

4. *Pick the right strategic partners.* Cisco was working with Microsoft to create an industry standard for security over the network, with MCI to deliver premium Internet services, and with HP to develop and sell Internet-based corporate computing systems built with each other's products.

If Chambers could successfully execute on this four-point plan, he believed that Cisco would be the lead architect and provider of technologies for the new Internet-based

---

[6]Geoff Baum, "Cisco's CEO: John Chambers," *Forbes ASAP,* February 23, 1998, p. 52.
[7]Brent Schlender, "Computing's Next Superpower," *Fortune,* May 12, 1997, p. 88.

EXHIBIT 2 How Information Is Routed through the Internet

Main Office → LAN Adapter Card (Not a Cisco product) → Work-group LAN switch → Back-bone LAN switch → WAN Switch → High-end Router → Low-end Router → Hub → LAN Adapter Card (Not Cisco products) → Branch Office

High-end Router → Mid-range router → Remote-access dial-up port → Modem (Not a Cisco product) → Home

High-end Routers
1999 Revenue:
$2,000,000,000
#1 in market;
88% market share

Mid-range Routers
1999 Revenue:
$1,400,000,000
#1 in market;
80% market share

Low-end Routers
1999 Revenue
$1,800,000,000
#1 in market;
72% market share

WAN Switches
1999 Revenue:
$873,000,000
#3 in market;
22% market share

Shared Hubs and LAN Switches
1999 Revenue: $4,800,000,000
#1 in market; 41% market share

Remote Access
1999 Revenue:
$1,100,000,000
#1 in market;
21% market share

How information is routed through the Internet

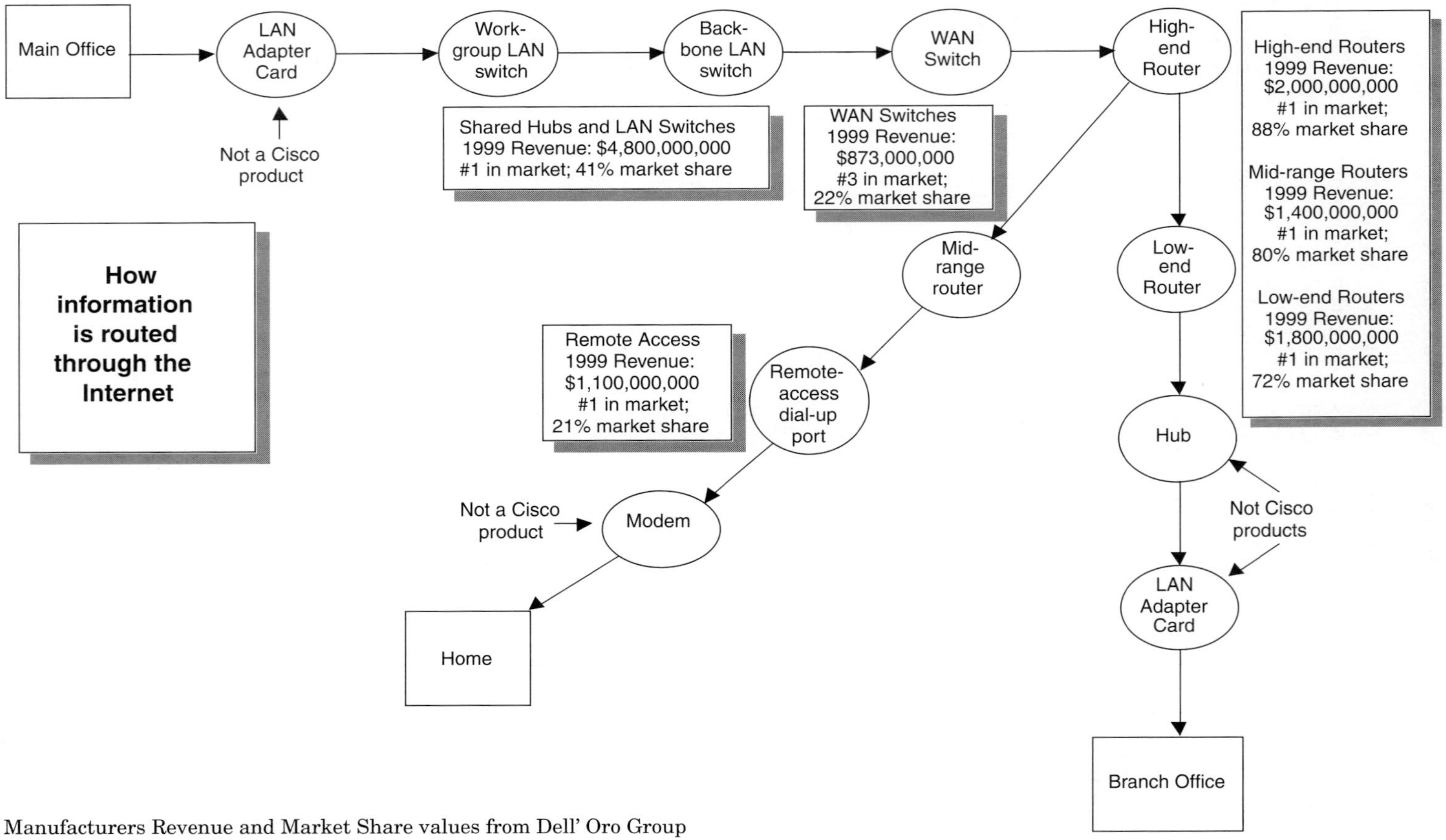

Manufacturers Revenue and Market Share values from Dell' Oro Group
Source: Case writer interpretation.

infrastructure in which voice, data and video will be delivered through one network. Further, Chambers believed that:

> . . . by providing the end-to-end network plumbing, we can change the way entire companies and industries operate. Only now are businesses beginning to realize how much the network will touch their people and customers and suppliers, and how much productivity and profitability can improve when they become truly global networked companies.[8]

In the end, Chamber's ultimate focus was on the customer, a fact that was emphasized by his directive to have the words "Dedication to Customer Success" on every Cisco worker's badge.

Building Cisco's IT Infrastructure

In January 1993, when Peter Solvik joined Cisco as their CIO, Cisco was a $500 million company, running traditional financial, manufacturing, and order entry systems. Solvik, who was fresh from Apple Computer, concluded that he had two key challenges. First, Cisco's Information Technology (IT) department was too traditional in the sense that it was viewed as a cost center that reported through the Finance department, and that it was too internally oriented. As a result, the potential contribution of IT to the business was much less than it could be and Solvik believed this had to change. Solvik's second challenge was that the current IT systems could not scale to support Cisco's growth, nor were they flexible and robust enough to meet management requirements.

To address the first challenge, three changes were made. First, the IT reporting relationship was changed from accounting to customer advocacy. Second, the IT budgets pertaining to specific functions were allocated to the func-

[8]John Chambers as quoted in Brent Schlender, "Computing's Next Superpower," *Fortune,* May 12, 1997, p. 88.

tions leaving just a small portion left as a General and Administrative (G&A) expense. This created a structure whereby all IT application projects were then client-funded. Third, the central IT steering committee was disbanded, and replaced with a structure that called for IT investment decisions on application projects to be pushed out to the line organization but the projects were still executed by central IT.

A Defining Moment

In January of 1994, Cisco's legacy environment experienced a major failure. An unauthorized method for accessing the core application database—a workaround that was itself motivated by the inability of the system to perform—malfunctioned, corrupting Cisco's central database. As a result, the company was largely shut down for two days. The failure was so dramatic that the shortcomings of the existing systems could no longer be ignored.

Cisco's struggle to recover from this major shutdown brought home the fact that the company's systems were on the brink of total failure. Solvik, Randy Pond, senior vice president of operations and a number of other Cisco managers came to the conclusion that the autonomous approach to systems replacement they had adopted was not going to be sufficient. An alternative approach was needed. Solvik described what they did:

> We said, "We can't wait casually by while Order Entry, Finance and Manufacturing go out and make three separate decisions." It would take too long to get those applications in place. We needed to take faster action. At that point we got sponsorship from the SVP of Manufacturing, Carl Redfield. He was with Digital before Cisco, in PC manufacturing. He took the lead and said, "O.K., let's get on with this . . . let's start from the manufacturing perspective, and see if we can get the Order Entry and Financial groups in the company interested in doing a single integrated replacement of all the applications instead of taking a longer time doing separate projects." And so in February, about a month after the [company shutdown], we went about putting together a team to do an investigation to replace the application.

Redfield understood from previous large-scale implementation experiences at Digital how "monolithic" IT projects could take on lives of their own. He echoed Solvik's concerns about project size and had strong views about how Cisco should approach a large implementation project.

> I knew we wanted to do this quickly. We were not going to do a phased implementation, we would do it all at once. We were not going to allow a lot of customization either. There is a tendency in MRP systems[9] for people to want the system to mirror their method of operation instead of retraining people to do things the way the system intended them. This takes a lot longer. Also, we wanted to create a schedule that was doable and make it a priority in the company as opposed to a second-tier kind of effort.

Selecting an ERP Product

Cisco's management team realized that implementing to meet *business* needs would require heavy involvement from the business community. This could not be an IT-only initiative. It was critically important to get the very best people they could find. Solvik elaborated:

> It was our orientation that in pulling people out of their jobs [to work on the project] if it was easy then we were picking the wrong people. We pulled people out that the business absolutely did not want to give up.

Consistent with the need for a strong Cisco team, the company would also need strong partners. Solvik and Redfield felt it was particularly important to work with an integration partner that could assist in both the selection and implementation of whichever solution the company chose. Great technical skills and business knowledge were prerequisites. Solvik explained the choice of KPMG as the integration partner:

KPMG came in and saw an opportunity to really build a business around putting in these applications. They also saw this as kind of a defining opportunity, to work with us on this project. As opposed to some other firms that wanted to bring in a lot of "greenies," KPMG was building a practice of people that were very experienced in the industry. For instance, the program manager that they put on the job, Mark Lee, had been director of IT for a company in Texas that had put in various parts of an ERP system.

With KPMG on board, the team of about 20 people turned to the software market with a multi-pronged approach for identifying the best software packages. The team's strategy was to build as much knowledge as possible by leveraging the experiences of others. They asked large corporations and the "Big Six" accounting firms what they knew. They also tapped research sources such as Gartner.[10] By orienting the selection process to what people were actually using and continuing to emphasize decision speed, Cisco narrowed the field to five packages within two days. After a week of evaluating the packages at a high-level, the team decided on two prime candidates, Oracle and another major player in the ERP market. Pond recalled that size was an issue in the selection. "We decided that we should not put Cisco's future in the hands of a company that was significantly smaller than we were."

The team spent 10 days writing a Request For Proposals (RFP) to send to the vendors. Vendors were given two weeks to respond. While vendors prepared their responses, the Cisco team continued its "due diligence" by visiting a series of reference clients offered by each vendor. Following Cisco's analysis of the RFP responses, each vendor was invited in for a three-day software demonstration and asked to show how their package could meet Cisco's information processing requirements. Cisco provided sample data and vendors illustrated

---

[9]MRP represents a class of systems, often thought of as predecessors of ERP that focus on planning the material requirements for production. Forecast or actual demand is fed to MRP either manually or from other types of systems. MRP functionality is embedded in the offerings of all leading ERP vendors.

[10]The Gartner Group is a leading industry resource for information on ERP and other information systems and manufacturing related research.

how key requirements were met (or not met) by the software. Upon completion of the process, Cisco selected Oracle as the vendor.

The selection of Oracle was based on a variety of factors. Redfield described three of the major decision points:

> First, this project was being driven pretty strongly by manufacturing and Oracle had a better manufacturing capability than the other vendor. Second, they made a number of promises regarding the long-term development of functionality in the package.[11] [Third was] . . . the flexibility offered by Oracle's being close by.[12]

Cisco also had reason to believe that Oracle was particularly motivated to make the project a success. Pond provided his impression of Oracle's situation:

> Oracle wanted this win badly. We ended up getting a super deal. There were, however, a lot of strings attached. We do references, allow site visits and in general talk to many companies that are involved in making this decision.

The Cisco project would be the first major implementation of a new release of the Oracle ERP product and Oracle had touted the new version as having major improvements in support of manufacturing. Thus, a successful implementation at Cisco would launch the new release on a very favorable trajectory.

It took the Cisco team 75 days, from project inception to the final selection on the project. Solvik described how the team made the vendor selection decision and how their decision was presented to the vendors:

> The team internally made the choice and informed the vendors. There was no major process we had to go through with management to "approve" the selection. We just said "Oracle you won, [other vendor] you lost." Then we went on to contract negotiations with Oracle and putting a proposal together for our board of direc-

tors. The focus immediately turned to issues of how long the project would take, and how much it would cost. The team decided "yes, we will do this and we ought to go forward with the project." So now at the very end of April we were putting the whole plan together.

Going to the Board

Before going to the board for approval, the team needed to answer two very important questions: How much would it cost and how long would it take? They knew their executives were worried that a big project might spin out of control and deliver sub-standard results. Despite the risks, the team took a pragmatic approach to estimating project requirements. Solvik described the process:

> Our quarters go August to October, November to January, February to April, and May to July.[13] So right here on May 1, beginning of the fourth quarter, we are asking "how long should it take to do a project to replace all of our core systems?" This is truly how it went. We said "you know we can't implement in the fourth quarter. The auditors will have a complete cow." If it takes a year we will be implementing fourth quarter, and that won't work. We thought it really should take 15 months, July or August a year later. Tom Herbert, the program manager, said there's no way we are going to take 15 months to get this done. That's ridiculous. So we started going in the opposite direction and said well can we do it in five months? That just didn't seem right. Understand we did not have a scope yet. In the end we basically settled that we wanted to go live at the beginning of Q3, so we would be completely stable for Q4. (See Exhibit 3 for a summary of milestone ERP implementation dates.)

That took care of setting a target date. Next came the task of estimating a project budget. Once again, Cisco was aggressive: "After we set a date, we estimated budgets. We put this whole thing together without really being that far into this program. We just looked at how much it touched" (Pete Solvik). Instead of developing a formal business case (i.e., a financial analysis) to demonstrate the impact

---

[11]Redfield later notes that not all of these promises were met in the time frame agreed to during contract negotiations.

[12]Oracle and Cisco world headquarters are both located in the Silicon Valley approximately 20 miles from each other.

---

[13]Cisco's financial year-end is July 31.

EXHIBIT 3   Summary of Milestone ERP Implementation Dates

Project Kickoff	June 2, 1994
Prototype Setup Complete	July 22, 1994
Implementation Team Training	July 31, 1994
Process, Key Data, Modification Designs Complete	August 31, 1994
Functional Process Approval	September 30, 1994
Hardware Benchmark and Capacity Plan Validated	October 15, 1994
Critical Interfaces, Modifications and Reports Complete	December 1, 1994
Procedures and End-User Documentation Complete	December 16, 1994
Conference Room Pilot Complete—Go/No Go Decision	December 22, 1994
End-User Training Beings	January 3, 1995
Data Conversion Complete	January 27, 1995
Go Live!	January 30, 1995

Source: Cisco ERP Steering Committee Report, October 20, 1994.

that the project would have on the company, the team chose to focus on the issues that had sparked the analysis in the first place. In Solvik's view, Cisco had little choice but to move. He explained his approach to the situation:

> We said that we had this big outage in January. That we were the biggest customer of our current software vendor and that the vendor was being bought by another company. It was unclear who was going to support our existing systems and we needed to do something. The reliability, the scalability and the modifiability of our current applications would not support our anticipated future growth. We needed either upgrades to the new version of the current application or we needed to replace it. If we replaced it, we could either do it in parts or do it as a whole. We evaluated those three alternatives, talked about the pros and cons of each alternative, and recommended that we replace our systems, big-bang, with one ERP solution. We committed to do it in nine months for $15 million for the whole thing. (See Exhibit 4 for a breakdown of project costs.)

Although Cisco was, to some extent, compelled to implement ERP, proceeding without a formal economic justification was also a matter of management philosophy. As Redfield put it:

> You don't approach this kind of thing from a justification perspective. Cost avoidance is not an appropriate way to look at it. You really need to look at it like "Hey,

we are going to do business this way." You are institutionalizing a business model for your organization.

At $15 million, the project would constitute the single largest capital project ever approved by the company. Members of the team prepared to take this number to senior management with some trepidation. The first meeting with CEO Morgridge did nothing to alleviate their concerns. Pond described the meeting with Morgridge this way:

> Pete Solvik, Tom Herbert, and I took the proposal to Morgridge and the reaction was pretty interesting. He made the comment "you know, careers are lost over much less money than this." Pete and I were as white as a sheet of paper. We knew that if we failed that we were going to get shot. Failure is not something the business took too well, especially with this kind of money.

But Morgridge okayed taking the project proposal to the board. Unfortunately for Pond and Solvik, the reception was not much warmer there. Pond described what happened:

> Before we even get the first slide up I hear the chairman speaking from the back of the room. He says "How much?" I said I was getting to it and he responded: "I hate surprises. Just put the slide up right now." After I put it up he said "Oh my God, there better be a lot of good slides. . . ."

EXHIBIT 4   Breakdown of Implementation Costs for Cisco ERP Implementation[a]

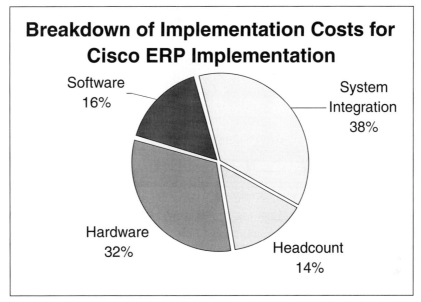

Breakdown of Implementation Costs for Cisco ERP Implementation

- Software 16%
- System Integration 38%
- Headcount 14%
- Hardware 32%

[a]The project budget estimate did not include estimates of the cost of Cisco personnel time beyond some members of the core team.
Source: Cisco ERP Steering Committee Report, October 20, 1994

There were a lot of good slides and the board ended up approving the project.[14] During the weeks and months following the meeting, Morgridge did his part by making it clear to the rest of Cisco that the ERP project was a priority. The project emerged as one of the company's top seven goals for the year. "Everybody in the company knew this was happening and it was a priority for the business" Pond explained.

The project was completed successfully and on time and formed the centerpiece of two-year, $100 million series of initiatives to replace all

IT applications and platforms worldwide within Cisco. Solvik describes the results:

> In a two-year period, we literally replaced every piece of technology in the company. We have a very low-cost/high-value technology architecture. We have no mainframes, no mini computers, and no legacy technology. Everything is current.

The IT platform architecture was standardized throughout Cisco: 100% UNIX at the server level, 100% Windows NT at the LAN level, 100% Windows Toshiba and HP PCs at the client level, 100% Oracle at the database level, and 100% TCP/IP (Transmission Control Protocol/Internet Protocol) for the worldwide network. Voice-mail, e-mail, meeting schedule software, desktop and server operating systems, and office productivity suites were all standardized. Virtually all business functions utilized single applications packages worldwide. Cisco's architecture is detailed in Exhibit 5.

[14]Pond adds that the cause for approval was aided by the fact that the legacy systems crashed on the day of the board meeting. "The day of the meeting, [the legacy system] went down. We were able to walk into the board meeting and say 'It's down again.' It was really a compelling story."

EXHIBIT 5   Cisco's IT Architecture

Technology Standardization

Common PC platform, O/S, Productivity SW, Email, Browser

Common Applications Packages Worldwide

Database Mgmt System: Oracle	Protocol: TCP/IP

Enterprise Servers: Unix	Workgroup Servers: NT

Worldwide Network, Voice PBX/Voicemail, Video Standards

= Reduced time to market
Reduced costs
Easier data integration

Being standardized to this degree had given the company a high level of flexibility. For example, when Cisco reorganized R&D and marketing from multiple business units into three lines of business, they completed all the changes required across all applications in less than 60 days for a cost of less than $1 million. Solvik feels "that without the IP and open-systems-based IT architecture and standardization, we would never have been able to accomplish such a feat in the short time that we did, and at an incredibly low cost."

Although standardization means flexibility, from a scalability perspective, distributing the company's systems and yet keeping a single system image remained a daunting task. Solvik explained:

> . . . the biggest and most challenging projects we have going on are distributing our centralized core systems. We have very big UNIX servers with huge, huge databases that just don't have the inherent reliability and scalability that the same size DB2 database would

have on a mainframe. A tremendous amount of our effort goes into designing our systems to be reliable and scalable. The whole UNIX platform has a much lower cost than mainframes so we're able to spend that money to have plenty of server capability.

Completion of their IP-based open standards architecture initiative provided the centerpiece of the Cisco IT architecture. It also provided the foundation for the next phase of Solvik's strategy—incorporating the Internet.

Internet and Intranet Applications and Benefits

Cisco began web development in the early 1990s when they discovered Mosaic, a public domain primitive web browser developed at the University of Illinois. Within six months of the discovery, Cisco had production and transaction web applications for itself and its customers, and a year after that they shifted from the Mosaic browser to the Netscape browser.

Solvik recalls that early on "when we purchased our applications, none were web-enabled. We had to web-enable them all. So we did that with a standard set of tools and a smart group of people."

The initial three-year investment in the Internet cost about $115 million. The following table details the key components for the Intranet and Internet applications.

Intranet	Internet
EIS (Executive Information Systems) and DSS (Decision Support Systems)	Extranet supply chain (information transparency)
Employee self-service	Customer self-service through web site
Communication and distance learning	Net commerce through the web
Collaboration and the workflow management	Marketing through the web
Web-enabled legacy systems	Any place access through the web

A very high percentage of Cisco customer, partner and supplier interactions with the company became network-based, and utilized Cisco's Home Page (see Exhibit 6). From the Cisco Connection Online (CCO), the user navigated to the information needed for the interaction work, or "publishes and subscribes"—that is, the user directly contributed information required to do business with Cisco, or enriched Cisco's intellectual asset base. This allowed users (both internally and externally) to do business more efficiently and effectively with Cisco.

Cisco has built its business processes on its own global intranet, and Cisco people deployed around the world interacted on this intranet to address business issues and customer needs. See Exhibit 7 for a screen of the "Cisco Employee Connection" home page. Links to strategic vendors and customers allowed Cisco to collaborate more efficiently with those outside the company. The intranet also provided a proving ground for new Cisco technologies and products, ensuring that they were ready for mission-critical applications before they were offered to customers.

Employee Self-Service: Internal Applications. The majority of Cisco's internal applications become web-enabled. For example, almost all functions that sales people performed on the computer were done using a web browser. EIS and DSS systems, training (including distance learning), and self-service HR were all web-based.

Cisco Systems' corporate intranet, Cisco Employee Connection (CEC), addressed the unique needs of its 40,000+ employees by providing centralized access to information, tools, and resources needed to streamline processes, facilitate knowledge exchange and maximize employee productivity.

Cisco had leveraged the web to truly revolutionize existing processes and create new, end-to end capabilities. Because the Web had integrated data and tools from a variety of sources under a unified user interface, Cisco's intranet was truly a key enabler of workforce optimization.

In addition to replacing its own custom-designed applications, Cisco worked with its vendors to help them convert their applications that Cisco has purchased for use within the company. By 2001, virtually every application in the company used a web browser as its only user interface.

Communication and Distance Learning. The network had continued to enhance the ability to communicate with employees and added an important dimension to training. Distance learning modules available to Cisco employees could be activated at the employee's desktop.

EXHIBIT 6   Cisco's Home Page

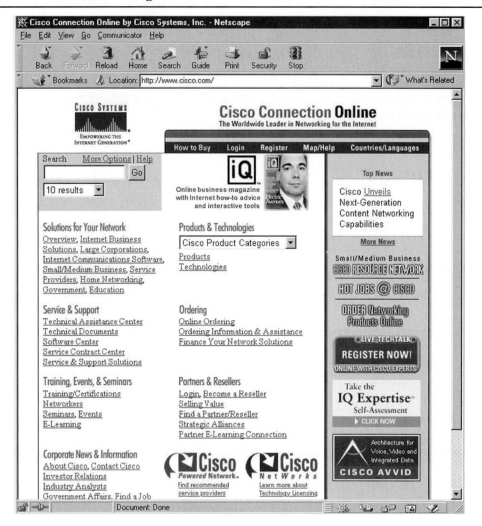

The use of these distance learning modules—as well as information about their effectiveness—could be easily tracked to determine the extent of use of the various education modules. Using the information gathered in the tracking system, the quality of the modules could be assessed to ensure high levels of effectiveness as the needs of the organization change.

An arrangement with Yahoo! (the search engine company) made available a Cisco-tailored version of "My Yahoo!." My Yahoo! was a type of "push" technology application whereby certain information is specified by the user, agents then search the Internet for the information and then "push" it out to the user's desktop. When the user signs onto the Internet, the information is waiting for them,

EXHIBIT 7   Cisco Employee Connection Home Page

tracking everything from late breaking news reports about competitors to up-to-the-minute information about worldwide financial markets (see Exhibit 8).

Chambers' addresses at Cisco's Quarterly Meetings could be viewed from employees' desktops in real-time. Thousands of employees tuned in to view the addresses in real-time or watched them in a delayed broadcast over the Intranet—using their PC to bring up a video window. This streaming of live video provided another capability that strengthen the Cisco culture by making the company "feel" closer to each of the employees.

Customer Self-service: Electronic Connection with Customers. Cisco management never missed a chance to reinforce that the customer

EXHIBIT 8   MyYahoo! at Cisco

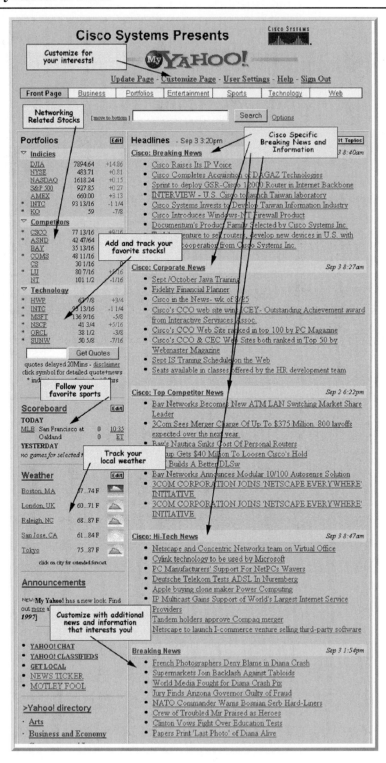

was the focal point of their business. The centerpiece of this strategy was Cisco.com, a comprehensive, web-based, online resource for information and networked applications. With about 590,425 active registered users from around the world, Cisco.com was accessed approximately 3.8 million times each month by registered users (as of January, 2001), making it the primary vehicle for delivering responsive, around-the-clock customer support.[15] Customers relied on Cisco.com to answer questions, diagnose network problems, and provide solutions and expert assistance worldwide. In fact, over 80% of Cisco's technical support for customers and resellers was delivered electronically, saving Cisco nearly $506 million annually and improving customer satisfaction.[16] For its international customers, portions of Cisco.com were translated into 17 different languages and were accessible through 68 different country pages.

Solvik reflected on the importance of the customer at Cisco:

> I have 600,000 registered Customers hooked up—those are Customers with a big "C"—compared to 42,617 Cisco employees. In contrast to most internally focused IT organizations in many other companies, my mission does not primarily focus on providing services and systems to meet the needs of the employees of the business. In fact, I refer to my employee users as clients, and not as Customers.
>
> Customers that are using our systems directly express higher satisfaction with us and enjoy a lower cost of doing business with us than those who do not use our systems. And of course, we also lower our cost of doing business.

---

[15]As of June 2000, there were 15 million hits per month against the Cisco.com web site and this number was growing by 3.6% per month. Seventy percent of these hits were not registered users but individuals visiting the Cisco.com website for general company information. Registered users have a special login that provides them access to specific Cisco information.

[16]"Ten Minutes with John Chambers," *NASDAQ: The International Magazine,* Issue 29, January 2001, pg. 18.

Seventy percent of the employees in Cisco have a very significant bonus multiplier tied to our annual customer satisfaction survey. The first thing we review at every senior staff meeting is the status of critical accounts. Every night Chambers gets a personal update on the status of every critical account. Any employee can put a Customer on the critical account list as an advocate of the Customer. So if I get a call from someone who knows me or has met me or has my business card, and they say "I'm having a problem with your company," I will find the relevant sales person and call the account team, to get the issue resolved or I can place the account on the critical account list. If you have an unhappy Customer, they stay on the critical account list until the problem is fixed.

Net Commerce—Shipping Product over the Internet.   Cisco was an early pioneer in using the Internet for full electronic commerce. Beginning more than five years ago with simple transactions, Cisco has since completed configuration and order placement for the company's entire product line. Solvik recalled their experience:

> We've learned an incredible amount in the 48 months of live e-commerce. We have racked up Internet shipments of product from 0% in July of 1996, to 2% of our revenue in August of 1996, to $800 million in calendar 1997, and to $1.5 billion each quarter in 1998. As of January, 2001, Internet Commerce based revenue represents 92% of our total revenue base, a run-rate of over $25 Billion annually. Cisco operates one of the biggest electronic commerce sites in the world.

Orders could be placed via the World Wide Web from anywhere in the world. After placing an order customers could use other applications to instantly check the status of pending orders. In addition, well over 90% of Cisco's software upgrades were then delivered via the Internet at a much lower cost and in a shorter time period than in the past when traditional distribution methods were used. For example, at Sprint it used to take 60 days from the signing of a contract to complete a networking project. Now, thanks partly to the efficiency of ordering Cisco equipment online, it takes 35 to 45 days. Sprint has also been able to cut its order-processing staff from 21 to 6, allowing the other 15 employees to work instead on installing networks.[17]

Productivity gains of 60% for Cisco and 20% for customers and resellers were being realized through online commerce.[18]

Cisco's Supply Chain Management Initiative. Beginning in 1992, Cisco outsourced much of its manufacturing to contract manufacturers while still performing final assembly and test. The supply chain functions were jointly performed by Cisco and its contract manufacturers, requiring them to exchange information and interact through labor-intensive processes.

As the company began implementing applications to extend to its suppliers and customers, Cisco decided that its core competencies were in design and fulfillment processes rather than physical transformation of product. As a result, Cisco chose to form partnerships with suppliers that performed physical transformation as their core competency. Central to Cisco's philosophy was to remove business barriers that would impede the flow of information within the company and with its business partners, further increasing the integration with its constituents and overall power of the supply chain.

Automating Cisco's supply chain involved five initiatives:

1. *Single Enterprise:* Cisco used networked applications to integrate suppliers into its production systems, creating in effect, a "single enterprise". This enabled key suppliers to manage and operate major portions of its supply chain. The electronic links across the single enterprise allowed Cisco and these

suppliers to respond to customer demand in real-time. Any change in one node of the supply chain was propagated throughout the supply chain almost instantaneously. Other improvements included the elimination of purchase orders and invoice processing.

2. *New Product Introduction (NPI):* A 1998 Cisco study revealed that as many as four to five iterations of prototype building were required, with each iteration taking, on average, one to two weeks. Two of the biggest drivers of costs and time delays in the prototype phase were the labor-intensive process for gathering and disseminating information and the delays caused by manufacturability design issues. In response to this problem, Cisco automated the process for gathering product data information, thereby reducing the amount of time required from as much as one day, to less than 15 minutes. By simulating the manufacturability of the product design prior to release to the factory, Cisco caught roughly 98% of all manufacturability issues upfront, reducing the number of interactions to 2½. The use of networked applications in NPI has reduced time to volume by three months and reduced total cost of NPI by $49 million in 1999.

3. *Autotest:* In 1992 Cisco began to build test cells that performed tests automatically with minimal labor and standardized product tests. Testing processes were made routine and embodied in software test programs that ran the test cells. Once testing had been automated and standardized it was outsourced entirely to the suppliers, allowing quality issues to be detected at the source. However, although testing

[17]Shawn Tully, "How Cisco Mastered the Net," *Fortune,* August 17, 1998, p. 210.
[18]Cisco 1997 Annual Report, p. 11.

was outsourced, the intelligence behind the testing was still supplied by Cisco.

4. *Direct Fulfillment:* Originally, orders were shipped to the customer exclusively from Cisco. Therefore, products configured by partners would have to go through two shipping legs: first from the partner to Cisco, and then from Cisco to its customer. Each of these legs took approximately three days. In 1997, the first step in moving toward global direct fulfillment was launched in the United States. The manufacturing partners who have transitioned completely represent about 60% of Cisco's unit volume.

5. *Dynamic Replenishment:* Prior to supply chain automation, Cisco manufacturers and suppliers lacked real-time demand and supply information, resulting in delays and errors. To compensate, inventory levels and overhead were higher than acceptable. The dynamic replenishment model allowed the market demand signal to flow through directly to the contract manufacturers without any distortion or delays. It also allowed contract manufacturers to track Cisco's inventory levels in real-time.

As a result of these five initiatives, Cisco had one of the most efficient supply chain models possible. In 1997 it improved responsiveness while improving profitability by $275 million. Network-enabled applications had been key to value maximization in Cisco's supply chain. This powerful new model of managing the supply chain was referred to as "the Global Networked Business Model."

EIS (Executive Information Systems) and DSS (Decision Support Systems). Cisco employees used the web browser as a front-end for access to all executive and decision support information in the company. The company's web-based EIS system (Executive Information Systems) was used by all sales managers and executives worldwide—a total of over 2,000 users including the CEO—and provided summary and drill down Bookings, Backlog, Revenue, Not Booked, Forecast and Plan for all products, customers, channels, geographies, and markets.

Sales tracking and reporting were also accessible via the Intranet. If a Cisco sales person wanted to track certain product sales in a region on a weekly basis, they merely called up the browser template and requested the information. After several clicks of the mouse, assuming that the salesperson had authority to access the information, the report would be automatically delivered their desktop at the level of detail and for the period of time requested.

Integrating Acquisitions into the IP-based IT Architecture

Acquisitions have been—and are expected to be for the foreseeable future—an important part of Cisco's strategy. Approximately two thirds of Cisco technology was from internally developed efforts, with the other one third from partnerships/acquisitions.[19] Approximately 70% of the CEO's from the acquired companies remain at Cisco following the acquisition.

Cisco seems to have mastered the acquisition process. There were no hostile takeovers and only companies with "market congruent" visions were considered. Because Cisco wanted to be assured of success, only 1 out of 10 acquisitions that Cisco considered is actually executed.

Once an acquisition is consummated, Cisco used a documented and repeatable process for integration. Generally, the acquired company

---

[19]Noel Lindsay, network analyst, Deutsche Morgan Grenfell.

was acquired for its R&D and developed products that would contribute to providing the network customer with an end-to-end solution. The R&D and Product Organizations of each acquired company were grafted onto the product side of the organization, which included Cisco branding, and product family integration. The manufacturing, sales, and distribution parts of the organization were integrated into Cisco's functional organization. Within Cisco's IT organization, a specific group handled acquisition integration and immediately eliminated non-standard technology, integrating the acquired company into all of Cisco's infrastructures and core applications. Because of Cisco's IP and standards-based IT architecture, the company was able to quickly and efficiently add the capacity required to handle the administrative processes of acquired businesses. Most acquisitions could be fully integrated within 60 to 100 days.

In August 1999, following a number of cooperative initiatives during its six-year relationship, Cisco announced that it would purchase a 19.9% stake in KPMG Consulting for $1.05 billion.[20] KPMG would own the remaining 80%. KPMG created KPMG Consulting as their global consulting arm with the goal of eventually taking the unit public.[21] In February 2000, KPMG spun off the unit with the intention of taking the unit through an Initial Public Offering (IPO).

KPMG global consulting planned to use the capital from the deal to build six technology centers that would be staffed with 4,000 of its consultants to deliver internet-based data, voice and video consulting services to Cisco's clients. With the new entity if a corporate customer wanted to transfer its business functions, such as accounting or financial reporting to the web, Cisco would provide the hardware and software systems, while KPMG would provide the software required to set-up the specific application and maintain it. For Cisco, the alliance with KPMG filled a gap to help customers install and maintain its systems. This was particularly important to Cisco as it was selling an increasing share of its systems to telecommunications providers, which were accustomed to more assistance from its equipment suppliers.[22]

Cisco gained a competitive advantage and increased shareholder value by implementing Internet business solutions across all functional areas (including marketing, employee, manufacturing, customer support, and commerce applications). The bottom line impact in FY2000, including increased revenue and margin, and reduced expenses, was conservatively calculated at $1.3 billion. Solvik observed that the benefits of moving to the new architecture could be thought of as either providing the company free IT services or alternatively, as allowing the company to invest $1 billion more in R&D than their competitors.

Beyond Cisco

It was clear that Cisco had been successful in what it had hoped to accomplish. In 2001, Chambers and Solvik believe that the principals at work at Cisco in using the Internet could apply to other organizations. Recently Solvik commented:

> The opportunity for Cisco to continue growing as a company is highly linked to the adoption of Internet-based infrastructures by other companies. We believe that we can continue to pioneer in the development and use of the Internet, and provide leadership to most traditional companies. These companies can find the same benefits that Cisco has enjoyed.

---

[20]Of the $1.05 billion, $420 million would be invested in the new unit, and the remainder would be paid to the KPMG audit and tax businesses.

[21]*The Wall Street Journal,* August 8, 1999, p. A3. To satisfy the SEC, KPMG agreed to give up control of the new entity minimizing their equity holding to around 30%. Two Cisco executives will sit on the Board of Directors of the entity.

[22]*The Wall Street Journal,* August 8, 1999, p. A3.

CASE 4–4
GENERAL DYNAMICS AND COMPUTER SCIENCES CORPORATION: OUTSOURCING THE IS FUNCTION (A)[1]

It was June 1991, just over a year since Computer Sciences Corporation (CSC) and General Dynamics (GD) had first come into contact at a conference on information systems outsourcing. Now, the two companies were attempting to negotiate what could be the largest information systems (IS) outsourcing deal in history, dwarfing the 1989 Kodak outsourcing mega-contract both in size and complexity.

In the proposed arrangement, General Dynamics would sell its information systems organization, the Data Systems Division (DSD), to Computer Sciences Corporation; in addition, the staff of DSD would be transferred to CSC to continue operating the data center assets. CSC would then use this capacity to provide information services to General Dynamics, as well as to other clients. It was an excellent opportunity for General Dynamics to continue to get superior information services at even lower cost while monetizing fixed assets and providing more flexibility for the future. In addition, General Dynamics considered the arrangement to be a valuable career opportunity for the employees of DSD to enter a growth business in information services by joining CSC.

Ace Hall, corporate vice president, information systems and administrative services, and Larry Feuerstein, vice president, planning and quality assurance, were the managers of the General Dynamics Data Systems Division who had been involved in developing the deal. Over 15 long months, they had learned about out-

sourcing and worked with CSC to develop a plan that could benefit both companies.

Now, they were entering more serious negotiations with CSC, and they focused on defining a plan for outsourcing DSD that they could present at the next General Dynamics Board of Directors meeting.

General Dynamics Company Background

General Dynamics, headquartered in St. Louis, Missouri, was the second-largest defense conglomerate in America. It provided tactical military aircraft, submarines, missile and electronics systems, armored vehicles, and space launch vehicles to the U.S. government. Its high-tech weapons systems included the Trident submarine, the M-1 tank, the F-16 fighter plane, and the Tomahawk cruise missile. In addition, General Dynamics owned and operated several smaller commercial subsidiaries. In the years of Cold War defense buildup, General Dynamics enjoyed a thriving defense market and sales grew to an all-time high of $10.2 billion in 1990.

In 1991, General Dynamics was composed of seven aerospace and defense divisions (see Exhibit 1). Its four core defense groups were Space Launch Systems, Missiles and Electronics, Military Aircraft, and Marine and Land Systems. In addition, the company had two nondefense operations—the Resources group and Cessna Aircraft. Finally, General Dynamics defined its own information systems organization as a separate division—the Data Systems Division.

- The Space Systems Division designed, manufactured, and supported space

[1]This case was prepared by Research Associate Katherine N. Seger under the supervision of Professor F. Warren McFarlan. Copyright © 1993 by the President and Fellows of Harvard College. Harvard Business School case 193-144.

EXHIBIT 1   General Dynamics Divisions, 1991

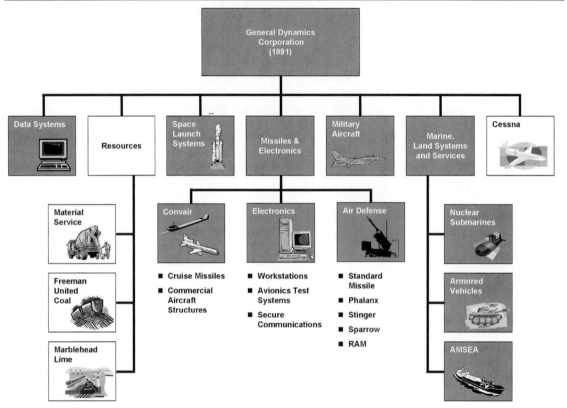

Source: General Dynamics Company records.

launch vehicles that carried defense and communications satellites into orbit around the earth.

• The Missiles and Electronics Group was mainly composed of two separate businesses. The Missile Systems business designed and manufactured air defense products such as the Tomahawk cruise missile, the Advanced Cruise Missile, the Sparrow, the Stinger, and the Phalanx gun system. The Electronics business produced avionics test equipment and provided information systems for the U.S. Air Force and radio systems for the Army. In addition, it designed and manufactured digital imagery and signal

processing equipment for intelligence information gathering.

• The Military Aircraft Group designed and manufactured tactical aircraft. Its strongest product was the F-16 fighter, which served as the backbone of America's tactical aircraft fleet and was sold to other nations around the globe. In addition, the division had an equal share with Lockheed and Boeing in the design of the F-22 fighter, the next generation of tactical aircraft.

• The Marine and Land Systems Group was composed of two businesses. The Electric Boat Division was the nation's leading designer and builder of nuclear

EXHIBIT 2   100 Years of U.S. Defense Spending

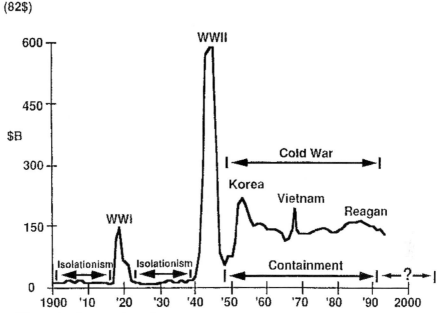

Source: General Dynamics Company Records.

submarines. In 1991, the U.S. Navy awarded Electric Boat the contract to build SSN22, the second ship in the *Seawolf* class. The Land Systems Division designed and built land defense systems such as M1A1 Abrams main battle tank.

- The Resources Group was composed of three commercial operations. The Material Service Corporation produced aggregates, ready-mix concrete, and concrete pipe. Marblehead Lime produced lime for use in the steel industry and building materials. Freeman United Coal was a coal mining operation.

- Cessna Aircraft was a subsidiary that designed and manufactured small private business jets.

- The Data Systems Division (DSD) supported the company's corporate information systems and provided information services to all of General Dynamics's aerospace and defense divisions. (See below for more detail on DSD).

The Board of Directors of General Dynamics totaled 16 members, comprised of 7 General Dynamics insiders, and 9 outsiders. The chairman and chief executive officer of the company was William A. Anders, who had joined General Dynamics in 1990 as vice chairman and then became chairman in January of 1991. Prior to joining GD, Anders had been an astronaut on the Apollo 8 mission around the moon, the executive secretary of the National Aeronautics and Space Council, chairman of the Nuclear Regulatory Commission, ambassador to Norway, and an executive at two large industrial manufacturing companies.

The fall of the Berlin Wall in 1989 marked the beginning of the end of the Cold War. In 1991, communism collapsed in the Soviet Union; by 1992, the Soviet Union had crumbled into a federation of independent states. With the end of the Cold War, a growing federal deficit, and a troubled domestic economy, the U.S. government began to reduce procurement spending on military power from a high of $96.8 billion in fiscal 1985 to $54.4 billion in fiscal 1993,[2] causing the market for defense products and weapons to shrink dramatically. (See Exhibit 2 for 100-year history of defense spending.)

This reduction in the defense market led to extreme overcapacity among suppliers and financial troubles for companies throughout the defense industry. In 1990, General Dynamics posted a loss from continuing operations of $674 million. (See Exhibit 3 for financial summaries.) There seemed to be two major strategies for surviving this sharp decline in the defense market: (1) diversify capacity into commercial markets or (2) downsize to a level that could be supported by a smaller defense market.

[2]Eric J. Savitz, "Hold the Taps for Defense Stocks," *Barron's*, Vol. 72, August 3, 1992.

EXHIBIT 3   General Dynamics Financial Highlights (dollars in millions, except per share and sales per employee amounts)

	1991	1990	1989
Summary of Operations			
Net sales[a]	$ 8,751	$ 9,457	$ 9,442
Operating costs and expenses	8,359	10,374	8,934
Interest, net	−34	−62	−73
Provision (credit) for income taxes	−43	−366	134
Earnings (loss) from continuing operation	374	−674	269
Net earnings (loss) per share			
Continuing operations[a]	8.93	−16.17	6.44
Discontinued operations	3.13	2.31	0.57
Capital expenditures[a]	$ 82	$ 306	$ 411
Research and development[a]			
Company sponsored	162	353	438
Customer sponsored[b]	601	510	506
Total	$ 763	$ 863	$ 944
At Year End			
Total backlog[a]	$ 25,597	$ 22,151	$ 27,688
Shareholders' equity	1,980	1,510	2,126
Total assets	6,207	5,830	6,049
Number of employees	80,600	98,100	$102,200
Sales per employee[a]	116,200	101,700	96,400
Other Information			
Purchases of property, plant, equipment	82	306	411
Depreciation, depletion, and amortization	303	370	352
Salaries and wages	$ 3,204	$ 3,433	$ 3,311

[a]Data excludes Cessna Aircraft Company.
[b]Data excludes A-12 R&D expenditures.

EXHIBIT 3 (CONTINUED)   **General Dynamics Consolidated Balance Sheet (dollars in millions)**

	December 31,	
	1991	*1990*
ASSETS		
Current Assets:		
Cash and equivalents	$ 513	$ 109
Marketable securities	307	–
	$ 820	$ 109
Accounts receivable	444	353
Contracts in process	2,606	2,843
Other current assets	449	288
Total current assets	$4,319	$3,593
Noncurrent Assets:		
Leases receivable—finance operations	$ 266	$ 287
Property, plant, and equipment, net	1,029	1,411
Other assets	593	509
Total noncurrent assets	$1,888	$2,237
	$6,207	$5,830
LIABILITIES AND SHAREHOLDERS' EQUITY		
Current Liabilities:		
Current portion of long-term debt	$ 455	$ 1
Short-term debt—finance operations	61	65
Accounts payable and other current liabilities	2,593	2,279
Deferred income taxes	–	326
Total current liabilities	$3,109	$2,671
Noncurrent Liabilities:		
Long-term debt	$ 168	$ 619
Long-term debt—finance operations	197	264
Other liabilities	753	766
Total noncurrent liabilities	$1,118	$1,649
Shareholders' Equity:		
Common stock	$ 55	$ 55
Capital surplus	25	25
Retained earnings	2,651	2,195
Treasury stock	−751	−765
Total shareholders' equity	$1,980	$1,510
	$6,207	$5,830

1991 General Dynamics Corporate Strategy

In 1991, Anders's top priorities for General Dynamics were to increase shareholder value and build financial strength and flexibility for the uncertain future. Anders wrote in his 1991 annual report:

> Studies by outside consultants and by us clearly show that diversification by defense companies into commercial enterprises historically has had unacceptably high failure rates. . . . We believe that the process of widespread conversion of defense resources to commercial use at General Dynamics, while an alluring concept, is generally not practical. Instead, we are sticking to what we know best, and are therefore focusing more sharply on our core defense competencies.

This policy was part of Anders' philosophy of defense industry rationalization that he had refined during his first year as General Dynamics's CEO. Anders believed that defense companies could survive the changing marketplace only if the industry sufficiently downsized to meet the reduced demand. Overcapacity must be shed (not merely diversified) and the industry must consolidate so that individual companies could obtain a "critical mass" of the market in order to maintain profitability.

In his 1991 letter to shareholders, Anders outlined three criteria for maintaining the strength of General Dynamics' individual businesses. For a business to remain viable, it must be within GD's core defense competency; it must be #1 or #2 in its field; and it must have a "critical mass" to ensure efficiency, economies of scale, and financial strength given the future business volumes available.[3] For businesses that did not fit these criteria, Anders' policy was "Buy, Sell, or Merge." In addition, Anders launched an aggressive campaign to increase General Dynamics's shareholder value. He instituted an executive com-

---

[3]From GD 1991 Annual Report.

pensation plan with heavy rewards for increased stock prices, and he sought out opportunities to monetize assets and generate more cash.

Larry Feuerstein commented on the power of Anders' corporate strategy within General Dynamics:

> Anders was *really* pushing his strategy out to all the executives and managers in the company. This was THE business strategy of General Dynamics, and it was reinforced daily for every employee Anders ever came in contact with. This was his singular focus.

It was with this corporate strategy in place that Larry Feuerstein and Ace Hall of GD's Data Systems Division began to look at outsourcing as a possible option for the future of the company's IS organization. As Feuerstein noted,

> General Dynamics is in the defense business, and data processing, admittedly, is not one of our core businesses. This is a great example of MIS really getting in line with corporate strategy. You read a lot about this, but rarely find such crisp examples of it really happening.

IT at General Dynamics: The Data Systems Division

Information technology (IT) was critically important to the operations of General Dynamics. Larry Feuerstein described computer technology as "the lifeblood" of GD's product units. Sophisticated computer systems were used in the operating units for product engineering, simulation, and manufacturing. Many of GD's products (such as "smart" cruise missiles) also had microcomputers installed directly within them. These proprietary embedded systems offered strategic advantage for GD's product lines. In addition, large computer systems were used to manage the company's business data in areas such as accounting, payroll, and inventory management. IT supported all aspects of General Dynamics operations; the quality and reliability of these information systems were crucial to the success of the company.

Prior to 1972, the information systems capabilities of General Dynamics were widely dispersed among the various business units of the company. In 1972, a study by Arthur Andersen recommended the consolidation of these facilities into regional centers to achieve more efficient and effective use of these resources. By 1976 the consolidation was complete, and the resulting organization—Data Systems Services—comprised three regional centers in San Diego, California; Fort Worth, Texas; and Norwich, Connecticut. At this time, the organization had 1,488 employees and was operated solely as a cost center. (See Exhibit 4 for DSD growth history.)

Larry Feuerstein joined the Data Systems Services management staff in 1976 at the Nor-

wich center as it was being formed. Feuerstein recalls his experience at this time of organizational change as being excellent preparation for his role in the CSC outsourcing decision and implementation: "There was major turmoil. I saw the pain of changing relationships, fundamental restructuring, and consolidation. It was an important experience which I've drawn on throughout this CSC deal."

In 1981, the Data Systems Services organization was elevated to the status of an operating business unit and its name was changed to Data Systems Division (DSD). The charter for the DSD stated:

> The Data Systems Division provides corporatewide guidance for, direction to, and management of the company's information resources and the information services required by the company's business units.

EXHIBIT 4   General Dynamics DSD Historical Perspective

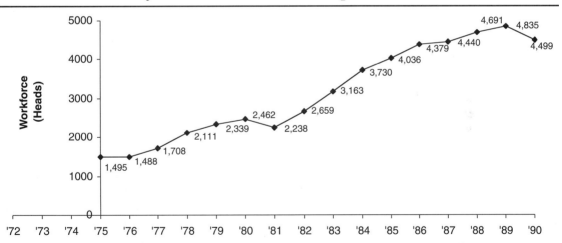

Significant Organizaitonal Events

- 11/72 Arthur Andersen EDP Consolidation Study Completed
- 5/73 Announcement of Data Systems Services
- 1/76 Consolidation of Data Systems Services Completed (3 centers)
- 7/81 Announcement of Data Systems Division

Source: General Dynamics company records.

The DSD Management Vision stated:

> Working together as part of the General Dynamics Team, our people are recognized leaders in providing high-quality, cost-effective, information solutions to make our Company's processes and products the best in the world, improve competitiveness, and enhance shareholder value.

DSD had two main areas of responsibility: (1) the companywide direction of information resource strategies, policies, procedures, and standards; and (2) the provision of a full range of information services to General Dynamics operating units, including computer systems development, data processing for business systems, computer-aided design and manufacturing systems (CAD/CAM), engineering systems, and development of software that is embedded and delivered in General Dynamics products.[4]

DSD facilities were located in the 3 large regional centers and 28 smaller service sites around the country. Hardware included 13 IBM mainframes, 3 Amdahl mainframes, a Univac mainframe, 2 Cyber scientific mainframes, a Cray scientific supercomputer, and 440 minicomputers. In addition, 3,700 engineering workstations and over 15,000 desktop micro-computers were scattered throughout the company's divisions. DSD operated three interconnected network layers—wide area, campus area, and work group. Capabilities included CAD/CAM, manufacturing, business applications, logistics, systems integration, electronic data interchange (EDI), distributed processing, and training. Total processing capacity for DSD was more than 1,000 MIPS (millions of instructions per second). The write-off lifetime for these fixed assets was a five-year accelerated depreciation for computer equipment and a five-year linear depreciation for software. In 1991, the DSD assets (including real estate, equipment, computer hardware, and licensed software) had a net book value of $140 million.

The staff of DSD consisted of highly-skilled professional computer technicians and programmers. Their educations and careers were in information systems, and their salaries and benefits were competitive with IS professionals in other companies and industries. The majority of the DSD staff was located at the three regional centers or satellite service centers, with only a few (2 to 50) information systems people at each of GD's product division sites. These people served primarily as liaisons to the DSD service providers in the regional centers. When Ace Hall came in from General Dynamics's Corporate Planning Department to become general manager of the division in 1984, DSD had grown to 3,730 employees. In 1989, DSD reached its peak of 4,835 employees. By 1991, the staff had been reduced to 3,400.[5] The DSD staff had been downsized in response to the shrinking defense market, mainly through attrition, reduced recruitment and hiring, and the elimination of selected positions. According to Larry Feuerstein, "We saw the market conditions, and we knew we were going to have to cut costs. We tried to manage downsizing in an orderly way, to avoid having to reduce the head count abruptly."

Each of the three regional data centers (West, Central, and East) served mainly the operating units in its region, giving each its own unique "clientele." A sophisticated charge-back billing system enabled the DSD to operate as a self-liquidating cost center. (See Exhibit 5 for DSD cost flow chart.) Larry Feuerstein commented on the meticulous accounting of costs in DSD's billing system:

> DSD was a cost center operation for General Dynamics, but it was organized and managed like an independent business. We knew where to charge every cost we incurred. Most "garden variety" in-house IS departments are not organized like this. They have all kinds of costs comingled and buried in the "overhead" category.

---

[4]From GD company records.

[5]Of this number, approximately 800 individuals were assigned specifically to the development and installation of technology directly embedded in GD's products.

EXHIBIT 5 General Dynamics DSD Sample Cost Flow Chart (1987)

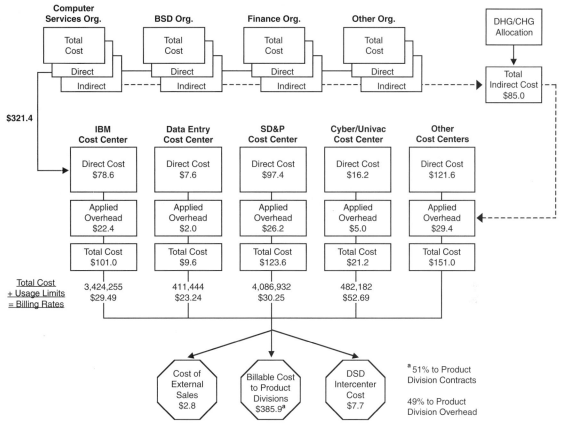

Notes:

Direct Costs are services directly consumed by GD business units.

Indirect Costs are DSD overhead costs.

The organizations across the top of the chart are departments of DSD that incur costs.

The **Computer Services Organization** manages the computer utility.

The **Business Systems Division (BSD) Organization** manages Professional Services.

The **Finance Organization** managed DSD finances, and is considered an overhead department; it thus had "direct costs" of zero.

The middle portion of the chart shows various cost categories for billing purposes.

The **IBM Cost Center** contains Computer Utility costs for GD business systems.

The **Data Entry Cost Center** contains nonprofessional data entry services. These costs are rated by labor-hour, in the same way as Professional Services.

The **SD&P (Systems Development and Programming) Cost Center** contains Professional Services costs.

The **Cyber/Univac Cost Center** contains Computer Utility costs for GD scientific and engineering systems.

The bottom of the chart shows the different consumers who are billed for DSD services.

The majority of DSD services are used by **GD Product Divisions.** Of these billed costs, 51% were charged directly to government contracts; the remaining 49% were considered product division overhead. This 51% figure was very favorable by industry standards.

DSD provided limited services to outside clients as **External Sales,** but these sales were negligible.

DSD Intercenter Costs accounted for work done by one DSD data center for another DSD data center. It was an accounting elimination tool to eliminate double charges.

DSD identified four main categories of costs within its structure—Professional Services, Computer Utility, Dedicated Resources, and Overhead Costs:

Professional Services included human services such as systems development, programming, consulting, and CAD/CAM.

Computer Utility was data processing on shared mainframe systems. These two categories were "rated"—GD divisions were charged at a given rate per unit of work for the amount of these resources consumed.

The rates in these categories were determined by dividing the total cost to DSD in each category by the total units used in each.[6] (The units used to define Professional Services rates were work-hours; the units used to define Computer Utility were volume units of processing resources.) The rate was then charged to each division for the particular amount of each cost category it consumed. These rates were reviewed monthly and adjusted at least quarterly by data center finance managers. Throughout the year, the divisions were charged at these *estimated provisional rates*. At the end of each year, the *actual rate* was calculated, and the divisions were charged or credited accordingly. Feuerstein stated, "The job of a good financial manager is to make sure the estimated rates are as close to the actual rate as possible. The division managers (our "clients") want the adjustment at the end of the year to be small—and they want it to be a credit, not a charge. Generally, our financial managers were good at their estimate adjustments."

Dedicated Resources included dedicated, division-unique (not shared) computer equipment and resources. These costs were "non-

rated"; each business unit was charged directly at DSD cost incurred for these specific devices.

Finally, DSD *Overhead Costs* were fully allocated to the divisions as a percentage of total direct costs in each cost category. DSD divided its total overhead costs by the total of their direct service costs to get the overhead percentage. All of DSD's overhead was then applied at this percentage to the other cost categories and included in the determination of rates charged to the divisions. In the nonrated category, overhead was applied as a percentage of the division's nonrated costs.

Describing the charge-out structure of DSD, Feuerstein commented on the success and importance of this complex system:

> This was a system that was well understood and accepted by the product division managers. They were used to it, they were generally comfortable with it, and it was predictable. In addition, the government accepted it. The Defense Contract Audit Agency looks over these charges with a fine-toothed comb, and they were comfortable with the existing structure.

DSD's total billable costs in 1991 were $375 million. Projected costs for 1992 were $370 million.[7] The breakdown of these 1992 costs by category (including overhead, which was projected to be 18% of direct costs) was as follows:

• Professional Services ("rated") systems development, CAD/CAM, consulting	$80 million
• Computer Utility / Processing Services ("rated") mainframe resources, tapes, disks	$82 million
• Dedicated Resources ("nonrated") dedicated division-unique resources and equipment	$208 million
TOTAL COST to GD	$370 million

---

[6]Within the Computer Utility cost category, DSD identified eight different rates for resources such as disk usage, tape drive usage, and processor usage. In the Professional Services category, however, DSD identified only one rate per hour of professional time without differentiating the skill level or specific task of the professional.

[7]These DSD cost figures did not include the 800 programmers located in GD product divisions who developed product-embedded software. These software engineers were considered product division overhead.

General Dynamics Data Systems Division was widely considered to be a highly successful operation. For example, in 1989 and 1990, *Computerworld Premier 100* rated DSD number one in the aerospace industry based on its "clearly stated IS management vision, strong commitment to IS quality, strong user role in defining applications, and advanced factory-automation applications."[8] In spite of its outstanding service, however, DSD suffered, along with the rest of General Dynamics, from the sharp decline in the defense market. The reductions in the DSD head count and billings reflected this downturn in the industry.

In 1990, with the new realities of the shrinking defense market, Hall began to evaluate the future viability of DSD. To address this issue, GD brought in a major general management consulting firm to do a strategic assessment of General Dynamics's information systems organizational structure.

Prior to the inception of this study, Ace Hall had sent Bob DeLargy, DSD vice president of finance, and Ken Wang, DSD director of systems integration, to a March 1990 conference on information systems outsourcing, which was emerging as an important trend in the information services field. Since the landmark 1989 Kodak outsourcing arrangement in which Kodak outsourced a large part of its business systems to three vendors, outsourcing had gained much attention and recognition as an important alternative solution for managing information services in the competitive economy of the 1990s. As more and more companies struggled to downsize and focus on their core businesses, outsourcing offered them a way to meet their information services needs without having to own and operate an information services business. Outsourcing was seen as an opportunity for companies to transform fixed overhead into variable costs, and free themselves from capital expenditures on information systems in an environment of rapidly changing technology. Companies found that they could receive better services at a lower cost while freeing up precious financial resources by outsourcing their IS needs to information systems experts.

At the outsourcing conference, DeLargy and Wang heard a presentation by a corporate senior vice president of Computer Sciences Corporation who introduced CSC's outsourcing framework. He explained that there were many vendors in the industry who offered "outsourcing," but had different definitions for the word. Most information services providers were "functional outsourcers" or "partial outsourcers;" they took on only one system or one portion of a company's overall information technology needs. CSC, on the other hand, defined itself as a "total outsourcer." In an outsourcing agreement, CSC would provide total information services to its clients by becoming a company's "information services partner." This presentation was so compelling that the DSD attendees invited CSC to address the next DSD strategic planning meeting later that month to present CSC's outsourcing framework as another potential option for the future of DSD.

Computer Sciences Corporation

Computer Sciences Corporation, headquartered in El Segundo, California, was a leader in the information technology systems and services industry, with clients in both the federal and private sectors. In its annual reports, the company described its business as follows:

> Computer Sciences Corporation (CSC) solves client problems in information systems technology. Its broad-based services range from management consulting in the strategic use of information and information technology to the development and operation of complete information systems. A leader in software development and systems integration, CSC designs, integrates, installs, and operates computer-based systems and

---
[8]Mitch Betts, *Computerworld Premier 100*, October 8, 1990.

communications systems. It also provides multidisci-plinary engineering support to high-technology operations and specialized proprietary services to various markets. The company manufactures no equipment.[9]

In 1991, CSC had over 23,000 employees and was composed of four major business groups: the Systems Group, the Industry Services Group, the Consulting Group, and CSC Europe.

The Systems Group was CSC's largest operating entity and major technological resource. It provided software, systems development, and systems operations primarily to the U.S. government. This federal client base consisted of hundreds of contracts with a wide range of the government's administrative, scientific, and military agencies, including NASA, the EPA, the National Weather Service, the Postal Service, the Air Force, the Navy, and the Army. The Systems Group had extensive experience specifically in the development of software for aerospace and defense systems, satellite communications, intelligence, logistics, and related high-technology fields. In 1990, the Systems Group's federal contracts accounted for 66% of CSC's total revenue. CSC was known as the premier contractor of information systems services to the U.S. government. With the Systems Group as its largest unit, the company had developed much of its expertise on large-scale government systems.

While the government provided a substantial and stable client base, CSC was also interested in expanding its private-sector client base and entering new commercial markets. According to its 1991 annual report, the company's goal in the commercial sector was to be one of the industry's top three professional services firms. CSC's commercial customers were served primarily by its Industry Services Group and its Consulting Group. The Industry Services Group handled information services, including facilities management and systems operations, for health care,

insurance, and financial-services customers. The Consulting Group (comprising subsidiaries such as CSC Index and CSC Partners) worked with businesses to develop strategic plans for information technology and to design and implement integrated systems that would fully support the customer's management objectives. (See Exhibit 6 for CSC organization chart.)

CSC was a successful and financially strong company. In 1991, the company set records in revenue and earnings from operations. World-wide commercial revenue increased 32% from $508 million to $668 million, and federal revenues increased 8% from $993 million to $1.07 billion, resulting in a total revenue of $1.74 billion in 1991, up 16% from the previous year's $1.5 billion. (See Exhibit 7 for financial summaries.) The company had made significant progress in achieving its stated goal of increasing its presence in commercial markets. In 1990, U.S. commercial revenue accounted for 21% of CSC's total revenue, with federal revenue making up 66% (the remaining 13% of revenue was accounted for by state and local government and international clients); in 1991, U.S. commercial revenue rose 3 percentage points to 24% of total. CSC also had an excellent record of capturing new business opportunities. Over the period from 1985 to 1990, the company won 54% of new federal contracts it bid on.

CSC's success was due to three decades of experience in software development and information systems management, combined with comprehensive knowledge of the information and application requirements of various industries and highly specialized government activities. The company had a deep and rich base of knowledge to bring to bear on information problems in both the public and private sectors. In addition, CSC differentiated itself in the information services market by its strong focus on quality and client satisfaction. According to William Hoover, chairman, president, and CEO,

---

[9]From CSC Annual Report, 1990.

EXHIBIT 6   Computer Sciences Corporation Organization Chart

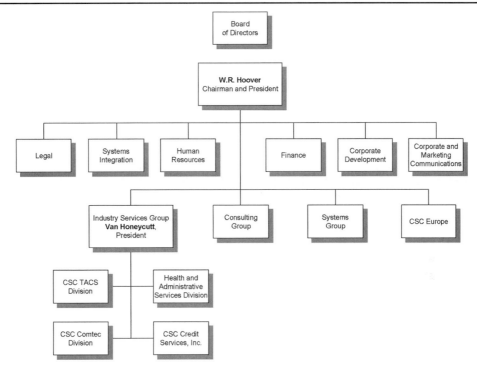

Performance management and client satisfaction are the dominant factors that have differentiated CSC in the industry. We have a high reputation for quality performance and delivering the systems that our clients ask us to build.[10]

In 1991, CSC was governed by an eight-person board of directors, comprised of three CSC insiders (President William Hoover, the chief financial officer, and the president of the Systems Group) and five outsiders.

The Outsourcing Decision

General Dynamics's interaction with CSC officially began after the March 1990 outsourcing conference, when CSC was invited to

---

[10]From an interview with William Hoover in *CEO Interviews,* May 1, 1989.

present its "total outsourcing" framework to DSD management at its strategic planning session later that month. After this meeting, DSD management was impressed with CSC, and agreed that outsourcing as a possible solution for General Dynamics's information services needs warranted further study.

1990.   Over the next several months, several key managers from CSC and DSD continued a dialogue on the subject of outsourcing, and eventually, the idea evolved into a proposed joint venture project between CSC and General Dynamics. In August of 1990, Van Honeycutt, president of CSC's Industry Services Group, formally presented the joint venture concept to Ace Hall. He proposed a shared-equity business venture of which CSC would have the majority interest; the new business

EXHIBIT 7   CSC Consolidated Balance Sheet (in thousands except shares)

	March 29, 1991
ASSETS	
Current assets:	
Cash and cash equivalents (note 1)	$ 73,304
Short-term investments, at cost	63,674
Receivables	443,447
Prepaid expenses and other current assets	37,403
Total current assets	$ 617,828
Investments and other assets:	
Excess of cost of business acquired over related net assets	$ 174,689
Purchased credit information files	34,664
Purchased software	9,918
Other assets	35,235
Total investments and other assets	$ 254,506
Property and equipment—at cost	
Land, buildings and leasehold improvements	$ 92,520
Computers and related equipment	104,297
Furniture and other equipment	54,709
	$ 251,526
Less accumulated depreciation and amortization	117,039
Net property and equipment	$ 134,487
	$ 1,006,821
LIABILITIES AND STOCKHOLDERS' EQUITY	
Current liabilities:	
Notes payable to banks	$ 28,864
Current maturities of long-term debt	3,828
Accounts payable	53,785
Accrued payroll and related costs	98,536
Other accrued expenses	56,611
Federal, state, and foreign income taxes	113,339
Total current liabilities	$ 354,963
Long-term debt, net of current maturities	$ 108,867
Other long-term liabilities	$ 16,765
Total stockholders' equity	$ 526,226
	$ 1,006,821

EXHIBIT 7 (CONTINUED)   **CSC Statement of Earnings (in thousands except per-share amounts)**

	Fiscal Year Ended		
	March 29, 1991	*March 30, 1990*	*March 31, 1989*
Revenues	$1,737,791	$1,500,443	$1,304,414
Expenses			
Cost of services	1,436,052	1,230,930	1,067,189
Operating overhead	131,512	118,594	98,885
Depreciation and amortization	40,203	34,014	31,090
	$1,607,767	$1,383,538	$1,197,164
Operating income	130,024	116,905	107,250
Corporate general and administrative expenses	23,376	20,945	19,416
Other expense (income)—net	4,106	(7,240)	3,370
	$ 27,482	$ 13,705	$ 22,786
Income before taxes	102,542	103,200	84,464
Taxes on income	37,551	37,668	31,982
Net earnings	$ 64,991	$ 65,532	$ 52,482
Earnings per common share	$ 4.02	$ 4.07	$ 3.28

would provide information services to General Dynamics and other clients. Through the end of 1990, Hall, Feuerstein, and other DSD managers remained interested in the CSC proposal and arranged several meetings with Honeycutt and other CSC managers to refine the details of the concept.

January 1991.   In January of 1991, William A. Anders became General Dynamics's new CEO after having spent a year as vice chairman. His top priorities as CEO were to increase shareholder value and build financial strength and flexibility to ensure the survival of General Dynamics in the shrinking defense market. Anders formed a Corporate Executive Council of GD's top executives and division heads for the purpose of driving his strategies throughout the company. For the Council's first meeting, in March of 1991, Anders assigned "home-

work" for each member—he asked them to bring to the meeting innovative ideas for implementing his corporate strategies and managing GD in the shrinking defense market of the future.

March 1991.   At this council meeting, Ace Hall presented the idea of a joint venture with CSC to provide information services to GD and other clients. Anders and the Executive Council were interested in the proposal, and Jim Mellor, GD president and chief operating officer, asked Hall to present the CSC option at an upcoming meeting in May, at which the consulting firm was scheduled to present their findings and recommendations for GD's future information services structure.

May 1991.   In what Larry Feuerstein described as "an *intense* six-hour session," Jim Mellor and other GD corporate managers heard first from the consulting firm. The consultants recommended maintaining the information systems facilities within General Dynamics, but eliminating the centralized Data Systems Division and returning the IS capabilities to the individual business groups. This plan was estimated to result in a cumulative savings of $243 million over a four-year period. Feuerstein noted, however, that he was skeptical of their numbers and wary of their plan:

> I thought their numbers were probably overstated, and their implementation plan made me nervous. They wanted us to go back to the IS structure we had in 1973, before we consolidated into a centralized data systems organization. But that kind of a structure wouldn't work for us today. Our IT capabilities had become so specialized that I doubted the operating units had enough expertise to manage them well. In addition, by being centralized, we had achieved economies of scale that would be lost if DSD was broken up and parceled out to the other divisions. Finally, it would not have been good for our people. Frankly, IS professionals are seen as "second-class citizens" by the product engineers in the operating units. Spread out across these units, they would lose the professional community and career development opportunities that DSD was able to offer. We would end up losing our best people to other companies that could offer them a better career path.

With the consulting team still at the conference table, Feuerstein then presented the CSC idea, which he called "Another Potential Option for Information Systems Structural Change." He explained the history of the joint venture proposal and gave background on CSC, highlighting its strong financial position and extensive experience in government information systems. He identified the benefits for GD as cost reductions for information services, a large cash infusion (since CSC would purchase GD's IS facilities for the new business), and the opportunity to participate in the growth market of commercial outsourcing. The risks, however, were the loss of GD's full control over its IS resources, the potential failure of the new business, and the

uncertain growth of the commercial outsourcing market. Feuerstein's main goal in this meeting was to learn whether or not there was enough interest on the part of corporate headquarters to explore this option further.

At the end of the meeting, and much to the surprise of the consultants, Mellor was very enthusiastic about the CSC option. As Feuerstein later noted, "It was critical that Mellor was positive. We would never have done this deal without operating management's buy-in." Mellor suggested that Hall and Feuerstein present the plan to Harvey Kapnick, GD vice chairman, whom Anders had brought in to drive his corporate restructuring strategy. As Feuerstein explained,

> Kapnick was Anders's shareholder-value-enhancement and divestiture guy. It was an incredible bit of fate, too, because Kapnick had been a top executive of another computer services firm, and so he understood the intricacies of MIS and was immediately drawn to this plan. This was an important subtle nuance in this whole process.

Kapnick was interested in the concept and agreed to meet with top CSC people to discuss the proposed business venture. On May 22, Ace Hall, Larry Feuerstein, and Harvey Kapnick met for dinner at the St. Louis Club with Van Honeycutt, CSC CEO William Hoover, and a CSC corporate senior vice president. As Feuerstein described it:

> It was a very positive meeting. Harvey [Kapnick] and Bill [Hoover] hit it off very well. And since Kapnick and a member of the CSC team had some mutual experience, there was instant common ground. They traded names and stories for a long time, helping to set a positive tone. The group was congenial; there was an immediate "fit." This was a critical "chemistry test." Had that meeting not gone so well, the whole idea might well have gone straight to the filing cabinet. After dinner, Harvey said to Ace and me, "These are good guys; I could work with them." And that was our go-ahead.

June 1991.   Throughout early June, various teams of GD and CSC people traded visits to one another's facilities. Feuerstein noted that:

CSC has an extremely good ability to muster a companywide team of great, intelligent, experienced people. The right individuals were there within 48 hours. They really know how to respond to a deal and pull it off.

Feuerstein invited a CSC review team to "come out and kick the tires" at DSD's regional data centers. According to Feuerstein, they were impressed with the IS facilities and personnel. Jim Mellor and several GD senior operations managers visited CSC offices and facilities to assess CSC operational capabilities. According to Feuerstein:

The GD operations guys came away satisfied that CSC had the capability to serve their information needs. They saw that CSC had not only the technological capability, but also the "product fit" because of their extensive experience with government clients and weapons systems. CSC grew up in the same defense business as we did. They know the regulations and the critical success factors. We would have had to teach other vendors the rules of the defense environment before they could do the work.

With their knowledge of the defense and high-tech industries, CSC was able to speak our language. This was another critical litmus test. Because IS runs throughout all of GD's operating units, we *had* to get the business units' buy-in. Mellor liked what he saw in the CSC facilities, and the operations managers were confident too. So he gave Kapnick the thumbs-up.

Later that month, Hall, Feuerstein, Kapnick, and GD's chief financial officer met with Honeycutt and Hoover to discuss terms for the proposed business venture. The main concern at this meeting was how to value the sale of GD's IS business. According to Feuerstein:

This was the point where the deal began to crash and burn. The problem is that there is no precedent for valuation of this kind. There is no "used-car blue book" to understand how to value these assets. The net book value for the assets was $140 million; but because of the award-winning service DSD maintained, we also expected some premium above book value. Harvey Kapnick had worked in information services before, so he was very familiar with computer systems and facilities. He looked at the data we had and estimated the value of our business at perhaps $200 million. We went in to the meeting with CSC

hoping to get near this amount. They offered us a 10-year contract with an annual charge for IS services that offered a slight savings over DSD's current charges. But the purchase price they offered us for the business was not acceptable.

Both sides left the meeting with this issue unresolved and the future of the joint venture uncertain.

Over the next month, Harvey Kapnick continued to think about the plan and finally decided that a joint-venture business was not the best solution at all—a 100% sale and pure outsourcing agreement would be better for both parties. In an outsourcing partnership, CSC could purchase outright all of GD's IS facilities and business (except product-embedded technology development)[11] and then provide information services to them. This solution fit beautifully with Anders's corporate strategy—General Dynamics would get a large cash infusion from this sale, could divest a noncore business division (DSD), and would not have to worry about the future risks of being involved in a new non-core high technology business. General Dynamics surmised that with CSC's interest in gaining more commercial clients, it would be eager to obtain the facilities for commercial outsourcing that GD could provide. Other GD top executives agreed with Kapnick that the better plan was an outsourcing agreement, and not a joint business venture. This change of mindset sparked renewed interest in the negotiation, but the purchase price was still an unresolved issue.

In order for this deal to go through, a purchase price for the business would have to be agreed upon, and then Hall and Feuerstein would have to work with CSC to put together a plan for outsourcing DSD that they could then present to the GD Board of Directors at their next meeting in August—less than two months away. If the Board approved the outsourcing concept, the two companies would then work to create a detailed contractual agreement.

---

[11]GD's product-embedded hardware and software technology was never up for sale in this negotiation. This proprietary technology was crucial for GD's innovative product strategies. As such, this technology fell under the auspices of GD "product development," rather than "information services."

At this point, Hall and Feuerstein had several critical issues on their minds: Clearly, the cash infusion generated by the sale of DSD would be very valuable to GD, but how much was "enough"? How much cash did they have to get for the sale of the DSD business to make the transaction worthwhile? In addition, the flexibility and savings afforded by outsourcing was a great advantage, but were the advantages of outsourcing worth the risks? How much cost savings should they demand? Or would it be enough for GD to pay CSC an amount equal to their own DSD charges for the benefit of cash and flexibility? How could GD maintain enough control over its information systems? How "operationally transparent" could this transfer be? How could they minimize the trauma to the organization and the people? How would employees be treated by this deal? Could they take their pensions, vacations, and fringe benefits with them as they transferred from GD to CSC? What would happen to the CSC contract in the future if GD decided, according to Anders's corporate policy, to divest any of its business units?

CONCLUDING THOUGHTS

Prediction is hard, especially of the future.
—Yogi Berra, *Hall of Fame Baseball Player and Manager*

In 1943, Thomas Watson, the venerable Chairman of the IBM Corporation, predicted that there would be a world market for "maybe five computers." Today, when there are literally hundreds of millions of computers worldwide, this colossal blunder reminds us how ill-prepared we are to see very far into the future. A quick glance backward reinforces the point. In 1992, there were no web browsers. Before 1995, Netscape was not yet a public company and Amazon had not been founded. Five years ago, who would have foreseen all that has since come to pass? Much has changed very quickly and nothing has happened to suggest that the IT industry is on the verge of a period of calm. There is surely more excitement ahead.

The objective of this book has been to provide readers with a better understanding of the influence of 21st century technologies on business decisions. This kind of understanding, when achieved, may help managers predict some of the wonderous things to come. But our aim here has not been to arm you to engage in predictions for prediction's sake. Instead we have focused on analytical frameworks and issues involved in using those frameworks to identify opportunities, design and deploy new technology-based businesses, and to create business value in the information age. These frameworks are based on concepts and theory that have withstood the test of time and remain relevant despite radical changes in the business environment. We have dealt with enduring practical questions, from the point of view of the executives who are grappling with them. Not long ago, many predicted the death of traditional economic and management principles. The subsequent fall in technology market stocks suggests that we should not be too quick to throw out those "old ideas" as we embrace the new.

Markets and models; capabilities, leadership, and organizations; infrastructure; and implementation and change management are the four enduring subject areas used to organize the management issues discussed in this book. As we have demonstrated, the effect of the new technologies on markets will be to alter competitive positions, to frame new strategic imperatives, and to suggest new IT-enabled strategies and ways of acquiring important capabilities. The new technologies have enabled new business models and improved the viability of old ones; executives in established firms that do not seize business model opportunities presented by new technologies will find their market positions threatened. As businesses seek to find value in the Information Age, they are forced to reexamine their capabilities, leadership and even the organizational structure itself. Infrastructure management includes all of those interwoven business-technical issues that general managers dread, but that ultimately make the difference between a rigid and constraining IT capability and a flexible and dynamic one; it is an area with many layers of relationships, technology models, and assurance processes that ultimately determines IT possibilities, that dramatically affects the ability to compete today and the business opportunities that can be pursued in the future. And finally, there is implementation and change management, areas that many companies cannot seem to solve; the projects grow larger and harder, and decisions must be made faster than some companies can learn. Yet this is an area that must be mastered if disasters are to be averted and if returns are to be realized from IT investments.

We conclude this book with a final case—Merrill Lynch—that provides an opportunity to analyze strategic decision making in the financial services industry and dovetails with the Schwab cases at the beginning of the book. The Merrill Lynch[1] case analyzes strategic reactions of this once-dominant established player in response to the launch of online Internet businesses by new entrants and established players that changed the power and the basis of competition within the financial services industry. A full service brokerage firm with $1.5 trillion in client assets, Merrill Lynch was under attack from both discount and electronic brokerage firms. It responded with Integrated Choice, a suite of products designed to capture clients from the do-it-yourself investor who does not want to use a broker to clients who want to rely completely on a broker. The high risk strategy requires massive organizational change.

---

[1]Weber, J. and McFarlan, F.W., *Merrill Lynch: Integrated Choice,* (HBS No. 301-081).

CASE C–1
MERRILL LYNCH: INTEGRATED CHOICE (ABRIDGED)[1]

We have put together the widest range of choice for our clients. Merrill Lynch can say to either you, your children, or your grandchildren, "How do you want to approach the market?" No matter how you respond, we will have a market offering to fit your needs.

David Komansky, Chairman & CEO, Merrill Lynch

The Wall Street Week, Oct. 15, 1999

We have moved forward like a bullet train and it is our competitors that are scrambling not to get run over.

John L. Steffens, *Vice Chairman & Head of U.S. Private Client, Merrill Lynch*

John L. (Launny) Steffens, vice chairman[2] and head of Merrill Lynch's U.S. Private Client Group, sat in his New Jersey office taking a brief moment to contemplate the frigid January landscape. Time, always at a premium in the retail brokerage business, was in especially short supply these days. Six months earlier, Merrill Lynch had stunned the financial services community by unveiling a new vision for the business called Integrated Choice. While it had been expected that the company, the market leader in full-service brokerage but under attack from discount and electronic traders, would make some kind of an "online move," the scope of the new offering and its pricing levels had raised the bar beyond anyone's expectations.

Integrated Choice made Merrill Lynch a one-stop source for financial services. The strategy was based on allowing customers to choose the products they wanted, the level of advice they wanted, and the way they wanted to transact their business.

Merrill Lynch announced its new direction on June 1, 1999, and products were rolled out over the next six months. U.S. Private Client was bullish on itself and established "choice" goals for 2005; specifically, it had set a target of being the Money Manager of Choice, with 20% of affluent relationships and $5 trillion in assets; the Advisor of Choice, with 17,500 financial consultants with high performance goals; the Bank of Choice, with $100 billion in deposits; and the Credit Card of Choice, with billions in VISA Signature transactions. As of 1998, Merrill Lynch had about 15% market share of affluent relationships, about $1.5 trillion in assets, and $6 billion in customer deposits.

Steffens knew that to achieve these goals, U.S. Private Client would have to successfully implement the Integrated Choice strategy and this would not be easy. His top three concerns were motivating the financial consultants to actively support the plan, managing a seamless transition, and determining the future role of the financial consultants.

Integrated Choice. As seen in Figure A with Integrated Choice, Merrill Lynch clients were offered a continuum of products from the fully self-directed (ML Direct) to the fully delegated

---

[1]This case was prepared by Senior Associate James Weber under the supervision of Professor F. Warren McFarlan. Copyright © 2000 by the President and Fellows of Harvard College. Harvard Business School case 301-081. It is an abridged version of an earlier case *Merrill Lynch: Integrated Choice* prepared by Professor Kasturi and Research Associate Marie Bell. HBS No. 500-090.

[2]During the course of writing this case Launny Steffens was promoted to chairman, U.S. Private Client.

FIGURE A Integrated Choice

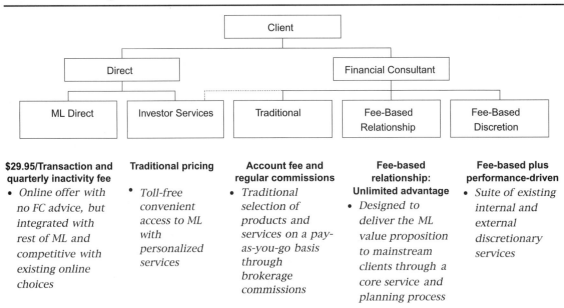

$29.95/Transaction and quarterly inactivity fee	**Traditional pricing**	**Account fee and regular commissions**	**Fee-based relationship: Unlimited advantage**	**Fee-based plus performance-driven**
• *Online offer with no FC advice, but integrated with rest of ML and competitive with existing online choices*	• *Toll-free convenient access to ML with personalized services*	• *Traditional selection of products and services on a pay-as-you-go basis through brokerage commissions*	• *Designed to deliver the ML value proposition to mainstream clients through a core service and planning process*	• *Suite of existing internal and external discretionary services*

(discretionary). Based on their individual needs and preferences, clients could opt for single or multiple accounts.

Clients who wished to invest online without the advice and guidance of a financial consultant could do so by opening a Merrill Lynch Direct account. ML Direct, a brand new offering from Merrill Lynch, offered online trading for as little as $29.95 per equity trade. Additionally, clients could purchase a range of fixed-income products through a Merrill Lynch Direct Service associate and participate in initial public offerings through the online IPO Center.

Next in the range of do-it-yourself products was Investor Services. Here, clients could access a Merrill Lynch representative 24 hours per day, seven days a week, for information, advice, and transactions via a toll-free telephone number. The reps, who were fully licensed and trained, worked on salary, not commissions. Although Investor Services was initially designed in 1997 to serve clients with assets of about $100,000 or less at Merrill

Lynch, experience showed that some clients with substantially larger assets preferred to be served this way. Investor Services clients had the option of selecting either fee-based pricing (% of assets) or traditional commission-based pricing ($ per trade).

There was a range of options available to clients that desired a relationship founded on advice from a financial consultant, the traditional brokerage relationship with a financial consultant being one. Clients opting for this paid on a fee-for-service basis based on the existing commission structures. The large majority of Merrill Lynch's five million private clients had this type of account.

Another choice was to establish an Unlimited Advantage account. For an annual fee, charged as a % of assets, starting at a minimum of $1,500, clients received personalized service from a financial consultant, a Financial Foundation (Merrill Lynch's comprehensive personal financial plan), virtually unlimited trading (by telephone, person-to-person, or online), and an array of other financial services, benefits, and products. Although clients received advice from their financial consultants, they could also execute transactions independently through Merrill Lynch Online or an automated touch-tone phone service.

Clients who wanted to minimize their involvement with investment decision-making could use Merrill Lynch's discretionary services and assign portfolio management responsibilities to a professional money manager. Merrill Lynch had access to hundreds of such money managers who, for a fee, would manage the client's portfolio. Such customers received customized asset-based pricing. About 100,000 of Merrill Lynch's clients chose this kind of service.

No matter which option clients chose, they gained access to a range of exclusive Merrill Lynch products and services. First in these services was access to proprietary Merrill Lynch analyst research, considered among the best in the industry. Other products and services included the Visa Signature credit card, check writing and electronic bill payment, and an exclusive electronic shopping site where over 400 retailers offered special promotions to Merrill Lynch customers.

Merrill Lynch's U.S. Private Client

Company Background.   Founded by Charles E. Merrill in 1914 with a belief that the financial markets should be accessible to everyone,

Merrill Lynch was often credited with bringing Wall Street to Main Street. In its modern form, Merrill Lynch's income was derived from operations in two main business segments: Wealth Management Group, with 1998 revenues of $11,331 million, and the Corporate and Institutional Client group (CICG), with revenues of $6,522 million. As seen in Table A below, Wealth Management had two broad product categories: brokerage and lending (e.g., securities transactions on behalf of clients, secured lendings, and asset allocation activities), and asset management and portfolio services. U.S. Private Client was part of the Wealth Management group.

Central to Merrill Lynch's Wealth Management strategy was asset gathering from millions of individual investors and small- and medium-sized businesses. Over the last 10 years, client assets had increased at a 16% compound annual rate to nearly $1,500 billion at the end of 1998. Included in these assets were $500 billion managed by the company's Asset Management Group. Thus, for example, if a Merrill Lynch client invested in a Merrill Lynch mutual fund, the brokerage transaction fee (in this case the "load") would show up as brokerage fee and the fee for management of the fund would show up as asset management fee. If, however, the client bought an outside security, then the only revenue source would be the brokerage transaction fee. U.S. Private Client managed nearly 80% of all assets, the

TABLE A   Wealth Management Revenues (worldwide)

($ in millions)	1996	1997	1998
Net Revenues	**$7,984**	**$9,505**	**$11,331**
Brokerage and Lending	$5,435	$6,328	$6,989
Asset Management and Portfolio Service	$2,431	$3,002	$4,202
Other	$118	$175	$140
Net Earnings	**$855**	**$1,056**	**$1,346**

Source: Company Documents.

rest coming from international operations. Approximately 66% of Merrill Lynch's Private Client assets were represented by equities (such as stocks and mutual funds), 22% by debt (fixed income vehicles) and 12% by cash. (See Exhibit 1 for Merrill Lynch's financial statements. Exhibit 2 shows client asset growth for Merrill Lynch and Charles Schwab, a key competitor.)

U.S. Private Client—All Things to Some People. U.S. Private Client served individuals, small businesses, and employee benefit plans using a planning-based approach to provide cash, asset, liability, and transition management services. Through nearly 14,000 financial consultants in approximately 750 offices throughout the United States, Merrill Lynch provided one of the widest arrays of financial services and products, sound advice, and effective execution. These financial consultants had strong relationships with five million households, ranging from high-net-worth individuals to young "next-generation" clients

(about 3 million clients), and with small- to mid-sized businesses and regional financial institutions (about 2 million clients).

Much of Merrill Lynch's strategy in the 1990s was based upon a visionary white paper written by Launny Steffens in the early 1980s. In that document, he described, "Why Becoming All Things to Some People," was so important:

All of our research has pointed toward a strategy of segmenting our client base, better identifying our target client groups, and then developing broader and stronger relationships with our key clients. It is obvious that the biggest payoff to Merrill Lynch does not lie in expanding our client base randomly across the entire spectrum of American households. Instead, the real profit potential rests with our ability to target and meet the financial needs of current and prospective affluent "A" individuals and small businesses that already provide the bulk of income to the financial services industry. Hence the goal is to become "All Things to Some People," . . . Thus the key to attracting such individuals to Merrill Lynch is to provide them with comprehensive, innovative solutions to their financial problems. We must package products like CMA to provide day-to-day convenience along with truly sophisti-

EXHIBIT 1A   Condensed Income Statement 1995–1998 ($ millions)

	1994	*1995*	*1996*	*1997*	*1998*
Revenue					
Commissions	$3,060	$3,308	$4,085	$4,995	$5,799
Interest and dividends	9,608	12,449	13,125	17,299	19,314
Investment banking & other revenues	5,905	6,303	8,503	10,205	10,740
Total revenues	18,573	22,060	25,713	32,499	35,853
Interest expense	8,614	11,445	12,092	16,243	18,306
Net revenues	9,959	10,615	13,621	16,256	17,547
Non-Interest Expenses					
Compensation and benefits	5,165	5,478	7,012	8,333	9,199
Communications and technologies	722	814	1,010	1,255	1,749
Other	2,325	2,487	2,971	3,604	4,627
Total non-interest expenses	8,212	8,779	10,993	13,145	15,451
Earnings before income taxes and dividends	1,747	1,836	2,628	3,111	2,096
Income tax expense	717	710	980	1,129	713
Net earnings	1,030	1,126	1,648	1,935	1,259

Exhibit 1B Condensed Balance Sheet ($ millions)

	1997	1998
Assets		
Cash and cash equivalents	$17,430	$19,120
Receivables	151,438	148,211
Trading assets at fair value	108,091	107,845
Other Assets	20,021	24,628
Total Assets	296,980	299,804
Liabilities		
Payables under repurchase agreements and securities loaned transactions	79,167	67,127
Commercial paper and other short-term borrowings	34,340	18,679
Trading liabilities at fair value	71,214	63,714
Long-term borrowings	43,143	57,563
Other liabilities	60,577	82,589
Total liabilities	288,441	289,672
Stockholders' Equity		
Equity	2,075	2,426
Retained earnings	9,579	10,475
Less treasury stock at cost and employee stock transactions	(3,115)	(2,769)
Total stockholders' equity	8,539	10,132
Total Liabilities and Stockholders' Equity	296,980	299,804

Exhibit 2 Client Asset Growth 1991–1998 ($ billions)

	1991	1992	1993	1994	1995	1996	1997	1998
U.S. household financial assets	$16,450	$17,294	$18,403	$19,081	$21,697	$24,039	$27,300	$30,633
Deposits	2,889	2,911	2,845	2,806	2,916	3,034	3,210	3,400
Total Securities Assets*	5,232	5,692	6,256	6,420	7,695	8,715	9,923	11,465
Merrill Lynch								
U.S. Private Client Assets	$422.2	$463.7	$527.4	$537.0	$664.8	$791.5	$979.0	$1,164.0
Assets under Mgt.**	123.6	138.5	161.0	163.8	196.4	234.1	446.4	501.0
% of Client Assets	29.3%	29.9%	30.5%	30.5%	29.5%	29.6%	45.6%	43.0%
Charles Schwab								
Total Client Assets	$47.5	$65.6	$95.8	$122.6	$181.7	$253.0	$354.0	$491.1
Mutual Fund Assets under Mgt.	14.6	22.9	40.7	54.3	81.7	93.0	160.4	210.6

*Corporate equities, fixed income, mutual funds, money market funds, and free credit balances
**Reflects the acquisition of Mercury Asset Management in 1997.
Source: Adapted from *Financial Services Retail Brokerage,* "The Bumpy Ride to Bigger, Better, Cheaper, Faster," Morgan Stanley Dean Witter, October 12, 1999.

cated financial planning and advice. The relationship between the client and the [financial consultant] is the central issue here, and must be the focus of our efforts.

Financial consultants worked with clients in managing their assets. The Cash Management Account (CMA), which Merrill Lynch pioneered for individuals in 1977, and the Working Capital Management Account for businesses were important tools for delivering a wide range of client services, including effecting trades in stocks, bonds, and other securities in financial markets around the world. For example, with the CMA account, Merrill Lynch clients could hold cash and write checks outside their bank accounts, and yet earn money market fund interest rates, which were higher than what they could get from bank deposits. Merrill Lynch also made available its investment research and offered various advisory programs.

Merrill Lynch financial consultants[3] were considered some of the best in the industry. A financial consultant's first two years were spent primarily in training and initial prospecting for clients. During this period, the firm supported the financial consultant's salary, but thereafter compensation was based on a complex formula that included commissions on traditional transactions (about 50% of brokerage commissions), client assets, and cash balances. Roughly 65% of a financial consultant's compensation came from brokerage fees, 25% on assets and asset growth, and the rest from performance against targeted marketing programs.

As a client's assets grew with Merrill Lynch, financial consultants directed their clients through a financial planning program, where clients filled out a detailed questionnaire, often with the help of the financial consultant, which was then processed at Merrill Lynch's centralized Financial Planning Resource Center. The outcome of the analysis, typically a substantial document with considerable detail, was sent back to the financial consultant who sat down face-to-face with the client to explain its implications and to redirect their savings, investments, insurance, estate planning and other such financial matters. Merrill Lynch financial consultants were considered very entrepreneurial and built their businesses through mailings, seminars, client referrals, cold calling, and word-of-mouth. There was no set rule on how they gained clients, some focused on doctors, some on ethnic groups, some on personal relationships in neighborhoods, and so on.

In the industry, brokers usually earned about $100–175K per year, but average compensation at Merrill Lynch was much higher, estimated at $300K,[4] with some earning in excess of $1 million. Recognizing the value of financial consultants in their relationships with clients, Merrill provided its experienced financial consultants some latitude in pricing its products. For example, they could discount brokerage transactions by as much as half the brokerage fee. Turnover was high with 20% to 40% of new hires leaving the organization within three years. Some who left the firm failed to meet Merrill Lynch's performance and quality targets while others found the work unappealing long-term. The firm prided itself on the very high standards it set for its financial consultants. On occasion, Merrill Lynch lost highly productive financial consultants to competitors, but at this level, the churn rate of experienced financial consultants was at about the industry average of 5%, which was very creditable given the large size of Merrill Lynch's salesforce. The strong stock market (see Exhibit 3 for market performance

---

[3]Even though we broadly refer to all members of Merrill Lynch's salesforce as financial consultants, in reality, they were designated as senior FC, assistant VP, VP, first VP, or senior VP.

[4]Charles Gasparino, "Wall Street is rocked by Merrill's online move," *The Wall Street Journal,* June 2, 1999, p. C1.

EXHIBIT 3   Dow Jones Industrial Average Performance 1970–1999

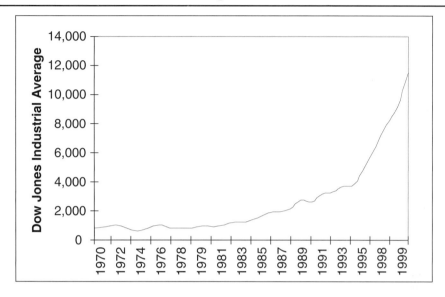

from 1970 to 1999) and the caliber of Merrill Lynch financial consultants made them a target for competitive firms anxious to hire proven high producers, with some "Wall Street securities firms offering upfront hiring packages of more than 100% of top brokers' commissions and fees for the past 12 months in order to persuade brokers to change firms."[5] Merrill Lynch's financial consultants were housed in 750 offices, reported to a manager who in turn reported to 180 regional vice presidents, who reported to 25 district managers and ultimately to two national sales directors.

Merrill Lynch actively used technology to enhance client service and leverage its financial consultants. Initiatives included Trusted Global Advisor (TGA), a technology platform for financial consultants which enabled them to view their clients' assets and transaction history online, thus making them more effective in advising their clients.

Merrill Lynch also served clients' diverse liability management needs. Through Merrill Lynch Credit Corporation (MLCC), financial consultants offered their clients a broad selection of first mortgage loans, home equity, and securities-based lines of credit and commercial real estate financing. The company was increasingly active in transition management. Its Insurance Group offered both fixed and variable annuities and variable life insurance products designed for retirement and estate planning. Through the Merrill Lynch Trust Company, the firm offered clients numerous trust and estate planning services designed to minimize estate taxes while preserving income in retirement. In addition, Merrill Lynch Group Employee Services provided 401(k) administration and investment services.

Competitive Environment. Until the late 1990s, firms in the industry competed against both other firms within their segment and

---

[5]Randall Smith, "Wall Street still spends big to court top stockbrokers," *The Wall Street Journal,* July 14, 1999, p. C1.

key firms in other segments. For example, Merrill Lynch would compete against other full-service brokers such as Prudential Securities and Morgan Stanley Dean Witter, while maintaining an awareness of the activities of discount brokerage leader Charles Schwab. Moreover, brokerage firms like Merrill Lynch competed with banks by drawing away their affluent customers' deposit accounts, which formed the entry point for many customers' use of securities firms.

In recent years, however, technological advances and other factors had begun to blur the differentiation between segments, and there was increased competition between the segments for the affluent individual investor. (Exhibit 4 shows projections for average client account balances, number of trades, and commission rates for brokerage segments.)

Schwab's recent advertising emphasized the affluent customer, suggesting that it was time for customers "to trade up to Schwab." Many industry observers also perceived Schwab's purchase of U.S. Trust (that managed $86 billion in assets mostly for clients

with investable assets of $2 million and up) in January 2000 as a means of furthering its initiatives with high-net-worth investors.

At the same time, while Schwab was targeting full-service firms' clients, full-service firms were becoming increasingly interested in discount brokers' higher-net-worth clients. Indeed, full-service firms had begun to focus more and more on Charles Schwab as a significant competitor, effectively turning the tables from "predator to prey."[6] One Merrill Lynch executive noted:

> In the past we viewed Schwab solely as a discount firm, believing that once its clients reached a certain level of affluence, about half a million dollars or so, that they would need more sophisticated analysis and advice and transition to a full-service firm, and indeed much research shows that at that stage most investors seek expert financial advice. However, with the blurring of competitive lines between full service and discounters, we are on the offensive and actively seeking to take affluent clients from Schwab.

----

[6]Rebecca Buckman, "Schwab, once a predator, is now prey," *The Wall Street Journal,* December 8, 1999.

EXHIBIT 4   Account Size, Number of Trades, and Commission Rates by Segment

	1998	*1999 (E)*	*2000 (E)*	*2001 (E)*	*2002 (E)*	*2003 (E)*
Discount (e.g., Etrade)						
Account size	$26,812	$28,957	$31,274	$33,775	$36,477	$39,396
Avg. # of trades	21.3	23.5	21.7	19.8	18.9	17.9
Avg. commission rate	$13.34	$13.27	$12.16	$11.09	$10.05	$9.05
Mid-tier (e.g., Schwab)						
Account size	$75,000	$84,000	$94,080	$104,429	$114,872	$126,359
Avg. # of trades	6.1	8.1	8.3	7.9	7.7	7.2
Avg. commission rate	$48.84	$39.06	$29.04	$24.37	$21.03	$18.79
Full Service (e.g., Merrill Lynch)						
Account size	$178,085	$185,944	$187,098	$191,007	$196,907	$204,497
Avg. # of trades	4.0	3.8	3.9	4.2	4.4	4.7
Avg. commission rate	$105.00	$99.75	$80.45	$62.88	$50.38	$41.57

Note: This table divides the industry into three segments: discount (e.g., Etrade), mid-tier (e.g., Schwab) and full service (e.g., Merrill Lynch)
Source: *Financial Services Retail Brokerage,* "The Bumpy Ride to Bigger, Better, Cheaper, Faster, Morgan Stanley Dean Witter," October 12, 1999

Merrill Lynch Continues to Lead

Although competitive forces pummeled the industry, Merrill Lynch commanded the largest share of household assets. As traditional competitive lines blurred, U.S. Private Client expanded its competitive set beyond traditional full-service firms. It paid special attention to two groups: competitors who posed clear threats to Merrill Lynch through their use of open architecture or the breadth and integration of their product lines; and a second class of competitors who posed a competitive threat because of their proven ability to re-shape the industry through innovations (see Exhibit 5).

Target Market

Merrill Lynch targeted the affluent individuals with investable assets of at least $100,000. Priority Clients with at least $250,000 in assets at Merrill Lynch were a key group of customers. On average they were about 60 years old, with assets of $650K, and traded about 6 times per year (see Exhibit 6 for a profile of Merrill Lynch's clients). Premier Priority Clients represented a generally higher level of affluence (greater than

---

EXHIBIT 5   U.S. Private Client Competitors

Competitors	*Rationale*
Top Tier Competitors	
American Express	Building retail client base by using like financial planners and accountants.
Bank of America/NationsBank	Largest bank in the U.S.
Charles Schwab	Innovator in discount brokerage. Moving beyond self-service model to aggressively compete for certain full service clients.
Citigroup	Pursuing universal financial service model. Global scale and presence.
Fidelity Investments	Leading mutual fund 401(k) provider in the U.S. Noted for exceptional performance of funds.
Morgan Stanley Dean Witter	Full service provider noted for integration of its operations and execution of the "Merrill Lynch" strategy. Aggressively competes for brokers.
Other Industry Shapers	
A. G. Edwards	Leader in customer satisfaction among full-service companies.
E*Trade	State of the art technology. Marking strides toward building a virtual universal financial services company.
First Union	State of the art technology to support cash management and identify cross selling opportunities.
Goldman Sachs	The "gold standard" for the delivery of products and services to high net worth clients.
KeyCorp	Creative use of strategic alliances to build an extensive product line.
USAA	Leader in back-office technology and customer service.
Vanguard	Mutual fund leader noted for indexing, low expenses, and self-help philosophy.

Source: Company records

EXHIBIT 6   **Merrill Lynch Client Profile**

	Total Merrill Lynch Clients	Merrill Lynch Priority Clients
1999 Demographic Profile		
Age (median)	53 years	63 years
% male	51%	53%
% retired	37%	62%
% self or spouse currently own a business	16%	16%
% with college degree or more	58%	63%
% married	67%	69%
Financial Profile		
1998 annual income (median)	$63K	$80K
Total household investable assets	$120K	$500K
% of household investable assets held at ML (median)	50%	75%
Work-related savings (e.g.,401 (k)) (median)	$50K	$120K
Years with Merrill Lynch (median)	10 years	15 years
# of total trades across firms used in the last 12 months (median)	3 trades	6 trades
Planning and Technology		
% with written financial plan	27%	42%
% use PC at home or work	68%	60%
% access Internet	54%	47%

Source: Company survey data based on a stratified random sample of 704 Priority clients, 504 Near Priority clients and 500 Low Asset clients.

$1 million in assets) and a generally greater use of products across product categories. Premier Plus Clients were wealthy individuals with even higher levels of investable assets that often required very specialized financial products and services. Overall, clients with more than $1 million in household assets accounted for about 5% of client households, but represented about 60% of assets. The top 15% of Private Client households represented three-quarters of assets. Table B below summarizes U.S. Private Client households by client segment.

Merrill Lynch Transforms Its Business Strategy

In early 1998, U.S. Private Client's Executive Committee established eight initiatives for further exploration. Of these initiatives, Launny Steffens believed that technology and pricing were the most pressing. On the technology side, the Internet, which had initially been no more than a 'gnat', was attracting increasing attention. In May 1998, Jupiter Communications reported that nearly 12% of U.S. households with incomes above $75,000 (i.e., 4.6 million households) conducted online financial transactions. By 2000, that number was projected to increase to 31%.

Without any pre-conceived bias towards change, Steffens established separate taskforces to analyze these issues. In June 1998, a taskforce, led by Madeline (Maddy) Weinstein, senior V.P. and director of U.S. Private Client (USPC) Business Innovation Group, was established with a mandate to look into the online

TABLE B   Households by Client Segment

Households (000s)	Existing Merrill Lynch Private Clients	Potential U.S. Market
Premier Plus	25	266
Premier Priority Clients	150	8,864
Priority Clients	825	10,495
Other Household Relationships	2,500	94,577
Group Employee Services Relationships	2,000	27,000

Source: Adapted from company records.

phenomena. In August 1998, Steffens charged another taskforce, led by Allen Jones, senior V.P., Private Client Marketing, with the pricing question.

The Online Taskforce.   The leaders of the pricing and the online taskforces were members of each other's taskforce. Outside consultants were connected as well. This cross-membership ensured that data were actively shared between the two groups. One member recalled:

> The recommendations of the online taskforce were unanimous. It was clear to us that there had been a rapid, significant change in investor attitudes toward electronic trading. We were seeing increasing pressure on margins, existing clients were opening online accounts with our competitors, and we were failing to attract newer customers at a fast enough rate. It was clear that we had to act.

While the online taskforce was solidly behind its recommendation, its work had only really begun. It needed to convince Merrill Lynch, one of the world's most successful firms, that it needed to change its business model. Utilizing the extensive amount of ongoing client feedback and quantitative data about the industry, the process began with a presentation to Launny Steffens. While acknowledging the validity of the data from the team, Steffens remained cautious about changing a highly successful business paradigm. He, like much of Private Client senior management, had originally come from

the field and thus was acutely aware of the value of the best-trained salesforce in the industry and the strength of its customer relationships. However, ten days later, Steffens and other members of the team flew to the Silicon Valley where they met with both financial consultants and clients to continue the dialogue about the online environment. When clients were asked at the focus group: "How many of you have online trading?" two-thirds of participants raised their hands. About the same proportion of the financial consultants at the later meeting also urged Merrill Lynch to go online.

That trip was followed by a second trip to Austin, Texas, where, once again, Steffens listened closely to clients explain their wants and needs. After weighing factors on all sides, on the way back to New York Steffens told his colleagues, "I'm convinced. We have to do a dot.com business."

Beginning in November 1998, the company began offering free access to its global stock research over the Internet for a four-month trial period. Many perceived this step as a watershed event for two reasons. First, Merrill Lynch was putting one of its most valued assets, its analyst reports, on the Web. Second, it proved that Merrill Lynch had "got the Internet" and was doing business differently—well before its full-service competitors understood the deeper impact of the Internet. Visitors to the website were able to create a "watch" list of stocks and pull up full-text research reports on over 1,500 companies covered by Merrill Lynch analysts across the globe, with Merrill Lynch then passing on leads to its financial consultants. Then, on December 28, 1998, Schwab's $25.5 billion market capitalization overtook Merrill Lynch's $25.4 billion. Schwab had increased its assets by 39% in 1998, while Merrill Lynch's grew only 18%. It was the moment "when Merrill got religion."[7] William Henkel, first vice president, senior director, Client Marketing and Strategy recalled, "That was an enormously difficult day for us. Here we were, with over a trillion dollars in client assets, to less than $500 billion for Schwab, and yet, our market cap was equal. That was a powerful market signal."

The Pricing Taskforce. Concurrent with the online taskforce, Allen Jones had formed the pricing taskforce under the leadership of Jeff Bennett, first vice president, director, Strategic Pricing, who had managed Unlimited Advantage's predecessor products, Asset Power and Merrill Lynch Financial Advantage. Asset Power, a fee-based program that charged 2% of assets under management, was launched in 1993. In 1997, Financial Advantage was launched with a 1.5% fee, about $300 to $500 in inclusive services and up to 17 free trades for an entry account. The product grew to $3 billion in its first year, and $8 billion by the second year. Both products, however, had met resistance from financial consultants reluctant to trade off commission revenue streams in favor of more in-depth client relationships and asset growth. As of 1998, Merrill Lynch's various fee-based products had attracted about $100 billion in client investments.

The role of the pricing taskforce was to thoroughly evaluate all aspects of the product/price

equation. Like its online counterpart, the pricing taskforce worked with consultants, conducted focus groups with financial consultants and clients, and conducted competitive comparisons. Jeff Bennett summarized the findings:

> It became very clear to us that our pricing structure was not aligned with how we delivered value to our clients. The execution component in the value chain had become a commodity, and we were putting a premium price on the execution of that commodity. For example, sometimes the best advice our financial consultants can give is not to trade. But when there was no trade we didn't get paid anything. It was like charging for the grocery bag, but not the groceries inside.

Looking outside the traditional brokerage firm, the taskforce also noted the rise of the RIAs (Registered Independent Advisors) that had been growing 40% per year, based on a price model that charged 1% of assets plus the costs of execution. Economic models were built to try to pinpoint the optimal pricing strategy. Within the traditional model, prices had been falling steadily, from 120 basis points (1.2% of assets) to approximately 80 basis points (0.8% of assets) within three to four years, and was expected to further fall to 50 basis points by 2003. Moreover, Merrill Lynch priced its asset-based products at above 100 basis points, which was on par with other full-service brokers charging 150 to 200 basis points. For many at Merrill Lynch, especially senior managers like Allen Jones, the taskforce research reinforced their drive to transform the business from "brokerage" to "asset gathering,"—only the company would now have to accelerate in that direction.

An Integrated Offer of Choice. As work progressed on both fronts, in February 1999, Merrill Lynch acquired D.E. Shaw Financial Technology, the developer of a real-time online trading system. This acquisition gave Merrill Lynch a cadre of developers, supplementing the existing technology team, to build a custom

---

[7]Leah Nathans Spiro, "Merrill's Battle," *Business Week,* November 15, 1999, p. 259.

online trading system for the brokerage. Another program, Microsoft's COM (Component Object Model), was being used to link the front-end system to Merrill Lynch's back-end systems. Additionally, while the front-end systems were to be based on clustered NT servers, Internet Information Server Web servers, and applications developed with Microsoft's Back office wares, Merrill Lynch also developed in-house "middleware" that would link those systems to its mainframes. As for communications, Merrill was also well into the deployment of an ATM backbone based on Cisco hardware and bandwidth from AT&T.

On March 4, 1999, Merrill Lynch became one of the first full-service firms to offer online trading. This move, however, was on a limited basis to 55,000 of its fee-based (MLFA and Asset Power) clients rather than commission clients. Indeed, in an attempt to offer online trading without undercutting their brokers' commission schedules, full-service firms such as Morgan Stanley Dean Witter and Paine Webber also planned to switch online customers from commission-based transactions to asset management fees (a percentage charge based on account size that covered a pre-set number of trades per year). For example, Paine Webber planned to charge $2,250 per year for a $100,000 account with up to 52 trades per year. On a per-trade basis, this was significantly higher than discount brokers or online trading companies ($43.27 per trade versus $29.95 or $8.00). The full-service firm maintained that customers received value such as customer profiling, planning, asset allocation, and research as well as trade execution.

While some within Merrill Lynch advocated the formation of an independent wholly owned online firm, Steffens was determined to keep all of Merrill Lynch's product offerings under the same brand. He recalled:

> Morgan Stanley set up its online brokerage operations as a separate business called Discover Brokerage. When it first started advertising the Discover name, it was huge and the only affiliation with Morgan Stanley was a very small line at the bottom of the ad. As we watched, the Morgan Stanley name became bigger and bigger. They spent tens of millions of dollars trying to build the Discover Brokerage brand without much success. It is difficult to build a no-name into a brand; many online startups have paid the price.

In March, Steffens made an eight-hour presentation to the 18-person Merrill Lynch & Co. Executive Committee, providing the outline of an Internet strategy that integrated the work of the online and pricing task forces. Steffens argued that "Merrill Lynch had to offer an online-only account or it would lose too many assets, not to mention the next generation of investors."[8]

Steffens advocated a transformation in Merrill Lynch's entire product-service portfolio. One significant change was the "Unlimited Advantage" service. Priced at 1% of assets or less depending on the asset mix, with a declining percentage as assets grew, the account was designed to be the best price/value equation in the industry. For an average Merrill Lynch client with a little over $200,000 in assets (66% in securities and 34% in fixed income), the fee would net out to $0.66 \times 1\% + .34 \times .3\% + .77\%$. Competitively, Merrill believed that it exceeded Prudential Securities offerings and was a better value than Schwab's outside advisor system, where customers could pay up to two percentage points on assets, plus commission on each trade. Jeff Bennett commented:

> Unlimited Advantage creates a "win/win" relationship between the financial consultant and the client. If the client's assets grow, the financial consultant's compensation grows. It effectively eliminates any suspicion that the broker's advice is based on the broker's desire to trade stock and earn a commission.

The second major change was the Merrill Lynch Direct channel that would offer online purchasing of equities and mutual funds, and

---

[8]Leah Nathans Spiro, "Merrill's Battle," *Business Week,* Nov. 15, 1999, p. 260.

telephone orders for fixed-income and other products at a basic charge of $29.95 a trade. Merrill Lynch research and a suite of portfolio management, cash management, and e-commerce services were also slated for online delivery. Additionally, the traditional broker relationships continued to be available to both new and existing clients.

The new strategy was perceived as high risk both internally and externally. An important challenge was the risk to the firm's revenue by effectively setting a fee ceiling at 1% of assets. Mitigating this factor was a long-standing strategic commitment to move towards operating like a major bank, beginning with the 1977 introduction of the CMA account. Anticipating the 1999 passage of Financial Service Modernization and the repeal of the Glass-Steagall Banking Act, Merrill's internal economic analysis showed that linking the Unlimited Advantage service to a Money Market Deposit Account (MMDA) would yield significant revenue to the firm. CMA accounts were currently linked to a Money Market Fund, but regulation prevented these balances from being invested in any instruments with average maturity exceeding 90 days. Merrill Lynch, however, could be more aggressive with MMDA deposits, thus delivering higher returns for its clients and a better spread than it was able to earn with the Money Market Funds. Consequently, although Unlimited Advantage exposed the firm to the possibility of adverse selection (because some clients could lower their cost without bringing in new assets), the MMDA strategy would minimize this risk. Merrill Lynch decided to apply this innovative idea to all its accounts, not just Unlimited Advantage, and this delayed the roll-out date to June of 2000 so that all clients could be properly notified and the strategy explained to FCs.

After the direct trading program was announced, observers speculated on the impact of online trading on Merrill Lynch's revenue— how much new business would be generated

versus how much would be lost due to the much lower commission structure. Adverse selection was an issue, as it was possible for a customer to keep the minimum balance in a brokerage account and use that advice to trade through the ML Direct Account. Internal models had indicated that a potential $400 million of earnings could be at stake. Moreover, while Merrill Lynch could be insulated while the market remained hot and online trading surged, many wondered what would happen if the bulls turned to bears and individual investors cut back on their trading. Conversely, while some were wondering if Merrill Lynch had made the right decision, others were concerned that they hadn't made it soon enough. "Merrill Lynch had created a highly successful business model," William Henkel astutely noted:

> One of the most difficult decisions for senior management is distinguishing short-term bumps from long term trends. As a market leader with $1.5 trillion in assets at risk, there needs to be a compelling reason to change, especially to change so profoundly and irrevocably. But once we reached our epiphany we moved dramatically—at Internet speed. We seized the initiative, and now people are reacting to us. After all, leadership is that difficult balance involved in trading off what is enduring for what is transient.

For Launny Steffens, Integrated Choice was not a revolutionary, but rather an evolutionary, step in a process begun several years earlier. He explained:

> Our fundamental business model of a universal financial services company has been the same for the past 15 years; we've just added two new rooms to our house. We began with a belief in asset gathering. At first our salesforce was incredulous but then began to see that once assets were at Merrill Lynch, we could help our clients with their full range of needs, be it managing their cash, investment decisions, liabilities, or the structure and disposition of assets over time. That led to our emphasis on financial planning and building a relationship with clients that allowed them to meet their goals. ML Direct, Unlimited Advantage, and electronic commerce are just additional ways to help clients increase their assets and meet their financial goals.

The Rubber Meets the Road

On June 1, 1999, Merrill Lynch publicly announced Integrated Choice, and the reaction of the market was immediate. While some in the business press saw it as a reactive move to stave off further intrusion into its client base, others in the business press and analysts were showering praise on Merrill Lynch's new strategy.

Merrill Lynch's move to a $29.95 trade price point seems almost designed to be something of a Schwab killer. . . . In our view, it is clearly a better value than Schwab's existing offering. . . . [Schwab's] Registered Investment Advisors average 194 bps vs. Merrill Unlimited Advantage at 85 bps!

Steve Galbraith (*Sanford Bernstein*)[9]

Further proof that Merrill Lynch had moved boldly in the right direction occurred in October 1999, when Morgan Stanley Dean Witter announced its new "iChoice" service with a range of products very similar to those in Merrill Lynch's Integrated Choice offering. Online trading was available for $29.95. Morgan Stanley offered a combination of human advice and online capabilities for fees ranging from 2.25% of assets to 0.2%, with fees decreasing as assets rose.

In making Integrated Choice a reality, however, Merrill Lynch faced several key challenges. The first was technology. Despite an annual IT budget of more than $2 billion and 6,000 IT people and 2,220 outside contractors, several hundred of whom were dedicated to the online project, bringing Merrill Lynch Direct to market effective December 1999 was a daunt-ing challenge. Failure to deliver would be risky. A June 1 announcement of services to be available six months later had given competitors (several of whom already offered more deeply discounted trading) time to counter Merrill Lynch's strategy even before it was fully implemented. Additionally, while the company seemed to have made the requisite technology investments, several firms wondered how Merrill Lynch's systems would react to the surges associated with online volumes, noting, "Merrill will have to work hard to convince those people that they should return to their father's stockbroker—particularly one like Merrill, whose computer systems haven't yet been seriously tested by big surges in online trading."[10]

In addition to the technical hurdles in offering online trading, Merrill Lynch also needed to bring its financial consultants (as well as other internal Merrill Lynch people) and clients on board. While the financial consultants had been told about Integrated Choice, they still needed to be sold. Unlike the upstart e-traders, Merrill Lynch's salesforce had been successful with the traditional business model and they were relative neophytes to the Internet and its potential. It took a combination of increasing online trading and flight of client assets from the field to create the need for change. As one observer noted:

> The firm had to wait until its brokers had accepted that the online world was here to stay. If Merrill had rolled out online trading in July 1999, 75% of its brokers would not have supported it. And Merrill stood the risk of having brokers and the assets they manage walk out. Because of the bull market for brokers and the practice of Wall Street firms paying multimillion-dollar signing bonuses, a successful Merrill broker could—and would—change jobs in a heartbeat.[11]

---

[9]Steve Galbraith is a leading industry analyst. Quotation from Merrill Lynch documents, combining remarks from Bernstein Research Call, October 8, 1999 and October 18, 1999.

[10]Rebecca Buckman, "Ambitious plan could result in lower fees," *The Wall St. Journal*, June 1, 1999, p. C1.

[11]Leah Nathans Spiro, "Merrill's Battle," *Business Week,* November 15, 1999.

For many, the initial reaction to Integrated Choice was that their personal incomes, dependent on trading commissions, would be dramatically reduced, and with that reaction, there was a risk that financial consultants would be lured to other firms. As Jeff Bennett pointed out, "The financial consultants had been insulated from many of the changes in the market. With the strongest market in memory, trading volumes were effectively shielding softening in commission rates."

To address this problem, Merrill Lynch executives launched a "full court press" with its financial consultants. While in the longer term Merrill Lynch expected that compensation would rise, particularly among financial consultants that executed the Private Client planning-based strategy and converted clients to the Unlimited Advantage, in the short term, some financial consultants could experience a near-term decline in compensation (of 10% to 15%). Key elements of a new plan were a "compensation bridge" for financial consultants for at least one year on assets converted to Unlimited Advantage and incentives for transitioning clients.

In addition to programs specifically targeted to financial consultants, Merrill Lynch had planned an extensive series of internal communications. The primary audience for these communications was the financial consultant and branch management; the secondary audience was the broader pool of Merrill Lynch domestic employees. The communications had three phases. The first, "Building the new Merrill Lynch," was focused on creating understanding, awareness, and excitement for the new business model. The second phase, "From Wall Street to Main Street to My Street," continued with employee education efforts, primarily through an Employee Channel delivered via Merrill Lynch's Intranet (WorldNet). The third communication phase, "Ongoing Communications," continued employee education efforts by providing information on how new events related to the business model. In conjunction with these efforts, "town hall" and business unit meetings and senior management "walk-arounds" were held to build employee excitement and commitment.

Perhaps the most important constituency that needed to understand and be converted to Integrated Choice was Merrill Lynch's clients. To reach out to its customers, the firm launched an extensive communication program that encompassed traditional media (television and print), as well as Internet-based media. Additionally, Merrill Lynch planned direct-mail programs with messages included in clients' statements.

Next Steps.   The success of Integrated Choice ultimately hinged on its execution, and Steffens had three items at the top of his agenda. First, was motivating the financial consultant community. There was a critical need to get Merrill Lynch's biggest asset, the financial consultants, converted from merely accepting the suite of Integrated Choice offerings to actively promoting the products—meeting with clients to identify the product that best matched client needs, preparing a financial plan with the client, and ultimately bringing a larger and larger share of that client's assets under the Merrill Lynch product umbrella.

A second issue was client transition and seamless service. Once clients met with their financial consultant and decided upon the optimal relationship for the client, Merrill Lynch needed a process for clients to be made aware of other products and services that might be appropriate. As one Merrill Lynch executive explained:

> Today a younger client with assets of, say, about $75,000, might be best served through ML Direct. However, as his or her assets and income grow, they may well want more advice and a relationship with a financial consultant. We need to establish a process so that we reach out to that client at the right time. Right now we've got discrete product offerings, but

we need proactive efforts to help clients make the best choices.

The third issue concerned the future role of the financial consultant. At present, financial consultants, often with the help of an administrative assistant, performed all facets of servicing the client relationship. This included a range of services from brokerage transactions and arranging financial planning, to administrative needs such as having checks certified for clients. Many at Merrill Lynch believed that there needed to be an evolution of the role, especially with its ambitious goal to be a full-service provider in all respects. Some suggested that the enhanced financial consultant might continue to manage the relationship, but expand access to specialists (such as estate planning) that was already available,

in addition to delegating more of the administrative tasks. Indeed, the entire structure of the selling operation would have to be carefully transformed to match the reality of the business situation.

While Integrated Choice was launched, its success was not yet guaranteed. As one industry observer noted:

The next nine months will prove to be a defining period in MER's history. The stakes are obviously quite high—if the company successfully reinvents itself where needed, MER's market cap could rise over 50%.[12]

Steve Galbraith (*Sanford Bernstein*)

_____

[12]First Call, November 19, 1999.

Index